The Survival Equation:

Man, Resources, and His Environment

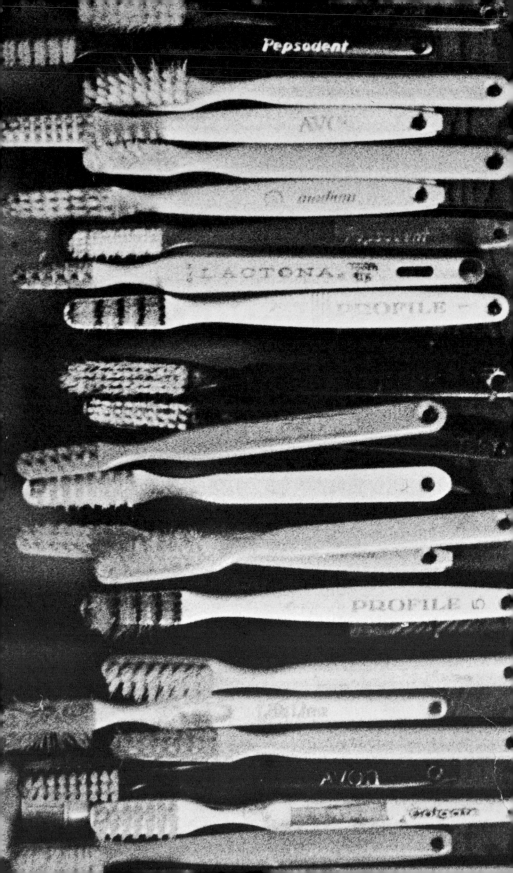

The Survival Equation:

Man, Resources, and His Environment

Edited by
Roger Revelle
Ashok Khosla
Maris Vinovskis

HOUGHTON MIFFLIN COMPANY · BOSTON
New York   Atlanta   Geneva, Illinois   Dallas   Palo Alto

Printed in the U.S.A.

Library of Congress Catalog Card Number: 79-140667

ISBN: 0-395-11243-5

Introduction

Most people nowadays agree with the poet's dictum that the proper study of mankind is man. But there are many ways to study man.

To the economist, man is economic man—the half-mythical creature whose wants are never satisfied and who must continually choose how to spend what he has in order to gain what he desires. To the sociologist, men are the bricks from which societies are built; to the political scientist they are political animals. The anthropologist and the humanist think of man as both *Homo faber*—man, the tool-maker—and *Homo ludens*—man who plays, dances, sings, and invents ritual, using his own body and the world around him as a medium of art and joy. To the historian, he is the time-binder, forever telling himself stories about his own past and peering vainly into the blank wall of the future. To the poet, he is the "... lord of all things, yet a prey to all; ... The glory, jest, and riddle of the world!" To some biologists man is simply one kind of living creature, part of the wonderful world of life. To the geneticist, individual men and women are basically devices for preserving and mixing the gene pool of the species, that one component of living things which seems close to immortality.

In this book we are concerned with still another aspect of man. Our theme is man and the earth—the relationship between the human species and its environment; in other words, human ecology. All the sciences that study man and the arts that reveal him are essential to understanding human ecology, but the ecologist must add something more. His task is to consider the whole environmental system in which people live, how it is shaped by the innate characteristics of human beings, and how it must change as human populations change, for when we speak of the environment, we think not only of the physical world, but also of the social world created by our fellow men, and we cannot forget that other living things share the surface of this planet with us.

Man as a species has many inherited characteristics that set him apart from other animals. Several of these are unique in themselves; others are unique in combination. Some of these characteristics are particularly important from the point of view of the ecologist.

Our females are highly fecund; the average woman is capable of giving birth to 12 to 15 children, even though this is about twice the number most women in the world actually bear. Our expected life span is long, compared with that of nearly all other animals. Our bodies are relatively large and strong, and we have great physical endurance; given enough time, a man in good condition can outrun and outwalk a horse. We can adapt ourselves to nearly the whole range of environments the earth presents. Some of our fellow men, the Polar Eskimos, live in the frozen wastes of Greenland: we have brothers in the tropical rain forests of Africa and South America. Even the rats and sparrows who share many of our wanderings with us cannot live in such extreme conditions. To stay alive, we must consume and produce a great deal of energy. Pound for pound, human beings radiate about 20,000 times as much energy as an equal mass of the sun. Our big adult brains must be encased in big heads, too large to pass through a mammalian birth canal. As a result, our brains and our heads grow for a long time after we are born, and human infants are helpless, half-formed creatures who must receive constant care. This requires the existence of families as the fundamental pattern of human social organization, and this in turn may determine the special nature of human sexuality. Because we possess voice boxes and mobile mouths, unlike our fellow primates, we are able to make a great variety of complicated sounds, and thus to give all things a name.

In one way we are truly unique. Unlike any other living creature, we are able to gain some understanding of the world we live in and of ourselves. It is this which makes it possible to say that man may be the beginning of a new form of matter—matter that can understand itself. More practically, it means that we are able to think and act in our own future interest, to take thought for the morrow even though we cannot foretell the future. Yet we are also highly irrational—creatures of joy and sorrow, emotion and fear, driven by half-remembered tribal experiences and subject to inherited urges we can neither control nor completely understand.

In these and other traits that underlie human ecology we are exactly like our ancestors thousands of years ago, because these characteristics are genetic ones, forged in a million years of evolution, and locked in our genes. We would not want to change them even if we could, since we think of them as especially human—those things which set us apart from other forms of life. But we have built on them another kind of inheritance which can change very rapidly. This is human culture—the collective memories of the race—and the societies which incorporate and preserve it. While our genetic traits have remained constant for many thousands of years, our cultures and societies have evolved with ever-increasing speed. Today's world would hardly be recognizable to a man of the eighteenth century.

As our societies have evolved, our numbers have increased beyond even the imaginings of our ancestors, until we have begun to press against the entire life support system of the planet. It is by no means certain that our ancient species, with its genetic inheritance shaped in a completely different world, can survive under the social pressures it has itself created. But we can be sure that the present pace of social change cannot continue for long, nor can its present direction remain unaltered. We are living in a time of tremendous transition—as some have said, at the hinge of history. The transition must soon cease; the swinging of the hinge must stop. This book deals with some of the reasons why this is so.

Ten thousand years ago, *Homo sapiens* was only one of several competing predatory animals; the numbers of lions and people were about the same. Today men have preempted the earth, in a manner and to an extent never before accomplished by any other kind of animal. In consequence, we must take into account not only the effects of the environment on man, but the effects of our actions on the earth and its other inhabitants. We must consider how the limitations and the resources of the earth influence individuals and shape their societies, and also how men, with their rapidly growing numbers and their ever more powerful technics, are changing the face of the earth.

In the perspective of human lives, the earth is a closed, finite system. Nothing material can be added or subtracted, and only energy enters and leaves, with the income and outgo of energy over any long time being in perfect balance. The moon voyages have helped us to realize, as nothing else could, these basic properties of our planetary home. The pictures of that beautiful sphere shining in the darkness, with its thin film of blue oceans and brown and green land and its veils of air and clouds, have helped many of us to see for the first time the true nature of the earth as a small and fragile place.

The earth from space is a single unitary sphere, the home of a single dominant species. But when we return to its surface, we find that species tragically divided. Two sets of nations face each other across the oceans: one rich and one poor, with a growing gap between them. In both groups of nations there is environmental degradation and decay, but for quite different reasons. In the rich countries, even though many of their inhabitants are poor and deprived, the resources of the earth are being used up in ways that cannot be sustained, and waste products and poisons foul the air, the water, and the land. In the poor countries, misery is multiplied by a growth in human numbers at rates never before experienced. Like so many other aspects of the modern world, the gulf between peoples is unique to the present time; it did not exist a few hundred years ago, and it cannot persist very far into the future.

In thinking about man and the earth, we must consider first the balance between human beings and the resources of earth, air, energy, and water on which men depend for their livelihood, and second how human actions are changing the life support system for all living creatures. From both points of view we are concerned with the most fundamental event of our times—the enormous growth of the world's population during the last twenty years and the prospects for continued growth in the future.

Many people believe, as Malthus did at first, though he later changed his mind, that the numbers of human beings will always increase up to a level set by the available food supply, or by enemies and disease. "Gigantic, inevitable famine stalks in the rear of misery and vice to limit the numbers of mankind." Even though death rates today are lower than they have ever been, and the proportion of the world's human population which is seriously malnourished is probably less than at any time since the Old Stone Age, the belief is widespread that uncontrolled population growth in the earth's poor countries is leading to catastrophe. It is possible, however, to take a different view, based on what we know about the history of human populations and on the behavior of many people at the present time. This is, that social inventions will be developed in the future, as they were in the past, which will lead to a deliberate limitation of fertility by individual couples. In the articles in the first third of this book, these questions are examined. The discussion emphasizes what we know about why people have the numbers of children they actually have, the consequence of today's rapid population growth, and the practical actions that can be taken to lower birth rates.

The other side of the population-resources equation is described in the second section of this volume. Because the earth is a closed system in which energy income and outgo are balanced, our material resources are not disappearing and indeed cannot disappear; they can only be chemically transformed or physically dispersed. But we are not sure that the quantity and quality of material and energy resources in the earth will be sufficient to maintain worldwide human civilization and to provide for the numbers of people who will live in times to come. The most fundamental question is the one mankind has always had to ask: Will there be enough food? The articles in this second section reflect the sharp diversity of opinion among specialists concerning the answers to these questions.

Even if we conclude that available land, water, air, and minerals are sufficient, another set of problems remains. Are we poisoning ourselves and our fellow creatures, degrading our environment, and destroying the delicate balance of life with our own waste products, dams, and other artificial structures, and the new chemical substances which we are deliberately or accidentally spreading in the environment? Many of these substances were never before present in nature; the birds and the fishes, and perhaps we ourselves, have no physiological defenses against them. These problems of environmental decay and ecological destruction may well be the most serious the world will face during the next hundred years. Yet as some of the authors in the third section of this book demonstrate, remedies can be found if we learn how to act in the common interest.

Once, long ago, I had a cardboard sign tacked to the wall of my office—"Fan the flames of controversy." The idea back of the sign was that in many human problems we are surrounded by a fog of uncertainty, and that the fog can be cleared a little if we brighten the fire of argument. When men passionately reason together, some truth will emerge. In this book we are dealing with just such uncertain problems. No one knows the answers, and no single point of view is likely to be more than half correct. This in one of the reasons why we have chosen to assemble the ideas and opinions of many different authors, rather than to write a textbook, which would reflect mainly our own biases and prejudices. We believe also that an assembly of original articles will allow for greater flexibility in teaching and will give the student a greater sense of involvement in the reality of the problems we are all facing today. The articles herein have not been filtered through the bland cheesecloth of summarization and reconciliation; they are the raw originals which state the facts and opinions on which real individuals base their beliefs.

Although we have tried to preserve a certain impartiality in our choice of authors, we are by no means neutral in our point of view. We believe that men will act rationally and in their own interest if they have a chance to do so; that technological means exist or can be found to solve the population and ecological problems of our time; that the real questions are political, social, and moral. How can we develop the political will, the social organizations, and the ethical concern for our fellow men that are essential to solve them?

Consider the problems of food and resources in the poor countries of Asia, Africa and Latin America: During the next 30 years the technical potentialities exist not only to feed all human beings, but greatly to improve the quality of human diets. And the natural resources available to present technology are sufficient to allow a vast improvement in the standard of living of all the people who will inhabit the earth 30 to 40 years from now. This is not to say that such an improvement in diets or standard of living will inevitably occur. It will depend on the maintenance and improvement of social and economic institutions, and on the growth of cooperation and interdependence among the peoples of the world. Large capital investments and massive transfers of technology are essential elements of such development, though a reduction in human fertility is also an important component.

If birth rates throughout the world can be lowered to between 15 and 20 per thousand per year by about the year 2000, the earth's human population could level off at less than 10 thousand million people in the latter half of the 21st century. This number may seem frighteningly large, but from the point of view of foreseeable resources of arable land, water, air, minerals, and energy, the life support capacity of the earth is probably sufficient to allow a moderately high material standard of living for this number of people.

If birth rates continue as at present for about another century, the earth's human population would rise to a level of around 50 thousand million people, but the leveling process would be a terrible one. It would result from an increase in death rates to match birth rates, due primarily to widespread malnutrition, and the chances of any future improvement would be minimal. The ghost of Malthus would join the Pale Horsemen of famine, pestilence, war, and death in a triumphant ride over the earth.

Assuming that a nuclear holocaust can be avoided, the all-encompassing problems of our times are, first, to arrive at a world in which human beings everywhere control their own fertility so that population does not rise beyond the point at which resources are adequate for all, and second, to create the social institutions and the shared human values which will make such a world a tolerable one.

Each of the authors represented here has his own partial vision of how the transition of our times will end, and of man's future fate. None can see clearly or very far because we have so little from the past to guide us.

Roger Revelle
Harvard University

Contents

Population Policy

RESOURCES, FOOD, AND DEVELOPMENT

Minerals and Energy

The World Food Problem

Enough Food for All?

Closing the Economic Gap

The Survival Equation:

Man, Resources, and His Environment

POPULATIONS—
HUMANITY'S PROBLEM

Population

ROGER REVELLE

ROGER REVELLE *is Professor of Population Policy and Director of the Center for Population Studies, Harvard University.*

This article presents a general introduction to the population problem. In it Revelle examines the two major demographic revolutions of the past with particular attention to the extent of the reasons for the population explosion during the last 250 years. Since much of the debate on the population dilemma today centers on predicting future population size, he also analyzes two of the most widely used population forecasts. Using them, Revelle shows how different estimates of future birth and death rates will yield very different estimates of world population in the year 2000.

In some senses population forecasts are the most basic of any that can be made. But however fundamental the number of people living in various regions of the world may be as a parameter, it is not an easy one to assess at the present time or to extrapolate into the future.

Like many other phenomena, changes in the size of human populations tend to follow an exponential or compound interest law over any short period. But over longer periods populations seem to grow in more or less sudden steps, from one stage of quasi-equilibrium to another. For example, consider the two major demographic revolutions in man's experience: the population growth that accompanied the development of agriculture, and the one that began in the 17th century in northern Europe and has since spread throughout the world.

Man has existed in substantially his present biological form for perhaps a million years yet, during all but the last one per cent of that time, the number of people was never more than a few million, not much greater than the number of lions. We know this was so from the estimated density of population among peoples who were still living in a stone age culture when they were observed or studied by Europeans—certain American Indians, African tribes, Australian bushmen, Papuans in New Guinea and

Science Journal, pp. 2–8, October 1967. Reprinted by permission.

others. Over most of the first million years, birth rates and death rates of the world's population must have been, on the average, almost exactly equal. The mean rate of natural increase, taken over any set of millennia, could not have been more than 0.05 per thousand per year, corresponding to a doubling time of 20,000 years or more. Of course, the books were never so nicely balanced. In every particular region there may have been wild fluctuations from century to century, and even from generation to generation, in death rates and population size, followed in many cases by parallel fluctuations in birth rates. But the long term average of population size against time must have been almost a level line.

Agriculture was invented 6000 to 9000 years ago. Its development over the next few millennia radically changed the human condition, and destroyed the previous equilibrium between birth rates and death rates. In the Fertile Crescent from the Nile to the Tigris-Euphrates, in China, India, Southern Europe, Middle America and Peru, human numbers may have increased a hundred fold in one or two thousand years, until a new quasi-balance between births and deaths was attained. It has been estimated that, by the time of Christ, the world population was 300 million, even though agriculture had barely begun, or had not even been started, over large areas.

Between the beginning of our era and the early part of the 17th century, the population slowly increased to somewhere around 600 million. Then it began to rise rapidly again and at an ever accelerating pace. Whereas the average annual rate of increase from 1 A.D. to 1600 had been less than 0.5 per thousand, it rose to 4 per thousand from 1750 to 1800, to 8 per thousand from 1900 to 1950, and is now probably nearly 20. The number of human beings has increased more than five fold in three and a half centuries. At the present rate it will double again by the end of our present century.

This remarkable change was brought about largely by a decline in death rates, although fertility did rise above previous levels at some times and places. Between 1700 and 1900 the overall rate of growth was two to three times as great in Europe and areas of European settlement as in the rest of the world. Today the situation has become almost exactly reversed. The underdeveloped countries are now growing more than twice as fast as the developed ones. At the beginning, infant and child mortalities everywhere were extremely high. In the 17th century, two-thirds of the children of English monarchs, from James I to Anne, died before they were 21 years old. Throughout the 18th century, only about half the children born in Brittany—one of the 'underdeveloped' provinces of France—lived past the age of 10; elsewhere in France, for example in the south west and in Normandy, two-thirds of the children reached their 10th birthday. In India, during the first decade of the 20th century, the expectation of life at birth was a little over 20 years, and perhaps half the children died.

Today, in all developed countries, between 97 and 99 per cent of the children survive the first year of life, and almost all these survivors live to adulthood. In India, the expectation of life at birth now exceeds 40 years, and probably at least three-quarters of the children grow up.

Even during the early stages of the modern epoch of population growth,

FIGURE 1. Population of the world has increased enormously in the past 300 years. By 1800—about a million years since his beginnings—man had built up a population of 1000 million. Since then, however, the periods between successive increases of 1000 million have progressively shortened. For the population to increase from 6000 million to 7000 million could take only seven years (1993-2000). Such explosive growth can be attributed at least in part to improved nutrition and standards of hygiene in the developing countries.

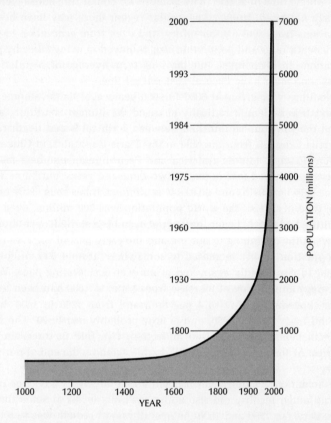

an effective 'social' mechanism for controlling fertility existed in Western Europe—the custom of relatively late marriage for women or even life-long spinsterhood. This mechanism began to be more widely used as individuals became concerned about having too many children. The age of marriage probably rose throughout the 17th and 18th centuries; for example in 1626, in Amsterdam, 61 per cent of brides were under 25 years of age, but only 35 per cent a century and a half later. By 1850, the average age of women at first marriage in the Netherlands and Belgium was between 28 and 29 years, and about the same for Switzerland. From 15 to 20 per cent of women were still single at age 50.

In several parts of Europe, a certain amount of deliberate control of fertility was apparently practised by married couples in the 17th and 18th centuries, but birth control began to be more and more widely used and effective during the 19th century, first in France and the United States and later in other countries of Europe. It was clearly regarded as an improvement over delayed marriage; as fertility among married couples declined, the age of women at first marriage also went down; it is now less than 23 years in France and Belgium. In Eastern Europe, which had never adopted the Western pattern of late marriage and spinsterhood, rigorous fertility control within marriage was evident in some provinces at least as early as the 1890s.

Low birth rates and low death rates, lower than those that prevailed anywhere at any time more than a century ago, characterize all developed countries—communist, capitalist, Catholic, Orthodox, Protestant or Buddhist. Conversely, birth rates that were widespread two centuries ago prevail in the less developed countries today, while death rates are about the same as those in the developed countries 40 to 60 years ago. The tragic question of our time is when and how this time gap will disappear—by a reversion to higher death rates or an advance to lower birth rates. The most far reaching practical task of students of human populations is to help define the biological, psychological, social and economic changes which will lead to a sufficient lowering of birth rates in the less developed countries.

As with any other science, the demographer's problem is to frame hypotheses that can be tested by prediction. His difficulty is similar to that of the forester or the climatologist; the events he is concerned with take a long time to happen; within one lifetime he cannot test many hypotheses by forecasting the future. In principle the difficulty could be overcome by testing hypotheses against past events—what geophysicists call 'hindcasting.'

But accurate data from the past exist over only a comparatively short time span, and are far from comprehensive. Although the Christian era began with a population count, and a few censuses were taken in Europe and North America toward the end of the 18th century, less than 20 per cent of the world's peoples were even moderately well counted before the middle of the 19th century. Even today, only about 70 per cent of human beings have been included in a census.

In this article I intend to discuss two population forecasts which have been made recently—one by the U.S. Census Bureau and one by the Population Division of the United Nations. Both illustrate the difficulties of forecasts and the value of the information they provide. First, however, I should say something of the pitfalls of population forecasting in general. To construct a population projection for a country or region, one should know the number of people at a particular point in time, their distribution by age and sex, their fertility, mortality and migration, and be able to make an educated guess about changes in these last three quantities during the time interval being spanned. But for large parts of the world the demographer must make do with much less information than this. Uncertainties about present size of population and rate of growth, and about future trends of mortality are three important sources of error in forecasting, and I shall discuss these in the next section. Future change in fertility is even more important, but because fertility is the more or less controllable variable in an otherwise uncontrollable situation I shall leave discussion of it till the end of this article.

The estimate of about 3300 million for the world's population as of the middle of 1965, used in both the projections I shall cite, is based on inadequate data for a number of countries. There are no recent censuses for many Asian, African and Latin American countries. Uncertainty about the size of China's population contributes a possible error of more than 100 million. Pakistan's population, according to one estimate, was undercounted by nearly 8 million (7.6 per cent of the total population) in the census of 1961. If the most probable value of about 3 per cent per year for the growth rate since 1961 is accepted, the estimate of the present population is understated by another 5 per cent. Supposing India's population to be underestimated in somewhat the same proportions as that of Pakistan, the error is more than 50 million. Taking account of the possibility of errors of a similar magnitude for many other less developed countries, the paucity of data for others, and estimates of undercounts of 2.5 to 3 per cent for some developed countries such as the United States, the world population of 1965 may be underestimated by more than 200 million.

The most serious problem arises from lack of satisfactory data for mainland China, which probably has nearly a quarter of the world's population. The only census of modern times was made in 1953, and gave a total of 583 million persons. There were no accurate data on the sex and age distribution of the population, and levels of fertility and mortality are unknown. Moreover, judging from experience in other countries, it is likely that the census was an undercount, probably by at least 5 per cent, and perhaps by as much as 10 or 15 per cent. The base estimates as of mid-1953 for the population of China would then be between 610 and 640, or even 670 million. On the other hand, if the published figure of 583 million is taken as the mid-point of the probable range, with uncertainty of plus or minus 10 per cent, the spread of possible population size in 1953 would be 525 to 640 million.

If all the possibilities for China's population are incorporated into alternate estimates and projections, the totals at the upper and lower limits describe an extremely wide range. Projections for 1985 have a spread of more than 500 million, with no guarantee that all possibilities have been covered. One demographer has estimated a possible range from 1000 million to 2000 million in the year 2000, while the United Nations projections give a minimun of under 900 million and a maximum of over 1400 million.

Of equal significance are the rates at which populations are now growing. Estimates of present growth rates for much of the world are of doubtful reliability or are simply not available. Very divergent values may be obtained by different techniques. For example, the rate of growth for Pakistan is 2.1 per cent per annum if one accepts the growth indicated by the censuses of 1951 and 1961, but about 3.2 per cent if one accepts the results of sample surveys conducted since 1962. A population increasing at 3.2 per cent annually will be 12 per cent larger at the end of ten years than one of the same initial size growing at an annual rate of 2.1 per cent.

Since the end of World War II, there has been a very sharp decline in mortality levels in many developing countries. This is usually ascribed to large scale public health measures, together with the widespread use of antibiotics and insecticides, although improved foods and better food distribution, particularly for children, have undoubtedly played a part. The pace of mortality decline has probably slackened in the past two or three years, at least in several developing countries. Major improvements in standards of living, and more equitable income distribution, may be necessary for a future marked reduction of mortality.

Nearly all countries are committed, in one degree or another, to further reductions. There is no certainty, however, that this commitment can or will be translated into markedly lower death rates. Population is already pressing hard on the food supply of a number of nations. Except for shipments of grain from the United States, Canada and a few other countries in 1966, death rates in India might have risen sharply.

As food requirements increase, the chances that a country will be able to forestall a major famine by importing food from abroad may diminish. The absence of large reserves, which characterizes the present situation in developed countries with surplus producing capacity, lessens the likelihood that a subsistence crisis in less developed countries, produced by drought or flood, can be met. Even if production in the developed countries could be increased to meet the need, their electorates might be unwilling to accept the economic burden of filling the food deficits of the poor nations.

Two series of projections of the population of India, Pakistan, Brazil and the world in 1985 have recently been made by the United States Census Bureau for President Johnson's Science Advisory Committee. The high series were based on the assumption that fertility will remain at present levels, while fertility was assumed to decline in the low series. It was assumed that mortality would decline at the same rate in both.

For the assumed growth rate of the world population in 1965, the United Nations estimate of 1.8 per cent per year for the rate of growth from 1960 to 1964 was used, but other sources were taken for estimating present growth rates in Brazil, Pakistan and India. The estimate for Brazil was about 2.9 per cent, for India about 2.6 per cent, and for Pakistan 3.2 per cent.

The level of mortality for the world in 1965 was taken as 16 per thousand population; the birth rate would then be 34 per 1000, about equal to that of Taiwan. A set of female age-specific rates was obtained by slightly modifying a schedule of known rates for Taiwan in 1960. For the high projection this was assumed to remain constant but for the low one it was postulated that fertility rates would decline to 90 per cent of the 1965 values by 1970, to 80 per cent by 1980 and to 70 per cent by 1985.

For both projections for Pakistan the expectation of life at birth was assumed to increase about 3.3 years per decade and the levels of fertility for East and West Pakistan were considered separately. East Pakistan's birth rate was assumed to be 53 per thousand in 1961 (the time of the last census) while that for West Pakistan was placed at 50. For the low series it was assumed that the intensified family planning programme introduced in 1965 would be gradually extended throughout the population, and that its maximum effectiveness would be reached by 1972, at which time the fertility rate would have decreased 28 per cent. After 1972 the family planning programme was assumed to expand at the same rate as the population; in other words, the proportion of the population practising family planning techniques would remain essentially constant.

FIGURE 2. Projections of population for the world (total colored area), developed (dark color)
and developing nations (light color) shown above are based on figures produced by the Population Division of the United Nations and the U.S. Census Bureau. The data for the year 2000
show the four variants—low, medium, high and continued fertility level—postulated by the
United Nations. At the present time one-third of the world's population lives at the high
standard of the present developed nations; by the end of the century only one-quarter of the
population will have this advantage.

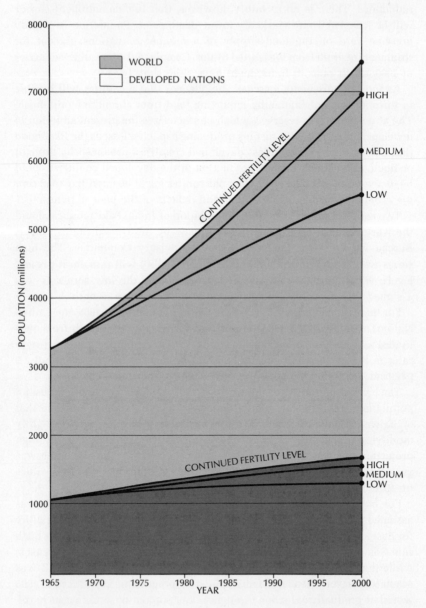

The Indian high projection was based on estimates by the Institute of
Applied Manpower Research in New Delhi. The average birth rate during
1961–65 was assumed to be 41 per thousand and this was taken as the 1965
birth rate. The expectation of life at birth was assumed to increase about
7 years per decade. For the low projection, the percentage decline in fertility
assumed for Pakistan was adopted.

FIGURE 3. Projections of the populations of Brazil, India, and Pakistan up to 1985 are illustrated above. The data were prepared by the U.S. Census Bureau for President Johnson's
Science Advisory Committee. The high series was based on the assumption that fertility will
remain at present levels, while fertility was assumed to decline in the low series. Mortality
was assumed to decline at the same rate in both. Extrapolation from the high series for India
and Pakistan suggests that by the year 2000 the population of the subcontinent could be over
1800 million—three times the present population of the region, more than half the 1965 population of the world and perhaps considerably higher than that of mainland China at the end
of the century.

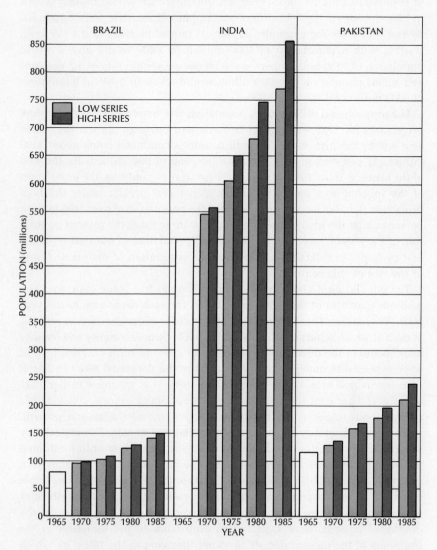

For Brazil, the United Nations Economic Commission for Latin America
estimated the birth rate during the period 1959–61 to be in the range of 40
to 43 per thousand. A birth rate of 41 for 1965 was therefore assumed to
establish the level of (constant) fertility for the high projection. For the low
projection, a modified version of the fertility model used for Pakistan was
employed.

The high projection shows an increase in the population of the world
from 3300 million in 1965 to 5030 million by 1985, or by 52 per cent. The

low projection gives a population of 4645 million by 1985, an increase of about 40 per cent above the 1965 figure. These correspond to average annual growth rates over the 20 year period of 2.1 per cent and 1.7 per cent respectively.

The difference between the high and low figure is only 385 million persons, about the same as the likely range of uncertainty in the projected population of mainland China in 1985. However, the difference would rapidly widen in later decades if the 1985 differences in rates of increase were to persist. By the year 2000, for example, an annual rate of increase of 2.4 per cent, starting with a population of 5000 million in 1985, would give a world population of 7150 million persons, whereas an annual rate of 1.7 per cent and a 1985 population of 4650 million would result in a world population of 6000 million by the year 2000.

The proportional difference in population size between the high and low projections for 1985 was greater in India and Pakistan than in the world as a whole; the high value for both countries combined being about 1100 million, 12 per cent greater than the low one of 980 million. By the end of the century, if the 1985 rates of increase were to continue, the population of the subcontinent would be nearly 25 per cent greater under the high projection than the low. In the year 2000, the population of over 1800 million persons under the high projection would be three times the present population of the region, more than half the 1965 population of our entire planet, and perhaps considerably higher than the population of mainland China at the end of this century.

The population division of the United Nations has made high, low and medium estimates of the world population for each decade up to the year 2000. To calculate these projections, the world was divided into 24 regions, in each of which separate estimates of probable future mortality and fertility were made. In the developed countries, the levels of birth and death rates were expected to undergo very little change; the decennial rate of natural increase, which was 11 per cent in the 1960s was assumed to decrease slightly to 9 per cent in the 1990s. In the developing regions, considerable changes were expected in the main components of population growth.

To project mortality levels, it was assumed that average life expectancy at birth of a population would rise annually by a half year until it attained 55 years; between 55 and 65 years, there would be a slightly higher gain each year, followed by a slow-down after 65 until the gain became negligible when life expectancy had risen above 74 years. On this basis, death rates in the poor countries, which currently average twice as high as in the developed nations, were expected to drop from 18 per thousand at the beginning of the present decade to 10 per thousand in the 1990s, by which time they would have attained the same average as those of the developed countries.

For many poor countries, fertility has not yet started to decline. In these it was assumed that once a decline begins, 30 to 45 years are needed to drop to half the original level. As to the date of onset, several assumptions were made for each region. These different dates, combined with different assumptions concerning the duration of decline, give rise to the high, medium and low projections. The medium projection gives an overall decrease of one-quarter in the average birth rate of the poor countries, from 40 per thousand in the 1960s to 29 in the 1990s, that is, from a little over twice the present birth rate of the developed regions to a little over 1.5 times this level.

In the medium projection, the world's population, totalling 3281 million in 1965, is estimated to rise by 87 per cent to 6130 million by the year 2000. The high and low projections, which the UN regards as equally plausible, might raise the world population by as much as 113 per cent at the century's end, to 6990 million, or by as little as 66 per cent, to 5450 million. (In the past, the UN high projections have turned out to be closer to reality than its medium projections.) If fertility remained at present levels in every region, the world total would be 7520 million by 2000, with ever accelerating growth, but this was regarded as unlikely. The increase during the remainder of the century would then be 129 per cent of the 1965 world total, 53 per cent in the developed regions and 164 per cent in the developing ones. Some demographers have taken a very much more optimistic view about possible future declines in fertility, and have projected an end of the century world total of between 4200 and 5000 million people. This demonstrates clearly the importance of fertility control and it is now time I dealt with the problems this involves in more detail.

Fertility rates in most human societies are well below the potential of human fecundity; the direct constraints on population growth are social ones and not, as Malthus at first thought, starvation and disease. As I have said, birth rates in Europe and North America began to fall below their previous levels more than 100 years ago. In the 17th and 18th centuries, there had been a growing tendency in Western Europe to postpone marriage and to increase celibacy. In the later 19th century married couples began to resort to abortion on a large scale and to practice contraception, in addition to the limitation of population by emigration.

In recent years, rapid declines in fertility have occurred in eastern Europe and Japan. Fertility rates went down by about 40 per cent in Hungary between 1954 and 1962, by 36 per cent in Rumania between 1955 and 1962, and by 30 per cent in Poland between 1955 and 1964. Japan experienced a fall of 44 per cent between 1950 and 1962. The conditions in these nations differed markedly from those that prevail today in the underdeveloped world. Literacy rates were high, many couples were already deliberately controlling fertility and they had strong motivations to limit family size.

Yet there are good reasons to believe that human fertility in most of the less developed countries will decrease during the next few decades, though when and how much cannot be predicted. In the past, high fertility has been an adjustment to high and unpredictable mortality, and has been well fitted to a community life built on family and kinship ties. Only one son may have been needed for ritual or economic purposes, but it was common to desire at least two for insurance against the death or incapacity of one. Families had to average four children to obtain two sons. Clan and tribal kinship systems enhanced the value placed on children, because they contributed to the power or status of the group. Today, as can be seen from surveys of individual husbands and wives, many couples in the less developed countries want no more children than they already have, and would like to know better ways of preventing further births. At the same time, these surveys show that the desired numbers of children are much higher than in the developed countries. The average is four children per couple, which, with present and prospective levels of mortality, would result in a doubling of population every 30 to 35 years.

Most people in developed countries want two to four children; in the less developed countries they want three to five. In the developed countries, actual family size is slightly less than desired family size, while the reverse is true in less developed ones. In the poor countries, favourable attitudes to family limitation are much more common among couples who already have four or more living children. Availability of contraceptive devices may not be very important until the desired number of living children is secure. Low infant and child mortality, and public awareness that mortality is low, may be one of the necessary preconditions for reducing fertility.

In developed countries, infant mortalities are nearly always less than 50 per thousand live births. But in the less developed countries, with very few exceptions, 50 to more than 150 children out of every 1000 die before the age of one. In a family of four or five children the probability that all will grow up is often less than 50 per cent.

When average infant and child mortality is high, the variance is also high; the chances in an individual family that several children will die are frighteningly large. Because parents desire a high degree of assurance that one of their sons will grow up to be a man, they are willing to assume the burden of having too many children in order to gain this assurance. We are faced with the apparent paradox that a reduction in mortality may reduce rather than raise the rate of population growth. The population problem of our time has been created by lowering death rates, yet an essential element in curing it may be to lower infant and child death rates further still, perhaps down to the levels existing in the Western world. If this is so, then the quickest possible increase of food supplies, both in quantity and quality, is of the utmost urgency for the long term as well as the short, because poor nutrition in the poor countries strikes fiercely at the children. In the developed countries, most human beings live to middle age, and cardiovascular diseases and neoplasms are overwhelmingly the leading causes of death. In developing countries, the main killers are diseases of childhood resulting from infection and malnutrition.

Only a small proportion of people in the less developed countries have even moderately good knowledge of modern methods of family planning; the poor and the uneducated need to learn what the well-to-do and the educated already know—that there are a number of safe, reliable and simple ways of limiting one's family. Knowledge of contraceptive methods is much rarer than the desire not to have more children.

The governments of developing countries are now adopting population control policies at a rate and in a climate of world approval unimaginable even a few years ago. Among the nations that have officially decided to foster family planning are India, Pakistan, mainland China, South Korea,

Ceylon, Singapore, Hong Kong, Malaysia, Turkey, Egypt, Tunisia, Morocco and Honduras. Taiwan has no formal policy, but the Government has given full co-operation to an island-wide programme that has already reached a substantial part of the population. In many countries, at least the beginning of government interest is visible. These include the Philippines, Thailand, Nepal, Afghanistan, Iran, Kenya, Mauritius, Chile, Colombia, Peru and Venezuela. The role of governments in reducing fertility is to exhort, inform and provide; decisions and actions must be taken by individual couples acting in accordance with their perceived interests. Even so, the governmental task is large and difficult, requiring a high degree of organization, adequate financial and logistic support, great flexibility in meeting changing conditions, and continuing objective evaluation of results.

Although there have been high hopes for family planning programmes using intrauterine devices, and birth rates appear to have gone down in some countries, notably Korea and Taiwan, the part played by these birth control programmes is not clear. Many of the devices may have been used by older women who were already controlling their fertility in other ways. Postponing the age at which women have their first child, and longer spacing between pregnancies, are now being recognized as important. In Japan, postponement of marriage has been one of the key factors (together with abortion) in the post-war fertility decline. In the Republic of Korea, an increase in the mean age at marriage of women from 19 years in 1935 to 24 years in 1960 has apparently accounted for a 16 per cent drop in total fertility rates.

We need to find, to learn how to bring about and how to help people recognize the changes in living conditions in the less developed countries that will lower the benefits to individual families of having more than two or three children, and increase their costs. At the same time, research is needed to develop methods of fertility control that are easier to introduce than the present oral contraceptives and mechanical devices. Much of this research can be done by the developed nations.

Norms for Family Size in Underdeveloped Areas

RONALD FREEDMAN

RONALD FREEDMAN *is professor of sociology and Associate Director of the Population Studies Center at the University of Michigan.*

The previous article by Revelle pointed out the difficulty of predicting the future rate of population growth because of changing birth and death rates. Freedman carries this analysis further by examining the importance of cultural norms in determining family size. He points out that although controls on fertility are available in all societies, the cultural norms in less-developed countries lead to high birth rates. Due to high infant mortality in the past, families in less-developed countries have needed high birth rates in order to insure that enough children survived to carry out necessary functions. The problem now is that while infant mortality has been greatly reduced since World War II, the cultural norms of those areas have not yet adjusted to the new situation.

It is a commonplace observation that fertility is high in the so-called underdeveloped societies. Sometimes this leads to the erroneous view that their fertility is limited only by what is biologically possible so that birth rates reach a mythologically high natural level. In this idealized view free and unrestrained sexual unions beginning at an early age produce very high fertility as an incidental result without deliberate intent and without much individual or social concern about family size.

A more plausible general proposition is that reproduction, whether at high or low levels, is so important to the family and to society everywhere that its level is more or less controlled by cultural norms about family size and such related matters as marriage, timing of intercourse, and abortion. In each society the cultural norms about these vital matters are consistent with social institutions in which they are deeply embedded. Changes in fertility

Proceedings of the Royal Society 159: 220–34, 1963. Reprinted by permission. Abridgment by the editors of the present volume.

are unlikely without prior or, at least, simultaneous changes in these institutions.

Before developing these ideas, it may be useful to consider briefly the variability in fertility among underdeveloped societies. A recent study of the Cocos Island population(1)* provides a unique example of exceptionally high fertility expected in the model of virtually unrestrained fertility. The Cocos Islanders, living between 1870 and 1947 under an exceptionally favourable paternalistic regime married early, and about two-thirds of their brides were pregnant at marriage. The birth rates between 1880 and 1947 averaged about 55 per thousand and reached 60 in several years. This may be contrasted with birth rates of about 35 per thousand in pre-industrial England. The gross reproduction rate for the Cocos Islands was about 4.2, perhaps the highest ever recorded with reliable data.

The range of fertility rates currently found among underdeveloped areas is wide enough to include rates which characterized Western Europe before its modern fertility decline but long after social and economic development were under way. For example the gross reproduction rate of 2.4 for England in 1861, shortly before fertility began to decline, is lower than the rates for most but by no means all of the high fertility societies today. Married women born in England in 1841–45 had just under six children on the average,(2) if they survived to the end of the child-bearing period. This is about the same as the figure reported for India now,(3) although it is significantly less than the average of more than eight children born to the Cocos Island mothers and the average of more than ten to the American Hutterite mothers.(4)

These selected data are intended only to illustrate the idea that fertility, however measured, varies from moderately to very high levels in underdeveloped societies, even after allowing for inaccuracies of base data.

Genetic differentials in fecundity eventually may be shown to account for some of the existing variation between societies, but I think they are unlikely to explain the major variations in time or between societies. They are unlikely to explain why fertility is relatively high in underdeveloped societies and declines with development.

As a more plausible explanation, I begin with the thesis that societal levels of fertility are related to variations in cultural norms about reproduction, and these, in turn, are related to the nature of society.

One of the fundamental principles of sociology is that when many members of a society face a recurrent common problem with important social consequences they tend to develop a normative solution for it. This solution, a set of rules for behaviour in a particular situation, becomes part of the culture, and the society indoctrinates its members to conform more or less closely to the norms by explicit or implicit rewards and punishments.

The problem of how many children a couple should have is so widely shared and has so many personal and social consequences that it would

---

*The numbers in parentheses refer to the collected notes at the end of this paper.

be a sociological anomaly if social norms regarding it did not develop. This is also true for such related problems as when to marry and when sexual intercourse is permitted. In view of the special importance attached to kinship ties in the underdeveloped societies, it would be particularly strange if the reproductive level of the familial unit were not a matter of normative concern.

Norms about family size are likely to be in terms of a range in numbers of children that are permissible or desirable. While specifying clearly that childlessness is an unspeakable tragedy and an only child very undesirable, the norm for a particular culture or group may be as vague as 'at least three or four children' or 'as many as possible.' But I know of no organized society, primitive or modern, in which the question of how many children are born is a matter of indifference either to the reproducing unit or to the community.

In various underdeveloped societies, a large number of sample interview surveys(5) have been made since the Second World War in which peasant populations have been asked such questions as how many children they want for themselves, how many are right for others, etc. In almost all of these studies only a small minority of the respondents found the questions ridiculous or meaningless or answered that such matters were up to fate or God, etc. Even where the answers invoke the Deity or fate, further inquiry frequently indicates that the respondent has rather firm ideas of what he desires that fate or divine providence should bring. In most such surveys the answers tend to be clustered about a moderate modal value rather than to be randomly distributed. Of special significance are data in a number of these studies indicating that a majority of those with three or four children want no more and many prefer a smaller number than they have.

There are a few studies in which it is reported that questions about the desired number of children are regarded by respondents as ludicrous. This is reported, for example, by Richards & Reining for the Bahaya of Africa.(6) But, the attitude expressed apparently does not result from the absence of a norm. The report is that, under existing conditions, most women do not have the four to six children in the household which they consider ideal and would approximate if they could. And even in this instance, the authors report that there are voluntary practices limiting reproduction during certain periods.

The exact meaning and accuracy of the answers obtained in such surveys is open to question, but there is little doubt that there is considerable consensus in such populations about desirable family size.

It must be admitted that much of the survey evidence is from societies that have been in touch with the West for many years, but some of the samples studied have been in village areas of India, the Near East and other places where illiteracy and immobility have isolated much of the population from modern ideas.

It is possible, but unlikely, that all of the populations studied through sample surveys have already been considerably influenced by modern Western values about reproduction. The same cannot be said for a large number of primitive societies whose ethnology with respect to sexual and reproductive behaviour was studied by Ford.(7) He concluded that childbirth is by no means universally accepted as either natural or inevitable. Many women are ambivalent about childbirth, so that considerable social pressure may be necessary to insure adequate reproduction.

Obviously, social norms encouraging reproduction at less than the physiological maximum can be implemented only if one or more practices for fertility reduction is fairly widespread in the population, so it is very relevant to ask what control practices are available. A variety of controls are possible and are used. In addition to such deliberate and obvious practices as contraception and abortion, there are a large number of others; for example, the age at first sexual union, timing and frequency of intercourse, voluntary or involuntary fecundity impairments, foetal mortality, etc.

Davis & Blake(8) have provided a useful classification of such control factors immediately determining the fertility level of a society. They call them 'intermediate variables' because they are the means of fertility control standing intermediate between the social institutions and norms on the one hand and actual fertility on the other. Any social influences on fertility can only operate by affecting one or more of these 'intermediate variables.' The Davis & Blake classification is shown in Appendix I. I will not duplicate the detailed discussion of these variables given in their excellent paper.

Different combinations of values for these intermediate variables may produce identical fertility levels. On the other hand, societies with very different fertility levels may have similar values on some though, of course, not all of the intermediate variables. It is unnecessary and often incorrect to assume that levels of these control variables always are manipulated deliberately to limit fertility. The limiting effect on fertility is often, probably usually, an unintended consequence of one or more cultural patterns that have no explicit connexion with fertility.

Contemporary data for high fertility societies make it evident that a combination of very different control variables may produce high fertility. Coale & Tye(9) have recently shown that high fertility in some Chinese populations results from late marriage followed by very high reproduction rates into the later child-bearing years. On the other hand, high fertility in India results from very early marriage and high reproduction rates in the early child-bearing years, with a sharp decline in the later years. While both types of controls may lead to similar average family size, the 'Chinese' pattern will result in a slower rate of population growth, other things being equal, because the length of a generation is greater.

Cultural norms controlling premarital intercourse and the age of marriage have been particularly important in reducing fertility levels in a number of pre-modern societies. Apparently, this explains the fact that fertility was only moderately high in pre-industrial Europe. Economic historians(10) have shown that property and labour arrangements in a number of West European areas encouraged celibacy or the postponement of marriage in order to maintain certain standards of what the economic unit should be, and of what a couple should have in order to marry and raise children. Together with controls on premarital intercourse such arrangements apparently kept fertility below the levels of other pre-industrial societies. The breakdown of these controls in the first stages of modern urban-industrial development apparently resulted in an increase in fertility in some places before the long-run decline in fertility set in. The fact that fertility was only moderately high in many areas of pre-industrial Europe is evidence that very high fertility is not a universal characteristic of such societies.

Davis & Blake point out that since having some children is very important in pre-industrial societies, a society with high and variable mortality often is likely to have built into its structure strong pressures for having children early in marriage before one or both of the parents die and also for having some 'extra' children as a safeguard against the catastrophic loss of the essential minimum number. If unfavourable economic conditions develop, this may result in 'too many' children. Therefore, there is likely to be a delicate balance of pressures toward higher fertility to insure at least a certain minimum number of children, and counterpressures to minimize an intolerable surplus of children under difficult subsistence conditions. Davis & Blake present the hypothesis that this necessary pressure in opposite directions accounts for the adoption in many pre-industrial societies of those control practices which insure a minimum fertility level but permit a reduction in the numbers of children late in the child-bearing process, principally abortion and infanticide. These counter-balancing pressures also may account for the failure to adopt contraception, which operates very early in the reproductive process.

It would be desirable to have a systematic classification of societies by the values of the intermediate variables. Then we could study how particular combinations of the control variables produce a particular fertility level, and how each pattern is related to social norms about family size and ultimately to the social structure. Unfortunately, the data for such systematic classifications are not available.

However, Carr-Saunders,(11) Himes,(12) Ford,(13) Devereaux(14) and others have assembled scattered evidence on the existence in many pre-industrial societies of a wide variety of fertility control measures including contraception, abstinence, abortion, infanticide and delayed marriage. In many cases the limiting practice is not perceived as having birth limitation as an objective. Most of the evidence demonstrates the existence of certain practices in a culture without specifying either the extent of use or the effect on fertility. Nevertheless, there is basis for the supposition that more or less effective methods of population control potentially were available in many pre-industrial societies and that this probably affected fertility levels in most of them. I venture the view that such practices might have had much wider use and greater effect were it not for the rewards derived from having children in such societies and the risk that these rewards would be lost because of unpredictably high mortality.

Contraception is not one of the potential control practices widely prevalent in any large underdeveloped society. An important unresolved question is whether this has been because adequate contraceptive technology was lacking or because normative pressures for high fertility precluded either the development of new methods or the adoption and dissemination of known methods beyond a small minority of the population.

Despite evidence that various types of contraception have been known and used by small numbers in many pre-industrial societies, there are very few examples of their adoption by sufficient numbers to affect the general fertility level. Coitus interruptus, requiring no mechanical or chemical materials, has been known in many societies for a long time. Potentially this practice might have diffused to a wider group from the small minority using it in pre-industrial societies with resultant impact on fertility levels. It is difficult to dismiss coitus interruptus as unsuitable for mass adoption, since this was the principal means by which the British and French drastically reduced their birth rates in the modern period.(15) Coitus interruptus is still one of the most important methods producing the relatively low birth rate in Britain.(16)

Many hypotheses have been advanced to explain why coitus interruptus and other possible methods were not adopted or why alternate methods were not developed before the modern period. Among various explanations two emphasize the internal structure of the family. The combination of male dominance and the lack of communication between husband and wife, especially on problems of family size and family planning, is said to retard the adoption of family planning. This might be especially true if, as has been suggested by some, the wife has the stronger interest in family limitation, while the husband is indifferent. Dominance of the husband combined with his indifference on the issue might be particularly important for such a male-dominated method as coitus interruptus. Hill, Stycos & Back(17) have provided some evidence from Puerto Rico that customary barriers to husband-wife communication may be related to failure to adopt family planning in Puerto Rico now.

Whether this type of explanation is valid is an open question. There is a *prima facie* case for the interest of the father, too, in limiting fertility in a subsistence economy, since children are consumers as well as producers. Some recent studies in underdeveloped areas indicate that the father's disinterest may have been exaggerated. Studies in India, Ceylon, Taiwan, Puerto Rico and elsewhere(18) indicate roughly similar attitudes on the part of husbands and wives on many issues about reproduction. If it is true that pre-industrial couples do not discuss fertility control or family size, this may be because a long-standing consensus on high fertility leaves little to discuss.

Other explanations for lack of use of contraception in some cultures centre on the idea that modern contraceptives were not available and that coitus interruptus was not acceptable in many cultures. Whether it was simply the availability of contraceptive means which determined fertility levels historically is currently of great practical importance. If fertility levels were high in pre-industrial societies simply because of inadequate contraceptive technology, then current programmes for reducing fertility in such areas can concentrate on making modern contraceptives available. This very simple solution is no longer widely espoused, because programmes for making contraceptives available in underdeveloped areas have not been very successful to date. While it is true that no country as yet has mounted an efficient all-out campaign to disseminate contraceptive supplies and information, the efforts made have been intensive enough in some places to indicate that the motivations to limit family size either are not yet very powerful or are restrained by powerful cultural counter-pressures.

While the issue is certainly very controversial, I take the position that a variety of control measures, including some forms of contraception, have been available potentially in underdeveloped areas and that past failure to use them more extensively has been a result of normative pressures for high fertility. On the individual psychological level this reduces to a simple statement that couples had many children because they wanted them, not because they were ignorant of how to avoid having them. This does not preclude the probability that ignorance about control methods was prevalent. Nor is it necessary to assume that the size of family achieved was deliberately planned. It does require an assumption that the values about family size and limiting practices, deliberate or not, were in rough correspondence.

Obviously, at the proper time and place provision of suitable contraceptive supplies and information is indispensable for fertility decline. I am questioning only whether this necessary cause is also a sufficient cause for a fertility decline.

Up to this point, I have been concerned mainly with indicating that control measures were available potentially in the underdeveloped areas so that their absence is not the explanation for high fertility. But to support the position that high fertility was normative, it is also necessary to consider why there have been normative pressures for large numbers of births.

I believe that most demographers and sociologists would agree on two very general explanations. From either the individual or the social point of view, high fertility has been an adjustment both to high and variable mortality and to the central importance in community life of familial and kinship ties.

In most pre-industrial societies a wide range of activities involve interdependence with kinsmen and especially with children. These include production, consumption, leisure activity, assistance in illness and old age and many other activities covered by non-familial institutions in modern societies. To simplify greatly: large numbers of children are desired if the values considered worthwhile are obtained through familial ties rather than through other social institutions. If kinship ties are very important in a society where mortality is high and variable, the number of births desired and produced will be especially high in order to insure the survival to adulthood of the essential minimum number of children. Selective experience favours the development of beliefs and practices encouraging fertility high enough to minimize the grave risks of few or no surviving children.

Because mortality is such an important consideration in underdeveloped areas, it is necessary to distinguish between norms for large numbers of births and norms for large numbers of children. A considerable number of studies in contemporary underdeveloped areas have found that three or four children are reported as desired by the populations studied. This is contrasted with the six or more births women actually have had by the end of the child-bearing period. A frequent interpretation of these results is that the number of children desired has sharply declined from higher earlier levels, evidence of a trend to modern small-family values. But, it is quite possible that the number of living children desired really is not much lower now than it was 100 or more years ago. With high mortality, six or more births are required if three or four children are to survive.

In India and elsewhere the finding that three or four children are considered desirable frequently is considered paradoxical, since the populations surveyed make little use of family planning information and supplies when these are available. However, wanting three or four living children in a high mortality country is quite consistent with the much higher average number of births. Even if mortality is declining, the peasant who has learned from his culture to depend on his children for labour on the farm, for old-age security, and for other essentials cannot be expected to extrapolate declining mortality with the demographer and to calculate a long-range need for fewer children. Significantly, several studies indicate that favourable attitudes to the practice of family limitation are much more common among those who already have three or four living children. This is consistent with the view that the availability of means for birth control is largely irrelevant until what is regarded as the essential minimum number of children is secure.

This suggests that known low mortality is one of the necessary conditions for an effective social policy for reducing fertility. Historically developed normative pressures for large numbers of births may persist for a long time after mortality has fallen, since they are closely tied to many aspects of the social structure. Housing allocation and other social arrangements in high fertility countries are developed on the implicit assumption that many of the family members, and especially many infants, will die. When mortality declines, increasing pressure is exerted on many traditional social arrangements, thus creating a ferment for change. But this takes time, and historically there has been almost always a considerable lag between the fall of mortality and the fall of fertility. It is likely to be particularly difficult to counter the traditional pressures for high fertility when the mortality decline is only prospective. This is what is being attempted in many underdeveloped areas today.

Compensation for high mortality does not account alone for the differences in fertility between developed and underdeveloped areas. After taking into account the effects of mortality, the number of children desired probably is still larger, on the average, than in more developed societies.

Why does the social norm prescribe a relatively large number of *living* children in underdeveloped countries? In seeking an answer, I begin with the premise that the norm depends on how having a particular number of children affects the ability of the familial unit to attain socially valued goals. This, in turn, depends on the division of labour between the family and other social institutions and on how much the performance of important functions by the family depends on the number of children produced in it. The assumption is that family size norms will tend to correspond to a number which maximizes the net utility to be derived from having children in that society. Obviously, different aspects of the society may exert opposing pressures on the norms, so a balance must be struck. Therefore, we must look for important aspects of the social organization which support the norms for family size by providing explicit or implicit social rewards or penalties depending on the number of children.

As already noted, the familial and kinship units are so important in underdeveloped societies that we may expect relatively high fertility in order to maintain them. This kind of global explanatory hypothesis lacks the precision to explain the existing and historical diversity ranging from moderately to very high fertility. But, if the general hypothesis is valid, then specific variations in kinship structure should help to explain the observed variations in fertility. Anthropological research reveals a rich diversity of kinship organization and functions in different societies. Unfortunately, systematic study of how these variations are related to variations in fertility, normative or actual, is not very advanced. Nevertheless, some broad speculative generalizations can be considered.

Corporate kinship systems involving an immortal clan with a patrilocal or matrilocal basis and affecting every aspect of life, even political organization and war, are seen by Lorimer(19) as greatly enhancing the valuation of children. Joint family systems combining several nuclear units but with periodic fission and reconstitution of the joint family make for somewhat lower fertility, since they encompass social relations less fully than the corporate system. Systems based on nuclear, neolocal familial units make for still lower fertility, since fewer routine functions are carried out within the family unit.

These broad generalizations greatly oversimplify a complex subject. Both the theory and the evidence are in a rudimentary state. Lorimer has placed emphasis on kinship organization and especially on the role of corporate kinship systems in producing high fertility in African societies. But his work gives little attention to how the corporate kinship system affects the intermediate variables so as to produce the high fertility. Davis & Blake illustrate(20) how variations in the kinship structure operate through particular intermediate variables to affect fertility. For example, they analyze the probable functional significance of the joint family system in India in inhibiting widow remarriage and, thus, reducing fertility. The idea that neolocal nuclear family systems may lead to relatively lower fertility levels even in pre-industrial societies has been discussed mainly with reference to pre-industrial Europe. The discussion particularly has centred on various economic arrangements leading to late marriage or non-marriage, as already mentioned.

Studies in India about the comparative fertility of couples living in nuclear and joint family units yield contradictory results, with some studies indicating that couples living in nuclear units have fertility at least as high as the fertility of couples in joint households.(21) One possible explanation is that high fertility increases the likelihood that joint households will split up. But such comparisons within a society are unlikely to provide relevant evidence of how a dominant family system affects the society's reproduction level. For this purpose, the units of comparison must be whole societies or societies at different time periods.

Recent Japanese data provide a striking illustration of the close relation between norms about dependence on adult children and the course of fertility. Between 1950 and 1961 the Japanese birth rate fell spectacularly from 28 to 17 per 1000. In the same period the biennial sample surveys by

the Mainichi press(22) posed to a representative cross-section of the population the question: 'Do you expect to depend on your children in your old age?' In 1950 a majority, more than 55%, answered 'definitely yes.' The proportion giving this answer declined steadily in five succeeding surveys, reaching 27% by 1961. It is rare that public opinion on a matter this vital changes so steadily and rapidly and just as rare that we have statistical data with which to document the trend.

These are only illustrative of theories and data about how kinship is related to fertility. No one has yet been able to assemble more than illustrative evidence relating levels and determinants of fertility under varying kinship systems, but it is unlikely that significant general explanations will emerge which do not take into account the role of kinship in the society.

This is not to deny that social norms about family size may be affected by non-familial aspects of the social organization. For example, emphasis in the religious system on the importance of a male heir for ritual purposes probably produces pressures over time in a high mortality society for at least two sons to guarantee the survival of at least one. This means that on the average each family will want at least four children. Such values, based on long tradition and embedded in many aspects of the society, persist long after mortality has fallen.

Taiwan is an interesting case in point of the persistence of such traditional values after mortality has fallen and even after there is an apparent willingness to adopt family planning.

Under present mortality conditions in Taiwan a single son is very likely to survive to adulthood, so having additional sons as 'insurance' is probably an anachronism, but the traditional preference for several sons persists. The family size and sex composition being sought are approximately what a traditional Chinese family might have achieved with luck under high mortality and high fertility, but fewer births are needed now to achieve this goal. The present goal of many Taiwanese appears to be to maintain traditional values in the face of the pressures of higher survival rates by using family planning.

While a preference for sons is frequently embedded in religious institutions, it may have its origin in the value of sons for agricultural labour or for other purposes. The religious sanction may sanctify and insure what has been needed traditionally for other essential purposes.

Religious or other emphases on the importance of sons is only one of a large number of values that may affect the norms for family size, either indirectly or directly in relation to the role of the familial unit in the society. All of these must be taken into account in applying the general principle that the additional children are desired if they provide rewards greater than their costs under the particular familial arrangements of that society.

In seeking explanations for high fertility in supportive institutions and values, it would be grossly incorrect to suggest that the norms about the intermediate control variables are finely consistent with the norms about family size. On balance and in the long run a rough consistency is probable. But discrepancies between ends and means may develop and persist when aspects of the social structure not even recognized as related to fertility affect the reproductive level by their effect on the intermediate variables. For example, many religious systems prescribe periods of abstinence which usually (though not always) will have the effect of reducing fertility.

Illustrative of another 'unintended restraint' on fertility is the possible reduction in fecundity resulting from poor nutrition and poor health in the whole society or a stratum of it. For example, several recent Indian studies find relatively low fertility for the poorest social stratum. It is plausible that this may be a result of poor health and nutrition conditions in the lower status groups, although other explanations are possible.

A variety of such unintended effects of cultural factors in pre-industrial societies contribute to keeping fertility below its maximum biological potential. We really do not know, from systematic evidence, to what extent these operate selectively to keep fertility near the normative values. It is only a reasonable assumption that, if norms about family size are very important, the intermediate control variables will tend to reach a balance consistent with these norms. But, where social change is very rapid, such a long-run balance may not be struck exactly, and for short periods a large discrepancy between means and ends is probable.

Another approach to finding the variables that supported early high fertility is to study the correlates of the declines in fertility that have already occurred in developed societies. First of all, it is clear that in almost every case a substantial decline in mortality preceded fertility decline.(23) In Japan the period of lag was much shorter than in Western Europe. The lag may grow still shorter if social policy succeeds in accelerating fertility decline in such countries as Pakistan, India, Egypt and Korea. But, in all the countries that have such policies at present, mortality already has declined for several decades, with little evidence of fertility decline.

Apart from lower mortality, what social and economic variables are associated with fertility decline? Given the preceding analysis there is no surprise in the plausible hypothesis that a shift of functions from family to other specialized institutions is important. There is illustrative evidence that this shift has decreased the value and increased the costs of more than a small number of children for attaining the goals men seek in the more developed society. But the demonstrable changes in family functions are difficult to disentangle from the larger complex of social and economic changes in the course of social development. Broadly speaking, development is associated with many variables: e.g., urbanization, industrialization, more complex technology, greater capital investment per worker, higher living standards, and greater literacy. There is an increase in the mass media of communication and in transportation facilities which go with larger markets and the linkage of local populations in larger political, social, and economic units. In these larger units, a more complex division of labour exists not only with respect to economic life but also in almost every other aspect. Thus, the tasks of an urban society are divided among a much larger number of institutions. As the economic unit ceases to be the family, recruitment of workers is less closely linked to reproduction.

Because the development process is so complex, I have postponed any definition of development until this late point. At least with reference to fertility decline, I suggest that what is essential in the development process is the shift from major dependence on relatively self-contained local institutions, to dependence upon larger social, economic and political units. Such a shift implies a change in the division of labour from one in which the kinship unit is necessarily central to a larger complex in which such local units as family and village give up many functions to larger, non-familial specialized units. In such a shift, greater literacy and the development of effective communication networks are essential.

I have purposely avoided proposing industrialization and urbanization as the essential developmental changes for lower fertility, although they are usually part of the change process, and I do not minimize their importance. But I think that the essential change is the expansion of the unit within which most social and economic interchange occurs.

Some evidence that urbanization and industrialization alone may not provide the explanation for fertility decline appears in some unpublished work by Knodel & Tangoantiang at the Princeton Office of Population Research.

Tracing fertility declines from earlier times to the present, the Princeton group found that in all of the countries in Europe, with the exception of Albania, there has been a decline in fertility of 50% or more and that, with the further exception of France, the decline began some time between 1860 and 1920. The timing and steepness of the decline is not conspicuously associated with proportions of the labour force engaged in agriculture or changes in these proportions, nor is it associated consistently with urbanization. The only index examined whose movement seems almost universally to parallel that of fertility measures is illiteracy. The level of illiteracy varied widely between countries at the beginning of the decline, ranging from 24% reported in England to 79% for Russia. Yet, in each case, fertility and illiteracy declined together. A striking example of the unexpected lack of association between industrialization as normally visualized and declining fertility is that the decline began in the 1880's in Italy, Hungary and Finland, as well as in England and Wales. Literacy and mass education appear to deserve special attention in relation to changing fertility, along with the more frequently stressed urbanization and industrialization.

How can literacy and broad educational gains affect fertility? One indirect way is by helping to reduce mortality which will later reduce fertility in ways already indicated. Obviously, literacy also will facilitate the dissemination of information about the idea and means of family limitation. But I think the role of education and literacy is more basic. I suggest that with increased education and literacy the population becomes involved with the ideas and institutions of a larger modern culture. If the individual is, or believes he is, part of a larger non-familial system, he begins to find rewards in social relationships for which large numbers of children may be irrelevant. If this thesis is correct, major expenditures for education in a development programme are justified not only for developing worker skills but also for their potential effect on the fertility level, if lower fertility is a social objective.

It is pertinent that in every country for which we have empirical evidence the spread of family planning practices to attain a smaller family has been associated with a literate audience influenced by the mass media and by a person-to-person communication of their message that transcends local boundaries. In no case up to now has a government or private programme designed specifically to disseminate family planning or small family values been the principal agency for information and change.

In the pilot study in Taiwan, referred to earlier, education and contacts with the mass media were more closely related to the actual practice of family planning than were occupation, income, or rural background. It is relevant that Taiwan, a high fertility country in which a significant fertility decline has begun and where just now the probability of fertility decline seems great, has a relatively high literacy rate and also has had a rapid expansion in the circulation of the mass media and in the use of the mails for personal and business correspondence. Indicative of the possible importance of wider communication, is the symbolic, if humorous, fact that long-distance calls per capita are one of the best predictors of the 1961 fertility level for the 22 local administrative units in Taiwan.

I do not believe that education about fertility and family planning alone, completely in advance of other changes in the society, can be very effective for changing fertility norms and behaviour. Such a single specialized educational programme alone does not affect the linkage of the local population to the larger units in the broad and continuing way which can lead to the essential growing dependence on non-local and non-familial institutions. General education and literacy probably are required to do this.

High fertility norms and behaviour are too deeply embedded in traditional, emotionally-supported institutions—especially the familial—to be affected much by education or informational programmes centred on fertility alone. This is not to deny the potential importance of such programmes, once development is under way. Probably, reduced mortality sets the stage, providing the minimal threshold level required before fertility will drop. But, in addition, there must be at least minimal changes in the institutions which motivate high fertility by rewarding parents of relatively large numbers of children. There must be reason to believe that those who have smaller families can meet their needs in ways differing from the traditional patterns.

This view does not preclude the possibility that broad gains in literacy and education can facilitate lower fertility levels in advance of some other changes in the society. The extent to which this is possible and what associated changes are required is still an open question. Significant studies with careful controls are possible in some of the countries introducing family planning to test whether particular levels of literacy or of other development indices are a necessary threshold to a fertility decline.

The existence of the mass media and of postal networks already involves, to some extent, the larger interaction system of which I am speaking. If the literate regard themselves as members of a larger and less parochial society, the adoption of behaviours appropriate to that society may be accelerated, if at least minimal threshold changes in society make their new self-image plausible.

Obviously, changes in literacy, education and communication networks are related to many other aspects of development. Changes in all of them probably are related in interaction to fertility decline. But it is unnecessary to assume that all aspects of development must move together. We know that there have been uneven rates of movement in the past. From a policy point of view it is desirable to look for some elements subject to social control which might lead the development process and decrease the time-gap between mortality and fertility decline. I have emphasized education because it might be such a leading variable and it is given less attention usually than economic variables or urbanization.

To recapitulate, I have reviewed briefly the evidence that social norms support the moderately to very high fertility found in the so-called under-developed societies. I have suggested that high fertility and high fertility norms are not a result of unrestrained maximum fecundity but rather are an adjustment mainly to the high mortality and to dependence on kin-ship-based local institutions. Variations in the kinship structure were seen as a major possible explanation of variations from moderate to very high fertility. The net effect of a large number of possible control variables determines the extent to which the social norms about fertility are approximated in behaviour. Finally, I have suggested that the complex continuum from underdeveloped to developed societies is best represented for our purpose by a continuum from major dependence on relatively small local units to increasing interdependence in larger social units in which kinship plays a decreasing part. In this shift to larger units of interdependence, education and literacy not only have an important part to play but may lead other elements in their effect on fertility.

APPENDIX I. CLASSIFICATION OF THE 'INTERMEDIATE' VARIABLES AFFECTING FERTILITY

Taken from K. Davis & J. Blake, "Social structure and fertility: an analytic framework," *Economic Development and Cultural Change* 4, No. 3 (April 1956), pp. 211–235.

I. *Factors affecting exposure to intercourse*

    A. Those governing the formulation and dissolution of unions in the reproductive period.

        1. Age of entry into sexual unions.

        2. Permanent celibacy: proportion of women never entering sexual unions.

        3. Amount of reproductive period spent after or between unions.

            (a) When unions are broken by divorce, separation or desertion.

            (b) When unions are broken by death of husband.

    B. Those governing the exposure to intercourse within unions.

        1. Voluntary abstinence.

        2. Involuntary abstinence (from impotence, illness; unavoidable but temporary separations).

        3. Coital frequency (excluding period of abstinence).

II. *Factors affecting exposure to conception*

    A. Fecundity or infecundity, as affected by involuntary causes.

    B. Use or non-use of contraception.

        1. By mechanical and chemical means.

        2. By other means.

    C. Fecundity or infecundity, as affected by voluntary causes (sterilization, subincision, medical treatment, etc.).

III. *Factors affecting gestation and successful parturition*

    A. Foetal mortality from voluntary causes.

    B. Foetal mortality from involuntary causes.

REFERENCES

1. Smith, T. E. November 1960. The Cocos-Keeling Islands: A demographic laboratory. *Population Studies* 14, no. 2: 94–130.
2. *Royal Commission on Population, Report.* 1949. London: H.M.S.O., p. 24. Women recorded as married in the fertility census of 1911 and born in the period 1841–45 reported an average of 5.71 live births.
3. For example, in the United Nations. *The Mysore population study.* 1962. New York: The United Nations; and in Sovani, N. V. and Dandekar, K. 1955. *Fertility survey of Nasik, Kolaba, and Satara Districts.* Poona: Gokhale Institute of Politics and Economics, Pub. no. 31.
4. Cf. Eaton, J. and Mayer, A. 1954. *Man's capacity to reproduce.* Glencoe: The Free Press, pp. 20 ff.
5. For example, Dandekar, K. 1959. *Demographic survey of six rural communities.* Poona: Gokhale Institute of Politics and Economics; Hatt, P. K. 1952. *Backgrounds of human fertility in Puerto Rico: A sociological survey.* Princeton: Princeton University Press; Hill, R., Stycos, J. M., and Back, K. W. 1959. *The family and population control: A Puerto Rican experiment in social change.* Chapel Hill: University of North Carolina Press; Mukherjee, S. B. 1961. *Studies of fertility rates in Calcutta.* Calcutta: Bookland Private Ltd.; Singh, B. 1958. *Five years of family planning in the country-side.* Lucknow: J. K. Institute of Sociology and Human Relations; Stycos, J. M. and Back, K. 1957. *Prospects for fertility reduction.* New York: The Conservation Foundation; Tabah, L. and Samuel, R. 1962. Preliminary finding of a survey on fertility and attitudes toward family formation in Santiago. In Milbank Memorial Fund. *Research in family planning.* Princeton: Princeton University Press; United Nations. 1962. *The Mysore population study.* New York: United Nations; Yaukey, D. 1961. *Fertility differences in a modernizing country.* Princeton: Princeton University Press.

   A more complete annotated bibliography of such studies appears in *The sociology of human fertility: A trend report and bibliography,* vol. 10/11, no. 2. 1961–62. In the series *Current Sociology* published by the International Sociological Association with the support of Unesco.
6. Richards, A. J. and Reining, P. 1952. Reports on fertility surveys in Buganda and Buhaya. In Lorimer, F. *et al.* 1954. *Culture and human fertility.* Paris: Unesco, pp. 351–404.
7. Ford, C. S. 1945. *A comparative study of human reproduction.* New Haven: Yale University Press, Yale University Publications in Anthropology, no. 32.
8. Davis, K. and Blake, J. April 1956. Social structure and fertility: An analytic framework. *Economic Development and Cultural Change* 4, no. 3: 211–35.
9. Coale, A. J. and Tye, C. Y. October 1961. The significance of age-patterns of fertility in high fertility populations. *Milbank Memorial Fund Quarterly* 39, no. 4: 631–46.
10. For example, Eversley, D. E. C. 1960. Population and economic growth in England before the 'takeoff.' In *contributions and communications to the First International Conference of Economic History.* Stockholm, pp. 457–73; Habakkuk, H. J. December 1958. The economic history of modern Britain. *J. Econom. Hist.* 18, no. 4: 486–501; Krause, J. T. January

1959. Some implications of recent work in historical demography. *Comp. Stud. Soc. Hist.* 1, no. 2: 164–88.

11. Carr-Saunders, A. M. 1922. *The population problem.* Oxford: Clarendon Press. The frame of reference of this work has influenced greatly the ideas presented in this paper.

12. Himes, N. E. 1936. *Medical history of contraception.* Baltimore: The Williams and Wilkins Co.

13. *Op. cit.* (see note 7).

14. Devereux, G. 1955. *A study of abortion in primitive societies.* New York: Julian Press.

15. For relevant evidence see Bergues, H. *et al.* 1960. *La prevention des naissances dans la famille.* Paris: Presses Universitaries de France; and Lewis-Faning, E. 1949. Report on an inquiry into family limitation and its influence on human fertility during the past fifty years. In *Papers of the Royal Commission on Population,* vol. I. London: H.M.S.O.

16. Pierce, R. M. and Rowntree, G. November 1961. Birth control in Britain, part 2. *Population Studies* 15, no. 2: 121–60.

17. *Op. cit.* (see note 5).

18. For a general discussion of this issue see Stycos, J. M. 1962. A critique of the traditional planned parenthood approach in underdeveloped areas. In Kiser, C. V., ed. 1962. *Research in family planning.* Princeton: Princeton University Press. References to Taiwanese data in this paper are all drawn from unpublished work of the Taiwan Population Studies Center in which participating personnel include Dr. C. H. Yen, Dr. J. Y. Peng, Dr. Y. Takeshita, Mr. T. H. Sun, and Mr. S. Y. Soong.

19. Lorimer, F. *et al.* 1954. *Culture and human fertility.* Paris: Unesco.

20. *Op. cit.* (see note 8).

21. For example, in the experimental study in Singur, India, described by Mathen, K. K., in Preliminary lessons learned from the rural population control study of Singur. In Kiser, C. V., *op. cit.,* pp. 33–50 (see note 18).

22. The Population Problems Research Council. 1959 and 1962. *Fifth public opinion survey on birth control in Japan* and *Sixth opinion survey on family planning and birth control.* Tokyo: The Mainichi Newspapers.

23. France and Spain are among possible exceptions.

Economic Development
and the Fertility Transition
DAVID M. HEER

DAVID M. HEER *is associate professor of demography at the School of Public Health, Harvard University.*

While the Freedman article described the effects of a large variety of cultural factors, Heer focuses on the relationship between income and family size. Using concepts proposed by Joseph J. Spengler, Heer argues that the expected rise in fertility due to increased per capita income and leisure in the United States and Western Europe has not occurred because of the increased costs of having children and changes in our preference system.

Population theorists have developed contrasting views concerning the effect that economic development, or increase in per-capita income, has on fertility. One school contends that economic development inhibits fertility. This view, perhaps predominant in recent years, is expressed most succinctly in the theory of demographic transition set forth by Warren S. Thompson, C. P. Blacker, Kingsley Davis, Frank Notestein, and others.[1] According to this theory, a nation's demographic process depends on its stage of industrialization and, by implication, its level of economic development. Warren Thompson and Kingsley Davis, for example, divide the nations of the world into three classes. Class I nations are highly industrialized, have low fertility and mortality, and show little or no population growth; Class II nations are beginning the process of industrialization, have declining although still high fertility, rapidly declining mortality, but, in net balance, a high rate of population growth; Class III nations are not yet industrialized, have both high fertility and high mortality, and, at most, only moderate population growth. The theory of demographic transition, popularized around the time of World War II, is congruent with the generally inverse association between fertility level and degree of industrialization among nations today. Indeed, fertility levels of industrialized nations are lower than they were before the nations became industrialized.

Daedalus 97(2): 447–62, Spring 1968. Reprinted by permission.

A second school of thought, however, argues that economic development promotes fertility. Perhaps the foremost representative of this viewpoint was the English economist T. R. Malthus. He believed that an increase in the demand for labor increased the proportion of persons marrying and reduced the average age at marriage, and that this change in marriage pattern led in turn to an increase in fertility.(2) Because Malthus lived during the middle of the Industrial Revolution in England, his views were presumably colored by what he conceived to be recent trends in fertility in his own country. Later critics of Malthus, considering his views on the relation between fertility and economic development to be erroneous, generally attributed the large acceleration in population growth which accompanied the Industrial Revolution exclusively to lowered mortality. Several historical demographers have, however, recently produced evidence indicating that fertility may well have increased during England's period of industrial development in the early nineteenth century(3), and that similar increases may have occurred in parts of the Netherlands.(4)

Support for the school of thought linking fertility increase to economic development has also been supplied by studies indicating a relationship between birth and marriage rates and business cycles.(5) Virginia Galbraith and Dorothy Thomas have demonstrated that business cycles in the United States between 1919 and 1937 affected both marriages and births. With an appropriate time lag, marriages and births of each parity increased when business conditions improved and declined when business fell off.(6) Dudley Kirk analyzed the situation in Germany during the 1920's and arrived at similar conclusions.(7) Researchers working with such data from other countries have in all cases shown a positive correlation between birth and marriage rates and the height of the business cycle.(8)

Evidence that economic development promotes fertility also comes from other types of studies. From his analysis of both the influence of general business conditions on fertility and the effects of the relative demand for labor on young persons of reproductive age, Richard Easterlin hypothesizes that the high wage and salary levels of persons twenty to twenty-nine years old was one of the prime factors sustaining the American baby boom of the 1950's. The number of persons in this age group was exceptionally low because of the small number of babies born during the Depression. The supply of new entrants to the labor force was, therefore, abnormally reduced during the 1950's, a period when demand for labor was high. Moreover, the group entering the labor force in the 1950's was exceptionally well educated in comparison with older age groups and thus had a competitive advantage in employment during a period in which educational qualifications became increasingly important.(9)

A recent study by W. Stys further supports the conclusion that a high economic level increases fertility. Stys has shown that for Polish peasant women born during the latter half of the nineteenth century, average completed family size varied directly with size of farm. Among landless peasants, the average number of births per mother was 3.9; on farms of more than seven hectares, the average number was 9.1. The difference in fertility by size of farm results mostly from variations in the mother's age at marriage. There was, nevertheless, some tendency for births per year of marriage to be slightly higher among women living on the larger farms.(10)

The results of surveys conducted by Gordon De Jong imply that respondents of each social class would increase their fertility as their economic circumstances improved and would reduce it were their economic circumstances to decline. De Jong asked respondents in the Southern Appalachian region of the United States what they considered to be the ideal number of children for the average young couple today, for a "well-off" young couple, and for a "not well-off" couple. The respondents in the study believed that the ideal number of children for the "not well-off" couple would be 1.5; for the average couple, 2.79; and for the "well-off" couple, 4.02. Similar results were obtained separately for respondents of each social class.(11)

Deborah Freedman has been concerned with the extent to which the husband's "relative income" affects fertility of individual married couples in the United States.(12) (By "relative income" she means the degree to which the husband's actual income exceeded or was exceeded by that of men in his socio-economic reference group—that is, men of similar age, occupation, income, and region of residence.) Her analysis was made with data from a national probability sample of fecund, white, nonfarm wives eighteen to thirty-nine years old married at least five years. After controls for thirteen other relevant variables, she found that the number of children born to the wife was positively related to the magnitude of the husband's relative income. After ten years of marriage, wives whose husband's relative income was low had .42 less children than would have been expected on the basis of the other variables; conversely, wives whose husband's relative income was high had .21 more children than would have been expected.

The two contrasting views concerning the effect of economic development on fertility obviously demand reconciliation. I have elsewhere hypothesized that economic development directly increases fertility, although various other factors usually accompanying the process of economic development serve to reduce fertility.(13) The indirect effects of economic development tending to reduce fertility are often, albeit not invariably, stronger than the direct effect tending to raise it. Thus, economic development frequently results in fertility decline.(14) Making use of data for forty-one nations during the 1950's, I found that the average level of national fertility was inversely associated with per-capita net national product when no other variables were held constant. The relation between the two variables was slightly positive, however, after instituting controls for other relevant variables—the level of infant mortality, per-capita newspaper circulation, population density, and the recent percentage increase in per-capita energy consumption. Controlling for these other variables, I found that per-capita newspaper circulation and population density were inversely related to fertility, and that infant mortality and recent increase in per-capita energy consumption were directly related. After control for other variables, infant mortality showed a stronger relation to fertility than any of the other four variables. Increase in educational attainment, for which per-capita newspaper circulation is a good index, and decline in infant and early childhood mortality are, of course, two of the most pervasive phenomena accompanying economic development.

An understanding of the biological factors which constrain fertility is necessary to any analysis of fertility change. Nevertheless, fertility cannot be fully explained unless voluntary decisions concerning future children are also considered. Biological factors clearly place an upper bound on the fertility of each individual. Below the limit of biologically maximum fertility (probably around twelve births for the average woman(15)), each individual is more or less free to choose how many babies to have. Excess fertility can always be avoided even though the price for doing so may be great. To consider two extreme examples, couples can refrain from sexual intercourse to avoid a further pregnancy, or the pregnant woman can decide to abort the fetus even at the risk of her own life.

Joseph Spengler has devised an excellent conceptual scheme for analyzing the factors affecting the decision to have children.(16) He considers the decision to have an additional child to be a function of three variables: the preference system, the price system, and income. Provided these terms are given a broader definition than they usually receive in economic literature, the three concepts provide a complete classification of all factors that affect such a decision. The preference system simply describes the value a married couple places on an additional child relative to the value of goals they might otherwise achieve. The price system delineates the cost of an additional child relative to the cost of attaining other goals that might be achieved were the decision to have another child not made. Costs must be broadly defined to include not only monetary costs, but expenditures of time and effort. Income, too, must be broadly defined so that it encompasses monetary income as well as the total amount of time and energy available to a couple in their pursuit of possible goals. (Because the term *resources* fits the definition more closely than the term *income,* I shall henceforth refer to the former rather than the latter.) Given these definitions, the probability of deciding in favor of another child will vary directly with the relative value anticipated from that child, inversely with the predicted relative cost, and directly with the amount of resources foreseen as available for all goals.(17)

Spengler's scheme should prove to be useful in analyzing the long-term changes in fertility in the now developed countries during the last century or so and in demonstrating further the thesis that economic development directly enhances fertility, but has indirect effects that lead to fertility decline. Any explanation of the variables accounting for the long-term fertility change in the developed nations should, however, be postponed until the magnitude of this change has been described. The accompanying graph shows, for example, the change in the total fertility rate for white women in the United States between 1800 and 1965. The total fertility rate for a given year is a summary measure of fertility, which can best be described as the total number of children a woman would have were she to live through the entire reproductive period and bear children at the average rate for that time. As one can see from this graph, the decline in the total fertility rate from 1800 to 1965 has been very pronounced. The

FIGURE 1.   Total fertility rate for the white population of the United States, 1800–1965. Sources: Ansley J. Coale and Melvin Zelnik, *New Estimates of Fertility and Population in the United States,* Princeton: 1963, p. 36; U.S. National Center for Health Statistics, *Monthly Vital Statistics Report* 15 (11 Supplement): February 1967. **Figures in column on left indicate total births per woman assuming every woman lives to the end of her reproductive period.**

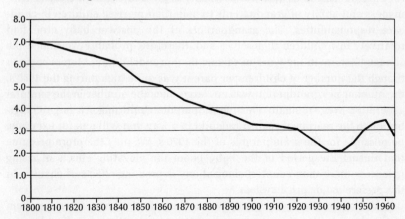

regularity of the decline, however, is distinctly marred by the dramatic fertility rise during the 1940's and 1950's. Since 1957, the trend of fertility decline has been renewed, and from 1964 to 1965 the United States experienced the sharpest annual percentage fertility decline in its entire history (almost 8 per cent).

It should not be supposed that the temporal pattern of fertility decline has been identical in all of the developed nations. The magnitude of the decline was greater in the United States than in Europe. Furthermore, fertility reduction began much earlier in France and the United States than in Great Britain, where decline dates only from 1876(18), even though England industrialized much earlier. Moreover, the baby boom following World War II was much more pronounced in the United States than it was in Europe.

The developed nations have a long history of increasing per-capita monetary income. According to Simon Kuznets, the average decennial rate of growth in per-capita national product in the United States between 1839 and 1960–62 was more than 17 per cent, a rate sufficient to increase per-capita product 4.9 times per century.(19) The developed nations also have a long history of decreasing hours devoted to gainful employment and increasing amounts of leisure time. Had there been no change in either the price or preference system, one might have expected that the long-term trend in fertility would have been upward. Since fertility has tended over the long run to go down rather than up, changes in the preference and price system must have discouraged rather than encouraged fertility to an extent that they counterbalanced the elevating effects of increased money and leisure time.

On the other hand, the developed nations which did not suffer severely from World War II (United States, Canada, Australia, and New Zealand) underwent a substantial rise in fertility during the 1940's and 1950's. As I have noted earlier, Easterlin has provided extensive documentation that this period of rising fertility was also one of rapid rise in monetary income for young adults in the United States.(20) During the period of the baby boom in the United States, the amount of time, money, and effort available for child-rearing activities was markedly expanded by the increased willingness and ability of grandparents to help their married children in child-care responsibilities. The grandparents of the postwar baby crop had relatively few children themselves and, therefore, probably welcomed the chance to share in the work of raising their grandchildren. Moreover, even though the number of children per parent was quite high during the 1950's, the number per grandparent was not large since the number in the parental generation was so small. Thus, grandparents could make a large contribution to the rearing of each grandchild in a way that will not, for example, be possible for the grandparents of the 1970's. We may therefore presume that during the period of the baby boom the elevating effects of rising resources more than counterbalanced any depressing effects of changes in the preference or price system.

In the last hundred years or so, several changes in the preference system of the developed nations have undoubtedly tended to reduce family size. One of the most important of these is the decline in mortality, which has of course been pronounced. In the United States for example, the mean expectation of life at birth increased from 47.3 years in 1900 to 70.2 years in 1964.(21) The secular (long-term) decline in mortality has had greater relative effect in infancy and childhood than adulthood. If fertility had not declined, the reduction in mortality would have tended to increase somewhat the number of living children per living parent. The United Nations estimates that for a population with high fertility (a Gross Reproduction Rate of 2.5) and very high mortality (life expectation at birth of twenty years), the ratio of population under fifteen years to that aged fifteen to fifty-nine years is 0.56. When the expectation of life at birth is increased to seventy years with no change in fertility, the ratio is increased to 0.83.(22) Thus one would expect the value of an additional birth to wane as the level of mortality declines.

There is also a possible connection between the level of mortality and the amount of emotional energy that parents invest in each of their children. It may be supposed that the pain of bereavement at a child's death is directly proportional to the amount of emotional energy that the parents have invested in the child. Where mortality levels are high, one might expect parents, in the interest of self-protection, to develop relatively little emotional involvement in any one child. A reduction in mortality encourages parents to place more libido in the existing children and thus should reduce their desire to have an additional child, since they have limited amounts of emotional energy.(23)

Lowering the mortality level should also reduce the desire for additional children because parents can be more certain of having a specified minimum number of children survive to maturity. When mortality is high, one cannot be sure that any of one's existing children will survive to maturity. When mortality is as low as it is in the developed nations, parents can be highly certain that their child will survive from birth to maturity. Thus, a decline in mortality reduces the value of an additional child as insurance against the possibility that one or more of the existing children may die. The effect of mortality reduction in this respect can be quantitatively measured. If one assumes that each couple is capable of bearing twelve children, that a perfect means of birth control is available and utilized, and that all couples want to be 95 per cent certain of having at least one son who will survive to the father's sixty-fifth birthday, the Gross Reproduction Rate will fall from 5.2 when the expectation of life at birth is twenty years to 0.95 when the expectation of life rises to seventy-four years.(24)

A second long-term change in the preference system relates to the value which parents can derive from the productive labor of their children. In the agrarian society of the United States in the eighteenth century, when the supply of land was practically unlimited, children could be productive assets to their parents at a very early age. As the amount of land per capita declined, as it did in the United States during the nineteenth century, the value to the farmer of the labor of an additional child probably declined correspondingly. In all of the developed nations, industrialization substantially reduced the value of child labor. Although such labor was quite common in many of the early factories, the situation of the child in the factory was much less satisfactory than it was when he worked under the direction of his father on the family farm. As a result, strong moral sentiment developed against child labor, and legislation restricting it emerged in all of the developed nations. In each nation, the development of this legislation was very gradual, and the early regulations were much less restrictive than later laws. The first such legislation in England, passed in 1817, merely banned children under nine years of age from working in cotton mills. In the United States, the first mildly restrictive legislation appeared in a few northern states about the middle of the nineteenth century.(25) Only in 1938 did the United States Federal Government enact child-labor regulations; these prohibited the employment of children under sixteen in manufacturing or mining and banned the employment of children under fourteen from all industry, except agriculture, which engaged in interstate commerce.(26)

The utility of child labor was further reduced by compulsory education laws which, as they increased in severity, also lowered the productive value to the parents of an additional child. Prussia, under the leadership of Frederick the Great, became in 1763 the first nation to legislate compulsory attendance at schools for all persons five to fourteen years of age. The first law establishing compulsory school attendance in England was enacted in 1876. In the United States, Massachusetts became in 1852 the first state to demand school attendance; similar legislation did not become universal until 1918, when attendance was finally made compulsory in Mississippi.(27)

The development of formal institutions to support the elderly has also brought about substantial changes in the value of an additional child. In the pre-industrial period and in the early stages of the Industrial Revolution, the elderly could expect to receive financial support only from their own kin—mainly from their sons. Gradually business corporations and governments developed social-security schemes for the aged and for widows. In the United Kingdom, legislation establishing old-age pensions for needy persons was first enacted in 1908, and in 1925 a contributory system covering all workers was established. In the United States, the first federal legislation concerning old-age, survivors', or disability pensions dates from 1935, although many private corporations provided pensions and insurance systems much earlier.(28) With the full development of social security, it became unnecessary for parents to bear children in sufficient number to assure that one or more sons would support them in their old age. Thus, the value to parents of additional children has been further diminished.

The preference system has also been altered by the decline in social rewards for bearing a large number of children. When mortality was high, a high rate of fertility was a positive necessity if the population was not to decline. Governmental and religious authorities who did not wish to see the nation's population reduced encouraged a high level of fertility. As mortality declined, however, a high level of fertility was no longer necessary to maintain the existing population level. As a result, many governments and religious bodies have shifted from a position favoring large families to one of neutrality or even opposition. A historic landmark was reached when the Church of England admitted at its Lambeth Conference of 1930 that mechanical or chemical means of contraception were not necessarily immoral.(29) Since that time, the Protestant churches have, for the most part, ceased to extol the virtue of large families, and in the present decade the Roman Catholic Church has been faced with a great internal struggle, as yet unresolved, concerning this question. Although no European government has become alarmed about problems of excess fertility—all, in fact, encourage large families through their programs of family allowances—the United States has for the first time, under the Johnson Administration, provided federal funds for the establishment of family-planning clinics, thus indicating that it no longer wishes to encourage large families, at least among the poor.

A fifth possible change in the preference system may be the result of a tendency for economic development to shift the criteria for social status from ascribed characteristics (such as birth into a particular family) to achievement. Where status is ascribed at birth, one need spend little effort in advertising one's status to others; where status is achieved, its level tends to be transitory, and individuals may develop an intense need for conspicuous consumption to demonstrate their rank. If the preference for conspicuous consumption increases, the preference for children, who do little to publicize one's status, should decline. J. A. Banks has provided extensive documentation to show that during the latter years of the Victorian Era, the British middle class felt an increasing need to engage in conspicuous consumption, and that English fertility first began its decline during this period.

The tremendous development of new and improved methods of birth control over the last century has not only reduced the relative preference for children, but has also increased their price relative to that of other goals. When available methods of birth control are crude and undeveloped, or knowledge of better methods is lacking, the decision not to have an additional child involves substantial inconvenience, interference with sexual pleasure, or even some hazard to health and life incurred by resort to a primitive means of abortion. Some of the major landmarks in the development of contraceptive technology during the last century were the manufacture of rubber condoms in the late-nineteenth century, the invention of a diaphragm by Mensinga in 1880, and in the 1930's the appearance of the latex condom, which was cheaper and better than its rubber predecessor.(30) Increasing use of the highly effective oral contraceptives in the United States and other nations during the 1960's reduced the penalties in deciding against another child and may have been one of the major reasons for sharp fertility decline. Although the "pill" was placed on the United States market only in 1960, by 1965 it was the most popular contraceptive, the method used most recently by 24 per cent of white wives eighteen to thirty-nine years of age.(31) Abortion has also been one of the principal means of birth control, and improvements in its technology have probably affected the preference for children. Little has been written about this, however, and it is difficult to ascertain the history of abortion techniques in those nations where the purposeful disruption of pregnancy is for the most part illegal.

Economic development has produced other changes in the price system affecting desired family size. Urbanization has been one of the most important concomitants of economic development. In the United States, the proportion of the population classified as urban increased from 5 to 70 per cent between 1790 and 1960.(32) In general, urbanization results in a rise in the relative price of living space. Since rearing of children demands considerable living space, the relative cost of children no doubt rises with each increase in the relative price of living space. Although the relative cost of living space has in general been increasing over the last hundred years, the rise has, perhaps, not been invariant. One may speculate that the increasingly widespread use of the automobile in the United States during the 1940's and 1950's, together with governmental policies which subsidized home-ownership, made possible the acquisition of suburban houses at a relative cost probably substantially lower than prevailed during previous decades. Part of the American baby boom of the 1940's and 1950's may be explained by this short-term change in the relative cost of living space.

The tendency for the labor cost of child care to rise relative to the labor cost of producing material goods no doubt is a factor affecting desired family size. While economic development makes possible a much larger production of factory goods per man-hour of labor, the number of man-hours necessary to supervise and socialize a child has certainly not declined and most probably has risen. When a married couple are deciding whether to have another child, they can assume that an additional child will burden the wife with the responsibilities of child care for about three years. Moreover, with another child to supervise, she will have to work harder during the period when the older children are still under her care. This increased effort must be set against the possible remuneration from a job. Since the amount of material goods which can be bought with each hour of labor outside the home has steadily increased with each advance in national economic

level, there has been a substantial long-term increase in the price of child-care services relative to the price of material goods.

A final long-term change in the price system affecting the decision to have children concerns the quality of education which parents demand for their children and which is socially imposed. A society more and more oriented to a complex technology requires that children be given an increasingly lengthy education. Parents recognize that their own child will be at a substantial disadvantage unless his education meets society's new norm. Even where the direct cost of education is met by the state, longer education increases the cost to the parent in terms of more years of child dependency. Hence the secular rise in the standard of education has no doubt helped to depress family size.

The factors connected with industrial development which I have listed have, in my opinion, tended to depress fertility to such an extent that the actual trend has usually been downward despite the elevating effect increased resources have had on fertility. It is not yet possible to evaluate the importance of the role each of these factors has played in the temporal changes in fertility in the developed nations during the past century or more. Although their relative importance may never be well established, further historical research may be of great value. I would recommend, in particular, detailed study correlating fertility change with such matters as the development of social-security systems, the decline in the prevalence of child labor, increases in the proportion of children attending school, changes in the relative cost of living space, and augmentation of the relative labor cost of child care.

Analysis of the past can be of some help in predicting the future course of fertility in both the more developed nations and in those currently less developed. For the economically advanced nations, certain of the factors which have operated in the past will in the future operate with much diminished force. It is, for example, impossible for infant and childhood mortality to drop much further. Again, provision for old-age security is now almost completely divorced from the extended kin-group, and little further shift from kin-group responsibility can be expected. Moreover, child labor has been practically eliminated, and additional change in this will be of no further importance to fertility. Thus, for the economically developed nations, at least three factors important in the past reduction of fertility will have little impact on the course of future fertility.

This might tempt one to predict that if per-capita income continues to rise in these nations, fertility will also rise. We should, however, be able to count on the continuation of certain trends which in the past have been inimical to high fertility. Most of these trends affect the price system. Since the ideal means of birth control has not yet been invented, we can anticipate some decline in fertility with each successive step toward this ideal. We can also predict that the mother's opportunity cost for spending time in child-rearing activities will continue to climb since the price of material goods will most probably continue to fall relative to that of providing child-care services. The demand for a higher level of education will in all likelihood also continue. Unless the cost of such education is completely socialized, this demand should constitute additional pressure for fertility decline. Barring unforeseen developments in transportation technology, increasing population density should make inevitable a further increase in the relative cost of living space, an important component of the total cost of rearing children. Finally, we can, I think, be fairly confident that public opinion will take an increasingly negative stance toward large family size. A withdrawal of social rewards for a large number of children might have a substantial effect on fertility preference. I believe that the public will be more and more aware of the taxes necessary to support population growth, of the ways in which a larger population aggravates urban congestion and crowds detract from the enjoyment of places of prime historic and scenic interest. If, however, the level of international tension is exacerbated, a contrary pressure in favor of larger families might ensue since each nation might fear that its power relative to other nations would diminish were its relative population size to fall.

The long-run fertility trend in the now industrialized nations will, I think, not be upward. Nevertheless, it is certainly plausible to assume that fertility may rise in several of these nations for certain short-run periods. For the less developed nations, it seems very probable that further progress in economic level should bring substantial fertility decline. In these nations, economic development should have all of the indirect effects that it had previously in Europe and North America. In many of these nations, there will also be governmental programs encouraging small families. Furthermore, the technology of birth control is now more advanced than it was when fertility first began to decline in the West; thus, the mere introduction of the new birth-control methods may bring moderate fertility reduction into populations only weakly motivated to reduce family size. The real question for the less developed nations is whether they will be able to attain a further measure of economic development. It is, of course, not impossible that in at least some of these nations population growth will outstrip the increase in the means of subsistence. If lower living standards ensue, the level of mortality may be greatly affected. Given a rise in infant and childhood mortality, it may then be impossible to obtain fertility decline.

REFERENCES

1. See Thompson, W. S. 1946. *Population and peace in the Pacific.* Chicago, pp. 22–35; Blacker, C. P. October 1947. Stages in population growth. *Eugenics Review* 39, no. 3: 88–102; Davis, K. 1949. *Human Society.* New York, pp. 603–08; Notestein, F. W. 1953. The economics of population and food supplies. *Proceedings of the Eighth International Conference of Agricultural Economists.* London, pp. 15–31.

2. Malthus, T. R. 1914. *An essay on population.* New York, vol. 1., pp. 167, 277–78; vol 2., pp. 27–28, 132, 140, 230–31.

3. Krause, J. T. January 1954. Some implications of recent work in historical demography. *Comparative Studies in Society and History* 1, no. 2: 164–88; Habakkuk, H. J. December 1953. English population in the 18th century. *Economic History Review* 6, no. 2: 117–33.

4. Petersen, W. June 1960. The demographic transition in the Netherlands. *American Sociological Review* 25, no. 3: 334–47.

5. In citing studies whose conclusions can be interpreted as lending support to the Malthusian theory of a direct relation between economic development and fertility, I do not wish to imply that the authors of the studies necessarily themselves subscribe in whole or in part to Malthus's views in this regard.

6. Galbraith, V. and Thomas, D. S. December 1941. Birth rates and the inter-war business cycles. *Journal of the American Statistical Association* 36: 465–76.

7. Kirk, D. April 1942. The relation of employment levels to births in Germany. *Milbank Memorial Fund Quarterly* 28: 126–38.

8. For further bibliography on this topic, see Freedman, R. 1961–62. The sociology of human fertility. *Current Sociology* 10/11, no. 2: 108.

9. Easterlin, R. 1962. *The American baby boom in historical perspective.*

New York.

10. Stys, W. November 1957. The influence of economic conditions on the fertility of peasant women. *Population Studies* 11, no. 2: 136–48.

11. De Jong, G. 1965. Religious fundamentalism, socio-economic status, and fertility attitudes in the Southern Appalachians. *Demography* 2: 540–48.

12. Freedman, D. S. June 1963. The relation of economic status to fertility. *American Economic Review* 53, no. 3: 414–26.

13. See Heer, D. M. 1966. Economic development and fertility. *Demography* 3, no. 2: 423–44, where I set forth a theory which attempts to harmonize these contrasting views and offer empirical evidence of a new theory's validity.

14. Actually there are four possible versions of this hypothesis. In the first version, we refer to one national population over time and examine the effect of aggregate economic development and the aggregate factors accompanying it on aggregate trends in fertility. In the second, we look at the effect of the aggregate level of economic development and its accompanying factors on the aggregate level of fertility in a set of national populations at a particular time. In a third version, we look at the effect of economic development and its accompanying factors on an individual basis—individual change in income and style of life associated with that income—on individual fertility for a group of persons over time. In the fourth version, we examine the effect of the individual level of economic development and its accompanying factors on individual fertility for a group of persons at a given moment in time. Ansley Coale has correctly pointed out that a demonstration of the truth of one of these versions does not necessarily constitute proof of any other version. My main interest in this paper is the first version of the hypothesis.

15. See Eaton, J. W. and Mayer, A. J. 1953. The social biology of very high fertility among the Hutterites. *Human Biology* 25: 206–63.

16. Spengler, J. J. 1966. Values and fertility analysis. *Demography* 3, no. 1: 109–30.

17. I shall ignore the possibility that children are an "inferior good" so that as income rises children are substituted for more desirable objects which give the same sort of satisfaction only in higher degree. I do not consider this to be a realistic assumption.

18. Carr-Saunders, A. M. 1964. *World population: Past growth and present trends.* London, p. 92.

19. Kuznets, S. 1964. *Postwar economic growth: Four lectures.* Cambridge, p. 64.

20. Easterlin, *The American baby boom in historical perspective.*

21. U.S. Public Health Service. *Vital statistics of the United States, 1964,* vol. 2, section 5, Life Tables, p. 12.

22. United Nations, Department of Economic and Social Affairs. 1956. *The aging of populations and its economic and social implications.* New York, pp. 26–27.

23. This idea was first advanced in an oral communication by Dr. Laila Sh. El Hamamsy, Director of the Social Research Center, American University, Cairo, Egypt.

24. Heer, D. M. and Smith, D. O. 1967. Mortality level and desired family size. *Indian Population Journal* 1, no. 1.

25. United States Children's Bureau. 1930. *Child labor: Facts and figures.* Washington, D.C., Pub. no. 197, pp. 2–5.

26. Taylor, F. 1950. *Child labor fact book: 1900–1950.* New York.

27. Good, H. G. 1960. *A history of western education.* New York, pp. 318, 356, 450; Education in the United States. 1959. *Collier's Encyclopedia* 7: 79–93.

28. Social security. 1967 *Encyclopedia Britannica* 20: 762–69.

29. Fagley, R. M. 1960. *The population explosion and Christian responsibility.* New York, 194–95.

30. For extensive accounts of the history of contraception, see Himes, N. E. 1963. *Medical history of contraception.* New York; and Draper, E. 1965. *Birth control in the modern world.* London.

31. Westoff, C. F. and Ryder, N. B. February 1967. United States: Methods of fertility control, 1955, 1960, & 1965. *Studies in Family Planning* no. 17.

32. U.S. Bureau of the Census. *United States census of population, 1960,* vol. 1, part 1, p. 4.

Negro Fertility and Family Size Preferences: Implications for Programming of Health and Social Services

ADELAIDE CROMWELL HILL and FREDERICK S. JAFFE

ADELAIDE CROMWELL HILL *is Director of Afro-American Studies and associate professor of sociology at Boston University.*

FREDERICK S. JAFFE *is Vice-President of Planned Parenthood and World Population.*

Both Freedman and Heer stressed the importance of taking into account societal and family preferences when investigating levels of fertility. However, the general public often allows its prejudices to distort the importance of some cultural or racial differences in order to reinforce its own myths. Hill and Jaffe analyze the stereotypes of negro fertility that are found among many whites today. They also discuss the actual demographic characteristics of nonwhite fertility in the United States and the availability of family planning programs for this segment of the population.

This paper appears in Talcott Parsons and Kenneth B. Clark, eds. *The Negro American.* Houghton Mifflin Company, pp. 205-24. Copyright © 1965, 1966 by the American Academy of Arts and Sciences. Reprinted by permission.

The authors wish to acknowledge with gratitude the suggestions and criticisms of Arthur A. Campbell, National Center for Health Statistics; Lisbeth Bamberger, Office of Economic Opportunity; Bruce Jessup, M.D., Department of Health, Education, and Welfare; Lincoln Day, Yale University; and the following staff members of Planned Parenthood Federation: Steven Polgar; Mrs. Naomi Thomas Gray; Mrs. Jeannie Rosoff; and Richard Lincoln.

*The subtlest and most pervasive of all
influences are those which create and
maintain the repertory of stereotypes.
We are told about the world before we
see it. We imagine most things before
we experience them. And those preconceptions, unless education has
made us acutely aware, govern deeply
the whole process of perception. . . .
There is another reason, besides
economy of effort, why we so often
hold to our stereotypes when we might
pursue a more disinterested vision.
The systems of stereotypes may be the
core of our personal tradition, the
defenses of our position in society. . . .
Any disturbance of the stereotypes
seems like an attack upon the foundation of the universe. It is an attack
upon the foundations of our universe,
and, where big things are at stake, we
do not readily admit that there is any
distinction between our universe and
the universe. A world which turns out
to be one in which those we honor are
unworthy, and those we despise are
noble, is nerve-racking. There is anarchy if our order of precedence is not
the only possible one. For if the meek
should inherit the earth, if the first
should be the last, if those who are
without sin alone may cast a stone,
if to Caesar you render only the things
that are Caesar's, then the foundations of self-respect would be shaken
for those who have arranged their
lives as if these maxims were not
true. . . .*
Walter Lippmann, Public Opinion

Several years ago, Cornell sociologist J. Mayone Stycos evaluated fertility control efforts in developing nations and found that a principal obstacle to acceleration of programs is rooted, not simply in objective conditions, but in the *subjective explanations* which the élite and ruling classes of most countries offer for the high fertility of lower-class groups. He identified a complex of related attitudes summed up in the expression, "procreation is the poor man's recreation." These attitudes have three major components:

(1) lower-class parents do not *care* how many children they have; or (2) they *want* many children; and (3) they have an *unusually active sex drive* uninhibited by a sense of morality or social responsibility, which derives from their basic "nature," variously defined as primitive, child-like, animal-like, amoral, and/or immoral. Stycos found that, although the evidence in the developing countries at that time (and since reinforced substantially) contradicted each of these postulates, the social policies advocated by the élites followed from their own unfounded preconceptions. Thus they placed less emphasis on measures aimed at modifying economic and social conditions (including the availability of family planning services). Rather, they advocated confronting high fertility among the lower classes primarily by "more direct" measures such as "teaching 'self-control,' reducing sexual frequency by state-provided avenues of sublimation, and the reduction of illegitimacy by legal, religious and social pressures." He concluded that "the initial and perhaps major hurdle" which must be surmounted for the expansion of fertility control in the developing countries is the attitude of their élite ruling classes.(1)

Stycos' model of upper-class stereotypes blocking the development of sound policies and programs is focused on experience with fertility control efforts, but has considerable relevance for a broader range of problems in both the developing countries and the United States. It offers an especially useful insight in the current discussion of the problems of impoverished Negro families stimulated by the Department of Labor study, *The Negro Family: The Case for National Action,* because (1) these problems are most frequently defined precisely in terms of the different fertility behavior of the Negro poor and (2) upper-class biases about lower-class fertility (which Stycos found to be universal in all societies) are in this case reinforced and augmented by racial biases as well.

The basic facts outlining the trend of white-nonwhite fertility changes since World War II are hardly in dispute. The postwar baby boom was the result of increased levels of fertility among all Americans, but was more pronounced among Negro families. Nonwhite fertility increased very rapidly in the late 1940's and continued at quite high levels until 1957, when it began to decline along a path parallel to the decline in white fertility. In the last several years, in fact, there has been a somewhat larger absolute decline in nonwhite fertility rates than in white rates. Nevertheless, in 1963 nonwhite fertility was still 40 per cent higher than white—144.8 births per thousand women aged fifteen to forty-four compared to 103.7.(2)

Through painful experience, demographers have learned to avoid offering simplistic explanations for complex changes over time in fertility behavior. Investigators are currently attempting to elucidate both the causes of the baby boom itself and the widening of fertility differentials by color, which is especially puzzling because it occurred at a time when the nonwhite population was becoming increasingly urbanized, achieving higher educational levels, and improving on some socio-economic indices. These are changes, of course, which in many societies have, in the long run, been associated with declining fertility levels.

To some observers, however, the postwar widening of the fertility gap is "proof" of nothing more or less than an all-prevasive pathology among impoverished Negroes—a pathology which has become internalized, is self-perpetuating, and has produced in "zoological tenements" of the urban ghetto a state of "biological anarchy."(3) Such a conclusion generates "remedies" quite similar to those which Stycos found were advocated by élites in developing nations: more efficacious exhortation of the poor to be more responsible, coupled with a variety of pressures, not excluding punitive and coercive measures (such as compulsory sterilization of mothers of out-of-wedlock children) which have thus far been regarded by most Americans as impermissible.

In the United States, as in the developing countries, the available evidence contradicts the essential premises of this kind of instant demography. A *detailed* examination of recent nonwhite fertility behavior reveals a far different picture—one of considerable underlying (but for the most part thwarted) aspiration for family limitation and upward mobility. It is our view that this is of the highest significance for structuring sound—and humane—programs in a variety of problem areas for those Negro families which are disadvantaged and economically deprived. In this paper, we shall attempt a closer look at nonwhite fertility, summarize research findings on the family size preferences of impoverished Negroes, and assess the fertility and family planning practices of Negro parents in the context of the actual medical services which have been available to them. From this analysis, hopefully, will emerge some implications for both short- and long-term programming of major health and social services to meet the needs of impoverished Negro families.

A CLOSER LOOK AT FERTILITY BEHAVIOR

Negro families in the United States are not divided simply into a group of relatively successful middle-class families, on the one hand, and a large, undifferentiated group of impoverished and disorganized families on the other. There is a growing group of well-to-do Negroes at the top and a wide variety of types of middle-class families within the Negro community. There are also significant socioeconomic sub-groups among low-income Negro families, as among all families, such as a stable blue-collar working class. Even in a slum, a great diversity of family structure is found.(4)

If likes are to be compared with likes, therefore, it is essential that differential fertility be analyzed among comparable groups. Thorough studies of postwar trends in white-nonwhite fertility reveal that, when various measures of socioeconomic status are held constant, white-nonwhite differences in fertility are either reduced very significantly, eliminated entirely, or, in some cases, even reversed. In Chicago in 1950, "almost all of the difference between white and nonwhite total fertility could be accounted for by differences in socio-economic status."(5) For the nation as a whole in the same year, when fertility rates were compared by educational status, the same result was found.(6) Ten years later, the 1960 census showed that nonwhites with four years of high-school education have about the same number of children as whites with the same amount of education, while those with four years of college have fewer than comparable whites. When fertility is compared by occupational status and income, there is still a gap between white and nonwhite rates. However, the gap is narrowed considerably in the occupation and income categories above the most impoverished level; while nonwhite mothers aged forty-five to forty-nine with incomes below $2,000 have one-third more children than comparable whites, in income brackets above $3,000 the difference is cut in half.(7)

These analyses strongly suggest that continuing high fertility is more a consequence of the Negro's disproportionately low socioeconomic status than of any other factor. This conclusion is reinforced when one unique variable—Southern farm background with its particular blend of rural and regional influences—is independently traced. Current higher fertility levels among nonwhites are the result partly of the *unusually* high fertility of the minority of nonwhite couples who presently live in the rural South and partly of the *moderately* high fertility of the many nonwhite couples who were born on Southern farms and have since emigrated. "When we come to nonwhite couples with *no* previous Southern farm residence, we find average past and expected numbers of births that do not differ significantly from those of white couples. *In other words, by the time nonwhite couples are one generation or more removed from the rural South, their fertility is very much like that of the white population.*"(8) This finding(9) of the 1960 Growth of American Families study is especially significant in light of the fact that Negroes who are one generation or more removed from the rural South are still subject to continuing discrimination in employment, income, housing, education, and health services which does not affect their white counterparts(10); as St. Clair Drake has so aptly put it, they continue to be victims of "a system of social relations [which] operates in such a way as to deprive them of a chance to share in the more desirable material and non-material products of . . . society [and which deprives them of] the same degree of access which others have to the attributes needed for rising in the general class system."(11)

In addition to the general improvements in economic and social conditions which sparked the overall postwar baby boom, the medical advances of the last several decades appear to have substantially affected the nonwhite rate of population growth in a manner not too different from the way in which sharp reductions in mortality rates have been the prime cause of the population explosion in developing countries. The medical advances which increased significantly the childbearing and infant survival potential of nonwhites include the greater proportion of nonwhite deliveries occurring in hospitals, an increase from approximately 18 per cent of births in 1935 to 89 per cent in 1964; the rapid fall in the incidence of diseases which often caused sterility; and the general decrease in maternal, neonatal, and fetal mortality since 1935.(12) The immediate effect of an increase in childbearing potential among a population "which is not widely employing sophisticated methods of birth control" is a very rapid increase in birth rates.(13)

Finally, much of the fertility differential is explained by a higher proportion of larger families among nonwhites. Fifth-order births or higher totalled nearly one-third of all nonwhite births—almost twice the proportion for white women.(14) (However, since 1960, nonwhite rates for fifth- and higher-order births have declined more rapidly than white rates for similar birth orders.) The significance of this finding is indicated by Mollie Orshansky's observation that "the larger the family, the greater the poverty hazard for children. . . . Of the 15 million children being reared in poverty, $6\frac{1}{2}$ million or 43 per cent were growing up in a home with at least 5 youngsters under age 18. Indeed the poverty rate among families rose sharply from 12 per cent when there was one child in the home to 49 per cent when there were 6 or more children. . . . *The poverty rate for all families with 5 to 6 children is three and a half times as high as for families with 1 or 2 children.*"(15)

Since 1957, both white and nonwhite fertility has declined, but there has been a slightly larger drop in nonwhite rates; between 1959 and 1963 there was a decrease of 11.2 births per thousand nonwhite women aged fifteen to forty-four compared to 10.2 per thousand white women.(16)

THE QUESTION OF ILLEGITIMACY

Detailed examination of white-nonwhite fertility trends also requires something better than mechanical repetition of the *registered* rates of out-of-wedlock births by color, which are often seized upon to support the image of widespread pathology, rampant sexuality, and galloping family disintegration among Negroes. Apart from the fact that even these registered rates are almost never analyzed by socioeconomic status (which would help to compare likes with likes), it is clear that knowledgeable population scholars have serious doubts of their validity. The expert committee convened by the National Center for Health Statistics and the Census Bureau to scrutinize all aspects of the collection and interpretation of fertility data points out that the published rates are certainly incomplete because some out-of-wedlock births are not registered as such; the committee concludes ruefully that "*the most that can be said* about the illegitimacy figures is that they indicate the minimum extent of illegitimacy."(17) Clearly the opportunity for under-registration and misstatement of legitimacy status is more available to whites than to nonwhites, if only because of the disproportionately greater reliance of nonwhites on public and charity hospitals where concealment is extremely difficult.

There has been one systematic study thus far which attempts to illuminate the extent of white-nonwhite differences in *out-of-wedlock conceptions* (an index that might be more indicative than *registered illegitimate births* of the actual state of differential unmarried sexual activity unprotected by contraception). In this careful study linking marriage certificates and birth records in Detroit, coupled with a mail survey, the ratio found in 1960 was one out-of-wedlock *conception* among whites to three among nonwhites, as compared to a ratio of one to eight for registered illegitimate *births*. The study also showed that while most pregnant whites married *before* the birth of the child, a substantial proportion of nonwhite "illegitimate" children are legitimized *after* birth by subsequent marriage of the natural parents. The investigator concluded that "the dramatic difference between white and nonwhite illegitimate births, then, is as much or more a function of fewer marital resolutions before the birth of the child [among nonwhites] as it is a function of higher illegitimate conceptions." In other words, precipitous marriages among whites and illegitimate births among nonwhites are largely different adjustments to the same underlying trend of rising out-of-wedlock conceptions.(18)

It should be pointed out that even this striking reduction in the color differential does not fully correct the impression given by the illegitimacy statistics, since this study does not take into account the considerably higher proportion of whites who resort to illegal abortion when they become pregnant out of wedlock(19), nor does it estimate illegitimate births to women *remaining* single which are registered as legitimate. It seems reasonable that if adequate data on differential utilization of abortion and concealment were combined with the findings of this study on forced marriages, the differential between white and nonwhite rates of out-of-wedlock *conceptions* would be reduced even further or might well become negligible, even without controlling for socioeconomic status.

This is not to dismiss the fact that a significant proportion of Negro children are born in a status branded illegitimate, nor to deny the serious social consequences which result. It suggests, however, that formation of sound policies aimed at equalizing the outcomes of out-of-wedlock conceptions can be based only on an honest confrontation of the total reality and not merely a fragment. Despite the vast expressed concern over the increasing incidence of illegitimacy, there is little demand for comprehensive studies which would illuminate the central operative factors: the extent of unmarried sexual activity among different socioeconomic groups, the true incidence of out-of-wedlock pregnancy, and the different adjustments (for example, abortion, concealment, forced marriage, illegitimate birth, adoption) to out-of-wedlock pregnancy. There is in fact considerable resistance to confronting the limited knowledge we do have, as can be seen in the opposition to extending publicly financed family planning services even to unmarried *mothers*, which would help somewhat to equalize access to contraceptive guidance between the unmarried poor and non-poor.

Indeed, perhaps nothing better illustrates élitist and class-biased attitudes, such as Stycos found in the developing countries, than our society's differential treatment of the issues of sexual morality and illegitimacy. Almost without exception, and whatever the author's point of view, books, magazine and newspaper articles, and television shows about sexual morality and/or immorality are concerned with what are regarded as lowered sexual standards in a middle- or upper-class setting (*Sex on Campus, Sex in Suburbia, Sex and the Single Girl, Sex in the Office,* and so on). It is the *changed nature* of the sexual activity itself which is criticized, approved, or explained, and the psychodynamic impact of this change on "relationships" of boy to girl, man to woman, husband to wife. It is striking that the question of illegitimacy is almost never raised in this setting since it is presumed (sometimes wrongly) that middle-class couples have access to effective contraception and, if they slip, to competent abortion. (A report by a distinguished group of psychiatrists on *Sex and the College Student* discusses, matter-of-factly, not merely the availability of contraception— "many college students view contraceptive information as a right that is due them"—but also the resort to abortion either at the hands of illegal practitioners or on dubious legal grounds or in a foreign country where the operation is legal. Apparently these alternatives, and precipitous marriage, dispose of most campus pregnancies since, the report states,"the few unmarried pregnant college women who decide to carry their babies to term usually then give them up for adoption."(20)

In the context of lower-class (and usually nonwhite) behavior, on the other hand, illegitimacy is *always* discussed; it is *never* seen as a different adjustment to the same sexual revolution which has changed the attitudes and practices of all Americans in the last forty years, but rather is presumed to be the outcome of a historic, unchanged, and unchanging lower-class promiscuity that can only be dealt with moralistically and punitively. Deluged by this veritable flood of double-standard literature (Freud and interpersonal relationships for the upper class, Calvin and judgmentalism for the lower), James Baldwin has been led to comment: "White people seem to ask us, if they ask us anything, 'Come into my nightmare with me; be like me; have abortions instead of illegitimate children.' " (21) To our knowledge, no one has yet responded to the policy implications of his observation.

FAMILY SIZE PREFERENCES

It is clear from the data that socioeconomic and educational status, and particularly the influence of fertility patterns of the rural South, continue to play a decisive role in shaping nonwhite fertility trends. Several investigators(22) suggest that the gap in white-nonwhite fertility will be narrowed as general socioeconomic conditions improve, as more Negroes move from the rural South, and as higher educational levels are achieved by nonwhites. These conclusions are reinforced by the findings of the 1960 Growth of American Families study which provides, for the first time, a nationwide view of the family size preferences of nonwhite parents. The study demonstrates that nonwhite wives want *fewer* children than white wives. The average number wanted by nonwhite respondents was 2.9, compared to 3.3 by the white wives. (Only the small number of nonwhite wives currently living on Southern farms expressed a desire for more children than their white counterparts; for the South as a whole, both groups wanted an average of 3.0). Furthermore, 46 per cent of nonwhites said they wanted no more than two children, compared to 29 per cent of whites.(23)

These findings are based on a national sample survey of married women of childbearing age now living with their husbands, but they are confirmed by numerous local studies which investigated family size preferences without regard to formal or present marital status: In Chicago, twice as many nonwhites as whites said they wanted only two children(24), and 90 per cent of a group of AFDC mothers of out-of-wedlock children said they did not want to have the child(25); in Florida, 70 per cent of a predominantly Negro group of public-health maternity patients said they wanted to have no more children(26); in New Orleans, 56 per cent of a sample of very low-income Negroes said they wanted no more than three children, 94 per cent said they thought family planning services should be made available to the medically indigent, and 75 per cent of those between fifteen and thirty-four expressed a desire for more information themselves.(27) Confirmation is also provided by the Greenleigh study of poverty in Detroit, which surveyed 2,081 low-income, largely Negro households to identify the services the impoverished families required to ameliorate poverty. The survey showed that family planning services ranked sixth in a listing of twenty-eight needed services, outranked only by such obvious needs as financial assistance, job training, help with children's school problems, and day care facilities.(28)

RESPONSE TO FAMILY PLANNING SERVICES

The above studies, though demonstrating that impoverished Negro parents almost uniformly express a strong desire for effective family limitation, may perhaps be viewed with skepticism because they represent mere verbal expression. They are, however, confirmed by the response of impoverished Negro parents in those communities where family planning services are made available to them with dignity, energy, and skill. Privately organized Planned Parenthood centers in some 120 communities are still the main birth-control clinics available to low-income families in the U.S.; among the 282,000 patients served by these centers in 1964, the largest single ethnic group—47 per cent—was Negro. The birth-control program initiated by the District of Columbia Health Department is described as "one of the most popular programs that we have."(29) In two hospital clinics operated by the University of Buffalo Medical School for low-income patients, 88 per cent of the patients are nonwhite—a significantly higher proportion than in the hospitals' other medical services.(30) Similar findings are reported from North Carolina(31), Grady Hospital in Atlanta, Georgia, and in the fourteen birth-control clinics located in New York City's municipal hospitals which have experienced a remarkable increase of more than 150 per cent in new patients seen during the last year alone.(32) In a hospital-centered maternity care project in Augusta, Georgia, a nurse tells of the response of patients to the offer of contraception: "Almost everyone who is told about it wants it."(33) In Chicago, nonwhite birth rates dropped 22 per cent in the last five years—an "extraordinary" decline—as a result of an intensive program of birth-control service and education; the differential between white and nonwhite fertility has declined by one-fourth.(34)

Perhaps the most significant finding to date is contained in a recently published study from the Chicago Planned Parenthood clinic of more than 14,000 low-income patients on oral contraception; 83 per cent of the patients were nonwhite, nearly half had not completed high school, one out of six were welfare recipients. Between 70 and 83 per cent of the patients (72 to 84 per cent of nonwhite patients) continued to take the pills regularly thirty months after they came to the clinic.(35) This is an astonishingly high retention rate for *any* procedure requiring continuous self-administration of medication, and is testimony to the readiness of the poor generally, and particularly the Negro poor, to respond to well-conceived, energetically-delivered voluntary programs employing modern contraceptive methods.

The operative consideration here lies in the combination of proper conception and energetic delivery of the service.(36) The most successful demonstration programs have, to one degree or another, been considerably different from the kind of medical care which impoverished Negroes normally receive. Instead of compelling patients to sit for hours on end in dingy waiting rooms, appointments are often scheduled (as in private practice) and efforts are made to offer a bright and cheerful atmosphere. Many clinics are located in the heart of impoverished neighborhoods, not halfway across town, and sessions may be scheduled at night or other unusual times to fit patients' needs. Staff members are urged to refrain from imposing their attitudes and values upon patients, and nonprofessional workers have been employed to interpret to potential patients how family planning can help them to realize *their* desires about family size. Baby-sitting services are sometimes provided. Fees are adjusted to what the patient can afford. And, perhaps most significant, clinics are not segregated by color.

MEDICAL CARE FOR THE NEGRO POOR

Through these and other fairly simple innovations, efforts have been made in the best clinics to approach the atmosphere of mutual respect and understanding which governs private medical practice, and impoverished Negro parents have responded. But they have not often been given the opportunity. While most Americans of higher income are easily able to secure competent and sympathetic guidance in fertility control from their private physicians, if they desire it, the Negro poor have to depend very heavily on charity or tax-supported medical facilities which for the most part still do not make family planning services available.

This denial is but one aspect of what Commissioner Alonzo S. Yerby has vividly described as "a two class system of health care" that gives the poor medical services which are piecemeal, inadequate, underfinanced, uncoordinated, and offered without compassion or concern for the dignity of the individual.(37) But the Negro poor do not share equally even in this inferior system of medical care, though there is ample evidence that their health needs are greatest. Citing current rates of perinatal mortality as an example, Yerby demonstrates that "in terms of health, there is a special disadvantage to being a Negro in the United States which transcends being poor."(38)

The net effect of this double discrimination is to discourage impoverished Negroes from seeking preventive and diagnostic medical care, and to confine their care to those emergency and chronic conditions which make medical services absolutely necessary.(39) Among those who do get some medical care, one out of three visits to a physician among Negroes occurs in a hospital outpatient clinic, compared to one out of ten among whites.(40) Even this understates the extent of the deprivation in regard to family planning services, since Negroes rely more heavily on public or charity medical facilities during the childbearing period when the subject of family planning normally comes up. Data from the National Center for Health Statistics shows that in 1963–4, 48.6 per cent of nonwhite hospitalizations for delivery were in government institutions, compared to 23.7 per cent of white hospitalizations.(41) In New York City between 1955 and 1959, 82 per cent of married nonwhites delivered their babies in municipal hospitals or on ward services of voluntary hospitals, compared with 14.5 per cent of whites.(42) In Washington, D.C. in 1961, 75 per cent of nonwhite births were staff cases.(43) In 1961, 57 per cent of Negro live births in California occurred in county hospitals, compared to 13 per cent of white.(44) The 1961 report of the Obstetrical Statistical Cooperative, based on 66,000 discharges at approximately twenty hospitals in New York, New Haven, Hartford, Philadelphia, San Francisco, Baltimore, and other cities, showed that nearly 94 per cent of nonwhite deliveries were on ward service, compared to 35 per cent of whites.(45)

These figures make clear that the vast majority of nonwhite mothers do not have ready access to a private physician during the childbearing period. They help explain the findings of the 1960 GAF study that, despite their expressed interest in family limitation, only 59 per cent of nonwhite couples had used *some* method of fertility control, compared to 81 per cent of whites, and that nonwhites relied much more on methods which are relatively low in effectiveness (douche, jelly, and vaginal suppositories) and do not require "medical advice which is generally less available to nonwhite than to white wives."(46) The 1960 study, of course, was conducted before the introduction of oral pills and intrauterine devices which, in the clinical reports noted above, have proved to be particularly acceptable to low-income couples generally(47)—but which require competent medical guidance and prescription.

Thus the denial of birth-control services to the Negro poor is an integral part of the denial of adequate medical services in general and during the child-bearing period in particular—a discrimination which has contributed to the continuation of doubled and quadrupled rates of infant and maternal mortality for nonwhites as compared to whites. Furthermore, the higher rate of nonwhite fertility, caused in part by unequal access to adequate fertility control services, in turn tends to keep these mortality rates high, since maternal and infant mortality and morbidity increase significantly with increasing parity and with shorter intervals between births.(48)

IMPLICATIONS FOR PROGRAMS FOR THE DISADVANTAGED NEGRO FAMILY

These, then, are some of the main features of the current Negro fertility picture. Fertility levels among Negroes are substantially higher than whites, reflecting the disproportionately low socioeconomic status of the Negro community and particularly the influence of Southern farm background. Negro parents in all socioeconomic groups (except the few now living on Southern farms) express a consistent desire for smaller families than do whites. In those few communities where skillful and sympathetic birth control services have been made available to impoverished Negroes, the response has been considerable. Adequate instruction in fertility control, however, is still beyond the reach of the poor because tax-supported and charity medical agencies do not yet generally offer these services. The Planned Parenthood Federation of America estimates that there are some five million American women in impoverished families—about one-fourth Negro—who are in their child-bearing years, fertile, and not pregnant or seeking a pregnancy at any given time, and who thus may be considered the minimum patient load for subsidized contraceptive services in the United States. Approximately 500,000 of these women are estimated to receive contraceptive services either from Planned Parenthood Centers or public agencies, leaving 4.5 million women not now being served.(49)

What are the implications of these related findings for programming of health and social services?

First, it seems clear that voluntary family planning services must be made available to impoverished Americans generally, including the Negro poor, in order to give them a genuine opportunity to carry out *their* desires in regard to family size. The implementation of comprehensive family planning services should result, fairly rapidly, in fewer unwanted conceptions and, over a longer term, in reduced rates of maternal and infant mortality and morbidity. Many observers believe that there would also be significant social consequences, such as a decrease in desertion and divorce, as more couples learn that it is possible to control at least part of their life circumstances.(50)

Family planning is not a panacea for all the problems of poverty and dependency, nor is it a substitute for massive social programs to enable impoverished Negroes to obtain jobs, increase income levels, enlarge educational opportunities, and otherwise improve their living conditions. But the reduction of poverty and dependency will be slowed significantly, no matter how comprehensive these programs, unless the poor, white and nonwhite, are also able to have only the number of children they want. In the spectrum of urgently needed programs, family planning is one which is achievable relatively quickly and easily: With modern methods, we have sufficient knowledge and technology; it is a relatively simple and inexpensive aspect of medical care; the number of patients to be served is quite limited; and, most important, the poor have shown considerable readiness to respond to this service.(51) It is not necessary to remold basic attitudes or develop new aspirations among many impoverished Negroes, but to provide the means of realizing aspirations they already have.

This does not mean that *any* kind of program will work automatically. If the program is proffered with racist overtones, if it is coupled with constant threats to sterilize unmarried mothers on welfare, if it is presented as a punitive means of reducing relief costs, and if the mere request for birth control is taken as *prima facie* evidence that there's a "man in the house," thus jeopardizing the woman's eligibility for public assistance, the response is likely to be negligible. Moreover, this kind of program gives credence to those groups in the Negro community who reject family planning as an effort by the white majority to reduce Negro power. In spite of these vocal attacks by some individuals and nationalist organizations, it is significant that militant Negro political figures have given outstanding leadership during the last several years in campaigns to modify restrictive laws or liberalize public policies on birth control in such states as New York, Illinois, Michigan, Maryland, and Wisconsin.

A second implication of this analysis is that the extension of birth-control services will require a very considerable expansion in the maternity care services—and in the full spectrum of health services—which are available to the Negro poor. This expansion must involve both the development of additional facilities and considerable improvements in the quality and comprehensiveness of the services provided, and in the arrangements for their organization and delivery. In other words, it will require significant movement toward ending the "two class system," certainly as far as maternity care is concerned.

THE MODERNIZATION PROCESS

Expansion of family planning services and improvements in maternity care would directly affect fertility itself. We believe, however, that there are less obvious underlying implications for a much wider range of services. Here it may be useful to draw on the understanding, which is emerging among students of population problems in the developing countries, of the "basic unity of the modernization process."(52) This concept, which means that economic and social development on the one side and declining fertility on the other are integrally related parts of the same process of modernization, may be of use in understanding the full significance of the expressed desires of the Negro poor for effective family limitation. For the concept is based upon the premise that social, cultural and psychological readiness for fertility control does not and cannot take place unless it is a part of social, cultural, and psychological readiness for general economic and social development. In simple terms, the readiness of parents for family planning reveals a desire to insure a better life for the children—a theme which is repeated continually in interviews among parents in all countries and ethnic groups who express an interest in fertility control. Thus the readiness of the Negro poor for family limitation confirms Hylan Lewis' finding that "a major aspiration of low-income parents for their children is to see that their children do better in life—especially in jobs, education and family behavior—than they have been able to do themselves."(53)

That impoverished Negroes have profound hopes for their children's futures ought to be obvious in the light of the civil rights revolution. Yet in most health, social and educational services, it is often maintained that the poor and the Negro poor are "unmotivated" to take advantage of services which they need and would benefit by. It is our view that the expressed and demonstrated readiness of the Negro poor for fertility control is but one aspect of a readiness for a wide variety of measures aimed at improving mobility, and suggests that the response will be considerable to genuine services which are properly organized and delivered.(54) The task is to use our intelligence, imagination and affluence to restructure existing service systems—health, welfare, education and so forth—in order to fulfill these hopes and not thwart them.

Far from revealing disintegration and unrelieved pathology, current trends in Negro fertility attitudes and behavior suggest a substantial reservoir of aspiration and indeed of strength on which positive service programs for impoverished Negro families can be based. In this country, as in the developing nations, such programs can be developed only with a genuine understanding of real human beings in the real world, and not with élitist stereotypes which, in the United States too, appear to be "the initial and perhaps major hurdle" to be surmounted.

REFERENCES

1. Stycos, J. M. February 1963. Obstacles to programs of population control—facts and fancies. *Marriage and Family Living* 25, no.1.
2. Lunde, A. S. September 1965. White-nonwhite fertility differentials in the United States. *Health, education and welfare indicators.*
3. White, T. H. 1965. *The making of the President 1964.* New York, pp. 221–42.
4. Cf. Lewis, H. Child rearing among low-income families. Reprinted in Ferman, L. A. *et al.*, eds. 1965. *Poverty in America.* Ann Arbor, Mich.; and The family: Resources for change. Agenda paper prepared for planning session for the White House Conference "To Fulfill These Rights," November 1965.
5. Kitagawa, E. M. and Hauser, P. M. Trends in differential fertility and mortality in a metropolis—Chicago. In Burgess, E. W. and Bogue, D., eds. 1964. *Contributions to urban sociology.* Chicago, pp. 74–75.
6. Lee, A. and E. March 1959. The future fertility of the American negro. *Social Forces* 37, no. 3: 229.
7. Lunde, *op. cit.*, p. 28.
8. Campbell, A. A. September 1965. Fertility and family planning among nonwhite married couples in the United States. *Eugenics Quarterly* 12, no. 3: 126, 131, emphasis added.
9. The 1960 census confirms the findings of sample surveys which show that the excess of nonwhite over white fertility is concentrated in the South. While all ever-married nonwhite women aged eighteen to thirty-nine, regardless of socioeconomic status, living outside the South had only 11 per cent more children than white women, the differential in the South was 42 per cent, ranging from 34 per cent in Southern urban areas to 64 per cent on Southern farms. *1960 Census PC (1)-ID, Table 249.*
10. It would be interesting to study comparable segments of the major immigrant groups—for example, Irish, Italians, Northern Europeans, Eastern Europeans, and Jews, who came from rural backgrounds—to determine how long it took these groups to approximate the childbearing patterns of urban America, and which groups achieved this adaptation within one generation after arriving in the United States.
11. Drake, St. C. 1966. The social and economic status of the negro in the United States. *The negro American.* Boston: Houghton Mifflin, p. 4.
12. Cf. especially Farley, R. April 1965. Recent changes in negro fertility. Paper presented at Population Association of America. The relative difference between white and nonwhite rates of maternal, neonatal and fetal mortality has in fact increased since 1950, but nonwhite rates were in absolute terms so high in the mid-30's that the decline was significant enough to enhance nonwhite childbearing potential; for example nonwhite maternal mortality declined from 875.8 per

100,000 live births in 1935–39 to 98.1 in 1963.

13. Farley, *op. cit.*

14. Lunde, *op. cit.,* p. 31.

15. Orshansky, M. July 1965. Who's who among the poor: A demographic view of poverty. *Social Security Bulletin,* pp. 14–15, emphasis added.

16. *Vital statistics of the United States, 1963,* vol I. Natality. Table 1–2, pp. 1–4.

17. National Center for Health Statistics. September 1965. *Fertility measurement: A report of the United States National Committee on Vital and Health Statistics,* p. 8, emphasis added.

18. Pratte, W. F. Premarital pregnancy in a metropolitan community. Paper presented at Population Association of America, April 1965. Since non-whites have repeated out-of-wed-lock births more often than whites, the published rates of illegitimate *births* give a misleading impression of the numbers of women involved. When repeaters are taken into account, the color differential is reduced even further: Pratt found that in Detroit the proportion of non-white *women* ever experiencing illegitimate conception is only about twice as high as among whites.

19. Gebhard, P. H., *et al.* 1958. *Pregnancy, birth and abortion.* New York.

20. Group for the Advancement of Psychiatry. 1965. *Sex and the college student.* New York, pp. 43–55.

21. *Life.* May 24, 1963.

22. Lunde, *op. cit.;* Lee and Lee, *op. cit.;* Farley, *op. cit.*

23. Whelpton, P. K., Campbell, A. A., and Patterson, J. 1966. *Fertility and family planning in the United States.* Princeton, N.J.

24. Blair, A. O. 1963. A comparison of negro and white fertility attitudes. Master's Thesis submitted at University of Chicago.

25. Greenleigh Associates. 1960. *Facts, fallacies and future.*

26. Browning, R. L. and Parks, L. L. November 1964. Childbearing aspirations of public health maternity patients. *American Journal of Public Health* 54:1831.

27. Beasley, J. D., M.D., Harter, C. L., and Fischer, A. October 1965. Attitudes and knowledge relevant to family planning among New Orleans negro females. Paper presented at American Public Health Association.

28. Greenleigh Associates. 1965. *Home interview study of low-income households in Detroit, Michigan.*

29. Grant, M., M.D. Testimony. *Hearings on District of Columbia appropriations for 1966—H.R. 6453.* Subcommittee of Committee on Appropriations, U.S. Senate, p. 590.

30. Lippes, J., M.D. and Randall, C. L., M.D. Participation of area hospitals in family planning. In Polgar, S. and Cowles, W., eds. January 1966. Public health programs in family planning. Supplement to *American Journal of Public Health.*

31. Corkey, E., M.D. November 1964. A family planning program for the low-income family. *Marriage and the Family* 26, no. 4.

32. Yerby, A. S., M.D. Personal communication.

33. Close, K. September-October 1965. Giving babies a healthy start in life. *Children* 12, no. 5: 181.

34. Bogue, D. (In press.) *West Side fertility report,* Community and Family Study Center, University of Chicago.

35. Frank, R., M.D. and Tietze, C., M.D. September 1, 1965. Acceptance of an oral contraceptive program in a large metropolitan area. *American Journal of Obstetrics and Gynecology* 93: 122. The difference between 70 per cent and 83 per cent is explained by assignment of the small number of patients lost to follow-up, with the lower figure representing the minimum number of continuing users and the larger the maximum.

36. Cf. Gray, N. T. 1965. *Recruiting low-income families for family life education programs.* Child Study Association; and Martin, J. S., M.D. October 30, 1965. The implementation of family planning: Experiences in an urban community. Paper presented at District V, American College of Obstetricians and Gynecologists. Cleveland.

37. Yerby, A. S., M.D. November 3, 1965. The disadvantaged and health care. Paper presented at White House Conference on Health, and The problems of medical care for indigent populations. August 1965. *American Journal of Public Health* 55: 1212. Cf. also Glasser, M. A. October 1965. Extension of public welfare medical care: Issues of social policy. *Social Work;* Berry, L. H., M.D. November 3, 1965. Disadvantaged populations. Paper presented

at White House Conference on Health; and Yankauer, A. September 1964. Maternal and child health problems. *The Annals.*

38. The disadvantaged and health care, *op. cit.*

39. Cowles, W. and Polgar, S. Winter, 1964. Health and communication in a negro census tract. *Social Forces* 10, no. 3.

40. National Center for Health Statistics. June 1965. *Volume of physician visits by place of visit and type of service—U.S. July 1963–June 1964,* p. 8.

41. Lawrence, P. S. Personal communication (special tabulation of data from National Center for Health Statistics).

42. Pakter, J., *et al.* May 1961. Out of wedlock births in New York City, no. 1—sociologic aspects. *American Journal of Public Health* 51, no. 5.

43. Oppenheimer, E. January 1961. Population changes and perinatal mortality. *American Journal of Public Health* 51, no. 2.

44. State of California, Department of Public Health Birth Records.

45. Obstetrical Statistical Cooperative, *1961 Combined report.*

46. Campbell, *op. cit.,* p. 129.

47. Workers in Planned Parenthood centers credit the doubling of patient loads in the last five years to the much greater acceptability of the new methods among low-income couples. For a discussion of the importance of type of contraceptive method in understanding family planning behavior of the poor, see Polgar, S. April 1965. The impact of new contraceptive methods in impoverished neighborhoods of New York. Paper presented at Population Association of America.

48. These relationships were demonstrated in classic studies by such investigators as Jacob Yerushalmy in the early '40's. The extensive recent literature has been summarized in Jaffe, F. S. and Polgar, S. 1964. Medical indications for fertility control.

Planned Parenthood Federation of America (mimeographed).

49. Jaffe, F. S. (In press.) Financing family planning services. *American Journal of Public Health.*

50. Without attempting to state a causal relationship for which adequate studies have not been done, Orshanky (*op. cit.,* p. 16) comments on the interaction between high fertility and family breakdown: "What cannot be said is how often the poverty itself may have antedated and even contributed to the family dissolution. Age for age, mothers without a husband present have borne more children than women still living with a husband. Knowing that it is often the worker with low earnings potential who has the larger family, one can only wonder about the possible relation between too many children, too little family income and the breakup of a marriage." See also Lewis, "The family: Resources for change," *op. cit.,* p. 7.

51. Cf. Jaffe, F. S. (In press.) Family planning, public policy and intervention strategy. *Journal of Social Issues.*

52. Taeuber, I. September 1965. Future population trends. Paper presented at United Nations World Population Conference.

53. The family: Resources for change, *op. cit.,* p. 18.

54. The potentially strategic role of medical agencies is suggested by Greenleigh (*Home interview study, op. cit.,* p. 10) and by Dean Julius Richmond who observes: "Health personnel with an interest and competence in dealing with the social problems of their patients, and operating in a setting providing personalized, dignified care, may find they have a unique entree to helping families to deal with their social and psychological problems." ("Infants and children," paper presented at White House Conference on Health, November 3, 1965).

Consequences of Rapid Population Growth in the Poor Countries

ROGER REVELLE

ROGER REVELLE *is Richard Saltonstall Professor of Population Policy and Director of the Center for Population Studies, Harvard University.*

The previous selections have discussed the nature and the determinants of rapid population growth. The next three essays examine some of the results of the current population explosion. Revelle points out the cost of rapid population growth for economic development as well as for social and political well-being. In addition, the effects of high fertility on the individual family are analyzed.

Rates of population growth in the poor countries of Asia, Africa, and Latin America are at least half the rates of growth of national income and in some cases almost equal the latter. Chiefly because of high birth rates in these countries, the ratios of the number of children to adults is very high in comparison to the rich countries. The numbers of children and of young people seeking employment are rapidly increasing.

The economic theory of the consequences of rapid population growth in the poor countries focuses on two factors: the high dependency burden (proportion of non-working consumers to workers) resulting from the high proportion of children, and the heavy investments required by the rapid growth in the labor force. During the next fifteen years, the size of the labor force will not be affected by changes in birth rates because all the new workers who will be seeking employment are already born. But with continuing high birth rates, the total national income must be divided among an ever larger number of persons, and, hence, per capita incomes will be smaller than would be the case with fewer births. Though a sharp decline in birth rates would result in higher per capita incomes, the calculated effects over the next twenty years (which is a long time-horizon for most politicians) are relatively small compared to the effects produced in different

This article is the revised and abridged version of a paper delivered to the 20th Pugwash Conference on Science and World Affairs, Fontana, September 9–15, 1970.

countries by differences in the rate of savings and investment, or in the productivity of labor and capital.

If, instead of concerning ourselves with economic theory, we look at what is actually happening in the poor countries, we see that rapid population growth is affecting human lives in many serious and often tragic ways. Even the agricultural revolution which must take place if the poor countries are to feed their growing populations may not succeed in reducing human misery unless birth rates can be quickly lowered. Problems of unemployment and underemployment, urbanization, child development, education, and ethnic conflict are greatly worsened by rapid population growth.

I. AGRICULTURE

The new agricultural technology is much better suited to some regions than to others. In India, whereas irrigation development is easy to accomplish in the Gangetic plain of Uttar Pradesh and Bihar, it is difficult and expensive in most of the Deccan plateau which covers central India. In the case of East Pakistan, particularly the thirty per cent of the country which is flooded for five months each year, existing new cereal varieties cannot be grown and chemical fertilizers cannot be used except for one crop during the dry season. National prices for farm produce will almost certainly fall because of greatly expanded production in the Gangetic plain and in other favorable regions where new technology can be successfully applied. As a result, farmers in the Deccan may then be unable to sell their crops at prices sufficient to pay for the water, chemical fertilizers, and other inputs needed for high-productivity agriculture, and they will thus be forced back to subsistence farming. However, this will be insufficient to feed the growing populations of their own villages, even though *total* national food production may be enough for everyone. Large numbers of poverty-stricken and unskilled countrymen will be driven out either to cities and towns or to more favored agricultural regions, where most of them will become landless laborers. The challenge to policy-makers, either to promote the development of new agricultural technologies for non-irrigated land, or to provide employment and a new way of life for these people is very great.

II. UNEMPLOYMENT AND UNDEREMPLOYMENT

The existence of large and rapidly growing supplies of cheap labor in many less-developed countries tends to hold back the adoption of capital-intensive, labor-saving technology in industry, and thereby slows down increases in productivity and in standards of living.

As we have noted, policies and programs to reduce the growth of the labor force by fertility control can have little effect during the next fifteen or twenty years. Therefore, for the near future emphasis needs to be placed on (1) retaining as many workers as possible in agriculture by government policies which favor hand labor and those kinds of mechanization, such as tube wells, small tillers, and grain dryers, that raise the demand for labor by fostering multiple-cropping; (2) service occupations; and (3) relatively small-scale, consumer-goods industries which in the aggregate can employ large numbers of workers. At the same time, efforts to increase productivity of these and other workers should be accelerated as rapidly as available resources allow, because only in this way can standards of living be raised. The productivity of labor in many less-developed countries is now so low that industries based on it often cannot compete with similar industries in the advanced countries, even when wages are held at a subsistence level. An extreme example of the rapidly accelerating problems of unemployment and underemployment in the less developed countries is seen in East Pakistan (see pages 328–348).

In 1985, with a population of about 125 million, some 42.5 million people will be seeking employment. If the population is to feed itself, the gross cultivated area should have risen to about 36 million acres. If we assume the same land/man ratio on the gross cultivated area in 1985 as in 1970 (on the average each farm worker cultivates 1.5 acres), there would be 24 million farm workers, and the non-agricultural labor force would be 18.5 million, or 43.5% of the total of 42.5 million employable. If cities and towns grow extremely rapidly, urban employment might be about 7 million. This leaves 11.5 million people who would need employment outside agriculture in the countryside, yet it is hard to see how more than 4 million of these could find jobs. Therefore, the rate of unemployment plus underemployment in the entire labor force would be about 18%. Either urbanization and industrialization must proceed much more rapidly than seems possible, or labor intensity on the farms must be considerably increased. For example, if the gross cultivated area per farm worker were reduced to 1.2 acres, the agricultural labor force would be 30 million and the non-agricultural workers in the countryside only 5.5 million, about the same proportion as in 1970.

A continuing increase in farm labor intensity is said to have taken place in Java with the rapid growth of its rural population. It may well have occurred during the past few decades in East Pakistan. But such "agricultural involution" may be incompatible with the modernization of agriculture which is essential if the people of these regions are to feed themselves.

III. URBANIZATION

In times to come, our century may be thought of as that point in history when the way of life of human beings changed from a primarily rural to a primarily urban one. In 1900 no more than a quarter of the world's population lived in cities and towns; by the year 2000 probably more than 60 per cent will be city dwellers. Just as populations are now growing more rapidly in the poor countries than they ever grew by natural increase in the presently rich ones, so the rate of growth of cities is now faster in the poor countries than it ever was during the period of most rapid urbanization in Europe, North America, and Japan. Not only are urban populations (as well as rural ones) growing because of the excess of births over deaths, but the cities and towns are also absorbing large numbers of rural immigrants. For example, between 1950 and 1960 in 24 countries with per capita incomes of less than $250 per year, cities of over 100,000 inhabitants grew

60 per cent more rapidly than the total population. The migration from the countryside was due at least in part to the diminishing size of farms and increasing difficulties of making a living in rural areas. Stagnant rural economies are unable to absorb their own population growth. Although living conditions for many migrants in the cities are appallingly bad, they are probably better from several points of view than in the villages.

In one carefully studied farming region of the Punjab in northwestern India, the rate of migration to the cities during the 1950's equalled half the rate of natural increase in population. However, with the increase of rural prosperity resulting from the "green revolution," the net migration has diminished by 50 per cent.

In East Pakistan, room must be found in cities and towns during the next 15 years for more than 10 million persons, twice the present size of the urban population. The difficulties of accommodating these numbers in existing cities would be enormous. New cities and towns and new industries must be created on a very large scale. Planners and policy makers will have hard choices to make in dividing scarce resources between investments to provide industrial and service jobs and construction of housing, roads, water, and sewage systems. Other choices must be made between developing many towns of 10–50,000 inhabitants and larger cities with hundreds of thousands or millions of people.

The forced migration from the countryside causes much hardship. Many of the new urbanites are young men between the ages of 20 and 35 who have left their villages to seek employment, leaving their wives and families behind. Census data for urban areas in East Pakistan show about three males for every two females. In crowded rural areas there are about three women for every two men in the 20 to 35-year-old age group, just the reverse of the sex ratio in the cities.

IV. DEPENDENCY RATIO AND FAMILY SIZE

The primary cause of the high proportion of children in the less-developed countries (usually from 40 to 50 per cent of the entire population aged less than 15 years old) is not rapid population growth, but the high birth rates which existed even when these populations were growing very slowly. Even before the post-World War II decline in mortality, these countries, because of their high fertility, had young populations.

If and when fertility rates decline in the future, the populations of the less developed countries will become older, reaching a maximum average age when the populations become stationary at a low mortality level, and the proportion of children will decline to less than 30 per cent. There will then be between two and three adults for every child under 15 years of age, instead of the present nearly one-to-one ratio of children to adults. The average size of families will sharply decrease, and the proportion of families with six or more children under 15 will become small. Today, this proportion is probably about 20 per cent. Studies of the effects of family size show that in families with many children there is more malnutrition and illness, higher mortality, slower physical growth, and less intellectual development of children than in small families. Family size is not the only cause of these effects, but it is an important element in the interacting network of causes.

A study of eleven villages of the Indian Punjab during 1955–1958 showed that in families where the mother had given birth to seven or more living children, 206 out of 1,000 children died during the first year after birth and another 95 died between the ages of one and two. In families of two children, infant mortality was only half as great, and only 16 out of every thousand children died between the ages of one and two years. In Candelaria, Columbia, more than 47 per cent of young children who had three or more siblings of pre-school age were seriously malnourished, whereas only 34 per cent of children who had no pre-school sibling were malnourished.

Large numbers of children in the family diminish not only physical growth but also linguistic skills, intelligence as measured by intelligence tests, and educational performance. These elements are to some extent interrelated. For example, heavier children mature earlier, and early maturers do better in school than late maturers. The child's greater contact with adults or with siblings considerably older than himself in small families is probably even more important, because such contact helps in learning necessary verbal skills and in developing the ability to think abstractly, qualities which underlie most kinds of human problem-solving.

Data from the British National Survey of Health and Development show that in every social class children from small families perform better in educational tests than those from large families. In the upper manual working class, "only" children and those in two-child families scored about 20 per cent higher than children in families of seven or more. The difference in the lower manual working class between "only" children and children in large families was about 17 per cent. In the upper middle class the difference was somewhat smaller, about 10 per cent. Similar differences were found in the average scores of army recruits on general, verbal, and special mechanical intelligence tests, showing that the effects on children of large and small families persist in adult life.

Many large families existed even in the old days of high mortality. The principal change brought about by the modern decline in mortality and the resulting high rates of population growth has occurred between generations; in a sense there has been an explosion in the number of families from one generation to the next. In rural areas where the supply of arable land is limited, this results either in a fragmentation of farms or in an enforced migration of younger sons and their families to towns and cities. The average size of farms in the Punjab of West Pakistan has decreased by about fifty per cent in one generation. The effects of farm fragmentation can be partially overcome by the formation of agricultural cooperatives among the small farmers, but experience shows that this usually occurs only under the impetus of strong government or outside encouragement.

V. EDUCATION

The number of children enrolled in the primary schools of the less-developed countries increased by 150 per cent during the fifteen years from 1950 to 1965, and the percentage of children 6 to 12 years old who were in school rose from less than 40 per cent to more than 60 per cent. These marked increases reflected the value placed on education by the people of all classes and income groups of the developing countries.

With rapid population growth, the numbers of children grow even more rapidly than the total population. The need for educating ever larger numbers increases the difficulty of raising enrollment ratios (the proportion of school age children in school) and improving the quality of education. Also, the high percentage of children in the population reduces the amount that can be spent per child out of any given educational budget, and because each cohort of the population is larger than the last, it is difficult to recruit sufficient numbers of teachers from among the adult population.

In 1965, the United Kingdom used 6 per cent of its Gross National Product for education, whereas Ghana used 5 per cent. However, the school age population (5–19 years) was about 37 per cent of the total population in Ghana and 22 per cent in the United Kingdom. Thus, Britain used nearly twice as large a percentage of its GNP per child of school age as did Ghana. In absolute terms, the United Kingdom, with a Gross National Product per capita of $1800, spent about $500 per child for education, and Ghana, out of a total GNP per capita of $300, spent about $40 per child.

In spite of the rapid expansion of education in the poor countries, the total number of illiterates increased from 1950 to 1965. This occurred because the number of children in the primary age group rose more rapidly than the number being educated. Educational planners are aiming to reverse this situation in the future by raising enrollment ratios to above 90 per cent during the next 2 to 3 decades.

Such an increase in enrollment ratios will be extremely difficult to accomplish in less than 20 to 30 years, even under the most favorable circumstances, and it will be much more difficult if the school age population continues to grow rapidly. Calculations for Pakistan show that unless birth rates are reduced, total enrollment would have to be increased by 517 per cent to raise enrollment ratios from 40 per cent to 95 per cent in 30 years. If fertility goes down by 50 per cent, the increase in enrollment would be 200 per cent. A 51 per cent saving in enrollment would thus be attained at the end of 30 years by the assumed rapid reduction in birth rates. The saving would be only 3 per cent at the end of the first 10 years, but it would be 30 per cent at the end of 20 years.

Total educational costs would also be much smaller if present fertility rates were rapidly lowered. Basically, this is due to the fact that the proportion of children to adults in the population would diminish. In 1995, the per cent of GNP required if the 1970 birth rates continue and enrollment ratios are raised would exceed that for a rapidly declining birth rate by 30 per cent. The amount saved each year if the birth rate goes down would be about 900 million dollars, more than four times the *total* expenditures on education in Pakistan in 1970.

The calculation for Pakistan assumes a growth in GNP of 6 per cent per year, or about 350 per cent by 1995. Even with this very high rate of growth, more than 8 per cent of national income would have to be devoted to education in order to accomplish the planned increase in enrollment ratios, unless there is a marked decline in birth rates. Practically no country today allocates such a high percentage of resources to education. If the economy grows at a slower rate than 6 per cent, the increase in enrollment ratios would probably be unattainable without a sharp reduction in fertility.

VI. POLITICAL CONSEQUENCES

In countries which do not have a homogeneous population, rapid population growth creates or aggravates political and economic conflicts between racial, cultural, religious, and linguistic groups. Numbers are an important element of political power, especially when an attempt is being made to introduce or to maintain democratic institutions. Ethnic groups usually differ from each other in birth and death rates and therefore their relative numbers change with time. The perception of these changes is usually magnified by conflicting groups, far beyond the reality.

Even in the rich countries, intergroup conflicts involving real or imagined differences in population growth often occur. Familiar examples are the rivalry between French Canadians and "Anglo-Saxons" in Canada, Walloons and Flemings in Belgium, Yankees and Irish Catholics in Massachusetts, Protestants and Catholics in Northern Ireland, "Whites" and "Non-Whites" in the United States, White Russians and other ethnic groups in the Soviet Union, English and immigrant Asians in Britain. But partly because of higher rates of population growth together with greater poverty, illiteracy, and political instability, intergroup conflicts are more intense and bitter in the poor countries. The civil war in Nigeria between the Ibos and the Yoruba, Hausa, and other tribal groups is the most tragic and recent example.

Conflicts between Chinese and Malays in Malaysia and Indonesia, Africans and descendents of Indian immigrants in Kenya, Moslems and Hindus in India and Pakistan, Ghanaians and natives of Upper Volta and Togo in Ghana, Whites and Bantus in South Africa, Jews and Arabs in Palestine, and Arabs and Negroes in the Sudan have also had disastrous consequences.

Inter-group relations may be further exacerbated by the large-scale migration from the country to the city, or from one region to another, which is one of the results of rapid population growth in most less-developed countries. One typical aspect of this migration is that people of one ethnic, linguistic, cultural, or religious group move into a region where other groups have previously predominated. Ordinary human hostility to "strangers" and "outsiders" is multiplied by the emotions of racism or religious antagonism.

The problems of ameliorating these conflicts have not been solved, and they represent a most serious threat to the existence of many states. In some cases, far-reaching measures such as mass migration or fragmentation of states into autonomous or semi-autonomous smaller units (as happened, for example in the division of the former Indian state of Punjab into two states, one Sikh and one Hindu) may be the only feasible policy options. But governments can do much by a more even handed treatment of different groups, providing not only equal but increased educational and employment opportunities and services for all, and by political and legal devices which protect minorities without jeopardizing the basic interests of the majority. These may require rather drastic but pragmatic departures from normal democratic procedures.

Contraceptive Technology:
Current and Prospective Methods

SHELDON J. SEGAL AND CHRISTOPHER TIETZE

SHELDON J. SEGAL *is Director of the Bio-Medical Division of The Population Council.*

CHRISTOPHER TIETZE *is Associate Director of the Bio-Medical Division of The Population Council.*

Unlike other animals, man has the ability to consciously limit the size of his population. Although the earlier article by Freedman pointed out that every society has had some method of controlling its population, it is only recently that such a wide variety of contraceptive devices has come into existence. Segal and Tietze describe and evaluate the effectiveness of these currently available contraceptives. They also speculate on the possible future development of different types of contraceptive devices.

INTRODUCTION

Until recently, the scientific basis of most contraceptive methods was the realization that the ejaculate represents or contains the male factor responsible for fertilization. For centuries, mankind attempted to prevent pregnancy by the simple and direct procedure of withdrawing the penis prior to ejaculation; by mechanical devices such as the condom and, later, the diaphragm; by a variety of chemical spermicides introduced into the vagina; and retroactively by postcoital douching. The effectiveness, or lack of it, of these procedures depends on their success in preventing sperm from making their way to the arena of fertilization, the fallopian tubes, on the occasion of a particular coitus. Permanent blockage of sperm passage was achieved by surgical procedures on the male genital organs.

Contraceptive technology caught up with the twentieth century when scientists turned their attention to the ovulatory cycle in the female and

---

Reports on Population/Family Planning, pp. 1–20, October 1969. Reprinted by permission. Abridgment by the editors of the present volume.

the hormonal control of reproduction in both sexes. The principle of periodic abstinence timed to avoid coitus near the day of ovulation was the first method of fertility regulation that had as its basis a modern scientific understanding of the reproductive process. That the rhythm method has never proven to be an effective contraceptive practice does not detract from its significance in focusing upon the ovulatory process as a key event for control of fertility. It was several decades before the necessary knowledge was marshalled to develop effective means to prevent ovulation, but when that moment came, the practice of contraception was revolutionized. The era of hormonal contraception was launched and, with it, the search for different ways to achieve the regulation of fertility by interfering with specific links in the reproductive chain of events.

Almost without exception, experimental efforts to inhibit fertility can be described as attempts to manipulate a key event in the endocrine control of reproduction. With the gradual elucidation of the normal hormonal requirements of the reproductive process, it becomes apparent that there are many steps in this sequence that are vulnerable to controlled interference.

This report will attempt to review the pertinent studies in this area, to point out types of work needed, and to project the kinds of control mechanisms that could evolve from our present knowledge of reproductive physiology. At the onset, a review is presented of the presently used methods of contraception.

CURRENTLY AVAILABLE CONTRACEPTIVE METHODS

The term contraception, as used in this report, includes all temporary and permanent measures designed to prevent coitus from resulting in pregnancy. This objective may be achieved by preventing ovulation, fertilization, or implantation. Interference with fetal survival following implantation is not included in the definition. The discussion covers the following ten methods which together account for virtually all contraceptive practice in the world today:

FOLK METHODS
  1. Coitus interruptus
  2. Post-coital douche
  3. Prolonged lactation

TRADITIONAL METHODS
  4. Condom
  5. Vaginal diaphragm
  6. Spermicides
  7. Rhythm method

MODERN METHODS
  8. Oral contraceptives
  9. Intrauterine devices

PERMANENT METHOD
10. Surgical sterilization

The scope of the evaluation encompasses effectiveness, acceptability, and safety (side effects).

Coitus Interruptus

History   Withdrawal of the penis prior to ejaculation, or coitus interruptus, is probably the oldest contraceptive procedure known to man. It is referred to in the Old Testament and has been noted by anthropologists among diverse tribes throughout the world. In western and northern Europe during the Middle Ages and early modern times, where relatively late marriages coexisted with close and frequent contacts between unmarried adults and where pregnancy out of wedlock was strongly condemned, coitus interruptus appears to have been the principal method for averting the consequence of premarital intercourse. Transfer of the practice into married life on a scale sufficient to influence the trend of the national birth rate occurred in France toward the end of the eighteenth century and in other countries of the region during the nineteenth century.

Mode of Action   Coitus interruptus results in the deposition of semen outside the female genital tract.

Advantages   The method requires no supplies and no particular preparation; it costs nothing.

Disadvantages   The successful practice of coitus interruptus makes great demands on the self-control of the male; some men are physically or emotionally unable to use the method. Unless the woman reaches orgasm prior to withdrawal, additional manual stimulation may be necessary for sexual satisfaction.

Effectiveness   The contraceptive effectiveness of withdrawal has been traditionally underestimated by the medical profession. Careful studies in the United States and the United Kingdom have revealed pregnancy rates only slightly higher than those achieved by the same populations using mechanical and chemical contraceptives.

Reasons for Failure   Escape of semen prior to ejaculation, delayed withdrawal, or deposition of semen in the woman's external sexual organs may result in pregnancy.

Side Effects   A wide variety of gynecologic, urologic, neurologic, and psychiatric ills have been attributed to the practice of coitus interruptus, but the cause-and-effect relationship has never been demonstrated. Many couples continue to use the method for years without apparent ill effect and with adequate sexual satisfaction for both partners.

Extent of Use   Coitus interruptus does not appear to be popular in the United States but apparently still occupies the first place in many countries of Europe and the Near East. In general, its use is inversely associated with socio-economic status.

Post-coital Douche

History   Post-coital douches with plain water, with vinegar, and with various products advertised under the name of "feminine hygiene" have long been used for contraceptive purposes. The bidet, presumably designed for ablution of the genitalia, made its first appearance in France early in the eighteenth century. The douche was the principal method recommended by Dr. Charles Knowlton (1883), one of the earliest American writers on family planning, and was widely used until World War II.

Mode of Action   It is intended to provide for the mechanical removal of semen from the vagina. Addition of vinegar, etc., is intended to produce a spermicidal effect.

Advantages   It is useful only as an emergency measure, e.g., if a condom breaks.

Disadvantages   It is ineffective and inconvenient.

Effectiveness   While the post-coital douche reduces the chance of conception to a limited degree, it is the least effective of the methods currently in use.

Reasons for Failure   Spermatozoa have been demonstrated in the cervical mucus within 90 seconds after ejaculation.   *too slow!*

Side Effects   Frequent douching and use of strong solutions may damage the bacterial flora of the normal vaginal mucosa.

Extent of Use   The use of the douche has declined markedly over the past thirty years, at least in the United States, where its employment for contraceptive purposes is concentrated among the poor and uneducated.

Prolonged Lactation

History   Since time immemorial, women have known that they are less likely to conceive after a delivery if they breast-feed their babies than if they do not. This awareness led to the deliberate extension of lactation in order to delay conception.

Mode of Action   It delays the return of ovulation.

Advantages   It costs nothing and requires no special preparation.

Disadvantages   See effectiveness.

Effectiveness   Breast-feeding prolongs post-partum amenorrhea but cannot do so indefinitely, nor is it possible to predict the extent of the prolongation. Ovulation may return at any time and may even precede the first post-partum menstrual period. If this happens, conception may occur while the woman is still amenorrheic.

Reason for Failure   See effectiveness.

Side Effects   If nursing is prolonged beyond the appearance of incisors in the baby, trauma to the mother's nipple may result. Exclusive reliance on lactation beyond infancy may result in malnutrition of the child.

Extent of Use   Breast-feeding over long periods is the rule in most of the developing countries, but it is not known to what extent this is done with the intention, or even the hope, of delaying conception.

Condom

History   The contraceptive sheath made its first appearance in England during the eighteenth century. Early condoms were made from the intestines of sheep and other animals. Since the latter part of the nineteenth century, these so-called skin condoms have gradually been replaced by the cheaper and more convenient rubber sheaths.

Mode of Action   The condom serves as a cover for the penis during intercourse and prevents the deposition of semen in the vagina.

Advantages   The condom offers reliable protection not only against pregnancy, but also against venereal infection. It can be used in almost any situation where coitus is possible. The evidence immediately after intercourse of an intact contraceptive barrier adds reassurance.

Disadvantages   Foreplay must be interrupted to put on the condom. Some men and some women perceive the rubber membrane as an obstacle to sexual sensations; some men do not like to use a condom with their wives because of its association with prostitutes.

Effectiveness   The manufacture of condoms requires a high level of quality control. In the United States, where these devices are under the jurisdiction of the Food and Drug Administration, about 997 out of every 1,000 condoms sold are free from defect demonstrable by current tests. Given a high quality product and consistent use, the condom is one of the most effective means of contraception.

Reasons for Failure   Pregnancy may result from a break or tear—estimated in one study to occur once in 150 to 300 instances of use—or from the escape of semen at the open end of the condom if withdrawal is delayed until after detumescence. The most common cause of failure is, however, "taking a chance." The risk of pregnancy associated with a single unprotected coitus, enjoyed at random during the menstrual cycle, is on the order of 2 to 4 per cent, which is probably more than the pregnancy rate during a full year of consistent use of the condom.

Side Effects   Extremely rare; an occasional individual may be sensitive to rubber or to the powder used for dusting the condom.

Extent of Use   Prior to the introduction of oral contraceptives, the condom was the most widely used method in the United States. According to a survey in 1955, about 27 per cent of all couples practicing contraception reported the condom as the method used most recently; the corresponding figure for 1965 was 18 per cent. Use of the sheath is also important in most countries of Europe, in Japan, and increasingly in developing countries where the method has been incorporated in national family planning programs.

Vaginal Diaphragm

History   The vaginal diaphragm, invented by Wilhelm P. J. Mensinga, a German physician, sometime before 1882, is still in use with minor modifications. Prior to the introduction of oral contraceptives, the diaphragm was the contraceptive method most often recommended both by physicians in private practice and in birth control clinics in the United States, the United Kingdom, and, indeed, throughout the world. The diaphragm is always prescribed in combination with a vaginal jelly or cream.

Mode of Action   The diaphragm serves as a mechanical barrier to the entry of spermatozoa into the cervical canal. The jelly or cream acts as a spermicide and as a lubricant for inserting the diaphragm.

Advantages   The vaginal diaphragm is a reliable method for the woman's use and is virtually without side effects.

Disadvantages   Because the diaphragm must be fitted, it requires a pelvic examination by a physician or other trained health worker. For this reason, it is not suitable in situations where such services are not available. Nor is it a suitable method if privacy is lacking, since it must be inserted either daily as a bedtime routine or before intercourse. The method makes great demands on purposeful behavior and is easily abandoned if poor motivation or neurotic behavior intervene. Some women object to the genital manipulation associated with the insertion of the device.

Effectiveness   Used consistently, the diaphragm offers a high level of protection against unwanted pregnancy, reflected by a failure rate of 2–3 pregnancies per 100 women per year. However, perfect use without any omissions is rarely achieved. In clinical practice a pregnancy rate of 10 per 100 women per year is quite satisfactory and much higher rates (20 to 30) have been reported for populations not yet accustomed to the practice of contraception.

Reasons for Failure   Even a well-fitted diaphragm may be incorrectly inserted so that it fails to cover the cervix, or it may be displaced during the orgastic expansion of the inner two-thirds of the vaginal barrel.

Side Effects   Reactions to rubber or to one of the components of jelly or cream have been reported in rare cases.

Extent and Continuation of Use   Prior to the introduction of oral contraceptives, the diaphragm was used by about one-fourth of all couples in the United States who used any form of contraception. By 1965 the share of the diaphragm in total contraceptive practice had dropped to about one-tenth of all users. It has always been less popular in Europe and in other regions for which information is available.

   In general, use of the diaphragm is directly associated with socioeconomic status. While middle-class women have found the method acceptable, rates of continuing use among the clientele of birth control clinics have been disappointingly low.

Spermicides

History   Jellies and creams and, more recently, vaginal foams, with highly spermicidal action, intended for use without a diaphragm, have been developed by the pharmaceutical industry in recent years. Other vehicles for the introduction of spermicidal substances are suppositories that melt in the vagina and tablets that crumble and dissolve on contact with moisture to release carbon dioxide, producing a dense foam.

Mode of Action   These materials immobilize sperm on contact with the ejaculate.

Advantages   Spermicides are relatively simple to use and do not require a pelvic examination; foam tablets, at least, are inexpensive.

Disadvantages   Many users complain of vaginal leakage ("messiness") and excessive lubrication. Suppositories and foam tablets require a waiting period of several minutes to allow for melting or disintegration.

Effectiveness   Spermicides used alone appear to be less effective than spermicides used in combination with the diaphragm. According to clinical trials in the United States, vaginal foams appear to be more effective than other types of spermicides.

Reasons for Failure   An inadequate quantity or quality of the spermicidal material is the most obvious reason for failure. Some spermicides dissolve or disintegrate slowly and are inadequately distributed throughout the vagina. Some couples fail to observe the waiting period.

Side Effects   Irritation and/or inflammatory changes of the mucous membrane have been reported in rare cases.

Extent of Use   The use of spermicides is of relatively minor importance in the United States, with vaginal foam and suppositories as the leading types. They are apparently more popular in Europe. In spite of many failures, foam tablets are still an important method in the family planning programs of some developing countries.

Rhythm Method

History   The notion that women are able to conceive during part of the menstrual cycle only is very old. However, early ideas of the fertile and sterile periods of the menstrual cycle were often the opposite of what is known today.

At the present time, two varieties of the rhythm method are practiced: calendar rhythm and temperature rhythm. Calendar rhythm was developed independently in the 1920's by Ogino in Japan and Knaus in Austria. According to these authors, the day of ovulation can be estimated by means of a formula based on the individual woman's menstrual history recorded over a number of months. Abstinence is prescribed for a few days before and after the estimated day of ovulation.

More recently, observation of the typical changes of basal body temperature during the menstrual cycle has been used to determine the fact that ovulation has occurred and conception is no longer possible during the cycle in question. Marital relations are permitted during the post-ovulatory phase only.

Mode of Action   The rhythm method is based on the avoidance of coitus on the days it could result in the simultaneous presence of a fertilizable ovum and motile spermatozoa.

Advantages   Rhythm is the only contraceptive method currently sanctioned by the Roman Catholic Church.

Disadvantages   Opportunity for coitus is greatly reduced, especially with temperature rhythm. It is unsuitable for women with grossly irregular menstrual cycles.

Effectiveness   The contraceptive effectiveness of the rhythm method has been the subject of much controversy. Correctly taught, correctly understood, and consistently practiced, the rhythm method may be quite effective, especially the temperature rhythm method. However, successful practice requires considerable self-control and an equally strong desire to control fertility. Self-taught rhythm, haphazardly practiced, is a very ineffectual method of contraception.

Reasons for Failure   Apart from "taking a chance" on a day known as "unsafe," the principal reasons for failure of calendar rhythm are errors in recording the menstrual history, errors in computation, the inherent variability of the menstrual pattern, and exceptionally long survival of sperm in the female genital tract. The principal reasons for failure of the temperature rhythm method are errors in reading the thermometer and errors in interpreting the temperature curve.

Side effects   None.

Extent of Use   The rhythm method is widely used among Roman Catholics to whom other methods are prohibited by their faith. According to a survey in 1955, rhythm accounted for about one-half of all contraceptive practice by Catholics in the United States. By 1965, the proportions had declined to about one-third. In general, use of the rhythm method among Catholics is directly proportional to socio-economic status.

Oral Contraceptives (OCs)

History   Oral contraception has long been an attractive solution to the problem of fertility control. Ancient manuscripts are replete with prescriptions for potions and other oral medications, whose exotic content and application appear to have no rationale to the modern reader. Over the past decade, the work of John Rock, the late Gregory Pincus, and other pioneers associated with the development of "the pill" has brought the concept of the somewhat mysterious early oral medicaments into the realm of reality. Following extensive investigation in the laboratory and some clinical study, field trials of oral contraceptives began in 1956. Four years later, the first oral contraceptive was approved for general distribution by the Food and

Drug Administration. Since then the use of these compounds has spread rapidly throughout the world.

Mode of Action The oral contraceptives discussed in this report are synthetic compounds, some of which are similar in structure to the natural hormones associated with the menstrual cycle and with pregnancy in the human female. In the dosages currently used, these compounds suppress ovulation. The nature and importance of additional antifertility effects is still under investigation.

The OCs now in general use are prescribed according to two distinct regimens—combined and sequential. Under the combined regimen, 20 (or 21) identical tablets, containing one of several synthetic progestins as well as estrogen, are taken from the 5th to the 24th (or 25th) day of the cycle. Under the sequential regimen, 15 (or 16) tablets, containing estrogen only, are followed by 5 tablets containing progestin and estrogen. Under both regimens, suspension of medication ordinarily results in withdrawal bleeding within a few days. Medication is then resumed on the 5th day of the new cycle. An alternative procedure is "3 weeks on the pill, 1 week off." The substitution of inert tablets for the "off" week may facilitate following the regimen.

Advantages The outstanding advantage of oral contraceptives is their almost complete effectiveness, according to available clinical studies. Women who faithfully adhere to the regimen can be completely free of the fear of an unwanted pregnancy. Another advantage is that its application is not immediately related to sexual activity.

Disadvantages See side effects.

Effectiveness Taken according to the regimen prescribed, OCs of the combined type are almost 100 per cent effective in preventing unwanted pregnancy. Major reports published since 1962 cover an aggregate of some 200,000 cycles of medication, accumulated by more than 13,000 women. During this period of use only 15 pregnancies occurred that were not associated with the omission of one or more tablets, according to the statements of the users. The corresponding pregnancy rate is 0.1 per 100 women per year.

Sequential OCs are somewhat less effective and have a pregnancy rate of 0.5 per 100 women per year, based on 70,000 cycles and 25 pregnancies, apparently resulting from method failure.

Reasons for Failure The only important reason for failure is the omission of one or more tablets during the prescribed cycle of medication. If patient failures are included, the pregnancy rate rises to about 0.7 per 100 women per year under the combined regimen and to 1.4 per 100 women under the sequential regimen, according to published reports.

Side Effects The early use of OCs is frequently associated with symptoms similar to those occurring during early pregnancy, such as nausea, vomiting, or breast engorgement, which are primarily related to the estrogen content of the tablets. Other common complaints are breakthrough bleeding during medication, weight gain, headache, dizziness, and a brownish discoloration of the facial epidermis known as chloasma. While most of these symptoms are usually relieved within a few months, some users are discouraged and turn to other methods or even abandon their efforts at family planning.

In addition to the relatively trivial complaints associated with early use, a wide range of adverse experiences has been observed, some of which have been attributed to the medication. The evaluation of these findings is extremely difficult because the conditions under consideration also occur among women who are not "on the pill" and may therefore be expected to occur to some extent among the millions of women taking these compounds regularly. Available observations have failed, as yet, to establish or to exclude a statistical association with oral contraception for most of the adverse experiences reported in the literature.

The one important condition for which an association has been established is thromboembolic disease, including its sometimes fatal outcome, pulmonary embolism.

Definitive statistical evidence was first provided by three major investigations in the United Kingdom, published in 1967–69. Each of these studies was based on a comparison of "cases" (with thromboembolic disease) and "controls" (without thromboembolic disease); each yielded statistically significant results.

A fourth investigation of the association of thromboembolic disease with the use of OCs was completed in the United States in 1969.

According to these studies, the incidence of thromboembolic disease of the venous system appears to be several times as high among women taking OCs as among otherwise comparable women not using these compounds.

The excess mortality from pulmonary embolism or infarction, attributable to the use of OCs, may be estimated at 3 deaths per year per 100,000 users. This excess mortality is reflected by increasing numbers of deaths due to thromboembolism among women of reproductive age in the United Kingdom and in the United States.

The significance of excess mortality from thromboembolic disease should be weighed against a current annual death rate in the United Kingdom from all causes of about 100 per 100,000 women of reproductive age, 15–44 years, and against a risk to maternal life resulting from or associated with pregnancy and delivery exclusive of death from illegal abortion, of about 25 per 100,000 pregnancies. The comparable rates in the United States are slightly higher.

In early 1970, a group of investigators in the United Kingdom, Sweden, and Denmark demonstrated a positive correlation between the amount of estrogen contained in OCs and the risk of pulmonary embolism, deep vein thrombosis, cerebral thrombosis and coronary thrombosis. No significant differences were found between combined and sequential preparations containing the same amount of estrogen, nor between the two estrogens, ethinylestradiol and mestranol. As a result of these findings, health authorities in a number of countries have taken steps to restrict the use of OCs with a high estrogen component.

The effect of prolonged suppression of ovulation on the pituitary gland

and on the ovaries is still under study. As a rule, the cycle of ovulation and menstruation is promptly restored when medication is discontinued and, with it, the capacity to conceive and bear. Laboratory studies of carbohydrate metabolism, hepatic and thyroid function, and other body functions have, in some instances, revealed deviations from normal values. The evaluation of the significance of these changes for the health of the individual requires further study.

In 1969 a survey of women attending the clinics of Planned Parenthood of New York City revealed a higher prevalence of epithelial abnormalities, diagnosed as carcinoma in situ, among women using OCs compared with those using the diaphragm. These women had never been subject to systematic cytologic screening prior to this study, but some of them may have had Papanicolaou smears done in other cancer detection programs. The diagnosis was made in each case on the basis of a biopsy, examined by two pathologists without knowledge of the contraceptive used.

Since the effect of all known carcinogens in humans is delayed, with a latent period of about a decade, it will not be possible to make a definitive statement on this point until substantial numbers of women have used OCs for prolonged periods.

On the basis of current experience, fertility is unimpaired among most women who discontinue the use of OCs in order to plan a pregnancy. Isolated cases of prolonged amenorrhea following discontinuation have been reported, but the available data do not permit an evaluation of the frequency of this phenomenon as compared with the general female population of reproductive age. While no increase has been noted in the prevalence of congenital malformations among children born to women taking OCs, there is a definite need for well-designed epidemiologic studies of the possible effect of long-term use on the individual and on her progeny.

Extent and Continuation of Use   The high acceptability of the OCs in the United States is attested by the fact that within five years of the approval of the first product by the Food and Drug Administration for general distribution throughout the country, current users reached about 3.8 million, accounting for close to one-quarter of all contraceptive practice in the United States. By mid-1968 the number of women "on the pill" in the United States had risen to more than 8 million. Other countries accounted for a slightly larger number of current users, with the highest rates of use reported from Australia and New Zealand, Canada, the United Kingdom and West Germany. The number of users in Latin America exceeds 2 million and appears to be growing rapidly.

While in the United States the OCs are most popular among younger women with better than average education, there is general consensus among clinicians that most women, including those with limited education, can be taught to take them with reasonable consistency and that this method of birth control has proved acceptable to many couples who had been unwilling to try the traditional methods or unable to use them successfully.

A major measure of the acceptability of a fertility regulating method is the continuation rate, indicating the proportion of couples still using the method at a given time after use was initiated. For the OCs, data from a national survey in the United States suggests a continuation rate of 73 per cent after 12 months and about 62 per cent after 24 months, excluding women who discontinued use because they wanted to plan a pregnancy. The continuation rate was higher among the younger women and those with a better education than among their older and less well-educated sisters, but the differences were not very large.

It is possible to improve the continuation rate by appropriate educational techniques. This is illustrated by an investigation in Chicago, based on the experience of 14,400 women for whom OCs had been prescribed at Planned Parenthood centers over a period of three years as a routine service procedure, and not as a research project, with special efforts to ensure maximum continuity. At least 72 per cent of the women and perhaps as many as 85 per cent, were still current users after 24 months, a substantially higher proportion than noted in the national sample.

Preliminary evaluations of recent attempts to introduce OCs into the national family planning programs of several developing countries have revealed lower continuation rates than had been expected on the basis of experience in the United States. It is reasonable to assume that small women, especially those suffering from malnutrition, react with severe vomiting and other gastrointestinal symptoms to amounts of estrogen that are easily tolerated by heavier and well-fed women. Nevertheless, since the OCs have proved themselves far superior to the traditional methods among low-income groups in the developed countries, it may be expected that they will also be more useful in the developing countries.

Intrauterine Devices (IUDs)

History   Various types of intrauterine or, more accurately, intracervical devices have been used, on a relatively small scale, since the nineteenth century. The better known early models were in the shape of collar buttons and wishbones. Although these devices had their advocates, the majority of gynecologists rejected them as abortifacients and also because their use, at least in untrained hands, was associated with inflammatory conditions of the pelvic organs which, in those days, were difficult to treat and not infrequently fatal.

In 1928, Gräfenberg of Berlin reported on his experience with an intrauterine ring, which he had first made of silkworm gut and later of silver wire. After a brief flurry of popularity, opposition to the new device developed rapidly and universally among gynecologists, the majority of whom had never had any experience with it, but judged it in terms of what they had been taught about its forerunners. For almost thirty years, textbooks of gynecology, if they discussed contraception at all, mentioned the Gräfenberg ring only to condemn it.

The era of the modern IUDs had to await the availability of new chemically inert materials, such as plastics and stainless steel, which could remain in the uterus indefinitely. In 1962, the Population Council inaugurated an intensive research program, which includes experimentation in the laboratory as well as clinical and field trials. The results of these trials have encouraged the adoption of IUDs as the method of choice in the national family planning programs of a number of countries.

Mode of Action The precise mode of action of the IUD remains uncertain in spite of intensive research during the past few years. An early theory, supported by experiments on super-ovulated and artificially inseminated monkeys, held that the movement of the ovum through the fallopian tube is greatly accelerated in the presence of an IUD and that the ovum is either not fertilized at all or, if fertilized, reaches the uterine cavity at a time when neither the ovum nor the endometrium is ready for implantation. This theory has been abandoned on the basis of findings in naturally ovulating and cohabiting animals.

In 1968 a scientific group convened by the World Health Organization agreed that the common denominator for the anti-fertility effect of the IUD in all mammalian species is a hostile uterine environment which either destroys or damages the sperm on its way to the arena of fertilization or interferes with the implantation of the fertilized ovum when it reaches the uterus. The common histological basis of the hostile uterine environment appears to be lencocytic infiltration of the endometrium.

The view that the IUD acts as a mild irritant on the endometrium is further supported by the observation that the anti-fertility effect can be greatly increased by the addition of a metallic element such as a length of copper wire tightly wound around the stem of the device. There is no evidence that the antifertility effect of the IUD involves interference with the implanted embryo.

Advantages The IUD is a method of contraception particularly suitable for large-scale programs where the intelligence and motivation of the individual members of the target population may vary considerably. The one action and the one decision that is required of a couple is to have an IUD inserted. For the majority of the couples, the IUD is effective, safe, and acceptable. Furthermore, the fact that its use is disassociated from the sexual act appeals to couples at all social levels. The IUD is economical, and national programs for mass application of its use are relatively easy to develop.

Disadvantages See side effects.

Effectiveness The largest body of clinical data on the effectiveness of IUDs has been assembled under the Cooperative Statistical Program (CSP). The most recent report of the CSP, as of 1968, covers more than 400,000 woman-months of use experienced by almost 24,000 women. This project represents the first attempt in the history of fertility regulation to evaluate a new method from its inception by the systematic analysis of pooled data, using uniform procedures and a sophisticated statistical approach. Other sources of data are independent investigations in Chile, Taiwan, Korea, Pakistan, and elsewhere.

Analysis of the CSP data has revealed pregnancy rates for the most effective IUDs on the order of 1.5 to 3.0 per 100 women during the first year and lower rates during subsequent years. Somewhat higher pregnancy rates can be expected under the conditions of a public health program, since the

IUD may be expelled without its being noticed by the wearer. The frequent checkups, customary in clinical studies, increase the chance of discovering an unnoticed expulsion before pregnancy occurs.

The contraceptive effectiveness of the IUD is largely independent of the patient's psychology and social background. Well-educated and emotionally well-adjusted couples should not expect a higher level of protection from the IUD than from the consistent use of traditional methods, such as the diaphragm or the condom, and they can certainly achieve lower pregnancy rates with OCs than with IUDs. The higher effectiveness of the IUD is most apparent in populations not accustomed to the consistent practice of contraception and among couples with emotional difficulties that interfere with the consistent practice of birth control.

Reasons for Failure Failures with the IUD are for the most part method failures since the majority of the few pregnancies that do occur are observed in women with the device *in situ*. A certain number of undesired pregnancies could have been avoided if all IUD wearers checked periodically for its presence.

Side Effects Among women using IUDs, the most common complaints are bleeding or spotting and pain, including cramps, backache, and similar discomforts. These symptoms most often occur soon after insertion and tend to disappear within a few months. In some cases, however, the bleeding and/or pain is sufficiently severe to require removal of the device.

A more important adverse experience associated with the use of IUDs is pelvic inflammatory disease (PID) reported in the CSP during the first year after insertion for 2 to 3 per cent of the women using the major types of IUDs. The incidence was higher in the first month after insertion than in later months. Comparable data on the incidence of PID in the general population are not available, but at least one study suggests that in a population with a high rate of PID the incidence is even higher among women wearing an IUD.

To a considerable extent, episodes of PID associated with an IUD have been interpreted as reactivations of pre-existing chronic or subchronic conditions brought on by the insertion procedure rather than by new infection. Whether the insertion of an IUD in a woman with healthy pelvic organs can produce PID is not known.

The majority of cases of PID among women wearing IUDs are relatively mild and can be treated successfully with antibiotics and without removing the device. However, some patients with PID, with or without an IUD, develop serious complications and a few women wearing IUDs have, in fact, died from PID.

Perforation of the uterus with translocation of the IUD into the abdominal cavity is an infrequent complication. Most perforations of the uterus are entirely asymptomatic and are discovered at a routine checkup, when removal is attempted, or after delivery. The incidence of this accident with the most widely used device was 1:2,500 insertions according to the CSP; a much higher rate (1:150) has been reported from Singapore for the same type of IUD. In a few instances, perforations involving closed IUDs are known to have caused intestinal obstruction. It is now accepted practice to remove closed devices immediately when a perforation is discovered. In the absence of symptoms, removal of a translocated open IUD is less urgent.

There is no evidence at the present time that the IUDs cause cancer in women. However, since the effect of all known carcinogens in humans is delayed, with a latent period of about a decade, it will not be possible to make a definitive statement on this point until substantial numbers of women have used IUDs for prolonged periods.

On the basis of current experience, fertility is unimpaired among women who discontinue the use of IUDs in order to plan a pregnancy. Nor has any increase been noted in the prevalence of malformations among the children born to women wearing IUDs.

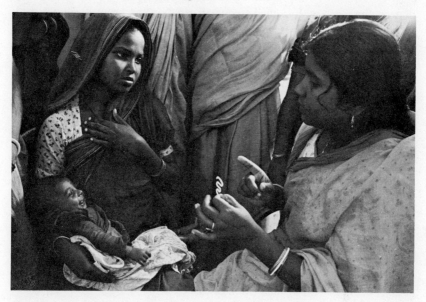

Extent and Continuation of Use   The number of IUD insertions in the United States is not known, but informed guesses suggest between 1 and 2 million as the order of magnitude. Abroad, the IUDs have become the mainstay of several national family planning programs, especially in Asia, with the largest numbers of insertions reported from India, Pakistan, South Korea, and Taiwan. The total number of women in the world currently wearing one of the modern IUDs is probably about 6 million.

Continued use of IUDs is primarily determined by the incidence of expulsions and of side effects that necessitate removal of the device. The incidence of expulsion varies markedly among the various IUDs, with about 10 per cent during the first year after insertion reported for the most widely used device. The expulsion rate tends to be higher among young women of low parity than among older women of higher parity, with age being the more important factor. Most expulsions occur during the early months after insertion; usually, but not always, during the menstrual flow. Expulsion after the first year is uncommon. While the risk of repeated expulsion after reinsertion is much higher than the risk of primary expulsion, about two out of five women who experience a first expulsion are eventually able to retain the device. The most important medical reasons for the removal of an IUD are bleeding and pain, including cramps, backache and other types of discomfort. Because the monthly rates of removal do not decline as rapidly as do the corresponding rates of expulsion, removal is the major cause of discontinuation.

According to the experience under the CSP, which reflects mainly clinical practice in the United States, 70 to 80 per cent of the users were still wearing an IUD one year after the first insertion and 60 to 70 per cent, two years after the first insertion. These figures include women who are wearing an IUD after one or more reinsertions. Continuation rates based on the experience of national family planning programs have been significantly lower than in the CSP, with typical two-year rates on the order of 50 per cent. The reasons for this less satisfactory performance are being investigated.

Surgical Sterilization

History   Surgical sterilization was originally used to protect women whose life or health was threatened by pregnancy or delivery. Dr. James Blundell of London is credited with having first suggested the procedure in 1823. Effective techniques were developed in the latter part of the nineteenth century when aseptic surgery and anesthesia became available. At about the same time, sterilizing operations began to be used on males, mainly in connection with surgery of the prostate gland.

Growing confidence in the efficacy and safety of surgical sterilization led to its use for eugenic purposes, i.e., to prevent persons suffering from hereditary disabilities from having offspring. In recent years, discussion has centered on the legality and/or propriety of voluntary sterilization as a method of family limitation and on the use of sterilization in countries where high birth rates and rapid population growth threaten to produce serious economic and social difficulties.

Mode of Action   Cutting, ligation, and removal of a portion of the fallopian tube in the female or of the spermatic duct in the male (vasectomy).

Advantages   The operation provides maximum protection. No further action is needed at any time.

Disadvantages   While it has been possible, in some cases, to restore fertility by a second operation, this cannot be counted on and the decision to undergo sterilization should in each case be considered definitive.

Effectiveness   It is virtually 100 per cent effective.

Reasons for Failure   Inadequate surgery and rare anatomical aberrations.

Side Effects   The risks of surgical misadventure and complications are very small, especially in the male, but they exist nevertheless. Adverse emotional reactions occur in predisposed individuals.

Extent of Use   The number of voluntary sterilizations in the United States during the late 1950's is estimated at 110,000 annually, including 65,000 operations on women and 45,000 vasectomies. Since that time, the numbers have probably increased. Sterilization of women has been popular in Puerto Rico since the 1940's and has gained wide acceptance in Japan. In India, Pakistan, and South Korea, vasectomy is encouraged by the government as a method of population control.

POSSIBLE MEANS OF FERTILITY CONTROL—DISTANT OR NEAR

It is possible to compile a list of potential methods to regulate fertility which have a realistic basis in terms of our present knowledge.

For Use By Female

1. *Once-a-month anti-ovulant pill.* Now under limited clinical evaluation; this is a modification in the manner of using estrogen-progestin combinations. The steroids used are absorbed from the gastrointestinal tract, stored in adipose tissue and released gradually over a month.

2. *Once-a-month anti-ovulant injection.* Now in clinical investigation; this is a modification in the manner of using estrogen-progestin combinations. Long-acting steroid esters are injected at a dose calibrated to last one month.

3. *Once-a-month vaginal ring.* Preliminary trials completed. This procedure is based on anti-ovulatory action of a synthetic progestin released from an elastomer and absorbed through the vaginal mucosa.

4. *Long-term anti-ovulant injection.* Extensively studied in clinical trials, this procedure is based on the anti-ovulatory action of a synthetic progestin without estrogen. Micro-crystallized suspensions of the steroid are injected in doses that will last 3 or 6 months.

5. *Long-term anti-ovulant implant.* Not yet studied clinically, this procedure would provide chronic release of estrogen-progestin to suppress ovulation and menstruation.

6. *Continuous low-dose progestin.* This provides an antifertility effect without inhibiting ovulation or the normal endometrial cycle.
   a. Pill or oil-filled capsule taken orally: one product is now marketed and others are under investigation.
   b. Subdermal implant: provides for continuous absorption from an elastomer at a constant rate. Now in earliest stages of clinical trial.
   c. Removable vaginal ring: provides for continuous absorption and may act locally on cervical mucus glands or systemically to give the low-dose progestin anti-fertility effect.
   d. Long-acting injection: requires the development of a preparation that would provide a depot effect that gives constant, low absorption below level that will affect pituitary or endometrium.

     e. Skin-contact absorption: requires the development of highly potent progestin, active at levels that could be absorbed through the skin—from a finger ring, for example, or by adding to a cosmetic.

     f. IUD-released: provides for continuous absorption and may act either locally in the uterus, or systemically to give the low-dose progestin antifertility effect.

7. *Long-term luteotrophin injection.* Requires a better understanding of the trophic control of the human corpus luteum. The purpose would be to lengthen the post-ovulatory phase of the cycle to perhaps 90 days so that a woman would have fewer ovulations per year.

8. *Corpus luteum maintenance by injection of LT-RF releaser.* Requires identification and purification of LT-RF active in human female. Objective same as in (7).

9. *Monthly oral preparation to cause luteolysis.* At least two compounds, active orally, have been claimed as having luteolytic activity in animals, and possibly in humans. Taken regularly, the drug would bring on menstruation whether or not the cycle had been fertile.

10. *Monthly injection to cause luteolysis.* This would be an application of the proposed uterine luteolytic factor. If active in the human, it will probably require injection since preliminary work indicates a peptide structure. Objective would be as in (9).

11. *Non-regular use of methods (9) or (10).* A variation in the use of methods (9) or (10) would be to instruct the woman to do nothing for contraception but on the infrequent occasion of a fertile cycle, as evidenced by a delay in menstruation, to use a luteolytic method.

12. *Once-a-month anti-progestational pill.* To be taken regularly at the time of the expected menses, to interfere with luteal maintenance of early decidua, and bring on endometrial sloughing whether or not the cycle has been fertile. Several compounds with a potential for this activity are available.

13. *Post-coital estrogen or anti-estrogen taken orally.* On the basis of limited human use, this procedure is claimed to be effective in preventing pregnancy following isolated exposures. Presumably, it affects the rate of ovum transport. Several compounds are active in animals.

14. *Post-coital anti-zygotic agent taken orally.* Work is required to seek compounds that would appear in the tubal fluid at adequate concentration to be toxic to the zygote without manifesting general toxicity.

15. *Immunization with sperm antigens.* The objective is to prevent deposited spermatozoa from achieving fertilizing capacity in the female tract. Success has been reported in animals, but considerable basic work, including safety studies, are needed before human trials are feasible.

16. *Injection of passively transferred antibodies to HCG.* This procedure would be employed on the occasion of a missed period, during the time that HCG stimulation of the corpus luteum is required to maintain a nascent implantation. Animal studies establish the feasibility of the approach.

17. *Immunization with steroid-binding proteins.* Recently described tis-

sue-specific intracellular binding proteins can be derived from the uterus. Active antibody production would prevent estrogenic changes from occurring in the uterus without interfering with the ovarian cycle.

18. *Improved methods to detect ovulation.* This is feasible on the basis of simplification in the method to detect either LH or progesterone, in urine, saliva, or blood (finger-prick sample).

19. *Reversible tubal occlusion.* Instead of sectioning the fallopian tube, a removable plug would be introduced, either trans-cervically or through an abdominal approach.

20. *Simplification of tubal ligation operation.* Now being tested by several surgeons, the tube is sectioned or electro-coagulated by a peritoneoscopic or culdoscopic instrument.

21. *Intrauterine infusion of cytotoxins.* Intrauterine infusion of cytotoxins has been reported as a means of inducing sterility. The safety and permanency of the procedure need further study. The objective is to occlude the intra-myometrial portion of the fallopian tube.

22. *Oral or parenteral preparation to assure multiple births at will.* Purified human pituitary gonadotropin can stimulate multiple ovulations; at least one synthetic compound has similar activity. Fine adjustment of dosage, on the basis of ovarian function tests, would provide assurance of multiple births, if desired.

23. *Sex determination at will by immunization with Y-sperm antigen.* There is some evidence that specific antigens from Y-sperm may be identifiable. If so, women could be immunized against this antigen in order to inactivate Y-sperm and assure female sex determination. No similar approach to male sex determination can be envisaged.

24. *Sex determination at will by artificial insemination.* There have been occasional claims of success in separating X-and Y-spermatozoa in an ejaculate by physical means (centrifugation, electrophoresis, sizing, column diffusion). By using only Y-bearing gametes in artificial insemination, male zygotes could be assured. No confirmed procedure has yet been established, however.

For Use By Male

1. *Subdermal implant to suppress spermatogenesis.* Release of an androgen from a silicone rubber capsule can occur at a low and constant rate for several years. This can provide a basis for gonadotropin suppression at levels of androgen therapy that may be medically acceptable.

2. *Periodic injections of long-acting androgen.* Testosterone enanthate, or other esters, can suppress sperm production while providing androgen replacement therapy. Depot injections can remain active for three to six months.

3. *Subdermal implant of progestin.* Low doses of progestin, below the threshold for pituitary suppression, can prevent maturation of epididymal sperm in some animals. A similar activity in the human male would prevent fertility without suppressing spermatogenesis.

4. *Oral tablet of synthetic spermatogenesis inhibitor.* Several compounds that act directly on the testis to prevent spermatocyte maturation have been reported. In animals, some compounds require continuous administration while others can be given for a few days each
   month. A non-toxic compound of this type is being sought.
5. *Oral tablet to alter biochemical constitution of seminal fluid.* Although no specific compound has yet been identified that can influence fertility by this mechanism, the possibility of this type of action
   exists. The appearance of exogenously administered substances in
   seminal fluid has been reported.
6. *Immunization with testis or sperm antigens.* This procedure can
   cause aspermatogenesis in animals. Purification of antigens, control
   over reversibility, and mode of immunization remain as problems to be
   investigated for human application.
7. *Reversible vas deferens occlusion.* The use of a liquid silicone rubber
   that vulcanizes into a pliable plug at body temperature has been
   attempted in animals.
8. *Reversible vas deferens ligation.* Procedures are being tested to
   modify the procedure for surgical vasoligation, in a manner that
   would improve prospects for reversibility.

For Use By Either Male of Female

1. *Immunization with gonadotropin-releasing factors.* The isolation of
   these substances, probably polypeptides, may provide a basis for
   specific LH or FSH suppression so that gamete production in either
   the male or female could be prevented.
2. *Immunization with enzymes specific for normal reproductive function.*
   There is evidence that specific iso-enzymes can be identified in go-
   nadal or placental tissue. Although this work is at a preliminary stage
   of development, it could lead to a source of highly specific antigens.
3. *Oral administration of chemical inhibitors of releasing factor production.* Monamine oxidase inhibitors, prostaglandins and other biological amines interfere with reproductive function in either male or
   female. These substances may act by interfering with the function of
   neuro-secretory cells in the CNS.
4. *Immunization with purified gonadotropins.* In either male or female
   animals gonadotropin antibody formation leads to the expected
   result of gonadotropin deficiency. In some animals, LH immunization prevents the maintenance of early pregnancy.
5. *Oral administration of anti-gonadotropic drugs.* Several antigonado-
   tropic agents, either synthetic chemicals or natural plant products,
   have been reported. Taken regularly, an active and safe preparation
   of this type could prevent sperm production in the male or interfere
   with reproductive function in the female in a number of ways.
6. *Topical application of pheromones.* Laboratory experiments demonstrate that volatile agents produced by one animal can influence
   reproductive functions in another. The role of such substances in
   human reproductive physiology remains to be established.

The Abortion Debate
RALPH B. POTTER, JR.

RALPH B. POTTER, JR. *is professor of social ethics at the Divinity School, Harvard University.*

The use of different methods of population control involves ethical questions as well as technological ones. This is particularly true in the United States where liberalization of abortion laws is at issue. Unfortunately, many of the ethical aspects of the abortion debate have been obscured by the heated rhetoric of both sides. Potter attempts to examine these issues and to assess the impact of this controversy on the churches.

Many individuals and groups in the United States want reform of the laws governing abortion. To gain political leverage, reformers must mobilize opinion within the massive Protestant community, for in the increasingly widespread political contests over abortion law reform the mainline Protestants generally constitute a "swing vote." What basic concepts shape Protestants' attitudes toward abortion? What arguments impress them?

Protestants traditionally have disapproved of the termination of any healthy pregnancy. Amidst the present ferment and strife, however, American Protestants are showing signs of confusion regarding the proper moral and legal status of abortion. Various streams of thought have been converging to form a theological and ethical blend which is eroding the inherited Protestant position of disapproving abortion in all circumstances in which the life of the mother is not seriously threatened.

BENEFITS OF THE STATUS QUO

The first clue to Protestant confusion is the extent of the silence of the churches on the question of abortion. No one knows the exact dimensions of the abortion problem, but it is a problem of no less significance than other matters on which the churches have invested great energies.

During the churches' participation in a variety of civic crusades in recent decades, the practice of nontherapeutic abortion has remained morally condemned and legally proscribed, but widely practiced and perennially ignored.

The best explanation appears unduly simple and circular: Protestants have been relatively content with the status quo. They seem to have concluded that it represents the best possible balance of their conflicting inclinations towards "law" and "grace." The untidy arrangement by which antiabortion laws are retained, but enforced only sporadically against criminal abortionists and never against their clients, has allowed Protestants to employ the didactic, educative power of the law to reinforce their strong negative judgment upon abortion itself; yet relief from the stringency of the rule is afforded in individual cases by tolerating the existence of a decentralized system of illegal abortion accessible to women equipped with the resources necessary for individual enterprise in any sphere—that is, motivation, information, and money. If the resulting inequities have been unattractive, the alternatives have seemed still less attractive. Enforcement of the law would forestall relief for "exceptional cases." A weakening of the law might imply an acceptance, in principle, of nontherapeutic abortion.

NEW RECEPTIVITY

The main elements of the abortion issue are not new; zeal for reform is not new; most of the arguments are not new. It is the receptivity of a broad segment of the "Protestant" public that is new.

Three factors have contributed most to this new receptivity. The first is the breakdown of old theological certainties which shaped Protestant opposition to nontherapeutic abortion. What has broken down is a constellation of beliefs about nature, man, and God which sustained the conviction that nascent life in the womb is, in every circumstance, a gift of God given for the realization of his mysterious purpose, and is, therefore, to be respected as inviolable from lawful human interference except in the tragic case in which the life of the fetus is pitted against the life of its mother.

The Protestant approach has rested upon the prevalence of Providence. When a new habit of mind now attributes new life to "rotten luck" in the practice of contraception rather than to the purposeful will of a merciful God, neglect of the countermeasure of abortion becomes irrational and superstitious retreat from the possibility of exercising control of one's destiny. Denial of accessibility to abortion comes to be seen by many as a violation of a civil liberty.

The second factor underlying the new receptivity consists of the abortion reform movement's forceful expression of themes taken from the Protestant tradition itself, particularly the themes of self-determination and rational control of nature. If men are unable to believe that God has carefully planned and ordained each pregnancy, they themselves must take measures to insure that procreation is not left to "blind nature" or to chance. The status of abortion is enhanced among Protestants when it is advertised as a means of implementing rational control over nature.

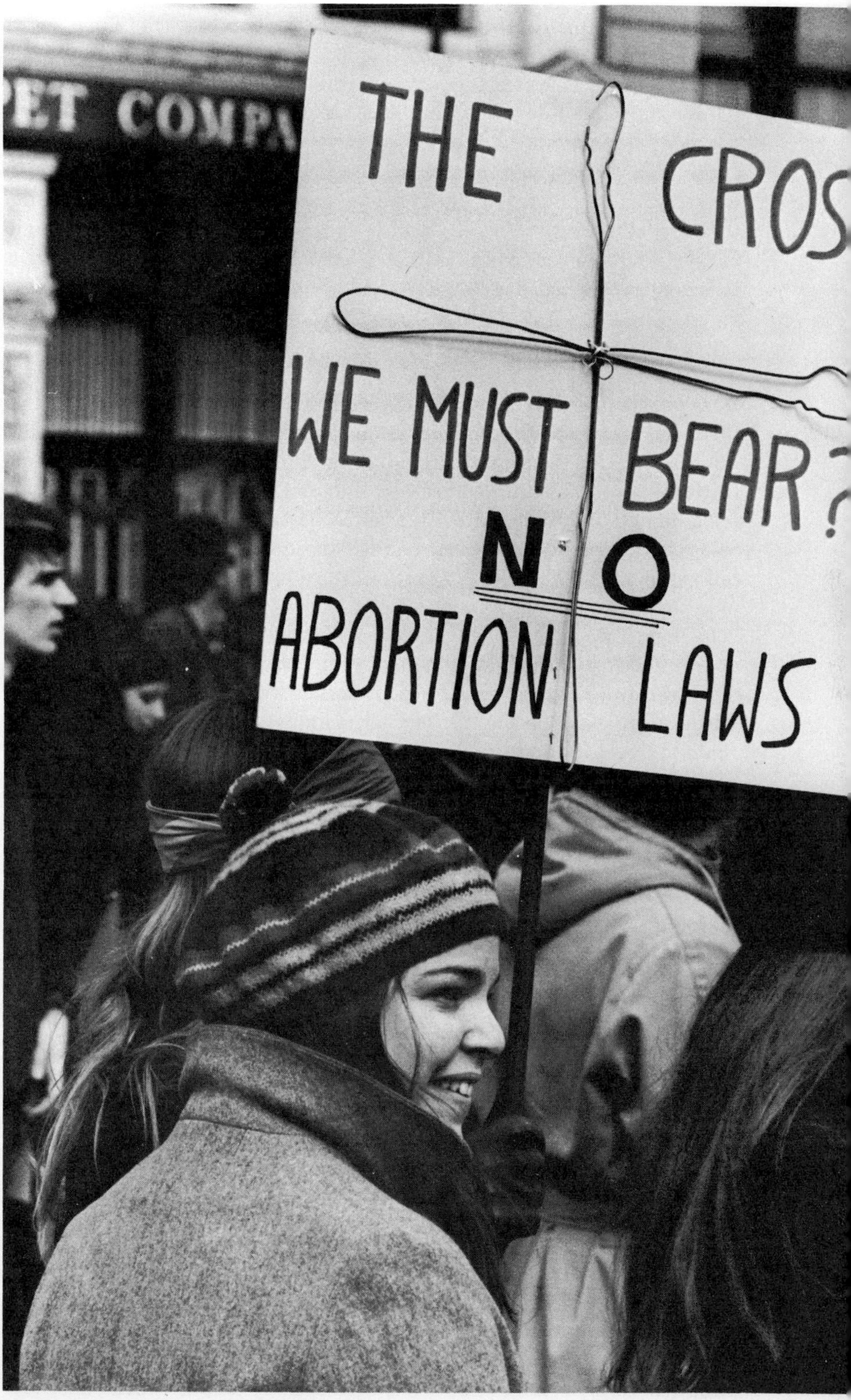
THE CROS
WE MUST BEAR?
NO
ABORTION LAWS

The third factor contributing to the new receptivity is the dimming of the vision of a Protestant American made to conform to the dictates of Protestant conscience. Protestants, convinced of the high value of control over nature and of self-determination, feel obliged, in a pluralistic society, to concede the exercise of these powers to all men. Those who disagree concerning the specific *content* of the imperatives of conscience must, nevertheless, be afforded the freedom necessary for self-determination through control over nature. By devotion to their own principles, Protestants are obliged to tolerate a gap between what is *morally* condemned and what is *legally* proscribed.

THE SPECTRUM OF CONTENDING VIEWS

If rational debate is to be promoted, careful distinctions must be made along the broad spectrum of recommendations put forward concerning abortional law reform. The spectrum may be divided into three major segments, three broad bands marking fundamentally different approaches to the issue. At the right end of the spectrum is a position that may be awkwardly referred to as "no abortion." At the left end is "abortion on demand." Those who fall within the middle range of the spectrum support the concept of "justifiable abortion."

In their style of argument, the members of the middle or "justifiable abortion" school differ from adherents of the two extreme positions by their willingness to require and to accept certain reasons or "indications" as adequate justification for the basically repugnant act of abortion. Within this middle school there is wide disagreement concerning which indications should establish acceptable grounds for abortion under the law. But all members agree that abortion may be justifiable for certain reasons and unjustifiable for other reasons. In contrast, neither of the extreme positions deals in reasons or "indications." Those who uphold the "no abortion" position deny that there is any reason that could render abortion morally and legally tolerable. Advocates of "abortion on demand" reject the notion that any reason should be required, since all decisions regarding the use of procreative powers must be left to the unrestricted private judgment of individual women.

THE LEFT WING: ABORTION ON DEMAND

The further one moves to the left along the spectrum, the stronger is the inclination to treat self-determination as an absolute value. It is the master theme in a medley of arguments drawn from a variety of sources. An argument for abortion on demand is likely to be composed of the following elements arranged in differing patterns of emphasis. Abortion on demand is necessary: (1) to protect the life and health of women by making medically safe abortion available to those who cannot be deterred by rigid laws or high risks; (2) to preserve the autonomy of the medical profession; (3) to insure that only wanted children will be born; (4) to guarantee that each child will receive careful nurture within a family able to expend adequate amounts of time, money and loving care upon it; (5) to help defuse the population explosion; (6) to enable women to attain equal status through escape from the risk of unwanted pregnancy; (7) to avoid discrimination by race and social class through making abortion equally available to all at low expense; (8) to realize the promise of full civil liberty by according women unquestioned control over the use of their bodies, and couples unchallenged right of privacy.

These themes are variously elaborated and supplemented; but they are invariably accompanied by strong emphasis upon the right of self-determination as a positive moral value which can be realized only through repeal of laws which presume to prescribe who may and who may not legally terminate her pregnancy.

These intellectual currents run so wide and deep that it is certain that the present legal and political contests focused upon the American Law Institute proposals for "justifiable abortion" represent only an initial phase of an inevitable conflict between the demand for unhampered self-determination and the tradition which asserts that there is a valid basis for public regulation of the practice of abortion. The impact of the left-wing school is strong enough that one may anticipate a significant shifting of the burden of proof. In many quarters, the central question of the abortion debate is gradually being rephrased. The question becomes: "What reasons can justify the refusal of the state to grant permission for an abortion?" The form of the question preserves the style of the middle; but the content reveals the influence of the left. Eventually, the question must be faced, "Why should there be any law governing who may undergo an abortion?"

THE RIGHT WING: REALIZATION OF THE GREATER GOOD

The right wing of the spectrum is defended most relentlessly in public debate by Roman Catholic spokesmen. It should not be overlooked, however, that some members of the Protestant and Jewish communities join in defense of the present laws regulating abortion. Nevertheless, most of the right-wing arguments stated here are to be attributed to Roman Catholic commentators who, by and large, have set the terms of debate over and against left-wing advocates.

As one moves toward the right end of the spectrum, certainty increases that it is the proper function of the state to intervene in the matter of abortion in order to prevent harm. The harm envisioned may be inflicted upon the mother, the medical profession, the family, society at large, the fetus, or what might best be described as "the cultural ethos."

The nub of the right-wing argument, as presented to contemporary Americans, is simple and stark: the condoning of widespread resort to abortion would undermine civilization. The argument is couched in theological terms; it leads, however, to conclusions in the realm of cultural anthropology. The constant goal is to convince hearers, by whatever arguments carry force in their generation, that the practice of abortion is incompatible with the attainment of man's true humanity. At stake in controversies over abortion law reform is the definition of the vision of what man should be. Urgency arises from the conviction that the content of that vision will shape the quality of human relationships in decades to come.

The profundity of the right-wing argument is its greatest weakness. Many of the injuries described by controversialists on the right take place in a dimension of existence unknown or unexplored by their fellow citizens.

The harm that is most vivid and imaginable to typical onlookers is injury to the health and welfare of the mother. Spokesmen for the left wing generate great dramatic impact by portraying very palpable injuries to mothers. They depict vivid harm to victims with whom readers can readily identify. A prompt remedy is offered through "legalization of abortion now." In the effort to recoup the title of "defenders of the public welfare," right-wing advocates are obliged, by contrast, to depict either very subtle injuries to real persons or somewhat less subtle harm to less vividly imaginable entities such as "society," "civilization," or "the fetus." Indeed, the attempt to overcome the seeming inability of many people to visualize the fetus as an object of real injury accounts for many of the intellectual and rhetorical maneuvers in the battle over abortion law reform.

The right wing's first line of defense—that abortion, as a medical procedure, is both dangerous and superfluous—seems to be crumbling under an avalanche of statistics from Eastern Europe and other regions where abortion is widely practiced and new techniques are being developed through research. The level of medical danger there is not high. Also, it can be argued that abortion is not totally superfluous. If it is seldom necessary, abortion may nevertheless be occasionally necessary, and the law should not bar physicians from attempting to preserve the life and health of their patients.

There is a second line of defense. The dangers of abortion may be more subtle. The unhappy effects may be delayed in time and buried in the recesses of the personality, accessible only to those armed with psychiatric skill.

A considerable body of literature deals with the psychiatric effects of abortion. From this literature adherents of the left wing extract evidence that the incidence of serious psychological aftereffects is relatively low. They go on to argue that the incidence would be much lower still if right-wing propaganda did not perpetuate the self-fulfilling prophecy that induces symptoms of guilt by contending that such symptoms are virtually inevitable. They hold that guilt over abortion is a cultural legacy that will become increasingly rare as societies adopt a more "enlightened" and therefore more tolerant attitude toward abortion.

The reply of those on the right wing is to make the injury from abortion appear more subtle still. They hold that some psychiatrists cannot detect the full extent of the harm to mothers because they maintain a superficial view of the full components of true health. True health involves more than "a state of complete physical and mental wellbeing." It has a spiritual dimension. The injury to the spirit of one who violates the law of nature and commandment of God by indulging in abortion may escape the notice of observers who employ less sensitive indices of affliction.

The third line of defense of the right-wing claim to be the true guardian of women is the claim that the practice of abortion frustrates the realization of man's true humanity. Evidence for this is not easily given. It is difficult to muster "hard empirical data" to convince those who, on other bases, do not already share a particular view of men. The difficulty exposes the true nature of the dispute and demonstrates the burden of profundity.

With regard to the protection of mothers, as on other issues, participants in the abortion controversy talk past one another. Reformers on the left gather statistics which purport to prove that, at least in certain nations, few women experience deep remorse after an abortion. But the statistics, even if acknowledged as accurate, have little effect upon right-wing commentators. Their arguments are not grounded in such observations. Their line can be defended with the aid of statistics that show abortion *does* have ill effects. But it cannot be overthrown by empirical evidence that abortion does *not* have bad medical or psychiatric consequences. Only the outer defenses can be endangered by the attack of epidemiologists and sociologists. The inner defense is founded firmly upon theological ground. The battle is being fought over questions of theological anthropology and ethics. The issue is: What ought man to be? What style of life represents the realization of true humanity?

HIGH STAKES

The central claim of the right wing is that abortion is evil because it deprives an individual of the greater good of becoming a more selfless creature. Abortion, in killing the actual self of the fetus, kills the potential higher self of the mother. Abortion is inimical to the attainment of "a generous spirit" which welcomes new life and accepts the occasion of redemptive suffering and sacrifice.

At stake in the abortion debate is not simply the fate of individual women or even the destiny of individual nations and cultures. It is difficult to demonstrate that acceptance of the most extreme proposal for abortion on demand would establish a clear and present danger to the civil harmony necessary for the maintenance of a tranquil state. Nations that have lenient abortion laws do function. But if abortion is not an actual threat to minimal public order, it may nevertheless be a symbolic threat to the ideal moral order espoused by Christians for two millennia. Abortion does not merely contradict specific mores and moral teachings pertaining to sexuality, marriage, and procreation or endanger a system of law built upon "respect for life." It implies the rejection of a world view which has sustained a way of life, a mode of being in the world, a pattern of response to the human condition.

For Christians, an entire system of meaning may be at stake in the abortion debate; but is anything at stake for a secular, pluralistic state?

SOURCES OF THE ABHORRENCE OF ABORTION

Christians frequently are delighted to take credit for instilling into the Western tradition a deep abhorrence of abortion. This affirmation of the historical relevance of Christianity may do wonders for Christian pride and morale, but it makes it more, rather than less, difficult to maintain anti-abortion laws in a secular, pluralistic setting.

The teaching of the church generated the sentiments expressed through the ban upon abortion. Abortion is a practice which seems incongruous with the profession of faith of those who live under the sign of the cross. But the nation does not live under the sign of the cross. Why, then, should there be laws restricting abortion? Do such statutes serve any secular purpose which may invest them with binding force in a society no longer willing to submit to the tutelage of the church?

WHAT VALUES DO ABORTION LAWS PROTECT?

The harm attributed to abortion by right-wing critics of legal reform is subtle and profound; it is the deprivation of man's greatest good—a character formed by charity and humble obedience to God's commandments. But the very nobility of the vision places it beyond the law's protective concern.

The state cannot command charity, but it can enforce justice. If it could be demonstrated that abortion did injury to some proper subject of the law's protection, a more solid foundation for antiabortion statutes could be constructed. This is the challenge to the right wing and to the middle: they must indicate a harm the law cannot ignore to a victim the law is bound to protect. The Christian commentator is goaded by a moral abhorrence of abortion derived from the charitable lesson of the Gospel. But to defend public laws against abortion he needs legal arguments derived from the universal norms of natural justice.

LATENT FUNCTIONS OF THE LAW

Society must have an appropriate and adequate reason for denying a woman legal access to a medical procedure she desires, oftentimes with great desperation. The protection of all men from the loss of the high moral stature considered by some to constitute man's greatest good is not, in itself, a suitable basis for restrictive legislation. What reasons can be given for such laws?

Left-wing spokesmen insist that the original intent of the American laws passed in the nineteenth century was to protect the prospective mother from the medical dangers of abortion which, given the state of medical art at that time, were extremely high. Now, as medical skill has increased, the same motive requires revision of the statutes so that women who cannot be deterred by the persuasion of counseling or the threat of law can have abortions in the safety of the hospital under excellent medical care. Right-wing historians hold that the intention of the law has been to preserve the life of the unborn child and that this purpose remains a valid and sufficient basis for laws restricting abortion.

The compromise established by the present laws realizes neither intention fully. The laws fail to deter women from risking life and health at the hands of criminal abortionists and, in failing to deter mothers, they fail to preserve the lives of the unborn children. Why then do the laws persist? Edwin Schur suggests that every social system must maintain its membership; hence, "no society has allowed uncontrolled termination of pregnancies. . . . It may be also that the members of our society feel some illusory satisfaction in maintaining a formal and ideal standard in this area, even if they are largely unable to conform to it."

THE PRESERVATION OF INDIVIDUAL CHARACTER

In order to provide a secular purpose for the legislative restriction of abortion, those sharing the inclinations of the right wing can argue that the ban on abortion functions not simply to uphold a particular code of behavior, let alone a peculiar code of sexual behavior. It upholds character, the type of character that is indispensable to good citizenship. The state has a stake in the promotion of self-restraint rather than self-indulgence, responsibility rather than irresponsibility, and selfless adaptability rather than selfish rigidity.

There is more to this phase of the argument than the cry that acceptance of abortion will lead to sexual promiscuity. The fear is rather that it will lead to a general decline of individual character through lax enforcement of responsibility. The issue is not whether sex is to be separated from procreation, but whether procreation can be divorced from the responsibility to nurture new life.

Right-wing commentators insist that the woman must bear the residual risk of pregnancy because her dismissal from that responsibility would bring on a widespread eagerness to evade every troublesome inconvenience which members of society must bear. To this, critics reply that the desire to escape the "natural consequences" of our actions is not only common and in most circumstances approved; it is, in fact, the stimulus to research and progress. The progress attained by permitting abortion as an emergency backstop to contraception would be the upgrading of parenthood and the realization of a happy family in a home in which every child would be wanted and welcomed. Men applaud the extension of human control into all other areas. Advocates of reform ask, "Why should this one act be set off as inaccessible to control?" The answer from the right wing is that life is present. No matter how tenuous the existence of a newly formed embryo, its creation is an event of moral import that cannot be totally ignored or despised.

The battle line is drawn at the point at which the relentless extension of self-determination and control over nature collides with the fundamental principle of "respect for life."

THE POPULATION ARGUMENT: A BOOMERANG

One attempt to ground antiabortion laws in concern for the common public interest of the secular state has backfired. Throughout most of the last hundred years the strong antagonism of the churches to abortion abetted the population policies of Western nations which aimed at increasing the birth rate in order to counter the threat of underpopulation. There was a convenient alliance of secular nationalism and ecclesiastical natalism. The moral evil of abortion was also a social evil which would deny the state a citizen, a soldier, a producer. Homilies on family life frequently placed strong emphasis upon the obligation of the Christian couple, when contemplating the number of children to be brought into the world, to consider the needs of the state.

Now the demographic situation has changed. Overpopulation rather than underpopulation is a menace. The argument that couples should consider the needs of the state in deciding about their procreative behavior can prove embarrassing when public policy seeks a reduction of the birth rate.

The response of the right wing has been to deemphasize the Christian's obligation to weigh the current demographic needs of the state as a significant factor in decisions regarding family size. Instead, much labor has been expended upon the construction of a high wall of privacy which would shelter decisions regarding procreation from the influence or intervention of any public authority. Here the right wing concurs with the left. In the abortion debate, the two extreme positions seem to agree that public authority must not tamper with decisions regarding procreation.

A decision to have an abortion is viewed on the left wing simply as a particular kind of "decision regarding procreation." It falls within the sphere of private acts sheltered from public interference. As a necessary backstop to fallible contraceptive measures, abortion is indispensable to the full realization of self-determination. On the right wing, however, abortion is categorized differently. It is a decision regarding procreation, but it can never be merely private because the taking of a life is entailed. The taking of life is always a matter of public concern. It is quite properly a matter of legal restriction. This is the ground upon which antiabortion laws must rest.

ABORTION AS A VIOLATION OF "THE RIGHT TO LIFE"

Opponents of abortion labor under the handicap of attempting to portray subtle harms to remote subjects. They find it difficult to offset the vividness of the case for abortion which can be presented on behalf of a forlorn woman whose plight can readily be discerned. There is one type of injury, however, that is vivid and is clearly within the duty of the state to prevent: murder. Right-wing authors habitually assimilate the destruction of life in abortion to the forensic category of murder. Abortion is held to violate a legally enforceable "right to life." A simple syllogism unfolds into a complex network of ideas. Human life is not to be destroyed; fetal life is human life; therefore, fetal life is not to be destroyed.

Resort to the legal vocabulary to capture the emotionally powerful term "murder" imposes an obligation to attain the linguistic precision appropriate to the legal sphere. Hence, the meaning of the major and the minor premises and the conclusion itself must be specified more closely.

The major premise represents a restriction of responsibility to protect life within confines more narrow than those implied by such terms as "reverence for life" or "respect for life." Not all life is included in the injunction, only human life. But, it is noted, even with regard to human life, the framers of the syllogism do permit exceptions. In imposing capital punishment, for example, society demands the life of one who, by his depradations upon his fellow men, is said to have forfeited his right to life. Thus the premise must be narrowed: *Innocent* human life is not to be destroyed. Again there are exceptions. In wartime, men acting in good conscience under the principle of double effect, may destroy the life of a civilian who, innocent both subjectively and materially, is tragically situated close to an important military target. A further specification is required: *Innocent* human life is not to be destroyed *by direct, purposeful attack.*

The minor premise requires not refinement but evidence of its truth in fact. Robert Drinan, S.J., former Dean of Boston College Law School, has asserted, "If the advocates of legalized abortion desire to have an intellectually honest debate about the fundamental change they seek in the moral and legal standards of American life, they should not fall back on the error of fact that a fetus is not a human being." What type of fact is it that a fetus is a human being? What evidence would count for or against such an assertion? What type of question is posed when one asks, "Is the fetus a human being?"

In the present context, the question is, in the first instance, a legal inquiry. It translates into the question, "Can a fetus be the victim of murder?" Murder requires a human victim. Even if the fetus is not taken to be *fully* human, a moral problem still exists. One can still ask whether or not it is right to destroy whatever it is that exists in the womb after conception and before birth. Arguments against such destruction can be given which do not hinge on the question whether murder has been committed upon a fully human fetus. If the fetus is not human, what is lost is not the moral quandary regarding abortion but the strong argument for public legislation grounded in the demands of justice. If there is no human victim to be murdered, opponents of abortion must revert to less stirring arguments.

How might one "prove" the statement that "the fetus is fully human"? In order to gain the semblance of certainty over against the seemingly arbitrary demonstration available through legal or moral discourse, many right-wing authors attempt to convert the question of when human life exists into a straightforward biological problem.

Such an attempt to surround a moral and legal judgment with an aura of biological factuality evades the truth that, in searching for signs of life, the biologist who does not aspire himself to be a theologian must rely upon the indices of life which the theologian has defined. If the theologian says that the drawing of breath is the sign of life, the biologist is likely to report that life is not present until a moment after birth. If human life is thought to begin when a human form is visually recognizable, the biologist must estimate the moment in gestation at which the fetus becomes so "formed." If life is defined in terms of the capacity to carry on certain biological functions, it is nevertheless the theologian who has determined that these shall serve as the appropriate criteria of life.

Nor can certainty about the fully human status of the fetus be gained by recourse to philosophical and religious thought about the soul as the animating principle or actuating cause of individual life. The question then becomes even less credibly an issue to be settled by embryologists. How would their scientific tools detect the creative act of God at the moment he animates the fetus with a living soul? Theologians again must be summoned to describe what to look for. But they have disagreed among themselves. In the last hundred years, authoritative Roman Catholic teaching has required the assumption that animation takes place at the moment of conception. But many respectable theologians, past and present, have held theories of successive animation according to which the soul develops gradually through vegetative and animal stages before the distinctively human rational soul appears. Moral theologians have disagreed precisely because there is no conclusive evidence to be brought to bear from biology or from any other discipline outside of their own field. They can neither escape the decision nor invest it with a factitious certainty. In determining what it is that is to be protected through restrictions upon abortion they define what is to be considered "human life."

In search of rhetorical power, right-wing publicists tend to disregard pertinent distinctions which have led to the discrimination in popular language and law between "murder" and "abortion." The lack of disciplined precision invites a counterindulgence by left-wing authors. The straining for effect is aggravated when the right wing claim that the fetus is truly human is logically extended and emotionally undergirded with a religious appeal that prospective "murderers" have concern for the eternal destiny of the soul of the fetus. The fragile fabric of argument begins to tear when stretched so far. Neither the church nor the state nor the family actually carries out the practices logically entailed by the affirmation that the fetus is fully human. The church does not baptize the outpouring spontaneously aborted soon after conception. Extreme unction is not given. Funeral rites are not performed. The state calculates age from the date of birth, not of conception, and does not require a death or burial certificate nor even a report of the demise of a fetus aborted early in pregnancy. Convicted abortionists are not subjected to the penalties for murder. The intensity of grief felt within a family over a miscarriage is typically less than that experienced upon the loss of an infant, an older child, or an adult.

It is not the fate of the fetus itself that is the troubling aspect of abortion. It is difficult for most people to imagine the fetus "suffering" either here or hereafter. Indeed, much of its vulnerability stems from men's inability to believe that the fetus has a self-conscious awareness of its own existence and prospective nonexistence.

Glanville Williams inadvertently provides a clue to the basis of the moral condemnation of abortion: "Our comparative indifference towards the natural death of the foetus contrasts strangely with the emotions traditionally released by its artificial termination." The significant distinction between spontaneous miscarriage and induced abortion is that the artificial termination of pregnancy involves the intervention of human agency. The natural death of the fetus is a natural evil. Induced abortion is a moral evil. It is the doing of evil, not the experiencing of evil, that is to be condemned. It is the effect that abortion is presumed to have upon the killers rather than upon the killed that makes abortion dreadful.

The inescapable difficulty, obscured but not erased by an overlay of biological, theological, and legal suppositions, is that many people do not consider the fetus to be fully human and there is no way that they can be logically compelled so to believe. There are undeniable differences between the nonviable fetus and the fully human adult or even the newly born infant. The nonviable fetus is physically bound to its mother and may constitute a threat to her life. It is unable to be adopted or removed to the care of another. It is totally dependent upon the mother. No other arrangement can be made for its continued life.

It is inappropriate for adherents of the right wing to deny that these basic facts are devoid of significance in reasoning about abortion. But it is equally inappropriate for those on the left wing to deny that even the newest conceptus is something more than "just another piece of the woman's tissue." It is a potential man. Abortion is not just another surgical procedure. Nor is it murder. Abortion is abortion. It is a peculiar moral problem that can neither be "solved" by clumsy analogies nor dissolved by some rhetorical sleight of hand. Abortion is the destruction of potential, potential which has already attained the form of nascent life. The rejection of abortion implies an affirmation of the goodness of creation. It gives testimony to the conviction that what is potential ought to be welcomed to actuality.

It can be replied that no one except a dyspeptic nihilist would argue that abortion is good because the destruction of life is desirable in itself. The claim of reformers is only that under extraordinary circumstances abortion may be justifiable as the lesser evil. The unknown potential of the fetus must be weighed against the actualized relationships and responsibilities of the mother. The mother, as well as her unborn child, has unrealized potential. When the balance between them must be struck how should the scales be weighted?

ASSESSING THE "VALUE" OF LIFE

Those who would indulge in such calculations can employ one of two patterns of reasoning. They may give weight to the very existence of actualized potential or to the anticipated quality of unactualized potential. The first approach could be described as the "labor theory of value." Garrett Hardin expresses an attitude that inevitably leads to preference for the mother: "The early stages of an individual fetus have had very little human effort invested in them; they are of very little worth."

As men become more godlike in the scope if not in the employment of their powers, surprising conclusions may be drawn by application of a second mode of reasoning which, in emphasizing the quality of unrealized potential, need not lead to the automatic preference of the mother over her unborn child. By shifting the unknowables in a not uncommon decision-making formula we may perform a thought experiment which, if medically improbable, is nevertheless ethically interesting. Suppose a situation late in pregnancy where it is medically possible to save either but not both the mother and child. Suppose, further, that the state of fetology has advanced so that it can be predicted confidently that the offspring will be of very superior endowment. The mother is, by universal agreement, a wretch. Considering the potential benefit to the community and the quality of individual life that could be attained, would it not be deemed suitable to kill the mother in order to insure the realization of the superior potential of her child?

Concern for the "quality of life" or "the full realization of human potential" can be used well to stimulate efforts to prevent the occurrence of lamentable defects and deficiencies so that all may enjoy a high quality of life. But it can also lead to an inclination to derogate life which, burdened with defects and deficiencies, does not seem capable of high quality. The application of "quality control" techniques to the production of new life is a constant temptation to some. An ominous note is sounded in an article by a Protestant layman and physician Dr. H. B. Munson, who writes, "these days it seems a questionable practice even to allow an irresponsible mother to take responsibility for the rearing of a child, much less force her to do so.... The fact that these days we not only allow her to keep her baby, but that to a large degree we force this state of affairs by denying her an abortion would seem to make us guilty of mismanagement." Dr. Munson, seems to be on the verge of proposing an indication for *involuntary* abortion which would be imposed for the sake of maintaining a well-managed society. One cannot repress the question, "Who will be the managers?"

It seems there are few who are able to sustain the theological beliefs necessary to give meaning to the realization of potential through self-sacrifice for the sake of the life of another. But Americans habitually do glorify the sacrifice of life in defense of the nation. And heroes frequently risk and not infrequently lose their lives in the rescue of fellow men. Yet the sacrifice of a mother to save the unknown, nascent, potential life contained in a tiny tissue is not heralded on civic occasions. It is the apparent disproportion of the sacrifice that seems objectionable. The more the life of the fetus is depreciated, the more glaring is the apparent disproportion.

Both the emphasis of "the labor theory of value" upon the degree of realized human potential, and the social engineering stress upon the quality of unrealized potential represent departures from the classical Christian account of the origin of the worth of each human life. Christians have proclaimed that God has bestowed upon man "an alien dignity." Man's worth is not to be assessed according to what he has become through social intercourse or by an estimate of what he may yet become. Rather, it is God's labor, his purpose, his economy which places the price of each life so high that no transient human value can serve as compensation. But, with the erosion of the theological foundations of the Christian view of man's alien dignity, the barriers to abortion built upon those foundations are crumbling in the hearts of individuals and in the statutes of the states. The trend may be lamentable, but the demands of Christian responsibility cannot be met by pouting and pining for an "age of faith." What must the churches do now in the face of a problem they will no longer be allowed to ignore?

OPTIONS FOR THE CHURCHES

The drift of the abortion debate is clearly to the left. An ironic benefit of the confusion which has beset the Protestant churches is that it has kept open several options. Different streams might be panned in the search for a new wealth of ideas.

The new receptivity of Protestants to arguments for abortion law reform has been attributed to a decline of the theological certainties which supported right-wing arguments; to the exploitation of latent Protestant themes to bolster the left-wing demand for self-determination and control over nature, including human nature; and to perplexity concerning the proper relationship between the moral beliefs of particular segments of the public and legal enactments imposed upon all of the citizenry. Alternative strategies might emerge through response to one or another of these factors.

One possibility is to attempt to reverse the tide and rebuild the eroded theological foundations of the ban on abortion so that narrow restraints might be enforced both within the church and within society. A second course is to proceed to the blessing and baptizing of the arguments of the left wing and a willing entry into a brave new world in the hope that churchmen, having supplied some of the building materials, might have a role in shaping the plan of the new city of man. A third option is to accede to the separation of the legal and the moral and withdraw into a sectarian absolutism, preserving the ban on abortion under the discipline of the church but relinquishing the determination of public policy to other voices.

Each of these three options has disadvantages. The first requires confidence in the possibility of theological reconstruction and the renewal of profound religious commitment throughout a broad segment of the American public. Even many who pray for such a revival would be startled by its occurrence. The second option entails a theological reconstitution involving the abandonment of significant elements of Christian teaching about the nature of human life and the obligation to preserve it. The discontinuity would be jarring to the churches. The changes would ramify throughout the entire system of Christian doctrine. Teaching upon related social and moral issues would have to be recast. The implications for Christian thought concerning the obligation to show respect for life in other settings might be unappealing even, or perhaps, especially to those who now advocate accommodation of Christians to the idea of abortion on demand. The third approach implies a sociological reformation of the relationship of the churches to matters of public policy in a variety of fields. If the churches withdraw from the struggle on behalf of the fetus to defend by law the most fundamental "right to life" how will they be brought back into the public arena to do battle on behalf of the rights of racial minorities, the poor, the persecuted, the victims of injustice and warfare? Whatever measure of grace, love, and justice the churches are able to mediate needs to be diffused throughout the public realm and not be confined within a sectarian enclave. It would be a bad bargain for all if the cost of removing "obstinate" churchmen from the abortion controversy were to be the diminution of their active public concern for abolition of poverty and the realization of civil rights, peace, and a more just world order.

A fourth option constitutes the most probable outcome of the churches' increasing concern with the problem of abortion. The mainline Protestant churches can be expected to provide spotty support for reform measures modeled on the American Law Institute proposals. It is doubtful that abortion law reform will become a cause promoted by a fervent Protestant crusade. But when the issue is thrust upon them, Protestants will respond with an uncoordinated but steady movement toward acceptance of moderate reform. When statewide controversies reach a critical stage in which debate is polarized between Roman Catholic spokesmen in the right wing and advocates of abortion on demand on the left, Protestants will gravitate toward the middle. They will be moved by political disposition rather than by theological exposition. After their arrival, they will need to fill in theological ground on which to stand.

By the time American Protestants are prepared to address the issue of abortion in its present manifestations it is likely that new developments will have recast the current questions. The development of an abortifacient pill that might be prescribed for simple, private, inexpensive, safe use at home will alter the pattern of debate over abortion. Issues that hinge upon estimates of effects of illegal abortion upon mothers, the medical profession, law enforcement agencies, and the poor will become less salient, as will controversies regarding the utility of procedural devices such as hospital abortion committees. A new phase of debate will evolve, a phase in which polarization will be increased. Self-determination will seem to be more readily within reach. Women could abort without risky dependence upon a shady underworld and without the reallocation of scarce medical resources necessary to provide abortion on demand under present medical conditions. But the violation of the "right to life" of the fetus will be the same.

CAN THE DEMAND FOR ABORTION BE REDUCED?

The prospect of a safe abortifacient pill available for self-administration at home quickens awareness of the inefficacy of all external sanctions against abortion. If the demand for abortion were high, effective suppression of the pill would be difficult to achieve. But even today, when most abortions require clandestine negotiations and a costly surgical procedure, those who seek to reduce the number of abortions cannot expect success merely through more aggressive enforcement of criminal provisions or the imposition of more strict administrative procedures in hospitals. They must seek to allay the demand for abortion through a variety of social innovations which might increase a pregnant woman's inclination to bear her child by (1) easing the burden of pregnancy through the provision of better medical care and opportunities for consultation, improvement in the status of illegitimate children, and greater tolerance of unwed mothers; (2) providing assurance of proper care for the child, either *apart* from the mother, through more adequate programs for foster homes and adoption, or *with* the mother through alleviation of poverty by improved programs of social welfare, family subsidy, or tax relief, and through the creation of day-care facilities. The most popular approach to the reduction of the demand for abortion is to reduce unwanted pregnancies through better sex education and the promotion of improved contraceptive practices.

The possible effectiveness of contraception as a means of forestalling the desire for abortion has been used within the Roman Catholic Church as an argument on behalf of a more liberal attitude toward birth control programs. But many Roman Catholic commentators agree with advocates of abortion on demand that contraception and abortion will inevitably be linked in practice. Both extremes consider the hope of having one without the other to be chimeric. Believers in justifiable abortion find consolation in the anticipation that more agressive promotion of contraception will diminish the demand for abortion by preventing unwanted pregnancies.

But the extreme schools join in the observation that, in order to motivate couples to use contraceptives, it is necessary to generate a strong intention not to have another child at a particular moment in time. By inducing this strong motivation, one simultaneously stimulates a latent demand for abortion should contraception fail.

It is not unreasonable to conclude that the high demand for abortion is stimulated not exclusively by social ills but by a disposition of the spirit of the age. The clientele of criminal abortionists includes the poor and the unmarried, but it consists primarily of married women, comfortably placed, who bear neither shame nor poverty, but are resolved to preserve or extend whatever comfort they have attained. No program or policy readily at the disposal of the public can quickly change the calculations that lead women to conclude that abortion is the most convenient solution to their awkward, but not tragic, circumstance.

Abortion can be seen as a medical, legal, social, and ethical problem. It also is to be seen as a problem involving the meaning of life. No external authority can reimpose respect for the law regulating abortion. Apart from such respect, the social costs of enforcement become exorbitant. If legal restraints are to function they must be buttressed by inner conviction. But the conviction has decayed that abortion is an offense against God, nature, the state, one's higher self, the common weal, and the right to life. Can it ever flourish again?

Those who, for one reason or another, would like to reduce the incidence of abortion, must ask, "How can 'respect for life' be regenerated?" The radical feeling of awe at the mystery of all human life can never be predictably induced. But it is best conveyed by demonstrating respect for life in all its forms through the courage of an institution or an individual to sacrifice wealth and prestige and station in defense of the poor, the sick, the homeless, the confused, the aged, the outcast in the ghetto, and the victims of war. Selective and painless opposition to evil is not impressive. The day of renewed inner restraints upon abortion will come sooner if churchmen and theologians exhibit in their relations with all men the same sacrifice of self in love which they have required of mothers menaced by their own offspring. A fetus may deserve respect because it is no less precious than a man. But neither should a man be less the object of ecclesiastical concern than a fetus. The churches must bridge their own credibility gap with costly grace, if they wish others to attain the grace to see the cost of each abortion.

The "cure" of the abortion epidemic can be no less profound than its causes. If, as right-wing critics affirm, its source is in the heart of man, its remedy must penetrate to similar depths. Neither cool debate nor heated polemics can move men at such levels. Only the example of sincere regard for others can rekindle the conviction that all life is sacred and bound together in mystery so that the death of the least diminishes each.

When a fetus is aborted no one asks for whom the bell tolls. No bell is tolled. But do not feel indifferent and secure. The fetus symbolizes you and me and our tenuous hold upon a future here at the mercy of our fellow men.

View from Louisiana

JOSEPH D. BEASLEY

JOSEPH D. BEASLEY *is Director of the Center for Population and Family Studies of the Tulane University School of Medicine and Director of the Louisiana Family Planning Program, Inc.*

There have been numerous family planning programs that have tried to incorporate the existing knowledge of the determinants of fertility change and of the effectiveness of available contraceptives. Most of these programs have met with only limited success. One of the most successful and widely publicized family planning programs in the United States today is taking place in Louisiana. Beasley describes how this program was developed despite initially formidable religious and political obstacles and analyzes ten principles which he considers useful guidelines for any community-wide family planning program.

In Louisiana, we have attempted to design and implement a system to offer high quality modern, medical family planning services to the estimated 130,000 medically indigent women of the State who want and need them, assuring the dignity, privacy and right of free choice of every patient. Our immediate goal is to have such a program operational in each of the State's 64 parishes (counties) by August 1970—just three years from the inception of our first large-scale service program in New Orleans.* Our ultimate objectives are substantially to reduce the incidence of unwanted pregnancies, infant deaths, stillbirths, premature births, abortions and illegitimate births, and to augment significantly the delivery of health care for the medically indigent.

Our experience has indicated that effective and large-scale services can be implemented rapidly when developed systematically, while preserving a high standard of medical care and respecting the right of free choice of

Family Planning Perspectives 1(1): 2-17, Spring 1969. Reprinted by permission. Abridgment by the editors of the present volume.

*The progress made in the Louisiana Program to date has been mainly due to the staff of the Louisiana Family Planning Program, the staff of the Center for Population and Family Studies, LSU and Tulane Departments of Obstetrics and the cooperating and coordinating agencies noted in this paper. J.D.B.

every patient. Recognizing the importance nationally of creating working community-wide service programs, we included in the Louisiana design a substantial research component, through which we hope to provide program development models for large and smaller urban centers, their suburbs, and rural areas elsewhere in the nation.

Some aspects of the development of the Louisiana program are possibly unique, and, indeed, no one community's experiences can be lifted wholesale and transferred uncritically to another. In Louisiana, for example, we began to lay the groundwork for our program in 1964, under conditions where it was a felony to disseminate family planning information; as a result, there were *no* organized family planning services in the state for the medically indigent. In order to secure community acceptance as well as a change in the law, we had to develop extensive data to prove that such services were supported by the overwhelming majority of the population, and that they were needed, wanted and would effectively be used by the indigent. On the other hand, since there were no pre-existing family planning services, it was possible to plan from scratch, without accommodating a variety of overlapping uncoordinated family planning programs, disparate in quality, degree of service, and with differing eligibility requirements.

In Louisiana there is a State operated and controlled Charity Hospital system with uniform criteria for eligibility. More than 95 per cent of indigent births occur in these hospitals. In addition, the State Board of Health operates health units in each of the 64 parishes, and the indigent population is used to coming to both of them for much of their health care. It seemed advisable, under these conditions, to conceive of this program, from the beginning, as State-wide in scope, and to relate it intimately with the Charity Hospital and Health Department Systems. In other communities, the structure of the health delivery system may suggest designing the program on a regional, SMSA,* city, or health district basis.

Regardless of such organizational specifics, there are a number of principles of operation which need to be observed to develop an effective community-wide program. These principles apply equally to a program serving a city, a county, a state or a nation. Their application may be illustrated through examples of our Louisiana experience.

PRINCIPLE #1: STUDY THE POPULATION

This study should minimally include information on the following matters:

    a. Who are those in need of service?
    b. What are their characteristics?
    c. Where are they located?
    d. Where do they receive their medical care?
    e. Where do they deliver their babies?

---

* Standard Metropolitan Statistical Tract Area (Eds.)

f. What family planning services now exist?

g. How many poor persons currently have access to effective family planning services?

Study Results

Only 26 per cent of the female population of reproductive age in New Orleans was poor but it accounted for: 56 per cent of live births; 88 per cent of illegitimate births; 68 per cent of births to women under 19; 72 per cent of stillbirths; 80 per cent of maternal deaths; and 68 per cent of infant deaths.

Half of the pregnancies among lower socio-economic group women culminating in infant or maternal deaths occurred to women who, on the basis of their previous medical histories, were predictably "high risk" *before they became pregnant,* i.e: they had experienced a previous stillbirth or infant death, or their last pregnancy resulted in a premature or out-of-wedlock birth. In contrast, very few of the upper socio-economic group women studied who had catastrophic outcomes of pregnancy had ever had a previous reproductive event which would make them predictably high risk.

Only 28 per cent of the poor used any form of contraception, compared to 85 per cent of the upper and middle income group.

More than 90 per cent of the poor showed marked ignorance about reproductive physiology, family planning and the causes of infertility.

Eight out of ten poor women in the study had their first child before the age of 18; they were five times as likely not to complete their high school education as those who delayed their first child until beyond the age of 18.

Despite the lack of knowledge of the poor about family planning and their low level of contraceptive practice, they expressed considerable motivation to limit and space their children. While they had an average of nearly five children each before they were 26 years old, 60 per cent of them had wanted no more than three children. Three-fourths of them did not ever want to become pregnant again; nine-tenths of them felt it was their right to plan the size of their families, and wanted their children to have information about birth control.

Of the population surveyed, consisting of all racial, religious and economic groups, 91 per cent thought family planning was a basic right, and 93 per cent favored offering services to the poor.

Armed with such findings we were able to work with the State Board of Health to secure a reinterpretation of the criminal code: a ruling by the State Attorney General in August, 1965, subsequently approved by the Governor, made it legally permissible to operate medical family planning clinics in Louisiana. Within a month, the Lincoln Parish Family Planning Clinic was in operation.

Lincoln Parish

The Lincoln Parish program was initiated primarily as a research laboratory for population and family planning studies in a rural setting, a major purpose of which was to design a program which would rapidly provide

all medically indigent mothers and their families with the information and services needed to plan their families. Since no organized family planning facilities existed in Louisiana, this program also served as a pilot study for our proposed State-wide system of publicly supported family planning clinics.

Our first step was to study the Lincoln Parish population, much as we had the New Orleans population. The results were amazingly similar.

On the basis of the study findings, we initiated actual clinical operations in Lincoln Parish on September 10, 1965 and had all phases in operation by March 1966, designed on the premise that the provision of adequate information and services would result in a high level of utilization by couples of lower socio-economic status.

Lincoln Parish Results

These premises were borne out by experience: in the first year of operation, over 75 per cent of post partum patients accepted and kept appointments at the clinic; and nearly 60 per cent of the rest of the indigent Lincoln Parish women who were available for services came to the clinic and accepted a family planning method.

The Lincoln Parish program is now three years old, and is still producing important information which is being fed into our family planning programs elsewhere in the State. But within the first 18 months, operations in Lincoln Parish gave us sufficient experience in offering services to all indigent women who could be identified from hospital and vital records to equip us to design and implement an effective program for New Orleans; this, in turn, provided the basis for our State-wide program, now in effect in more than half of the State's parishes.

Knowledge, attitude and practice studies as extensive as were undertaken in Louisiana in 1964–65 are no longer necessary as a prerequisite for the development of effective community-wide family planning programs in other communities in the United States. Today, responsible citizens should recognize the readiness of the poor to accept family planning services,[1] and the intimate relationship which exists between the denial of such services to the indigent and the social and health problems associated with poverty.[2]

What must be obtained during the program planning period, however, is an appraisal of the characteristics of the population, the level of unmet family planning need and the actual and potential resources capable of delivering family planning services.

PRINCIPLE #2: DEVELOP A STRONG LEADERSHIP ORGANIZATION WITH AUTHORITY AND RESPONSIBILITY

Armed with relevant data about the population and having evaluated existing and potential resources for service delivery, it is next essential to establish or identify a strong leadership organization—a group capable of sophisticated planning (or able to acquire it) which can proceed to develop a systematic goal-oriented program design for operation of a community-wide family planning program. One of the most important functions of this leadership organization is to examine and evaluate the community's total approach to family planning; it must seek to achieve the active participation and cooperation of the various interest groups within the community, help them understand how their interests are identified with the goals of the program and enlist, where appropriate, their direct and joint efforts toward achievement of the program goal. Once a plan is agreed upon, then funding must be secured. Frequently it is necessary to use many different sources of funds for a single program. It is essential, therefore, that the tedious details of pertinent legislation and funding mechanisms be thoroughly understood.

In Louisiana, the leadership organization has taken the form of a new, independent non-profit corporation, Louisiana Family Planning Program, Inc. The corporation mechanism may be useful elsewhere; or in other communities the leadership organization could be an existing voluntary agency, a health department, a hospital, a medical school or a health planning committee. It could also be one organization or a group of institutions which agree to operate under unified leadership. Whatever the organizational specifics, however, there must be early agreement that one central organizational entity will take primary responsibility for the development, implementation and administration of the program plan decided upon, including the central collection of data, and the evaluation and reporting of whether or not program goals are being met. It should have sufficient control of program funds to assure performance of agreed-upon program functions.

PRINCIPLE #3: DESIGN A GOAL-ORIENTED PRELIMINARY PLAN

Once established, the leadership organization should proceed with formulation of a preliminary plan designed to offer service on a systematic basis to all of the indigent population in the community within a designated period of time. The plan should be drawn up in such a way that agreement can be obtained from local agencies and institutions which should participate in, cooperate with or support the program.

In so far as possible, the plan should be designed to integrate family planning services within the community's health delivery structure in a manner which enhances maternal and child health services for the entire indigent population.

Criteria for Eligibility
As to eligibility, our own experience in New Orleans and elsewhere suggests that the financial criterion for "Near Poor" families ($4,345 for a non-farm family of four) developed by the Social Security Administration(3) is the only national standard available which can serve as a minimum index of medical indigency. Unfortunately there are differences between OEO and Children's Bureau guidelines as to financial eligibility for services—and even more significant differences among state-run Medicaid programs; in the long run we need a national standard applicable everywhere for all programs. In Louisiana, a woman is financially eligible for the program if she meets OEO standards of indigency, has delivered in a Charity Hospital in the previous five years, or is currently eligible for maternity services in a Charity Hospital (a slightly higher standard of indigency than the Social Security Administration near-poverty index).

For a family planning program to be maximally effective, all fertile, medically indigent women should be eligible for family planning services. In Louisiana, all married women and all women, including minors, who have been pregnant were offered family planning services from the beginning. Family planning education was offered to women over 21 who were never married and had never been pregnant, but they were not eligible for clinic services until 1969. Unmarried minors who had not been pregnant could receive counseling and now are getting clinic services, with parental consent. (At the present time, we are receiving numerous requests for service from minors whom we know to be sexually active and who are not willing to ask for parental consent. We are trying to come to a consensus as a community as to how we can meet this need in a reasonable way, and to establish a mechanism for handling complications which might ensue.) In some other communities, it may be possible to achieve consensus as to establishment of a much wider range of eligibility for service* at an earlier stage. Such consensus should be achieved before proceeding to implementation, however, no matter how desirable the social goal. Otherwise we risk endangering acceptance of the whole plan. On the other hand, we should move forward vigorously to achieve such consensus as rapidly as possible in order to bring competent services to all who want and need them. In the matter of extending service to the unmarried never-pregnant woman, including the sexually active minor, it may be necessary to demonstrate to the community's satisfaction that the availability of birth control services does not lead to an increase in promiscuity, but does indeed salvage the lives of numerous women and children from the stigma and disabilities of illegitimacy. (4)

Identify Target Group; Locate Clinics and Set Priorities for Service

From Census Bureau data, the 1965 Metropolitan New Orleans Survey, and examination of vital records we were able to estimate that in New Orleans there were about 30,000 women potentially eligible for the program. From a detailed examination of birth records we could see that most indigent mothers lived in six areas of the City. These were also the areas where health indices showed the highest proportions of infant and maternal mortality. This helped us to determine where we would set up our central clinic (near Charity Hospital and accessible to the major areas where the indigent lived), and where our priority areas for satellite clinics should be.

The Lincoln Parish experience, supported by previous studies(5), indicated that post partum women are most highly motivated to use family planning. Our plan therefore gave first priority to reaching women who delivered or aborted in Charity Hospital. Thus we were assured of reaching the largest number of women in the shortest possible time at the lowest logistical and financial cost.

---

*See "Birth control, teenagers and the law," page 29.

Patient Contact and Follow-Up

Our next step was to develop a patient contact and appointment system, and a method of outreach and follow-up, capable of systematically locating the groups identified above, educating them about family planning and reproductive physiology, offering them a medically sound birth control method of their choice, and helping them to maintain that method while they chose not to be pregnant.

Record System

The Louisiana Family Planning Program has developed a precise, functional record system which provides information needed for clinic administration, evaluation and research. It was designed and installed (based on the Lincoln Parish experience and before a single patient was admitted to service) at a relatively low cost for securing information on patient characteristics, clinic load, outreach and follow-up.

PRINCIPLE #4: LOCATE AND COORDINATE
ALL EXISTING FACILITIES AND SERVICES

From both a political and religious point of view, Louisiana may have been (and is) a particularly sensitive workshop for the initiation and implementation of a large-scale family planning program. Perhaps for this very reason, our own experiences have been particularly useful in negotiating a community consensus by underlining the vital importance of identifying existing community interests with the goals of the program, and enlisting their cooperation and joint participation. The politics of confrontation may or may not be useful in shaking up or breaking down entrenched power structures which are unresponsive to community needs; in my opinion, however, such tactics alone are unlikely to be very useful in implementing a program which requires the coordinated efforts of existing agencies and institutions, and their support and assistance in introducing new—and what may at least superficially appear to be threatening and competitive—services.

It may be possible, and even necessary, in some communities to introduce family planning as an isolated service without support of other community institutions. It is highly unlikely, however, that any one agency adequately can provide the services needed by all low income couples in the community.

Thus, in addition to studying the population and designing a preliminary plan, the leadership organization must at a very early stage obtain from established agencies approval of the program design and active support for its implementation. In addition to those institutions which will actually provide facilities and staff for delivery of the services (e.g., hospitals and health departments), approval should also be sought from professional and medical societies, governmental agencies and civic and religious groups.

Indeed, "trouble shooting" or education is a prime function of the leadership organization. The support of the various groups depends to a large extent upon the manner in which they are informed of the program's purposes and progress, and in which their cooperation is solicited. The value of investing considerable effort in initial contact, groundwork, and coordination cannot be overemphasized.

PRINCIPLE #5: ALLOW TIME FOR DEVELOPMENT AFTER FUNDING

Once the preliminary plan has been worked into a detailed program design through agreement among participating, cooperating and supporting agencies, obviously it is necessary to obtain funding. Our own funding pattern in Louisiana is not typical, since it contains such a large research component. The major Federal resources for funding of family planning programs at the present time are through the OEO and the Children's Bureau.

Matching local funds are required on a 20–25 per cent basis. The patterns of Federal funding are likely to undergo considerable change in the future, and it is not necessary to go into them in detail here. It is important, however, to note that the Louisiana Family Planning Program is receiving funding from 11 different public and private sources, at this writing, and we hope soon to increase this to 20 different sources—most of them local. Diversification of funding sources, with a strong local base, is highly desirable to assure long-term continuity.

Funding agencies are often impatient to see the work get started; and it is usual, given these pressures, to try to open the clinic doors to patients almost as soon as the ink is dry on the contracts. This can be a tragic error; a considerable amount of development time—usually from two to five months, depending upon the extent and sophistication of the program design—is necessary to provide the proper organizational framework and to hire and train program staff and orient the staff of cooperating agencies as to the program's purposes and operations.

The Orleans Parish program, for example, was funded April 1, 1967, but we did not see our first patient in the central clinic facility until July 1, three months later. These are some of the things we had to do in this interim:

Having developed a manning table in the program design, we began to recruit a staff capable of handling the first phase (post partum) of the program. These included: administrators (our first two staff members were an administrator and an accountant), physicians (under contract from LSU and Tulane), nurses, social workers, data analysts and clerks.

New staff was trained in the objectives and operations of the Orleans Parish program and in the State-wide program of which this was to be a part.

Every Welfare Department caseworker and Public Health nurse—some 225 staff members—was oriented to our program, and arrangements were made with the Departments of Health and Welfare for referral of eligible women.

The central clinic facility was renovated and equipped to handle the anticipated patient load during the first phase, so as to assure a high quality of service, as well as patient privacy and dignity. (This included cheerful patient waiting rooms, private examining rooms with curtained dressing rooms, etc.) A capability was developed for rapid expansion as we moved into succeeding phases, so that convenient, dignified, quality care would be maintained.

We set up an appointment system and worked out logistics to implement it, so that patients would not be kept waiting for inordinate periods of time.

We developed, staffed and equipped a computer-based central record system capable of quickly delivering accurate patient and administrative data needed for medical and program decisions, as well as statistical data required to evaluate whether the goals of the program were being met and to test our various hypotheses. (The record system was designed for eventual expansion to encompass the entire State-wide program.)

PRINCIPLE #6: CONTACT ALL ELIGIBLE PATIENTS WITHIN SPECIFIC TIME LIMIT

Having identified a considerable number of the patient-eligible population, it is vital that the actual implementation of the program be vigorous and systematic enough to assure contacting all eligible women within the specific pre-determined time limit.

As stated earlier, in New Orleans we set a time limit of two years to contact—on a phased priority basis—and offer family planning services to all of the patient-eligible population who were post partum, or who could be identified from vital records. We hypothesized that the great majority of women contacted would accept and keep family planning appointments.

In point of fact, we were able to contact all of the post partum patients within the first year(6), and all of the identifiable high risk and low risk mothers within the first 18 months of the Program's operation. What is even more significant is the fact that 85 per cent of those contacted made and kept an initial appointment, and more than 90 per cent of those were current with scheduled appointments at the end of 12 months.

In terms of numbers, we served 9,210 patients in the first year of the Program's operations, and we will be serving more than 18,000 New Orleans patients by June 30, 1969, the end of the second year, if current rates of patient acceptance continue. This means that we will have contacted an estimated 75 per cent of New Orleans' medically indigent women in need of family planning within two years, and will be providing service to some two-thirds of them. Since we have only recently instituted an outreach program to reach the so-called non-identifiable segment, and we are now providing service for the first time to never-married nulliparous women, we expect to be providing family planning services for almost all of the low income population of New Orleans who want and need it by the end of 1969.

It is not only the numbers of patients accepting service that are significant, but the effectiveness of the family planning methods which they chose after coming to the clinic (where the advantages and disadvantages of all methods, and the attitudes of the major religious groups towards them, are carefully explained). Prior to their participation in the Program, 75 per cent of the patients had used either no birth control method or were using nonprescription methods, often irregularly. After coming to the clinic, 82 per cent of the patients chose either the orals or the IUD, while only 17.1 per cent chose a non-prescription method.

Follow-Up
About 40 per cent of patients miss an appointment at some time. All are promptly followed up, first with a reappointment letter and then a home visit from an auxiliary worker. Within the follow-up procedure, highest priority is placed on reaching any patient who has a positive Pap smear suggesting cancer of the cervix, or some other medical indication that an immediate visit is vitally necessary for her life or health. In such cases, a reappointment letter is dispensed with, and a home visit is made immediately—often involving extensive "detective" work in locating the patient. In routine cases, highest priority for follow-up is given to current pill patients, since they are most in danger of suffering an unwanted pregnancy if they do not get new supplies, followed by patients who fail to appear for their post partum examinations, and third, non-post partum patients on contraceptive methods other than the pill.

We are able to contact 95 per cent of patients who miss an appointment. Of those contacted, 22 per cent are found to be already pregnant, have moved, or wish to become pregnant; 89 per cent of the remainder accept an appointment, and about half of these keep their appointment at the clinic. The rapidity with which a follow-up contact is made dramatically affects the outcome. *Therefore, prompt contact results in considerably improved follow-up effectiveness.*

The Auxiliary System
The auxiliary staff members are mature, intelligent women from the poorer segment of the population who had little formal education but have a high capacity for learning. They are recruited through the OEO, newspaper ads, the State Employment Service, and—most important—the "grapevine." (Many of the auxiliaries ultimately employed were patients in the Program or friends of patients.)

The role of the family planning health workers is to act as intermediaries between the patient and the Program. On a follow-up visit, for example, they will introduce themselves to the patient, tell her they have come because she made an appointment with the clinic but did not keep it, and ask if she is still interested and wants another appointment. The family planning worker also tries to find out if the patient had some contact with the Program which she felt was unpleasant or demeaning. Such incidents are documented and reported back to the supervisor, who, in turn, refers them to the coordinator of patient services. Each such complaint is carefully investigated. If the patient is undecided about whether to make another appointment, but requests further information, additional education about family planning and reproductive physiology is provided by the family planning worker in the patient's home.

A carefully designed program of curriculum development, education and training of auxiliaries is carried out under the close supervision of professional social workers and medical personnel. The formal training program lasts three weeks, with close continuing supervision by professional personnel after that time. Role playing has been found to be one of the most useful training and teaching techniques. Several of the auxiliaries have advanced to the point where they have become supervisors in the outreach program.

Satellites

Prior to putting the auxiliaries in the field to contact the first high risk patients, we opened three satellite clinics (in an OEO sponsored neighborhood center, a Health Department unit, and a hospital) in neighborhoods with high concentrations of potential patients. We also opened a night clinic in our central facility. Both of these steps were taken to provide expanded, convenient facilities capable of handling the increased patient load which would be generated from implementation of this phase of the Program.

PRINCIPLE #7: EXPANSION OF FAMILY PLANNING SERVICES CAN BE CRITICAL FIRST STEP IN IMPROVING TOTAL HEALTH CARE

Because family planning services are in themselves so cost-effective in reducing poverty and infant mortality, their introduction under established health auspices on a systematic basis can often be the first step in improving a community's total maternal and child care pattern.

In New Orleans, for example, introduction of family planning in the first year more than doubled the post partum return rate among Charity Hospital maternity patients, and resulted in a vastly improved quality of post partum care. From the beginning, all of our family planning patients received a regular physical examination, including Pap smear and breast check for cancer. A highly trained social work staff works individually with all girls in the Program aged 17 or under to help them solve overwhelming life problems of continuing education for themselves, care of their babies, and often blighted home situations. In January of this year, through an arrangement similar to the post partum service, the Program accepted responsibility for delivering all routine prenatal care for Charity Hospital, and we expect quickly to see the same kinds of improvements as with post partum care. Most recently, we have extended our program to include a visit by a health auxiliary to the home of every patient who delivers her baby in Charity Hospital who cannot currently be visited by a Public Health nurse. She will reinforce with the mother the necessity for a post partum appointment, and appraise the ability of the home environment to sustain the life of the child.

Should the auxiliary worker find conditions in the home insupportable for the life of the child, she will report the condition to her Public Health Nurse supervisor, who will take appropriate steps to correct the conditions, or to remove the child from so dangerous an environment. Prior to this time the caseload of the Public Health Nurse was so great she could visit homes only where patients had premature babies, or there was some special condition. Now the auxiliary conducts a home visit routinely under the careful supervision of Program nursing staff.

Thus, while our action design was directed primarily to offering of family planning services, we recognized that, ideally, family planning should be part of an educational and health care process which should begin with family life and sex education in the schools, followed by premarital counseling, family planning service at the time sexual relationships are begun, prenatal clinics, maternal and delivery care, post partum care, and infant care. By working closely with the health, welfare, educational, religious and civic organizations of the community, family planning was the instrumentality through which all of these programs have been considerably enhanced—and, in some cases, instituted for the first time.

We have now created in New Orleans a system to provide total maternal health care, and established a structure whereby we may proceed to the next step—the incorporation of services for well and sick children.

PRINCIPLE #8: VALUE THE INDIVIDUAL PATIENT'S PRIVACY, DIGNITY, AND RIGHT TO CHOOSE

Poor patients receiving care under tax-supported auspices frequently have their privacy, dignity or right to choose disregarded. If those rendering service believe that their patients are "too dumb to learn," "not interested," "poor protoplasm or they would not be poor," then it is unlikely that patients will maintain a sustained relationship with the program.

To overcome these attitudes, constant supervision and constant in-service education at all levels of service delivery must be maintained. One cannot just write into a proposal that the dignity of the patient will be respected. Systematic and continuing supervision is necessary to insure this.

We believe that the fact that 85 per cent of our patients remained with the Program over an 18-month span, and that 82 per cent, after thorough education, chose the most effective methods of contraception, are due in large measure to scrupulous observance of this principle. And the high level of acceptance by black women of our voluntary services* indicates a very strong motivation by black couples for family planning in terms of their own perceived desires and aspirations—a motivation which is reinforced by the high quality of services maintained, careful observance of the right of free choice and continued respect for patient privacy and dignity.

---

*Conversely, acceptance by the low income white population has been disappointing—less than six per cent of our patients—and reflects their resistance apparently to an integrated service. We are studying how we may bring services to this extremely needy section of the populace while maintaining integration on a patient and professional level.

PRINCIPLE #9: USE MODERN MANAGEMENT TECHNIQUES TO DEVELOP AND MAINTAIN ADMINISTRATIVE EFFICIENCY

Cost accounting, flow charts, time effort studies, and other aspects of systems analysis should be applied to problems of program design and administration. A program must be concerned with providing the most effective service to the patient for the least amount of money.

For example, a well-run hospital may add family planning services for less than $20 per patient per year; but in an area with no facilities or few and inadequate systems of delivery of health services to the poor, as much as $50 to $100 per patient per year may be required.

It must be remembered that the purpose of efficient administration is to serve the objectives of the program, not vice versa. But the most well-intentioned program is almost certain to falter if a proper investment of time and money is not put into efficient management.

PRINCIPLE #10: OBTAIN, EVALUATE AND REPORT PROGRAM RESULTS

A goal-oriented program must be capable of evaluating its results at various stages. This is important not only to test hypotheses and make internal program judgments, but to provide witness for other incipient programs in just what way family planning can and does work. The two-year data from our initial Lincoln Parish study showing the correlation between provision of family planning services and declines in the indigent birth and illegitimacy rates provided an important spur, not only to our State-wide program in Louisiana, but to family planning programs around the country. Similarly, analysis of the data generated by the Orleans Parish program has confirmed, if further evidence were necessary, the validity of the original hypotheses advanced here—namely, that the poor want and will effectively utilize medically approved modern contraception when it is offered conveniently, systematically and with dignity.

Indications from the preliminary data suggest that we are experiencing in New Orleans a significant decline in indigent births and out-of-wedlock births as a result of the Program. While it is too early for definitive results, the response to the Orleans Program has been substantially higher than in Lincoln Parish, and it would not be surprising if the Orleans results are as good as in Lincoln(7) where:

In 1967, the first year in which the Program's impact could be expected, the number of indigent births in Lincoln Parish decreased by 32 per cent from the previous year. In four surrounding control parishes (which were similar to Lincoln in all respects except that they had no organized family planning programs) the decrease was only six per cent.

In the same year, the number of medically indigent out-of-wedlock births *dropped* 40 per cent in Lincoln Parish, compared to a two per cent *increase* in the control parishes. (Indeed, no parish in the State reported a change of the magnitude experienced in Lincoln.)

The decline significantly affected the entire illegitimacy picture; for indigent and well-to-do alike, the illegitimacy ratio in Lincoln Parish was *reduced* in 1967 by 23 per cent compared to a 13 per cent *increase* in the control parishes.

Since the family planning program in Lincoln was at that time restricted to women who were married or already had given birth, a study of its effect on second out-of-wedlock births was particularly significant. In Lincoln Parish, these *declined* by 41.5 per cent in 1967, compared to an *increase* of 6.2 per cent in the control parishes.

Since there were no significant changes in the health delivery system during this time in any of the parishes except for inauguration of Lincoln's family planning program, it seemed reasonable to assume that the family planning program was directly connected with the decline in indigent and out-of-wedlock births.

AFTERWORD: THE STATE-WIDE PROGRAM

Although this article has drawn from the Orleans Parish experience to exemplify principles of family planning program design and methodology we believe to be generally applicable, it would probably be useful here to outline the progress of the rest of the Louisiana State-wide program.

Of the State's 64 parishes, family planning programs are now operative in 33, where 70 per cent of the State's population resides. Our priorities were determined by analysis of where the largest number of people lived, modified by the availability of funding in the various regions.

Our objective, State-wide, is to develop family planning programs which offer coverage to the entire medically indigent population in need—an estimated 130,000 women—in every parish of the State by the Summer of 1970. We believe that this is an administratively feasible, realistic goal, and indeed the only reasonable outcome of the organizational and service framework we have been building throughout the State since the Orleans Parish program was initiated.

If we can accomplish this goal within three years, it should not be unrealistic—as proposed by the President's Committee on Population and Family Planning—to provide services nationwide within five years.(8)

For some time, while family planning programs were hardly acceptable, much less fashionable, several states claimed to offer family planning services to all of their indigent population, and continuing high birth and illegitimacy rates were usually blamed on the reluctance of the poor to use them. On close examination, the services offered proved minimal, almost non-existent; but the damage done by these false claims was significant and long-lasting. In today's atmosphere of acceptance and even growing enthusiasm about family planning, we must be especially careful not to repeat those early mistakes, and boast of "total coverage" when we have barely opened a clinic door. For waiting grimly in the wings (and in some instances already onstage) are numerous "taxpayers" and their legislative representatives who remain seized by the conviction that "procreation is the poor man's recreation," and that coercive measures beyond voluntary family planning are necessary to cope with such problems as illegitimacy and increasing AFDC rolls.(9) Long sensitive to this kind of anti-poor (and especially anti-black) "taxpayer" vigilantism, a counter-force is developing among some segments of the poor (and especially among some segments of the black poor) themselves, who are suspicious of governmental family planning programs as possibly concealing a hidden agenda to coerce the poor through such measures as punitive sterilization, deprivation of welfare, seizure of children and even jailing of unwed parents.

The development of systematic, workable programs is vital, therefore, for the implementation of effective community-wide services, and as a bulwark against coercion. Our experience in Louisiana has given strong backing to earlier findings that the poor want and will use family planning consistently and effectively, when services are properly designed and implemented.

REFERENCES

1. Cf., e.g., Freedman, R., Whelpton, P. K., and Campbell, A. A. 1959. *Family planning, sterility, and population growth.* McGraw Hill; Whelpton, P. K., Campbell, A. A., and Patterson, J. E. 1966. *Fertility and family planning in the U.S.* Princeton; Bogue, D. J., ed. 1967. *Sociological contributions to family planning research.* Chicago; and Westoff, C. F. and Ryder, N. B. 1969. Recent trends in attitudes toward fertility control and in the practice of contraception in the United States. *Fertility and family planning, a world view.* U. Michigan Press.

2. *Bull. of the New York Acad. of Med.* Oct. 1946, p. 555; Committee on Public Health. 1965. *Bull. New York Acad. of Med.* 41: 410; *J.A.M.A.* 1964. 190. United States Department of Health, Education and Welfare. 1966. *Child Health Care Programs.* Washington, D.C.: Government Printing Office; Yerushalmy, J., Palmer, C. E., and Kramer, M. 1940. *Pub. Health Rep.* 55: 1195; Newcombe, H. B., and Tavendale, O. G. 1964. *Mutation Res.* 1: 446; Day, R. L. 1967. *Am. J. Dis. Child.* 113: 179; Butler, N. R. and Bonham, D. G. 1963. *Perinatal Mortality.* Edinburgh and London: E. & S. Livingstone, Ltd; Heady, J. A. and Morris, J. N. 1959. *J. Obst. & Gynec. Brit. Emp.* 66: 577; Morris, J. N. and Heady, J. A. 1955. *Lancet* 1: 343; Yerushalmy, J., et al. 1956. *Am. J. Obst. & Gynec.* 71: 80; Eastman, J. H. and Hellman, L. M. 1961. *Williams' Obstetrics,* ed. 12. New York: Appleton-Century-Crofts; Heady, J. A., Daly, C. and Morris, J. N. 1955. *Lancet* 1: 395; U.S. Public Health Service. 1956, 1958 and 1960, 1961. *Vital Statistics of the United States,* vol I and II; Yerushalmy, J. 1945. *Human Biol.* 17: 65; Israel, S. L. and Bishop, E. H. 1967. *A. J. Obst. & Gynec.* 97: 623; Jaffe, F. S. and Polgar, S. Medical indications for fertility control. Unpublished paper. Planned Parenthood World Population; Hendricks, C. H. 1967. *Am. J. Obst. & Gynec.* 97: 608; Pakter, J., et al., 1961. *Am. J. Pub. Health* 51: 846; United States Department of Health, Education and Welfare. 1967. *International comparison of perinatal and infant mortality: The United States and six West European countries.* National Center of Health Statistics, series 3, no. 6, Government Printing Office.

3. Orshansky, M. March 1966. The shape of poverty in 1966. *Social Security Bulletin,* Table 4.

4. Beasley, J. D. and Parrish, V. W. June 1969. Epidemiology and prevention of illegitimate births in the rural south. *Journal of Social Biology.*

5. International Post Partum Family Planning Program. August 1967. *Studies in Family Planning,* no. 22.

6. Orleans Parish first year report. June 1969. *Milbank Memorial Quarterly.*

7. Beasley, J. D. and Parrish, V. W., *op. cit.*

8. Report of the President's Committee on Population and Family Planning. Nov. 1968. Population and family planning: The transition from concern to action.

9. Paul, J. August 1968. The return of punitive sterilization proposals. *Law and Society Review* VIII, no. 1.

India's New Departure in Mass Motivation for Fertility Control

FRANK WILDER AND D. K. TYAGI

FRANK WILDER *is a Ford Foundation Consultant in mass communications for family planning to the government of India.*

D. K. TYAGI *is Assistant Commissioner (Media) for the Department of Family Planning.*

Availability of contraceptives is usually not sufficient by itself to reduce the rate of population growth. Often people have to be shown the benefits of reducing their family sizes before they will voluntarily use contraceptive devices. However, this is a very difficult administrative undertaking—particularly in the less-developed countries. Wilder and Tyagi suggest ways in which the mass media might be used in these countries to publicize family planning programs. The authors describe the efforts of the Indian government to utilize the mass media for this purpose. They analyze the obstacles to the use of the mass media in these countries as well as the advantages of the current Indian program.

Imagine that we could construct a "success scale" along which we might rank the several major development fields in which aid-giving agencies (notably of the United States) have sought to assist the developing countries over the past two decades. On such a scale the field of Mass Communications—also known under the aliases of Communications Media, Information, Mass Media Development, Publicity, Propaganda, Mass Education, Audio-Visual Aids and Mass Motivation—would surely land near, and likely at, the bottom.

Perhaps in no other field have we achieved so little, although we seem to have so much to offer; we invested meagerly and sometimes aimlessly, although the potential development return was, and still is, promising.

It is not the purpose of this paper to examine and analyze the unhappy record of the developed countries in assisting the buildup abroad of mass media facilities, techniques, and competence to support national and inter-

Demography 5(2): 773–79, 1968. Reprinted by permission.

national development goals. Our purpose is to record the evidence in India of a new and unusual mass communications strategy in that country's family planning program. India's brave radical departures in mass motivation techniques are worth study because they hold promise of unprecedented payoffs at reasonable cost, within the pressing time limits of national fertility control programs in the crucial developing countries. There may also be lessons, both for foreign aid agencies and host governments, in any development effort where success depends on wide public understanding and participation. However, if only to set the background of the recently implemented Indian formula, let us state some important facts and circumstances in that dark history of efforts to apply mass media techniques in development programs, including family planning:

1. Most development planners recognize at last (albeit 21 years after Gen. George C. Marshall enunciated the European postwar recovery plan that opened an era of global "foreign aid") that the free flow of information and knowledge to and from the people in a developing society is a requisite for (and indeed a spur to) economic and social development.

2. Nonetheless, thus far, no developing country has been assisted to develop resources for mass media development that are commensurate with the enormity and urgency of development needs or responsive to the special non-Western setting in which development must be made to occur—notably in truly traditional rural societies. The gravest deficiency, in both the aid-giving community and the host countries, is a lack of working experts attuned to the special local audience settings that must govern selection of media, mode of presentation and message content.

3. The evidence is overwhelming that no developing country (with the apparent new exception of India) has put into motion a wide-scale mass motivation program whose messages are so contrived and presented that they hit the target tellingly and result in widespread new knowledge necessary for timely mass adoption of a new practice. Commercial firms, it is true, have successfully promoted product sales through mass media (largely to literate and urban and semi-urban audiences). It is true also that extension methods, together with radiation from personal experience, have brought spectacular results in agricultural innovation. But mass media utilization, for the spread of awareness, interest, and (possibly) acceptance has been universally marked in the developing countries by one or both of the following disastrous conditions:

   a. The public did not receive message.—Insufficient penetration of the audience results from either (1) a dearth of the standard major media outlets (newspapers, radios and movie facilities) in the target areas; (2) insufficient governmental investment in the personnel and facilities needed, informational materials (posters, pamphlets, exhibits and filmstrips, as well as items for distribution through the press, radio stations and motion picture facilities);

(3) a message that lacked luster and prominence, or, most likely, (4) all three.

b. The public did not understand the message.—This condition is uniquely the result of that great intellectual distance between message-maker and audience. The message-maker is all too frequently an administrator or an artist, and not a trained and seasoned communicator whose concern should be primarily getting the message across. By definition, the message can be got across only within the audience's frames of reference. To make matters worse, most persons designated as mass communications officers themselves shape messages to meet their own sophisticated tastes and those of their colleagues and supervisors. In short, mass communications messages in development programs have suffered the two extremes of inutility—ineptness or Madison Avenue aptness.

4. Three options in mass media development, or combinations of the three, seem to be available to the developing countries:

a. To continue developing the standard media—that is, the press, radio, motion pictures, posters, pamphlets, exhibits, and (for the more developed developing countries) television. (In the light of Indian departures from exclusive use of these media, which will be described later, one may now regard these once-modern media as "traditional.")

b. To introduce new communications technology developed in the West thereby hurdling years of Western communications evolution. Included here are satellite-based television, electronic typesetting, facsimile transmission, microfiche for libraries, laser beams and the like.

c. To exploit massively as media those widely existing facilities and societal accoutrements with which the public is already intimately familiar and is in frequent day-to-day contact. Some of these facilities and accoutrements are already in use as media—e.g., traveling troupes of entertainers. Some can be transformed into media—e.g., the outsides of railroad rolling stock. Most are characteristically visual, local, and outdoors. None has been effectively used by national development programs.

THE INDIAN FORMULA

India herself, by virtue of the massive attention she has received from aid-giving countries, exemplified diagrammatically the unhappy record of mass communications at work in a national development program. Then, in the summer of 1966, the Department of Family Planning (within the Ministry of Health and Family Planning) examined its allocations for the use of radio, films, press, exhibitions and printed materials and decided that no amount of investment in these media would bring the message to India's 560,000 villages in time. Mr. Govind Narain, Secretary of the Department of Family Planning, speaking in August 1968 at the Indian Institute of Mass Communications, described the Department's motivation in these words:

> *Perhaps it is the special nature of family planning that forced upon us the need for re-examining our traditional ways of communicating with the public and of devising new ways to accomplish a communications job that seemed almost impossible. In the first place the success of our total population control programme depends primarily on the individual's acceptance of the idea of preventing pregnancy for his own good. This means that many crores (tens of millions) of individuals must have sufficient information and be highly motivated to adopt one of the several family planning methods. The difficulty here is that we are dealing with the most intimate aspect of human life. The practice of family planning means a radical change in behaviour, ranging from the frequent use of a conventional contraceptive device to submission to a surgical procedure such as vasectomy or tubectomy. In dealing with such an intimate and difficult situation, you will appreciate that many of our people, especially in the rural areas, will readily listen to and accept rumours and misinformation about family planning. When you realise that we do not have at our command the benefit of instantaneous dissemination of information, such as through the radio, to the remote villages of our country, you will appreciate our concern to try to find different ways to spread the message of family planning as far and wide as possible.*

It should be added that Departmental moves toward more rapid and effective spread of family planning messages were made possible by the unusual phenomenon of a top administrator (the Secretary himself) sensitive to the role of mass communications in development and willing to take risks. In turn, the "education" of such program leaders to the urgency of the mass communications job had been the first priority of the Department's man heading the "Mass Education and Media Section." This office is under the Commissioner, the technical head of the program (and himself a prime target in the crucial early internal "education" drive).

The Indians opted, then, for a combination of the "standard" media (press, radio, motion pictures and printed materials) and any "outdoor" visual medium they could lay their message on. The noteworthy features of the revolutionary Indian strategy, however, are not confined to the add-on of these new media (which, in some cases, amounts to a return to older, truly traditional, media). Two other elements in the Indian strategy differ radically from earlier approaches—the *message* and the use of a special *symbol*.

THE MESSAGE

First, let us consider the special treatment of the content, or messages, of the information program. To begin with, the Indians chose to ignore those Indian and foreign specialists in advertising, publicity, and mass communications who counselled a changing, phased campaign that would run the gamut in both presentation and message. Slogans would change: designs would change; appeals would change from "What is Family Planning?" to reproductive biology to "What is the Best Method for Me?" Instead, sizing

up the bad void in media coverage in villages and the prospect of bureaucratic delays, they decided to find a message that would be a *direct exhortation to have a specific number of children;* to present this message
in the same form in all media; to keep it *simple and understandable;* and
to *stay with it* until everyone knew, through this message, that family
planning is legitimate and what it means. And in sudden realization that
no literate Indian in the target group does not know his own language,

materials for mass consumption are no longer produced in English; only the 13 major languages are used. The basic design presents visually the stylized front-view faces of a smiling mother and father, a son and a daughter. The message, in words no Indian can fail to understand, says simply: "Have Only Two or Three Children. . . That's Plenty." (The message is warmer and more engaging in the Indian languages than it is in that English translation.) The colors are always the same, bright and attractive. The faces are drawn always in the same style. The same message is verbalized in an appealing song by a popular Indian songwriter and recorded by a singer whose voice is as familiar to Indians as Bing Crosby's once was to Americans.

It should be noted, in passing, that adoption of the 2-or-3-children slogan was itself a bold and risky step. There is a strong Indian tradition that insists on sons, no matter how many pregnancies it takes. Worse, high officialdom was then concerned with high-parity couples, not the newly married or low-parity couples. Only those few Department officers who forced through the 2-or-3 slogan knew that the fourth child spells death to India's goal of a 2-per-thousand birth rate by 1978.

One obvious major pay-off of simplicity and repetition is that they help to hurdle the barrier of illiteracy (which is near-total in many Indian villages). It takes no more than a day or so for an illiterate to know the meaning of that distinctive design he seems to see at every turn. We are convinced that the studies the Indians are planning will show this approach has an overwhelming advantage over the use of several messages in press, radio and films. A high-ranking state family planning official, recently visiting New Delhi, decried the validity of the technique, because "you have put up hundreds of billboards in New Delhi, and we could never do that in the rural areas." He was then told that there are a mere 17 billboards to cover Delhi population of two million. Repetition had created the illusion of saturation.

The largest payoffs, for a fertility control program that lacks time and talent, result from the use of the exhortative message specifying the limits of a "small" family, rather than the loose appeal "Practice Family Planning" or the abstract declaration "A Small Family is a Happy Family." Given normal long delays in message dissemination, why not spell out the meaning of "family planning" in the first awareness message? Can we expect that the words "family planning" in a local language means "birth prevention?" (It certainly does not in any Indian language.) Does the small-family-happy-family message transmit the specific action to be taken? Can fertility programs succeed if people are left to "Have Only Those Children You Can Afford?" And are these not rather elusive concepts for a villager whose personal aspirations do not parallel those of the educated program administrator or the foreign communications advisor?

Finally, the repetition of the simple direct exhortation in the same form, in different "outdoor" media, seen everyday by the population at large, provides an illusion of legitimation and, by "airing" the subject of birth control, stimulates public discussion of it.

THE MEDIA

It would seem prosaic, even backward, in our television age, to turn to village walls, buses and billboards to carry a motivational message. However, employing the message techniques already described on such handy media, the Indians appear to be reaping large communications benefits (widespread awareness, considerable primary knowledge and some inclination toward birth control) with these "new" media.

The first important fact that struck the Indians in their examination of their mass media program was that the press, radio and films reach only an estimated 20–25 per cent of the population, mainly in the urban and semi-urban concentrations—where the need for motivation is least.

Equally revealing was a realistic look at the well-known mobile audiovisual unit as a means of bringing information and knowledge to villagers. In India, the Government's total public information program (both for support of development and for straight information) had at its command a mere 140 such mobile units, known as "cinema vans." That means one unit to cover 4000 villages. The Department of Family Planning, already seized with the need for a massive mass communications effort, had won a fund appropriation for 335 mobile units exclusively for family planning— that is, one for each District (average population 1.6 million). It would be another few years before these 335 additional family planning mobile units would be functioning. Whether all or most of them will be efficiently and effectively functioning at that time is still doubtful. Given full effect operation of these new audiovisual vehicles—meaning a large, trained, and hard-working staff, availability of power, no breakdowns of vehicle or equipment, and sustained logistic support—it would take *eight years for each vehicle to visit each of its 1700 villages once.* (At India's present growth rate, the addition to the population would, by then, be more than 100 million.)

Another old communications media standby, the ordinary printed paper poster, provided another goad that sent the Department searching for other ways to reach their far-flung audience. Posters, they observed, took many months from conception to printing, and sometimes two years or more to the moment of actual public display. Public display itself rarely occurred, since the quantity of posters printed brought only two or three to each clinic, hospital administrator or other appropriate office. The posters were then usually used for display in those very places, where motivation obviously is least needed. When publicly displayed, they found, the average life of posters is about three days: they are either mutilated by children, washed away by rain or used as a smooth foundation for a fresh movie poster. The cost-benefit ratio was clearly so disadvantageous that no one in the busy Department of Family Planning ventured to suggest a specific study to measure it.

In the new strategy, therefore, the Indians began to exploit—in addition to the "standard" media—billboards, buses, matchboxes, rickshas, pocket calendars, newspaper and magazine advertisements, carnival banners, shopping bags, official village civic registers, telephone directories and—

most important—the exterior walls of buildings for huge lasting paintings of the basic design. Also, permanent enamelled metal signs are being distributed to the country's 100,000 post offices, and, after traditional railroad conservatism was painfully overcome, the broad sides of locomotive tenders are being used as traveling billboards.

THE SYMBOL

The third major departure in the Indian mass communications strategy is the *Red Triangle*—a symbol that communicates even as it identifies and represents. It is unadorned, in solid vermillion, and equilateral, with its apex pointed downward.

A development program seeking widespread public participation need not be much concerned with a symbol as a decorative emblem for letterheads and office doors. Where masses of people are as yet untouched by modern contraceptive methods, a symbol should and can act to strengthen the program. The Indians eschewed selection of the conventional sign that attempts to convey meaning through *graphic* representation—that is, a design that seeks to *depict* the idea of family, few children or, somehow, population control. Instead, they sought a design with no prior meaning or connotation, in the belief (now proved correct) that it would soon produce, distinctively and exclusively, an association in the public mind's eye with Family Planning—indeed, would convey awareness of the concept of limiting the number of one's children to two or three.

History's best example of such a non-representational symbol is the Red Cross. This famous symbol, however, has two obvious defects, of which the Red Triangle is free. One is that the Red Cross is suggestive of Christianity, and for this reason it is not used in some Moslem countries. The other is that the Red Cross has come to be recognized widely as representing not only the Red Cross organization (its original purpose), but also medical services, hospital, first aid, drugs, doctors, and facilities or products unrelated to the original purpose. While the Red Triangle is expected to be identified later with products as well as clinics, it will remain, hopefully, within the world of population control programs.

The Indian program must reach out to the minds of some 400 million persons. Illiteracy is widespread, incomes are low, and there is little built-in motivation toward family planning. Effective mass media in the vast rural areas are insufficient. Under those conditions, the special characteristics of the Red Triangle seem to help advance the program significantly. First, it is distinctive. This means it will be identified in people's minds only with family planning and with family planning services and products. (Some intellectuals have read into the Red Triangle the suggestion of images or ideas peculiar to their own conscious and subconscious experience. But the mass of people do not seem to have such established connotations in their minds concerning a vermillion equilateral triangle, its apex pointed downward.) In India, the Red Triangle always appears with the 2-or-3 children message and the "four faces" design.

Second, and more important, the Red Triangle is easy to reproduce anywhere. No artistic talent is needed; it can be quickly painted in the remotest areas by local personnel. It already appears, painted large and prominent, on most of the country's clinics. For use on the clothing of family planning workers, it is easily cut from a piece of red cloth and sewn on. Nor is there any difficulty in making metal or plastic badges.

Because of its bright color, the Red Triangle is clearly visible at some distance. The Red Triangle will soon be displayed wherever contraceptive supplies are sold or distributed, even at drug stores, grocery stores, and tea and cigarette stalls.

But probably of greatest importance is the fact that, unlike elaborate graphic emblems, the Red Triangle can be verbalized in any language in the world. It can be called by name—"The Red Triangle"—even spontaneously by illiterates in their own particular language. This makes it easy for persons to inquire about the location of a clinic and to converse about family planning. They can ask for contraceptives without embarrassment, especially if contraceptive products carry the symbol in their packaging or carry the brand name, "Red Triangle."

There is no scientifically gathered data to gauge the economic and programmatic soundness of the Indian strategy, although the Department of Family Planning, at this writing, is mapping several needed studies. Nonetheless, informal assessment of results thus far lead us to commend it unqualifiedly for adaptation and application in other developing countries. This apparently visceral conclusion rests only on our conviction that mass communications methods, in their nature and in these settings—unlike clinical methods, for example—lend themselves to sufficiently valid assessment through daily intimate professional (if only visceral) observation. This would be a dangerous premise in a modern marketing situation wherein wide use is made of the press, radio, television and motion pictures, aimed at an audience that is able to buy, is informed and discriminating, and has several choices. Where all those conditions do *not* exist, and where the primary and urgent goal of mass media utilization is widespread positive public inclination toward contraception, it makes no sense to question the possible pay-off of large, bright paintings of a crisp, meaningful, graphic message (at 13 cents a square foot) on outdoor walls in villages.

In the cold light of print, this three-part Indian strategy in mass communications will seem to some of us to be undeserving of the labels, "imaginative," "new," or "revolutionary." Yet, it is all of those. It is imaginative in its insistence on thinking primarily in terms of its audience; it is new in its departure from the "standard" media, although it turned stubbornly to the old and the obvious; it is revolutionary in its upset of existing thinking and trends in mass communications for development. The entire approach is unheard of elsewhere. But it promises to work.

Poor Black Women

Not all people are agreed that family planning programs are a desirable service. The charge of genocide has been sporadically raised against family planning programs in the United States and abroad. Those suspicious of the motivations of family planning advocates sometimes jump to the conclusion that fertility control is simply another way of minimizing potential opposition to the ruling classes. The following two selections discuss this issue in the context of a family planning program in Peekskill, New York.

BIRTH CONTROL PILLS AND BLACK CHILDREN: A STATEMENT BY THE BLACK UNITY PARTY (PEEKSKILL, N.Y.)

The Brothers are calling on the Sisters to not take the pill. It is this system's method of exterminating Black people here and abroad. To take the pill means that we are contributing to our own *GENOCIDE*.

However, in not taking the pill, we must have a new sense of value. When we produce children, we are aiding the REVOLUTION in the form of NATION building. Our children must have pride in their history, in their heritage, in their beauty. Our children must not be brainwashed as we were.

PROCREATION is beautiful, especially if we are devoted to the Revolution which means that our value system be altered to include the Revolution as the responsibility. A good deal of the *Supremacist* (White) efforts to sterilize the world's (Non-whites) out of existence are turning toward the black people of America. New trends in Race Control have led the architects of *GENOCIDE* to believe that Sterilization projects aimed at the black man in the United States can cure American internal troubles.

Under the cover of an alleged campaign to 'alleviate poverty,' white supremacist Americans and their dupes are pushing an all-out drive to put rigid birth control measures into every black home. No such drive exists within the White American world. In some cities, Peekskill, Harlem, Mississippi and Alabama, welfare boards are doing their best to force black women receiving aid to submit to *Sterilization*. This disguised attack on black future generations is rapidly picking up popularity among determined genocidal engineers. This country is prepared to exterminate people by the

New England Free Press, pp. 1–2, 1968. Reprinted by permission.

pill or by the bomb; therefore, we must draw strength from ourselves.

You see why there is a Family Planning Office in the Black Community of Peekskill.

THE SISTERS REPLY

Here is the sisters' reply:

September 11, 1968

Dear Brothers:

Poor black sisters decide for themselves whether to have a baby or not to have a baby. If we take the pills or practise birth control in other ways, it's because of poor black men.

Now here's how it is. Poor black men won't support their families, won't stick by their women—all they think about is the street, dope and liquor, women, a piece of ass, and their cars. That's all that counts. Poor black women would be fools to sit up in the house with a whole lot of children and eventually go crazy, sick, heartbroken, no place to go, no sign of affection—nothing. Middle class white men have always done this to their women—only more sophisticated like.

So when whitey put out the pill and poor black sisters spread the word, we saw how simple it was not to be a fool for men any more (politically we would say men could no longer exploit us sexually or for money and leave the babies with us to bring up). That was the first step in our waking up!

Black women have always been told by black men that we were black, ugly, evil, bitches and whores—in other words, we were the real niggers in this society—oppressed by whites, male and female, and the black man, too.

Now a lot of the black brothers are into a new bag. Black women are being asked by militant black brothers not to practise birth control because it is a form of whitey committing genocide on black people. Well, true enough, but it takes two to practise genocide and black women are able to decide for themselves, just like poor people all over the world, whether they will submit to genocide. For us, birth control is freedom to fight genocide of black women and children.

Like the Vietnamese have decided to fight genocide, the South American poor are beginning to fight back, and the African poor will fight back, too. Poor black women in the U.S. have to fight back out of our own experience of oppression. Having too many babies stops us from supporting our children, teaching them the truth or stopping the brainwashing as you say, and fighting black men who still want to use and exploit us.

But we don't think you are going to understand us because you are a bunch of little middle class people and we are poor black women. The middle class never understands the poor because they always need to use them as you want to use poor black women's children to gain power for yourself. You'll run the black community with your kind of black power—you on top!

Mt. Vernon, N.Y.

Patricia Haden—welfare recipient
Sue Rudolph—housewife
Joyce Hoyt—domestic
Rita Van Lew—welfare recipient
Catherine Hoyt—grandmother
Patricia Robinson—housewife and psychotherapist

Population Policy:
Will Current Programs Succeed?

KINGSLEY DAVIS

KINGSLEY DAVIS *is professor of sociology and Director of International Population and Urban Research at the University of California, Berkeley.*

The early advocates of national family planning programs often exaggerated their effectiveness in order to generate interest and to obtain sufficient funds to carry them out. Davis examines the current population policies of the 30 nations now trying to curb their population growth and presents grounds for skepticism in regard to the effectiveness of these programs because they ignore the issue of the motivations of the couples involved. He then analyzes in detail the experience of Taiwan as a case study of the effort to reduce population growth in the less-developed countries.

Throughout history the growth of population has been identified with prosperity and strength. If today an increasing number of nations are seeking to curb rapid population growth by reducing their birth rates, they must be driven to do so by an urgent crisis. My purpose here is not to discuss the crisis itself but rather to assess the present and prospective measures used to meet it. Most observers are surprised by the swiftness with which concern over the population problem has turned from intellectual analysis and debate to policy and action. Such action is a welcome relief from the long opposition, or timidity, which seemed to block forever any governmental attempt to restrain population growth, but relief that "at last something is being done" is no guarantee that what is being done is adequate. On the face of it, one could hardly expect such a fundamental reorientation to be quickly and successfully implemented. I therefore propose to review the nature and (as I see them) limitations of the present policies and to suggest lines of possible improvement.

Science 158 (3802): 730–39, November 10, 1967. Copyright 1967 by the American Association for the Advancement of Science. Reprinted by permission. Abridgment by the editors of the present volume.

THE NATURE OF CURRENT POLICIES

With more than 30 nations now trying or planning to reduce population
growth and with numerous private and international organizations helping,
the degree of unanimity as to the kind of measures needed is impressive.
The consensus can be summed up in the phrase "family planning." President
Johnson declared in 1965 that the United States will "assist family planning
programs in nations which request such help." The Prime Minister of India
said a year later, "We must press forward with family planning. This is
a programme of the highest importance." The Republic of Singapore created
in 1966 the Singapore Family Planning and Population Board "to initiate
and undertake population control programmes" (1).

As is well known, "family planning" is a euphemism for contraception.
The family-planning approach to population limitation, therefore, concen-
trates on providing new and efficient contraceptives on a national basis
through mass programs under public health auspices. The nature of these
programs is shown by the following enthusiastic report from the Population
Council (2):

> No single year has seen so many forward steps in population con-
> trol as 1965. Effective national programs have at last emerged, inter-
> national organizations have decided to become engaged, a new
> contraceptive has proved its value in mass application, . . . and sur-
> veys have confirmed a popular desire for family limitation. . .
>
> An accounting of notable events must begin with Korea and Taiwan
> . . . Taiwan's program is not yet two years old, and already it has
> inserted one IUD [intrauterine device] for every 4–6 target women
> (those who are not pregnant, lactating, already sterile, already using
> contraceptives effectively, or desirous of more children). Korea has
> done almost as well . . . has put 2,200 full-time workers into the field,
> . . . has reached operational levels for a network of IUD quotas,
> supply lines, local manufacture of contraceptives, training of hun-
> dreds of M.D.'s and nurses, and mass propaganda. . .

Here one can see the implication that "population control" is being
achieved through the dissemination of new contraceptives, and the fact that
the "target women" exclude those who want more children. One can also
note the technological emphasis and the medical orientation.

What is wrong with such programs? The answer is, "Nothing at all, if
they work." Whether or not they work depends on what they are expected
to do as well as on how they try to do it. Let us discuss the goal first, then
the means.

GOALS

Curiously, it is hard to find in the population-policy movement any explicit
discussion of long-range goals. By implication the policies seem to promise
a great deal. This is shown by the use of expressions like *population control*
and *population planning* (as in the passages quoted above). It is also shown
by the characteristic style of reasoning. Expositions of current policy usually

start off by lamenting the speed and the consequences of runaway population growth. This growth, it is then stated, must be curbed—by pursuing a vigorous family-planning program. That family planning can solve the problem of population growth seems to be taken as self-evident.

The promised goal—to limit population growth so as to solve population problems—is a large order. One would expect it to be carefully analyzed, but it is left imprecise and taken for granted, as is the way in which family planning will achieve it.

When the terms *population control* and *population planning* are used, as they frequently are, as synonyms for current family-planning programs, they are misleading. Technically, they would mean deliberate influence over all attributes of a population, including its age-sex structure, geographical distribution, racial composition, genetic quality, and total size. No government attempts such full control. By tacit understanding, current population policies are concerned with only the *growth* and *size* of populations. These attributes, however, result from the death rate and migration as well as from the birth rate; their control would require deliberate influence over the factors giving rise to all three determinants. Actually, current policies labeled population control do not deal with mortality and migration, but deal only with the birth input. This is why another term, *fertility control,* is frequently used to describe current policies. But, as I show below, family planning (and hence current policy) does not undertake to influence most of the determinants of human reproduction.

The ambiguity does not stop here, however. When one speaks of controlling population size, any inquiring person naturally asks, What is "control"? Who is to control whom? Precisely what population size, or what rate of population growth, is to be achieved? Do the policies aim to produce a growth rate that is nil, one that is very slight, or one that is like that of the industrial nations? Unless such questions are dealt with and clarified, it is impossible to evaluate current population policies.

The actual programs seem to be aiming simply to achieve a reduction in the birth rate. Success is therefore interpreted as the accomplishment of such a reduction, on the assumption that the reduction will lessen population growth. In those rare cases where a specific demographic aim is stated, the goal is said to be a short-run decline within a given period. The Pakistan plan adopted in 1966(3, p. 889) aims to reduce the birth rate from 50 to 40 per thousand by 1970; the Indian plan(4) aims to reduce the rate from 40 to 25 "as soon as possible"; and the Korean aim(5) is to cut population growth from 2.9 to 1.2 per cent by 1980. A significant feature of such stated aims is the rapid population growth they would permit. Under conditions of modern mortality, a crude birth rate of 25 to 30 per thousand will represent such a multiplication of people as to make use of the term *population control* ironic. A rate of increase of 1.2 per cent per year would allow South Korea's already dense population to double in less than 60 years.

One can of course defend the programs by saying that the present goals and measures are merely interim ones. A start must be made somewhere. But we do not find this answer in the population-policy literature. Such a defense, if convincing, would require a presentation of the *next* steps, and these are not considered. One suspects that the entire question of goals is instinctively left vague because thorough limitation of population growth would run counter to national and group aspirations. A consideration of hypothetical goals throws further light on the matter.

Industrialized nations as the model. Since current policies are confined to family planning, their maximum demographic effect would be to give the underdeveloped countries the same level of reproductive performance that the industrial nations now have. The latter, long oriented toward family planning, provide a good yardstick for determining what the availability of contraceptives can do to population growth. Indeed, they provide more than a yardstick; they are actually the model which inspired the present population policies.

What does this goal mean in practice? Among the advanced nations there is considerable diversity in the level of fertility(6). At one extreme are countries such as New Zealand, with an average gross reproduction rate (GRR) of 1.91 during the period 1960–64; at the other extreme are countries such as Hungary, with a rate of 0.91 during the same period. To a considerable extent, however, such divergencies are matters of timing. The birth rates of most industrial nations have shown, since about 1940, a wavelike movement, with no secular trend. The average level of reproduction during this long period has been high enough to give these countries, with their low mortality, an extremely rapid population growth. If this level is maintained, their population will double in just over 50 years—a rate higher than that of world population growth at any time prior to 1950, at which time the growth in numbers of human beings was already considered fantastic. The advanced nations are suffering acutely from the effects of rapid population growth in combination with the production of ever more goods per person(7). A rising share of their supposedly high per capita income, which itself draws increasingly upon the resources of the underdeveloped countries (who fall farther behind in relative economic position), is spent simply to meet the costs, and alleviate the nuisances, of the unrelenting production of more and more goods by more people. Such facts indicate that the industrial nations provide neither a suitable demographic model for the nonindustrial peoples to follow nor the leadership to plan and organize effective population-control policies for them.

Zero population growth as a goal. Most discussions of the population crisis lead logically to zero population growth as the ultimate goal, because *any* growth rate, if continued, will eventually use up the earth. Yet hardly ever do arguments for population policy consider such a goal, and current policies do not dream of it. Why not? The answer is evidently that zero population growth is unacceptable to most nations and to most religious and ethnic communities. To argue for this goal would be to alienate possible support for action programs.

Goal peculiarities inherent in family planning. Turning to the actual measures taken, we see that the very use of family planning as the means for implementing population policy poses serious but unacknowledged limits on the intended reduction in fertility. The family-planning movement, clearly devoted to the improvement and dissemination of contraceptive devices, states again and again that its purpose is that of enabling couples to have the number of children they want.

Logically, it does not make sense to use *family* planning to provide *national* population control or planning. The "planning " in family planning is that of each separate couple. The only control they exercise is control over the size of *their* family. Obviously, couples do not plan the size of the nation's population, any more than they plan the growth of the national income or the form of the highway network. There is no reason to expect that the millions of decisions about family size made by couples in their own interest will automatically control population for the benefit of society. On the contrary, there are good reasons to think they will not do so. At most, family planning can reduce reproduction to the extent that unwanted births exceed wanted births. In industrial countries the balance is often negative—people have fewer children than they would like to have. In underdeveloped countries the reverse is normally true, but the elimination of unwanted births would still leave an extremely high rate of multiplication.

Actually, the family-planning movement does not pursue even the limited goals it professes. It does not fully empower couples to have only the number of offspring they want because it either condemns or disregards certain tabooed but nevertheless effective means to this goal. One of its tenets is that "there shall be freedom of choice of method so that individuals can choose in accordance with the dictates of their consciences"(8), but in practice this amounts to limiting the individual's choice, because the "conscience" dictating the method is usually not his but that of religious and governmental officials. Moreover, not every individual may choose: even the so-called recommended methods are ordinarily not offered to single women, or not all offered to women professing a given religious faith.

Thus, despite its emphasis on technology, current policy does not utilize all available means of contraception, much less all birth-control measures. The Indian government wasted valuable years in the early stages of its population-control program by experimenting exclusively with the "rhythm" method, long after this technique had been demonstrated to be one of the least effective. A greater limitation on means is the exclusive emphasis on contraception itself. Induced abortion, for example, is one of the surest means of controlling reproduction, and one that has been proved capable of reducing birth rates rapidly. It seems peculiarly suited to the threshold stage of a population-control program—the stage when new conditions of life first make large families disadvantageous. It was the principal factor in the halving of the Japanese birth rate, a major factor in the declines in birth rate of East-European satellite countries after legalization of abortions in the early 1950's, and an important factor in the reduction of fertility in industrializing nations from 1870 to the 1930's(9). Today, according to *Studies in Family Planning*(10), "abortion is probably the foremost method of birth control throughout Latin America." Yet this method is rejected in nearly all national and international population-control programs. American foreign aid is used to help *stop* abortion(11). The United Nations excludes abortion from family planning, and in fact justifies the latter by presenting it as a means of combating abortion(12). Studies of abortion are being made in Latin America under the presumed auspices of population-control groups, not with the intention of legalizing it and thus making it safe, cheap, available, and hence more effective for population control, but with the avowed purpose of reducing it(13).

Although few would prefer abortion to efficient contraception (other things being equal), the fact is that both permit a woman to control the size of her family. The main drawbacks to abortion arise from its illegality. When performed, as a legal procedure, by a skilled physician, it is safer than childbirth. It does not compete with contraception but serves as a backstop when the latter fails or when contraceptive devices or information are not available. As contraception becomes customary, the incidence of abortion recedes even without its being banned. If, therefore, abortions enable women to have only the number of children they want, and if family planners do not advocate—in fact decry—legalization of abortion, they are to that extent denying the central tenet of their own movement. The irony of anti-abortionism in family-planning circles is seen particularly in hair-splitting arguments over whether or not some contraceptive agent (for example, the IUD) is in reality an abortifacient. A Mexican leader in family planning writes(14):

> One of the chief objectives of our program in Mexico is to prevent abortions. If we could be sure that the mode of action [of the IUD] was not interference with nidation, we could easily use the method in Mexico.

The questions of sterilization and unnatural forms of sexual intercourse usually meet with similar silent treatment or disapproval, although nobody doubts the effectiveness of these measures in avoiding conception. Sterilization has proved popular in Puerto Rico and has had some vogue in India (where the new health minister hopes to make it compulsory for those with a certain number of children), but in both these areas it has been for the most part ignored or condemned by the family-planning movement.

On the side of goals, then, we see that a family-planning orientation limits the aims of current population policy. Despite reference to "population control" and "fertility control," which presumably mean determination of demographic results by and for the nation as a whole, the movement gives control only to couples, and does this only if they use "respectable" contraceptives.

THE NEGLECT OF MOTIVATION

By sanctifying the doctrine that each woman should have the number of children she wants, and by assuming that if she has only that number this will automatically curb population growth to the necessary degree, the leaders of current policies escape the necessity of asking why women desire so many children and how this desire can be influenced(15, p. 41; 16).

Instead, they claim that satisfactory motivation is shown by the popular desire (shown by opinion surveys in all countries) to have the means of family limitation, and that therefore the problem is one of inventing and distributing the best possible contraceptive devices. Overlooked is the fact that a desire for availability of contraceptives is compatible with *high* fertility.

The family planners do not ignore motivation. They are forever talking about "attitudes" and "needs." But they pose the issue in terms of the "acceptance"of birth control devices. At the most naive level, they assume that lack of acceptance is a function of the contraceptive device itself. This reduces the motive problem to a technological question. The task of population control then becomes simply the invention of a device that *will* be acceptable(17). The plastic IUD is acclaimed because, once in place, it does not depend on repeated *acceptance* by the woman, and thus it "solves" the problem of motivation(18).

But suppose a woman does not want to use *any* contraceptive until after she has had four children. This is the type of question that is seldom raised in the family-planning literature.

In viewing negative attitudes toward birth control as due to ignorance, apathy, and outworn tradition, and "mass-communication" as the solution to the motivation problem(19), family planners tend to ignore the power and complexity of social life. If it were admitted that the creation and care of new human beings is socially motivated, like other forms of behavior, by being a part of the system of rewards and punishments that is built into human relationships, and thus is bound up with the individual's economic and personal interests, it would be apparent that the social structure and economy must be changed before a deliberate reduction in the birth rate can be achieved. As it is, reliance on family planning allows people to feel that "something is being done about the population problem" without the need for painful social changes.

Designation of population control as a medical or public health task leads to a similar evasion. This categorization assures popular support because it puts population policy in the hands of respected medical personnel, but, by the same token, it gives responsibility for leadership to people who think in terms of clinics and patients, of pills and IUD's, and who bring to the handling of economic and social phenomena a self-confident naiveté.

Similarly, the Janus-faced position on birth-control technology represents an escape from the necessity and onus of grappling with the social and economic determinants of reproductive behavior. On the one side, the rejection or avoidance of religiously tabooed but otherwise effective means of birth prevention enables the family-planning movement to avoid official condemnation. On the other side, an intense preoccupation with contraceptive technology (apart from the tabooed means) also helps with family planners to avoid censure. By implying that the only need is the invention and distribution of effective contraceptive devices, they allay fears, on the part of religious and governmental officials, that fundamental changes in social organization are contemplated. Changes basic enough to affect motivation for having children would be changes in the structure of the family, in the position of women, and in the sexual mores. Far from proposing such radicalism, spokesmen for family planning frequently state their purpose as "protection" of the family—that is, closer observance of family norms. In addition, by concentrating on *new* and *scientific* contraceptives, the movement escapes taboos attached to old ones (the Pope will hardly authorize the condom, but may sanction the pill) and allows family planning to be regarded as a branch of medicine: overpopulation becomes a disease, to be treated by a pill or a coil.

We thus see that the inadequacy of current population policies with respect to motivation is inherent in their overwhelmingly family-planning character. Since family planning is by definition private planning, it eschews any societal control over motivation. It merely furnishes the means, and, among possible means, only the most respectable. Its leaders, in avoiding social complexities and seeking official favor, are obviously activated not solely by expediency but also by their own sentiments as members of society and by their background as persons attracted to the family-planning movement. Unacquainted for the most part with technical economics, sociology, and demography, they tend honestly and instinctively to believe that something they vaguely call population control can be achieved by making better contraceptives available.

THE EVIDENCE OF INEFFECTIVENESS

If this characterization is accurate, we can conclude that current programs will not enable a government to control population size. In countries where couples have numerous offspring that they do not want, such programs may possibly accelerate a birth-rate decline that would occur anyway, but the conditions that cause births to be wanted or unwanted are beyond the control of family planning, hence beyond the control of any nation which relies on family planning alone as its population policy.

This conclusion is confirmed by demographic facts. As I have noted above, the widespread use of family planning in industrial countries has not given their governments control over the birth rate. In backward countries today, taken as a whole, birth rates are rising, not falling; in those with population policies, there is no indication that the government is controlling the rate of reproduction. The main "successes" cited in the well-publicized policy literature are cases where a large number of contraceptives have been distributed or where the program has been accompanied by some decline in the birth rate. Popular enthusiasm for family planning is found mainly in the cities, or in advanced countries such as Japan and Taiwan, where the people would adopt contraception in any case, program or no program. It is difficult to prove that present population policies have even speeded up a lowering of the birth rate (the least that could have been expected), much less that they have provided national "fertility control."

Let us next briefly review the facts concerning the level and trend of population in underdeveloped nations generally, in order to understand the magnitude of the task of genuine control.

RISING BIRTH RATES IN UNDERDEVELOPED COUNTRIES

In ten Latin-American countries, between 1940 and 1959(20), the average birth rates (age-standardized), as estimated by our research office at the University of California, rose as follows: 1940–44, 43.4 annual births per 1000 population; 1945–49, 44.6; 1950–54, 46.4; 1955–59, 47.7.

In another study made in our office, in which estimating methods derived from the theory of quasi-stable populations were used, the recent trend was found to be upward in 27 underdeveloped countries, downward in six, and unchanged in one(21). Some of the rises have been substantial, and most have occurred where the birth rate was already extremely high. For instance, the gross reproduction rate rose in Jamaica from 1.8 per thousand in 1947 to 2.7 in 1960; among the natives of Fiji, from 2.0 in 1951 to 2.4 in 1964; and in Albania, from 3.0 in the period 1950–54 to 3.4 in 1960.

The general rise in fertility in backward regions is evidently not due to failure of population-control efforts, because most of the countries either have no such effort or have programs too new to show much effect. Instead, the rise is due, ironically, to the very circumstance that brought on the population crisis in the first place—to improved health and lowered mortality. Better health increases the probability that a woman will conceive and retain the fetus to term; lowered mortality raises the proportion of babies who survive to the age of reproduction and reduces the probability of widowhood during that age(22). The significance of the general rise in fertility, in the context of this discussion, is that it is giving would-be population planners a harder task than many of them realize. Some of the upward pressure on birth rates is independent of what couples do about family planning, for it arises from the fact that, with lowered mortality, there are simply more couples.

UNDERDEVELOPED COUNTRIES WITH POPULATION POLICIES

In discussions of population policy there is often confusion as to which cases are relevant. Japan, for instance, has been widely praised for the effectiveness of its measures, but it is a very advanced industrial nation and, besides, its government policy had little or nothing to do with the decline in the birth rate, except unintentionally. It therefore offers no test of population policy under peasant-agrarian conditions. Another case of questionable relevance is that of Taiwan, because Taiwan is sufficiently developed to be placed in the urban-industrial class of nations. However, since Taiwan is offered as the main showpiece by the sponsors of current policies in underdeveloped areas, and since the data are excellent, it merits examination.

Taiwan is acclaimed as a showpiece because it has responded favorably to a highly organized program for distributing up-to-date contraceptives and has also had a rapidly dropping birth rate. Some observers have carelessly attributed the decline in the birth rate—from 50.0 in 1951 to 32.7 in 1965—to the family-planning campaign(23), but the campaign began only

TABLE 1. Decline in Taiwan's fertility rate, 1951
through 1966.

YEAR	REGISTERED BIRTHS PER 1000 WOMEN AGED 15-49	CHANGE IN RATE (PER CENT)*
1951	211	
1952	198	−5.6
1953	194	−2.2
1954	193	−0.5
1955	197	+2.1
1956	196	−0.4
1957	182	−7.1
1958	185	+1.3
1959	184	−0.1
1960	180	−2.5
1961	177	−1.5
1962	174	−1.5
1963	170	−2.6
1964	162	−4.9
1965	152	−6.0
1966	149	−2.1

*The percentages were calculated on unrounded
figures. Source of data through 1965, *Taiwan* Demographic Fact Book (1964, 1965); for 1966, *Monthly
Bulletin of Population Registration Statistics of Taiwan* (1966, 1967).

in 1963 and could have affected only the end of the trend. Rather, the decline
represents a response to modernization similar to that made by all countries
that have become industrialized(24). By 1950, over half of Taiwan's population was urban, and by 1964 nearly two-thirds were urban, with 29 per cent
of the population living in cities of 100,000 or more. The pace of economic
development has been extremely rapid. Between 1951 and 1963, per capita
income increased by 4.05 per cent per year. Yet the island is closely packed,
having 870 persons per square mile (a population density higher than that
of Belgium). The combination of fast economic growth and rapid population
increase in limited space has put parents of large families at a relative
disadvantage and has created a brisk demand for abortions and contraceptives. Thus the favorable response to the current campaign to encourage
use of the IUD is not a good example of what birth–control technology can
do for a genuinely backward country. In fact, when the program was started,
one reason for expecting receptivity was that the island was already on
its way to modernization and family planning(25).

At most, the recent family-planning campaign—which reached significant
proportions only in 1964, when some 46,000 IUD's were inserted (in 1965
the number was 99,253, and in 1966, 111,242) (26; 27, p. 45)—could have
caused the increase observable after 1963 in the rate of decline. Between
1951 and 1963 the average drop in the birth rate per 1000 women (see Table
1) was 1.73 per cent per year; in the period 1964–66 it was 4.35 per cent.
But one hesitates to assign all of the acceleration in decline since 1963 to
the family-planning campaign. The rapid economic development has been
precisely of a type likely to accelerate a drop in reproduction. The rise in
manufacturing has been much greater than the rise in either agriculture

FIGURE 1. Births per 1000 women aged 15 through 49 in Japan and Taiwan.

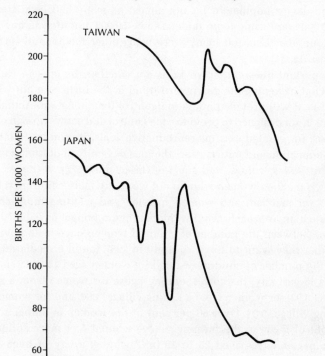

or construction. The agricultural labor force has thus been squeezed, and migration to the cities has skyrocketed(28). Since housing has not kept pace, urban families have had to restrict reproduction in order to take advantage of career opportunities and avoid domestic inconvenience. Such conditions have historically tended to accelerate a decline in birth rate. The most rapid decline came late in the United States (1921–33) and in Japan (1947–55). A plot of the Japanese and Taiwanese birth rates (Fig. 1) shows marked similarity of the two curves, despite a difference in level. All told, one should not attribute all of the post-1963 acceleration in the decline of Taiwan's birth rate to the family-planning campaign.

The main evidence that some of this acceleration is due to the campaign comes from the fact that Taichung, the city in which the family-planning effort was first concentrated, showed subsequently a much faster drop in fertility than other cities(27, p. 69; 29). But the campaign has not reached throughout the island. By the end of 1966, only 260,745 women had been fitted with an IUD under auspices of the campaign, whereas the women of reproductive age on the island numbered 2.86 million. Most of the reduction in fertility has therefore been a matter of individual initiative. To some extent the campaign may be simply substituting sponsored (and cheaper) services for those that would otherwise come through private and commercial channels. An island-wide survey in 1964 showed that over

150,000 women were already using the traditional Ota ring (a metallic intrauterine device popular in Japan); almost as many had been sterilized; about 40,000 were using foam tablets; some 50,000 admitted to having had at least one abortion; and many were using other methods of birth control(27, pp. 18, 31).

The important question, however, is not whether the present campaign is somewhat hastening the downward trend in the birth rate but whether, even if it is, it will provide population control for the nation. Actually, the campaign is not designed to provide such control and shows no sign of doing so. It takes for granted existing reproductive goals. Its aim is "to integrate, through education and information, the idea of family limitation *within the existing attitudes, values, and goals* of the people"[27, p. 8 (italics mine)]. Its target is *married* women who do not want any more children; it ignores girls not yet married, and women married and wanting more children.

With such an approach, what is the maximum impact possible? It is the difference between the number of children women have been having and the number they want to have. A study in 1957 found a median figure of 3.75 for the number of children wanted by women aged 15 to 29 in Taipei, Taiwan's largest city; the corresponding figure for women from a satellite town was 3.93; for women from a fishing village, 4.90; and for women from a farming village, 5.03. Over 60 per cent of the women in Taipei and over 90 percent of those in the farming village wanted 4 or more children(30). In a sample of wives aged 25 to 29 in Taichung, a city of over 300,000, Freedman and his co-workers found the average number of children wanted was 4; only 9 per cent wanted less than 3, 20 per cent wanted 5 or more(31). If, therefore, Taiwanese women used contraceptives that were 100-per cent effective and had the number of children they desire, they would have about 4.5 each. The goal of the family-planning effort would be achieved. In the past the Taiwanese woman who married and lived through the reproductive period had, on the average, approximately 6.5 children; thus a figure of 4.5 would represent a substantial decline in fertility. Since mortality would continue to decline, the population growth rate would decline somewhat less than individual reproduction would. With 4.5 births per woman and a life expectancy of 70 years, the rate of natural increase would be close to 3 per cent per year(32).

In the future, Taiwanese views concerning reproduction will doubtless change, in response to social change and economic modernization. But how far will they change? A good indication is the number of children desired by couples in an already modernized country long oriented toward family planning. In the United States in 1966, an average of 3.4 children was considered ideal by white women aged 21 or over(33). This average number of births would give Taiwan, with only a slight decrease in mortality, a long-run rate of natural increase of 1.7 per cent per year and a doubling of population in 41 years.

Detailed data confirm the interpretation that Taiwanese women are in the process of shifting from a "peasant agrarian" to an "industrial" level of reproduction. They are, in typical fashion, cutting off higher-order births at age 30 and beyond(34). Among young wives, fertility has risen, not fallen.

In sum, the widely acclaimed family-planning program in Taiwan may, at most, have somewhat speeded the later phase of fertility decline which would have occurred anyway because of modernization.

Moving down the scale of modernization, to countries most in need of population control, one finds the family planning approach even more inadequate. In South Korea, second only to Taiwan in the frequency with which it is cited as a model of current policy, a recent birth-rate decline of unknown extent is assumed by leaders to be due overwhelmingly to the government's family-planning program. However, it is just as plausible to say that the net effect of government involvement in population control has been, so far, to delay rather than hasten a decline in reproduction made inevitable by social and economic changes. Although the government is advocating vasectomies and providing IUD's and pills, it refuses to legalize abortions, despite the rapid rise in the rate of illegal abortions and despite the fact that, in a recent survey, 72 per cent of the people who stated an opinion favored legalization. Also, the program is presented in the context of maternal and child health; it thus emphasizes motherhood and the family rather than alternative roles for women. Much is made of the fact that opinion surveys show an overwhelming majority of Koreans (89 per cent in 1965) favoring contraception (35, p. 27), but this means only that Koreans are like other people in wishing to have the means to get what they want. Unfortunately, they want sizable families: "The records indicate that the program appeals mainly to women in the 30-39 year age bracket who have four or more children, including at least two sons . . ."(35, p. 25).

In areas less developed than Korea the degree of acceptance of contraception tends to be disappointing, especially among the rural majority. Faced with this discouragement, the leaders of current policy, instead of reexamining their assumptions, tend to redouble their effort to find a contraceptive that will appeal to the most illiterate peasant, forgetting that he wants a good-sized family. In the rural Punjab, for example, "a disturbing feature . . . is that the females start to seek advice and adopt family planning techniques at the fag end of their reproductive period"(36). Among 5196 women coming to rural Punjabi family-planning centers, 38 percent were over 35 years old, 67 percent over 30. These women had married early, nearly a third of them before the age of 15(37); some 14 percent had eight or more *living* children when they reached the clinic, 51 percent six or more.

A survey in Tunisia showed that 68 percent of the married couples were willing to use birth-control measures, but the average number of children they considered ideal was 4.3(38). The corresponding averages for a village in eastern Java, a village near New Delhi, and a village in Mysore were 4.3, 4.0, and 4.2, respectively(39, 40). In the cities of these regions women are more ready to accept birth control and they want fewer children than village women do, but the number they consider desirable is still wholly unsatisfactory from the standpoint of population control. In an urban family-planning center in Tunisia, more than 600 of 900 women accepting contraceptives had four living children already(41). In Bangalore, a city of nearly a million at the time (1952), the number of offspring desired by married women was 3.7 on the average; by married men, 4.1(40). In the metropolitan area of San Salvador (350,000 inhabitants) a 1964 survey(42) showed the number desired by women of reproductive age to be 3.9, and in seven other capital cities of Latin America the number ranged from 2.7 to 4.2. If women in the cities of underdeveloped countries used birth-control measures with 100-percent efficiency, they still would have enough babies to expand city populations senselessly, quite apart from the added contribution of rural-urban migration. In many of the cities the difference between actual and ideal number of children is not great; for instance, in the seven Latin-American capitals mentioned above, the ideal was 3.4 whereas the actual births per women in the age range 35 to 39 was 3.7(43). Bombay City has had birth-control clinics for many years, yet its birth rate (standardized for age, sex, and marital distribution) is still 34 per 1000 inhabitants and is tending to rise rather than fall. Although this rate is about 13 per cent lower than that for India generally, it has been about that much lower since at least 1951(44).

IS FAMILY PLANNING THE "FIRST STEP" IN POPULATION CONTROL?

To acknowledge that family planning does not achieve population control is not to impugn its value for other purposes. Freeing women from the need to have more children than they want is of great benefit to them and their children and to society at large. My argument is therefore directed not against family-planning programs as such but against the assumption that they are an effective means of controlling population growth.

But what difference does it make? Why not go along for a while with family planning as an initial approach to the problem of population control? The answer is that any policy on which millions of dollars are being spent should be designed to achieve the goal it purports to achieve. If it is only a first step, it should be so labeled, and its connection with the next step (and the nature of that next step) should be carefully examined. In the present case, since no "next step" seems ever to be mentioned, the question arises, is reliance on family planning in fact a basis for dangerous postponement of effective steps? To continue to offer a remedy as a cure long after it has been shown merely to ameliorate the disease is either quackery or wishful thinking, and it thrives most where the need is greatest. Today the desire to solve the population problem is so intense that we are all ready to embrace any "action program" that promises relief. But postponement of effective measures allows the situation to worsen.

The need for societal regulation of individual behavior is readily recognized in other spheres—those of explosives, dangerous drugs, public property, natural resources. But in the sphere of reproduction, complete individual initiative is generally favored even by those liberal intellectuals who, in other spheres, most favor economic and social planning. Social reformers who would not hesitate to force all owners of rental property to rent to anyone who can pay, or to force all workers in an industry to join a union, balk at any suggestion that couples be permitted to have only a certain number of offspring. Invariably they interpret societal control of reproduction as meaning direct police supervision of individual behavior. Put the word *compulsory* in front of any term describing a means of limiting births—*compulsory sterilization, compulsory abortion, compulsory contraception*—and you guarantee violent opposition. Fortunately, such direct controls need not be invoked, but conservatives and radicals alike overlook this in their blind opposition to the idea of collective determination of a society's birth rate.

That the exclusive emphasis on family planning in current population policies is not a "first step" but an escape from the real issues is suggested by two facts. (i) No country has taken the "next step." The industrialized countries have had family planning for half a century without acquiring control over either the birth rate or population increase. (ii) Support and encouragement of research on population policy other than family planning is negligible. It is precisely this blocking of alternative thinking and experimentation that makes the emphasis on family planning a major obstacle to population control. The need is not to abandon family planning programs but to put equal or greater resources into other approaches.

REFERENCES

1. *Studies in family planning, no 16.* 1967.
2. *Ibid, no. 9.* 1966, p. 1.
3. U.S. Congress, Senate, Subcommittee on Foreign Aid Expenditures, *Hearings on S. 1676,* 89th Cong., 2d sess., April 7, 8, 11, 1966, pt. 4.
4. Raina, B. L. In Berelson, B., *et al.,* eds. 1966. *Family planning and population programs.* Chicago: Univ. of Chicago Press.
5. Kirk, D. 1967. *Ann. Amer. Acad. Polit. Soc. Sci.* 369: 53.
6. As used by English-speaking demographers, the word *fertility* designates actual reproductive performance, not a theoretical capacity.
7. Davis, K. 1959. *Rotarian* 94: 10; *Health Educ. Monographs.* 1960 9: 2; Day, L. and A. 1964. *Too many Americans.* Boston: Houghton Mifflin; Piddlington, R. A. 1956. *Limits of mankind.* Bristol, England; Wright.
8. Gardner, J. W., Secretary of Health, Education, and Welfare. Jan. 1966. Memorandum to heads of operating agencies. Reproduced in *Hearings on S. 1676, op. cit.,* p. 783.
9. Tietze, C. 1964. *Demography* 1: 119; *J. Chronic Diseases.* 1964. 18: 1161; Muramatsu, M. 1960. *Milbank Mem. Fund Quart.* 38: 153; Davis, K. 1963. *Population Index.* 1963. 29: 345; Armijo, R. and Monreal, T. 1964. *J. Sex Res.* 1964: 143; Proceedings World Population Conference, Belgrade, 1965; Proceedings International Planned Parenthood Fed.
10. *Studies in family planning, no. 4.* 1964, p. 3.
11. Bell, D. (then administrator for Agency for International Development). In *Hearings on S. 1676, op. cit.,* p. 862.
12. United Nations. 1964. *Asian population conference.* New York, p. 30.
13. Armijo, R. and Monreal, T. In Milbank Fund. 1965. *Components of population change in Latin America.* New York, p. 272; Rice-Wray, E. 1964. *Amer. J. Public Health* 54: 313.
14. Rice-Wray, E. In Intra-uterine contraceptive devices. 1962. *Excerpta Med. Inter. Congr. Ser. No. 54,* p. 135.
15. Blake, J. In Sheps, M. C. and Ridley, J. C., eds. 1965. *Public health and population change.* Pittsburgh: Univ. of Pittsburgh Press.
16. Blake, J. and Davis, K. 1963. *Amer. Behavioral Scientist* 5: 24.
17. See Panel discussion on comparative acceptability of different methods of contraception. In Kiser, C. V., ed. 1962. *Research in family planning.* Princeton: Princeton Univ. Press, pp. 373–86.
18. "From the point of view of the woman concerned, the whole problem of continuing motivation disappears, . . ." (Kirk, D. In Muramatsu, M. and Harper, P. A., eds. 1965. *Population dynamics.* Baltimore: Johns Hopkins Press.)

19. "For influencing family size norms, certainly the examples and statements of public figures are of great significance . . . also . . . use of mass-communication methods which help to legitimize the small-family style, to provoke conversation, and to establish a vocabulary for discussion of family planning." (Freymann, M. W. In Muramatsu, M. and Harper, P. A., eds. 1965. *Population dynamics.* Baltimore, Johns Hopkins Press.)

20. Collver, O. A. 1965. *Birth rates in Latin America.* Berkeley, Calif.: International Population and Urban Research, pp. 27–28; the ten countries were Colombia, Costa Rica, El Salvador, Ecuador, Guatemala, Honduras, Mexico, Panama, Peru, and Venezuela.

21. Rele, J. R. 1967. *Fertility analysis through extension of stable population concepts.* Berkeley, Calif.: International Population and Urban Research.

22. Ridley, J. C., *et al.* 1967. *Milbank Mem. Fund Quart.* 45: 77; Arriaga, E. Unpublished paper.

23. "South Korea and Taiwan appear successfully to have checked population growth by the use of intrauterine contraceptive devices." (Borell, U. *Hearings on S. 1676, op. cit.,* p. 556.)

24. Davis, K. 1963. *Population Index* 29: 345.

25. Freedman, R. 1965. *Ibid* 31: 421.

26. Before 1964 the Family Planning Association had given advice to fewer than 60,000 wives in 10 years and a Pre-Pregnancy Health Program had reached some 10,000, and, in the current campaign, 3650 IUD's were inserted in 1965, in a total population of $2\frac{1}{2}$ million women of reproductive age. See *Studies in family planning, no 19.* 1967, p. 4, and Freedman, R., *et al.* 1963.

27. Gillespie, R. W. 1965. *Family planning on Taiwan.* Taichung: Population Council.

28. During the period 1950–60 the ratio of growth of the city to growth of the noncity population was 5: 3; these ratios are based on data of Shaohsing, Chen, S. 1963. *J. Sociol. Taiwan* 1: 74, and data in the United Nations *Demographic yearbooks.*

29. Freedman, R. 1965. *Population Index* 31: 434. Taichung's rate of decline in 1963–64 was roughly double the average in four other cities, whereas just prior to the campaign its rate of decline had been much less than theirs.

30. Chen, S. H. 1963. *J. Soc. Sci. Taipei* 13: 72.

31. Freedman, R., et al. 1963. *Population Studies* 16: 227; *ibid.,* p. 232.

32. In 1964 the life expectancy at birth was already 66 years in Taiwan, as compared to 70 for the United States.

33. Blake, J. 1967. *Eugenics Quart.* 14: 68.

34. Women accepting IUD's in the family-planning program are typically 30 to 34 years old and have already had four children. (*Studies in family planning no. 19,* 1967, p. 5.)

35. Cha, Y. K. In Berelson, B., *et al.,* eds. 1966. *Family planning and population programs.* Chicago: Univ. of Chicago Press.

36. Ayalvi, H. S. and Johl, S. S. 1965. *J. Family Welfare* 12: 60.

37. Sixty percent of the women had borne their first child before age 19. Early marriage is strongly supported by public opinion. Of couples polled in the Punjab, 48 per cent said that girls *should* marry before age 16, and 94 per cent said they should marry before age 20 (Ayalvi, H. S. and Johl, S. S. *ibid.,* p. 57). A study of 2380 couples in 60 villages of Uttar Pradesh found that the women had consummated their marriage at an average age of 14.6 years (Rele, J. R. 1962. *Population Studies* 15: 268).

38. Morsa, J. In Berelson, B., *et al.,* eds. 1966. *Family planning and population programs.* Chicago: Univ. of Chicago Press.

39. Gille, H. and Pardoko, R. J. Ibid., p. 515; Agarwala, S. N. 1961. Med. Dig. Bombay 4: 653.

40. United Nations. 1961. *Mysore population study.* New York, p. 140.

41. Daly, A. In Berelson, B., *et al.* 1966. *Family planning and population programs.* Chicago: Univ. of Chicago Press.

42. Goméz, C. J. 1965. Paper presented at the World Population Conference, Belgrade.

43. Miro, C. In Berelson, B., *et al.* 1966. *Family planning and population programs.* Chicago: Univ. of Chicago Press.

44. *Demographic Training and Research Centre (India) Newsletter* 20: 4. Aug. 1966.

Beyond Family Planning

BERNARD BERELSON

BERNARD BERELSON *is Vice-President of the Population Council.*

The Davis article set forth reasons why the current family planning programs are inadequate in accomplishing the goals they seek. Berelson analyzes the numerous proposals that go beyond the current efforts of national programs based on voluntary cooperation. He examines these suggestions on the basis of six criteria: (1) scientific/medical/technological readiness, (2) political viability, (3) administrative feasibility, (4) economic capability, (5) moral/ethical/philosophical acceptability, and (6) presumed effectiveness.

This article rests on four propositions: (i) among the great problems on the world agenda is the population problem; (ii) that problem is most urgent in the developing countries, where rapid population growth retards social and economic development; (iii) there is a time penalty on the problem in the sense that, other things being equal, anything not done sooner may be harder to do later, due to increased numbers; and accordingly (iv) everything that can properly be done to lower population growth rates should be done, now. The question is, what is to be done? There is a certain agreement on the general objective (that is, on the desirability of lowering birth rates, though not on how far and how fast), but there is disagreement as to means.

The first response to too high growth rates deriving from too high birth rates is to introduce voluntary contraception on a mass basis, or try to. Why is family planning the first step taken on the road to population control? Probably because, from a broad political standpoint, it is the most acceptable one; since it is closely tied to maternal and child care it can be perceived as a health measure beyond dispute, and since it is voluntary it can be justified as a contribution to the effective personal freedom of individual couples. On both scores, it ties into accepted values and thus achieves political viability. Moreover, it is a gradual effort and an inexpensive one, both of which features contribute to its political acceptability.

How effective have family-planning programs been as a means toward

Science 163(3867:533–43, February 7, 1969. Copyright 1969 by the American Association for the Advancement of Science. Reprinted by permission.

population control? There is currently some controversy among qualified observers as to its efficacy (1), and this is not the place to review that issue. There is agreement, however, that the problem is of such magnitude and consequence that additional efforts are needed to reach a "solution," however that is responsibly defined.

For the purpose of this article, then, let us assume that today's national family-planning programs, mainly based on voluntary contraception, are not "enough"—where "enough" is defined not necessarily as achieving zero growth in some extended present, but simply as lowering birth rates quickly and substantially. "Enough" begs the question of the ultimate goal and only asks that a faster decline in population growth rates be brought about than is presently being achieved or in prospect—and, within the range of the possible, the faster the better (2,3). Just to indicate roughly the order of magnitude, let us say that the proximate goal is the halving of the birth rate in the developing countries in the next decade or two—from, say, over 40 births per thousand per year to 20 to 25(4). For obvious reasons, both emigration and increased death rates are ruled out of consideration.

What is to be done to bring that reduction about, beyond present programs of voluntary family planning? I address that question in two ways: first, by listing the programs or policies more or less responsibly suggested in recent years for achieving this end; second, by reviewing the issues raised by the suggested approaches.

PROPOSALS BEYOND FAMILY PLANNING

Here is a listing of the several proposals, arranged in descriptive categories. The list includes both proposals for consideration and proposals for action.

A. *Extensions of voluntary fertility control.*
  1) Institutionalization of maternal care in rural areas of developing countries: a feasibility study of what would be required in order to bring some degree of modern medical or paramedical attention to every pregnant woman in the rural areas of five developing countries, with professional backup for difficult cases and with family-planning education and services a central component of the program, aimed particularly at women of low parity(5).
  2) Liberalization of induced abortion (6; 7, p. 139; 8).
B. *Establishment of involuntary fertility control.*
  1) Mass use of a "fertility control agent" by the government to regulate births at an acceptable level. The "fertility control agent," designed to lower fertility in the society to a level 5 to 75 per cent below the present birth rate, as needed, would be a substance now unknown but believed to be available for field testing after 5 to 15 years of research work. It would be included in the water supply in urban areas and administered by "other methods" elsewhere (9). A related suggestion is the "addition of temporary sterilants to water supplies or staple food"(10).
  2) "Marketable licenses to have children," given to women and perhaps men in "whatever number would ensure a reproduction rate of one"

(say, 2.2 children per couple). For example, "the unit certificate might be the 'deci-child,' and accumulation of ten of these units, by purchase, inheritance or gift, would permit a woman in maturity to have one legal child"(11).

3) Temporary sterilization of all girls by means of time-capsule contraceptives, and of girls and women after each delivery, with reversibility allowed only upon governmental approval. Certificates of approval would be distributed according to national popular vote on desired population growth, and saleable on the open market(12).

4) Compulsory sterilization of men with three or more living children (13); a requirement of induced abortion for all illegitimate pregnancies(6).

C. *Intensified educational campaigns.*

1) Inclusion of educational materials on population in primary and secondary school systems(6, 14, 15).

2) Promotion of national satellite television systems for directly disseminating information on population and family planning and for indirectly promoting acceptance of modern attitudes and practices in general(7, p. 162; 16; 17, especially pp. 13–14; 18).

D. *Incentive programs.* As used here, the term *incentive programs* refers to payments, or their equivalent, made directly to couples who use contraceptives or to couples who do not have children for specified periods. It does *not* refer to payments to field workers, medical personnel, volunteers, and others, for securing acceptance of contraceptive practice.

1) Payment, or the equivalent (for example, the gift of a transistor radio), for accepting sterilization(6, 19–21) or for the effective practice of contraception(21–24).

2) A bonus for child spacing or nonpregnancy(25–28); a savings certificate to couples for each 12-month period in which no child is born(29); a lottery scheme for preventing illegitimate births among teenagers in a small country(30); "responsibility prizes" for each 5 years of childless marriage or for vasectomy before the birth of a third child, and special lotteries, with tickets available to the childless(7, p. 138).

E. *Tax and welfare benefits and penalties*—that is, a system of social services that would discourage childbearing rather than encourage it, as present systems tend to do.

1) Withdrawal of maternity benefits, perhaps after the birth of N(3?) children(6, 21, 26) or in cases where certain limiting conditions, such as adequate child spacing, knowledge of family planning, or attainment of a given level of income, have not been met(31, pp. 130–31).

2) Withdrawal of child or family allowances, perhaps after the birth of N children(6; 26; 31, pp. 131–36).

3) Levy of tax on births after the Nth child (21; 26; 28, p. 30).

4) Limitation of governmentally provided medical treatment, housing, scholarships, loans, subsidies, and so on, to families with fewer than N children(6, 26).

5) Reversal of tax benefits, to favor the unmarried and the parents of

fewer rather than more children(6; 7, pp. 136–37; 21; 26; 31, p. 137; 32).

6) Provision by the state of N years of free schooling, at all levels, to each family, to be allocated among the children as desired(33).

7) Pensions for poor parents with fewer than N children, as social security for their old age(21, 34, 35).

F. *Shifts in social and economic institutions*—that is, broad changes in fundamental institutional arrangements that could have the effect of lowering fertility.

1) Raising the minimum age at marriage, through legislation or through imposition of a substantial fee for marriage licenses(6, 32); through direct payment of bonuses for delayed marriage(25); through payment of marriage benefits only to parents of brides over 21 years old(31, p. 130); through government loans for wedding ceremonies when the bride is over a given age, or with the interest rate inversely related to the bride's age(36); through a "governmental 'first marriage grant' . . . awarded each couple in which the age of both [sic] partners was 25 or more"(7, p. 138); or through establishment of a domestic "national service" program for all men for the appropriate 2-year period in order to develop social services, inculcate modern attitudes toward (among other matters) family planning and population control, and delay marriage(37).

2) Measures to promote or require the participation of women in the labor force (outside the home), in order to provide roles and interests for women that are alternative or supplementary to marriage(6, 32, 38).

3) "Direct manipulation of family structure itself—planned efforts at deflecting the family's socializing function . . . or introducing non-familial distractions . . . into people's lives," specifically through employment of women outside the house(39); "selective restructuring of the family in relation to the rest of society"(6).

4) Promotion of "two types of marriage, one of them childless and readily dissolved, and the other licensed for children and designed to be stable"; marriages of the first type would have to constitute 20 to 40 percent of the total in order to allow free choice of family size for marriages of the second type(16, 40).

5) Encouragement of long-range social trends leading toward lower fertility—for example, "improved and universal general education, or new roads facilitating communication, or improved agricultural methods, or a new industry that would increase productivity, or other types of innovation that may break the 'cake of custom' and produce social foment"(41); improvement in the status of women(42).

6) Efforts to lower death rates even further, particularly infant and child death rates, in the belief that lower birth rates will follow(43).

G. *Political channels and organizations.*

1) U.S. insistence on "population control as the price of food aid," with highly selective assistance based thereon, and exertion of political pressures on governments or religious groups that impede "solution" of the population problem(7, pp. 161–66; 44).

2) Reorganization of national and international agencies to deal with the population problem: within the United States, "coordination by a powerful governmental agency, a Federal Department of Population and Environment . . . with the power to take whatever steps are necessary to establish a reasonable population size"(7, p. 138; 45); within India, creation of "a separate Ministry of Population Control" (46, p. 96); development of an "international specialized agency larger than WHO to operate programs for extending family limitation techniques to the world . . . charged with the responsibility of effecting the transfer to population equilibrium"(16).

3) Promotion of zero growth in population as the ultimate goal, and acceptance of this goal now in order to place intermediate goals of lowered fertility in proper context(6).

H. *Augmented research efforts.*

1) More research on social means for achieving fertility goals(6).

2) Focused research on practical methods of sex determination(47).

3) Increased research directed toward improvement of the contraceptive technology(48).

PROPOSALS: REVIEW OF THE ISSUES

Here are 29 proposals beyond family planning for dealing with the problem of undue population growth in the developing world. Naturally I cannot claim that these are all the proposals that have been made more or less responsibly toward that end, but my guess is that there are not many more and that these proposals are a reasonably good sample of the total.

Since several of the proposals tend in the same direction, it seems appropriate to review them against the criteria that any such proposals might be required to meet. What are such criteria? There are at least six: (i) scientific, medical, and technological readiness; (ii) political viability; (iii) administrative feasibility; (iv) economic capability; (v) moral, ethical, and philosophical acceptability; and (vi) presumed effectiveness. In other words, the key questions are: Is the scientific, medical, technological base available or likely? Will governments approve? Can the proposal be administered? Can the society afford the proposal? Is it morally acceptable? And, finally, will it work?

Scientific, Medical, Technological Readiness

Two questions are involved: (i) is the needed technology available? and (ii) are the medical or paramedical personnel needed in order to assure medical administration and safety available or readily trainable?

With regard to temporary contraception, sterilization, and abortion, not only is the needed technology available now, but it is being steadily improved and expanded. The intrauterine device (IUD) and the oral pill have been major contraceptive developments of the past decade, and several promising leads are now being followed up(49), though it cannot be said with much confidence that any of the efforts will produce measures suitable for mass use within the next few years(50). Improved technologies for sterilization, both male and female, are being worked on, and there has been a recent development in abortion technique, the so-called suction device.

However, neither Ehrlich's "temporary sterilants" nor Ketchel's "fertility control agent" (B-1) is now available or on the technological horizon, though that does not mean that the research task ought not to be pursued against a subsequent need, especially since any such substance could be administered to individuals on a voluntary basis as well as to the population as a whole on an involuntary basis. In the latter case, if administered through the water supply or a similar source, the substance would have to be medically safe and free of side effects for men and women, young and old, well and ill, physiologically normal and physiologically marginal, as well as for animals and perhaps plants. As some people have remarked, the proposal that such a substance be added to a water supply would face far greater difficulties of acceptance, simply on medical grounds, than the far milder proposals with regard to fluoridation to prevent tooth decay.

Though a substantial technology in fertility control does exist, that does not necessarily mean that the techniques can be applied where they are most needed; this is true partly because of limitations in the number of trained personnel. In general, the more the technology requires the services of medical or paramedical personnel (or, what is much the same, is perceived as requiring them), the more difficult it is to administer in the developing countries. In the case of sterilization and abortion, the medical requirement becomes more severe. For example, when the policy of compulsory vasectomy of men with three or more children was first being considered in India(see 13), it was estimated that the policy would affect about 40 million males: "one thousand surgeons or parasurgeons each averaging 20 operations a day for five days a week would take eight years to cope with the existing candidates, and during this time of course a constant supply of new candidates would be coming along"(51)—at present birth rates, probably some 3.5 million a year. A program of large-scale abortion (provided such a program was legal and acceptable) might also require hospital beds, which are in particularly short supply in most developing countries. However, the newer abortion technique might not require hospitalization—theoretically, the abortion "camp" may be feasible, as the vasectomy "camp" was, though the problems are substantially greater.

In short, the technology is available for some but not for all current proposals, and the case is similar for properly trained personnel.

Political Viability

The "population problem" has been increasingly recognized by national governments and international agencies over the past decade, and policies for dealing with it have been increasingly adopted: national family-planning programs in some 20 to 25 countries; positive resolutions and actions within the United Nations family; large programs of support by such developed countries as the United States and Sweden; the so-called World Leaders' Statement, in which 30 heads of governments endorsed efforts to limit population growth. There is no reason to think that the trend toward population limitation has run its course.

At the same time, the political picture is by no means unblemished. Some

favorable policies are not strong enough to support a vigorous program, even one limited to family planning on health grounds; in national politics, "population control" can become a handy issue for a determined opposition; internal ethnic balances are sometimes delicately involved, with political ramifications; national size is often equated with national power, from the standpoint of international relations and regional military balances; the motives behind the support and encouragement of population control by the developed countries are sometimes perceived as neocolonialist or neoimperialist; and on the international front, as represented by the United Nations, there is still considerable reluctance based on both religious and political considerations. In short, ambivalence on the part of the elite and recognition of the issue as a political liability are not absent even in the countries that favor population limitation.

Any social policy adopted by government rests on some minimum consensus concerning goals and means. They need not be the ultimate goals or the final means; the socioeconomic plans of developing countries are typically 5-year plans, not 20- or 40- or 100-year plans. Indeed, the ultimate goal of population policy—that is, zero growth—need not be agreed upon or even considered by officials who *can* agree upon the immediate goal of lowering growth by a specified amount or by "as much as possible" within a period of years. And since there are always goals beyond goals, one does not even need to know what the ultimate goal is—only the direction in which it will be found (which is usually more readily agreed upon). Would insistence *now* on the acknowledgment of an *ultimate* goal of zero growth advance the effort or change its direction?

To start with, the proposal of compulsory controls in India in 1967 (B-4) precipitated "a storm of questions in Parliament"(52); the proposal was withdrawn, and the issue resulted in a high-level shift of personnel within the family-planning organization. No other country has seriously entertained the idea. Other considerations aside, in many countries political instability would make implementation virtually impossible.

Social measures designed to affect the birth rate indirectly—for example, tax benefits, social security arrangements, and so on—have been proposed from time to time. In India there have been several such proposals: for example, by the United Nations mission(53, chap. 11), by the Small Family Norm Committee(26), by the Central Family Planning Council(54), and in almost every issue of such publications as *Family Planning News, Centre Calling,* and *Planned Parenthood.*

As Samuel reports, with accompanying documentation(21), "the desirability of imposing a tax on births of fourth or higher order has been afloat for some time. However, time and again, the suggestion has been rejected by the Government of India." In some cases action has been taken either by the central government [for example, income tax "deductions for dependent children are given for the first and second child only"(53, p. 87)] or by certain states ["Maharashtra and Uttar Pradesh have decided to grant educational concessions and benefits only to those children whose parents restrict the size of their families"(55)]. Indicative of political sensitivity is the fact that an order withdrawing maternity leave for nonindustrial women employees with three or more living children—at best a tiny number of educated women—was revoked before it went into effect(56). There is a special political problem in many countries, in that economic constraints on fertility often turn out in practice to be selective on class, racial, or ethnic grounds, and thus exacerbate political tensions. Moreover, the promotion of female participation in the labor force runs up against the political problem that such employment would be competitive with men in situations of already high male unemployment and underemployment.

Whether programs for eliminating population growth are or are not politically acceptable appears to depend largely upon whether they are perceived as positive or negative; where "positive" means that they are seen as promoting not only population limitation but other social benefits as well, and where "negative" means that they are seen as limited to population control. For example, family planning programs, as noted above, are often rationalized as contributing to both maternal and child health and to the effective freedom of the individual family; a pension for the elderly would have social welfare benefits as well as indirect impact upon family size, in countries where a large family has been the traditional "social security system"; contraceptive programs in Latin America are promoted by the medical community as a medical and humanitarian answer not to the population problem but to the extensive illegal and dangerous practice of abortion. On the other hand, imposing tax liabilities or withdrawing benefits after the birth of the Nth child, not to mention involuntary measures, can be attacked as punitive means whose only purpose is that of limiting population.

It would thus require great political courage, joined to very firm demographic convictions, for a national leader to move toward an unpopular and severe prescription designed to cure his country's population ills. Indeed, it is difficult to envisage such a political move in an open society where a political opposition could present a counter view and perhaps prevail.

The governmental decisions about measures to be taken to deal with undue population growth must be made mainly by the countries directly involved; after all, it is their people and their nation whose prospects are most centrally affected. But in an interconnected world, with peace and human welfare at issue, others are properly concerned, for reasons both of self-interest and of humanitarianism—other governments from the developed world, the international community, private groups. What of the political considerations in this connection?

A recommendation (G-1) that the United States exert strong political pressures to effect population control in developing countries seems more likely to generate political opposition abroad than acceptance. It is conceivable that such measures might be adopted here, but it is hardly conceivable that they would be agreed to by the proposed recipients. Such a policy seems likely to boomerang against its own objective, quite aside from ethical or political considerations.

The proposal (G-2) to create an international superagency seems more likely of success, but is not without its difficulties. The World Health Organization, UNICEF, and UNESCO have moved some distance toward family planning, if not population control, but only slowly and in the face of considerable political restraint on the international front (57). A new international agency would find the road easier only if its efforts were restricted to the convinced countries. Certainly the international organizations now concerned with this problem would not be expected to abdicate in favor of a new agency. If it could be brought into being and given a strong charter for action, then, almost by definition, the international political climate would be such as to favor action by the present agencies, and then efficiency and not political acceptability would be the issue.

Administrative Feasibility

Given technical availability and political acceptability, what can actually be done? This is where several "good ideas" run into difficulties in the developing world, in the translation of a theoretical idea into a practical program.

It is difficult to estimate the administrative feasibility of several of the proposals listed above, if for no other reason than that the proponents do not put forward the necessary organizational plans or details. How are "fertility control agents" or "sterilants" to be administered on an involuntary mass basis in the absence of a central water supply or a food-processing system? How are men with three or more children to be reliably identified in a peasant society and impelled to undergo sterilization against their will; and what is to be done if they decline, or if a fourth child is born? What is to be done with parents who evade the compulsory programs, or with the children born as a result of this evasion? How can an incentive system be honestly run in the absence of an organized network of offices, positioned and staffed to carry out the regulatory activity? How can a system of social benefits and penalties, including incentives to postpone or forego marriage, be made to work in the absence of such a network?

These questions are meant only to suggest the kinds of difficulties that must be taken into account if proposals are to be translated into programs. It would seem desirable that every responsibly made proposal address itself to such administrative problems. Some proposals do move in that direction. The feasibility in administration, personnel, and costs of the plan (A-1) to institutionalize maternal care in rural areas, with family planning attached, is currently under study in several developing countries.

The plan (C-1) to include population as a subject in the school curriculum has been carried forward as far as the preparation of educational materials, and in a few cases beyond that(58). The plans for incentive programs sometimes come down to only the theoretical proposition that people will do anything for money (in this case refrain from having children), but in some cases the permissible payment is proposed on the basis of an economic analysis, and in a few cases an administrative means is also proposed(59). The plan for governmental wedding loans scaled to the bride's age recognizes that a birth-registration system might be needed to control against misreporting of age(6).

Thus the *why* of population control is easy, the *what* is not very hard, but the *how* is difficult. We may know that the extension of popular education or an increase in the number of women in the labor force or a later age at marriage would all contribute to population control in a significant way. But there remains the administrative question of how to bring those developments about. In short, several proposals assume workability of a complicated scheme in a country that cannot now collect its own vital statistics in a reliable manner. Moreover, there is a limit to how much administrative burden the typical developing country can carry; it cannot manage many large-scale developmental efforts at a time, either within the field of population or overall. After all, population is not the only effort; agriculture, industry, education, health, communications, the military— all are important claimants. And, within the field of population, a country that finds it difficult to organize and run a family-planning program will find that harder when other programs are added. So, difficult administrative choices must be made.

Economic Capability

From the standpoint of economic capability there are two questions: (i) is the program worthwhile when measured against the criterion of economic return, and (ii) if worthwhile, can it be afforded from present budgets?

Most of the proposals probably pass the second screen. If a fertility-control agent suitable for mass administration becomes available and politically and administratively acceptable, such a program would probably not be prohibitively expensive; incorporation of population materials into the school curriculum is not unduly expensive; imposing of taxes or withdrawing of benefits or increasing fees for marriage licenses might even return a net gain after administrative cost.

But a few proposals are costly in absolute if not relative terms. For example, the institutionalization of maternal care (proposal A-1) might cost some $500 million for construction and $200 milion for annual operation in India, or, respectively, $25 million and $10 million in a country with a population of 25 million(5) (although recent estimates are substantially lower). The plan for a "youth corps" in India would cost upward of $450 million a year if the participants were paid only $50 annually. The plan for payment of pensions to elderly fathers without sons could cost from $400 million to $1 billion a year, plus administrative costs(35). The satellite television system for India would cost $50 million for capital costs only, on a restricted project(17, p. 23), with at least another $200 million needed for receiving sets, broadcast terminals, and programming costs if national coverage were to be secured. All of these proposals are intended to have beneficial consequences beyond population control and hence can be justified on multiple grounds, but they are still expensive in absolute amounts.

The broad social programs of popular education, improved methods of agriculture, and increased industrialization (F-5) already absorb even larger sums, and they could no doubt utilize even more. Here the question is a different one. At present, in such countries as India, Pakistan, South Korea, and Turkey, the funds allocated to family-planning programs constitute less than 1 per cent—in most cases, much less—of the total funds devoted to economic development. Would that tiny proportion make a greater contribution to population control, over some specified period, if given over to education or industrialization or road-building than it makes when utilized directly for family planning(60)? From what we now know, the answer is certainly "No."

Beyond family planning, the situation is still less clear. On the assumption that some level of incentive or benefit would have a demographic impact, what would the level have to be to cut the birth rate by, say, 20 per cent? We simply do not know: the necessary experiments on administration and effectiveness have not been carried out. Let us review what has been proposed with respect to incentives. On the ground that incentives for vasectomy are better than incentives for contraception—since vasectomy is a one-time procedure and is likely to be more effective in preventing births—Pohlman(20) proposes for India a range of money benefits depending upon parity and degree of acceptance—from $7 to a father of four or more children if half the villagers in that category enter the program up to $40 to a father of three children if 75 per cent enter. If the 50 per cent criterion were met in both categories throughout India, the current plan would cost on the order of $260 million in incentives alone, apart from administrative costs. The decline in the birth rate would be slightly over a fourth, perhaps a third—roughly equivalent to $35 to $40, per prevented birth(61).

Simon proposes an incentive of half the per capita income "each year to each fertile woman who does not get pregnant"(23). Here a special problem arises. In a typical developing population of 1000, about 25 to 30 per cent of the married women of reproductive age give birth each year: a population of 1000 means from 145 to 165 such women, and a birth rate of, say 40. Thus, the incentives paid to about three-fourths of the married women of reproductive age would have no effect on the birth rate, since these women would not be having a child that year in any case; thus the cost could be three to four times the amount "needed" for a desired result. Even if the incentive were fully effective and really did prevent a birth, a cut of ten points in the Indian birth rate would cost on the order of $250 million (or 5 million prevented births at $50 each). The cost would be substantially larger if the women (including the nonfecund or the semifecund) who would not have had a child that year in any case, could not be screened out effectively.

But these and other possibilities are only speculations: to data we simply do not know whether incentives will lower a birth rate, or rather, we do not know how large the incentives would have to be in order to do so. These illustrations show only that an incentive program could be expensive. In any case, incentive systems would require a good amount of supervision and record keeping; and, presumably, the higher the incentive (and hence the greater the chance of impact), the greater the risk of false reporting and the greater the need of supervision—which is not only expensive but difficult administratively.

Moral, Ethical, and Philosophical Acceptability

Next, is the proposal not only politically acceptable but considered right and proper—by the target population, government officials, professional or intellectual elites, and the outside agencies committed to aid in its administration?

Coale states(3, 62), "One reason the policy of seeking to make voluntary fertility universal is appealing—whether adequate or not—is that it is a natural extension of traditional democratic values: of providing each individual with the information he needs to make wise choices, and allowing the greatest freedom for each to work out his own destiny. The underlying rationale is that if every individual knowledgeably pursues his self-interest, the social interest will best be served." But what if "stressing the right of parents to have the number of children they want . . . evades the basic question of population policy, which is how to give societies the number of children they need?"(6). The issue rests at the center of political philosophy: how best to reconcile individual and collective interests.

Today, most observers would acknowledge that having a child is theoretically a free choice of the individual couple. However, for many couples, particularly among the poor of the world, the choice is not effectively free in the sense that the individual couple does not have the information, services, and supplies needed to implement a free wish in this regard. Such couples are restrained by ignorance, not only of contraceptive practice but of the consequences of high fertility for themselves, their children, and their country; they are restrained by religious doctrine, even though they may not accept the doctrine; they are restrained legally, as in the case of people who would choose abortion if that course were open to them; they are restrained culturally, as in the case of women subject to a tradition that reserves for them only the childbearing and childrearing roles. Hence effective freedom of choice in the matter of childbearing is by no means realized in the world today, as recent policy statements have remarked(63).

To what extent should a society be willing to compromise its ethical standards for the sake of solving a great social problem? Suppose a program for population control resulted in many more abortions in a society where abortion is morally repugnant and where, moreover, abortion by acceptable medical standards is widely unattainable; how much fertility decline would be "worth" the result? What of infanticide under the same conditions? How many innocent or unknowing men may be vasectomized for a fee (for themselves or for others who obtained their consent) before the practice calls for a moral restraint? How large an increase in the regulatory bureaucracy, or in systematic corruption through incentives, or in differential effect by social class to the disadvantage of the poor(64) is worth how much decrease in the birth rate? How much association of childbearing with monetary incentive is warranted before "bribing people not to have children" becomes contaminating, with adverse long-run effects on parental responsibility(65)? How much "immorality," locally defined as extramarital sex, outweighs the benefits of contraceptive practice (assuming that there is an association)? How much withholding of food aid is ethical, judged against degree of fertility decline? If it were possible to legislate a later age at marriage, would it be right to do so against the will of young women, in a society in which they have nothing else to do? In countries, like our own, where urbanization is a serious population problem, is it right to tell people *where* to live, or to impose heavy economic constraints that in effect "force" the desired migration? Is it right to withdraw educational benefits from children in "too large" families? Such withdrawal would not only be repressive from the standpoint of free education but in the long run would be unfortunate from the standpoint of fertility control. In the balance—and this is a question of great but neglected importance—what weight should be given the opportunities of future generations as against the ignorance, the prejudices, or the preferences of the present one?

Guidance on such ethical questions is needed. For further consideration, these propositions are put forward. (i) "An ideal policy would permit a maximum of individual freedom and diversity. It would not prescribe a precise number of children for each category of married couple, not lay down a universal norm to which all couples should conform"(3). (ii) "An ideal program designed to affect the number of children people want would help promote other goals that are worth supporting on their own merits, or at least not conflict with such goals"(3). (iii) An ideal program would not burden the innocent in an attempt to penalize the guilty—for example, would not burden the Nth child by denying him a free education simply because he *was* the Nth child of irresponsible parents. (iv) An ideal program would not weigh heavily upon the already disadvantaged—for example, by withdrawing maternal or medical benefits or free education from large families, policies that would tend to further deprive the poor. (v) An ideal program would be comprehensible to those directly affected and hence subject to their response. (vi) An ideal program would respect present values concerning family and children, values which some people may not be willing to bargain away in a cost-benefit analysis. (vii) An ideal program would not rest upon the designation of population control as the final value justifying all others; "preoccupation with population growth should not serve to justify measures more dangerous or of higher social cost than population growth itself"(3).

Presumed Effectiveness

If proposals are scientifically ready to be implemented, politically and morally acceptable, and administratively and financially feasible, to what extent will they actually work in bringing population growth under control? That is the final question.

To begin with, the compulsory measures would probably be quite effective in lowering fertility. Inevitably in such schemes, strongly motivated people are ingenious enough to find ways "to beat the system"; if such people were numerous enough the system could not be enforced except under conditions of severe political repression(66). Otherwise, if the scheme was workable, compulsion could have its effect.

What about the proposals for the extension of voluntary contraception? Institutionalizing maternal care in the rural areas, with family planning attached, does promise to be effective within, say, 5 to 10 years, particularly in its potential for reaching younger women and women of lower parity. The International Postpartum Program did have that effect in the urban areas(67), and presumably the impact would extend to the rural areas, though probably not to the same degree because of the somewhat greater sophistication and modernization of the cities.

A liberalized abortion system—again, if workable—could also be effective in preventing unwanted births, but it would probably have to be associated with a contraceptive effort; otherwise there might be too many abortions for the system, as well as for the individual woman (who might need three a year to remain without issue).

Free abortion in cases where contraception had failed would probably make for a decline in fertility, but how large a one would depend upon the quality of the contraceptive program. With modern contraception (the IUD and the pill) the failure rates are quite small, but women who only marginally tolerate these two methods could fall back on abortion. Free abortion has certainly lowered fertility in Japan and in certain countries of eastern Europe(68) and, where medically feasible, such free abortion would do so elsewhere as well; as a colleague observes, in this field one should not underestimate the attraction of a certainty as compared to a probability.

The large question of the impact of the various incentive and benefit or liability plans (D and E) simply cannot be answered: we have too little experience to know much about the conditions under which financial factors will affect childbearing to any substantial degree. Perhaps everyone has his price for everything; if so, we do not know what would have to be paid, directly or indirectly, to make people decide not to bear children.

Such as it is, the evidence from the pro-natalist side on the effectiveness of incentives is not encouraging. All the countries of Europe have family allowance programs of one kind or another(69), most of them legislated in the 1930's and 1940's to raise the birth rate; collectively Europe has the lowest birth rate of any continent. The consensus among demographers appears to be that such programs cannot be shown to have effected an upward trend in the birth rate where tried.

As in the case of abortion for illegitimate pregnancies, several of the benefit or liability proposals would affect only a trivial fraction of people in much of the developing world. However, because the impact of incentive and benefit or liability plans is uncertain and may become important, we need to become better informed on the possibilities and limitations, and this information can come only from experimentation under realistic circumstances and at realistic levels of payment.

A higher age at marriage and a greater participation of women in the labor force are generally credited with effecting fertility declines. In a recent Indian conference on raising the age at marriage, the specialists seemed to differ only on the magnitude of the fertility decline that would result: a decline of 30 per cent in the birth rate in a generation of 28 years if the minimum age of the women at marriage were raised to 20(70), or a decline of not more than 15 per cent in 10 years(71). I say "seemed to differ" since these figures are not necessarily incompatible. In either case, the decline is a valuable one. But an increase in the age at marriage is not easy to achieve, and that must come before the fertility effect.

Similarly, an increase in the proportion of working women would have its demographic effect, but could probably come about only in conjunction with other broad social trends like education and industrialization, which themselves would powerfully affect fertility, just as a decline in fertility would assist importantly in bringing these trends about(72). Both compulsory education and restrictions on child labor would lower the economic value of children, hence tend to produce a decline in fertility. The question is, how are they to be brought about?

Finally, whether or not research would affect fertility trends depends of course upon its nature and outcome. Most observers believe that, under the typical conditions of the developing society, any improvement in contraceptive technology would lead toward the realization of present fertility goals and might help turn the spiral down. Indeed, several observers believe that this is the single most important desideratum, over the short run. Easy means of determining sex should have some effect upon the "need for sons" and thus cut family size to some extent. Research on the social-economic side would probably have to take effect through programs of the kinds discussed above.

The picture is not particularly encouraging. The measures that would work to sharply cut fertility are politically and morally unacceptable to the societies in question (as with coercion), and in any case unavailable; or they are difficult of attainment in any foreseeable future, as in the case of broad social trends or a shift in age at marriage. The measures that might possibly be tried in some settings, like some version of incentives or benefit or liability plans, give uncertain promise of results at the probable level of operation. Legalization of abortion, where the needed medical facilities are available, would almost certainly have a measurable effect, but acceptability is problematic.

TABLE 1. Illustrative appraisal of proposals, by criteria.

PROPOSAL	SCIENTIFIC READINESS	POLITICAL VIABILITY	ADMINISTRATIVE FEASIBILITY	ECONOMIC CAPABILITY	ETHICAL ACCEPTABILITY	PRESUMED EFFECTIVENESS
A. Extension of voluntary fertility control	High	High on maternal care, moderate-to-low on abortion	Uncertain in near future	Maternal care too costly for local budget, abortion feasible	High for maternal care, low for abortion	Moderately high
B. Establishment of involuntary fertility control	Low	Low	Low	High	Low	High
C. Intensified educational campaigns	High	Moderate-to-high	High	Probably high	Generally high	Moderate
D. Incentive programs	High	Moderately low	Low	Low-to-moderate	Low-to-high	Uncertain
E. Tax and welfare benefits and penalties	High	Moderately low	Low	Low-to-moderate	Low-to-moderate	Uncertain
F. Shifts in social and economic institutions	High	Generally high, but low on some specifics	Low	Generally low	Generally high, but uneven	High, over long run
G. Political channels and organizations	High	Low	Low	Moderate	Moderately low	Uncertain
H. Augmented research efforts	Moderate	High	Moderate-to-high	High	High	Uncertain
Family-planning programs	Generally high, but could use improved technology	Moderate-to-high	Moderate-to-high	High	Generally high, but uneven, on religious grounds	Moderately high

CONCLUSION

This review leaves us with some conclusions concerning proposals that go beyond family planning.

1) There is no easy way to achieve population control. If this review has indicated nothing else, it has shown how many obstacles stand in the way of a solution to the population problem. Table 1 shows, by way of recapitulation, how the various proposals seem to fit the several criteria(73). That is only one observer's judgment of the present situation, but, whatever appraisal is made of specific items, it would appear that the overall picture is mixed.

2) Family-planning programs do not compare unfavorably with other specific proposals, especially when one considers that any *actual* operating program is at a disadvantage when compared with any competitive *ideal* policy. Indeed, on this showing, if family-planning programs did not exist, they would have to be invented; it appears that they would be among the first proposals to be made and the first programs to be tried, given their generally acceptable characteristics.

In fact, when such proposals are made, it turns out that many of them call for *more* family planning, not less, but in a somewhat different form. In the present case, at least a third of the proposals listed above put forward, in effect, simply another approach to family planning, often accepting the existing motivation as to family size. In any case, family-planning programs are established, have some momentum, and, importantly, would be useful as the direct instrument through which other proposals would take effect. So, as a major critic(74) acknowledges(6), "there is no reason to abandon family-planning programs."

What is needed is the energetic and full implementation of present experience. Much more could be done on the informational side, on encouraging commercial distribution of contraceptives, on the use of paramedical personnel, on logistics and supply, on the training and supervision of field workers, on approaches to special groups of individuals, ranging from women after childbirth to young men drafted into the armed forces. If workers in this field did well what they know how to do, that in itself would in all likelihood make a measurable difference, competitive in magnitude with the probable effects of other specific proposals—not to mention the further impetus of an improved contraceptive technology.

3) Most of the proposed ideas are not new; they have been around for some time. So, if they are not being tried, it is not because they have not been known but because they have not been accepted—presumably, for reasons like those discussed above. In India, for example, several of the social measures being proposed have been, it would seem, under almost constant review by one or another committee for the past 10 to 15 years. So it is not correct to imply that it is only new ideas that are needed; the ideas are there, but their political, economic, or administrative feasibility are problematic.

4) All of the proposers are dissatisfied to some degree with present family-planning efforts, but that does not mean that they agree with one

another's schemes for doing better. Thus, Ohlin believes that "the demographic significance of such measures [maternity benefits and tax deductions for children] would be limited"(34). Ketchel eloquently opposes several "possible alternatives to fertility control agents"(9). Meier argues against the tax on children on both humanitarian and political grounds(16). The U.N. Advisory Mission to India comments(53, p. 87), "it is realised that no major demographic effects can be expected from measures of this kind [maternity benefits], particularly as only a small proportion of families are covered . . . but they could contribute, together with a family-planning programme, to a general change in the social climate relating to childbearing." Earlier, in supporting a family-planning effort in India, Davis noted that "the reaction to the Sarda Act [the Child Marriage Restriant Act of 1929] prohibiting female marriage [below age 14] shows the difficulty of trying to regulate the age of marriage by direct legislation"(75). Myrdal warns against cash payments to parents in this connection and supports social awards in kind to the children(76). Kirk believes that "it might prove to be the height of folly to undermine the existing family structure, which continues to be a crucial institution for stability and socialization in an increasingly mobile and revolutionary society"(77). Finally, Ehrlich is contemptuous of the professors whose "idea of 'action' is to form a committee or to urge 'more research.' Both courses are actually substitutes for action"(7, p. 191).

5) In a rough way, there appears to be a progression in national efforts to deal with the problem in population control. The first step is the theoretical recognition that population growth may have something to do with the prospects for economic development. Then, typically, comes an expert mission from abroad to make a survey and report to the government, as has occurred in India, Pakistan, South Korea, Turkey, Iran, Tunisia, Morocco, and Kenya, among others. The first action program is in family planning, and most of the efforts are still at that level. Beyond that, it apparently takes (i) some degree of discouragement about progress combined with (ii) some heightened awareness of the seriousness of the problem to move the effort forward. To date, those conditions have been most prominently present in India—and that is the country that has gone farthest in the use of incentives and in at least consideration of further steps along the lines mentioned above.

6) Proposals need to be specific—proposals both for action and for further research. It is perhaps too much to ask advocates to spell out all the administrative details of the way their plan is to operate in the face of obstacles and difficulties, or even to spell out how it is to get permission to operate; the situations, settings, opportunities, and personalities are too diverse for that. But it does seem proper to ask for the fullest possible specification of actual plans, under realistic conditions, in order to test out their feasibility and likely effectiveness. Similarly, advocates of further research ought to spell out not only what would be studied, and how, but also how the results might be applied in action programs to affect fertility. Social research is not always readily translated into action, especially into administrative action; and the thrust of research is toward refinement, subtlety, precision, and qualification, whereas the administrator must act

in the large. Short of such specification, the field remains confronted with potentially good ideas, such as "raise the age of marriage" or "use incentives" or "substitute pension systems for male children," without being able to move very far toward implementation.

7) Just as there is no easy way, there is no single way. Since population control will at best be difficult, it follows that every acceptable step that promises some measure of impact shoud be taken. The most likely prospect is that population control, to the degree it is realized, will be the result of a combination of efforts—economic, legal, social, medical—each of which has some effect but not an immediately overwhelming one(78). Accordingly, it is incumbent upon workers in the professional fields concerned to look hard at various approaches, including family planning itself, in order to screen out what is potentially useful for application. In doing so, it may be the path of wisdom to move with the "natural" progression. Some important proposals seem reasonably likely of adoption—institutionalization of maternal care, population study in the schools, the TV satellite system for disseminating information, a better contraceptive technology, perhaps even liberalization of abortion laws in some settings—and we need to know not only how effective such efforts will be but, beyond them, how large a money incentive would have to be to effect a given amount of fertility control and how effective those indirect social measures are that are morally acceptable and capable of realization. It may be that some of these measures would be both feasible and effective—many observers 15 years ago thought that family-planning programs were neither—and a genuine effort needs to be made. The "heavy" measures—involuntary measures and political pressures—may be put aside for the time being, if not forever.

8) In the last analysis, what will be scientifically available, politically acceptable, administratively feasible, economically justifiable, and morally tolerated depends upon people's perceptions of consequences. If "the population problem" is considered relatively unimportant or only moderately important, that judgment will not support much investment of effort. If it is considered urgent, much more can and will be done. The fact is that, despite the large forward strides taken in international recognition of the problem in the 1960's, there still does not exist an informed, firm, and constant conviction in high circles that this is a matter with truly great implications for human welfare(79). Such convictions must be based on sound knowledge. Here it would appear that the demographers and economists have not sufficiently made their case to the world elite—or that, if made, the case has not sufficiently commanded their attention and support. Population pressures are not sharply visible on a day-to-day or even year-to-year basis, nor, short of major famine, do they show themselves in dramatic events. Moreover, the warnings of demographers are often dismissed, albeit unfairly and wrongly, on the basis of past forecasts that were not borne out(80). After all, only a generation ago we were being warned about a decline in population in the West. Asking government leaders to take steps toward population control is asking them to take very substantial steps indeed—substantial for their people as well as for their own political

careers—hence the case must be virtually incontrovertible. Accordingly, the scientific base must be carefully prepared (and perhaps with some sense of humility about the ease of predicting or urging great events, for the record is not without blemishes). Greater measures to meet the problem—measures which exclude social repression and needless limitation of human freedom—must rely on heightened awareness of what is at stake, on the part of leaders and masses alike.

What is beyond family planning? Even if most of the specific plans are not particularly new, that in itself does not mean that they are to be disregarded. The questions are: Which plans can be effected, given such criteria? How can they be implemented? What will be the outcome?

This article is an effort to promote the discourse across the professional fields concerned with this important issue. Given the recent stress on family planning programs as the "means of choice" in dealing with the problem, it is natural and desirable that counter-positions be put forward and reviewed. But that does not in itself settle the critical questions. What can we do now to advance the matter? Beyond family planning, what?

REFERENCES

1. See, for example, Davis, K. 1967. *Science* 158: 730; Potter, R. G., Freedman, R. and Chow, L. R. 1968. *Ibid.* 160: 848; Notestein, F. W. Fall 1968. Population growth and its control. Paper presented before the American Assembly on World Hunger.

2. See, for example, the section on "Goals" in Davis, K. 1967. *Science* 158: 730.

3. Coale, A. J. 1968. Should the United States start a campaign for fewer births? Presidential address presented before the Population Association of America.

4. For current targets of some national family-planning programs, see Berelson, B. November 1967. National family planning programs: Where we stand. Paper presented at the University of Michigan Sesquicentennial Celebration. The paper concludes: "By and large, developing countries are now aiming at the birth rates of Western Europe 75 years ago or the United States 50 years ago."

5. Taylor, H. C., Jr. and Berelson, B. 1968. *Amer. J. Obstet. Gynecol.* 100: 885.

6. Davis, K. 1967. *Science* 158: 730.

7. Ehrlich, P. R. 1968. *The population bomb.* New York: Ballantine.

8. Chandrasekhar, S. 1966. *Population Rev.* 10: 17.

9. Ketchel, M. M. 1968. *Perspect. Biol. Med.* 11: 687; Ketchel. October 18, 1968. *Med. World News*, p. 66.

10. Ehrlich appears to dismiss the scheme as unworkable (7, p. 136), though two pages later he advocates "ample funds" to "promote intensive investigation of new techniques of birth control, possibly leading to the development of mass sterilizing agents such as were discussed above."

11. Boulding, K. E. 1964. *The meaning of the twentieth century: The great transition.* New York: Harper & Row, pp. 135–36.

12. Shockley, W. B. in a lecture delivered at McMaster University, Hamilton, Ontario, December 1967.

13. Chandrasekhar, S. as reported in the New York *Times,* July 24, 1967. Just as the present article was being completed, Chandrasekhar proposed (*ibid.*, Oct. 21, 1968) "that every married couple in India deny themselves sexual intercourse for a year.... Abstinence for a year would do enormous good to the individual and the country." The reader may wish to consider this the 30th proposal and test it against the criteria that follow.

14. Wayland, S. In Berelson, B., et al., eds. 1966. *Family planning and population programs.* Chicago: Univ. of Chicago Press, pp. 353–62; Wayland, S. in Ross, J. and Friesen, J., eds. In preparation. *Family planning programs: Adminstration, education, evaluation;* Columbia University. 1965. *Teaching population*

dynamics: *An instructional unit for secondary school students.* New York; Columbia University. 1965. *Critical stages in reproduction: Instruction materials in general science and biology.* New York. The two last-named publications are pamphlets prepared under Wayland's direction at Teachers College.

15. Visaria, P. August 8, 1964. *Economic Weekly,* p. 1343.

16. Meier. R. L. and G. New directions: A population policy for the future. Unpublished manuscript.

17. UNESCO Expert Mission. 1968. *Preparatory study of a pilot project in the use of satellite communication for national development purposes in India.*

18. Schramm, W. and Nelson, L. 1968. *Communication satellite for education and development—the case of India.* Stanford, Calif.: Stanford Research Institute, pp. 63–66.

19. Chandrasekhar, S. July 19, 1967. As reported in the New York *Times.*

20. Pohlman, E. (Central Family Planning Institute, India). Incentives for 'non-maternity' cannot 'compete' with incentives for vasectomy. Unpublished manuscript.

21. Samuel, T. J. 1966. *J. Family Welfare* 13: 11.

22. Simon, J. Money incentives to reduce birth rates in low-income countries: A proposal to determine the effect experimentally. Unpublished manuscript; The role of bonuses and persuasive propaganda in the reduction of birth rates. Unpublished manuscript.

23. Simon, J. Family planning prospects in less-developed countries, and a cost-benefit analysis of various alternatives. Unpublished manuscript.

24. Enke, S. 1960. *Population Rev.* 4: 47.

25. Young, M. 1967. The behavioral sciences and family planning programs: Report on a conference. *Studies in Family Planning,* no. 23, p. 10.

26. Bhatia, D. 1967. Government of India small family norm committee questionnaire. *Indian J. Med. Educ.* 6: 189. As the title indicates, this is not a proposal but a questionnaire soliciting opinions on various ideas put forward to promote "the small family norm."

27. Enke, S. 1960. The gains to India from population control. *Rev. Econ. Statist.* 42: 179, 180.

27a. Leasure, J. W. 1967. *Milbank Mem. Fund Quart.* 45: 417.

28. Spengler, J. J. May 1967. Agricultural development is not enough. Paper presented before the Conference on World Population Problems, Indiana University.

29. Balfour, M. C. 1962. A scheme for rewarding successful family planners. *Population Council Mem.*

30. Mauldin, W. P. 1967. Prevention of illegitimate births: A bonus scheme. *Population Council Mem.*

31. Titmuss, R. M. and Abel-Smith, B. 1960. *Social politics and population growth in Mauritius.* London: Methuen.

32. David, A. S. 1968. *National development, population and family planning in Nepal,* pp. 53–54.

33. Fawcett, J. Personal communication.

34. Ohlin, G. 1967. *Population control and economic development.* New York: Development Centre of the Organisation for Economic Co-operation and Development, p. 104.

35. Davison, W. P. Personal communication. Davison suggests a good pension (perhaps $400 a year) for men aged 60, married for at least 20 years, with no sons.

36. Davis, K. Personal communication.

37. Berelson, B. and Etzioni, A. Brief formulations, 1962 and 1967, respectively.

38. Hauser, P. M. 1967. In The behavioral sciences and family planning programs: Report on a conference. *Studies in family planning,* no. 23, p. 9.

39. Blake, J. In Sheps, M. C. and Ridley, J. C., eds. 1965. *Public health and population change: Current research issues.* Pittsburgh: Univ. of Pittsburgh Press, p. 62.

40. For the initial formulation of the proposal, see Meier, R. L. 1959. *Modern science and the human fertility problem.* New York: Wiley, chap. 7.

41. Hauser, P. M. 1967. *Demography* 4: 412.

42. United Nations Economic and Social Council, Commission on the Status of Women. 1968. Family planning and the status of women: Interim report of the Secretary-General. New York, especially p. 17 ff.

43. Revelle, R. quoted by Viorst, M. Summer 1968. *Horizon,* p. 35; Heer, D. M. and Smith, D. O. April 1967. Mortality level and desired family size. Paper presented before the Population Association of America.

44. Ehrlich makes the same point in *New Scientist.* Dec. 14, 1967, p. 655:

"Refuse all foreign aid to any country with an increasing population which we believe is not making a maximum effort to limit its population. . . . The United States should use its power and prestige to bring extreme diplomatic and/or economic pressure on any country or organization (the Roman Catholic Church?) impeding a solution to the world's most pressing problem."

45. In an earlier article Ehrlich calls for a "Federal Population Commission with a large budget for propaganda," presumably limited to the United States.

46. Chandrasekhar, S. In Chandrasekhar, S., ed. 1967. *Asia's population problems.* New York: Allen & Unwin, p. 96; Chandrasekhar cites a suggestion made in 1961 by Julian Huxley.

47. Polgar, S. 1967. In The behavioral sciences and family planning programs: Report on a conference. *Studies in family planning,* no. 23, p. 10.

48. National Academy of Sciences, Committee on Science and Public Policy. 1963. *The growth of world population.* Washington, D.C., pp. 5, 28–36. This recommendation has of course been made on several occasions by several people. For an imaginative account of the impact of biological developments, see Berry, P. C. 1966. Appendix to *The next thirty-four years: A context for speculation.* Croton-on-Hudson, New York: Hudson Institute.

49. See, for example. Segal, S. J. November 1967. Biological aspects of fertility regulation. Paper presented at the University of Michigan Sesquicentennial Celebration.

50. It is worth noting that such expectations are not particularly reliable. For example, in 1952-53 a Working Group on Fertility Control was organized by the Conservation Foundation to review the most promising "leads to physiologic control of fertility," based on a survey conducted by Paul S. Henshaw and Kingsley Davis. This group did identify a "lead" that became the oral contraceptive (then already under investigation) but did not mention the intrauterine device. It was searching specifically for better ways to control fertility because of the population problem in the developing world, and considered the contraceptive approach essential to

that end: "It thus appears imperative that an attempt be made to bring down fertility in overpopulated regions without waiting for a remote, hoped-for transformation of the entire society. . . . It seems plausible that acceptable birth control techniques might be found, and that the application of science to developing such techniques for peasant regions might yield revolutionary results" (Conservation Foundation. 1953. *The physiological approach to fertility control, report of the working group on fertility control.* New York.)

51. Parkes, A. S. 1967. *New Scientist* 35: 186.

52. New York *Times.* Nov. 17, 1967. The then Minister had earlier suggested a substantial bonus (100 rupees) for vasectomy, the funds to be taken from U. S. counterpart funds, "but both Governments are extremely sensitive in this area. Yet in a problem this crucial perhaps we need more action and less sensitivity" [S. Chandrasekhar (46)].

53. United Nations Advisory Mission. 1966. *Report of the family planning programme in India.* New York.

54. Demographic Training and Research Centre. 1968. *Implications of raising the female age at marriage in India.* Chembur, India, p. 109; *Centre Calling.* May 1968, p. 4.

55. *Planned Parenthood.* Mar. 1968, p. 3.

56. *Ibid.* April 1968, p. 2.

57. For a review of this development see Symonds, R. and Carder, M. 1968. *International organisations and population control (1947–67).* Brighton, England: Institute of Development Studies, Univ. of Sussex.

58. At present, population materials are being included in school programs in Pakistan, Iran, Taiwan, and elsewhere.

59. See, for example, Balfour (29), Mauldin (30), and Pohlman (20) and, for the economic analysis, Enke (27) and Simon (22).

60. For the negative answer, see Enke (27) and Simon (22). Data are from family-planning budgets and national development plans.

61. E. Pohlman, "Incentives in birth planning," in prepartion.

62. Coale, however, does point out that "it is clearly fallacious to accept as optimal a growth that continues until overcrowding makes additional births intolerably expensive."

63. See, for example, the World Leaders'

Statement (*Studies in family planning*, no. 26. 1968) and the Resolution of the International Conference on Human Rights aspects of family planning, adopted May 12, 1968, reported in *Population Newsletter*, no. 2. 1968. (Issued by the Population Division, United Nations) p. 21 ff. Incidentally, the issue of population policy was apparently a live one in classical times, and resolved by the great philosophers in ways not fully consonant with modern views. Plato, in the *Republic* (Modern Library edition, pp. 412, 414), says, "the number of weddings is a matter which must be left to the discretion of the rulers, whose aim will be to preserve the average of population and to prevent the State from becoming either too large or too small"—to which end certain marriages have "strict orders to prevent any embryo which may come into being from seeing the light; and if any force a way to the birth, the parents must understand that the offspring of such a union cannot be maintained, and arrange accordingly." Aristotle, in *Politics* (Modern Library edition, p. 316) says, "on the ground of an excess in the number of children, if the established customs of the state forbid this (for in our state population has a limit), no child is to be exposed, but when couples have children in excess, let abortion be procured before sense and life have begun. . . ."

64. After noting that economic constraints have not been adopted in South Asia, though often proposed, Gunnar Myrdal continues: "The reason is not difficult to understand. Since having many children is a main cause of poverty, such measures would penalize the relatively poor and subsidize the relatively well off. Such a result would not only violate rules of equity but would be detrimental to the health of the poor families, and so of the growing generation" (*Asian drama: An inquiry into the poverty of nations*, vol. 2. 1968. New York: Pantheon, pp. 1502-03).

65. Notestein, F. W. In Berelson, B. et al., eds. 1966. *Family planning and population programs*. Chicago, Univ. of Chicago Press, pp. 828-29: "There is a real danger that sanctions, for example through taxation, would affect adversely the welfare of the children. There is also danger

that incentives through bonuses will put the whole matter of family planning in a grossly commercial light. It is quite possible that to poor and harassed people financial inducements will amount to coercion and not to an enlargement of their freedom of choice. Family planning must be, and must seem to be, an extension of personal and familial freedom of choice and therby an enrichment of life, not coercion toward its restriction."

66. In this connection see the novel by Burgess, A. 1963. *The Wanting Seed*. New York: Ballantine. At the same time, Myrdal, a long-time observer of social affairs, remarks that "the South Asian countries . . . can, to begin with, have no other principle than that of voluntary parenthood. . . . State direction by compulsion in these personal matters is not effective . . ." (Myrdal, G. 1968. *Asian drama: An inquiry into the poverty of nations*. New York: Pantheon, p. 1501.

67. Satuchni, G. I. 1967. International postpartum family planning program: Report on the first year. *Studies in family planning*, no. 22, p. 14 ff.

68. For example, the repeal of the free abortion law in Rumania resulted in an increase in the birth rate from 14 in the third quarter of 1966 to 38 in the third quarter of 1967. For an early report, see Pressat, R. 1967. *Population* 22: 1116.

69. See U.S. Department of Health, Education, and Welfare. 1964. *Social Security programs throughout the world*. Washington, D.C.

70. Agarwala, S. M. In Demographic Training and Research Centre. 1968. *Implications of raising the female age at marriage in India*. Chembur, India, p. 21.

71. Chidambaram, V. C. *Ibid*, p. 47.

72. Actually, recent research is calling into question the prior need of such broad institutional factors for fertility decline. If further study supports the new findings, that could have important implications for present strategy in the developing countries. See Coale, A. J. 1965. In *Proc. U.N. World Population Conf.* vol 2, pp. 205-09, and Coale, A. J. 1967. The decline of fertility in Europe from the French Revolution to World War II. Paper presented at the University of Michigan Sesquicentennial Celebration.

73. As the roughest sort of summary of Table 1, if one assigns from 5 for "high" to 1 for "low," the various proposals rank as follows: family-planning programs, 25; intensified educational campaigns, 25; augmented research efforts, 24; extension of voluntary fertility control, 20; shifts in social and economic institutions, 20; incentive programs, 14; tax and welfare benefits and penalties, 14; political channels and organizations, 14; establishment of involuntary fertility control, 14.

74. Davis was a strong advocate of family planning in India, and quite optimistic about its prospects even in the pre-IUD or pre-pill era. See Davis, K. In Milbank Memorial Fund. 1954. *The interrelations of demographic, economic, and social problems in selected underdeveloped areas.* New York. Davis concludes (pp. 87–88): "Although India is already well-launched in the rapid-growth phase of the demographic transition, there is no inherent reason why she should long continue in this phase. She need not necessarily wait patiently while the forces of urbanization, class mobility, and industrial development gradually build up to the point where parents are forced to limit their offspring on their own initiative and without help, perhaps even in the face of official opposition. . . . Realistically appraising her situation, India has a chance to be the first country to achieve a major revolution in human life—the planned diffusion of fertility control in a peasant population prior to, and for the benefit of, the urban-industrial transition."

75. Davis, K. In Milbank Memorial Fund, 1954. *The interrelations of demographic, economic, and social problems in selected underdeveloped areas.* New York, p. 86.

76. Myrdal, G. 1968. *Asian drama: An inquiry into the poverty of nations.* New York: Pantheon, p. 1503.

77. Kirk, D. August 1968. Population research in relation to population policy and national family planning programs. Paper presented before the American Sociological Association.

78. It begins to appear that the prospects for fertility control may be improving over the decades. Kirk, after reviewing several factors that "favor a much more rapid [demographic] transition than occurred in the West"—changed climate of opinion, religious doctrine, decline of infant mortality, modernization, fertility differentials, grass-roots concern, and improved contraceptive technology—shows, in a remarkable tabulation, that the later a country began the reduction of its birth rate from 35 to 20 births per thousand, the shorter the time it took to achieve this reduction: from 73 years (average) for the period 1831–60, for example, to 21 years after 1951; the trend has been consistently downward for over a century (Kirk, D. 1967. Natality in the developing countries: Recent trends and prospects. Paper presented at the University of Michigan Sesquicentennial Celebration.

79. Nor, often, does such a conviction exist among the general public. For example, in midsummer of 1968 a national sample of adults was asked in a Gallup poll, "What do you think is the most important problem facing this country today?" Less than 1 percent mentioned population growth (Gallup release, 3 Aug. 1968, and personal communication).

80. For an old but enlightening review, see Dorn, H. 1950 *J. Amer. Statist. Ass.* 45: 311.

RESOURCES, FOOD,
AND DEVELOPMENT

The Myth of Our Vanishing Resources
HAROLD J. BARNETT

HAROLD BARNETT *is professor of economics at Washington University in St. Louis.*

Prophecies of imminent and total depletion of the stocks of natural resources have sometimes been made in the past. Historically, they have rarely been fulfilled. Does the future promise to be different? The law of diminishing returns predicts that other factors being unchanged, further use of a resource must draw on poorer stocks and therefore incur greater expense. After a time the expense becomes so great that the resource is essentially "exhausted." Other factors, however, are not always unchanged. Important among these for resource development are technology and knowledge. Barnett suggests that, as in the past, advances in these spheres will continue to rescue man from resource depletion. He points out, however, that a conscious effort will have to be made to improve or even preserve the quality of life.

". . . We have timber for less than 30 years, . . . anthracite coal for but 50 years. . . . Supplies of iron ore, mineral oil, and natural gas are being rapidly depleted. . . ." Or so thought Gifford Pinchot in 1910 when he argued in *The Fight for Conservation* that America was gorging itself to death on a diet of natural resources.

Obviously, the nation did not choke nor later starve from its ravenous appetite. More than 10 billion cubic feet of timber were cut in 1965, for example, while about 15 million tons of anthracite and 500 million tons of soft coal were mined that same year. Nor has a scarcity of iron ore, oil, or gas developed. Taconite iron resources are now economical, proved oil reserves in 1965 were 24 per cent higher than 15 years earlier, while natural gas reserves were 55 per cent greater than those known in 1950.

Yet only recently, Lord Robens, chairman of England's National Coal Board, raised the same specter again. Present proved worldwide resources of oil, gas, and uranium, he warned, will not meet "more than 20 years

TRANS-action, pp. 7–10, June 1967. Copyright © June 1967 by TRANS-action, Inc. New Brunswick, New Jersey. Reprinted by permission.

consumption at the established rates of growth." Population experts like Robert C. Cook see an exploding world population imploding on agricultural resources. Some conservationists and ecologists believe that a scarcity of natural resources not only hinders economic growth, but that we should change the "basic philosophy, indeed, religion of modern man" with respect to growth. Pinchot was wrong, and these modern-day prophets of resource doom may also be.

According to classic economic reasoning, a scarcity of natural resources leads to diminishing incremental returns for economic effort. Thus, for example, it tends to cost more and more over the years, in terms of labor and capital, to mine another ton of coal or to grow another bushel of wheat. This view of diminishing returns, however, is not justified by the facts. Since 1870 in the United States the record shows *increasing* returns, averaging 1 to 2 per cent a year. Moreover, the favorable trend in natural resource industries is stronger in the past 40 years than in the earlier period when the nation's natural resources were less fully utilized.

The voices of the past—and perhaps some of the present ones too—overlooked the cornucopia of scientific advance and technological change. These have created a virtually unlimited "knowledge bank" for an endless stream of new cost-saving innovations. There has operated what Gunnar Myrdal calls the principle of "circular and cumulative causation," or change fostering further change in the same direction. This new reality sharply contrasts with the classical school's contention that natural resources are "fixed" or unchangeable.

Mechanical transformation of resources, moreover, is no longer the principal means of using them. Atoms and molecules and their energies, not fields and trees and fossils, are the building blocks of our time. Nature's availability should be measured in these units, not in acres or tons. The new technology is able to tap resources—including low-grade mineral deposits or sea water—with a skill and level of productivity never conceived 100 years ago. And the world's oceans are a vast farmland, waiting to be developed and harvested if needed.

This is why the long-term upward trend of economic growth will not be halted by availability of extractive goods, as Pinchot and many others before him predicted. And why new, cheap contraceptive devices could bring a timely end to the specter of unabated population growth.

THE PERSISTENCE OF PESSIMISM

It is not surprising, however, that the natural resource scarcity "conventional wisdom" has persisted so long. "The ideas of economists and political philosophers, both when they are right and when they are wrong, are more powerful than is commonly understood," wrote John Maynard Keynes.

The persistence of such ideas about resources is understandable on two accounts. First, because there is extensive interest in the social problems stemming from the relation of natural resources to man's welfare. There are more than 500 private and public bodies, including the massive agriculture and interior departments, concerned with the conservation of natural resources. In addition, the list of publications and research studies is seemingly endless. (The Pinchot collection alone in the Library of Congress includes about one million papers.) Established public policy, buttressed in platform statements every presidential election year, is based on the view that natural resources play a significant role in the nation's welfare.

Second, the authors of the classical school of economic reasoning are impressive in their logic. And their premises have not been proved wrong for all time, nor can they be. Thomas Malthus' now legendary dilemma, first advanced in 1798, held out the gloomy prospect of a rapidly expanding population pressing on limited agricultural land. Future generations, he warned, would be afflicted with diminishing returns when all farm land was in use.

About two decades later, David Ricardo observed that natural resources varied in physical properties. It followed, Ricardo reasoned, that society would employ those resources in the order of declining economic quality—richer farm land would be cultivated before marginal acres. Thus, growth would be hampered long before the Malthusian limits were reached, by the need to resort to inferior acres as population grew.

John Stuart Mill subsequently restated the now two-pronged doctrine. The Malthusian limit was the ultimate problem, Mill agreed, but Ricardian limitations of declining quality resources were operating even as Mill wrote in the mid-nineteenth century. These predictions of the classical economists gave to the growth theory of economics its essential character and reputation as "the dismal science."

In the 1860's W. Stanley Jevons extended the Ricardian-Mill conceptions of agricultural land in a study of coal—the chief reason, in his opinion, for Britain's economic growth. Jevons foresaw coal depletion as creating a Ricardian-type problem of declining quality of resources. Thus minerals exhaustion became another powerful force in the doctrine of natural resources scarcity.

At the same time, George Perkins Marsh observed that man's influence had greatly damaged the limited and ecologically balanced natural resource environment. This, in turn, was the door opener for the American conservation movement of 1890–1920 led by Pinchot and later by President Theodore Roosevelt.

THE U.S. AS AN EMERGING NATION

Let us examine the record from 1870 to 1957. At the beginning of the period, the U.S. was an "underdeveloped" country with a population of under 40 million. Since then, population has multiplied fourfold, the annual output of goods and services is roughly 20 times as great, and consumption of the products of agriculture, mining, and forests is six times larger.

During this period, the U.S. also passed from an underdeveloped to an advanced economic status by the close of World War I. While the process was continuous, the decade of World War I stands out as a landmark. The war effects were significant. The first conservation movement ended about then, final homestead entries hit a peak and declined thereafter, immigration dropped off sharply, and the nation ceased to be a net exporter of extractive products.

Look at the record in agriculture, where the net output expanded better than threefold in the period 1870–1957. According to the scarcity doctrine, increasing resource scarcity would force the "unit cost" of farm output—the cost of a bushel of grain, for instance—to rise. We mean by cost man-days plus capital resources to get a unit of output. But not only did unit cost fail to rise, it actually declined by more than half—whether measured in terms of labor-plus-capital costs or in labor cost alone. What about the hypothesis that scarcity increases with economic growth and time? In the period from 1870 to 1919, the unit cost of agricultural goods declined by a compounded annual rate of 0.4 per cent, but in the 1919–1957 period it declined by 1.4 per cent a year. Contrary to the natural resource scarcity hypothesis, our economic advance is accelerating.

What about minerals? These have been subject to depletion; demand has increased about 40 times over since 1870. The answer: Over the entire period, cost of a unit of minerals has fallen to a level only one-fifth as large. Again, the declines in unit costs (which mean an increase in productivity) were more rapid in the latter half of the period than in the earlier segment—a 1-plus per cent yearly drop to World War I versus a 3-plus per cent annual decline from 1919 to 1957.

The record in forestry, a small segment of the economy or of the extractive sector, *does* give support to the doctrine of natural resource scarcity. Unit costs of forestry products doubled, an average increase of about 1 per cent annually in the 87-year period. Almost all of the increase occurred before World War I. There has been a more favorable cost record in the post-1920 period, with real costs approximately stable and a fairly constant output. There have been major substitutions of metals, plastics, and masonry for lumber due to more favorable costs.

The scarcity doctrine receives no support from a view of the extractive industries as a whole. The labor-plus-capital input necessary to produce a unit of extractive goods output declined by two-thirds.

TECHNOLOGICAL COST CUTTERS

Why the declining trend in the real cost of extractive goods? Is the decline in cost general among commodities?

Have some goods gone up in cost and others down? In agriculture there is a pronounced downward trend in unit costs for all crops, feed grains, oil crops (soybeans), sugar crops, cotton, hay and forage, fruits and nuts, vegetables, and tobacco but a less rapid decline in livestock and products, particularly meat animals. The same holds true for individual minerals. Each of the fuels has experienced a major decline in unit cost. Each of the metallic minerals examined has declined in unit cost, except lead and zinc which have had a level trend.

A pervasive and significant factor in declining costs of extractive products has been the substitution of minerals for land. For example, if the U.S. had to rely on work animals for its farm "horsepower," their feed alone would require 20 to 50 times as many acres of crop land as is cultivated today. If synthetic fibers from minerals and fuels were replaced by cotton, the additional land required would equal or exceed acreage now planted in cotton.

To what extent have imports been responsible for averting cost increases in extractive products? At the beginning of the test period, the U.S. was a net exporter but gradually shifted to being an importer by the 1930's. Since then, imports have ranged from 2.5 per cent of consumption of extractive goods in 1937–1939 to about 4 per cent in the 1951–1957 period. The bulk of agricultural imports are "exotic" crops not grown in this climate, like coffee and cocoa.

The foreign trade influence on minerals is quite different. Since World War II imports have increased to where they now account for about 10 per cent of domestic minerals consumption. In certain commodities partial substitution of imports facilitated the decline in unit costs of domestic production by moderating demand pressures on our resources. This is true in petroleum, which accounts for the largest share of mineral imports, to the regret of domestic producers who are producing at far less than capacity in order to maintain prices. As for minerals like copper, lead, zinc, and bauxite, imports were significantly responsible for declining or level costs.

Technological change has been *the* dynamic factor in the declining cost trend for agricultural and mineral commodities. In addition to the substitution of mechanical power for animal and human effort, the discovery and introduction of improved breeds, fertilizers, weed killers, and other agricultural methods have fostered the long-term trend of declining costs. In forestry the use of the power saw and log-pulling tractor has augmented important technical advances in the development of substitutes for saw timber.

In minerals the advances are particularly striking. New domestic reserves of minerals have been found or have become economically accessible because of advances in geological knowledge and search techniques. Strip mining of coal has more than doubled daily output per worker. Long distance gas pipelines have opened markets for previously useless gas wells. Taconite pellets, concentrated to 60 or more per cent iron content, are no less efficient than high-grade hematite ore in blast furnaces.

Yet knowledge advance and technological change have been lightly regarded in the natural resources "conventional wisdom." Implicitly, they are fleeting phenomena which might not persist, which might evaporate at any moment. Indeed, Alfred Marshall, the great neoclassical economist, believed diminishing returns to be a historical law, because improvements in production "must themselves gradually show a diminishing return."

This is not the case. Natural resource scarcity and diminishing returns through time are not a curse that society must bear. An examination of the historical record and an awareness of the multiplier effect of technological change argue against hoarding these resources. Of course, society has an obligation to future generations. But the natural environment is only part of what one generation passes on to another. Knowledge, technology, capital instruments, and economic institutions—these are more significant

for economic welfare because they are, in fact, the determinants of real income per capita and economic growth. Higher production today, if it also means greater knowledge, research, and development, will serve the economic interest of future generations better than preservation of resources and lower production. In the United States, for example, the economic magnitude of the estate each generation passes on—the income per capita the next generation enjoys—has been approximately double that which it received, over the period for which data exist.

But if the U.S. no longer needs to be concerned about diminishing returns and natural resource scarcity, there is an even more important resources problem still facing this society. Have we learned how to protect the *quality* of life? Indeed, it might be said that diminishing qualitative, rather than quantitative, returns are really the central issue. Averting a deterioration in the quality of life may be more challenging than finding ways to circumvent increases in the economic scarcity of certain natural resources.

Preservation of natural beauty, urban agglomeration, waste disposal and pollution, changes in income distribution, water supply, land use—these are a few of the social problems related to natural resources and the quality of life. The modern natural resources problem is not one of facing up to diminishing returns, but rather one of social adjustment to a variety of effects of technological change and economic growth upon the nature-man relationship. If not solved, these social problems can undermine the quality of life. This should be our contemporary social concern with natural resources in this country, not the classical economics problem of scarcity and subsistence. Even in such nations as India the dilemma is not primarily obdurate natural resources. Rather, it is an inefficient ratio of population to productive capital and a culture not yet fully subjugated to the goals of economic growth. Man's relations to nature are not governed by uncontrollable natural forces. It is, rather, man's relations to man which in our time have become crucial for handling his relation to the natural environment.

FURTHER READING SUGGESTED BY THE AUTHOR

Landsberg, H. H. 1964. *Natural resources for U.S. growth.* Baltimore: Johns Hopkins Press.
Fisher, J. L. and Potter, N. 1964. *World prospects for natural resources.* Baltimore: Johns Hopkins Press.
Jarrett, H., ed. 1966. *Environmental quality in a growing economy.* Baltimore: Johns Hopkins Press.

Realities of Mineral Distribution

PRESTON E. CLOUD, JR.

PRESTON CLOUD *is professor of geology at the University of California at Santa Barbara.*

The hardware of society is, in large measure, made up of materials derived from nonrenewable resources. The quantities of estimated recoverable reserves of some, for example lead, phosphorus, and helium, are extremely limited. Extraction, refining, and processing of natural resources often have effects destructive to the environment which are only beginning to be considered. There is, moreover, a highly uneven world-wide distribution of many important minerals. Proponents of the technological fix promise that indefinite extensions of mineral lifetimes are possible in some cases by use of substitutions, synthetic materials, recycling, and extraction from more dilute sources such as rocks and the oceans. Preston Cloud suggests, however, that in the absence of large supplies of cheap energy, which itself is often obtained from natural resources, such promises should be viewed with skepticism.

INTRODUCTION

Optimism and imagination are happy human traits. They often make bad situations appear tolerable or even good. Man's ability to imagine solutions, however, commonly outruns his ability to find them. What does he do when it becomes clear that he is plundering, overpopulating, and despoiling his planet at such a horrendous rate that it is going to take some kind of a big leap, and soon, to avert irreversible degradation?

The inventive genius of man has got him out of trouble in the past. Why not now? Why be a spoil-sport when brilliant, articulate, and well-intentioned men assure us that all we need is more technology? Why? Because the present crisis is exacerbated by four conditions that reinforce each other in a very undesirable manner: (1) the achievements of medical technology which have brought on the run-away imbalance between birth

The Texas Quarterly, 11: 103–26, 1968. Reprinted by permission. Abridgment by the editors of the present volume.

and death rates; (2) the hypnotic but unsustainable national dream of an ever-increasing real Gross National Product based on obsolescence and waste; (3) the finite nature of the earth and particularly its accessible mineralized crust; and (4) the increased risk of irreversible spoilation of the environment which accompanies overpopulation, overproduction, waste, and the movement of ever-larger quantities of source rock for ever-smaller proportions of useful minerals.

Granted the advantages of big technological leaps, therefore, provided they are in the right direction, I see real hope for permanent long-range solutions to our problems as beginning with the taking of long-range views of them. Put in another way, we should not tackle vast problems with half-vast concepts. We must build a platform of scientific and social comprehension, while concurrently endeavoring to fill the rut of ignorance, selfishness, and complacency with knowledge, restraint, and demanding awareness on the part of an enlightened electorate. And we must not be satisfied merely with getting the United States or North America through the immediate future, critical though that will be. We must consider what effects current and proposed trends and actions will have on the world as a whole for several generations hence, and how we can best influence those trends favorably the world over. Above all, we must consider how to preserve for the yet unborn the maximum flexibility of choices consistent with meeting current and future crises.

Rhetoric, however, either cornucopian or Malthusian, is no substitute for informed foresight and rational action or purposeful inaction.

What are the problems and misconceptions that impede the desired progress? And what must we invest in research and action—scientific, technological, *and* social—to assure a flexibility of resource options for the long range as well as for the immediate future? Not only until 1985, not only until the year 2000, not only even until the year 2050, but for a future as long as or longer than our past. In the nearly five billion years of earth history is man's brief stay of now barely a million years to be only a meteoric flash, and his industrial society less than that? Or will he last with reasonable amenities for as long as the dinosaurs?

NATURE AND GEOGRAPHY OF RESOURCES

Man's concept of resources, to be sure, depends on his needs and wants, and thus to a great degree on his locale and place in history, on what others have, and on what he knows about what they have and what might be possible for him to obtain. Food and fiber from the land, and food and drink from the waters of the earth have always been indispensable resources. So have the human beings who have utilized these resources and created demands for others—from birch bark to beryllium, from buffalo hides to steel and plastic. It is these other resources, the ones from which our industrial society has been created, about which I speak today. I refer, in particular, to the nonrenewable or wasting resources—mineral fuels which are converted into energy plus carbon, nuclear fuels, and the metals, chemicals, and industrial materials of geological origin which to some extent can be and even are recycled but which tend to become dispersed and wasted.

All such resources, except those that are common rocks whose availability and value depend almost entirely on economic factors plus fabrication, share certain peculiarities that transcend economics and limit technology and even diplomacy. They occur in local concentrations that may exceed their crustal abundances by thousands of times, and particular resources tend to be clustered within geochemical or metallogenic provinces from which others are excluded. Some parts of the earth are rich in mineral raw materials and others are poor.

No part of the earth, not even on a continent-wide basis, is self-sufficient in all critical metals. North America is relatively rich in molybdenum and poor in tin, tungsten, and manganese, for instance, whereas Asia is comparatively rich in tin, tungsten, and manganese and, apparently, less well supplied with molybdenum. The great bulk of the world's gold appears to be in South Africa, which has relatively little silver but a good supply of platinum. Cuba and New Caledonia have well over half the world's total known reserves of nickel. The main known reserves of cobalt are in the Congo Republic, Cuba, New Caledonia, and parts of Asia. Most of the world's mercury is in Spain, Italy, and parts of the Sino-Soviet bloc. Industrial diamonds are still supplied mainly by the Congo.

Consider tin. Over half the world's currently recoverable reserves are in Indonesia, Malaya, and Thailand, and much of the rest is in Bolivia and the Congo. Known North American reserves are negligible. For the United States, loss of access to extra-continental sources of tin is not likely to be off-set by economic factors or technological changes that would permit an increase in potential North American production, even if present production could be increased by an order of magnitude. It is equally obvious that other peculiarities in the geographical distribution of the world's geological resources will continue to encourage interest both in trading with some ideologically remote nations and in seeking alternative sources of supply.

Economic geology, which in its best sense brings all other fields of geology to bear on resource problems, is concerned particularly with questions of how certain elements locally attain geochemical concentrations that greatly exceed their crustal abundance and with how this knowledge can be applied to the discovery of new deposits and the delineation of reserves. Economics and technology play equally important parts with geology itself in determining what deposits and grades it is practicable to exploit. Neither economics, nor technology, nor geology can *make* an ore deposit where the desired substance is absent or exists in insufficient quantity.

ESTIMATED RECOVERABLE RESERVES OF SELECTED MINERAL RESOURCES

Consider now some aspects of the apparent lifetimes of estimated recoverable reserves of a selection of critical mineral resources and the position of the United States with regard to some of these. The selected resources are those for which suitable data are available.

Figure 1 shows such lifetimes for different groups of metals and mineral

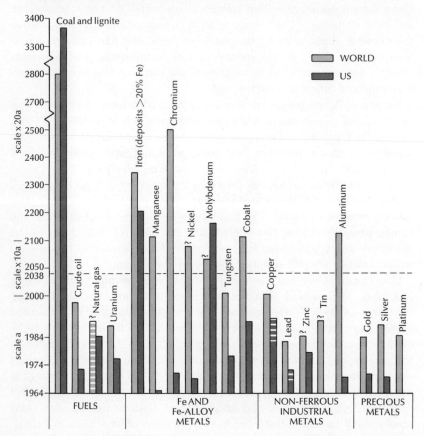

FIGURE 1. Lifetimes of estimated recoverable reserves of mineral resources at current mineable grades and rates of consumption (no allowance made for increasing populations and rates of consumption, or for submerged or otherwise concealed deposits, use of now submarginal grades, or imports). Data from Flawn, 1966.

fuels at *current* minable grades and rates of consumption. No allowance is made for increase of populations, or for increased rates of consumption which, in the United States, tend to increase at twice the rate of population growth. Nor is allowance made for additions to reserves that will result from discovery of submarine deposits, use of submarginal grades, or imports—which may reduce but will not eliminate the impact of growth factors. Data are from the U.S. Bureau of Mines compendia *Mineral Facts and Problems* and its *Minerals Yearbooks*, as summarized by Flawn (*Mineral Resources*, Rand McNally, 1966). The light lines represent lifetimes of world reserves for a stable population of roughly 3.3×10^9 at current rates of use. The dark lines represent similar data for a United States population of about 200 million. Actual availability of some such commodities to the United States will, of course, be extended by imports from abroad, just as that of others will be reduced by population growth, increased per capita demands, and perhaps by political changes. The dashed horizontal line represents the year 2038. I have chosen this as a reference line because it marks that point in the future which is just as distant from the present as

FIGURE 2. Estimated recoverable reserves of minerals (above sea level) for which U.S. reserve estimates exceed, equal, or fall only slightly below those of the USSR plus Mainland China. Data from Flawn, 1966.

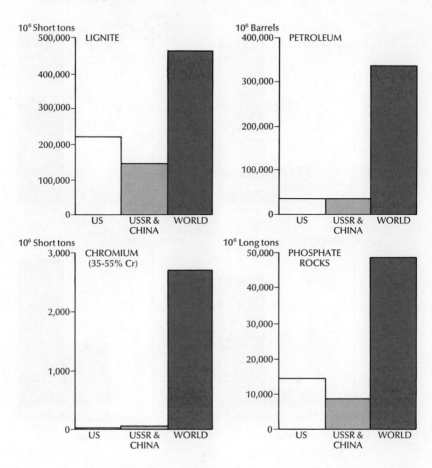

the invention of the airplane and the discovery of radioactivity are in the past. I might have used 2089, which is only as far from the present as the admission of Texas to the Union in 1845.

The prospect is hardly conducive to unrestrained optimism. Of the nineteen commodities considered, only fourteen for the world and four or five for the United States have assured lifetimes beyond 1984; only ten for the world and three for the United States persist beyond the turn of the century; and only eight for the world and three for the United States extend beyond 2038. I do not suggest that we equate these lines with revealed truth. Time will prove some too short and others perhaps too long. New reserves will be found, lower-grade reserves will become minable for economic or technological reasons, substitutes will be discovered or synthesized, and some critical materials can be conserved by waste control and recycling. The crucial questions are: (1) how do we reduce these generalities to specifics; (2) can we do so fast enough to sustain current rates of consumption; (3) can we increase and sustain production of industrial materials at a rate

FIGURE 3.　Estimated recoverable reserves of minerals (above sea level) for which U.S. reserve estimates are less than those of the USSR plus Mainland China. Data from Flawn, 1966.

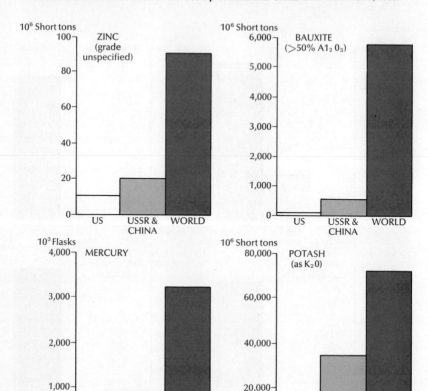

sufficient to meet the rising expectations of a world population of nearly three and one-half billion, now growing with a doubling time of about thirty to thirty-five years, and for how long; and (4) if the answer to the last question is no, what then?

A more local way of viewing the situation is to compare the position of the United States or North America with other parts of the world. Figures 2 to 4 show such a comparison for sixteen commodities with our favorite measuring stick, the Sino-Soviet bloc. Figure 2 shows the more cheerful side of the coin. The United States is a bit ahead in petroleum, lignite, and phosphate, and neither we nor Asia have much chromium—known reserves are practically all in South Africa and Rhodesia. Figure 3, however, shows the Sino-Soviet bloc to have a big lead in zinc, mercury, potash, and bauxite. And Figure 4 shows similar leads in tungsten, copper, iron, and coal.

Again there are brighter aspects to the generally unfavorable picture. Ample local low grade sources of alumina other than bauxite are available with metallurgical advances and at a price. The United States' coal supply

FIGURE 4. Estimated recoverable reserves of minerals (above sea level) for which U.S. reserve estimates are less than those of the USSR plus Mainland China. Data from Flawn, 1966.

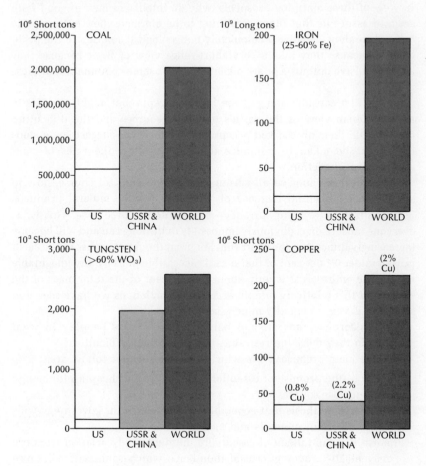

is not in danger of immediate shortage. Potassium can be extracted from sea water. And much of the world's iron is in friendly hands, including those of our good neighbor Canada and our more distant friend Australia.

No completely safe source is visible, however, for mercury, tungsten, and chromium. Lead, tin, zinc, and the precious metals appear to be in short supply throughout the world. And petroleum and natural gas will be exhausted or nearly so within the lifetimes of many of those here today unless we decide to conserve them for petrochemicals and plastics. Even the extraction of liquid fuels from oil shales and "tar sands," or by hydrogenation of coal, will not meet energy requirements over the long term. If they were called upon to supply all the liquid fuels and other products now produced by the fractionation of petroleum, for instance, the suggested lifetime for coal the reserves of which are probably the most accurately known of all mineral products, would be drastically reduced below that indicated in Figure 1—and such a shift will be needed to a yet unknown degree before the end of the century.

THE CORNUCOPIAN PREMISES

In view of these alarming prospects, why do intelligent men of good faith seem to assure us that there is nothing to be alarmed about? It can only be because they visualize a completely nongeological solution to the problem, or because they take a very short-range view of it, or because they are compulsive optimists or are misinformed, or some combination of these things.

Let me first consider some of the basic concepts that might give rise to a cornucopian view of the earth's mineral resources and the difficulties that impede their unreserved acceptance. Then I will suggest some steps that might be taken to minimize the risks or slow the rates of mineral-resource depletion.

The central dilemma of all cornucopian premises is, of course, how to sustain an exponential increase of anything—people, mineral products, industrialization, or solid currency—on a finite resource base. This is, as everyone must realize, obviously impossible in the long run and will become increasingly difficult in the short run. For great though the mass of the earth is, well under 0.1 per cent of that mass is accessible to us by any imaginable means (the entire crust is only about 0.4 per cent of the total mass of the earth) and this relatively minute accessible fraction, as we have seen and shall see, is very unequally mineralized.

But the cornucopians are not naive or mischievous people. On what grounds do they deny the restraints and belittle the difficulties?

The five main premises from which their conclusions follow are:

Premise I—the promise of essentially inexhaustible cheap useful energy from nuclear sources.

Premise II—the thesis that economics is the sole factor governing availability of useful minerals and metals.

Premise III—the fallacy of essentially uninterrupted variation from ore of a metal to its average crustal abundance, which is inherent in Premise II; and from which emanates the strange and misleading notion that quantity of a resource available is essentially an inverse exponential function of its concentration.

Premise IV—the crucial assumption of population control, without which there can be no future worth living for most of the world (or, worse, the belief that quantity of people is of itself the ultimate good, which, astounding as it may seem, is still held by a few people who ought to know better—see, for instance, Colin Clark, *Population Growth and Land Use*, Macmillan, 1967).

Premise V—the concept of the "technological fix."

Now these are appealing premises, several of which contain large elements of both truth and hope. Why do I protest their unreserved acceptance? I protest because, in addition to elements of truth, they also contain assumptions that either are gross over-simplifications, outright errors, or are not demonstrated. I warn because their uncritical acceptance contributes to a dangerous complacency toward problems that will not be solved by a few brilliant technological "breakthroughs," a wider acceptance of deficit economy, or fall-out of genius from unlimited expansion of population. They will be solved only by intensive, wide-ranging, and persistent scientific and engineering investigation, supported by new social patterns and wise legislation.

I will discuss these premises in the order cited.

PREMISE I

The concept of essentially inexhaustible cheap useful energy from nuclear sources offers by all odds the most promising prospect of sweeping changes in the mineral resource picture. We may be on the verge of developing a workable breeder reactor just in time to sustain an energy-hungry world facing the imminent exhaustion of traditional energy sources. Such a development, it has been persuasively stated, will also banish many problems of environmental pollution and open up unlimited reserves of metals in common crustal rocks. There are, unhappily, some flaws in this delightful picture, of which it is important to be aware.

Uranium 235 is the only naturally occurring spontaneously fissionable source of nuclear power. When a critical mass of uranium is brought together, the interchange of neutrons back and forth generates heat and continues to do so as long as the U^{235} lasts. In the breeder reactor some of the free neutrons kick common U^{238} over to plutonium 239, which is fissionable and produces more neutrons, yielding heat and accelerating the breeder reaction. Even in existing reactors some breeding takes place, and, if a complete breeding system could be produced, the amount of energy available from uranium alone would be increased about 140 fold. If thorium also can be made to breed, energy generated could be increased about 400 fold over that now attainable. This would extend the lifetime of visible energy resources at demands anticipated by 1980 by perhaps 1000 to 3000 years and gain time to work on contained nuclear fusion.

The problem is that it will require about 275,000 short tons of $6.00 to $10.00 per pound U_3O_8 (not ore, not uranium) to fuel reactors now on order to 1980, plus another 400,000 tons to sustain them until the turn of the century, burning only U^{235} with currently available enrichments from slow breeding (Charles T. Baroch, U.S. Bureau of Mines, oral comment). Only about 195,000 of the 675,000 tons of uranium needed is known to be available at this price, although known geologic conditions indicate the possibility of another 325,000 tons. Thus we now appear to be about 155,000 tons short of the U_3O_8 needed to produce the hoped-for 150,000 megawatts of nuclear energy on a sustained basis from 1985 until the end of the century without a functioning breeder reactor. Unless we find a lot more uranium, or pay a lot more money for it, or get a functioning complete breeder reactor or contained nuclear fusion within ten or fifteen years, the energy picture will be far from bright. There is good reason to hope that the breeder will come, and after it, contained fusion, *if* the U^{235} and helium hold out—but there is no room for complacency.

If and when the breeder reactor or contained fusion does become available as a practicable energy source, however, how will this help with mineral resources? It is clear immediately that it will take pressure off the fossil "fuels" so that it will become feasible, and should become the law, to reserve them for petrochemicals, polymers, essential liquid propellants, and other special purposes not served by nuclear fuels. It is also clear that cheap massive transportation, or direct transmittal of large quantities of cheap electric power to, or its generation at, distant sources will bring the mineral resources of remote sites to the market place—either as bulk ore for processing or as the refined or partially refined product.

What is not clear is how this very cheap energy will bring about the extraction of thinly dispersed metals in large quantity from common rock. The task is very different from the recovery of liquid fuels or natural gas by nuclear fracturing. The procedure usually suggested is the break-up of rock in place at depth with a nuclear blast, followed by hydrometallurgical or chemical mining. The problems, however, are great. Complexing solutions, in large quantity also from natural resources, must be brought into contact with the particles desired. This means that the enclosing rock must be fractured to that particle size. Then other substances, unsought, may use up and dissipate valuable reagents. Or the solvent reagents may escape to ground waters and become contaminants. Underground electrolysis is no more promising in dealing with very low concentrations. And the bacteria that catalyze reactions of metallurigical interest are all aerobic, so that, in addition to having access to the particles of interest, they must also be provided with a source of oxygen underground if they are to work there.

Indeed the energy used in breaking rock for the removal of metals is not now a large fraction of mining cost in comparison with that of labor and capital. The big expense is in equipping and utilizing manpower, and, although cheap energy will certainly reduce manpower requirements, it will probably never adequately substitute for the intelligent man with the pick at the mining face in dealing with vein and many replacement deposits, where the sought-after materials are irregularly concentrated in limited spaces. There are also limits to the feasible depths of open pit mining, which would be by all odds the best way to mine common rock. Few open pit mines now reach much below about 1,500 feet. It is unlikely that such depths can be increased by as much as an order of magnitude. The quantity of rock removable decreases exponentially with depth because pit circumference must decrease downward to maintain stable walls.

It may also not be widely realized by non-geologists that many types of ore bodies have definite floors or pinch-out downward, so that extending exploitative operations to depth gains no increase in ore produced. Even where mineralization does extend to depth, of course, exploitability is ultimately limited by temperature and rock failure.

Then there is the problem of reducing radioactivity so that ores can be handled and the refined product utilized without harm—not to mention heat dispersal (which in some but not all situations could itself be a resource) and the disposal of waste rock and spent reagents.

Altogether the problems are sufficiently formidable that it would be fool-hardy to accept them as resolved in advance of a working efficient breeder reactor plus a demonstration that either cheap electricity or nuclear explosions will significantly facilitate the removal of metals from any common rock.

A pithy comment from Peter Flawn's recent book on *Mineral Resources* (Rand McNally, 1966, p. 14) is appropriate here. It is to the effect that "average rock will never be mined." It is the uncommon features of a rock that make it a candidate for mining! Even with a complete nuclear technology, sensible people will seek, by geological criteria, to choose and work first those rocks or ores that show the highest relative recoverable enrichments in the desired minerals.

The reality is that even the achievement of a breeder reactor offers no guarantee of unlimited mineral resources in the face of geologic limitations and expanding populations with increased per capita demands, even over the middle term. To assume such for the long term would be sheer folly.

PREMISE II

The thesis that economics is the sole, or at least the dominant, factor governing availability of useful minerals and metals is one of those vexing part-truths which has led to much seemingly fruitless discussion between economists and geologists. This proposition bears examination.

It seems to have its roots in that interesting economic index known as the Gross National Product, or GNP. No one seems to have worked out exactly what proportion of the GNP is in some way attributable to the mineral resource base. It does, however, appear that the dollar value of the raw materials themselves is small compared to the total GNP, and that it has decreased proportionately over time to something like 2 per cent of the present GNP, as I recall. From this it is logically deduced that the GNP could, if necessary, absorb a several-fold increase in cost of raw materials. The gap in logic comes when this is confused with the notion that all that is necessary to obtain inexhaustible quantities of any substance is either to raise the price or to increase the volume of rock mined. In support of such a notion, of course, one *can* point to diamond, which in the richest deposit ever known occurred in a concentration of only one to twenty-five million, but which, nevertheless, has continued to be available. The flaw is not only that we cannot afford to pay the price of diamond for many substances, but also that no matter how much rock we mine we can't get diamonds out of it if there were none there in the first place.

Daniel Bell (1967, Notes on the Post-industrialist Society II: in the *Public Interest,* no. 7, p. 102–118) comments on the distorted sense of relations that emerges from the cumulative nature of GNP accounting. Thus, when a mine is developed, the costs of the new facilities and payroll become additions to the GNP, whether the ore is sold at a profit or not. Should the mine wastes pollute a stream, the costs of cleaning up the stream or diverting the wastes also are added to the GNP. Similarly if you hire someone to wash the dishes this adds to GNP, but if your wife does them it doesn't count.

From this it results that mineral raw materials and housework are not very impressive fractions of the GNP. What seems to get lost sight of is what a mess we would be in without either!

Assuming an indefinite extension of their curves and continuance of access to foreign markets, economists appear to be on reasonably sound grounds in postulating the relatively long-term availability of certain sedimentary, residual, and disseminated ores, such as those of iron, aluminum, and perhaps copper. What many of them do not appreciate is that the type of curve that can with some reason be applied to such deposits and metals is by no means universally applicable. This difficulty is aggravated by the fact that conventional economic indexes minimize the vitamin-like quality for the economy as a whole of the raw materials whose enhancement in value through beneficiation, fabrication, and exchange accounts for such a large part of the material assets of society.

In a world that wants to hear only good news some economists are perhaps working too hard to emancipate their calling from the epithet of "dismal science," but not all of them. One voice from the wilderness of hyperoptimism and overconsumption is that of Kenneth Boulding, who

observes that, "*The essential measure of the success of the economy is not production and consumption at all, but the nature, extent, quality, and complexity of the total capital stock, including in this the state of the human bodies and minds included in the system*" (p. 9 in K. E. Boulding, 1966, "The economics of the coming spaceship Earth," p. 3–14 in *Environmental Quality in a Growing Economy*, Resources of the Future, Inc., The Johns Hopkins Press). Until this concept penetrates widely into the councils of government and the conscience of society, there will continue to be a wide gap between the economic aspects of national and industrial policy and the common good, and the intrinsic significance of raw materials will remain inadequately appreciated.

The reality is that economics per se, powerful though it can be when it has material resources to work with, is not all powerful. Indeed, without material resources to start with, no matter how small a fraction of the GNP they may represent, economics is of no consequence at all. The current orthodoxy of economic well-being through obsolescence, over-consumption, and waste will prove, in the long term, to be a cruel and a preposterous illusion.

PREMISE III

Premise III, the postulate of essentially uninterrupted variation from ore to average crustal abundance is seldom if ever stated in that way, but it is inherent in Premise II. It could almost as well have been treated under Premise II; but it is such an important and interesting idea, whether true or false, that separate consideration is warranted.

If the postulated continuous variation were true for mineral resources in general, volume of "ore" (not metal) produced would be an exponential inverse function of grade mined, the handling of lower grades would be compensated for by the availability of larger quantities of elements sought, and reserve estimates would depend only on the accuracy with which average crustal abundances were known. Problems in extractive metallurgy, of course, are not considered in such an outlook.

This delightfully simple picture would supplant all other theories of ore deposits, invalidate the foundations of geochemistry, divest geology of much of its social relevance, and place the fate of the mineral industry squarely in the hands of economists and nuclear engineers.

Unfortunately this postulate is simply untrue in a practical sense for many critical minerals and is only crudely true, leaving out metallurgical problems, for particular metals, like iron and aluminum, whose patterns approach the predicted form. Sharp discontinuities exist in the abundances of mercury, tin, nickel, molybdenum, tungsten, manganese, cobalt, diamond, the precious metals, and even such staples as lead and zinc, for example. But how many prophets of the future are concerned about where all the lead or cadmium will come from for all those electric automobiles that are supposed to solve the smog problem?

Helium is a good example of a critical substance in short supply. Although a gas which has surely at some places diffused in a continuous spectrum of concentrations, particular concentrations of interest as a source of supply appear from published information to vary in a stepwise manner. Here I draw on data summarized by H. W. Lipper in the 1965 edition of the U.S. Bureau of Mines publication *Mineral Facts and Problems.* Although an uncommon substance, helium serves a variety of seemingly indispensable uses. A bit less than half of the helium now consumed in the U.S. is used in pressurizing liquid fueled missiles and space ships. Shielded-arc welding is the next largest use, followed closely by its use in producing controlled atmospheres for growing crystals for transistors, processing fuels for nuclear energy, and cooling vacuum pumps. Only about 5.5 per cent of the helium consumed in the United States is now used as a lifting gas. It plays an increasingly important role, however, as a coolant for nuclear reactors and a seemingly indispensable one in cryogenics and superconductivity. In the latter role, it could control the feasibility of massive long-distance transport of nuclear-generated electricity. High-helium low-oxygen breathing mixtures may well be critical to man's long-range success in attempting to operate at great depths in the exploration and exploitation of the sea. Other uses are in research, purging, leak detection, chromatography, etc.

Helium thus appears to be a very critical element, as the Department of the Interior has recognized in establishing its helium-conservation program. What are the prospects that there will be enough helium in 2038?

The only presently utilized source of helium is in natural gas, where it occurs at a range of concentrations from as high as 8.2 per cent by volume to zero. The range, however, in particular gas fields of significant volume, is apparently not continuous. Dropping below the one field (Pinta Dome) that shows an 8.2 per cent concentration, we find a few small isolated fields (Mesa and Hogback, New Mexico) that contain about 5.5 per cent helium, and then several large fields (e.g., Hugoton and Texas Panhandle) with a range of 0.3 to 1.0 per cent helium. Other large natural gas fields contain either no helium or show it only in quantities of less than 5 parts per 10,000. From the latter there is a long jump down to the atmosphere with a concentration of only 1 part per 200,000.

Present annual demand for helium is about 700 million cubic feet, with a projected increase in demand to about 2 billion cubic feet annually by about 1985. It will be possible to meet such an accelerated demand for a limited time only as a result of Interior's current purchase and storage program, which will augment recovery from natural gas then being produced. As now foreseen, if increases in use do not outrun estimates, conservation and continued recovery of helium from natural gas reserves will meet needs to slightly beyond the turn of the century. When known and expected discoveries of reserves of natural gas are exhausted shortly thereafter, the only potential sources of new supply will be from the atmosphere, as small quantities of He^3 from nuclear reactor technology, or by synthesis from hydrogen—a process whose practical feasibility and adequacy remain to be established.

Spending even a lot more money to produce more helium from such sources under existing technology just may not be the best or even a very feasible way to deal with the problem. Interior's conservation program must be enlarged and extended, under compulsory legislation if necessary. New sources must be sought. Research into possible substitutions, recovery and re-use, synthesis, and extraction from the atmosphere must be accelerated—*now* while there is still time. And we must be prepared to curtail, if necessary, activities which waste the limited helium reserves. Natural resources are the priceless heritage of all the people; their waste cannot be tolerated.

Problems of the adequacy of reserves obtain for many other substances, especially under the escalating demands of rising populations and expectations, and it is becoming obvious to many geologists that time is running out. Dispersal of metals which could be recycled should be controlled. Unless industry and the public undertake to do this voluntarily, legislation should be generated to define permissible mixes of material and disposal of "junk" metal. Above all the wastefulness of war and preparation for it must be terminated if reasonable options for posterity are to be preserved.

The reality is that a healthy mineral resource industry, and therefore a healthy industrial economy, can be maintained only on a firm base of geologic knowledge, and geochemical and metallurgical understanding of the distribution and limits of metals, mineral fuels, and chemicals in the earth's crust and hydrosphere.

PREMISE IV

The assumption that world populations will soon attain and remain in a state of balance is central to all other premises. Without this the rising expectations of the poor are doomed to failure, and the affluent can remain affluent only by maintaining existing shameful discrepancies. Taking present age structures and life expectancies of world populations into account, it seems certain that, barring other forms of catastrophe, world population will reach six or seven billion by about the turn of the century, regardless of how rapidly family planning is accepted and practiced.

On the most optimistic assumptions, this is probably close to the maximum number of people the world can support on a reasonably sustained basis, even under strictly regularized conditions, at a general level of living roughly comparable to that now enjoyed in Western Europe. It would, of course, be far better to stabilize at a much smaller world population. In any case, much greater progress than is as yet visible must take place over much larger parts of the world before optimism on the prospects of voluntary global population control at any level can be justified. And even if world population did level off and remain balanced at about seven billion, it would probably take close to one hundred years of intensive, enlightened, peaceful effort to lift all mankind to anywhere near the current level of Western Europe or even much above the level of chronic malnutrition and deprivation.

This is not to say that we must therefore be discouraged and withdraw to ineffectual diversions. Rather it is a challenge to focus with energy and realism on seeking a truly better life for all men living and yet unborn and on keeping the latter to the minimum. On the other hand, an uncritical optimism, just for the sake of that good feeling it creates, is a luxury the world cannot, at this juncture, afford.

A variation of outlook on the population problem which, surprisingly enough, exists among a few nonbiological scholars is that quantity of people is of itself a good thing. The misconception here seems to be that frequency of effective genius will increase, even exponentially, with increasing numbers of people and that there is some risk of breeding out to a merely high level of mediocrity in a stabilized population. The extremes of genius and idiocy, however, appear in about the same frequency at birth from truly heterogeneous gene pools regardless of size (the data from Montgomery County, Maryland, are really no exception to this). What is unfortunate, among other things, about overly dense concentrations of people is that this leads not only to reduced likelihood of the identification of mature genius, but to drastic reductions in the development of potential genius, owing to malnutrition in the weaning years and early youth, accompanied by retardation of both physical and mental growth. If we are determined to turn our problems over to an elite corps of mental prodigies a more sure-fire method is at hand. Nuclear transplant from various adult tissue cells into fertilized ova whose own nuclei have been removed has already produced identical copies of amphibian nucleus-donors and can probably do the same in man (Joshua Lederberg, 1966, *Bull. Atomic Scientists,* v. 22, no. 8, p. 9). Thus we appear to be on the verge of being able to make as many "xerox" copies as we want or need of any particular genius as long as we can get a piece of his or her nucleated tissue and find eggs and incubators for the genome aliquots to develop in. Female geniuses would be the best because (with a little help) they could copy themselves!

The reality is that without real population control and limitation of demand all else is drastically curtailed, not to say lost. And there is as yet not the faintest glimmer of hope that such limitation may take place voluntarily. Even were all unwanted births to be eliminated, populations would still be increasing at runaway rates in the absence of legal limitation of family size, as Dr. Erlich has so passionately argued. The most fundamental freedom should be the right not to be born into a world of want and smothering restriction. I am convinced that we must give up (or have taken away from us) the right to have as many children as we want or see all other freedoms lost for them. Nature, to be sure, will restore a dynamic balance between our species and the world ecosystem if we fail to do so ourselves—by famine, pestilence, plague, or war. It seems, but is not, unthinkable that this should happen. If it does, of course, mineral resources may then be or appear to be relatively unlimited in relation to demand for them.

PREMISE V

The notion of the "technological fix" expresses a view that is at once full of hope and full of risk. It is a gripping thought to contemplate a world set free by nuclear energy. Imagine soaring cities of aluminum, plastic, and thermopane where all live in peace and plenty at unvarying temperature and without effort, drink distilled water, feed on produce grown from more distilled water in coastal deserts, and flit from heliport to heliport in capsules of uncontaminated air. Imagine having as many children as you want, who, of course, will grow up seven stories above the ground and under such germ-free conditions that they will need to wear breathing masks if they ever do set foot in a park or a forest. Imagine a world in which there is no balance of payments problem, no banks, or money, and such mundane affairs as acquiring a shirt or a wife are handled for us by central computer systems. Imagine, if you like, a world in which the only problem is boredom, all others being solved by the state-maintained system of genius-technologists produced by transfer of nuclei from the skin cells of certified gene donors to the previously fertilized ova of final contestants in the annual ideal-pelvis contest. Imagine the problem of getting out of this disease-free world gracefully at the age of 110 when you just can't stand it any longer!

Of course this extreme view may not appeal to people not conditioned to think in those terms. But the risk of slipping bit by bit into such a smothering condition as one of the better possible outcomes is inherent in any proposition that encourages or permits people or industries to believe that they can leave their problems to the invention of technological fixes by someone else.

Although the world ecosystem has been in a constant state of flux throughout geologic time, in the short and middle term it is essentially homeostatic. That is to say, it tends to obey Le Chatelier's general principle—when a stress is applied to a system such as to perturb a state of near equilibrium, the system tends to react in such a way as to restore the equilibrium. But large parts of the world ecosystem have probably already undergone or are in danger of undergoing irreversible changes. We cannot continue to plunder and pollute it without serious or even deadly consequences.

Consider what would be needed in terms of conventional mineral raw materials merely to raise the level of all 3.3 billion people now living in the world to the average of the 200 million now living in the United States. In terms of present staple commodities, it can be estimated (revised from Harrison Brown, James Bonner, and John Weir, 1947, *The Next Hundred Years,* Viking Press, p. 33) that this would require a "standing crop" of about 30 billion tons of iron, 500 million tons of lead, 330 million tons of zinc, and 50 million tons of tin. This is about 100 to 200 times the present annual production of these commodities. Annual power demands would be the equivalent of about 3 billion tons of coal and lignite, or about ten times present production. To support the doubled populations expected by the year 2000 at the same level would require, of course, a doubling of all the above numbers or substitute measures. The iron needed could probably be produced over a long period of time, perhaps even by the year 2000, given a sufficiently large effort. But, once in circulation, merely to replace losses due to oxidation, friction, and dispersal, not counting production of new iron for larger populations, would take around 200,000 tons of new iron every year (somewhat more than the current annual production of the

United States), or a drastic curtailment of losses below the present rate of 1 per cent every two or three years. And the molybdenum needed to convert the iron to steel could become a serious limiting factor. The quantities of lead, zinc, and tin also called for far exceed all measured, indicated, and inferred world reserves of these metals.

This exercise gives a crude measure of the pressures that mineral resources will be under. It seems likely, to be sure, that substitutions, metallurgical research, and other technological advances will come to our aid, and that not all peoples of the world will find a superfluity of obsolescing gadgets necessary for the good life. But this is balanced by the equal likelihood that world population will not really level off at 6.6 or 7 billion and that there will be growing unrest to share the material resources that might lead at least to an improved standard of living. The situation is also aggravated by the attendant problems of disposal of mine wastes and chemically and thermally polluted waters on a vast scale.

The "technological fix" is not a panacea but an anesthetic. It may keep the patient quiet long enough to decide what the best long-range course of treatment may be, or even solve *some* of his problems permanently, but it would be tragic to forget that a broader program of treatment and recuperation is necessary. The flow of science and technology has always been fitful, and population control is a central limiting factor in what can be achieved. It will require much creative insight, hard work, public enlightenment, and good fortune to bring about the advances in discovery and analysis, recovery and fabrication, wise use and conservation of materials, management and recovery of wastes, and substitution and synthesis that will be needed to keep the affluent comfortable and bring the deprived to tolerable levels. It will probably also take some revision of criteria for self-esteem, achievement, and pleasure if the gap between affluent and deprived is to be narrowed and demand for raw materials kept within bounds that will permit man to enjoy a future as long as his past, and under conditions that would be widely accepted as agreeable.

The reality is that the promise of the "technological fix" is a meretricious premise, full of glittering appeal but devoid of heart and comprehension of the environmental and social problems. Technology and "hard" science we must have, in sustained and increasing quality, and in quantities relevant to the needs of man—material, intellectual, and spiritual. But in dealing with the problems of resources in relation to man, let us not lose sight of the fact that this is the province of the environmental and social sciences. A vigorous and perceptive technology will be an essential handmaiden in the process, but it is a risky business to put the potential despoilers of the environment in charge of it.

THE NUB OF THE MATTER

The realities of mineral distribution, in a nutshell, are that it is neither inconsiderable nor limitless, and that we just don't know yet in the detail required for considered weighting of comprehensive and national long-range alternatives where or how the critical lithophilic elements are concentrated.

Stratigraphically controlled substances such as the fossil fuels, and, to a degree, iron and alumina, we can comprehend and estimate within reasonable limits. Reserves, grades, locations, and recoverability of many critical metals, on the other hand, are affected by a much larger number of variables. We in North America began to develop our rich natural endowment of mineral resources at an accelerated pace before the rest of the world. Thus it stands to reason that, to the extent we are unable to meet needs by imports, we will feel the pinch sooner than countries like the U.S.S.R. with a larger component of virgin mineral lands.

In some instances nuclear energy or other technological fixes may buy time to seek better solutions or will even solve a problem permanently. But sooner or later man must come to terms with his environment and its limitations. The sooner the better. The year 2038, by which time even current rates of consumption will have exhausted presently known recoverable reserves of perhaps half the world's now useful metals (more will be found but consumption will increase also), is only as far from the present as the invention of the airplane and the discovery of radioactivity. In the absence of real population control or catastrophe there could be fifteen billion people on earth by then! Much that is difficult to anticipate can happen in the meanwhile, to be sure, and to place faith in a profit-motivated technology and refuse to look beyond a brief "foreseeable future" is a choice widely made. Against this we must weigh the consequences of error or thoughtless inaction and the prospects of identifying constructive alternatives for deliberate courses of long-term action, or inaction, that will affect favorably the long-range future. It is well to remember that to do nothing is equally to make a choice.

Geologists and other environmental scientists now living, therefore, face a great and growing challenge to intensify the research needed to ascertain and evaluate the facts governing availability of raw material resources, to integrate their results, to formulate better predictive models, and to inform the public. For only a cognizant public can generate the actions and exercise the restraints that will assure a tolerable life and a flexibility of options for posterity. The situation calls neither for gloomy foreboding nor facile optimism, but for positive and imaginative realism. That involves informed foresight, comprehensive and long-range outlooks, unremitting effort, inspired research, and a political and social climate conducive to such things.

Every promising avenue must be explored. The most imperative objective, after peace and population control, is certainly a workable breeder reactor—with all it promises in reduced energy costs, outlook for desalting saline waters and recovering mineral products from the effluent wastes, availability of now uselessly remote mineral deposits, decrease of cutoff grades, conservation of fossil "fuels" for more important uses, and reduction of contaminants resulting from the burning of fossil fuels in urban regions.

But, against the chance that this may not come through on schedule, we should be vigorously seeking additional geological sources of U^{235} and continuing research on controlled nuclear fusion.

A really comprehensive geochemical census of the earth's crustal materials should be accelerated and carried on concurrently, and as far into the

future as may be necessary to delineate within reasonable limits the metallogenic provinces of our planet's surface, including those yet poorly-known
portions beneath the sea. Such a census will be necessary not only in seeking
to discover the causes and locations of new metalliferous deposits, but also
in allowing resource data to be considered at the design stage, and in
deciding which "common rocks" to mine first, should we ever be reduced
to that extreme. Of course, this can be done meaningfully only in context
with a good comprehension of sequence and environment based on careful
geologic mapping, valid geochronology, perceptive biogeology, and other
facets of interpretive earth science.

Programs of geophysical, geochemical, and geological prospecting should
meanwhile be expanded to seek more intensively for subglacial, subsoil,
submarine, and other concealed mineral resources in already defined favorable target areas—coupled with engineering, metallurgical, and economic
innovation and evaluations of deposits found.

Only as we come to know better what we have, where it is, and what
the problems of bringing it to the market place are likely to be will it be
feasible to formulate the best and most comprehensive long range plans
for resource use and conservation. Meanwhile, however, a permanent,
high-level, and adequately funded monitoring system should be established
under federal auspices to identify stress points in the mineral economy, or
likely future demands, well in advance of rupture. Thus the essential lead
time could be allowed in initiating search for new sources or substitutes,
or in defining necessary conservation programs.

Practices in mixing materials during fabrication and in disposal of scrap
metal should be examined with a view to formulating workable legislation
that will extend resource lifetimes through more effective re-use.

Management of the nation's resources and of wastes from their extraction,
beneficiation, and use should be regarded in the true democratic tradition
as national problems and not left entirely to the conscience and discretion
of the individual or private firm. Where practices followed are not conducive to the national, regional, or local welfare, informed legal inducement
should make them so.

Research into all phases of resource problems and related subjects should
be maintained at some effective level not dependent on political whimsey.
It would be a far-sighted and eminently fair and logical procedure to set
apart some specific fraction of taxes derived from various natural resources
to be ploughed back into research designed to assure the integrity of the
environment and the sufficiency of resources over the long term.

Much of the work suggested would naturally be centered in the U.S.
Department of the Interior and in various state agencies, whose traditionally
effective cooperative arrangements with the nation's universities should be
enlarged.

Scholarly institutions are central to the problem of sustaining a healthy
industrial society. For they are the source of that most indispensable of all
resources—the trained minds that will discern the facts and evolve the
principles via which such a society comes to understand its resources and
to use them wisely. The essential supplements are adequate support and a

vision of the problem that sweeps and probes all aspects of the environmental sciences the world over. The times cry for the establishment of schools and institutes of environmental science in which geologists, ecologists, meteorologists, oceanographers, geophysicists, geographers, and others will interact and work closely together.

I can think of no more fitting way to close these reflections than to quote the recent words of Sir Macfarlane Burnet (p. 29, in "Biology and the appreciation of life," The Boyer Lectures, 1966, ABC, 45p)—*"There are three imperatives: to reduce war to a minimum; to stabilize human populations; and to prevent the progressive destruction of the earth's irreplaceable resources."* If the primary sciences and technology are to be our salvation it will necessarily be in an economic framework that evaluates success by some measure other than rate of turnover, and in the closest possible working liaison with the environmental and social sciences.

ACKNOWLEDGMENTS

I am obligated to literally scores of people whose brains I have picked and whose ideas, data, and words have influenced me or have even been appropriated in formulating the above statement. Among these I acknowledge a special debt to T. S. Lovering, M. K. Hubbert, Peter Flawn, H. L. James, A. L. Weinberg, Frank Forward, and Walter Hibbard, Jr.

I also had the advantage in preparing this paper of having been the Chairman of a Committee on Resources and Man of the National Academy of Sciences, whose final report was being prepared for publication as I was working on this. The views expressed above, of course, are not the official views of that Committee. They are also cast in a more hortative vein than would be appropriate in a report by such a Committee.

Energy

PREPARED FOR THE U.S. GOVERNMENT
INTERDEPARTMENTAL STUDY ON ENERGY RESEARCH
AND DEVELOPMENT BY THE ENERGY STUDY
GROUP UNDER THE DIRECTION OF
ALI BULENT CAMBEL

Extensive use of energy—heat, light, electricity—is a characteristic of modern civilization. Few human activities exist without it: manufacturing industries, extraction of resources, refrigeration, transportation, communications, all require vast amounts. The standard of living is closely related to energy usage. Supplies of energy from such sources as fossil fuels, hydroelectric power, the sun, and nuclear fission are not infinite. Where these are large, conversion to useable forms may be inefficient and costly. This selection presents some of the findings and conclusions on this subject by the U.S. Government Interdepartmental Study on Energy Research and Development (R&D).

INTRODUCTION

The Problem
Advanced industrial societies have developed a high standard of living by utilizing energy on a large scale and replacing human and animal energy with mechanized energy for both industry and personal consumption.

Annual energy consumption in the United States has increased rapidly in the past and is expected to rise from 250 million (2.5×10^8) Btu's* per capita in 1960—45 quadrillion (4.5×10^{16}) Btu's in total—to about 400 million Btu's per capita or 135 quadrillion Btu's in total in the year 2000 (see Fig. 1). The total estimated cumulative consumption of 3 quintillion (3×10^{18}) Btu's over the 40-year span from 1960 to 2000 is much less than the known recoverable domestic reserves—estimates of which range from about 5 to nearly 25 quintillion Btu's of energy depending on the utilization factors

Energy R&D and National Progress: Findings and Conclusions, An Interdepartmental Study, September 1966, Washington D.C.: U.S. Government. Abridgment by the editors of the present volume.

*One British Thermal Unit (Btu) is the energy needed to lift a hundred pound load through approximately eight feet.

FIGURE 1.   United States energy consumption. Sources: U.S. Bureau of Mines, 1920–1980; *Resources in America's Future,* 2000.

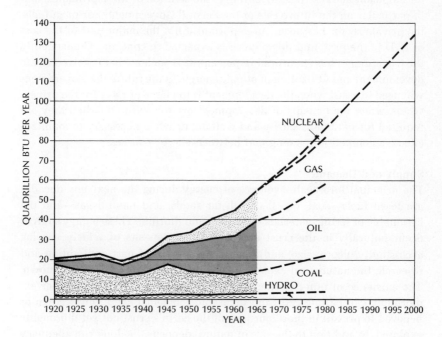

assumed for uranium and thorium. For the projected increase to take place, however, energy must be available at reasonable costs.

From the most reliable information, it seems fairly clear that presently foreseeable total resources will indeed be adequate to meet total energy needs without major cost increases for the remainder of this century, and for a considerable time thereafter. The committee has confined its detailed considerations to the period ending in the year 2000. It has done so with awareness that this is a short period on the scale of human history, but with confidence that critical problems are far enough removed in time so that human ingenuity and imagination can cope with later circumstances as newer information develops. *The main problem is how to meet the growing need in the most effective and least costly way,* both in the immediate future and for the long run.

Secondly, *problems arise in matching energy sources for particular purposes and in assuring competitive availability.* Coal was once the principal energy source for household heating, industrial use, transportation, and electrical power. Today it has been replaced widely by petroleum and natural gas in household heating and industrial uses, and by petroleum for transportation—truck, rail, ship, air, and automobile. It also now shares the market for electric generation with natural gas, oil, nuclear fuel, and waterpower. The economy should retain and expand its flexibility to choose among energy sources for particular application.

In addition, Americans wish to minimize pollution and preserve natural beauty in the course of developing and using energy resources.

The focus of the Energy Study has been on the role of research and development activity in contributing to the solution of these problems, and in particular on the future role of the Federal Government. For most fuels, the private sector has borne an important if not the major part of the cost of R&D in the past, and this pattern is expected to continue. Concurrently the Government has sponsored important R&D such as that involved in the development and utilization of atomic energy. In the future the Government will need to assist when the development is too large or risky for the private sector, when the benefits of development are too diffused, when they are required for national security and welfare, or when necessary to maintain effective competition among and between energy sources.

Supply and Demand

The principal foreseeable sources of energy during the next few decades are fossil fuels—coal, oil, shale oil, tar sands, and natural gas—and the fissionable or fertile materials—uranium and thorium. These energy sources occur naturally in the crust of the earth in deposits of widely varying accessibility, depth, size, and quality. As a result of past exploration and research, the nature and extent of some of these deposits are well known. The existence of other similar deposits, discoverable through further exploration, can be inferred from favorable geological conditions known or believed to prevail in those portions of the earth's crust not yet thoroughly explored. In addition to the size of natural deposits, the long-run adequacy of energy resources depends on other factors such as accessibility, quality gradations, processing and extraction techniques, and, importantly, on the particular needs of each consumer. A substantial part of the energy sources contained in both known and unappraised deposits is of submarginal quality, not economically exploitable with present technology, but it is reasonable to assume that technological gains will bring such deposits within economic reach in the future.

The long-run adequacy of our energy resources, therefore, will depend not only on the extent of presently known minable deposits but on R&D that:

improves knowledge of geology and exploration capability;
improves processes for extraction from grades now considered marginal
   and submarginal;
reduces transportation costs;
improves efficiency in use; and
develops substitutes for resources which are being depleted or are increasing in cost.

Also, some energy resources are available abroad at less cost than in the United States. America can benefit from foreign supplies of energy resources, giving in exchange goods in which the United States holds a comparative advantage. Ideally, the appraisal of a nation's total energy resources should reflect its ability to share in the use and production of world energy resources. In order to keep its scope manageable, however, the appraisal here is confined largely to domestic resources, and the conclusions reached are accordingly conservative.

TABLE 1.   Comparison of U.S. energy resources with projected requirements, 1960–2000. Derived primarily from Cambel, *Energy R&D and National Progress,* with some modifications in assumptions as to recovery of energy from uranium. Other estimates from competent sources may differ from those used here.

[Expressed in terms of energy content, where the unit is 1 Q = 1 quintillion (10^{18}) Btu]

	COAL	CONVEN- TIONAL LIQUID HYDRO- CARBONS	SHALE OIL	OIL IN BITUM- INOUS ROCKS	NATURAL GAS	URANIUM	THORIUM
1. Known reserves recoverable under present economic and technologic conditions	4.6	0.3	—	—	0.3	0.3	—
2. Undiscovered deposits recoverable (when found) under present technologic conditions	—	1.3	—	—	1.2	0.8	—
3. Additional known and undiscovered resources possibly recoverable in the future	84	2.3	945	0.07	0.9–25	224,000	336,000
4. Total resources (sum of lines 1, 2, and 3)	88.6	3.9	945	0.07	2.4–26	224,000	336,000
5. Cumulative projection of energy requirements 1960–2000, by source	0.6	1.4			1.0	¹0.2	
5.a. As per cent of known recoverable resources, assuming present conditions (line 5 divided by line 1)	13%	470%	—	—	333%	67%	—
5.b. As a per cent of total recoverable resources (line 5 divided by the sum of lines 1 and 2)	13%	87%	—	—	67%	18%	—
5.c. As per cent of total resources (line 5 divided by line 4)	1%	36%	0.1%	2,000%	42–3.8%	—	—

Energy Resources of the United States

Domestic energy resources and requirements are projected by source from 1960 to 2000 in Table 1. The projection must be qualified because estimates from various competent authorities differ substantially, and also are quickly outdated by new or improved information. It is evident nonetheless that the Nation's known energy resources are large, and that even greater supply is undiscovered or cannot now be exploited economically. Anticipated requirements exceed "known recoverable resources" from liquid hydrocarbons and natural gas; but "total resources" far exceed anticipated requirements for any and all energy sources. Undoubtedly, the fruits of research and development programs can assure economical and physically exploitable energy resources throughout the 20th century. The well-being of the Nation in the 21st century, however, may well depend on advances made in the efficiency of resource utilization and discovery of new resources.

TABLE 2. **Estimated energy resources of the United States and the world (as of 1962).** Derived from Cambel, *Energy R&D and National Progress*, except the larger world resources of uranium and thorium which are extrapolated from U.S. resources. Pore space gas in coal and shale not included in estimates of world resources. Assumptions as to recovery are the same as those used in Table 1.

[Expressed in terms of energy content, where the unit is 1 Q = 1 quintillion (10^{18}) Btu]

	KNOWN RECOVERABLE RESOURCES		UNITED STATES AS PER CENT OF WORLD	ADDITIONAL POTENTIAL RESOURCES[1]		UNITED STATES AS PER CENT OF WORLD
	UNITED STATES	WORLD		UNITED STATES	WORLD	
Coal	4.6	18	26%	84	320	26%
Liquid hydrocarbons	0.3	1.9	16%	3.6	26	14%
Natural gas	0.3	1.9	16%	2.1–26	20	10%
Shale oil	—	—	—	945	12,000	8%
Oil in bituminous rocks	—	0.2	0%	0.07	6.1	0.1%
Uranium	0.3	0.9–1.2	33–25%	224,000	4,000,000	6%
Thorium	—	—	—	336,000	5,600,000	6%

[1] Includes undiscovered resources assumed to be recoverable under present economic and technologic conditions, together with additional known and undiscovered resources possibly recoverable in the future.

Energy Resources of the World

Energy resource estimates for the United States and the world are shown in Table 2. The data indicate that the U.S. proportion of known recoverable reserves is 25 per cent for coal, 15 per cent for oil and natural gas, and 43 per cent for uranium. In terms of all resources, the United States is endowed with approximately one-fourth of the coal, one-seventh of the oil, possibly one-tenth of the natural gas, one-twelfth of shale oil, and one-seventeenth of the uranium and thorium.

While the United States is relatively well endowed with energy resources, it is also a relatively large consumer of energy, especially energy from oil and natural gas—the fuels for which world supplies are the smallest.

Implications

The foregoing comparison of the U.S. energy resources and projected requirements has the following implications:

1. In the light of present day technology, the Nation's total energy resources seem adequate to satisfy expected energy requirements through the remainder of this century at costs near present levels, but technological advances will be required to reduce costs and extend the supply base into the more distant future.

2. Future sources of electric power, especially coal and nuclear fuels, are abundant. All of the estimates indicate that *either* coal or uranium resources *alone* are adequate to take us through the year 2000 and longer.

3. Oil and gas, which now supply 73 per cent of our total requirements for energy, are the fuels for which there are the smallest known and potential resources, even on a world basis.

4. In addition to domestic resources, the energy resources of other countries offer increased potential supplies for the United States in exchange for other products of the U.S. economy.

OPPORTUNITIES AND INCENTIVES IN
RESEARCH AND DEVELOPMENT

The objectives of energy research and development programs are to provide adequate and diverse sources of energy at low costs. The incentives for research and development vary among different fuels, but opportunities for improving technology and extending supplies exist for all of them.

Oil

As previously shown, potential domestic resources are ample for increased production for many years; the question therefore, is whether exploration and development costs can be reduced sufficiently to attract enough investment to generate this production domestically, or whether needs are to be

met from lower cost foreign or synthetic sources. Increased R&D might yield cost-cutting benefits in each of the principal fields related to production—exploration and drilling technology, subsurface geologic mapping and analysis, and secondary recovery.

Gas
What is said for oil generally applies to natural gas, which is often associated with oil. In addition, some formations not favorable for oil—such as shales and coaly rocks that contain occluded gas—may be favorable for gas. Some of these formations are already yielding gas under artificial fracturing.

Oil Shales and Bituminous Rocks
Industrial research on the enormous domestic oil shale deposits is increasing with some prospect for competitive production within a few years. Since shale oil is a likely substitute for both gas and oil in some applications, its development is of great importance in extending the supplies of these fuels. Since large-scale production from oil shale faces serious obstacles due to its impact on the natural environment, it is desirable to explore mining and recovery systems that will be compatible with sound principles of environmental management and that might reduce costs as well. *In situ* extraction methods and advanced mining systems offer the most promise.

Further exploration of bituminous rocks, similar to the tar sands of Canada, may also lead to significant discoveries. Some R&D on recovery processes applying to such deposits is in progress and more would appear to be rewarding.

Coal
Until recently, coal R&D proceeded at low tempo; but the pressure of competition from oil, gas, and most recently nuclear energy, has led to increased expenditures. There has been progress in nearly every phase of the industry—mining, processing, transportation, and utilization—resulting in an overall decrease in the average price of coal. Opportunities for continued advance in extraction and transport technology are still great, and there are gains to be made also from studies of the distribution and quality of coal resources. Also, research and development on processes for extracting substitutes for crude oil and natural gas from coal have progressed in recent years.

Uranium and Thorium
Uranium constitutes a major energy resource for the United States and the world, even with the relatively low fuel efficiency in present reactors. Current commercial types of nuclear reactors are capable of utilizing only about 1.5 per cent of the fission energy contained in uranium, principally because little use is made of uranium-238. This fraction can be vastly increased, perhaps by as much as 50 times, when "breeder" reactors are developed in which more fissionable material is produced from uranium-238 or thorium than is consumed (up to the limits of available uranium-238 or

thorium). Such a potential improvement in efficiency and cost constitutes a strong incentive for research and development. In particular, as the efficiency of use is increased, fuel cost would become much less important in determining energy cost, so that more expensive ores would become more economic.

Although the development of reactors to use thorium is not as far along as the development of uranium fueled reactors, thorium nonetheless constitutes another major potential long-range nuclear fuel resource. Development of thorium energy sources will ultimately become important because of the desirability of extending the supply of low-cost nuclear fuel. In addition, research on exploration methods, recovery technology, and general knowledge of the geology of uranium and thorium ores would also be rewarding.

Controlled Nuclear Fusion
Development of controlled fusion of deuterium, which is abundantly available in the oceans, appears as an attractive means for removing virtually all limitations on the long-run availability of energy. Fusion also produces much less radioactive waste than the fission process. Unfortunately, the feasibility of physical control or economic utilization of this theoretical energy resource has not been determined and requires additional basic research. There is very small economic incentive for private research, although some is being done. Although practical payoffs are not now in sight, the enormous potential for the future justifies a continuing Federal research effort. Federal programs are pursuing a number of the most promising new ideas as they are generated.

Other Potential Resources
Energy can be extracted from sources arising from local features of topography, geology or climate—falling water, tides, wind, heat of the earth, and sun. R&D on these sources has proceeded at relatively low rates, and probably will continue to receive far less emphasis than the more significant fossil and fissile fuels. There are many opportunities, however, for lowering the costs and enlarging the magnitude of these usable sources. The possibility of using "bulb" type hydroelectric turbines in tidal estuaries and major rivers is an example.

Utilization Efficiency
Research and development which improves the efficiency with which energy is converted and consumed extends existing inventories of resources and may reduce total costs. Some improvements that show promise in this direction include fuel cells, storage batteries, central station components, thermoelectric devices, as well as those already mentioned in discussing particular resources.

The magnetohydrodynamic (MHD) generator—in which ionized gas at high temperature replaces the conventional rotating copper coil—combines the functions of prime mover and generator in a device with no moving parts, and may offer efficiency gains as high as 10 to 15 per cent in converting the energy of burning fuel directly into electricity. Progress has been slow because of uncertainties in computing both cost and benefits, because of severe material limitations and because even experimental devices are relatively large and expensive. Another new device which may hold promise, but is now in the speculative stage, is the coal-fired electrogasdynamic (EGD) process, in which a high-temperature ionized gas operates in an electrostatic field to generate electricity with no moving parts.

Development of high-voltage, long-distance electrical transmission lines is important to realize the benefits of lower costs associated with large unit size in many types of power plants. Steady progress toward increasingly high voltages has occurred with existing research and development programs. The greater efficiencies of large-scale central stations interconnected by extra-high voltage transmission systems can be realized from research and development in such areas as computer-control dispatching and improved control reliability. Private incentives seem to be adequate to insure satisfactory progress where alternating-current transmission systems are concerned. Direct-current transmission systems may require Government encouragement of R&D. Underground high voltage lines which replace unattractive surface powerlines may become increasingly important. It is not yet technically feasible to transmit electricity underground at very high voltages, and even at lower voltages underground transmission is much more expensive than overhead transmission. Government encouragement or support of R&D may be required.

Abatement of Damage to Health and Environment

In the future, development and use of fuel resources will be strongly influenced by the urgent necessity to control critical increases of environmental pollution—such as automobile exhaust gases, SO_2 and other products of fossil fuel burning; excessive heating of rivers and estuaries by powerplant water cooling; acid mine drainage; radioactive wastes; and damage to scenic and land values through mining. Research and development programs aimed at both the assessment of hazards to health and environment and the economical abatement of damages are urgently needed. Atmospheric carbon dioxide is not poisonous but in the long run may affect the temperature of the earth and the weather; research directed toward understanding thoroughly the implications of atmospheric carbon dioxide buildup is particularly necessary to determine with greater certainty the effects that can be anticipated if we continue our present usage of fossil fuels for the next several decades.*

Automobile exhaust gas pollution may ultimately limit the use of conventional automotive engines unless a sharp improvement in control is

---

*At our projected world rate of fossil fuel consumption, the Panel on Environmental Pollution of the President's Science Advisory Committee, in its report: *Restoring the Quality of Our Environment,* estimates an increase in carbon dioxide content of the atmosphere of 25 per cent by the year 2000. It is not yet known whether this would have undesirable consequences. (Tukey, John W., et al., *Restoring the quality of our environment.* 1965. Washington, D.C.: U.S. Government Printing Office.)

developed. Present technology for limiting pollution, developed in response to official regulation, is inadequate to keep pace with the rate of increase in the number of automobiles. The fuel cell or improved storage batteries may, with sufficient development, provide an alternative power source, even if continuing vigorous research on control of present sources should not be successful.

Nuclear reactors, which do not produce carbon dioxide or other combustion products, provide a potential means of decreasing future air pollution. However, they produce other kinds of deleterious wastes; and continued care will have to be exercised to avoid radioactive contamination in reactor operation, waste product handling, and fuel processing.

Food and Nutrition

REPORT OF THE PANEL ON THE
WORLD FOOD SUPPLY

Perhaps the most important resource is food. Diseases caused by hunger or malnutrition kill, cripple or debilitate large segments of the world's population. This selection, extracted from the U.S. President's Science Advisory Committee report *The World Food Problem,* gives some indication of the magnitude of this problem and presents some possible solutions for the near future.

This report defines and directs attention to a threatening problem of the global environment in which the United States and all nations must dwell together—the declining condition of more than two-thirds of the human race.

The Panel's detailed analysis of the world food problem has led to four basic conclusions:

1. The scale, severity, and duration of the world food problem are so great that a massive, long-range, innovative effort unprecedented in human history will be required to master it.

2. The solution of the problem that will exist after about 1985 *demands* that programs of population control be initiated now. For the immediate future, the food supply is critical.

3. Food supply is directly related to agricultural development and, in turn, agricultural development and overall economic development are critically interdependent in the hungry countries.

4. A strategy for attacking the world food problem will, of necessity, encompass the entire foreign economic assistance effort of the United States in concert with other developed countries, voluntary institutions, and international organizations.

The Nature of the World Food Problem

The world's increasingly serious nutritional problem arises from the *uneven distribution* of the food supply among countries, within countries, and

The World Food Problem: A Report of the President's Science Advisory Committee,
May 1967, The White House. Abridgment by the editors of the present volume.

among families with different levels of income. Global statistical surveys, based upon total food produced per person, suggest that there is no world-wide shortage of food in terms of quantity (calories) or quality (protein) at the moment. But in the developing countries, where two-thirds of the world's population live, there is overwhelming clinical evidence of under-nutrition (too few calories) and malnutrition (particularly, lack of protein) among the people. Clearly, millions of individuals are *not* receiving the amounts of food suggested by average figures.

Many South Asian and Latin American countries, for example, have average diets which are nutritionally inadequate according to minimum standards of the United Nations Food and Agriculture Organization (FAO). In these regions, surveys show that the poorest 25 per cent of the people consume diets with caloric and protein contents that are only about three-fourths of the country average and fall far below calculated nutritional requirements. It is in these low income groups that overt malnutrition is found, particularly among the most susceptible groups: infants and pre-school children, pregnant women, and nursing mothers.

Nutrition, Infant Mortality, and Family Planning

That reduction of population growth is essential to achieving a balance between food supply and food need is an obvious, easily understood, and widely appreciated fact.

There is, however, another more complex, less well-known, and crucially important relationship between nutritional needs and family planning. Surveys of the attitudes of married couples in developing countries show that the numbers of children desired are higher than in the developed nations. Furthermore, the average number of live births per woman in the developing countries is 30 per cent greater than the desired number of children.

Emphasis on the desire for heirs leads to large families. Only one son may be needed for ritual or economic purposes but it is common to want two sons to insure against the death or incapacity of one. Couples must average four children to obtain two sons.

Availability and efficacy of pills, intra-uterine devices and other technical means for birth control are largely irrelevant until couples have secured the desired number of living children.

If we assume the necessary preconditions for reducing fertility rates in the developing countries are low infant and child mortality and a public awareness that mortality is low, then *we have the apparent paradox that a reduction in childhood mortality will reduce rather than raise the rate of population growth.*

In the United States, approximately 25 of every 1,000 liveborn infants fail to survive to the age of one year and most of the deaths result from prematurity or congenital defects. In the poor countries of Asia, Africa, and Latin America, published infant mortality rates range from 100 to nearly 200 per 1,000 live births. *Much of the higher death rate is the direct or indirect result of protein-calorie malnutrition.*

Protein-calorie deficiency, in the form of a disease called *kwashiorkor,* is a great killer. Acute diarrhea can be a dangerous illness for a well-nourished American baby; in the malnourished infants of the developing countries, it has an appalling mortality. Common childhood diseases are catastrophic in protein-deficient children. In 1960, for example, the fatality rate from ordinary measles was more than 100 times greater in Chile than in the United States.

If lowered infant and child mortality is a precondition to acceptance of family planning, and the major underlying cause of excessive childhood deaths in the developing nations is malnutrition, it follows that an increase in both quantity and quality of food in these countries is essential to achieving stability of population growth.

Viewed in this light, alleviation of the world food problem must be accorded the highest priority in planning for the developing nations.

THE NEED FOR FOOD

The prevention of malnutrition throughout the world by providing adequate diets for the rapidly expanding population is a task of staggering proportions. FAO has estimated that at least 20 per cent of the population in the developing countries is undernourished (receives too few calories) and about 60 per cent receives diets that are inadequate in nutritional quality (commonly a deficiency of protein). Kwashiorkor is the most widespread deficiency affecting preschool children, the most vulnerable group in the population. Childhood malnutrition causes retardation of physical growth and development and recent evidence suggests that mental development may be impaired also. In malnourished preschool children, mortality and morbidity are extremely high and the common infectious diseases of childhood are catastrophic.

Nutrition has a vital role in the health of adults, also, and influences socio-economic and cultural development profoundly. Malnutrition leads to deterioration of physical fitness and mental efficiency, to emotional and personality disturbances, and to reduction in the capacity to perform work.

In the developing countries, increased supplies of calories and high quality protein are needed urgently. In many areas, vitamin and mineral deficiencies are prevalent and foods furnishing these specific nutrients must be made available. Anemias, endemic goiter (iodine deficiency), and xerophthalmia (vitamin A deficiency) are frequently encountered and beriberi (thiamine deficiency) and ariboflavinosis are observed in some countries.

Caloric Needs for the Future

In computing the nutritional requirements of a population, consideration must be given to the distribution by age and sex and the average body size of males and females at different ages in addition to the number of individuals in the population. There are marked variations in average body weights among different peoples. Data for seven Asian and seven Latin American countries show that the average Indian weighs nearly 15 per cent less than the average Malayan; the East Pakistani weighs about 20 per cent less than the West Pakistani; the range between the relatively small Indians and Vietnamese at one extreme, and Uruguayans and Chileans at the other, is approximately 40 per cent. The differences in body weight between the peoples of the Asian and the Latin American countries are probably partly genetic, but several lines of evidence suggest that nutrition can be a determining factor in fulfilling genetic potential. Hence, a sustained improvement in the nutrition of children in poor countries can be expected to increase the average body weight of adults 10 per cent or more during the next two decades, with a corresponding increase in food needs.

There are more females than males in the developed countries, while the reverse is often true in the developing ones. This difference in sex ratios would raise the per capita nutritional requirements of the developing countries except that they also have a larger proportion of children under 15, whose nutritional requirements are much less than those of adults.

The most serious nutrition problem of the developing countries arises from the uneven distribution of food, both in quantity and quality, among families with different levels of income. In India and South America, surveys show that the poorest 25 per cent obtain a diet with an energy and protein content that is usually less than 75 per cent of the average for the population, and is considerably below the calculated nutritional requirements. Among these low income groups, there is clear clinical evidence of malnutrition, particularly among the children.

Caloric needs of the World and of India, Pakistan, and Brazil were estimated from caloric requirements listed by the Food and Agriculture Organization (FAO) of the United Nations. In applying these standards, it was apparent that the average body sizes of children and adults were less than those suggested by FAO. Accordingly, current estimates of caloric needs were calculated at two levels, one for the FAO reference body weights, and the other, for the current body weights. Lack of satisfactory data on body weight in these countries introduces uncertainties as to accuracy. In projecting caloric demands for the future, it was assumed that children would receive sufficient calories to achieve normal growth to age 14 (FAO reference child weights) and that, because of better nutrition during childhood, the body weight of the adult population would increase three kilograms per decade.

Caloric needs for the world for 1965, based on FAO standard body weights, were 7,787 billion kilocalories, or 2,354 kilocalories per caput, per day. In 1985, the estimated caloric needs of the world will increase 52 per cent or 43 per cent above 1965, to 11,823 billion kilocalories, or 2,350 kilocalories per caput, per day, if fertility rates remain *unchanged* and 11,118 billion kilocalories, or 2,393 kilocalories per caput, per day, if fertility rates *decrease* by 30 per cent. Current estimates of caloric needs are probably high since the scanty information available indicates that many population groups are of smaller body size than FAO standards. Projections based on these standards seem justified as much of the world population is suffering from impairment of physical growth due to inadequate caloric and protein intake.

In 1965, estimates of caloric needs for India were 1,138 billion kilocalories per day or 2,352 kilocalories per caput for FAO body weights and were 937 billion kilocalories per day or 1,936 kilocalories per caput for the average body weights recorded in India. The lower estimate is in close agreement with caloric availability calculated by FAO in recent years for Far Eastern countries. In 1985, the needs will be 108 per cent more than present at the higher projection and will be 88 per cent more than the present at the lower projection.

In Pakistan, if present fertility rates continue, the population will more than double in 1985 and current caloric needs of 212 billion kilocalories

TABLE 1.   Needs for calories and proteins in 1985 expressed as per cent increase over needs estimated for 1965.

NEEDS	POPULATION ESTIMATE	WORLD	INDIA[2]	PAKISTAN[2]	BRAZIL[2]
Calories	High	52	108	146	104
	Low	43	88	118	92
Protein[1]	High	52	110	145	109
	Low	45	93	121	98

[1] Protein needs are for FAO "reference" protein.

[2] Based on estimated body weights in 1965.

per day will be increased by 146 per cent. If fertility declines, needs will still be 118 per cent more than estimates of current needs.

In Brazil, the lower level of estimated caloric needs in 1965 was 2,164 kilocalories per caput per day. A recent estimate of caloric availability for that country as a whole is 2,650 kilocalories per caput per day. This emphasizes the importance of food distribution as a factor in caloric availability since undernutrition is common in some parts of Brazil. Assuming no change in fertility, caloric needs for Brazil will increase 104 per cent between 1965 and 1985, from 176 to 360 billion kilocalories per day. With some decline in fertility, the increase will be 92 per cent. If needs are to be met, a more equitable distribution of calories within the country must be achieved.

Protein Needs for the Future

In estimating protein requirements, the procedures utilized were those proposed by the Joint FAO-WHO Expert Group on Protein Requirements. Protein needs were estimated in terms of FAO "reference" protein.* These values were then converted to an intake of protein from food sources in proportion to the amounts available in the national food supply of the population in question. This was done by estimating the net protein utilization (NPU) of these diets. NPU affords an index of digestibility of protein and of the biological values of the amino acid mixture absorbed from the intestine. Protein requirements were expressed as grams per kilogram of body weight for various age groups.

The estimated caloric and protein requirements for India, Pakistan, Brazil, and the World in 1985, relative to the needs for 1965, are summarized in Table 1.

The Panel has translated the calculated requirements for calories and protein into foods and commodities that will be needed to provide food for the world and the three selected countries. It should be emphasized that these requirements are for food that is consumed and not for food that is produced, which must be much greater to allow for various types of losses and for an even distribution among and within households.

Special problems exist in meeting protein needs in countries where single

---

*Defined as protein that is completely utilized for anabolic purposes, i.e., protein that has an NPU of 100.

foods provide most of the food energy, or where food resources are not equitably distributed. Attention must be given to mechanisms of food distribution within a country and within households to assure adequate intake of protein of young and growing children and other groups that are vulnerable to malnutrition. When food supplies are limited in quantity or variety, it may be necessary to provide additional protein to meet the requirements of vulnerable groups in the population.

The General Protein Problem

Statistical surveys, notwithstanding, there is abundant and unequivocal clinical evidence that large numbers of the world's people suffer from protein malnutrition. Clearly, these malnourished individuals are not getting the amounts of protein suggested by surveys. The reason for this apparent discrepancy is that the "average" daily per capita ration of protein does not quantitatively and qualitatively consider the requirement of three groups: *preschool children, pregnant women, and nursing mothers*. The protein needs of children of weaning age are particularly high in relation to caloric requirements, and unless these are satisfied, physical development and growth are impaired. Aggregate surveys of a global type also fail to consider the many individuals in different regions who are under nutritional stress due to crop failure, sickness, or natural catastrophe.

Supplying adequate nutrition to a developing area is not an isolated problem of providing adequate amounts of protein. Each region of the world has available to it certain foodstuffs; the people who live in each region have specific food habits and taboos. The choice of corrective action for a "target" population is dependent upon assessing local production and distribution and pinpointing the requirements for the specific acceptability patterns of the population. It is imperative that programs to alleviate protein deficiency be designed to produce results in a relatively short time. Since even the most vigorous efforts probably will fall short of the goal, consideration should be given to any program which shows promise of achieving significant results. Nutritional programs, however, differ greatly in the speed with which they can be initiated and developed as well as in their ultimate impacts. Present donations of grain and mixtures of protein (weaning foods) to the developing countries have an immediate but small-scale effect on protein malnutrition.

Future Needs for Other Nutrients

The needs for *thiamine, riboflavin, and niacin* are related to caloric intake. Accordingly, the relative increase in needs for the next 20 years will be about the same as indicated for calories. The Panel used the recommended intakes of these three vitamins suggested by the Joint Expert Committee of FAO-WHO. In many of the developing countries, cereal grain furnishes a large percentage of the diet. The thiamine and riboflavin content of grains is markedly reduced by milling. Since there is little reason to believe that food patterns will change, consideration should be given to the enrichment of cereal products with thiamine and riboflavin. The latter vitamin appears to be in short supply in many parts of the world. The niacin requirement can be met in two ways, by the vitamin itself and by conversion of the amino acid tryptophan to niacin in the body. This makes calculation of niacin availability and requirements difficult because of a paucity of information on the tryptophan content of many foods and because there are uncertainties about the efficiency of the biological conversion process. If protein needs are met by good quality protein, it can be assumed that niacin needs will be fulfilled also.

The world needs for *vitamin A,* if it is obtained largely (90 per cent) in the form of carotene, will increase 50 per cent between 1965 and 1985. In India, Pakistan, and Brazil, requirements will almost double during this period at the higher population projection and will increase by 80 per cent or more at the lower projection. Since there are areas in these and other developing countries in which vitamin A-containing foods are not widely used, ways in which this vitamin can be added to existing foods must be considered.

Estimation of *calcium* requirements is difficult and uncertain. Based on conservative estimates, the needs for calcium in India, Pakistan, and Brazil will double or more than double by 1985. On a world basis, requirements will increase 50 per cent at the high population projection and about 40 per cent at the low projection. Where milk and milk products are not available, careful selection of foods is necessary to meet even minimal allowances for calcium.

Numerous limitations exist in interpreting projections of food and population need. There are uncertainties in population numbers and characteristics, uncertainties in estimating caloric and protein requirements, inadequate information on home food production and consumption, and insufficient knowledge of food losses and nutrient composition of foods. Furthermore, averages should be interpreted cautiously in judging adequate and inadequate diets. Averages do not reflect inequities in distribution, the incidence of malnutrition, lack of food availability or purchasing power, local customs or ignorance.

Meeting the Need for More Food

For the next several years, any major expansion of the world food supply will be dependent on increased production from conventional sources and upon more efficient utilization of available foodstuffs through reduction of waste and spoilage. *The vast majority of the increased production must take place within the developing countries themselves.*

There is No Panacea Periodically, the news media draw attention to ongoing research on systems which offer possibilities as new sources of human food. Because there is a strong tendency to portray these as possible "solutions" to the world food problem and because the public is drawn understandably to such panaceas, this publicity undoubtedly lessens concern about the seriousness of the food supply in the developing nations.

The Panel has examined carefully and in detail the several new processes which are under current study. "Single cell protein" derived from fermentation by yeasts or bacteria of carbohydrates, hydrocarbons, or cellulose is particularly promising. A great advantage of single-cell protein is that it can be produced independently of agriculture or climatic conditions. However, there are major unsolved problems of scale of production, processing characteristics, nutritive quality, consumer acceptance, and cost which remain to be worked out. It will be several years, *at least,* before even a decision concerning the possible usefulness of such materials in the food supply can be made.

Methods for extraction of protein directly from green leaves have been devised and deserve careful consideration and further research since the materials utilized are frequently wasted or are fed to animals. Again, many problems of nutritive quality, scale, cost, and acceptability must be solved before evaluation of the usefulness of this material will be possible.

Investigations of the processing of algae as human food have been unrewarding thus far because of the excessive cost of deriving a product that is safe for human consumption. It now appears that the usefulness of algal materials economically derived as a by-product of reclaiming sewage and other waste waters will be as a feed for livestock.

In summary, some nonconventional sources of food appear to offer great potential for the long term but in the judgment of the Panel none of these can be expected to lessen the problem of increasing food production from conventional sources during the next two decades.

Furthermore, the magnitude of the world's food problem is so great that nonconventional sources, when and if they become available, may be needed to supplement rather than supplant modernized agriculture. The problem will be with us for so long, however, that every effort must be made now to invent new processes and develop known ones to produce novel foodstuffs. In order to provide a reasonable probability that the long-range potential of unconventional food sources may be realized within two decades, we must accelerate research on these methods now.

Animal Sources   There are good opportunities for improved production of livestock and increased utilization of fishery resources, including fish farming (aquiculture), in the developing countries. These deserve emphasis and exploitation because animals are capable of converting to food different types of by-products and forages that cannot be consumed directly by people and for the significant contribution that they can make to improving the quality of protein in diets and earning foreign exchange. A process of producing fish protein concentrate (FPC) appears to hold promise for the future although major problems of scale, technologies for different species, and consumer acceptability must be solved before its usefulness can be evaluated.

Agricultural Production   It is, therefore, evident that the *bulk of the increase in food supply must come from increased production of farm crops.* There are two ways in which agricultural production can be increased: by bringing more land under cultivation or by increasing yields of land under cultivation.

Until the present time, most of the increase in food production in the developing countries has been achieved by extending traditional farming methods over a larger area of cropland. Substantial opportunities remain to bring additional land under cultivation in the less densely populated areas of Latin America and of Africa, but the vast majority of arable land in Asia is already in use. While there are marginal possibilities for using small additional areas, it is clear that as the population continues to grow, the amount of cropland per person in the Asian countries will diminish progressively.

In Asia, a shift to increasing crop production by intensifying agriculture and using modern methods to improve annual yields on land under cultivation will be mandatory. Even in Latin America and Africa, the increasing cost of clearing additional land may well make it more economical in many regions to concentrate on elevating yields rather than expanding cultivated areas.

To increase yields, a major expansion of irrigation facilities will be necessary to make multiple cropping possible independent of wide variations in seasonal rainfall. It also will be necessary to develop and utilize new, high-yielding varieties of plants, to develop and utilize plants with a higher quality of protein, to increase the use of fertilizers and pesticides, and to employ improved farm machinery. Increased capital investments and increased expenditure on the part of farmers will be required to make these tools of modern agricultural technology available. These are the techniques that have been employed so successfully in the developed countries to transform farming into a *business.*

The transition from traditional farming to modern agriculture will be difficult and expensive for the hungry nations but it is absolutely essential if their food needs are to be met. There is no alternative.

On the Relative Importance of Calorie Deficiencies and Protein Deficiencies

SIR JOSEPH HUTCHINSON

SIR JOSEPH HUTCHINSON *teaches at the School of Agriculture, Cambridge University.*

Much is already known about nutrition, the nutritious content of foods, and the nutritional requirements of man. The practical problems of providing him with an adequate diet, however, have not always been solved in the past—even when it has technically been possible to do so. Often the solution is one of agricultural economics, knowledge and financial resources. Hutchinson, drawing on his experience in Africa and India, discusses the relative merits of different foods and points out some of the practical difficulties of improving the diet of a society.

The greater part of my experience has been in the agricultural botany of an industrial crop—cotton—and not with food crops. My interest in the latter arose late in my research career in Uganda, when kwashiorkor was discovered to be due to chronic protein malnutrition. Not unnaturally, the medical profession turned to the agriculturists with a demand for a change in agricultural practice that would make possible the elimination of kwashiorkor as a hazard to infant life. The agriculturists' response was that, in a country like Uganda, there was nothing technologically difficult about providing the farm produce on which to base an adequately balanced diet. I believe that this is so, not only in Uganda, but also in most countries of the world in which the climate is such that agriculture can be carried on free of serious climatic hazards. If this is true, and if, as I believe, man is like most animals in his ability to choose a satisfactory diet if the materials are available, how is it that he is malnourished in so many parts of the earth?

Let us first consider the repertoire of crops and stock available to man-

R. A. McCance and Elsie M. Widdowson, eds., *Calorie Deficiencies and Protein Deficiencies*, 1968, London: J. & A. Churchill Ltd., pp. 351–56. Reprinted by permission.

kind. Early man chose for domestication only a small number of plant and animal species, and we know from the archaeological record that of those plants with which he experimented he retained only a proportion, and discarded the rest as less suited to his needs than those that gave rise to our modern crop plants.

Agriculture began, both in the Old World and the New, in open country with extensive areas of grass and open woodland. One of the chief incentives to the development of agriculture must have been the need to harvest and store an adequate food supply to carry over the period of dry late summer and cool winter when food was not available for gathering at will. On the grasslands the material for a stored food supply was at hand, and the abundance of grass seeds at the end of the growing season, and the ease with which they could be stored, led to the extensive use of grasses and eventually to the domestication of the most suitable grass species. And in the Old World, as the early farming people prospered and spread, they adopted new grasses in new areas. Wheat and barley were the original cereals of the Old World. The farming colonists of Europe and the Mediterranean added oats and rye. Those who spread south and south east domesticated sorghum and finger millet in Africa, and rice in India. The farmers of the New World domesticated only one cereal, but that—maize—ranks with wheat, rice, and sorghum among the four most important of the world's cereal crops.

Cereals are a major source of calories, and an important source of protein, but they do not alone provide a totally adequate supply. Presumably the early farmers continued to depend on wild game for a part of their protein supply, and in the Old World the domestication of livestock took place at about the same time as the beginnings of crop production. But early man also discovered a major source of vegetable protein. The seeds of the members of the family *Leguminosae* have a high protein content, and a considerable number of leguminous species were domesticated. In the Old World, the peas and beans of western Asia spread through the Mediterranean and Europe. Lentils, pigeon pea, chick pea and a range of other such seeds were domesticated in middle Asia. And in Africa the cowpea, the lubia of the Sudan, and minor species such as the Bambara groundnut are all leguminous species, deriving their value as crop plants from the high protein content of their seeds. In the New World also, legumes were domesticated, giving us four species of beans, and the peanut.

In cereals and legumes, the farmers of both hemispheres selected from the same plant families. Not all plant families were available in both hemispheres, and the third great group of related crop plants, species of the genus *Brassica*, were only to be found in the Old World. There they gave rise on the one hand to a group of oilseed crops, and on the other to the great range of vegetables that dominates our greengrocery—turnips, rutabagas, cabbage, kale, cauliflower, broccoli, brussels sprouts, to name the commoner ones. Every vegetative part that could possibly hypertrophy has been monstrously developed to give us this diversity of salads, greens and roots. There are no native *Brassicas* in the New World, but their place was somewhat taken by the *Cucurbitaceae*, giving us pumpkins and squash.

Among our crop plants, those from the New World rank in importance, though not in number, with those of the Old. In domestic livestock, the Old World has made the major contribution. Cattle, sheep and goats were native in the grasslands of western Asia and southern Europe. Horses belonged to the grasslands of Europe and Asia. Pigs were brought in from the woodlands. Little was added as farming people spread. The camel from the deserts and the water buffalo from the swampy tropics are important, but not to be compared with cattle. The only major addition to our livestock was the jungle fowl, which gave us the domestic hen. The New World contributed only the turkey, the guinea pig, and the Andean cameloids.

It will be apparent that in the Old World the early farmers supplied themselves with an adequate range of crops and livestock to make up a well balanced diet. In the New World they depended primarily on leguminous crops for their protein, and were consequently not so well supplied with high-quality protein as in the Old World, except in so far as they were able to get animal protein from hunting and fishing. In both hemispheres the farming system was based essentially on a grassland ecology, and on the grasslands, dietary balance has on the whole been good. Food quality has been a much more important problem to the peoples who invaded forest lands, especially tropical forest lands. In temperate regions, as typified by Britain, it has been possible to clear woodlands and impose a grassland ecology. This has not been so easy in forested tropical regions, and agricultural development has followed a different course. A range of tropical plants has been domesticated that provides a large supply of calories, but is very deficient in protein. They are mostly roots and tubers, the circumtropical yams, the New World cassava and sweet potatoes, and the colocasias of Oceania. In the same category, though the edible material is a seedless fruit and not a root, is the starchy banana. These plants are often associated with communities that lived on or near the coasts. Cassava and sweet potatoes provided most of the calories of the Indian communities of the West Indies and the Spanish Main, but fish must have been of great importance in maintaining a dietary balance. Similarly, the bananas, sugar cane, and colocasias of New Guinea and the Pacific could be supplemented with fish in all the coastal and island regions.

As populations increase and farming communities colonize new lands it is the sources of protein that are most frequently overlooked or neglected. A farmer thinks first in terms of weight of food produced. In gross weight per acre, and indeed in calories produced, pulses yield less than cereals, and cereals less than root crops. It takes a degree of sophistication to appreciate that in yield of protein the order is reversed. Fish are only to be had where there are seas, rivers or lakes, and a community spreading inland leaves its source of fish behind. Game gives place to crops as human populations grow, and a community pressing on its resources in land cannot provide for domestic livestock. Indeed it is not unreasonable to regard malnutrition as the first stage of the Malthusian decline. The sequence of the growth of a population followed by a decline in the protein it can obtain can be seen in Africa today. In the Zande country in the southern Sudan the improvement of crop production was greatly hindered by the practice of giving up all agricultural activity in favour of hunting at the end of the dry season. Game had been reduced to the point at which an extensive hunt might yield only a few small mammals, but the desire for meat was such that all else was given up for the chase. In Uganda, in the banana-eating areas, the diet may well have been reasonable when the human population was small and the game abundant. In the grain-eating areas, one can see now the deterioration in dietary standards that follows the substitution of cassava for finger millet. It is an unfortunate fact that the success of the agricultural botanists in clearing cassava of virus diseases vastly increased its attractiveness as a food crop. The work of cultivation is much less than with finger millet, and the return in terms of starchy food very much greater. The decline in protein production goes unnoticed save by the medical service.

One of the most important lessons to be learnt from the Farming and Dietary Improvement Scheme at Gayaza High School in Uganda, was that a good diet costs more than a poor one. It is one of those facts of life that ought to be apparent to any well informed agriculturist, but it is often overlooked. I first experienced this problem in India in the 1930s. We were concerned with the relative importance of jowar (*Sorghum*) and tur (*Cajanus*) in the farming system, and I set out to obtain an objective estimate by a calculation of the monetary return per acre from the two crops. It was immediately apparent that any farmer working solely on the cash return from his crops would never grow any pulses at all. Yields were always below those of grain crops, and the price premium was a quite inadequate compensation for the yield differential. I was not then concerned with nutrition, and did not pursue the matter, but looking back, it is evident that the inadequacy of the differential is a reflexion of the impact of poverty and ignorance on the food market. The first requirement of the poor town dweller is enough to eat, and he can satisfy that at least expense by buying grain. He is ignorant of his own and of his children's need for protein, so the demand for the more expensive pulses is not great enough to create a price differential sufficient to make it worth a farmer's while to increase his pulse crops for the market. We may note in passing that the same inadequate differential exists in this country. Our subsidy system is based on the needs of the siege economy during and immediately after the war, when getting enough to eat was the first consideration, and the cereal prices were consequently set high. Though we now wish to obtain a better quality of protein in our diets, we still support cereals much more heavily than meat or milk, or eggs and poultry.

Looking at the matter as an agriculturist, malnutrition is the result of poverty and of ignorance. There are leguminous crops suited to all agricultural areas of the world, and an increase in groundnuts, soya, beans and other pulses is agriculturally straightforward. The reason these crops are not grown in adequate quantity is first that there is still widespread ignorance of their dietary importance, and second that poor people are not able to pay the differential necessary to induce farmers to increase their acreage at the expense of the higher-yielding grains or starchy vegetables.

If this is so as between crops, it is the more so as between crops and livestock. Only the most productive ways of keeping livestock can match the growing of crops in monetary return on land that is suitable for cropping. In an advanced agriculture such as that of the United Kingdom, the balance is kept by the concentration of livestock enterprises on land less suited for arable crops, and by the restriction of livestock in arable areas to the more intensive forms of production. Of these, only dairying uses land. Pigs and poultry are intensively kept in buildings occupying no more land than a factory. Recent experimental work indicates that it may be possible in the tropics also to develop livestock enterprises on land unsuitable for crop production. In the wet tropics such starchy crops as cassava and yams are cultivated for short periods in long-term systems of rotation. Any intensification leads immediately to degeneration of the soil. Recent work, particularly in Puerto Rico, has shown that there is a great potential for both dairy and beef production on intensively managed pastures in these hot, humid tropics. There is therefore a new potential for the provision of high value protein in those areas hitherto suffering the most serious protein deficiency.

It has seemed right first to discuss the provision of a balanced diet. Having made the point that we have now the knowledge of what is required and of the means whereby our needs may be met, it is necessary to turn to the problem of providing enough food. The problems of ensuring a sufficiency are different from those of ensuring a proper balance. The dominant factor in the provision of adequate quantities of food is the rate of increase in the population to be fed. This is not a new problem, and it is important to remember that, in Britain for instance, the improvement of agriculture went on sufficiently rapidly to ensure the food supply of the entire British population as it increased from 4 million at the end of the seventeenth century to 17 million in the mid nineteenth century, with no more imports than were necessary to balance seasonal fluctuations.

It is, of course, a truism to say that agricultural production has kept pace with population increase, since population increase must be limited absolutely by the rate at which food for more people can be produced. Thus, the rate of population increase is an index of the rate at which agricultural production has increased. Moreover, in those limited sections of the world in which a massive increase in production has been achieved, this has created a surplus followed either by an agricultural depression, or a heavy burden of State support. This emphasizes the delicacy of the balance between shortage and surfeit. A community needs an assured supply of food every day in the year. It cannot deal with a surplus by matching the fall in prices with a rise in consumption.

In considering the adequacy of food supplies, this inelasticity in demand must always be borne in mind. Simple agricultural communities have simple ways of dealing with it. The African subsistence farmer cultivates an area that will give him an adequate food supply in a bad year. In most years, therefore, he has a surplus. This he makes into beer and drinks, or gives it or throws it away. Only recently, with the advent of money and the building of towns, has there been a market for his surplus, and in good years now he sells it. In bad years he keeps all he has, and the town suffers a shortage before the next harvest, of the same kind as the towns in western Europe used to feel in the year following a bad harvest.

The real problem in the maintenance of the balance between population and food supply is the problem of seasonal variation. It is not solved simply by increasing production to the point where there is an adequate supply in all years. This can be done by the individual household at subsistence level, but at a more advanced level the surpluses that are generated become unmanageable. Seasonal variation can be met by storage—going back as early as Joseph and Pharaoh—and by transport, and under the British raj in India, food production was increased enormously by the provision of irrigation, and transport was greatly improved by the building of railways. By irrigation in the valley of the Indus and its tributaries, Karachi became a major wheat-exporting port. The increased supplies went to England, not

India, and the control of famine became the responsibility of the transport system rather than the departments of agriculture. In this respect, we have made very great advances in recent years. Food can be shipped cheaply over great distances. Sudden disasters like the famine in the Congo can be dealt with by the use of aircraft. So the need for local surpluses is reduced, and the effectiveness of a surplus in any part of the world as an insurance against famine somewhere else is enormously increased.

We are left with the most intractable problem of all, poverty. It is poverty in terms of foreign exchange that makes it impossible for India to buy food in the world market. And it is poverty in local currency that restricts the effectiveness of demand for food in Indian cities. Even in such densely populated countries as India and Pakistan, the rate at which food production can be increased with profit to the peasant is limited by the rate of increase in the ability of the urban population to buy food.

For the present, the technology of how to increase food production is not our major problem. Crop yields in both India and Africa are at levels surpassed by Britain in the eighteenth century, and the techniques of increasing yields very substantially have been demonstrated on an experimental scale. The barriers are political, social and cultural. Nevertheless, since the area of land available for agriculture is limited, there must come a time when it will no longer be possible to match an expansion of the population with an increase in agricultural production. And since every child born has to be fed for more than half a century, we would do well to plan now to stabilize our populations if our children and grandchildren are to enjoy an adequate share of the fruits of the earth.

Present Status of the Supposition that Malnutrition Causes Permanent Mental Retardation

ROSE E. FRISCH

ROSE E. FRISCH *is at the Harvard School of Public Health and is a research associate in the Harvard Center for Population Studies.*

Much recent literature has dealt with the consequences of hunger and malnutrition. The effects of a poor diet on physical and mental growth have often been said to be not only damaging but permanent. The possible human and policy implications of such a supposition can be tragic. Frisch discusses the constraints and limitations of many of the studies in this field and questions the validity of some of their conclusions.

The supposition that malnutrition causes permanent mental retardation is currently stated as a proven fact in newspapers, magazines, speeches of government officials, and even in semiscientific studies such as *Hunger USA 1968*: "protein deprivation between the ages of six months and a year and one-half causes permanent and irreversible brain damage to some young infants"(1). This trend is unfortunate since at the present time there is little conclusive scientific evidence to support such a supposition, as this paper will attempt to show.

The literature has been reviewed by Cravioto et al.(2) and Coursin(3) and extensive bibliographies accompany the papers in Scrimshaw and Gordon(4). The only evidence to be discussed here is direct, i.e., it includes actual tests of the mental or motor abilities of malnourished children. This seems a fundamental requirement for the judgment that malnutrition has caused permanent—or reversible—mental retardation in human beings. Experiments with malnourished animals have shown both reversible and irreversible effects of malnutrition on the subsequent development of the central nervous system and mental and motor behavior. When applying conclusions from animal experiments to human beings, however, there is

American Journal of Clinical Nutrition, 23(2): 189–95, February 1970. Reprinted by permission.

the very large reservation, pointed out by Dobbing(5), that the period of fastest growth of the human brain (when the brain is most vulnerable to environmental influences) is in the last few weeks of intrauterine life and the first few months after birth, a period very different from the critical period of brain growth of the animals most used in the experimental research in this field, the rat and the dog. (The pig has a period of rapid brain growth most similar to man.) The results of experimental malnutrition in animals, therefore, while suggestive, cannot be considered conclusive evidence for human beings.

The evidence from studies of acutely and chronically malnourished children will be discussed in that order. It is well established that acute protein-calorie malnutrition—kwashiorkor—produces extreme mental apathy in its victims(2), but whether even this extreme state of malnutrition causes a permanent mental deficiency is still not known. When the motor, adaptive, and personal-social behavior and language ability of 20 children being nutritionally rehabilitated in the hospital after suffering third degree protein-calorie malnutrition were tested, 14 children, ages 15–42 months on admission, all showed improvement on test scores when followed for 6 months; the gap between the theoretical normal and the actual performance of the child progressively diminished. "It is possible that the initial deficit will completely disappear if other relevant factors do not interfere"(6). (Cravioto and Robles quote similiar results of a Venezuelan study: 20 rehabilitated cases older than 2 years 10 months at the start of the study showed normal intelligence quotients when tested 2 years after discharge from the hospital(7).) Six infants, 6 months of age or below on admission, failed to show improvement in adaptive behavior with nutritional rehabilitation over a 6-month period. The authors(6) cautiously state: "If it is accepted that the adaptive behavior of the infant can be considered as analogous to the later intelligence of the adult, there is a high possibility that at least the children severely malnourished during the first 6 months of their lives might retain a permanent mental deficit." The *if* is a large one since intelligence measured at age 1 has a zero correlation with intelligence at age 17(8). The conclusion from this much quoted (and misquoted) study then is that children above 15 months of age are most probably not permanently retarded by extreme malnutrition and the evidence is inconclusive for children below 6 months of age. Nothing is known about children of ages 6 to 15 months.

The apparent difference in reversibility of the effect of malnutrition according to the age of the child at risk raises the question whether current infant feeding practices in the developing countries expose children to possible central nervous system damage during the postnatal vulnerable period. In most developing countries babies seem to be protected, since they are still nursed up to 6 months of age and grow normally up to that time(9). (The milk of women on seemingly inadequate diets is of satisfactory quantity and has the same protein content as that of well-nourished mothers although the concentration of vitamins A, B_2 (riboflavin), and C is lower(10). The protein needed for such adequate milk secretion by a malnourished woman must be derived from her own tissues(11).) Where nursing is still customary, it is after 6 months of age, when breast milk alone is inadequate for normal growth and children are given high calorie–low protein supplements—if any—that the risk of protein-calorie malnutrition rises and remains high through the weaning period, the weaning foods usually being gruels of cereals or starchy roots. (The mortality of the 1- to 4-year-old age group in underdeveloped countries is 10–30 times that of the United States while infant mortality, deaths in the 1st year, is three to five times that of the United States (Frisch, unpublished data).)

In some developing countries, however (particularly in Latin America), there has been a recent, alarming trend to a very early cessation of nursing and a substitution of artificial feeding, inadequate in both nutrition and hygiene(12, 13). If further work confirms the finding that infants severely malnourished at or below 6 months of age do not show mental rehabilitation with nutritional rehabilitation, inadequate artificial feeding in those early months could expose babies to possible brain damage. Infants inadequately nursed in the first 6 months would, of course, also be at risk; these may include the later-born children of malnourished mothers of large families, since such mothers may not have the physiological resources to nurse their infants normally.

Given the critical period of human brain growth (the peak near birth) the children most at risk of brain damage in developing countries may be those who suffer deprivation before birth, for example, the "small-for-dates" babies who suffer some placental restriction at the relevant time. Such babies are also found in privileged societies(5).

Chronically malnourished children—malnutrition severe enough to retard physical growth but not necessarily requiring hospitalization or resulting in clinical symptoms—present another aspect of the mental development problem. Such children test poorly on mental tests compared to well-nourished children(2, 14–16). These children also usually come from culturally and economically destitute environments, as do those who suffer acute malnutrition, but unlike the latter, chronically malnourished children do not suffer the extreme mental apathy—the complete absence of response to environmental stimuli—known to be caused by kwashiorkor. The question now becomes: does the poor showing of the chronically malnourished child on mental tests result from poor brain growth or brain damage, reversible or irreversible, due to malnutrition, or does it reflect the maternal and cultural deprivation usually concurrent with extreme poverty and the fatigue and lack of concentration which can accompany chronic malnutrition(17).

Differences in general intelligence are thought likely to be related to: *a*) stimulation provided in the environment for verbal development; *b*) extent to which affection and reward are related to verbal reasoning accomplishments; *c*) encouragement of active interaction with problems, exploration of the environment, and the learning of new skills(18), in addition to genetic factors. Consequently, the home environment can be a crucial factor in achievement on an intelligence test and the interpretation of test results can be difficult.

Stoch and Smythe(14) studied 20 chronically undernourished Cape Colored children of ages 10 months to 3 years and a control group for a period of 11 years. Thirteen children of the test group were illegitimate and all lived under "atrocious" conditions; their mothers appeared "lazy and too apathetic to care for the well-being of their children." The control children, while of the same socioeconomic background (the two groups of parents did not differ in IQ), were all legitimate; they lived in good municipal housing and attended an all-day nursery school where they received adequate meals. At the end of the 7 years of observation, the malnourished group had significantly smaller head circumferences (2.46 cm) than the control, were 7.95 cm shorter and 2.35 kg lighter, and tested significantly lower on a majority of the mental tests. It was concluded then that the effect of maternal neglect and emotional deprivation on the intellectual development was impossible to assess and that the findings were suggestive that malnutrition can retard brain growth(14). A second paper(15) after 11 years follow-up gave essentially the same evidence on head circumference, height, weight, and mental tests as at the end of 7 years, with the addition of electroencephalogram data; all but two of the test group were "benign within normal limits." The conclusion at this time is that evidence is cumulative and impressive that severe undernutrition during the first 2 years of life, when brain growth is most active, results "in permanent reduction of brain size and restricted intellectual development."

The validity of such a conclusion can be questioned. For example, what is the significance of the reduction in head circumference size in relation to brain size? Stoch and Smythe(15) state that head circumference is an index of brain mass and growth, which it is, but it is also an index of scalp size, temporal muscle, bony skull, and body height and weight—tall and fat children have big heads, short and thin children have small heads(19). In addition, in the severely malnourished child there can be reduction of thickness of all bones of the skull, skull base, and face(19, 20). That reduced head circumference size accompanying growth failure does not necessarily mean inhibition of brain growth is shown by the data from 16 children who died of congenital heart disease and whose growth had been seriously impaired since birth. Their head circumference sizes were 8.2% below the mean for their age (the deficits in body height and weight were 63.0% and 35.9%, respectively), but their brain weights on autopsy were found normal for their age(19).

The possibility of a maturational lag in head circumference growth must also be considered. Stoch and Smythe(15) speak of the head circumference and brain as "at maturity" at 11 years of age, but there is good evidence from measurement of school children in Berkeley, California, that there is an adolescent spurt in head circumference(21) even though about 96% of the adult value is attained by age 10(22). (In the Berkeley study, head circumference increased in males through age 21(21).) Whether the brain takes part in the growth spurt or whether it is due solely to thickening of the skull and its coverings is not known(22).

Finally, how much can be deduced about brain function from the association of reduced head circumference size and significantly lower scores on IQ tests? (Actually the Cape Colored malnourished children did not differ significantly from controls on comprehension, verbal reasoning, memory and absurdities(15).) Normally there is apparently no correlation between head size and intelligence(23). Within the group of malnourished children no correlation between head circumference size and intelligence levels was found either(15). The inferior performance of the malnourished children in this study could be explained by either cultural deprivation or brain damage (reversible or irreversible); there is no way at present of deciding which is the explanation.

Mönckeberg(13) studied 14 Chilean children hospitalized with marasmus at ages 3 to 11 months, given free milk monthly on discharge, and then tested for mental ability at ages 3 and 6 years. Height and head circumference of the experimental children were below the Iowa Reference Standards, which were used as the normal standard. Mental ability test results were significantly lower than the average Chilean preschool child of the low socioeconomic class(13). All the questions raised by the Stoch and Smythe study can be asked of this study. In addition one may ask: a) How meaningful are comparisons of height, weight, and head circumference of Chilean children with those of the Iowa Reference Standard, since the Chilean population is 65% mestizo(24), and this percentage is probably even higher in the lowest socioeconomic class? b) Did the children actually drink the milk after discharge from the hospital? The author notes that he cannot be certain that nutrition was optimal during the follow-up period but that weights were normal for age (Iowa Reference Standard) and even excessive relative to the short stature of the children. Considering the questions raised by the data, Mönckeberg's(13) conclusion that "brain damage in infancy is permanent at least up to the sixth year of life, despite improving nutritional conditions" hardly is warranted.

Thirty-six Serbian children aged 4–24 months at the time of hospital admission for malnutrition were assessed at ages 7–14 years for physical and mental growth. Their heights and weights were found to be normal, but their mean IQ was significantly lower than the mean IQ of children of nearby Serbian towns. No conclusion can be drawn from this study since nothing is known of the home environments of the controls and subjects. The possibility of parental neglect of some of the subjects is high since one-third of the parents were army officers or in professions and presumably had the economic means to feed their children(25).

A study(26) correlating stature and visual, haptic, and kinesthetic ability also presents the brain damage versus environment dilemma. Two groups of Guatemalan children from the same village and common ethnic background, aged 6–11 years, one including the shortest, and the other the tallest quartile for age, were tested for intersensory function. To control the possibility of maturational lag of the short children, a second sample of upper class urban children with equivalent differences in height, but no likelihood of exposure to nutritional risk, were tested. In the rural children a difference in height was accompanied by a greater number of errors on the intersensory tests; no such difference was found in the upper class urban sample. Cravioto and De Licardie(26) recognize that the results can be interpreted to mean: a) social impoverishment results in children who have poor intersensory development and who are malnourished and, therefore, of low stature or b) social impoverishment results in children who are malnourished and, therefore, of low stature and poor intersensory development (i.e., malnutrition has affected the central nervous system). They conclude that the available evidence does not permit the rejection of either hypothesis.

A rise in IQ of 10 and 18 points, respectively, took place when 91 mal-nourished, mentally retarded children and normal children aged 2–9 years were given proper nourishment for a period averaging 2 to 3 years. Well-nourished children tested at the same intervals showed no change in test scores(16). No conclusions can be drawn from this study since there is no information on the criteria for the judgment of malnourishment, or the method of rehabilitation, or the socioeconomic background of the children.

That social-environmental factors—particularly the role of the mother or mother-surrogate—can be very important in influencing the level of mental functioning and development is clearly shown in a study by Skeels(27). Thirteen children under 3 years of age, all mentally retarded at the beginning of the study, were transferred from an orphanage where physical care was adequate but completely impersonal, to a state school for the mentally handicapped. The children were placed by two's or small groups in wards of older, brighter girls and women who "adopted" them. Attendants also gave them much attention and the opportunity to play with toys and go on excursions. "The consistent element seemed to be the existence of a one-to-one relationship with an adult who was generous with love and affection, together with an abundance of attention and experimental stimu-lation from many sources." Length of the experimental period was from 6 to 52 months depending on the individual child's rate of development. As soon as a child showed normal intelligence scores he or she was either placed in an adoptive home or returned to the orphanage. A control group of 12 children (initially higher in intelligence than the experimental group) remained in the orphanage. In 2 years the experimental group gained an average of 28.5 IQ points, the control group lost an average of 26.2 IQ points. Eleven of the experimental group maintained and increased their earlier gains in IQ after being placed in adoptive homes. The two children of this group who remained in the orphanage declined in rate of mental growth. Twenty-one years later the entire experimental group was found to be self-supporting and had completed the 12th grade at school. The 12 controls completed a median of less than 3rd grade at school and 8 were in institu-tions for the mentally retarded(27).

Long-term studies which attempt to differentiate between the effects of environment on mental growth and possible effects of malnourishment on the central nervous system in children are now in progress or in the planning stage. (It might be illuminating if these studies report the data by sex, since it is known that adverse circumstances affect the growth and development of boys more than girls(28).) "It is to be hoped that in the next decade we shall have a body of detailed information which will convert our surmises about the relation of malnutrition to mental development into strongly based facts"(29). Until that time, surmises should not be treated as facts and millions of malnourished children should not be condemned as perma-nently retarded mentally. Of course, the humanitarian and practical need to ensure that malnourished children of all ages are properly fed is the same whether malnutrition has temporary physical and mental effects which must be reversed or permanent effects which must be prevented.

REFERENCES

1. Citizens Board of Inquiry into Hunger and Malnutrition in the United States. 1968. *Hunger USA 1968.* Washington, D.C.: New Community Press, p. 8.
2. Cravioto, J., DeLicardie, E. R., and Birch, H. G. 1966. Nutrition, growth and neurointegrative development: An experimental and ecologic study. *Pediatrics* 38: Suppl., part II, 319.
3. Coursin, D. 1967. Relationship of nutrition to central nervous system development and function: overview. *Federation Proc.* 26: 134.
4. Scrimshaw, N. S. and Gordon, J. E., eds. 1968. *Malnutrition, learning and behavior.* Cambridge: M.I.T.
5. Dobbing, J. Effects of experimental undernutrition on development of the nervous system. In Scrimshaw, N. and Gordon, J. E. *Op. cit.,* p. 181.
6. Cravioto, J., and Robles, B. 1965. Evaluation of adaptive and motor behavior during rehabilitation from kwashiorkor. *Am. J. Orthopsychiat.* 35: 449.
7. Barrera-Moncado, G. 1963. *Estudios sobre alteraciones del crecimiento y del desarrollo psicológico del síndrome pluricarencial (kwashiorkor).* Caracas: Editora Grafos.
8. Bloom, B. S. 1964. *Stability and change in human characteristics.* New York: Wiley, p. 57.
9. Scrimshaw, N. S., and Béhar, N. 1965. Malnutrition in underdeveloped countries. *New Engl. J. Med.* 27: 137, 193.
10. Gopalan, C., and Belevady, B. 1961. Nutrition and lactation. *Federation Proc.* 20: Suppl. 7, 177.
11. Gopalan, C. 1958. Effect of protein supplementation and some so-called "galactogogues" on lactation of poor Indian women. *Indian J. Med. Res.* 46: 317.
12. Kevany, J. In Yankauer, A. 1966. Appendix 7 of A health care program for mothers. *Pan-Am. Health Organ. Publ. 130.* Washington, D.C., p. 95.
13. Mönckeberg, F. Effect of early marasmic malnutrition on subsequent physical and psychological development. In Scrimshaw and Gordon. *Op. cit.,* p. 269.
14. Stoch, M. B., and Smythe, P. M. 1963. Does undernutrition during infancy inhibit brain growth and subsequent intellectual development? *Arch. Disease Childhood* 38: 546.
15. Stock, M. B. and Smythe, P. M. Undernutrition during infancy, and subsequent brain growth and intellectual development. In Scrimshaw and Gordon. *Op. cit.,* p. 278.
16. Kugelmass, I. N., Pouli, L. E. and Samuel, E. L. 1944. Nutritional improvement of child mentality. *Am. J. Med. Sci.* 208: 631.
17. Keys, A., *et al.* 1950. *The biology of human starvation,* vol. II. Minneapolis: U. of Minn. Press, p. 835.
18. Bloom, B. S. 1964. *Stability and change in human characteristics.* New York: Wiley, p. 190.
19. Robinow, M. Field measurement of growth and development. In Scrimshaw and Gordon. *Op. cit.,* p. 409.
20. Garn, S. M. 1966. Malnutrition and skeletal development in the preschool child. In Pre-school child malnutrition: Primary deterrent to human progress. *Natl. Acad. Sci.-Natl. Res. Council Publ. 1282.* Washington, D.C., chapt. 5.
21. Eichorn, D. H., and Bayley, N. 1962. Growth in head circumference from birth through young adulthood. *Child Develop.* 33: 257.
22. Tanner, J. M. 1962. *Growth at adolescence* (2nd ed.). Oxford: Blackwell. p. 14.
23. Barnicot, N. A. Biological variation in modern populations. In Harrison, G. A., *et al.,* eds. 1964. *Human biology.* Oxford: Clarendon, p. 210.
24. Coon, C. S. 1965. *The Living Races of Man.* New York: Knopf, p. 294.
25. Cabak, V., and Najdanvic, R. 1965. Effect of undernutrition in early life on physical and mental development. *Arch. Disease Childhood* 40: 532.
26. Cravioto, J. and DeLicardie, E. R. Intersensory development of school-age children. In Scrimshaw and Gordon. *Op. cit.,* p. 252.
27. Skeels, H. M. 1966. Adult status of children with contrasting early life experiences: a follow-up study. *Monogr. Soc. Res. Child Develop.* 31, no. 3, Ser. 105.
28. Tanner, J. M. 1962. *Growth at adolescence* (2nd ed.). Oxford: Blackwell, p. 127.
29. Birch, H. G. Field measurement in nutrition, learning and behavior. In Scrimshaw and Gordon. *Op. cit.,* p. 503.

Agriculture—Technical and Resource Opportunities

REPORT OF THE PANEL ON THE WORLD FOOD SUPPLY

For agriculture to be successful, the farmer must have available a variety of inputs. Important among them are land, water, fertilizer, seeds, labor, capital, pesticides, tools and machines. The reading below focuses on a few of these, and describes some of the problems faced by farmers in different parts of the world.

TECHNICAL AND RESOURCE OPPORTUNITIES

Availability of Land

The area of potentially arable land on the earth is much larger than estimated previously, being 24 per cent of the total ice-free area and considerably more than twice the land that has been cultivated at one time or another during the last few decades. It is more than three times the area actually harvested in any given year. More than half of the potentially arable land, amounting to more than 4 billion acres, lies in the tropics, and about a sixth of it is in the humid tropics. Another 20 per cent of this land is in the subhumid tropics where a season of abundant rainfall alternates with a relatively dry season. Outside the tropics, there are large areas of potentially arable land in temperate parts of North America and in Australia.

In contrast to the principal areas of *potentially* arable land, most of the *presently* cultivated land is in the cool—temperate zone. The largest areas of potentially arable land lie in Africa and South America which, outside of the relatively small continents of Europe and Australia, have the smallest cultivated areas. The potential for increasing net cultivated area is very small in Europe and Asia and relatively small in the Soviet Union.

In Asia, if we subtract the potentially arable land area in which water is so short that one four-month growing season is impossible, there is essentially no excess of potentially arable land over that actually cultivated.

The World Food Problem: A Report of the President's Science Advisory Committee, May 1967, The White House. Abridgment by the editors of the present volume.

To increase food supplies in Asia, therefore, it will be necessary either to increase yields per unit area or to increase the gross harvested area through double or triple cropping, often but not always, based on irrigation development. The Panel estimates that the potential for increase in irrigated area in the Indian subcontinent and Southeast and Southwest Asia is over 200 million acres. The total capital costs to develop irrigation in these regions would be approximately $80 billion.

In Latin America and Africa, the limiting factors in agricultural development are not potential land and water resources, but economic, institutional, and social problems.

The very large and ever-increasing disparity between population size and potentially arable land in Asia, on the one hand, and the still-unused potential in Latin America, North America, and Africa, on the other, suggests that very large-scale intercontinental migrations, such as characterized much of the 19th century, might occur in the future. Human migrations within different countries will almost certainly be required in the crowded agricultural lands in Asia. The marginal productivity of agricultural labor is approaching zero in these countries. It will be difficult to apply modern technology to raise agricultural production without moving large numbers of people off the land into the cities. For this, and other reasons, *agricultural development must be accompanied by general economic improvement and particularly by large-scale urbanization.*

Problems of Tropical Agriculture

The present technology for agricultural production is inadequate for the humid tropics and for most of the subhumid tropics. *New plant varieties must be developed and new methods of fertilization, pest control, soil conditioning, and water management must be found.* Even the basic data on soil properties and climatic conditions are scanty or lacking for most of this region. Major emphasis should be given to research and development of tropical agricultural technology.

In much of the tropics, crops must be grown on soils which are severely leached of nutrients and with high infestation of pests whose depredations never are interrupted by winter. The lands are cultivated by tradition-bound peasants who often are controlled by a political system which has its power base in cities and is unfamiliar or unconcerned with problems of farming and with measures needed to improve its productivity.

In the tropics, there are large areas of uncultivated land whose general climatic and soil characteristics suggest a vast unused potential for food production. But to realize this potential, we must:

1. Obtain knowledge of tropical soils and of practical soil and crop management systems needed for sustained high yields.
2. Provide technological and economic inputs of the kind and size now available to producers in temperate regions.

Tropical soils range from highly leached ones of the rain forest, through alkali-saturated soils of the desert, rich volcanic soils of Java, alluvial soils of the Nile delta, to impoverished soils of the Ancient uplands. On a few of these soils, cultural methods similar to those employed in temperate zones have been successful in giving annual yields far in excess of those of temperate regions. In other areas, these same cultural methods have failed completely and often have resulted essentially in the destruction of the soils. Unfortunately, up to now, farming techniques imported from the temperate zone have usually been inferior to those of the indigenous cultivators for management of soils in the tropics.

A common agricultural system of the humid tropics is the slash and burn method. The forest is cut and burned, the soil is cultivated until the natural fertility is gone, and then the leached infertile land is abandoned for a number of years while forest vegetation is established again.

The local cultivators may be uninformed, but they do not lack intelligence. They have made adaptations needed in the tropics. For example, to obtain fertilizer, cattle are released to forage in the daytime and penned at night— manure is then collected from the pens and put on the kitchen gardens. Primitive farmers in some countries have used human manure for centuries. As a result, the soil in some places, especially in China, is reasonably fertile within walking or bullock-cart distance of the villages.

Technology and cropping systems must be devised within each developing nation. A vast effort will be required to learn what technologies are applicable in the tropics. Some particularly important areas suggested for investigation are soil science, mineral deficiencies, high-temperature physiology and biochemistry, weeds, diseases, insects, and adaptation of temperate zone plants, especially legumes, to provide proteins. The United States should take effective leadership with interested governments to develop agricultural research and educational institutions in tropical areas to focus on the problems of production, storage, processing, and marketing of food crops.

Water Supplies for Irrigation
Wherever there is arable land which experiences periods during the growing season in which evapotranspiration exceeds precipitation by an amount greater than soil moisture storage, the opportunity to increase production by irrigation exists. Irrigation may be applied to the desert, where rainfall is totally inadequate for any agriculture, as in Egypt or Southern Iraq; it may replace or supplement rainfall agriculture as in the dry farming regions of the United States; it may make possible multiple-cropping in areas where only single-cropping is possible because of wet and dry seasons as in Bengal; or it may serve as insurance against damaging, short-time sporadic droughts, as in the eastern United States.

Adequacy of irrigation in terms of providing a full water supply for evapotranspiration potential is highly variable, ranging from sporadic spreading of meager spring flood waters in the deserts of the Middle East to sprout a thin crop of wheat, to carefully controlled, optimal applications under the sophisticated technology of the southwestern United States. Besides the temperate and subtropical deserts, large areas of subtropical and tropical lands experience long, dry seasons where rainfall is nonexistent or exceedingly short. It is in these areas that the use of irrigation could

provide the basis for rapid expansion of food supply through intensive, year-round cropping and could make attractive the use of increased fertilizer, pest control, and the other inputs of modern agricultural technology.

Presently Irrigated Lands The origins of irrigation are buried in antiquity. History makes many references to the practice of irrigation. It is well-established that several once-flourishing civilizations were based upon the practice. Remnants of irrigation systems built hundreds and even thousands of years ago are present today. However, until about the beginning of the 19th century, irrigation systems were small and most failed eventually because they did not provide for salinity control. Gulhati estimates that the area of irrigated land in the world was about 20 million acres in 1880. During the 19th century, larger and more sophisticated irrigation projects were constructed mainly in India, Russia, the United States, and Egypt, increasing the total area of irrigated land in the world to about 100 million acres by 1900. Experience gained during the latter part of the 19th century in the planning, construction, and operation of irrigation projects together with continuing advances in civil engineering and in the agricultural sciences has led to a nearly fourfold increase in the world's irrigated area during the first two-thirds of this century.

Of the approximately 3.43 billion acres of cultivated land in the world, about 0.38 billion acres or 11 per cent are presently irrigated. The small percentage of the world's arable land under irrigation suggests that irrigation agriculture plays only a minor role in the world food budget. However, when the distribution of irrigated and arable land over the world is related to the distribution of world population, it becomes apparent that a large fraction of the earth's people, living mainly in diet-deficient countries, are heavily dependent upon irrigation for food. In these areas, increasing the food supply will require extensive irrigation development. On the Indian subcontinent, with one-fifth of the population of the world, water supply seriously limits agricultural production on 65 per cent of the arable land and prevents year-round production on another 29 per cent. Nearly two-thirds of the world population lives in diet-deficient countries having less than half of the arable land but about three-fourths of the irrigated land. It has been estimated that by 1975 the total irrigated area in the world may exceed 500 million acres and that by the year 2,000 the area may well approach 750 million acres. If, as predicted, the world population is over 6 billion in the year 2,000, then the ratio of world population to world area of irrigated land will be approximately the same as at present.

Ground Water   In irrigation development, much more attention needs to be paid to ground water resources and their use, particularly in the Indian subcontinent.

In general, ground water reservoirs are integral with the continuous river system and are in dynamic balance with precipitation, evaporation, and drainage to the sea. Even so, the amount in storage is relatively large. The volume of ground water stored at depths of less than one-half mile is estimated to be 3,000 times as large as that contained in all rivers. There are also extensive ground water deposits which are not in dynamic equilibrium with the current surface hydrology but which have been stored from past ages. In the first instance, allowing for the impedance of the system, use of ground water for irrigation is reflected eventually in a reduction of the surface or the underground flow to the sea or in reduction of non-economic vegetation drawing on the water table; in the second instance, the water, in essence, is "mined" and is not replaced by nature within non-geological time spans.

Ground water supplies frequently may provide relatively fast and inexpensive development in contrast to surface supplies, as in the Central Valley of California, in southern Arizona, and in West Pakistan. If the supply is to be permanent, the draft over a period of time must not exceed the replenishment. However, overdraft of ground water supplies may well be justified as a means of providing rapid development, especially if these are to be replaced by eventual development of permanent surface supplies. This will occur, unplanned, in southern Arizona if the Central Arizona project or some other long distance transfer is completed, and, in Israel, where gound water overdrafts since about 1960, by deliberate action, have sustained a growing agricultural activity during the period of construction of the diversion from Lake Tiberias to the coastal valleys of Palestine. Ground water development, as in West Pakistan, may make extensive electrification feasible also, with consequent additional benefits to agriculture and industry. In West Pakistan, cost of well development and electrification in former Punjab and Bahalwalpur was $41 per acre; capital costs of drainage, fertilizer, pest control and educational facilities raised this to $81 per acre.

It is probable that extensive ground water supplies exist within those heavily populated areas of the sub-arid world where surface supplies have been exploited already or where their rapid development is inhibited by the magnitude of the task or by international complication; for example, in the Ganges Basin, other Indian subcontinental coastal basins, and Southeast Asia. *An intensive effort should be made to identify potential areas of available ground water, particularly in these areas of the world, and to assess their economic potentials.*

Ground water development should be planned conjunctively with surface water. The use of underground reservoirs by artificial recharge methods saves the cost of expensive surface reservoir development and avoids evaporation losses.

Development of ground water reserves *could* provide the quickest, easiest and least expensive means to enhance water supply and develop food supplies in large areas of the world. Overdraft or mining in the earlier stages of comprehensive development can provide the economic impetus on which later, more comprehensive development might be founded but there must be foreseeable replacement from surface supplies. *Emphasis should be placed on initiating development in those areas or in nearby heavily populated regions where ground water resources are reasonably available.*

Fertilizers, Seeds, Pesticides, and Machinery

Where adequate water is available, the optimum return on the investment and effort in food production comes through the development of improved farming systems involving more fertilization, better seeds, better machinery, and improved cultural practices, including water management.

Problems of water management and the interaction of water with other production inputs should be emphasized also. Whenever irrigation removes the moisture ceiling on crop yield, other management practices such as fertilization, liming, improved seeds, and insect and disease control become much more critical to success. *Failure to follow through with all required practices can easily offset the advantages of irrigation.* It is important to note that most major irrigation projects are concerned with only a small part of the total picture. Such projects normally are limited to storage dams, diversion structures, canals and laterals, and, in some cases, to tubewells. All who are involved in project planning, project authorization, and project operation should recognize the vital necessity of providing adequately, not only for water, but for all of the inputs and processes that agriculture requires if an irrigation scheme is to make a major contribution to increased agricultural productivity. Only if all of the inputs required to make an irrigation project fully productive are provided in a timely manner can the high capital cost of such projects be justified.

Fertilizers account for most of the capital investment required to produce these inputs, as well as two-thirds of the cost to the farmer, and are an absolute necessity for improved yields. The effectiveness of fertilizers can be increased greatly, often more than doubled, by the concomitant use of improved plant varieties, adequate pesticides, improved machinery, and proper water management.

The quantities of these physical inputs required to provide for the food needs of the developing world, outside of Mainland China, by the year 1985 have been projected for the Panel. Estimates of requirements were related to specific percentage increases of food production on land now in cultivation.

Estimates of fertilizer needed to *double* agricultural production in the developing countries indicate an increase in the usage of plant nutrients from the six million metric tons used in 1966 to 67 million metric tons. It is anticipated that, by the year 1985, capital totaling approximately $17 billion will be required for mining, manufacturing, and distribution of fertilizers, and it should be noted that immediate, as well as future, needs for capital are quite large. Manyfold increases in intercontinental shipping will be needed to serve international trade in fertilizers, since efficient nitrogen plants, potash mines, and phosphate mines are necessarily quite large and the needed raw materials are by no means uniformly distributed around the world.

Of the inputs needed to improve agricultural production of developing countries, seeds and improved plant varieties are important components. The new varieties must not only be developed but also be used as a part of improved farming practices. Experience has shown that, for some plant crops, production has been doubled when 25 per cent of the seed planted is of the improved type. The capital investment that will be required is relatively low—about $300 million.

Large increases in the use of pesticides are necessary to increase food production. All types of insecticides, fungicides, herbicides, nematicides, and rodenticides are needed. At the present time, only 120 thousand metric tons are used in the developing world, excluding Mainland China. If food production is to be doubled, 700 thousand metric tons will be required. To provide this quantity of pesticides will require $1.2 billion in capital for manufacturing plants and $670 million for formulation and distribution facilities. It is suggested that most pesticides should be manufactured in the developed nations where skilled manpower, utilities, and raw materials are easily available, but trade and monetary restrictions and excessive nationalism, of course, may be limiting factors. Formulation of pesticides, a relatively simple operation, can be carried out locally in the country of use.

In the developing free world, more machinery is badly needed—not as a labor-saving device, but to increase productivity. At the present time, machine power available to the farmers of Asia, Africa, and Latin America averages only a fraction of the more than one horsepower per hectare utilized by the farmers of Europe and the United States. This lack of power makes it difficult to prepare seedbeds efficiently and in time and to place seed and fertilizer accurately, both of which can contribute markedly to improved yields and to the economical utilization of these inputs. Although there are one or two exceptions, an analysis of yields in various countries indicates that a power level approaching 0.5 horsepower/hectare is needed for an efficient agriculture. It is estimated that $500 million will need to be invested by the end of this century in plants for the production of farm machinery in the developing countries. The total capital investment, including components which can best be imported, will approximate $2 billion.

It is estimated that the annual cost to farmers of improved inputs—fertilizers, seeds, pesticides, and machinery—will amount to approximately $14 billion by 1985. This will make it necessary to provide systems for farm credit on a scale manyfold greater than is available today.

Fisheries

REPORT OF THE PANEL ON THE
WORLD FOOD SUPPLY

The ocean never has and probably never will provide but a fraction of the world's food. In some societies, however—in many coastal regions, for example—sea food is an essential source of nutrition, especially protein, vitamins, and minerals. The importance of sea food throughout the world will continue to increase with new techniques of fishing, ocean farming, processing and distribution. Harvesting the oceans at lower levels in the food chain for example, plankton and algae, can also give much greater yields; but this requires additional expense for the energy needed in the gathering and processing of the more diffusely located and less palatable food. This reading discusses the potential and actual yield of both ocean and inland fisheries and concludes with a brief comment on the possibilities of obtaining protein from algae.

THE FISHERY POTENTIAL OF THE OCEAN

Taken as a whole, the seas contain a tremendous potential for world feeding. Only a few dozen of the 20 to 25 thousand species of fish are used directly or indirectly as food by man. The potential, however, is but the beginning. In order to achieve even a part of this potential, large expenditures of money on boats and equipment to catch and process the fish will be required and this will entail time as well as money. The problem of whether acceptable fish are available off the coast of certain developing countries remains as does the acceptability of fish in some of these cultures. With concerted efforts and large expenditures for boats, fishing gear, docks, and preservation equipment, it is estimated that in 5 to 10 years a substantial increase in harvest and preservation of the ocean's potential could be achieved.

There is little doubt that the potential productivity of fish is considerably larger than the 1964 harvest of 56 million tons. Many species are not harvested today for lack of specialized gear and for lack of a market; yet, many of these species are not only of nutritive value equal to that of the few

The World Food Problem: A Report of the President's Science Advisory Committee, May 1967, The White House. Abridgment by the editors of the present volume.

that are presently caught, but exist in unknown although in probably vast quantities. The estimates of potential fish catch are many and vary widely, mainly due to lack of adequate data and understanding of biological processes in the oceans. It is important to be aware of their range and the reasoning employed to arrive at the estimates. Some, although made quite recently by recognized experts, appear to be too low, some others appear to be fantastically high. It is generally agreed, however, that the catch of fish can be increased markedly.

One type of estimate (by Graham and Edwards) was based on the potentially productive area of the continental shelves and the output per acre of known fishing grounds (Table 1). It was concluded that an annual harvest of 20 pounds of fish per acre was a conservative average estimate for the known continental shelves, covering over 6 billion acres. This estimate led to a figure of 120 billion pounds of (presumably known and commonly used) fish per year, or 55 million metric tons. The estimate assumed that the catch of pelagic fish, not associated with the continental shelves, is negligible, and was only for bony fishes; whales, sharks, and invertebrates were not included. It is significant that at the time when Graham and Edwards made this calculation, the Peruvian catch was very small. It is now 350 pounds per acre or 9 million metric tons annually.

Graham and Edwards also made another estimate of fishery potential of 115 million metric tons of marine fishes and invertebrates annually. This second type of estimate is based on the production of plants in the sea. Kesteven and Holt estimated that the net production of plants was between 12 and 15 billion tons of carbon per year; or 500 billion tons of phytoplankton. If this plant matter is fully harvested by herbivores and if a conversion efficiency of about 20 per cent is assumed, the annual production of herbivores is 100 billion tons. If the conversion efficiences of primary and secondary carnivores are 10 per cent, then 1 billion metric tons of bony fish are produced, of which 50 per cent or 500 million metric tons might

TABLE 1. Total sustainable annual fisheries harvest, as estimated by various authors.

	ESTIMATED TOTAL SUSTAINABLE ANNUAL HARVEST IN MILLION METRIC TONS
Author:	
Graham and Edwards[1]	55
Pike and Spilhaus[2]	190
Schaefer[3]	200
Larkin[4]	500
Kesteven and Holt[5]	500
Chapman[6]	2,000
Schmitt[7]	2,000

[1]Graham, H. W., and Edwards, R. L., The world biomass of marine fishes. In: Heen, E., and Kreuzer, R. (eds). Fish in nutrition. London, Fishing News, 1962. 477 p. pp. 3–8.

[2]Pike, S. T., and Spilhaus, A., Marine resources. A report to the Committee on Natural Resources of the NAS/NRC. Nat. Res. Council Publ. 100-E:1–8. 1962.

[3]Schaefer, M. B., The potential harvest of the sea. Amer. Fish. Soc. Trans. 94(2):123–128. April 1965.

[4]Larkin, P. A. What is the potential of North American Fisheries? The Fish Boat 10(7):21–23, 1965.

[5]Kesteven, G., and Holt, S. J., A note on the fisheries resources of the Northwest Atlantic. FAO Fishery paper No. 7. 1955.

[6]Chapman, W. M., Ocean fisheries—status and outlook. Paper presented to Marine Technological Society, Washington, D.C., 1966.

[7]Schmitt, W. R., The planetary food potential. New York Acad. Sci. Ann. 118 (art. 17):645–718. Mar. 5, 1965.

constitute a sustainable annual harvest. Based on the estimate that 19 billion tons of carbon are fixed annually into living matter in the oceans, it was postulated that 2 billion tons of animals are available annually that are "large enough and useful enough to form the basis of practical commercial harvesting." A conversion efficiency of 10 per cent was used in this estimate but it was assumed that some of the catch would be primary as well as secondary carnivores.

Of all the estimates, some of which are as great as two billion tons (Table 1), only the first estimate of Graham and Edwards(1) for bony fishes will be realized in the near future. The catch of bony marine fishes was 40 million tons in 1964 or 75 per cent of their estimate of potential annual yield.

In the past decade the fish catch has increased about 7 per cent annually. At this rate of increase, the catch of bony fishes by 1969 would be as great as Graham and Edwards estimate. It is generally concluded that this estimate is conservative and that the annual yield will continue to increase as new fishing areas and new stocks are utilized.

It is evident on the other hand that, if the catch of fishes continues to increase at 7 per cent annually, the estimated catches of 2 billion metric tons would not be realized for about 50 years. It is apparent that if the highly publicized potential of the oceans is to be utilized, there will have to be a significant improvement in the amount and type of fishing effort. This effort will have to include research and development of new fishing methods for pelagic species and, ultimately, to change fisheries harvest from hunting and capturing to herding and cultivating.

That marine and fresh-water fisheries could supply more protein and calories to diets in the lesser developed countries is discussed below. Fish now provide a significant source of protein in some countries as shown in Table 2 which presents some statistics on the per capita consumption of fish and fish products.

PROTEIN FROM INLAND FISHERIES

The growing of fish in ponds, in rice paddies, and in natural man-made impoundments represents a realistic means of rapidly providing large quantities of animal protein in tropical climates.

Most of the inland fishery products are fishes with an annual catch estimated at 15 million metric tons live weight. This estimate includes noncommercial landings and is therefore greater than the 1964 fresh-water commercial catch of 6.6 million metric tons.(2) In some countries, the fresh-water catch is a larger fraction (Table 3). The catch is derived from natural waters and man-made impoundments, from harvesting natural populations, and from farming and culturing desired species.

Usage of the Catch

Most of the catch is sold locally as fresh fish, with a minor, but increasing, amount processed as frozen fish. Fresh-water fish, for the most part, are used in the diet as a source of high quality protein.

In the developing countries where there is no refrigeration, particularly in Asia and offshore Pacific islands, fish are processed by old techniques and sold dried, salted, smoked, and as sauce. These methods of processing

TABLE 2. **Per capita consumption of fish and fish products.** From Christy, F. T., and Scott, A., The common wealth in ocean fisheries: some problems of growth and economic allocation. Baltimore, Johns Hopkins Press, 1966. 296 pp. Reference p. 19.

COUNTRY	FAO, 1957–59 EDIBLE WEIGHT (KILOGRAMS PER YEAR)	USDA, 1957–58 LANDED WEIGHT (KILOGRAMS PER YEAR)	TOTAL ANIMAL PROTEIN 1954–57 (PER CENT)	TOTAL CALORIES 1958 (PER CENT)
Japan	22[1]	40	72	3.0
Portugal	20	35	59	2.4
Norway	19	44	19	2.3
Sweden	18	20	12	1.2
Philippines	15	24	NA	1.9
Denmark	15	22	13	1.2
Taiwan	11	22	54	1.5
Finland	11	14	11	.8
Spain	11	21	NA	1.4
United Kingdom	10	19	9	1.0
Thailand	9	28	NA	6.2
Greece	8	14	16	.9

[1]22 kg. per year of fresh edible weight is equivalent to about 9 g. of protein per day (based on protein content of 16 per cent).

TABLE 3.   Fresh-water fish as per cent of total fish catch in 1962.
From Christy, F. T., and Scott, A., The common wealth in ocean
fisheries: some problems of growth and economic allocation.
Baltimore, Johns Hopkins Press, 1966. 296 pp. Reference p. 23.

	PER CENT
Country:	
Mainland China (1959)	40
Indonesia	43
Pakistan	66
India	34
Thailand	20
Philippines	3
Japan	1
U.S.S.R.	10
United States	2
West Germany	2
Italy	6

preserve catches in excess of the current demand for fresh fish and make
it possible to transport fisheries products to distant markets. Fish too small
to market fresh can be processed into fish sauce. The basic process consists
of placing alternate layers of fresh fish and salt in a tank and allowing
enzymatic autodigestion to proceed until a clear liquid is produced. Sauces
of this type are widely used over rice and other cereals to improve taste
and to provide supplemental proteins and vitamins. Sauces can be produced
very easily which is one advantage over such products as fish protein
concentrate (FPC) that require extensive processing equipment, although
such sauces have a somewhat lower nutritive value and a high salt content.

Amount and Origin of the Catch

The inland fishery catch from rivers, streams, lakes, swamps, reservoirs,
fresh-water ponds and brackish-water ponds, excluding brackish bays and
estuaries, is estimated at 30 per cent of the world total. The annual catch
from rivers and natural lakes varies from about 5 to 170 pounds per acre,
with the average being about 20 pounds per acre. The overflow swamp
fisheries along the great rivers of Asia and Africa are more productive
because most of the crop can be harvested as the annual flood waters recede.
The catch varies, depending upon the extent and length of time the swamps
are flooded, from 30 to 400 pounds of fish per acre with the average being
100 pounds per acre. The annual catch is 270 thousand metric tons from
the Mekong River Swamps, 3 thousand metric tons from the Nile flood-
fisheries, and 45 thousand metric tons from the Middle Niger. These catches
will decrease as rivers are impounded for irrigation, power, and other
purposes and as swamp lands are claimed for agriculture. The total catch
from all natural waters is estimated at 13.2 million metric tons or 88 per
cent of the total inland catch.

The catch per acre in reservoirs ranges from 5 to more than 100 pounds
per acre, with an average of about 25 pounds per acre. About 5 per cent
of the total inland catch or 0.75 million metric tons come from reservoirs.

More intensive fishing probably could increase the catch by 50 to 100 per
cent. The fish populations in reservoirs result from expansion of the riverine

fish populations and often contain a large percentage of less desirable fish. Because of depth, the harvest of fish in most reservoirs is difficult with the primitive methods presently in use. Better management techniques are needed for poisoning or eliminating undesirable species, for stocking with desirable species, and increasing productivity with nutrient additions; and improved harvesting methods could be used to increase the catch significantly. Fishcultures have been developed for a variety of conditions and for different intensities of management. They are estimated to supply more than 7 per cent of the world catch of fresh-water fish or about one million tons annually.

ALGAE

The use of microscopic algae as a protein source has often been suggested and a great deal of work has been carried out on these plants, much of it with the aim of providing a food source during extended space flights.

Although the composition of algal protein is comparable in composition to other plant proteins, the major question concerning its use as food is economic. Early estimates of the cost of *Chlorella* were $0.25–0.30 per pound of algae, about $0.60–0.75 per pound of protein. A recent estimate was $0.06 per pound of algae (about $0.15 per pound of protein), but this was for a product, grown on sewage, that would not be suitable for human food. A credit against this cost, however, would be the water which would be reclaimed. A similar process has been described by the group working at Berkeley.

Though the economic factor is a major one, there are other unanswered questions concerning the use of algae as a protein source for humans. These are concerned with digestibility, palatability, and toxicity. These problems could be avoided if algae were used as animal feed.

It would appear that the major contribution of microscopic algae to human nutrition would be through serving as an animal feed stuff produced during the process of reclaiming sewage and other waste streams, and in which a major part of the production cost would be borne by the water treatment process.

REFERENCES

1. Graham, H. W. and Edwards, R. L. The world biomass of marine fishes. In Heen, E. and Kreuzer, R., eds. 1962. *Fish in nutrition.* London: Fishing News, pp. 3–8.
2. Food and Agriculture Organization of the United Nations. 1965. *Yearbook of fishery statistics, 1964,* vol. 18.

Losses and Protection of Food

REPORT OF THE PANEL ON THE
WORLD FOOD SUPPLY

Losses of food to pests, deterioration and damage are extensive throughout the world. The largest losses occur, however, in countries least able to afford them. Many techniques are available for the protection and preservation of food, but often the costs associated with protecting a given quantity are comparable to the costs of harvesting it again. The following reading, also excerpted from *The World Food Problem,* discusses in some detail the nature of these losses and suggests some methods useful for the protection of conventional foods as well as techniques for the production of new ones.

POST-HARVEST AND POST-SLAUGHTER LOSSES
IN DEVELOPING COUNTRIES

One of the functions of food marketing systems is the collection of produce from farmers, the processing and storage of these materials and, finally, the distribution of foods to consumers. It is important that the system operate efficiently and that food losses, both in terms of quantity and quality, be kept at a minimum. The nature and extent of these losses are important reasons for consideration of changes in the marketing systems and marketing techniques.

Causes of Food Losses

Losses in food supplies following harvest of crops and slaughter of animals occur because initial quality is poor or because of improper or inadequate treatment during the marketing process. The initial quality of food resources is affected by climatic conditions, production practices, the prevalence of insects and diseases, and other factors. The extent to which the initial quality is retained is conditioned by handling, storage, processing, transportation, and distribution procedures. Some of these factors are discussed below and where possible, data have been presented to illustrate the significance of each kind of loss.

The World Food Problem: A Report of the President's Science Advisory Committee, May 1967, The White House. Abridgment by the editors of the present volume.

Micro-organisms A large number of pathogenic bacteria, fungi, and viruses attack fruits and vegetables causing spoilage or blemishes after harvest. Following unfavorable growing conditions such post-harvest diseases may become unusually severe. Physiological disorders also cause storage problems. At harvest, most food grains are contaminated with a wide variety of micro-organisms. The organisms most likely to cause deterioration in grain are fungi that become active when the moisture content of the grain or the atmosphere is too high. Moldy grain is unsatisfactory for food or feed. It is costly to mill and it may contain toxic materials injurious to humans and animals. The viability of moldy grain is impaired, rendering it useless for seed purposes. The quality of oil and seed protein is affected when oil seeds become moldy. The high atmospheric temperatures and the high relative humidity of the wet tropics are particularly conducive to mold development. FAO has estimated that 1.0 per cent of the world's grain production is lost from mold activity.(1)

The rapid spoilage associated with highly perishable foods, such as fruits, vegetables, meats, and other animal products, is also caused by micro-organisms. The extent of losses sustained by such highly perishable food is unknown for developing countries. It is probably very large because facilities for short-term storage under refrigeration or long-term storage by appropriate techniques are not available. Highly perishable foods tend to be consumed seasonally and locally. Animals may be moved long distances on foot and slaughtered under primitive conditions where there are no facilities for utilizing by-products. Lack of refrigeration commonly necessitates consumption of meat within 24 hours of slaughter.

Insects In warm, humid climates insect infestations in grain may begin in the field, and additional species of insects appear after the grain is stored. Studies in Louisiana have shown that 10 per cent of corn kernels may be infested at harvest time. After six months storage the infestation may increase to 17 per cent, and after nine months more than 30 per cent of the kernels may be attacked.(2) The record of farm storage efficacy in developing countries is meager and contradictory. It is reported that Bantu tribes in Southern Africa have stored sorghum safely for four years in mud-plastered baskets. In Cameroun, farmers' storages for sorghum, peanuts, corn and beans were not infested until purchased food grains were stored in the same facilities.(3) A study of grain storage in underground mud-brick ghattis of India showed that deterioration occurred in these structures.(4)

Available data on storage losses in developing countries from insects can be divided into two categories: (a) estimates based on controlled experiments, and (b) estimates based on surveys and expert judgment. Losses based on experimental evidence obtained in different parts of Africa are shown in Table 1. Losses of a similar magnitude have been reported for other tropical countries. Estimates of losses in India and Africa at different points in the storage and marketing system are shown in Table 2. Weight loss is the usual basis for reporting, but this can be misleading because in some cases insect fragments, frass, and other debris were not removed. The loss of rice in Sierra Leone, for example, rose from 25 to 41 per cent when

TABLE 1. Storage losses caused by insects for 5 crops in Africa based on experiments.

COMMODITY	WEIGHT LOSS[a] PER CENT	STORAGE PERIOD MONTHS	COUNTRY
Corn	23.1	6	Kenya.
	9–22	7	Uganda.
	[b]7(14)	24	Nyasaland.
	8.8	5	Southern Rhodesia.
Sorghum	50	12	Congo.
	[b]19.7(23)	11	Tanganyika.
Beans	20	12	Congo.
	13.3	5	Southern Rhodesia.
	6–7	6	Uganda.
Peanuts	15	12	Congo.
	4.5	12	Nigeria.
	3.0	—	Gambia.
Rice (parboiled) (rough)	[b]25(41)	12	Sierra Leone.
	[b]4–5(14–15)	12	West Africa.

[a] Based on results of untreated controls.

[b] Insect fragments and trash removed.

this correction was made. Some insect species preferentially attack the germ and thus destroy a disproportionate amount of nutrients. For these reasons figures in Tables 1 and 2 may considerably underestimate losses in nutritive value.

Rodents Rats are a serious pest to the farmer and storage operator. Individual rats consume 20–30 grams of dry food daily and their caloric consumption is 6–8 times as great and food consumption 16 times as great as humans in terms of body weight. In addition to the amounts of food consumed, large quantities are contaminated. Rats feed on grains, dried fruit, peanuts, oil and many partially and fully processed foods.

In India, rodents are reported to cause losses of up to 20 to 30 per cent of stored grains.(5,6)

Losses in other tropical areas range from 5 to 60 per cent. In some regions losses fluctuate, depending upon sudden and unexplained rat population explosions. World-wide, it is estimated that 33 million tons (3.55 per cent of the 1961–62 production) of bread grains and rice are lost to rodents each year.(7)

Mycotoxins Some species of fungi that normally occur on stored grain and oil seeds produce toxic substances that have been implicated in human and animal diseases. One such toxic material is aflatoxin, a heptatoxin and a carcinogen to certain mammals and fish. It has been found in peanuts grown throughout the world, but it occurs most commonly where warm, moist post-harvest conditions prevail. This problem has limited the use of this protein-rich seed for food and feed purposes. It has created economic problems in developing nations which had good export markets for peanuts and peanut meal for animal feed. No completely adequate solution has been developed for the aflatoxin problem.

Toxins produced by fungi are important only when environmental conditions are favorable for growth of the fungi. Favorable conditions are

TABLE 2.   **Storage losses caused by insects for several crops in Africa and India based on survey data.**   Source: Hall, D. W. 1963. FAO Informal Working Bulletin No. 24, 176 pp. NAL. Rice in India, A Techno-Economic Review. Mysore, Central Food Technological Research Institute, 1965. 27 pp. Report of the Working Group for the Formulation of the 4th 5-year Plan Proposals on Plant Protection, Ministry of Food and Agriculture, Government of India.

PLACE OF STORAGE AND COMMODITY	APPARENT LOSS (IN PER CENT)		STORAGE PERIOD (MONTHS)	COUNTRY
	AVERAGE NUMBER OF DAMAGED GRAINS AND KERNELS	AVERAGE WEIGHT LOSS		
Producer storage:				
Beans	38–69	6	6	Uganda.
"	3.6	—	4	Northern Rhodesia.
"	80.7	—	12	"
Cowpeas	13.0	—	4	"
"	81.6	—	12	"
Corn	0.3–30.6	—	12	Matabeleland.
"	—	20+	8	Ghana.
"	30–50	—	5	Dahomey.
"	30	—	5	Togoland.
"	45–75	20+	7	Uganda.
"	90–100 (30 and 40)	—	12	Northern Rhodesia.
Corn (cobs)	5–10	—	12	Ivory Coast.
Millet (finger)	0	—	12	Matabeleland.
Bulrush (or pearl)	15	—	12	"
Sorghum	0.3–29.0	—	12	"
Sorghum (unthreshed)	3.78	1–26	9	North Nigeria.
	2.33	0–13	6	"
	2–62	3–13	14	"
Sorghum	11–88	6–37	26	"
General produce	—	5	—	India.
Trader storage:				
Beans	35–44	6	12	Uganda.
Corn	20	—	—	Togoland.
"	—	5–10	6	Uganda.
"	16.7	4	3	"
General produce	—	10–15	12	Zanzibar.
Central depot storage:				
Corn	—	5–6	11	Southern Rhodesia.
"	—	12–19	24	"
"	35–38	10	9	Uganda.
Rice (rough)	—	11–12	9	India.
Rice (milled)	—	13	9	"

generally high relative humidity and unsanitary storage situations. Species of *Fusarium*, *Aspergillus* and *Penicillium* have been associated with production of mycotoxins in cultures or on feeds. Strains of *Aspergillus flavus* produce aflatoxin at maximum levels at 23 to 25 degrees C. A shift of 6 degrees will reduce toxin production markedly. In addition to peanuts, mycotoxins have been found in cottonseed and rice among the food crops.

Improper Maturity   Mandatory maturity standards are used for fruits and several other crops in the developed countries because immature produce has poor flavor and lower nutritional value. Immature grain and pulses have a high moisture level and are more susceptible to spoilage from microorganisms. Immature grain may shrivel and be of low nutritional value.

Over maturity also tends to increase susceptibility of plant products to spoilage. The importance of maturity is particularly apparent in the case of peanuts. Peanuts that remain in the soil too long are more likely to be invaded by the fungi that produce aflatoxin.

Mechanical Damage Bruising and other kinds of mechanical damage tend to accelerate deterioration in storage. For example, mechanical clipping rather than hand picking citrus fruit facilitates the entry of fungi that induce storage diseases. Injury and cracking of seed coats of grain and oil seeds increase their susceptibility to invasion of insects and micro-organisms. Injury of this type may reduce viability of seeds to be used for planting purposes substantially.

Significance of Losses
In the developing countries, grains are the major food. In Asia, grains provide 70 per cent of the food supply, in Africa, 45 per cent, and in Latin America, 50 per cent of the food supply. Potatoes, yams, cassava, pulses, and peanuts are the other important items in the food supplies of Africa and Latin America.

Inadequate storage facilities and poor storage practices result in massive losses of grains from spoilage, contamination, and deterioration. Surveys in India show minimum storage losses from all causes of 10 per cent for cereals and oil seeds, 30 per cent for pulses, and 12 per cent for rice.(8, 9)

If only half of the estimated world loss of food grains was prevented, it would represent an additional 55 million tons or enough to make the diet of 500 million people in developing countries adequate in total calories.

Good storage practices could reduce these losses to 5 per cent or less.(10) Further reduction could be accomplished by prevention of spillage, better harvesting procedures to prevent grain breakage, and more prompt delivery of grains to storages.

From a study of thousands of storage sites, the United States Department of Agriculture found that proper storage could maintain grain quality at a high level at a cost of one cent per bushel loss in shrinkage, handling and deterioration per year. To keep losses at this level required an expenditure of five cents per bushel per year for maintenance, operation and fixed expenses. These data illustrate the cost and the effectiveness of proper storages and probably are indicative of the results that might be achieved in developing countries. A simple system for bean storage in jute bags fitted with a plastic film liner and treatment with ethylene dibromide would cost less than 2 per cent of the value of the beans stored.

Another source of loss in developing countries is the use of primitive processing techniques. Primitive cane crushers leave up to 50 per cent of the sugar in the bagasse. Hand-pounded rice has a high percentage of cracked kernels. In some areas of India a third more rice could be secured by replacing antiquated rice mills.(11)

One of the most commonly quoted estimates of world-wide losses for all cereals, pulses and oilseeds is the 10 per cent figure provided by FAO.(12) A United Nations estimate gave losses as high as 35 per cent in six Latin American countries from insects in stored cereals and pulses.(13) An AID report from Brazil indicated losses of 15 to 20 per cent in stored grains.(14) Storage experts familiar with conditions in Africa indicate that one-third of the harvested cereal is lost to pests.(15)

The shortage of suitable transportation and lack of refrigeration leads

to poor utilization of locally produced fruits and vegetables. In developing countries as much as 50 per cent of the harvested fruits and vegetables are lost from spoilage in market channels. Losses of meat, poultry, fish and dairy products are not adequately reported, but indications are that they amount to 15 to 25 per cent.(16)

In one state in India where losses of fruits and vegetables range from 25 to 60 per cent, utilization of the material produced would supply an additional 3 ounces of fruits or vegetables per person per day.(17)

FOOD PROTECTION TECHNOLOGY

Importance of Food Preservation

Preservation of foods that are now lost because of spoilage or waste would very significantly increase world food supplies. It is believed that the technology of food production that exists presently is adequate to meet world needs for many years. These techniques will need to be adapted to local conditions and special situations. Forceful programs will need to be initiated promptly if the available technology is to be used effectively.

Rural populations can subsist at some level on food produced locally, but urban populations depend upon the market place for their food supplies. The larger the urban population and the farther such populations are from primary sources of food, the greater the need for modern food protection techniques.

About 73 per cent of the rural population in India and 16 per cent of the urban population live at a subsistence level.(18) For these large segments of the population, processed foods now represent an unimportant share of their food purchases. Thus, for roughly three-fourths of the population of India there is no immediate prospect for use of processing methods if they increase food costs.

Methods of Food Protection

Foods are preserved by creating a physico-chemical environment wherein spoilage organisms cannot grow or by sterilizing the foods in sealed containers so that they cannot become recontaminated. A number of methods are used to establish an environment in food products that is unfavorable to spoilage organisms.

Dehydration   Sun drying and artificial dehydration can reduce moisture in foods to levels below which microorganisms cannot grow. Dry foods are relatively stable and provide a major part of the stored food supply throughout the world. Those preserved by natural field curing in the sun (for example, cereal grains and legumes) will constitute a major food resource in the future as they do now. Immediate attention must be given to preventing losses of such foods in storage and distribution by protecting them from rodents, insects, microbial spoilage, and spillage.

Where dry foods are held in numerous small stores rather than in large centralized storages, application of technical knowledge is difficult. Grain-handling practices vary from conditions in the Yaqui Valley of Mexico, where there is substantially no farm storage for wheat, to the subsistence-level rural economy of India, where grains and pulses are kept on the farm in quantities amounting to as much as 70 per cent of India's entire food supply. Traditional knowledge for keeping grain and legume supplies dry has been passed on by generations of populations requiring such knowledge to survive.

Dry food products can be preserved more efficiently in larger storages operated by the private sector of commerce, by cooperatives, or under government control. The value of larger holdings of food can justify the cost of training skilled operators and technicians in good handling practices and the use of pesticides. Capitalization of storage facilities and costs of rodenticides, fumigants, and other supplies must be met.

Suitable packaging for distributing food from storage centers to consumers involves further costs, ultimately borne by consumers or governmental subsidies. Grain and other dry foods in developing nations are distributed to many small outlets. Small quantities are sold from open sacks or bags to be carried away by consumers in their own containers. Bulk handling of dry foods may be cheaper than handling food in individual packages if physical losses in transport can be minimized. Handling dry foods in bulk and distributing them to the ultimate consumers in inexpensive paper or film packages are steps that might be taken to improve distribution of foods in urban areas, thus reducing spoilage and spillage and controlling adulteration and pilferage.

Refrigeration   Fruits and vegetables, animal and dairy products, and sea foods are more perishable than dry foods. Refrigeration extends the shelf-life of these foods and the distances over which they can be conveyed to markets. Refrigeration inhibits development of microorganisms and also prevents insects from damaging foods. Mechanical refrigeration is used for temporary protection of foods at reduced temperatures and for preservation of foods by freezing. The knowledge required to preserve most types of foods by freezing has been well worked out and can be applied where appropriate.

Refrigerated warehouses in the producing areas, refrigerated train and truck transport, and refrigerated storage facilities and display cabinets in the marketing areas could prevent substantial spoilage of perishable foods. Unfortunately, the development of a refrigerated marketing chain for such products would be extremely costly and is applicable only in limited areas in the developing world at this time.

Refrigerated transport implies improved highways and rail systems. Maintenance of refrigeration systems for trucks requires skilled mechanics whose availability in the near future is doubtful. Refrigerated trucks traveling on roads that are poorly maintained will require extra attention for maintenance. Liquid nitrogen refrigeration, under such circumstances, would have an advantage over mechanical systems because of an inherently simpler maintenance requirement but its present high cost would preclude its use. In one area in Brazil where the market can be reached by an overnight haul, frozen beef carcasses are shipped in insulated trucks without refrigeration. While this method is obviously much less expensive than shipping by refrigerated truck, it restricts severely the distance that can be reached from a food-producing area.

As urbanization increases, refrigeration will become more widely used and economic forces will be brought to bear to reduce its cost. For example, in an important potato-growing area in India when only one cold storage unit was in operation in the early 1940's, rental of refrigeration space was $51 per metric ton per season. A second unit was introduced in 1946 and rental dropped to $45. Continued addition of more cold storage units reduced the cost to less than $23 in 1960.(19)

Heat Sterilization   Heat preservation in hermetically sealed containers (canning) provides a major means for food preservation. Costs, however, may be high. In many parts of the world, metal containers are beyond the economic resources of a large fraction of the population. Glass containers can be made with native materials and labor in many regions of the world and can be used for preserving foods in place of metal containers. Glass breakage, however, may be a considerable factor of cost. Some of this disadvantage might be overcome in areas where hand-labor could provide pads and bottle sleeves of native materials to cushion glass jars in shipping containers. New innovations, such as plastic containers, may prove particularly useful.

Radiation   Radiation treatment to prolong storage life of perishable foods under refrigeration, to control insects in exported fruits and vegetables and stored grains, and to preserve perishables in hermetically sealed containers is technically possible, but not yet an efficient commercial reality. Recent studies suggest that harmful radiation effects may be transmitted by stable, toxic intermediate products in foods. The significance of these studies cannot be ascertained until extended feeding studies are completed. These

and other problems indicate that radiation is not likely to have a significant application for food preservation in the foreseeable future.

Fermentation, Brining and Smoking Fermenting, brining, and smoking are techniques known in most areas of the world. They were all developed in prehistoric times and have been well advanced even in some aboriginal cultures. Modern technology has provided advances in control of these methods and an explanation of how they work.

UTILIZATION OF FOOD PROTECTION TECHNIQUES

In developed countries losses of dry food resources are kept at reasonable levels by use of well designed and effectively operated, large storage facilities. Rodents are excluded or controlled with rodenticides, insects are controlled by fumigation with appropriate insecticides, and moisture is held at levels to prevent spoilage from microorganisms. Spoilage is controlled by artificial drying, by determining moisture content of each lot before storage, and by monitoring stored grain temperatures for evidence of heating. Processed dry food products are packaged to prevent damage from insects and microorganisms and to prevent spillage and waste in retail outlets or in homes.

In developed countries, highly perishable fruits, vegetables, meats, dairy products, eggs, etc., are refrigerated, dehydrated, canned, pickled, or frozen to minimize spoilage and to facilitate distribution. In terms of the purchasing capabilities of consumers, the costs are low because the necessary kinds and amounts of raw materials are available, and the knowledge and physical facilities are available to process goods efficiently. Moreover, competition among food storage operators and among food processors and market outlets has resulted in an efficient, high volume operation that functions with low profit margins.

In developing countries processed foods are a luxury beyond the purchasing capacity of most people. This situation exists for a number of reasons:

a The proper facilities are not available to store, prepare, and distribute processed foods in large quantities.

b Large volume markets are not available to support a large and efficient food processing operation.

c Dependable supplies of uniform and high quality raw materials suitable for processing have not been developed.

d Operational skills required to process and distribute processed foods are not available.

e High import duties designed to protect local industries result in increased costs for containers, processing equipment, etc.

f Distrust among people is so prevalent that large scale purchases of raw materials without quality standards would be impractical.

The organization of the public and private sectors in developed countries to provide grain storage, food processing, food distribution, research and education cannot be applied unchanged to the developing countries. Many of these programs and organizations involve objectives and techniques that are too sophisticated and too expensive to warrant consideration in developing nations. In the sections that follow, consideration has been given to the kinds of food protection techniques that should be applied in developing countries and the sequence of developments that could be programmed.

Home and Community Storage and Processing

For the farmer in India who subsists mainly on the grain and pulses that he can produce and store, the immediate problem is to protect these food resources in sufficient quantities to last until the next harvest. Rodent-proof storage bins are needed that will also provide protection against insects. If the stored grains are not sufficiently dry, the storage must have ample ventilation. The small operator cannot afford much of an investment in storage facilities and it may be more effective to develop better designed and efficiently operated facilities for community use on a cooperative basis.

Educational programs are needed to encourage the use of simple food preservation methods such as dehydration by sun drying, pickling, and preserving with sugar. Greater utilization of these techniques could increase the variety and amounts of food available in communities where shortages and surpluses occur seasonally. Some community canning projects have been initiated in India. In six communities in Uttar Pradesh, 45,000 pounds of preserved fruit were produced after the third year of operation.(20) While this is a trivial amount of food relative to needs, it is illustrative of the kind of educational program that would encourage food conservation and protection. Moreover, such programs could absorb surpluses that cannot be disposed of profitably at local markets.

Industrialization of Storage, Processing, and Distribution of Foods

As agriculture changes from a subsistence to a market orientation, an opportunity is afforded for the markets to specialize and to expand. Local grain collecting stations ultimately must be established close enough to farms to permit delivery. The collecting agencies may be operated as a private enterprise or as a cooperative. In either case, management should be able to provide credit or payment for the grain delivered. The village cooperative or the trusted merchant buying the grain will need a basis for their transactions with farmers that will reflect quality and value of the commodity in larger markets. Factors such as moisture content and prevalence of insect and mechanical damage will be important characteristics to describe. The units of measurement will need to be established. The Government will be required to develop grades of grain and to describe these grades in terms of specifications that reflect the value of the grain for storage and for processing. The government will also need to adopt a system of weights and measures that can be used in regional, national, and international trade. With these services it becomes possible for grain or other products to be sold to remote markets in terms of units of measure and quality criteria established by an unbiased third party. If the buyer and seller can relate prices to objectively determined quality and quantity criteria, they can transact business even though separated by many miles.

At all stages in the post-harvest handling procedures, farm produce must be transported and stored in a manner that will keep losses and spillage at a minimum. There should be premium prices paid to farmers for premium quality produce and the storage system should permit segregation in terms of quality until it reaches the processor or consumer. Such price incentives will tend to improve quality and the adoption of better farming practices.

In areas where perishable products such as meat, fish, fruit, and vegetables can be produced, the marketing procedure will become complex. The first step in the development of such markets might involve transportation of surplus fresh produce to adjacent communities. Utilization of more distant markets for perishables would require transportation facilities and refrigeration. Local and terminal refrigerated storages can be used as markets expand to prolong the season of availability and to control the flow of produce that otherwise might cause gluts and excessive losses. Again, uniform and realistic quality criteria must be developed as a government service and utilized in a manner that permits buyers and sellers to conduct business with confidence. The same or similar quality criteria will be useful to consumers to identify superior produce at retail levels.

As economic conditions develop, commercial dehydration, canning and freezing plants can be constructed in areas where the quantity and quality of perishable products are adequate. Before industrial preservation can be developed, there must be reliable supplies of good quality raw material, adequate supplies of good water, processing equipment, packaging materials, fuel, waste disposal facilities, and proper storages for finished products. Distribution systems for the processed products must be developed and the consumer must be educated to use new and different foods. The development of fruits and vegetable varieties and better cultural practices to provide more dependable supplies may be major problems because processing quality criteria are often very different than the quality characteristics desired for fresh market purposes.

If costs of preserved foods are to be low enough to benefit a significant segment of the population in developing countries, the scale of operation must be large enough to keep unit costs low. Cost inputs that can be supplied domestically are generally inexpensive, but imported equipment and containers are usually costly. While governments may need to provide financial support or even operate processing plants in early stages, there is ample evidence that private enterprise will operate them more efficiently, particularly if there is competition for raw materials and for sales of finished products.

Food preservation operations on a large scale have an important advantage in that by-products can be utilized. For example, the slaughter of individual animals for immediate sale of fresh meat results in the loss of blood, bones, and other useful animal products. These materials are recoverable for food or feed products in large slaughter houses. Primitive equipment for milling grain, for extracting cane sugar, or for pressing oil from seeds needs to be efficient to reduce losses and to permit utilization of by-products.

The marketing, processing, and distribution of processed foods require specialized knowledge and experience. The development of personnel with technical training and experience needed in the developing countries for food processing and distribution may be as difficult as development of material resources. The kinds of knowledge and experiences that will be required include (a) production of raw materials for processing, (b) movement of materials from farm to factories, (c) processing procedures, (d) development of auxiliary supplies and services, (e) treatment and disposal of waste materials, (f) utilization of by-products, and (g) distribution and marketing of finished products. Such knowledge in the developing countries is mainly limited to a few firms exporting such items as coffee, tea and bananas.

Programs for technological training and institutions for basic and adaptive research must be developed if the needed expansion in food preservation and food distribution is to be accomplished. Attention also must be given to the development of mechanical skills that handicap the introduction of modern techniques on a large scale.

DEVELOPMENT AND MARKETING OF NEW FOOD PRODUCTS

It is generally agreed that a major nutritional problem of developing countries is the inability of pre-school children to obtain the proper quantities and quality of protein. This problem has attracted the attention of numerous public agencies and a number of high protein foods have been developed specifically for young children. The nutritional value of these foods has been established in laboratories and hospitals. Several commercial organizations have been interested in the possibilities of marketing these high protein foods. The experiences of some of these commercial efforts have been well documented and clearly illustrate the complexity of developing an entirely new food, constructing facilities for manufacture of such foods, and the development of consumer demand for such an unusual product.

High protein foods have been developed for commercial distribution in Guatemala, Colombia, Peru, Brazil, Nigeria, West Africa, Hong Kong, and perhaps other areas. A number of high protein products also have been developed by institutions in India, but these products apparently have not been used for commercial purposes. There are some situations where commercial concerns have been interested in high protein foods only if manufacturing and distribution rights for a specific product could be held exclusively in a nation. Even with exclusive distribution rights it has been difficult to build distribution to a point where these foods have had an important impact on the quality of food consumed by pre-school children. Most organizations that have attempted to develop a high protein food business have been able to utilize an existing food distribution system, but there have been some attempts to develop a business with a high protein food product exclusively.

Creation of High Protein Foods

It has been demonstrated by a number of research agencies that nutritious mixtures of certain oil seed meals and cereals can be prepared. These mixtures generally contain about 25 per cent protein with the essential amino acids in proper balance. Vitamins and minerals have been added in some instances. It has been demonstrated that children fed these high protein foods to supplement their normal diet will be cured of severe protein malnutrition. In view of the great need for more and better proteins in the diets of pre-school children and the demonstrated effectiveness of the protein mixtures from vegetable sources, it would appear that foods of this sort should have important commercial possibilities.

One of the first considerations in the development of a high protein food is the local availability and quality of protein-rich ingredients. Oilseeds are particularly useful as one ingredient because a high protein residue remains after the oil is extracted. Oilseeds are commonly processed for animal feeds and are not handled with the care and sanitation considered necessary for human food. Such problems as excess fiber, toxic substances such as gossypol in cottonseed meal, or aflatoxin in peanuts, or antitryptic factors in soy beans, must be anticipated and corrected. Care must be taken to see that the methods used are consistent with domestic food regulations. Another large volume ingredient in the mixtures will generally be a locally available cereal such as rice, wheat, corn, milo, etc. Certain vitamins and minerals may be added as needed. The blended ingredients must result in a palatable, acceptable, and economical food that is not too greatly different from some important native food in appearance or form.

Most of the high protein foods developed to date have been designed for consumption in the form of a biscuit, liquid or semi-liquid formulation and similar forms resembling foods already in use in the countries involved. It is likely that formulation of high protein foods can be greatly improved by giving more emphasis to palatability, acceptance by children, appearance, and methods of preparation in the home. It is also likely that high protein foods should be made available in a variety of forms to avoid monotony of diet.

Collection and Processing of High Protein Food Components

The principal ingredients in high protein foods are selected because of their nutritional value, availability and cost. Sources of each ingredient will need to be developed and it will need to be ascertained that the nutritional quality is reasonably uniform. Quality requirements of oilseeds and cereals as regards moisture content, varieties, insect damage and similar factors may be more rigid than local farmers are accustomed to meeting. This situation may require the processor to engage in grower education and to participate in the development of quality criteria or government grades to serve as a basis for purchases.

Some raw materials may have to be imported. There are only a few places where cottonseed meal is commonly available that has been treated to remove gossypol and soy beans can be grown only in the temperate climates. Government assistance will be essential so that these critical materials can be imported on a duty free basis.

Special equipment will be needed for ingredient handling, storage, processing, blending, and packaging. An investment in manufacturing plants and storage facilities for raw and finished products will be required. Government assistance may be obtained in the form of reduced import duties on equipment and reduced taxes on capital investments.

Without the proper manufacturing and marketing skills the food processing venture would have scarcely any prospect for survival. These production and marketing talents are unavailable in the developing countries and even in short supply in developed countries. The people who would do the actual manufacturing and marketing work must be selected and trained from available nationals. A consortium of companies from the developed countries might be able to provide the necessary management talent easier than a single company. Such a consortium would have the added advantage of greater knowledge of food processing and marketing in the event the initial venture should develop into a major food industry.

Development of Consumer Demand

The successful commercialization of a high protein food has not yet been accomplished even though the basic technology has been available to create and manufacture the kinds of products needed, and it has been demonstrated that such foods will fulfill a prevalent need. There are several organizations engaged in marketing high protein foods in developing countries, but none of these products has had a dramatic effect in alleviating protein deficiencies on the large scale that will be necessary.

The programs followed by the different commercial concerns to develop consumer demand have been similar. These programs will be described here because they illustrate how difficult it has been to introduce new and needed foods in developing countries. These experiences clearly show that a huge gap separates our knowledge of food formulation and food marketing and our understanding of desires of uneducated, poor people in developing countries.

Food processors interested in developing and marketing high protein foods have first secured the support of local governments. This has been done to secure duty concessions applicable to the importation of equipment and ingredients, and tax concessions for the proposed business. In several instances the governments have made bulk purchases of the high protein foods for distribution to publicly supported children's institutions. In addition to the official support of government and its institutions, the products have been widely distributed to pediatricians and hospitals for research and educational purposes. In some cases international organizations, such as UNICEF, have supported product development financially and through educational material.

Market development for the products usually has been directed to the urban areas of the developing countries where there are retail outlets and where malnutrition of children is particularly serious. Attention has been given to attractive packaging, instructions for use by illiterate people, package size and the possibility of deterioration of the product after the package is opened. Care has been given to ascertain that unit costs are within the consumer's purchasing ability. All conventional advertising media have been utilized, including posters, radio, movies, and publications. Demonstrations and educational programs have been staged in mobile vans, in clinics, schools, hospitals, and other public places. Some campaigns have been purposely directed to upper or middle class segments of the population so that the product would not have the stigma of being known as food for "poor children." Changes have been made in flavors, and formulas have been modified to create a product with more appeal.

The experiences of food processors with the development and marketing of high protein foods suggest that one of the great unsolved problems is how to formulate a product for which the demand is related to need. A greater impact might have been made initially in some cases if the foods had been distributed to children by the local government. On the other hand, a successful commercial development will provide a greater incentive to continue product development and promotion. Another factor favoring manufacture and distribution through private enterprise is the possible development of a financially sound food processing industry that can also produce and market foods for other segments of the population.

A survey was conducted recently(21) in which 165 food processing companies were queried about their interest in a study relating to the production and marketing of a high protein food in Peru. There were 85 responses to the inquiry. All indicated no interest in supporting such a study. The reasons for lack of interest were belief that (a) a poor profit potential must exist because consumers do not have money with which to buy a special food, (b) local governments would not permit business a profit from making and marketing food for needy people, hence there would be no money for promotion, and (c) little consumer demand and uncertain government support would be available for such a project. The survey indicated that

United States industry will require some substantial encouragement before companies will enter the high protein food production field on a scale necessary to meet immediate needs.

REFERENCES

1. International Symposium on Mycotoxins in Foodstuffs, Massachusetts Institute of Technology, 1964, 1965. *Mycotoxins in foodstuffs, proceedings.* Cambridge, Mass.: M.I.T. Press.
2. Floyd, E. H., Oliver, A. D., and Powell, J. D. August 1959. Damage to corn in Louisiana caused by stored-grain insects. *J. Econ. Ent.* 52, no. 4: 612–15.
3. Nonveiller, G. 1965. Storage problems in North Cameroun (abstr.). *Food & Agr. Org. United Nations Plant Prod. and Protect. Div. Grain Storage Newsletter & Abstrs.* 7, no. 3: 49.
4. Hapur. Grain Storage Research and Training Institute. *Progress report (1958–62).* India: Ministry of Food and Agriculture.
5. Dykstra, W. W. October 1966. Seminar on rodents and rodent ectoparasites. Geneva, Switzerland: WHO.
6. Abiya, S. S. October 1961. All about rats. *Farmer* (Bombay) 12, no. 10: 3–5.
7. Ling, L. 1961. Man loses a fifth of the crops he grows. *Atlantic.* Special issue for FAO for Freedom from Hunger.
8. Central Food Technological Research Institute. 1965. *Rice in India, a techno-economic review.* Mysore.
9. Food and Agriculture Organization of the United Nations. Regional Conference for Asia and the Far East.
10. Faukner, R. and B. September 1963. *Increasing milling returns of rice from paddy in India.* New Delhi: The Ford Foundation.
11. *Ibid.*
12. FAO Expert Committee. 1946. *Report Nu/Wa.* WP 3.
13. Joint ECLA/FAO Working Party. 1950. *Agricultural requisites in Latin America,* Rev. 1. Lake Success: United Nations Dep. Econ. Affairs. (U.N. E/CN 12/83, U.N. publications. 1950. II.G.l.)
14. Weitz-Hettelsater Engineers. 1963. *Economic and engineering study-marketing facilities for grain and tuberous crops* (an economic survey for ETA). Weitz-Hettelsater.
15. Hall, D. W. 1963. *FAO. Informal Working Bulletin* no. 24. Jordan, R. C. 1963. *U.N. conference on the application of science and technology for the benefit of the less developed areas,* vol. 5. Geneva.
16. Jordan, R. C. 1962–63. New techniques for temperature control of perishable goods in transport and storage applicable to the less developed areas. In *United Nations conference on the application of science and technology for the benefit of the less developed areas,* vol. 5. Science, technology, and development. United States papers. Washington: U.S. Govt. Printing Office.
17. Food & Agr. Org. United Nations. 1958. *A community canning and food preservation project.* Expanded Tech. Assistance Program FAO Rep. no. 786.
18. Unpublished FAO data.
19. U.S. Department of Agriculture, Economic Research Service. November 1965. Changes in agriculture in 26 developing nations 1948 to 1963. *U.S. Dep. Agr. Econ. Res. Serv. Foreign Agr. Econ. Rep.* no. 27.
20. FAO Report no 786. *Op. cit.*
21. Milner, M. May 11–13, 1964. The need for food processing industry in developing countries. Talk before Food Industry Advisory Committee of Nutrition Foundation.

The New Seeds

LESTER R. BROWN

LESTER BROWN *is a Senior Fellow of the Overseas Development Council.*

Together with the success of programs to limit population, perhaps the greatest short-term hope for mankind lies in the discovery and development of the new varieties of grains. Much of the world's protein and calories is derived from cereals. Increased yields and higher nutritious content can do much to alleviate hunger and malnutrition. Because of the efforts of agricultural scientists and plant breeders, a silver lining is beginning to show through the clouds of poverty. Brown tells of the rapid acceptance of the new seeds.

Until recently, virtually all of the major breakthroughs in agricultural technology originated in the temperate zones. Even though a great deal of research has been devoted to plantation agriculture in the tropics, the prime beneficiaries have been outsiders, those in the rich countries to whom the commodities are sold. Those in the tropics were at best residual beneficiaries, forced to make do with an agricultural technology developed in northwestern Europe, the United States, or Japan, a technology admirably adapted to the temperate climates but usually poorly suited to the tropics.

The new seeds were designed to capitalize on the unique natural advantages of tropical-subtropical areas, particularly the wealth of solar energy available only in such climates. On bright, sunny days, land close to the Equator receives 56 to 59 per cent of the potential radiant energy, as compared with only 47 per cent at 40 degrees latitude (Washington, D.C.). These new seeds are the product of the first systematic attempt to devise a technology to capitalize on this and to help improve the lot of hundreds of millions of people who live in material poverty.

THE ENGINEERING PROBLEM

Plant breeders are biological engineers. Just as Henry Ford designed the Model-T to meet the varied needs of middle-class America, so the plant

---

Seeds of Change, 1970, Praeger Publishers, Inc., pp. 15–23. Reprinted by permission.

breeders designed the new wheat and rice varieties to meet the varied needs of peasant farmers in the poor regions of the world. The real challenge to the designers of the new seeds was to develop cereal varieties that were not only responsive to fertilizer but also adaptable throughout the poor regions of the world. If the poor countries have the advantage of a great supply of solar energy, they have the disadvantage of great variation in soil conditions. Just as the Model-T had to be able to run on all kinds of roads in all kinds of weather, so the new seeds had to be able to grow under a wide variety of soil and climatic conditions.

In the tropics, traditional food varieties are the result of centuries of natural selection, undisturbed by any scientific attempt to control the plant's environment. Left to its own devices, nature chooses strains that will survive under prevailing growing conditions. These traditional strains have to fight for survival against weeds and in heavy rains and floods. This makes for a tall, thin-strawed plant that can keep its head above water when there is flooding and can compete successfully with weeds for its share of sunlight.

Introducing fertilizer into this natural environment is a complex task. Traditional strains are not responsive to fertilizer; when it is applied liberally, they become topheavy with grain and fall over, or "lodge," before the grain is ripe. Their tall straw, so necessary for survival in nature's environment, is too weak to carry the added load of grain generated by the application of fertilizer.

This problem was overcome first in Japan and then in the United States. The Japanese isolated a dwarfing gene which produced a sturdy, short-strawed wheat capable of carrying a heavy head of grain. The new dwarf wheats owe their existence to this technological breakthrough. However, mass application came to the poor countries in a roundabout way.

The dwarfing gene was brought to the United States in 1947 by Dr. S. C. Salmon of the United States Department of Agriculture. The Japanese variety did not travel well, however. It was only when another USDA scientist, Dr. Orville Vogel, incorporated the Japanese dwarf gene into his own local breeding materials that a successful dwarf variety was developed. The resulting variety, called Gaines wheat, produced world-record yields in the irrigated and high-rainfall growing conditions of the Pacific Northwest.

Meanwhile, Dr. Norman Borlaug, Director of the Rockefeller Foundation's wheat-breeding program in Mexico, heard about Dr. Vogel's work and obtained some of Dr. Vogel's breeding materials containing the dwarfing gene. He refined Gaines wheat to make it more suitable for use in Mexico. In the process, he achieved a second major breakthrough in plant breeding.

Dr. Borlaug wanted to develop a dwarf wheat that would perform well under the varied growing conditions of Mexico. He amassed germ plasm from Japan, the United States, Australia, and Colombia and then began growing two alternate crops of wheat each year at two different sites, a summer crop just south of the United States border, and another crop in winter near Mexico City, some eight hundred miles away. The two sites differed in day length, or photoperiod, as well as in many other environmental factors. Given the cosmopolitan ancestry of his seeds, Dr. Borlaug was able to produce a dwarf wheat variety that was remarkably adapted to a range of growing conditions. The Mexican dwarf wheats today are growing successfully in latitudes near the Equator, where days are of uniform length and also in higher latitudes, such as Turkey, where day length varies greatly by season. This adaptability was something new. Hitherto, the dwarf wheats had performed well only under conditions comparable to those in which they were first bred.

FROM WHEAT TO RICE

Buoyed by the success of the Mexican wheats, and keenly aware that most of the world's poor eat rice, the Rockefeller and Ford Foundations joined forces in 1962 to establish the International Rice Research Institute on land provided by the Philippine government at Los Banos, near Manila. A crack team of scientists was assembled from the United States, the Philippines, Taiwan, and elsewhere under the direction of Dr. Robert Chandler, formerly President of the University of New Hampshire. The objective was to produce a cosmopolitan dwarf rice strain comparable to the Mexican wheats.

The team assembled some ten thousand strains of rice from every corner of the world and began a patient process of crossbreeding. Success came early when a tall, vigorous variety from Indonesia, called Peta, was combined with a dwarf rice from Taiwan; called Deo-geo-woo-gen, to produce the "miracle rice," IR-8. When properly managed, IR-8 has proved easily capable of doubling the yield of most local rices in Asia.

IR-8 and an increasingly popular new strain, IR-5, have already proved responsive to fertilizer in a wide range of growing conditions in several countries. IR-8 and its cousins can effectively absorb up to 120 pounds of fertilizer per acre without lodging, while traditional varieties usually lodge after the application of 40 pounds.

Not only do the new varieties respond to much heavier dosages of fertilizer, they are far more efficient in its use. One pound of nitrogen applied to the old varieties would yield close to 10 additional pounds of grain. David Hopper, a Rockefeller Foundation economist in New Delhi, calculates that a pound of nitrogen applied to the new seeds can yield up to 20 pounds of grain.(1)

In addition to being highly adaptable, the new rices are early maturing. IR-8 matures in 120 days, as compared with 150–180 days for traditional varieties. This shorter growth cycle often means an extra crop, if not of rice, of something else. It means that the new seeds are not only more efficient users of sunlight but of land itself.

A WINDFALL GAIN

The new seeds have been supplied to the poor countries on a virtually costless basis; millions of farmers who are planting them are reaping huge windfall gains in production. Countries such as India, Pakistan, and Turkey imported samples of Mexican wheats for testing. Once the seeds' adaptability to local conditions was established, these countries imported them from Mexico by the shipload (see Table 1), and at prices only marginally higher than world market prices for wheat. Since these countries were already importing wheat, the real additional cost was only the modest difference between the cost of the Mexican wheat seed and the world market price.

Not only was the new technology essentially free but, because the seeds could be imported in bulk, the time required for seed multiplication was greatly reduced. Normally the development of a new variety begins with a small handful of seed which is multiplied to a half bushel, then a quarter

TABLE 1. Imports of high-yielding Mexican wheat seed into Asia. Source: Dana Dalrymple, *Imports and Plantings of High-Yielding Varieties of Wheat and Rice in the Less Developed Nations*, Washington, D.C.: International Agricultural Development Service, U.S. Department of Agriculture, 1968, mimeo, pp. 2–3.

COUNTRY	CROP YEAR	TONNAGE IMPORTED
Afghanistan	1967	170
India	1965	250
	1966	18,000
Nepal	1966	38
	1967	450
Pakistan	1965	350
	1966	50
	1967	42,000
Turkey	1967	60
	1968	22,000

ton, ten tons, four hundred tons, eventually producing enough to release the seed commercially. Pakistan imported 42,000 tons of the new wheat seeds in 1967–68, enough to plant more than a million acres. When this crop was harvested, it provided enough seed to cover all of Pakistan's wheat land, thus telescoping into two years a process normally requiring several years.

Imports of seed rice from the Philippines similarly accelerated the diffusion of the high-yielding dwarf rices, such as IR-8. Since a ton of rice plants several times as much land as a ton of wheat, the imported tonnages are far lower for rice than for wheat.

Perhaps more important than the actual tonnage of the dwarf wheats and rices imported is the prototype they represent, which local plant breeders can refine and modify specifically for local growing conditions. The new seeds are thus raising the sights of agricultural scientists, ushering in a renaissance in agricultural research. Two promising rices, released in Eastern India during 1969, are Jaya and Padma, both local modifications of the dwarf prototype. Other local modifications are being released in Ceylon, Malaysia, and Thailand. Local improvements on the dwarf wheat prototypes are already in widespread use in India and Pakistan. As plant-breeding efforts continue, the first generation of high-yielding varieties will be replaced with a second generation. In some countries this process is already under way.

It is, of course, not the scientists and technologists who are responsible for the vast and rapid acceptance of the new seeds but the millions of farmers, particularly in Asia, who decided to plant them and in so doing found their incomes increasing two-, three-, and even fourfold. The area planted to high-yielding cereals in Asia in the 1964–65 crop year was estimated at 200 acres, and that largely for experimental and trial purposes.

By 1968–69, 34 million acres were covered. The expansion progressed as
follows:

1964–65	200 acres
1965–66	37,000 acres
1966–67	4,800,000 acres
1967–68	20,000,000 acres
1968–69	34,000,000 acres

This acreage consists largely of Mexican wheats and IRRI rices, but it
also includes locally developed high-yielding rices, such as ADT-27 in India
and H-4 in Ceylon, as well as limited plantings of high-yielding corn and
sorghum. Because they proved so profitable to farmers, adoption of the new
varieties spread far more rapidly than was anticipated, raising cereal
production at an unexpected rate. If it is assumed that replacement of local
varieties with high-yielding seeds raised output by a half-ton per acre—a
conservative assumption—the 34 million acres planted in 1968–69 expanded
the Asian food supply by 17 million tons, roughly the equivalent of two
billion dollars' worth of grain!

PLANT BREEDERS' AGENDA

Table 2 shows how the new seeds have spread in selected countries. At
present, less than one seventh of the wheat and rice land in Asia, excluding
Mainland China, is planted to the new seeds. Because this land is relatively
well irrigated and fertile, it produces a disproportionately large share of
the region's food. In Africa and Latin America the new seeds are not being
used so widely as in Asia, but they are being successfully introduced in
some countries, and a considerable amount of experimentation is taking
place in others. Introduction of the Mexican wheats into Morocco and
Tunisia, though more recent than in Asia, is proceeding successfully. Acreage is expected to expand rapidly in the early seventies.

The process of replacing traditional varieties of grain with high-yielding
ones in Asia will continue for the foreseeable future, but probably not at
the pace of the past few years. Although they are adapted to a wide range
of growing conditions, the Mexican wheats have a pronounced yield advantage over local wheats only when they are grown under irrigated or
high-rainfall conditions. Under dryland farming conditions, where little or
no fertilizer can be used, they offer little if any advantage. The dwarf rices,
conversely, perform poorly and sometimes fail completely in conditions of
natural flooding or in rainfed fields where they may be submerged for some
time. Expansion of the area planted to high-yielding wheats is already
slowing somewhat in both India and Pakistan, for example, as the additional
land with suitable water supply diminishes. But there is likely to be considerable expansion into countries that are not yet using the new seeds; Iran
and Iraq, for example, have just begun to plant the new wheats. But in
the parts of the continent where the high-yielding varieties are well established, water supply and water control will act as the principal constraints
to further spread.

TABLE 2.   Area planted to high-yielding Mexican wheats.
Source: Dalrymple, *op. cit.,* p. 2.

COUNTRY	CROP YEAR	PLANTED AREA (ACRES)
Afghanistan	1967	4,500
	1968	65,000
	1969	300,000
India	1966	7,400
	1967	1,278,000
	1968	6,681,000
	1969	10,000,000
Nepal	1966	3,500
	1967	16,200
	1968	61,300
Pakistan	1966	12,000
	1967	255,000
	1968	1,800,000
	1969	6,000,000
Turkey	1968	420,000
	1969	1,780,000

The biological engineers are at work on these problems, developing wheats that will raise yields under low rainfall conditions and rices that are more tolerant of flooding. At the same time, both farmers and governments are steadily expanding and intensifying irrigation and flood-control systems. Only a minor part of the cereal-producing land in Asia can be planted profitably with the seeds that exist now, but still more effective seeds are constantly being developed.

Farmers in the poor countries increasingly view the future in terms of new seeds, new techniques, and a more productive life. Symbolizing this attitude is the response of the Filipino Farmer of the Year, 58-year-old Andres de la Cruz, when asked what variety of rice he was going to plant next season. "I don't know," he unhesitatingly answered. "I'm still waiting for a newer variety."

REFERENCES

1. Hopper, W. D. April 1968. *Strategy for the conquest of hunger.* New York: Rockefeller Foundation, p. 107.

Ironies of India's
Green Revolution

WOLF LADEJINSKY

WOLF LADEJINSKY *is an agricultural economist at the International Bank for Reconstruction and Development.*

The demands of the green revolution, using the new seeds, are not trivial. The agricultural inputs—land, water, seeds, fertilizer, labor, technology— require relatively large amounts of capital and know-how. Distribution of the products and income cannot take place effectively without modern marketing and financing. The consequences, too, can be revolutionary. Surpluses can adversely affect prices and incentives and upset traditional trade relations. The total income of a region or a nation goes up, but so does the inequality in individual incomes, often leading to political and social upheaval. Ladejinsky discusses the credits and debits of the balance sheet of the green revolution in the particular case of India.

For nearly five years the "green revolution" has been under way in a number of agriculturally underdeveloped countries of Asia. Its advent into tradition-bound rural societies was heralded as the rebuttal to the dire predictions of hunger stalking large parts of the world. But more than that, those carried away with euphoria at the impending changes saw in them a remedy for the poverty of the vast majority of the cultivators. They were correct in assuming that the new technology stands for vastly increased productivity and income to match. However, the propitious circumstances in which the new technology thrives are not easily obtainable and hence there are inevitably constraints on its scope and progress. Apart from this, where it has succeeded, the revolution has given rise to a host of political and social problems. In short, the green revolution can be, as Dr. Wharton correctly pointed out in *Foreign Affairs* in April 1969, both a cornucopia and a Pandora's box.

Reprinted by permission from *Foreign Affairs*, 48(4): 758–68, July 1970. Copyright © Council on Foreign Relations, Inc.

This is seen very decisively in India's experience. There, extravagant anticipations have been replaced by a more sober and meaningful appreciation of its accomplishments and of the possibilities for expanding the scope of the technology beyond its current narrow limits. It has become obvious that many more farmers must be drawn in to share the benefits of the revolution. The polarization of income between the rich and the poor farmers and the erosion of the position of the tenantry which has been accentuated by the increases in productivity should not be part of the model of the new agricultural strategy. While self-sufficiency in foodstuffs is indeed a welcome—and likely—prospect for India, concern is rising that for all its technological feasibility it may fall short in helping solve some of the grave problems of a good many village poor. (The views expressed here and elsewhere in this article are, of course, those of the author alone.)

Indian political and economic problems are currently as numerous and grave as usual, but for once food shortages do not claim the headlines. The first two years (1965–66, 1966–67) of the new agricultural strategy were dried away by some of the worst monsoon failures recorded. Three years later, with favorable climatic conditions accompanying the new agricultural technology, the food position of India is "comfortable." In 1969–70 output of foodgrains was a record 100 million tons, or 11 million tons more than in 1964–65, which was the best year before the revolution. Since agricultural development *is* the basis of the country's economic growth, this is a very significant gain. The annual rate of growth so far is closer to 2.5 than the anticipated five per cent, giving rise to doubts about the attainment of the projected 130 million tons in 1973–74—the last year of the Fourth Five-Year Plan. But statistical trends do not tell the whole story of the program's effectiveness.

Despite the serious social and technological limitations of the new agricultural strategy, one thing is clear: the wheat revolution is a reality, way beyond any expectation. Second, where the ingredients for the new technology are available—new high-yielding varieties, concentrated doses of fertilizers, assured sources of perennial irrigation—no farmer denies their effectiveness. Third, agriculture in the late 1960s has benefited from a guaranteed minimum price for wheat and a general improvement of terms vis-à-vis other sectors. Fourth, the desire for better farming methods and a better standard of living is growing not only among the relatively small numbers using the new technology, but also among countless farmers still outside looking in. This mental attitude, though too seldom supported by the necessary resources, cannot be overemphasized. At long last, in India too, the power of ideas to bring about change is being demonstrated. To those concerned with purely physical entities of economic growth, a psychological change of this sort is not subject to numerology and is probably of no moment as a developmental factor. But it cannot be denied that a new, if unquantifiable, factor of growth has been introduced. Finally, the progress in agriculture is a result of major official and private efforts at several strategic points, which have slowly created a milieu radically different from that of the 1950s and early 1960s. These are considerable achievements, regardless of the growth rate.

II

This said, and viewing the new developments as a technological phenomenon, what stands out at this point is the unevenness of their application and the need for patient attention over a considerable period of time in order to achieve basic agricultural changes. Nothing makes this clearer than comparing the progress made with the two pivotal foodgrain crops of India, wheat and rice.

Whereas wheat has been a success story par excellence, rice can claim no such distinction. Between 1964–65 and 1968–69 all the basic indicators of agricultural growth in rice have remained almost unchanged; in contrast, the respective increases in wheat acreage, production and productivity were 19, 52 and 28 per cent. But the character of the technological changes is best seen in the hotbed of the green revolution, in the state of Punjab, India's traditional wheat basket. There, an innovation-minded group of farmers has in a few years succeeded in translating larger crops and income into a new way of life. More precisely, they planted 80 per cent of the land with "miracle" wheat varieties; increased the number of tubewells for irrigation from 7,000 to 120,000; virtually tripled the consumption of fertilizers within four years—moving, during the last decade, from a mere two to three kilograms per acre to as high as 40 to 60 kilograms in 1968–69—and almost doubled the yield. For this the Punjab farmers deserve much credit, but they were fortunate in a remarkable set of partners: the Ford Foundation, which pioneered and demonstrated the utility of the new "package of practices" idea; the Rockefeller Foundation, with its invaluable work in developing the Mexican "dwarf" wheat varieties upon which the wheat revolution is based; the Punjab Agricultural University, which has rapidly become the center of dissemination for new varieties; and finally, the great effort of the central and state agencies which in a variety of ways helped to provide the inputs upon which the upswing in productivity rests.

At the moment, the same cannot be said for rice, despite significant pockets of progress in Kerala, Tamil Nadu, parts of Andhra Pradesh and West Bengal. Since wheat accounts for 15 per cent of the total acreage in foodgrains as against 31 per cent in rice, the latter is most important in determining the overall rate of agricultural growth. If rice productivity had shown anything comparable to that of wheat, India would have been self-sufficient in foodgrains now. The principal reason for the disparity in performance is that tested and proved new varieties are still in the making, and that, generally speaking, rice varieties demand a great number of favorable environmental conditions; they are susceptible to pest and disease, the knowledge of which still is inadequate. The quality of the new strains leaves something to be desired and it markets at a considerable discount. Unlike Punjab, with its successful irrigation program, the lack of irrigation and absence of drainage facilities in some of the major rice-growing parts of the country are serious constraints. In such conditions, with few notable exceptions, the much talked about "miracle" strains from the Philippines and Taiwan have so far met with limited responses. Additionally, the problems of the "new" rice, especially in the eastern belt of the country, extend beyond the technological lag: a much larger proportion of the cultivated rice area is in small holdings whose proprietors lack credit and are often tenants on the land, and these impose limitations of their own. For this very reason, if the improved rice technology could become a reality it would achieve something beyond higher productivity.

Dramatic and speedy solutions to the problems with the existing rice technology cannot be expected. But it would be an error to conclude that they are insurmountable. From the few successes and many more failures much has been learned. The early assumptions about the miraculous performance of the new varieties overlooked the importance of their environment. (Even in wheat, unless the cropping of "Kalyan Sona"—the principal variety—is diversified, there is a danger that rust might affect the entire belt where the variety is grown. Much will depend upon the ability of agricultural science to ward off such setbacks.)

Now, however, Indian research institutions are deeply involved in propagating strains suitable for Indian contexts. They are equally involved in research about soils and water in the huge dry land areas of India. Whatever the time lag, the responsibility for failure to solve these difficult problems quickly in a country as vast as India and as varied in soil, climate and water management cannot be ascribed to the new agricultural strategy itself but only to its vulgarization as a "do-all."

Nor is the green revolution only a wheat revolution, as its critics taunt; this first stage is a spectacular development in itself but more importantly it will serve as a useful organizational testing ground for general changes in agricultural technology. Only a blind enthusiast could have conceived that the passage from traditional to modern agricultural practices would be effected as if by magic—even in the United States hybrid corn came into its own after much trial and error, and more than a decade after the initiation of the process.

That the changeover is a long-drawn-out affair, or that coarse grains and nonfood crops have hardly been touched by the transformation, or that the total rate of output is still only half of that anticipated is partly in the nature of things and partly a matter for concern. A monsoon failure to which India is so prone might slow down the progress of the new strategy still further, but it would not be fatal. And the most encouraging part about the recent technological developments is not so much the physical output as the use of inputs, or the willingness of the farmers to invest and take risks. Inputs have been sharply and steadily rising, as in the use of chemical fertilizers, improved seed, minor irrigation facilities, plant protection devices, tractors, etc., and the remarkable degree of monetization of the farm economy and the big array of industrial consumption goods increasingly in demand by the farmers. Another sign of the profitability of modern agriculture is the appearance on the scene of a new breed of farmers made up of a motley crowd of retired military and civil servants, doctors, lawyers and businessmen. Not a few of them have "unemployed" rupees acquired through undeclared earnings, and most of them look upon farming as a tax-haven, which it is, a source of high supplementary income free of any tax burdens.

The breakthrough in agriculture is far from a full-fledged revolution. For the time being, however, Indian agriculture has acquired some muscle. All its benefits cannot yet be estimated, but their gradual and cumulative effects on the purely productive side of the economy are inescapable. That for the time being this holds true only for a minority of India's 60 million farm families does not vitiate the significance of the changes in the making. In some parts of the countryside the new sense of initiative and optimism is palpable. That this is indeed so is attested by islands of progress even in a state like Bihar, which is still characterized by agricultural primitivism and almost unrelieved proverty.

III

Without minimizing the significance of the accomplishments, however, one must say that the revolution is highly "selective," even if its spread effect is not inconsiderable in certain areas. Such revolutions must often go slowly under the most propitious circumstances, which are not present in India. It is enough to recall that three-fourths of India's cultivated acreage is not irrigated, and "dry" farming predominates. If for no other reason, vast parts of the country have not been touched by the transformation at all and equally vast parts can boast only of "small islands within." Even in Punjab, with all its advantages, not every small farmer—not to speak of remaining tenants—practices the new technology and much less so in other developing parts of the country. The green revolution affects the few rather than the many not only because of environmental conditions but because the majority of the farmers lack resources, or are "institutionally" precluded from taking advantage of the new agricultural trends. The changes engendered by the new agricultural strategy have brought these and other handicaps

into sharp focus at a time when aspirations for betterment are widespread among all classes of farmers, and when most of them need no persuasion that modernization, which stands for bigger crops and higher income, is good for them. Waiting to be part of it and yet not getting there create potentially disturbing social, economic and political issues. And this is the other side of the coin in any assessment of the course of the green revolution.

In typical Indian conditions of great inequality of land ownership, resources and marketed surpluses, income inequality is the normal state of affairs. The seriousness of the inequalities in income distribution may be judged from the Prime Minister's remark that there are only two genuine majorities in India—the young and the poor. It is estimated that in 1969 out of a total rural population of 434 million, 103 million owned no land at all and another 185 million operated less than five acres per family. Taken together they represented 67 per cent of the total rural population, and of these an estimated 154 to 210 million lived in abject poverty, or at a level of 200 rupees ($21) per capita per year.

If the widening gap between the benefits to large and small holdings is to be reduced and the scope of the new technology enlarged, the less privileged cultivators must be enabled to secure the highly productive new inputs. Since it takes 10,000 to 12,000 rupees to reëquip a seven- to 10-acre holding, it is not normally within the reach of the farmer unless he can secure coöperative credit. More often than not he can get only insufficient credit and, on occasion, none at all, for the distribution of credit and inputs in an Indian village reflects a power structure very much biased in favor of the affluent. But whatever the causes, the argument is not against modernization for making the rich farmers richer still, but against the limited scope and that the growing disparity leaves the poor peasants relatively poorer. Many would-be innovators can be likened to tenants who receive land under a reform but nothing else to go with it. They are excluded from the purview of the green revolution altogether, or participate in a limited way at best. For reasons only partly attributable to the new technology, many farmers in areas of great potential are now pointing enviously to better production, higher income and better living "over there" in their neighbors' fields. India can ill afford any growth in social discontent.

The situation of the multitude of tenants is even more difficult than that of the small farmers. In areas where the agricultural transformation is a potent force—Punjab and the Purnea district of Bihar—the accomplishments are marred by its adverse effects on the already troublesome tenurial conditions. Where the new farm practices are in vogue, land values have risen three, four, or fivefold, and unrestricted land control has never been more prized. As a consequence, not only have rents risen from the traditional (though illegal under the reforms) 50/50 to as high as 70 per cent of the crop, but security of tenure and other rights in land a tenant might claim have also been perceptibly weakened. Now that green-revolution land is practically invaluable, the owners would like to get rid of tenants altogether and resume the land for self-cultivation, making use of the plentiful supply of hired labor which has no claims on the land whatsoever. There are too many tenants or sharecroppers to deal with them summarily without courting a good deal of trouble, but the old squeeze whereby tenants are reduced to sharecroppers and eventually to landless workers is being accelerated as more of the bigger owners become involved with the new technology. The basic provisions of tenancy reforms are less attainable than before the advent of the green revolution.

And the landless farm laborers, though their lot is temporarily improved, are eventually due for a setback. The new type of agriculture is labor-intensive, employing more labor due to double-cropping and other labor-demanding practices it is introducing. Not surprisingly, therefore, it has been hailed as a solution of the large problem of unemployment among rural landless. It appears, however, that even in the most advanced state like Punjab this is not as promising as anticipated because the technology is both labor-absorbing and labor-displacing. In recent years, wages have risen sharply, and so to a degree has the number of days of employment; on balance, and despite a steady rise in the cost of living, farm labor in Punjab is somewhat better off. Not so in Purnea, where higher productivity and higher prices have caused a shift in wage payments from kind to cash. This is a distinct disadvantage to the farm laborer, whose wages in kind have insured him a minimum food supply. And looking ahead, additional employment and better wages are not forever, for new farm practices are bringing in a host of labor-saving devices such as tractors and threshers and much in between.

Mechanization in India will never reach the science-fiction dream level where tractors will be guided by remote control. Most "farmer-revolutionaries" are more modest in their expectations, but economy of operation and increasing returns through mechanization are uppermost in their minds. Judging by the scheduled imports and contemplated increase in the domestic production of tractors and other equipment, the advocates of "go-slow" mechanization as a social policy measure have had their last ineffectual word on the subject, certainly for the life of the current Fourth Five-Year Plan.

In short, farm mechanization is as irreversible as the green revolution which fathered it, although much of it will not apply to nearly the same degree in the principal rice areas of India. Events are beginning to catch up with Nehru's lament against farm mechanization as a threat to peasant welfare. Agricultural labor has received none of the organizational and legislative benefits which have helped industrial labor. Even at this early stage of modernization of the bigger farms of Punjab the drive is for more equipment and fewer hands. The estimated 35 to 40 million landless laborers are bound to grow in numbers and their rate of employment in any other field of activity is not promising; thus the outlook is for an overcrowded, low-wage farm market regardless of the scope of the green revolution.

IV

The new technology is not the primary cause of the accentuated imbalances in the countryside. They are the result of all the social, religious, economic and political forms which govern the village, and which admittedly are mirrored in the shape which the new technology has assumed. It is not the fault of the green revolution that the credit service does not serve those for whom it was originally intended, that the extension service is falling behind expectations, that the village "panchayats," or councils, are essentially political rather than developmental bodies, that security of tenure is not given to the many, that rentals are exorbitant, that ceilings on land ownership are notional, that even rising wage scales are hardly sufficient to satisfy the basic essentials of the farm laborer, or that generally speaking in those conditions economic necessity and social justice of and for the village poor do not ride in tandem.

To a considerable extent these are man-made issues of long standing. Modernization of agriculture should include a combination of technical factors geared to higher production *and* improvements in the institutional framework to benefit the rural underprivileged. The current emphasis is on productivity, to the exclusion of social imperatives: the first will bring India to self-sufficiency; the second is beginning to yield great vexations. Self-sufficiency will also give rise to a variety of technical and economic problems, principally reduction in counterpart funds to finance parts of the country's developmental programs which will accompany the gradual elimination of foodgrain imports under PL 480. A much more serious matter, however, could well be a lack of effective demand for the increased output resulting from the insufficient income of a substantial number of rural people.

Under the leadership of leftist parties, the village poor are not averse to forcible occupation of land, harvesting standing crops and violent attempts to secure better wages. According to the Ministry of Foreign Affairs, in the first nine months of the past year 346 incidents of forcible occupation of land (totalling 100,000 to 300,000 acres) with many murdered and injured have taken place in West Bengal alone. That this could be only a foretaste of an enormous "law-and-order" problem is well understood, and the government of India is deeply disturbed by it. In late November 1969 an emergency conference was held on how to place the agrarian reforms back on the rails. The Prime Minister addressed the Chief Ministers of all the states with an unmistakable sense of urgency, saying: "The warning of the times is that unless the green revolution is accompanied by a revolution based on social justice the green revolution may not remain green." The Prime Minister wanted the Chief Ministers to "act now when there is still time and hope" to implement the reforms properly as part of the new agricultural strategy, because "no single program so intimately affects so many millions of our people as land reforms." This is the issue and the question is whether at long last the Prime Minister's exhortations will find their mark.

If past performance of the states in legislating and enforcing reforms is any guide to the future, it would be idle to expect smooth sailing for the Prime Minister's modest but useful package of "should-be-dones." In fact, the split of the ruling Congress Party has increased the political hurdles in state legislatures already dominated by the top class of the farmers. The reforms the party could not achieve in its heyday of undisputed authority are much more difficult of attainment now when the bargaining involved and the price paid become crucial to the governing power. It is possible, however, that the conflict of economic and social necessity and the tide of rising tension may force some politicians to rise above politics. Recent legislative enactments in a few states are new straws in the wind, although enforcing them is something else again, and the skeptics may be pardoned if they prefer to wait and see. A positive outgrowth of the new technology is the Small Farmers' Development Agency, which was created to provide some two million farmers with inputs and services which would enable them to share in the benefits of the new agricultural policy. For the first time in the country's agricultural history, members of this particular class of farmers have been singled out for rehabilitation. But in this instance, too, the guiding spirit behind this measure, Mr. B. Venkatappiah, noted that "the Agency will be virtually inoperative in various sectors . . . unless a number of measures are first undertaken . . . in regard to land records and land reforms."

India is not in a position to endow all or most of its frustrated small farmers, tenants and agricultural laborers with suitable means to share in the agricultural New Deal. In the ultimate analysis, the answer lies in the rapid growth of the entire economy *and* a high rate of employment. But to the extent that this lies in the distant future, India, and more particularly the states of India, could, if they so politically willed, see the present as an opportunity to remedy the worst features of rural inequities, thereby extending also the scope of the new technology. It must be reiterated that the issue is not one of solving all or most of the problems but of obtaining the minimum of security to mitigate the bias against institutional change and point the way to interdependence between technology and socioeconomic reform. In practical terms, it would mean providing a large number of farmers willing to innovate with the wherewithal to dig a well, buy fertilizer, obtain credit. This is part of "distributive justice" complementary with the need of growth, factors which cannot be looked at in isolation. Even failing this, an "explosion in the country"—in the sense of peasant rebellion and chaos—is unlikely, for the kind of poverty that wouldn't be tolerated in many another country is still tolerated in India. On the other hand, it cannot be doubted that the festering existing tensions will grow apace, and an agricultural revolution geared only to new techniques and higher productivity, a model extolled by most students of economic development, will unwittingly contribute to that very end.

Whether events will belie this gloomy assessment remains to be seen. But this much may be ventured. While on the face of it a confrontation between progress and poverty may be inevitable, poverty itself is not an immutable Indian condition laid down for ever from on high. Is it not just possible that, in order for India to maintain social peace and provide a measure of economic contentment, at the critical moment the worm may turn after all, and the miracles of the new technology will find the congenial company of political will and ensuing policies and actions bent on a steadfast attack on rural poverty?

Foreign Aid:
A Report on the Reports

WILLARD L. THORP

WILLARD L. THORP *is professor emeritus of economics at Amherst College.*

One of the most important resources available to a nation in the process of industrializing is financial capital. Capital is required not only for factory equipment, but, as described in the previous readings, is also needed in large quantities for agriculture and to build a national "infrastructure" — roads, transportation, communications, power, and irrigation networks — so necessary for both industry and agriculture. The predicament of today's poorer countries contrasts with the experience of the West which industrialized during a period when large international financial resources were available at low interest. Much has been written recently on the question of foreign aid. Thorp analyses several of the more influential studies, and discusses the political difficulties facing large transfers of capital to the economically less developed areas of the world.

The phrase "foreign aid" has been used to cover many activities— missionary enterprises, disaster relief, general postwar rehabilitation, aid to refugees, defense support, market expansion, foreign investment, political intervention, cultural extension and multilateralism. However, with the breakup of empires and the acceptance of the relatively new concept of government responsibility for social and economic conditions, aid has become focused on the development of the less developed world.

At first, there was full confidence that this could easily be done. Since there already were advanced countries, all that was needed was to follow in their footsteps. And the extraordinary success of that fortunate improvisation, the Marshall Plan, was also a source of optimism. But where the Marshall Plan involved the rehabilitation of societies already modernized, a repair job rather than a transformation, the less developed countries started off with few of the essential requirements for a modern society. Nor

Reprinted by permission from *Foreign Affairs,* 48(3): 561–73, April 1970. Copyright © Council on Foreign Relations, Inc.

were they homogeneous but large and small, new and old, far and near, rich and poor in physical resources. They differed in traditions, religions, languages, unity and character of leadership. Some already were in the process of changing while others had hardly started.

Both the League of Nations and the United Nations had procedures for a temporary, tutelary status to deal with situations where preparation was needed between the colonial condition and full independence. However, after World War II, with India as the exemplar, the insistence on instant independence in colony after colony was so strong that almost all skipped any transitional stage. And they wanted to parallel the sudden political change with a similar social and economic mutation.

Nor were the developed countries much better prepared for giving assistance. There existed no body of recorded experience and knowledge to provide answers to the obvious questions of how, where, how much, and on what terms, or to the more subtle problems created by national sensitivities and pride of sovereignty and by uncertainties about the development process itself. Aside from anthropologists, social scientists had paid little attention to the problems of less developed areas. And the colonial powers were equally at a loss. They had considered their main function to be preserving order rather than inducing widespread change.

During the forties and fifties, foreign aid was regarded as a temporary phenomenon. The metropolitan powers often agreed to give assistance to the newly independent for a few years. The initial Common Market agreement with former colonies was for five years. And in the United States, not only has the central foreign aid legislation always been of one-year duration, but in extending the Mutual Security Act in 1953 Congress stipulated that economic aid was to end within 24 months and military aid within 36. That particular death sentence, however, was commuted and the early years of the sixties saw economic assistance at much higher levels for nearly all supplier countries. Under United States leadership, they formed the Development Assistance Committee in 1961, agreeing "to secure an expansion of the aggregate volume of resources made available to less-developed countries and to improve their effectiveness."

II

The last twenty years have greatly increased the awareness of the difficulties of speeding up the growth process in the less developed countries. The disappointment of exaggerated expectations has led to a sense of frustration in many quarters. Aid itself has been increasingly challenged as ineffective and unjustified. As a consequence, a number of full-scale appraisals of foreign aid have recently been appearing.

The most comprehensive examination is that by the Commission on International Development, sponsored by the World Bank and headed by Lester B. Pearson. The Commission assembled a staff of experts and held regional meetings with some 70 governments to assess the results of 20 years of assistance and offer policies for the future. Its report was published in September 1969. There is also the report of the U.N. Committee for Development Planning, a group of experts with Professor Jan Tinbergen as chairman, which has been working on guidelines for the Second United Nations Development Decade. Supplementing these overall reviews is a study of the U.N. Development System carried out by Sir Robert Jackson at the request of the Administrator of the U.N. Development Programme.

Since its initiation, the U.S. program has been reviewed by at least a dozen official groups. The President's General Advisory Committee on Foreign Assistance Problems (James A. Perkins, Chairman) addressed a series of recommendations to the new administration in October 1968. President Nixon on September 24, 1969, appointed a Presidential Task Force on International Development (Rudolph A. Peterson, Chairman) to develop "a new U.S. approach to aid for the 1970's." The Rockefeller Presidential Mission for the Western Hemisphere submitted its report August 30, 1969 and it was released to the public on November 10, 1969. This should be read in connection with another report—the Latin American Consensus of Viña del Mar, which discusses Western Hemisphere coöperation.

A number of independent studies were made by private groups in 1969. Perhaps the most comprehensive are those of the National Planning Association, "A New Conception of U.S. Foreign Aid," March 1969, and by the Committee for Economic Development (CED), "Assisting Development in Low-Income Countries: Priorities for U.S. Government Policy," September 1969. Each of these reports was the result of initial staff work revised and approved by committees of businessmen and scholars.

These studies vary considerably in emphasis, but they all are reports of progress and agendas of unfinished business. They stress the immense magnitude of the problems of development, the interaction of economic, social and political change, and the diversity of experience and achievement. Taken out of context, their frank criticisms of past procedure and policies might be regarded as throwing doubt on the whole enterprise, but the authors would be the first to deny any such conclusion. Their deep concern for the needs of the less developed countries has led them to seek ways of increasing the effectiveness of the efforts of the less developed countries themselves and of the aid provided by the richer nations. The talk is not of withdrawing but of reorganizing and revitalizing.

III

As to why foreign aid should be provided, only the Rockefeller Report gives much weight to cold-war considerations. In general, the others present plural objectives, including economic, cultural, social and moral concerns as well as security interests. The Pearson Commission paraphrases President Kennedy's dictum by declaring "that it is only right for those who have, to share with those who have not," and supports the moral argument with a discussion of the increasing interdependence of the world community. "If we wish the world to be secure and prosperous, we must show a common concern for the common problems of all peoples." The rich will benefit from the greater availability of resources, expansion of trade and more friendly political relationships.

The President's Advisory Committee, in addition to stressing humanitarian considerations, maintains that more rapid material progress in less developed countries will lower tensions caused by hunger and other misery and reduce the risk that violent political instability will disturb world peace. Development efforts will direct energy to constructive activities rather than international grievances and adventures. Joint efforts by advanced and developing countries provide opportunities for more contact and improved understanding of each other's interests. Finally, the Committee points out the danger of ignoring the frustrations of poverty abroad as well as at home.

All the reports make it clear that rapid growth will not necessarily win friends or insure peace and stability in the less developed world. However, profound changes in these countries are inevitable, and, as the CED report puts it, "the long-term political rationale for aid . . . rests on the calculated risk that accelerating the modernization process, and reducing the sacrifice required to achieve it, will enhance the odds in favor of an earlier evolution of responsible and independent states." Creation of a sense of common purpose is an important instrument of foreign policy. And since foreign policy is a form of national expression, the American image of itself as generous, peace-loving, and all for the underdog requires the demonstration of these characteristics beyond national boundaries.

The reports deal in various ways with specific criticisms by arguing that the domestic cost is small compared with the possible gain in reduced world tension; the effect on the balance of payments is very limited; there is no evidence that economic aid leads to military entanglement; the evolution of procedures has made assistance more and more effective; and the cases of corruption and mismanagement are relatively few. As to the criticism that aid has failed to win friends and influence peoples, all the reviewers agree that assistance should be primarily directed at development, and not at short-run political or economic objectives.

Thus, the stated objectives range from the simple purpose of reducing hunger, disease, ignorance and poverty to economic, cultural and social benefits—the desire to help channel change toward higher living standards, more open and liberal societies and a stronger world community.

IV

While the reports emphasize difficulties and obstacles, they tend to be basically optimistic about the possibilities; they point out that extraordinary progress is being made by the two-thirds of the world's people who are struggling with post-colonial instability, racial bitterness, ignorance and massive poverty, and assert that the prospects for their further development are brighter than ever because of the improved performance of both donors and receivers of aid. In fact, the U.N. Committee for Development Planning would step up the economic growth target from the annual rate of 5 per cent set for the sixties to 6–7 per cent for the seventies. To be sure, the overall percentage figure creates too favorable an impression—due to the cases where high growth rates have resulted from circumstances which are not likely to be generalized—Libya, Korea, Taiwan, Israel, Mexico and Iran.

In fact, many unfortunately fell below the 5 per cent rate, and per capita progress was much lower.

The reports discount the use of simple growth rates as a measure of progress, pointing out that development is a matter of quality as well as quantity and involves the building of institutions necessary for the future, such as expanded educational systems. To be sure, they admit social change is not easy since it requires altering established traditions and institutions. And political change raises the specter of external interference in the most sensitive area.

While the reports emphasize social needs, especially with respect to population and its growing concentration in cities, they do not give enough weight to the political problems and uncertainties in the less developed countries. They recognize the key position played by governments and talk about the importance of effective planning, policies and performance. But they pay little attention to the disintegrating influence on the political structure of tribalism, religion, language or rigid class distinctions. Likewise, the specter of massive unemployment is kept in the wings.

It is a common criticism that foreign assistance has failed to set social and political objectives, although that was the central idea of the Alliance for Progress, which endorsed not only economic and educational development but agrarian and tax reforms. Probably these sectors have not been stressed because of the problems involved in trying to influence them from the outside. However, foreign aid can contribute readily to economic change through technical assistance and capital flows, and the economy is not isolated from society. Roads and electric power and education are great revolutionary forces. Feudal systems were built on isolation and ignorance. Social and political change is the inevitable consequence of economic expansion.

No one can predict the form of the institutions which will finally emerge but our ability to influence the patterns of the future depends in large part upon the aid relationship. In the early years of aid, most of the less developed countries had great expectations but were not ready to plan and carry out a development program. Often the requirements for infrastructure such as roads, power, schools, health facilities and civil service were so obvious that the problem was less one of planning than of mobilization. At that time, the international and national agencies played a very active role.

The reports are opposed to any such paternalistic or tutorial position. The word appearing most often is "partnership," although even this is probably too strong. The infancy of the 70 or more new nations is rapidly disappearing into the past. They not only are capable of assuming greater responsibility for shaping their own development but it is inevitable that they will do so, a point stressed particularly by the National Planning Association Report. To be sure, they were part of a larger world and they have important needs that must be supplied from outside, but their social and economic development cannot be imported. It will be the result of their policies and the way they organize and use their own resources. "Assistance" is the right word, for much can be done from outside to help in the process, but the influence and importance of foreign countries are limited.

It follows that one must not be surprised when the less developed countries move in directions which are contrary to Western experience—and this may be the course of wisdom for them.

This does not mean that the reviewers favor handing over assistance funds nonchalantly. They recommend that each recipient and its suppliers work closely together so that domestic policies and foreign assistance can be fully coördinated. The U.N. Committee for Development Planning proposes that both developed and less developed countries make commitments as to what they propose to do, and that a review and evaluation procedure be established to keep track of performance.

One way of reducing the national element in the aid relationship is to increase the flow through multilateral institutions. This receives universal support, though with a caveat by Jackson as to their present capacity. The Pearson Report calls for 20 per cent of the official flow from donor countries to go to the multilateral agencies, especially urging the expansion of IDA because of its soft lending. The Pearson formula for total volume combined with this recommendation would increase contributions to international agencies from the $618 million average for 1966–1968 to $3.2 billion in 1975. In addition, some of the agencies would raise additional funds in private markets. The President's General Advisory Committee urges increased contributions as rapidly as the managements can expand their competence, but would want other countries also to step up their contributions. Rockefeller urges the shifting of much of the policy responsibility to various regional organizations. In addition to expansion in lending activity, it is generally felt that the World Bank and IMF should provide more coördination to the assistance given to individual countries through consortia and consultative groups.

The Jackson Report deals with the capacity of the United Nations Development System. While stressing the importance of the work being done, particularly technical assistance and pre-investment activity, the author suggests that it needs stronger central control, that planning must be focused on the individual country, and that an improved organization could make an exceptional contribution, given substantially more money and sufficient management talent and supporting manpower.

V

The reports show surprising agreement on development strategy. Family-planning programs, while limited in their foreign requirements, would probably top the list, followed closely by agriculture and by education and vocational training. Of special interest is the possible use of aid to backstop a desirable national program, say of tariff reduction or exchange adjustment or land reform, where the local government recognizes the need for action but is dependent on technical help or financial underwriting.

Technical assistance is emphasized, though less is said, except by Jackson, about the problems of manpower and effective operation. In early 1969 a report was issued by a Task Force of the National Association of State Universities and Land-Grant Colleges, drawing on their own experience in developmental assistance and emphasizing the importance of technical assistance in human resource development and institution-building, as well as the need for a much greater research effort.

The reports dwell extensively on the impediments of procedural encumbrances and unrelated policy restrictions, including: requirements for expenditure in the aid-supplying country (tied aid), freight rates and shipping restrictions, unrelated policy positions by the recipient (expropriation, fishing rights, nonrecognition of this or that country), the use of engineers or other specialists from the supplying country, and elaborate inspection procedures. While each requirement may seem reasonable, they often increase the administrative and annoyance costs and make aid appear to be a payment on account. Tying is particularly criticized for reducing the area of choice and increasing the cost of aid programs. On this subject, the Pearson Commission makes an interesting suggestion for parallel untying of aid by donors in such a way as to leave the balance of payments of each virtually unaffected.

There is also considerable criticism of the gradual shift from grants to loans. In 1968 about one-half of the official commitments were either outright grants or loans with payment to be made in local currency, which would be used again in the country for development purposes. The regular loans vary greatly in their terms, but it is estimated that in total they are sufficiently below capital market terms so that they can be regarded as about half grant and half loan. The troublesome debt-service situation is aggravated by the fact that there is a large and growing volume of high-cost export credits and payments related to private capital flows. To be sure, the resources which the loans provided have been in use and may have added to the foreign exchange available for debt service. Nevertheless, the backflow may create a transfer problem. In general, the experts recommend softer loans and earlier efforts to deal with situations which may require debt relief.

The problem of the wide variety of expanded requirements and payments to outside countries which development requires is never put in its full perspective. To be sure, recommendations for the expansion of trade are common but they are usually expressed in terms of substituting trade for aid. In fact, added means of payment are required not only for growing debt service but also for increased supplies of non-indigenous raw materials, spare parts, more varied technical advice, increasing representation costs abroad, and growing import demands resulting from rising consumer incomes.

The trade recommendations are directed largely at the richer countries, urging them to reduce as soon as possible tariffs and excise taxes on possible imports from less developed countries. Less developed countries are also advised to extend tariff concessions to each other. The idea of preferential tariffs for less developed countries, as distinct from broader most-favored-nation cuts, was put forward most strongly in the Rockefeller Report, where it was recommended that the United States should lower tariffs to the less developed countries of Latin America if it could not obtain agreement with the European importers to give more general preferences.

VI

With respect to volume of foreign aid, the most frequent recommendation is for each supplier to bring its aid at least to the U.N. target of one per cent of gross national product. Pearson and the CED set 1975 as the goal, while the U.N. Committee for Development Planning prefers 1972. CED remarks "that the proposition that the United States can afford a substantially larger aid program cannot be reasonably doubted." The President's Advisory Committee proposes a goal to be reached in 1973 of one per cent of national income, which is about 20 per cent smaller than GNP.

No one is entirely satisfied with this target, especially since it disregards quality (for example, the proportion of grants) and makes no allowance for the principle of progressive taxation, whereby the richer countries would make a relatively larger contribution. Since it combines official and private flows, Pearson proposes as a supplemental target that official aid shall be .70 per cent of GNP by 1975 or at latest 1980.

The OECD Secretariat has made an estimate of the probable size of this target for official aid. Allowing for growth in GNP, the .70 per cent figure in 1975 would be $16.3 billion. To reach their individual goals, seven countries would merely have to maintain the rate at which their aid was increased from 1964 to 1968—Canada, Denmark, Italy, Japan, Netherlands, Norway and Sweden. For the four largest, the annual rate of increase would have to be: United States, 13.8 per cent; United Kingdom, 12.5 per cent; Germany, 12.0 per cent; France, 5.6 per cent.

While recommending "that greater and more assured resources be made available to the U.S. foreign aid agency," the National Planning Association concentrated its thinking on restructuring the aid effort because it sees little prospect of a substantial increase in appropriations. The Rockefeller Report makes no comment as to the volume of aid but proposes a number of procedural changes to increase its effectiveness.

Suggestions for increasing the official volume other than through direct appropriation include applying part of the new SDR purchasing power to this purpose, subsidizing interest payments so that high-cost private borrowing can be turned into low-cost lending, and setting up special arrangements for offsetting depressed primary export earnings. However, the most usual approach is to seek the further expansion of private investment. Its value lies not only in providing capital, but in the technical and management skills which are part of the investment process.

While it is recognized that private aid will not replace official aid for infrastructure purposes, and that its distribution among countries is related more to resource availability than development objectives, the process of growth inevitably opens up increasing opportunities for private foreign investment. The problem is how to do it, since the carrot must be provided by the less developed country and private investment depends upon private decisions. The source government can stop private flows but cannot turn them on. The most that can be done by government is to make the process more attractive.

In late 1968 the International Private Investment Advisory Council reported to AID on ways and means to increase the flow of private investment. Its central proposal was the organization of an overseas private enterprise development corporation funded by the U.S. Government. The President presented the proposal in somewhat limited form to the Congress, which has approved an Overseas Private Investment Corporation (OPIC) with a mixed board of public officials and private businessmen, a proposal strongly endorsed also by Rockefeller. It will take over the existing insurance and guarantee programs and have the debt service on AID loans plus some newly appropriated funds to invest in private projects.

VII

A favorite exercise of American systems analysts is to propose some scheme of reorganization. Rockefeller suggested the transfer of aid programs to the Executive office and much more coöperative decision-making by CIAP. The President's General Advisory Committee advocated the replacement of AID by the Development Coöperation Fund, the transfer of military assistance to the Defense Department budget, and an overseas investment corporation to promote private foreign investment. The National Association of State Universities and Land-Grant Colleges proposed the establishment of a quasi-autonomous group for technical assistance. The Congress has recently authorized the establishment of an Inter-American Social Development Institute for technical assistance to Latin America through private channels.

So far as the United States is concerned, these organizational rearrangements do not add new functions, though changed and fresh personnel might bring imaginative and energetic activity into old patterns. Actually, most of the suggestions run counter to general expert opinion that closer coördination is needed rather than fragmentation. However, there are two new proposals which may have a considerable positive effect: one is some reduction in the exhaustive procedure of annual authorization legislation; the second is the provision of more of the assistance through funding arrangements not requiring annual appropriations.

Reorganization is not only an American phenomenon. The Pearson Commission calls for strengthening the U.N. machinery for coördination on an individual country basis, and for a centralized means of reviewing development policies in all fields—aid, trade, monetary policy and private capital movements. It stresses the need for some means of making reasonably authoritative estimates of development objectives and aid requirements, of assessing regularly the performance of the less developed countries, and of reviewing donor aid policies and programs. The fact is that on each subject listed, progress has been made in the last decade. The greatest advance in coördination is being made by the less developed countries themselves as they strengthen their administrative structures and their civil services. Coordination is an attractive concept, but the learning process is not yet complete and there is much to be said for multiple participation and responsibility.

VIII

One can find books and articles which are hostile to foreign aid but most experts on the subject give it strong support. The reports described above generally conclude that, broadly speaking, substantial progress is being made, that the productive capacity of developing countries has increased significantly, that much has been learned so that both developed and less developed countries have improved their performance and that the record justifies an even greater effort in the future. To be sure, the experts make many suggestions for improvement, a large number of which are widely recognized and often already are being put into effect. The chief actions recommended for the developed countries are that they regard the objective as development and not immediate economic or political reward, that they increase substantially the flow of technical assistance and financial resources on softer terms, and that they open up their markets to exports from less developed countries.

In startling contrast to this picture of foreign aid is that painted by the U.S. Congress, where aid is seen as obsolete, outmoded and unrealistic, mindless, a boondoggle, a giveaway by Uncle Santa Claus, and a bureaucratic maze beyond comprehension, consisting of waste, frauds, sham, friends lost, enemies made and hopes dashed. To be sure, some defend the program with words of praise, but the proof of the matter is that the appropriation for economic assistance, not including amounts for the Food for Freedom program or the Export-Import Bank, reached a post-Marshall Plan high level in the early '60s but has dropped steadily since 1964–1965.

It is important to make some distinction between the attitudes of the executive and legislative branches of the government. While some Presidents have given higher priority to foreign aid than others, they have all declared its significance in messages to Congress. However, recently the recommendations by the President have been less year after year until President Nixon without apology described his recommendation for 1969–1970 as "the lowest proposed since the program began." The shrinking recommendations have been received by Congress without applause, then cut substantially and enacted reluctantly.

Since 1965, the proposals for foreign aid put forward by the President have met with more and more difficulty. In 1968, long before the program reached the floor of the Congress, it was common talk that the aid program was in trouble. The debate that year concerning the authorization did not begin until July. As always, there was considerable talk about rat-holes, dictatorships, corruption, balance of payments, the threats of communism, the brotherhood of man, India, and the responsibilities of global leadership. However, a new emphasis was evident. By July, the size of the 1967–1968 budget deficit stirred Cassandras in and out of government to predict imminent financial disaster. At the same time, interest in foreign affairs other than defense fell very low on a list of priorities featuring rising violence in the cities, lagging development in education, new health commitments and the realization that poverty existed at home. And pent-up dismay over the Vietnam situation found an outlet in attacking foreign aid.

Although Committee hearings were held earlier in 1969, the authorization debate did not begin until November and final action was taken December 19. The appropriation was taken up immediately but, despite Senator McGee's appeal to the Senate that "we hold our noses and adopt the conference report," it was rejected just before the Christmas adjournment because of disagreement over the inclusion of $54.5 million for Taiwan in the military assistance title of the bill.

It was finally agreed to eliminate this item, and the appropriations for 1969–70 were $1,462 million for economic aid and $350 million for military assistance, compared with $1,381 million and $375 million for 1968–69. These appropriations for the last two fiscal years, namely, $1,756 million for 1968–69 and $1,812 million for 1969–70, are less than half the amounts appropriated for the first three years of the '60s, which averaged $4,080 million. These are the figures which best indicate the attitude of Congress, although total foreign aid disbursements include funds for the Food for Freedom program, the Export-Import Bank, the Peace Corps and special appropriations for international agencies.

The 1969 debates were more limited than usual, most Congressmen evidently feeling that they were considering an interim proposal, with President Nixon yet to come forward with a really revised program. More time was devoted to the question of whether or not to earmark military assistance to South Korea and Taiwan and to certain special aids to Israel ($20 million for a prototype desalting plant and $5 million for Hadassah's health work in Israel) than to any basic policy issues. Congress did establish the Inter-American Social Development Institute "to stimulate people-to-people channels for aid" and the Overseas Private Investment Corporation. More important is that the authorization legislation was made to apply for two years. This was justified on the basis of the difficulty of approving a completely new aid program when the Peterson Report was not yet completed and the coming year included an election campaign. Some supported the idea because it would hold the program to its present low level at least for the duration of the present Congress.

IX

Clearly there is a wide gap between the judgment of the experts and the action of the Congress on foreign aid. There are a number of reasons for this. In the first place, the problem appears to each in quite a different perspective. The concern of the expert is focused on development. He examines it in terms of whether it is going well or badly. He seeks ways of accelerating the process by improving the performance of the less developed countries and the effectiveness of the aid from the developed countries. He feels that this endeavor is much more important than many items for which public funds are spent, but does not endeavor to establish specific priorities.

To the legislator, priorities are all important. Foreign aid is basically a budgetary problem, competing with all the other claimants. If he looks to the polls for guidance, he finds foreign aid far below such domestic interests as education, roads and health. But the polls are too simple and represent impressionistic reactions to undefined programs and inadequate information. A decision might be easier if it were possible to say that money saved here would be used there, but the appropriations procedure does not work that way. To be sure, a few members of Congress know a great deal about the subject, and the related committees usually hold several days of hearings. But in the last analysis, the pressure of immediate domestic needs is paramount. To be sure, the public can influence the situation as it did in connection with the enactment of President Truman's Point Four, or a President can shift the balance as President Kennedy did in 1961. But, much of the time, so far as the Congress is concerned, foreign aid is a political orphan.

The gap between expert and legislator is widened by differences in the source and kind of information to which each is exposed. The expert is most often someone who has had a direct connection with the development process. He knows the complexity of the problem through the diversity of his own experience. Aid matters to him.

The legislator is beset by hundreds of issues affecting government action on which he must record his judgment. He is likely to regard the experts in the executive branch of the government as prejudiced witnesses. He assumes that the proposed program has been padded to allow for Congressional cuts. And as far as public information is concerned, he, like the public at large, is the victim of the general principle that bad news drives out good. The vicissitudes of India's Congress Party are followed much more closely in the news than its extraordinary progress in family planning or agricultural yields. And the misbehavior in Antwerp of four persons on the AID payroll is more newsworthy than the proper performance of all the rest.

Sometimes the difficulty is that of the incomplete picture. The legislator and the public might be less disturbed by cocktail glasses sent to a Caribbean country if they knew that it was a tourist hotel which was being equipped. In the 1969 debates, several Congressmen were upset that the United States had borrowed $135 million from Thailand, Korea and Taiwan yet nevertheless was giving them aid. The missing piece in that picture puzzle is that these countries were substituting U.S. bonds for other assets in their monetary reserves, an objective which we have pursued for some years with many countries.

Another form of information which has quite a different impact on the two groups is the comparison of the U.S. program with that of other countries. The expert views development assistance as a common effort in which all the rich countries should participate. One of his interests is the comparative performance of aid donors as well as that of the recipients. He is impressed that, among the 16 members of the Development Assistance Committee, the United States ranked thirteenth in 1968 in terms of its public and private foreign aid disbursements when measured as a per cent of gross national product (0.65 per cent of GNP, as compared with 0.92 per cent of GNP for all other DAC members) and eighth if only official flows were considered. France and the United Kingdom, both also beset by inflation and international balance-of-payments problems, have nevertheless scheduled future increases in foreign aid. And Germany, by doubling her foreign aid in the last two years, has moved into second place in total volume.

The member of Congress is sure that the United States is really number one. If others seem relatively higher, it is because they have some special selfish interest, or perhaps the statistics are open to challenge. But in any event, in his view this is not a contest among countries, but among interests in and of the United States.

The expert and legislator also have differing attitudes toward foreign relations and foreign policy. The expert sees the aid process as one in which various countries are working together coöperatively and tending to reduce their hostilities in the process. He feels that a proper aid relationship will contribute to the easier handling of the many other unrelated problems involved in foreign relations, and that in a world of many countries, a nation whose behavior is ungenerous and inward-looking will have increasing difficulty.

On the other hand, the legislator is worried about excess foreign commitments which may be implied by, and be the consequence of, foreign aid. Senator Fulbright quotes former Secretary Rusk as having said that "one of the reasons justifying our involvement in Vietnam was the aid program; that the aid bill indicated Congress approved of the climate of intervention in that country." The President's Advisory Committee examined this proposition, and found no support for it in the evidence, pointing out that Korea and Vietnam had been security problems from the start, aid to the Dominican Republic had been ended before its revolution, and many other armed conflicts had occurred between or within countries where we had substantial economic assistance programs without our becoming militarily involved.

The Congressman, like the public, does not think of foreign aid as an important instrument of foreign policy. He is likely to feel that the richest and strongest country in the world should have no difficulty in dealing with the small, poor and weak. But national pride is no respecter of size or strength, and international leadership is much more a matter of demonstration, performance and the effective presentation of one's case than of arm-twisting or the distribution of largesse.

It has clearly been a disappointment to members of Congress that foreign aid has not caused countries to follow the position of the United States in international meetings or to behave with gratitude. They are disturbed by aid-recipients engaging in anti-American speeches, expropriating American properties and refusing to support us in Vietnam. The legislator wants specific results to report back to his constituents. He is under the pressure of the immediate and is looking at a one-year appropriation for a program with no permanent authorizing legislation.

This suggests one of the greatest differences—the time dimension. The expert groups do not expect instant development or current subservience, but they are frightened about the future. They fear that the same strains and stresses may develop internationally because of poverty as are now appearing within countries. In the words of the Pearson Report: "Who can now ask where his country will be in a few decades without asking where the world will be?"

It seems clear that there will be little change in the American aid posture until 1971. The President will then present a "new program" to be approved by Congress, presumably taking effect in the fiscal year 1971–1972. But if the expert reports discussed above are to be given any weight, there is no need for revolutionary change. Many improvements are desirable, but what is needed most is a clear commitment to the future—to increase greatly our efforts to assist the poor countries in their struggle against ignorance and poverty. The reorganizing and revitalizing would surely follow. Then the United States would be reflecting its true image.

An Introduction to Neo-Colonialism

JACK WODDIS

JACK WODDIS *is a journalist and writer on political affairs.*

The lack of financial resources is not the only disease which plagues the
economies of poorer countries. Traditional trade practices, in many instances
left over from former colonial relationships, also work to the detriment of
these countries. To build sound, healthy and viable economies, some of these
practices will have to be changed. Woddis gives here a view from the political
left of some of the inequities and barriers which continue to hinder the
development of many nations.

At the centre of all the activities of neo-colonialism lie its economic
policies. These are directed to assisting the profit-making functions of the
big monopolies, to providing the Western powers with the necessary economic power in the new states so as to be able to wield political influence
over the governments there, and to foster a certain growth of capitalism
in order to nourish a class which will co-operate with imperialism and
hinder the advance to socialism. All these three inter-linked objectives lie
behind the economic policies of the Western powers towards the countries
of the Third World.

In a brief introductory study such as this, it is not possible to make a
comprehensive examination of all the economic institutions and forms of
activity practised by Western Governments and Western monopolies in
Africa, Asia and Latin America; nor is it possible to provide a complete
picture of the results of these policies. But certain essential features should
be noted, for they help to throw a light on the general phenomenon of
neo-colonialism.

One of the aims of neo-colonialism is to retain essentially the same
economic relationship between imperialism and the developing countries
as has existed up until now. Some changes will be encouraged in order
to set these countries on to the path of capitalist development. This will

mean some modification in existing structures, a degree of industrial development, some changes in land tenure and agrarian systems—but essentially, in the plans of neo-colonialism, these territories are to remain as producers of raw materials (some degree of processing to be allowed), providing minerals, industrial crops, and foodstuffs for Western industry and commerce, and acting as markets for Western manufactured goods. This pattern of economic relationships, it is hoped, will also serve to protect imperialist political and strategic interests since it will keep the developing countries economically weak and dependent on imperialism. "He who pays the piper calls the tune," and especially is this likely to be so when the particular local government is composed of feudal, bourgeois and petty-bourgeois strata who accept that their countries remain weak semi-capitalist dependencies rather than strike out in the direction of socialism.

Western investments, loans, trading policies and "aid" schemes are all directed to the aim of keeping these territories as primary-producing hinterlands of imperialism which import the bulk of their machinery and manufactured goods from the metropolitan countries.

Private investments, for example, are directed mainly to mining and plantations, which are sources of huge profits for imperialism. Most U.S. investment, for example, points out Richard J. Barber(1), is "in the extractive industries, oil, copper, iron ore, cobalt, rubber, bauxite, uranium and other minerals. . . . Very little capital is invested in manufacturing facilities(2), with the result that the underdeveloped countries fail to acquire the skill necessary for development. As things stand, the emerging nations are caught in a serious bind: they sell their oil and minerals under conditions distinctly favourable to the buyers and purchase finished goods on terms favourable to sellers, with their predicaments aggravated by the ocean shipping conferences which are prone to rig transport rates in a fashion that still further disadvantages the new nations."

Such investments are, of course, immensely profitable for these big firms. In fact, available figures for the United States show that the net income from these investments each year exceeds the net outflow in the form of new investments. For the years 1950 to 1961, the total net direct investment capital outflow from the United States was 13,708 million dollars, while the total income from these investments was 23,204 million dollars(3). A report of the American National Industrial Conference Board, which continues the examination of American overseas investment beyond 1961, states that with the exception of a single year "profits repatriated from direct foreign investments have exceeded the new capital outflows in every year since 1950. In 1964, for example, foreign investments returned $3.6 billion to the U.S.A., compared with a new capital outflow of $2.3 billion—for a net gain to the U.S. of $1.3 billion. In 1965, preliminary Administration figures indicate that the return from the U.S. direct investments was slightly over $4.0 billion compared to about $3.0 billion of fresh capital sent abroad."

These figures in themselves reveal only part of the truth, since they state *net* gains. Gross profits from these investments are now estimated to be running at over $8,000 million a year. Most of this is derived from the more industrially developed countries (Canada, Europe, Australia), but a substantial amount comes from the developing countries. For Britain, too, overseas investments are a lucrative source of profit for the big monopolies. By 1965, overseas interest, profits and dividends amounted to £1,003 million(4). Again, as in the case of the U.S., most of this comes from more developed countries, but a considerable share comes from newly independent ones. For the period 1956–62, it has been estimated that the western monopolies exported over $30,000 million to 56 developing countries, but received back in interest and profits $15,000 million. In other words, in a mere six years they derived benefits equivalent to half of their export.

It is therefore evident that whatever may be the benefits to the developing countries from foreign investments, the benefits to the investors are far greater. In fact, the above figures indicate that foreign investment, far from being a means of assisting developing countries, is mainly a form of transferring wealth from the Third World to the imperialist states, while making it easier for the latter to increase their economic stranglehold on the former.

Foreign loans (usually through State agencies) serve the same purposes. First, there is the question of their direction. Foreign loans, when they go to governments in the Third World, are usually ear-marked for improving the infrastructure—for building roads, ports, airfields. These are not entirely useless for the developing country but the reasons why foreign State loans are used in this way are that such developments require the expenditure of vast sums for which there is not the quick and large return to attract private investors; the construction of such lines of communication is not without its military-strategic purposes; and the new facilities make possible a more speedy and large-scale export of raw materials to the imperialist centres. Thus, the iron ore of Fort Gouraud, Mauretania, of Mount Nimba, Liberia, and of Swaziland, is being heavily exploited by foreign monopolies. In each case, the governments are building railways and port installations to carry away the ore—in the first two cases to the West, in the last-named to Japan. The same has happened with the rich iron ore of Venezuela, which is being exploited by U.S. companies.

A second feature of the loans (and this is often connected with various "aid" schemes), is that the lending country usually stipulates that they must be used neither to construct heavy industry, nor to assist the State sector of the economy at the expense of private enterprise. That the open encouragement of private capitalist development is their aim in the developing countries is not hidden by official circles in the United States. "It is a basic policy of the ICA (International Co-operation Administration) to employ U.S. assistance to aid-receiving countries in such a way as will encourage the private sector of their economy."(5) Secretary of State, Dean Rusk, has himself declared: "We are increasing our efforts to stimulate the private sector in the developing countries and increase the role of U.S. private enterprise in our assistance programme."(6) What this can mean in terms of a particular country is illustrated by Liberia. In the past quarter of a century, the big American rubber firm, Firestone, has taken $160 million worth of rubber out of Liberia; in return the Liberian Government has received a paltry $8 million. The average net profit made by this American company is three times the entire Liberian revenue(7).

The third feature of foreign loans from the West is their high interest rates. The result has been the placing of an impossible burden on the developing countries, to such an extent that many of them can no longer "afford" to "receive" a loan. The high interest charges (often 6 to 7 per cent, and with the capital to be repaid in a relatively short time, too), combined with the conditions under which the loans are made, and their use for undertakings which do not produce large or quick returns, mean that the receiving country has to spend more and more of its gross national product not for its own development but in paying overseas money-lenders for their pound of flesh. World Bank figures for 1962 showed that 71 countries of Asia, Africa and Latin America owed foreign debts to the tune of $27,000 million, on which they paid interest and service charges of $5,000 million. In May, 1963, Mr. George Thomson, Minister for Foreign Affairs in the British Government, said that 28 per cent of British "aid" goes to pay back the interest on former aid. On January 7, 1966, the *Financial Times* wrote that "between now and the early 1970's the under-developed countries as a whole are due to repay from a quarter to a half of their foreign debt. And as this is estimated to be in the region of £9,800 million, it is not difficult to imagine what this is going to mean for countries whose combined annual export earnings do not usually amount to much more than £13,000 million."

The latest figures show quite clearly that the amount pumped out from the underdeveloped countries in profits and interest on loans rises year by year, and steadily becomes an increasing proportion of the total amount of "aid" provided. Thus a recent report of the Secretary General to the United Nations Conference on Trade and Development (UNCTAD) showed that the indebtedness of the developing countries had increased from 9,000 million dollars in 1955 to 33,000 million in 1964. This means that over half of the total international flow of financial "aid" to developing countries is now offset by interest on their debts, and outflow of profits and dividends to the foreign monopoly firms which have invested in their countries.

The furtherance of this trend will put the developing countries in an impossible position. The President of the International Bank for Reconstruction and Development, George D. Woods, has stated that "the under-developed countries as a whole must now devote more than a tenth of their foreign-exchange earnings to debt service . . . These payments are continuing to rise at an accelerating rate, and in a little more than fifteen years, on present form, *would offset the inflow completely*."(8) (Emphasis added.)

Loans from imperialist countries have clearly become a means of placing developing countries further in thrall and making them utterly dependent on Western Governments and banking institutions.

Robbery through profits and interest on loans is not the only burden which the developing countries have to bear. There is a third channel through which the wealth of the developing countries is drained away, and that is the unfair price relationship between the prices of their primary goods exports and the prices of the machinery and manufactured goods which they import from the West.

A special U.N. study in 1949 showed that between 1897 and 1938 the average prices of primary products fell by approximately a third in relation to those of manufactured goods. A further U.N. study (*Economic Problems,* No. 600, June 20, 1959) points out that the increase in prices of industrial goods and the decline in prices of raw materials represented a loss in import capacity for underdeveloped countries of approximately "the equivalent of six years of loans to underdeveloped countries by the International Bank for Reconstruction and Development, on the basis of 1956-7 prices." Pierre Moussa(9) calculates that, on the basis that the export of basic products by the non-industrialised areas of the world amounts to about £25 billion, "an adjustment of prices of 14 per cent would therefore suffice to increase the annual income of the *Tiers-Monde* (Third World) by £3.5 billion, the present total of all public aid to underdeveloped countries." A United Nations Report in 1961 (*International Economic Assistance to the Less Developed Countries*) reveals that between 1953-5 and 1957-9 the loss through the worsening in terms of trade for underdeveloped countries was nearly twice the total amount of public aid funds these countries received.

Between the years 1954-1962, the production and export of cocoa in Nigeria went up by 120 per cent—yet for more than doubling her export of cocoa, Nigeria received only £29 million, as against £30 million in 1954. If she had received in 1962 the same price for her cocoa as she had received in 1954, she would have been paid £70 million—in other words, she was robbed of £41 million. But the robbery does not end there, because during this same period the prices of the machines and the manufactured goods she had to import went up considerably.

Similarly, in 1952, Ghana was being paid £467 a ton for her cocoa. After independence in 1957 she estimated her planned economic development on the assumption that she could rely on the modest price of £200 a ton for several years. In fact, the large western importers had more or less given such an assurance. By 1965, however, the price was down to £85 a ton. This played havoc with Ghana's economic development and was one of the causes of the economic difficulties and discontent which were part of the background to the coup against President Nkrumah.

When one considers that Ghana received £85.5 million in 1954/5 for 210,000 tons of cocoa, compared with only £77 million in 1964/5 for 590,000 tons, and after spending £30 million on fighting cocoa disease (swollen shoot, pests, etc.), one can begin to realise how much the developing countries suffer through the ability of the Western powers to dominate the capitalist market and to manipulate prices in their own favour and to the detriment of the Third World.

These examples indicate the problem of the under-developed countries. Over a period of years the prices of the raw materials—whether minerals or cash crops—tend to fall or to rise very slowly and always to fluctuate, in comparison with the prices of the manufactured goods and especially machinery, which they have to import.

The amount of this robbery is so great that the gap between the western industrialist countries and the countries of the Third World grows wider and wider. For Latin America, according to the International Monetary Fund, the losses resulting from the non-equivalent exchange forced on it by the United States amounted for the period 1951–1962, to some 20,500 million dollars. For Africa, Professor Dumont has noted: "From 1955 to 1959 export prices went down 15 per cent, entailing a loss to tropical Africa of 600 million dollars, twice the annual amount of foreign aid."(10) For all the developing countries it was estimated at the United Nations Conference on Trade and Development in 1965 that, at the present rate of robbery arising from the unequal exchange, the total loss in the year 1970 for these territories would be 7,000 million dollars (£2,800 million).

To present the problem in another way we give the following table:

Unequal Exchange

To buy 1 ton imported steel	1951	1961	Increase
Ghana (lbs cocoa)	208	571	283%
Brazil (lbs coffee)	158	380	240%
Malaya (lbs rubber)	132	441	334%

Thus the amount of steel these countries imported has had to be paid for by increasing quantities of their main exports. This is sheer robbery.

This obvious cause of difficulty for the developing countries and the necessity to provide them with more equitable trading relations has led them to press for fair trading rather than aid. The Western powers have replied by constantly opposing every measure which would make things easier for them.

When the United Nations Conference on Trade and Development took place in Geneva between March and June 1965, 121 countries were present including 77 countries of the Third World. The *Financial Times* commented at that time that Britain, in common with the United States and other Western countries, was "opposed to the Conference from the start."

The voting at the Conference certainly bears this out. The Conference voted on fifteen General Principles and thirteen Special Principles. On issue after issue, we find the overwhelming majority of the countries, including the representatives of Asia, Africa and Latin America, together with the Soviet Union and other socialist countries, sometimes joined by some of the smaller west European countries, voting in favour of progressive resolutions against the opposition or abstention of a handful of countries, mainly the major Western powers and invariably including both the United States and the United Kingdom. A specific proposal dealing with the loss to the developing countries resulting from the unequal price relationship, Special Principle Number 7, urged that "extra measures should be taken to correct falls in prices in primary products in order to protect primary producers from loss of income." Eighty-five countries voted for this proposal, but thirteen voted against, including the United States and Britain.

While the industrially developed Western powers have, over recent years, taken more from the developing countries in profits, in interest on loans and capital repayment, and through the advantages they gain as a result of the unequal price relationships, the amounts allocated by them in various so-called "aid" schemes has steadily declined. The combined total economic aid of the O.E.C.D. countries (thirteen West European countries, together with Canada and the United States) dropped from £2,282 million in 1963 to £2,222 million in 1964.

The United States, which accounts for about 60 per cent of the total, made the biggest cuts. United States official "foreign aid" schemes have dropped from an annual average of £2,000 million in the late 1950's to roughly £1,200 million for the current year—which is about 40 per cent of the current profits from overseas investment. This "aid," includes military assistance to "countries bordering on the Soviet Union and China." This year's projected £1,200 million is to be divided between £880 million for economic purposes, and £327 million for military aid. The latter figure, however, is irrespective of the war in Vietnam and of other military actions. The journal *Fortune* has calculated that the Vietnam war in 1966 was costing the United States £5,480 million a year, and that in the next fiscal year it would be £7,600 million(11). The purposes of American aid, and the extent to which military and political considerations determine its scope and direction, are openly admitted in the United States. Commenting on the report of the Clay Committee which had been appointed by the late President Kennedy to examine U.S. foreign aid, the London *Times* wrote editorially:

> American aid is not just aid, but part of foreign policy. The Committee calculated that 44 per cent of American aid was military and economic support for allied countries bordering the communist bloc, and if the sums spent in Vietnam and Laos are included, the share of total appropriations comes to 72 per cent(12).

In some instances, the proportion of the "aid" which is actually spent on undertakings of economic value to the recipient country is almost negligible, and sometimes completely so. For example, in the case of Laos, a report appearing in the *Tribune des Nations* in 1957, stated "Official American aid to Laos is running at $74 million a year. This aid is apportioned as follows: 7 million dollars for the police and state security organisations, 7 million for the administration, 50 million for an army of 25,000 men and another 10 million for the keep of 250 American advisers and experts." A quick calculation shows that the above items take up the whole of the 74 million dollars. Not a single dollar is left for economic development, neither industrial nor agricultural. What makes it even more damaging—and the same applies generally to other countries receiving this form of "aid"—is that the money is used to prop up political systems which resist the kind of social changes which would enable the people to build up independent economies and overcome their underdevelopment.

There are other ways in which "aid" schemes benefit the donor. Invariably a high proportion of the funds loaned is used on purchases by the recipient from the donor at prices higher than those prevailing on the world market. A report of Dr. Franz Pick, who visited Pakistan in 1963, pointed out that U.S. assistance is a veiled form of what he termed "self-financing," and was, in fact, "a subsidy to the U.S. domestic industry."(13) His study revealed that 90 per cent of the $4,500 million advanced annually by the United States to developing countries is spent in the United States itself. In summarizing this study, the *Financial Times* Karachi correspondent commented: "Certainly, over 90 per cent of the aid that the U.S. offers to Pakistan as loans is ploughed back to the U.S. economy in the form of commodity purchases made in the U.S.—at higher than world market prices—consultants' fees, salaries of experts, freight and insurance charges, and interest and loan servicing charges."(14) In the 1966–7 "aid" programme of the United States, one-third of the 500 million dollars allocated for agriculture is for the purchase of American fertilizers(15).

Thus, in a variety of ways the imperialist powers, even after they no longer wield direct state power in colonial territories, continue to exploit their manpower and resources. In fact, the extent of robbery increases. The newly independent states, standing on shaky legs and taking their first hesitant steps to construct independent and balanced economies, find themselves confronted not solely by one imperialist power as hitherto during the days of colonial rule but by a series of imperialist states, each of which is anxious to obtain the maximum profit. In particular, they are faced with the United States, the most economically powerful and ruthless of the imperialist states.

It is a specific feature of neo-colonialism that, in addition to providing new opportunities for each imperialist power, it also makes possible their *joint* exploitation of the developing countries. The term "collective colonialism" has been used to describe these new joint efforts. Sometimes they take the form of the establishment of giant financial consortia by international monopolies, such as the Iron Ore Company of Mekambo, comprising French, West German, Italian, Dutch, Belgian and American capital, which is operating in Gabon; Miferma (British, French, West German and Italian capital) exploiting the iron ore of Mauretania; Fria (American, British,

French and Swiss capital) exploiting the bauxite of Guinea.

The Development Fund, set up by the European Common Market ostensibly to assist the economic growth of the associated African states, has, in fact, become an obstacle to such advance. In the first five years, 1958–62, some £200 million was allocated to the fund. Spread over fifty million people in the then sixteen associated states, the sum to be spent over five years was sufficient only for a halfpenny a head per day. By December 31, 1962, when the term of the first five years had expired, less than 63 per cent of the funds for development had been spent. Apart from the insufficient amount allocated for development, the control of it is in the hands of the Common Market powers themselves. As a result most of the money goes on infrastructure and agriculture rather than on basic industrialisation. "The Fund authorities spend the money first and foremost in the interests of foreign capital."(16)

When the Upper Volta suggested utilising a portion of the Funds for piping oil and natural gas from the Sahara fields to West Africa, in order to assist African industrial development, this was rejected. The same fate has met almost every other proposal put forward by the associated states. By January 1, 1962, of two hundred projects submitted by the African states, more than half had been rejected outright, and work had begun on only six, totalling about £600,000. For the period 1963 to 1967 the Development Fund will have over £260 million. Nearly one third of this is for agriculture. Over 80 per cent of the funds to be allocated are to be handed out in the form of grants. This may appear, at first sight, to be very generous. But the aim of these funds is that they should be used to pave the way for private enterprise. A statement of the Economic and Social Committee of the European Common Market makes this quite clear:

> In view of the importance of private capital investment for industrialising associated countries and of the difficulty of an exact assessment of the political risks incurred in investing capital in those countries, the committee considers it necessary to offer a security restricted exclusively to political risk . . . Moreover, non-repayable grants should largely be used for the infrastructure so as to attract private capital(17).

By the end of 1965, about 30 per cent of the Fund for the five-year period had been distributed. So once again, it would appear that the substantial sum announced is, in part, intended as a carrot. As *The Economist* has commented cynically: "This kind of money is enough to keep the associated states generally friendly for the present towards Europe." And if they do not remain "friendly," they have been warned what to expect by the Common Market Council of Ministers which, according to the minutes of their meeting on December 18, 1962, declared:

> Should any of the associated countries take measures designed to menace the friendly relations between that country and the EEC or any of their member states, the Council of Ministers will consider the situation and decide what measures should be adopted under the convention(18).

REFERENCES

1. See Barber, R. J. April 30, 1966. *The New Republic.*
2. This was well illustrated in an outstanding paper on Neo-Colonialism read by Ali Yata, General Secretary of the Moroccan Communist Party, at a special seminar on *Africa—National and Social Revolution,* held in Cairo, October 1966. Ali Yata stated that out of 1,629 million dollars invested by the United States in Africa in 1964, only 225 million were for manufacturing industries—and of this total 192 million were invested in the Republic of South Africa. This left only 33 million dollars for the rest of the continent. In other words, only about 2 per cent of U.S. investment in Africa (apart from the industrialised, white-dominated South Africa) went on manufacturing; and in relation to the population this meant only about seven dollars per head per year.
3. Table compiled by Baran and Sweezy from U.S. Department of Commerce. *Survey of current business.* Quoted in Roy A. 1966. *Economics and politics of U.S. foreign aid.* Calcutta, p. 51.

4. *Balance of payments report.* 1966.
5. Krause, W. 1961. *Economic development—underdeveloped world and the American interest.* San Francisco, p. 407.
6. *Department of State bulletin.* April 18, 1966. Washington, D.C.
7. Nkrumah, K. 1965. *Neo-Colonialism, the last stage of imperialism.* London.
8. *Foreign Affairs.* January 1966, pp. 211-12.
9. *Les nations proletaires.* 1960, p. 20.
10. Dumont, R. 1966. *False start in Africa,* London.
11. See *Financial Times.* May 20, 1966.
12. March 28, 1963.
13. See *Financial Times.* July 20, 1965.
14. *Ibid.*
15. *Newsweek.* February 14, 1966.
16. *African trade and development.* September 1962, p. 13
17. *Bulletin of the European Economic Community.* April 1966. Brussels, p. 49.
18. Cited by Brendel, G. 1966. Economic relations of EEC countries to African associations. *German Foreign Policy* no. 5, p. 360.

Herewith Is a Proposal for the Use of American Food: "Triage"

WILLIAM and PAUL PADDOCK

WILLIAM PADDOCK *is an agronomist and former Director of the Iowa State College Guatemala Tropical Research Center, Antigua, Guatemala.*

PAUL PADDOCK *served in the U.S. Foreign Service for 21 years.*

Everyone agrees that the population problem is a serious one. However, there is considerable disagreement on the question of how much time is left to solve this problem before we suffer the worst consequences of it. This selection is typical of writings by those individuals who feel that the present rate of population growth will lead to a famine in the next few years. The Paddocks suggest how the United States should allocate its scarce food resources during that famine period. Paul Ehrlich has called this work "one of the most important books of our age" and has incorporated the concept of "triage" in his own best-seller, *The Population Bomb.*

I now propose a course of action which I believe to be a feasible procedure to achieve maximum benefits from the distribution of our food stocks, both for the United States and for the world as a whole. It is my alternative to an unplanned escalation of food aid, an alternative to an aimless frittering away of this precious food resource. It requires no new law but can be carried out under the existing Food for Peace bill.

To summarize what I have emphasized earlier:

a. The exploding populations in the hungry nations combined with their static agricultures make famines, in many, inevitable. Their future contains a mounting increase of civil tensions, riots and military take-overs as the growing scarcity of food forces prices higher and higher.

b. The timetable of food shortages will vary from nation to nation, but

William and Paul Paddock. *Famine 1975! America's Decision: Who Will Survive.* Little, Brown and Company, pp. 205–29. Copyright © 1967 by William and Paul Paddock. Reprinted by permission. Abridgment by the editors of the present volume.

by 1975 sufficiently serious food crises will have broken out in certain
of the afflicted countries so the problem will be in full view. The Time
of Famines will have begun.

c. The stricken peoples will not be able to pay for all their needed food
imports. Therefore, the hunger in these regions can be alleviated only
through the charity of other nations.

d. Only bulk food can alleviate this hunger, which means grain. Yet the
only grain available in sufficient quantity is wheat, except insofar as
corn is sent to certain parts of Latin America and Africa. Only four
countries produce enough wheat to play a major role in the Time of
Famines, countries I term "The Granary."

e. However, three of these countries, Canada, Australia and Argentina,
have in the past given only small amounts of food as charity to the
hungry nations, and it is unlikely they will do more in the future. They
will sell their stocks on the international market to anyone with cash
in hand. Whatever these three countries may give to the needy will
be only a token gesture.

f. This leaves the United States as the sole hope of the hungry nations.

g. Yet the United States, even if it fully cultivates all its land, even if
it opens every spigot of charity, will not have enough wheat and other
foodstuffs to keep alive all the starving.

Therefore, the United States must decide to which countries it will send
food, to which countries it will not.

THE THESIS OF "TRIAGE"

"Triage" is a term used in military medicine. It is defined as the assigning
of priority of treatment to the wounded brought to a battlefield hospital
in a time of mass casualties and limited medical facilities. The wounded
are divided on the basis of three classifications:

1. Those so seriously wounded they cannot survive regardless of the
treatment given them; call these the "can't-be-saved."

2. Those who can survive without treatment regardless of the pain they
may be suffering; call these the "walking wounded."

3. Those who can be saved by immediate medical care.

The practice of triage is put into effect when the flow of wounded fills
the tents of the battlefield hospitals and when it becomes impossible for
the available medical staff to give even rudimentary care to all. Furthermore,
the number allowed to be sorted into the third group for immediate treatment must be limited by the number of doctors available. The marginal
cases must then also be selected out into the other two groups.

It is a terrible chore for the doctors to classify the helpless wounded in
this fashion, but it is the only way to save the maximum number of lives.
To spend time with the less seriously wounded or with the dying would
mean that many of those who might have lived will die. It would be a misuse
of the available medical help.

Call triage cold-blooded, but it is derived from the hard experience of medical humaneness. In fact, if there is time before the battle starts, the medical staff prepares in advance the facilities to sort out these three groups.

TRIAGE APPLIED TO THE TIME OF FAMINES

President Johnson has proposed "that the United States lead the world in a war against hunger."(1) On the battlefields of this forthcoming war the practice of triage will be vital because choices must be made as to which wounded countries will receive our food.

The leadership in Washington comprises the medical staff. The stricken ones in need of medical attention (American food aid) are the hungry nations. To provide maximum effective treatment the medical staff must divide them into the three classifications of triage:

1. Nations in which the population growth trend has already passed the agricultural potential. This combined with inadequate leadership and other divisive factors make catastrophic disasters inevitable. These nations form the "can't-be-saved" group. To send food to them is to throw sand in the ocean.
2. Nations which have the necessary agricultural resources and/or foreign exchange for the purchase of food from abroad and which therefore will be able to cope with their population growth. They will be only moderately affected by the shortage of food. They are the "walking wounded" and do not require *food* aid in order to survive.
3. Nations in which the imbalance between food and population is great but the *degree* of the imbalance is manageable. Rather, it is manageable in the sense that it can give enough time to allow the local officials to initiate effective birth control practices and to carry forward agricultural research and other forms of development. These countries will have a chance to come through their crises provided careful medical treatment is given, that is, receipt of enough American food and also of other types of assistance.

The stocks of American food will be limited. Therefore, the extent of aid to the nations in the third group must be limited proportionately.

Call it a sieve. Adjust the size of the openings to the amount of food available to be shipped. The smaller the openings (of food), the fewer can be treated.

Unfortunately, it is not that simple. The size of a nation can itself be the determining factor against it or for it. If the available food is sent to the few big, politically important nations, then nothing will be left over for the smaller ones. Or vice versa.

Decisions that take into account all the assorted, highly complex factors affecting differently each nation cannot be made in a vacuum. Political, economic and psychological factors must be considered. This calls for the careful analysis by experts studying the actual food capacity of the U.S. as set against the food needs and *survival capabilities* of the individual nations.

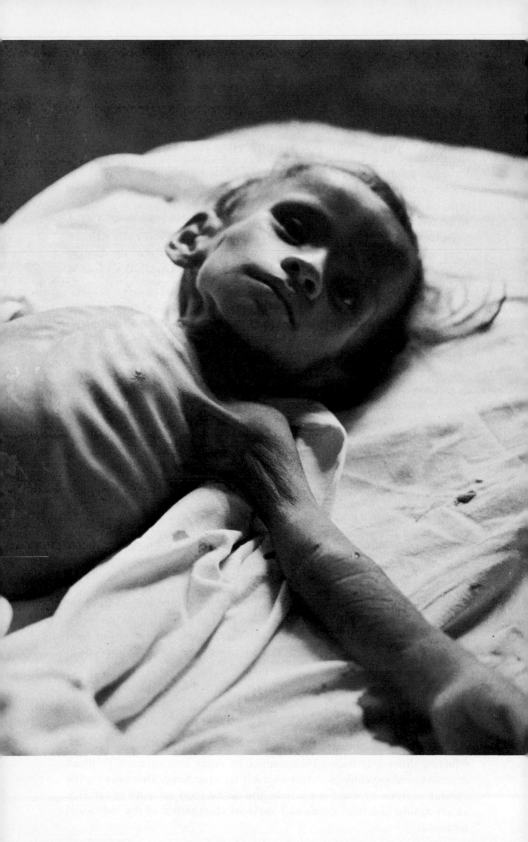

One delusion must be fought. Because each of these nations is hungry it is easy to jump to the conclusion that all internal problems can be solved by sending in enough food. Unfortunately, the affected nations have an assortment of wounds from an assortment of causes in addition to the food shortage. Ceylon has its language division. Sudan has its racial conflict. Bolivia has its class schism. Many have stifling corruption and graft.

In certain cases no amount of food can prevent political and social upheavals and continued, steady degeneration. Food sent to these will by itself not heal the wounds, wounds already festered.

Nor can the national interests of the United States be excluded, whether political, military or economic. American officials when applying triage decisions and shipping out *American* food are surely justified in thinking beyond only the food requirements of the individual hungry nations. They are justified, it seems to me, to consider whether the survival of a specific nation will:

a. help maintain the economic viability and relative prosperity of the United States during the Time of Famines.
b. help maintain the economic stability of the world as a whole.
c. help create a "better" world after the troubles of the Time of Famines have ended.

No nation lives on an island all alone. Each is a part of the whole. Thus, if two nations are equal in their need for American food to increase their chances for eventual self-sufficiency but there is not enough food to send to both, then, assuredly, the one must be chosen which is better able to contribute to the foregoing three goals.

And when overall demand for food in the hungry world catches up with the American capacity to produce food (the Department of Agriculture officially forecasts this will be by 1984 and I maintain it will occur by 1975), then America's own consumption of food will have to be curtailed or altered in order to maintain the same level of food aid. For instance, curtailment of meat. Every pound of grain-fed meat that a person eats takes four to twelve pounds of feed grain. "How much grain-fed meat will the heavy meat eaters in the United States and Europe be willing to forgo in order to feed hungry people thousands of miles away?"(2)

Now is the time to recognize the implications of this. For when such shortages and/or high prices do force the American public to change their diet, it is certain that our citizens will become dead serious about this food, food which they will forgo in order to feed distant foreigners. When this happens, I take for granted that American public opinion will demand that this food be distributed in a manner which will give them their "money's worth." But unless we begin *now* to concentrate our food aid on those who can be saved during the Time of Famines, our future efforts may be ineffective. By the next decade today's savable nations may have passed beyond the point of help.

What will Americans, ten years from now, consider to be their "money's worth"? What will be a legitimate return on the food they are sending to others?

The ultimate answer, I am sure, will be stated in terms of American economic and political aims. Some can criticize this as selfish, as unhumanitarian and as unchristian. Yet the continued stability and relative prosperity of the United States during the coming decades is, surely, the single most important guarantee to insure:

—*that the world as a whole, and especially the selected hungry nations themselves, will survive the Time of Famines without sinking into chaos, and*

—*that the world will evolve into that "better" life which we hope will come to all peoples afterwards; a "better" life (both spiritual and material) is difficult to visualize as coming to fruition without the support of American capital goods which today nearly equal all those possessed by the rest of mankind.*

Therefore, I emphasize the following pertinent aspects which American officials must consider when they make their decisions as to which countries will receive our food:

(1) *Ignore the prospect that if food is withheld from a country it will "go communist."*

If a nation needs food aid to survive, then its political stability does, to a degree, depend upon that food. Like Samson's hair, when the food aid is cut off weakness will result. Assuming that the Cold War with Russia and/or China continues throughout the 1970's at its present heat (and that can be only an assumption), it is hard to see any one of these hungry nations being so vital to the United States that disaster would overwhelm our interests if it does, in fact, "go communist."

(2) *Ignore the short-range political changes in these countries:*

My own guess is that the single greatest weakness of Washington in its conduct of foreign affairs since the last war has been its pusillanimous dashing to and fro, like a mouse in a cage, whenever a government is overthrown by revolution, by assassination or by correct election. Aid is rushed in or pulled out. Diplomatic recognition is quickly given on a silver platter or fitfully held back. Perhaps this is a part of the United States' becoming accustomed to its new role as the dominant world power. Whatever the reason, this has been a major cause in preventing stable foreign policies with a single nation or with a continent. During the Time of Famines revolution and turmoil will be the order of the day in most of the affected countries. To help pull a nation through the Time of Famines Washington itself must remain stable in its policies toward that nation.

(3) *Take into consideration the quality of local leadership.*

In an earlier chapter I posed the question, "In times of stress do people retrogress?" In applying the thesis of triage, that is, in selecting one country but not another to receive American food (and other forms of technical assistance), the quality of a nation's leadership must be taken into account. Without effective leaders the populace will indeed retrogress. Thus, whenever the rare quality of imaginative leadership is found, then surely it is the duty of outsiders, such as the American government, the international organizations and others, to give support in whatever manner can be extended. This support can be in the form of trade benefits or military assistance or whatever. And food—unless the nation is hopelessly in the "can't-be-saved" category or, hopefully, in the "walking wounded."

(4) *Give maximum* NON-FOOD *aid to those nations where we wish short-range political advantages.*

If we do not have enough food to supply a nation or if we have already decided it is a "walking wounded" case, then we still will have at hand the full range of our non-food resources and technical assistance with which to help it. If administered wisely this often ought to be enough to help maintain those leaders and governments whom we wish to stay in power. For instance, we have the large funds of local currencies from the "sale" of our P.L. 480* food and other supplies, i.e., the "funny money."

(5) *Favor nations which have raw materials required by the American and the world economy.*

Some countries, depending on how the Lord scattered, or failed to scatter, His largesse, produce agricultural and mineral materials which have a strategic value in today's industrial economy, while other countries do not. If a choice must be made between two equally deserving hungry nations then, certainly, the importance of keeping production lines open for a key product must be the deciding factor.

(6) *Favor nations which have military value to the United States.*

"Strategic military value" is an elusive and transitory factor amid the kaleidoscope shiftings of international politics. But it cannot be ignored by the decision-makers.

EXAMPLES OF HOW TO APPLY TRIAGE

The clearest way to understand a theory is, of course, to apply it to specific examples. So now I present certain nations most of whom, I am sure, will make strident calls during the coming decade for American food and assistance above the levels they may already be receiving.

To bring home the painful responsibility of the official when he must himself sign the paper that will give one applicant nation priority over another, I provide a blank space where the reader can insert his own considered view of what the decision should be.

Afterwards, I give my own opinion and I recognize that my presentation of each "case" is colored by that opinion. Nevertheless, the adverse facts I state must be faced up to by the American official judging the case; and the local officials anxious to present only their country's good points must refute these same adverse facts.

---

*Public Law 480, passed by Congress in 1954, authorized the donation of surplus food to international relief organizations and the sale of food to needy countries for the nonconvertible currency of those countries, (Eds.)

Haiti

Its population long ago exploded beyond the level of what the nation's resources can provide for a viable economy. There is nothing whatever in sight that can lift up the nation, that can alter the course of anarchy already in force for a century. At one time Haiti was one of the most agriculturally productive regions in the world, but now its fecundity has outstripped the country's resources (432 persons per square mile).(3) Now it is too late for an energetic, nationwide birth control program. (The nation is 90 per cent illiterate and has only one doctor for each 11,000 persons).(4) It is too late for intensive agricultural research efforts. The people are sunk in ignorance and indifference, and the government is entrapped in the tradition of violence.

Can't-be-saved ☐

Walking Wounded ☐

Should Receive Food ☐

Egypt

Its population will double in twenty-three years.(3) A birth control program is being organized, but in no sense is it an all-out effort. Agricultural research and food production are static. All faith is placed in the Aswan Dam, but the production from the new land thereby opened up will be absorbed by the population born during the ten-year construction period of the dam. The area of agricultural land per Egyptian is one-fifth that for each Haitian. Meanwhile, Egypt continues to put almost no effort or money into modernizing its agriculture.(4)

Currently, Egypt has a stable government, but it is anybody's guess what conditions will prevail since Nasser is gone. Certainly, there is no tradition within the people of being able to govern themselves and to solve their own problems—and the blame cannot be laid on the Turkish and British colonialisms.

Today, the latest contract (1966) for P.L. 480 food to Egypt stipulates shipment of 538,000 metric tons over a six-month period.(5) Egypt has been the third largest recipient of American food, loans and grants. The value of this food is, in fact, almost double what Russia has contributed to the Aswan Dam.(6) Egyptian leaders give great publicity to the Russian gift but press the lid on publicity about the food from the United States.

Although Egypt has been, to repeat, the third largest recipient of our food program, Nasser consistently, year after year, did all in his power to abort American policies in the Middle East, the Congo and elsewhere through deliberate acts of subversive plots, alleged attempted assassinations of neighboring leaders friendly to the United States and open, active support of anti-American regimes throughout the area.

In the interplay of international politics there is, of course, the importance of assuring that the Suez Canal is kept open to world shipping. In fact, this seems to be about the only specific point of interest that the United States has within Egypt. If worst comes to worst (that most dire of vague phrases) the Canal could be kept open to world shipping by militarily occupying the canal strip and cordoning it off from the rest of Egypt. In today's political context such action would rightly be considered an example of fantasy; in tomorrow's chaos of the Time of Famines it could be another matter.

The Egyptian problem is, probably, within the capabilities of United States resources. To control a problem of this size, however, would mean to curtail or cancel food shipments to other needy nations. The Egyptians themselves, if current trends remain, will never in the foreseeable future be able to feed themselves or to generate enough foreign exchange with which to buy the food.

Can't-be-saved ☐
Walking Wounded ☐
Should Receive Food ☐

The Gambia

Perhaps no country has such artificial boundaries as The Gambia, either economically or politically. Yet, oddly enough, the population (300,000) and the national economy seem to be in balance with their sliver of land, twenty miles wide and three hundred miles long. It has no more agricultural land per person than does Haiti, but all the land borders on a navigable river.

A few years ago I traveled in a small boat the length of the Gambia River. My chief impression was of the relaxed, full life of the people within the traditions of their culture. Outsiders and also the elite of the capital city can argue that progress in the country is hopeless until those same traditions are thrown aside and replaced with the "modern" life. My only answer is that the Gambians probably will be glad they have not yet progressed into the "modern" life when they see the crises and turmoil of those countries around them which attempted development beyond the base of their resources. The chief problem of The Gambia now is to hold back its population increase and to hold back its capital, Bathurst, to its present size—without it exploding into the usual city slum so typical of other African capitals and thereby overpowering the government with city problems.

With only one doctor for every 16,000 persons and a population 80 per cent illiterate(7), The Gambia will need foreign aid and technical assistance, but should this include an allotment of American food, even the small amount needed for this small nation?

Can't-be-saved ☐
Walking Wounded ☐
Should Receive Food ☐

India

India is the example that cuts across all the political and economic guide rules I have been using for the other nations. Also, more than in any other country, if the United States should today cut off its food aid, or even curtail it, immediate turmoil and possible catastrophe would result.

Today India absorbs like a blotter 25 per cent of the entire American wheat crop. Nearly all of this is sent as P.L. 480 food.

No matter how one may adjust present statistics and allow for future increases in the American wheat crop, for future shipments of rice and corn to India and for a possible increase of India's own production of grains, today's trends show it will be beyond the resources of the United States to keep famine out of India during the 1970's. Indian agriculture is too antiquated. Its present government is too inefficient to inaugurate long-range agricultural development programs. Its population tidal wave is too overwhelming, more than 11,500,000 are added each year to the current half-billion population.(8)

Thus far, the Indian leadership, beginning with Nehru, appears to have botched just about every effort at progress in local food development and population control that has been offered to it. "As one Indian farmer puts it, 'The bureaucrats aren't hungry, so they just won't get excited.' "(9)

Of all the national leaderships the Indian comes close to being the most childish and inefficient and perversely determined to cut the country's economic throat. But, except for a degree of graft, it is not an evil leadership like those of some other nations. It is not looting the country or threatening rapine on its neighbors. It is just childish. There is little reason to believe that future American help will result in a more responsible Indian leadership than our past help has effected.

So the famines will come. Riding alongside will surely be riots and other civil tensions which the central government will be too weak to control.

In retrospect it is hard to see any positive, direct advantage the United States has received from its $6.5 billion of aid to India, other than the negative one of, so far, bolstering a sort of stable nation. Although the vituperative blasts against all things American that the Indian representative used to shout in the United Nations are now muted, the present government continues to work actively against many American policies in the assorted chancelleries of the world. Yet this has done little harm, one way or another, to the United States.

If we cut off the food to India we are not losing a reliable friend. Nor do we gain an enemy able to do us serious hurt.

On the other hand, we do condemn a segment of the human race to disastrous suffering, people who, in the end, may be as worthy to receive our limited food aid as other, perhaps equally neuter, nations.

> Can't-be-saved   ☐
> Walking Wounded   ☐
> Should Receive Food   ☐

Pakistan

On the surface it suffers from the same troubles, the same malaise, as the rest of the undeveloped world. It is indeed a candidate for mass starvation in the 1970's. Its population of 115,000,000—which will double in twenty-five years(10)—makes effective aid from the United States a stupendous job and one which must perforce divert our energies and resources away from many smaller nations.

Birth control programs are not yet intensive, but they have had a firm background in the efforts since 1953 of the Family Planning Association of Pakistan to popularize family planning. Also, since 1958 they have had the strong support of President Ayub Khan who has made them a part of the national development plan and even included his advocacy in his election platform manifesto.(11) This fifteen-year history, combined with Ayub's type of government, may indeed have an effect on the birth rate within the next couple of decades.

Most important of all, Pakistan has a unique asset now working for it: it is one undeveloped country whose top leadership seems to have faced up to the problem of feeding the exploding population. So far, apparently, the effort is concentrated primarily on expanding the wheat production of West Pakistan, thus for the most part letting the rice of East Pakistan and other types of crops remain in their time-worn ruts. Nevertheless, it is so unusual for the key men in an undeveloped country to give full support to even one part of the agriculture that Pakistan is today special. And, of course, success with the wheat crop may spill over and favorably affect the rest of the agriculture.

Nevertheless, despite the optimism of everyone connected with this program, can even maximum success meet the food demands of an additional 115,000,000 persons rolling in on the tide of the next twenty-five years? This wheat may in time be the salvation of West Pakistan, but it is doubtful that East Pakistan will receive similar hope until its own agriculture is accelerated. In fact, the true moment of crisis will come for Pakistan when the one half of the nation retains hope of adequate food but the other half sinks without hope into famine. It is hard to see how West Pakistan, even with the most sincere sacrificing of its own food stocks, can itself transport enough wheat to East Pakistan to save that region, a thousand miles away across a hostile, equally hungry India or three times as far by sea.

Through the years Pakistan has been, next to India, the largest recipient of American aid. Yet the leaders of all parties blithely ignore this in their active opposition to most American international policies and they ignore the omens that their nation must continue to be dependent on this aid.

Politically and militarily Pakistan has value to the United States because of accumulated activities and installations resulting from CENTO and SEATO. Actually, however, it is about as queasy an ally as France is to NATO.

If the United States continues to send P.L. 480 food to this elephant-sized, apathetic "ally," it may be possible to keep East Pakistan quiescent for a decade or so and thus, perhaps, give West Pakistan enough time to press forward birth control and to increase food production in order to prevent at least that part of the nation from foundering. As for East Pakistan it must surely sink into famine unless drastic and comprehensive programs for agriculture are immediately started; this the national leadership, the majority of whose background is in the West, seems unable to initiate.

Although one can say that the saving of a half a loaf, namely West Pakistan, is better than giving up the entire loaf, nevertheless the size of American food shipments, directed to the nation as a whole, would probably have to remain at the present gigantic scale.

Can't-be-saved   ☐
Walking Wounded   ☐
Should Receive Food   ☐

My own opinion as to the triage classification of these sample nations is:

Haiti	Can't-be-saved
Egypt	Can't-be-saved
The Gambia	Walking Wounded
India	Can't-be-saved
Pakistan	Should Receive Food

These examples seem to me to adhere closely to the basic triage divisions for the use of American *food* up to and during the Time of Famines. Those that I say should receive our shipments have within the foreseeable future a valid chance to obtain self-sufficiency in food or, at least, to achieve an important improvement in self-sufficiency. This will be due primarily to their own efforts and resources. They are far enough along with their population control and agricultural research and development programs to hope that they eventually will hold their own. Furthermore, political factors are adequately stabilized to give these programs a chance for success.

But what about the countries which are doing little or nothing to overcome their population growth and static agriculture and yet which are, for some specific reason, vital to the economy of the United States and the rest of the world? I call these "The Exceptions." For example:

Panama

Not only does the United States have a vital interest that the Panama Canal be kept open, but so has the rest of the world. Unlike the Suez Canal, it cannot be isolated from the rest of the country.

Panama's population explosion (one of the world's highest) versus its static agriculture is as serious as that in any Latin American country. This adverse ratio must be resolved before the country can ever achieve tranquillity. Yet so far little is being done. The country is continuing to drift passively along the brink of chaos. The not-so-latent anti-American feeling is all-pervasive. Even though the chief cause of this, the once abrasive American staff of the Panama Canal Company, is now less conspicuous, it is doubtful that the feeling against the U.S. will decrease materially.

Meantime, the cost and logistics of sending food to this miniature nation (1,200,000 population)(12) is minimal and the amount of food required in the decades ahead will not appreciably affect other food aid programs qualifying under triage. Therefore, put Panama on the dole and consider it a form of subsidy for the Canal.

Bolivia

If a nation is fortunate to possess a resource vital to the world's needs, that nation often can market it at a high enough price to buy with the proceeds the amount of food it needs. There are countries, however, where the value of the product, although vital, is not enough to do this.

Venezuela probably throughout this century ought to be able to buy the food it needs from its oil receipts. On the other hand, the world demand for the equally vital tin has failed to keep Bolivia solvent. If, as the Time of Famines approaches, civil unrest cuts off the tin from export to the outside world, should the United States send in the large amount of food necessary to keep the country stable and the flow of tin open?

The population of Bolivia is 3,700,000 but fortunately it is growing at a rate (1.4 per cent per year)(13) even lower than that of the United States. The agriculture of the *altiplano* (where the population is centered) is surely among the most difficult and unrewarding in the world; it is hard to see how even unlimited capital or a large research program, if one is ever started, could produce adequate results there. This puts the future hope of the country in the now sparsely inhabited tropical areas; here, as in the rest of the tropical world, the research must start from scratch in order to bring forth, some day, successful new techniques which, years later, can be put into operation in the area.

In the meantime, the social unrest and the revolutions that have spasmodically disrupted the country for a generation will undoubtedly continue. It is easy to understand and sympathize with the causes of the social tensions, but it is hard to predict how the country can ever get on its feet economically, even with maximum income from tin, until the tropical areas become farmable.

Thus, American food support would be needed far into the future. It would be an open-end obligation once the responsibility is accepted. Yet I am told by officials that the uninterrupted export of the tin is a strategic necessity. Accordingly, I would place this case among the exceptions to receive American food.

IN THE END THE RESPONSIBILITY
LIES WITH AMERICA'S OFFICIALS

The weakness of triage lies in its implementation by a democratic government like that of the United States. The democratic process does not lend
itself to thinking through coldly and logically a complex problem such as
American food versus the world's hungry, trying to formulate a practical
program before the crisis strikes and then sticking with it through several
administrations. The strength of triage is that it satisfies what I assume will
be the demands of:

a. *the humanitarians:* to save the maximum number of lives during the
   Times of Famines.
b. *the patriots:* to safeguard the economic stability of the United States.
c. *the diplomats:* to safeguard the political, economic and strategic interests of the United States on all continents.
d. *the realists:* to keep our goals within the limits of our resources.

Equally important, triage fits existing legislation. It gives a jumping-off
point for the leaders in Washington to begin their analysis of what our
government will do with our foodstuffs that soon will be forthcoming from
the land under the new Food for Peace concept of "turning the farmers
loose." Today's India has alerted one and all to the magnitude of the problem
created by the population explosion in the face of static agriculture.

Washington may dally and shuffle and procrastinate, but the Moment of
Truth will come the morning when the President must make a choice
whether to save India or to save Latin America, when he must sign a piece
of paper to send available food to one of two neighboring countries but
not to the other, though both are equally friendly to the United States, both
equally worthy of help.

Let us hope that before this Moment of Truth arrives there has been wide
discussion of this problem in the press, in church councils, in Congress and
in the departments of the government. The many-faceted problems of the
choices of triage, the most far-reaching problem of the coming generation,
cannot be resolved on the spur of the hour or, worse, on a fluctuating
day-to-day, crisis-to-crisis basis.

This is so because during this discussion in the open forum of a democracy, the following compromises must be reached:

a. The humanitarians must come to realize it will be impossible to save
   everyone, that choices must be made, that logical, thought-out choices
   are themselves the essence of humanitarianism.
b. The patriots must come to realize that the economic stability of the
   United States is weakened, not strengthened, by a policy of isolation-
   ism.
c. The diplomats must come to realize that although the Time of Famines
   will last for several decades it will indeed end some day; and when
   it does end then the interests of the United States will be served best
   by independent friends, not subordinate retainers.

d. The realists must accept the policy of utilizing our resources to the maximum, not the minimum, in behalf of the hope, the quite practical hope, of a "better" world when the Time of Famines gives way to the Next Age.

Finally, everyone—the Bolivians, the Indians, the Gambians, the Zambians, the Trinidadians and, most of all, the Americans—must realize that when a 10,000-ton freighter loaded to the scuppers with Food for Peace wheat sails out of New York or Baltimore or Seattle or Buffalo or Houston a specific component of American wealth is shipped out, wealth in the form of 200 tons of nitrogen, 41 tons of phosphorus and 50 tons of potassium.(14) Multiply these figures by the approximately 14,600 freighter loads shipped out from 1954 to July 1965 and one sees that the portion of our soil's fertility thus lost forever is a significant part of our national resources, resources which we are denying to our children and grandchildren.

Also carried within the freighter is American wealth in the form of the farmers' labor, the depreciation of the tractors, the consumption of the diesel fuel, the use of the transportation system which moved the wheat to the ports and the labor that loaded the ships. The shiploads of food (and currently we are rushing to India 1,000,000 tons a month, or three to four ships *each day*) are not a gift which "has cost nobody nothing." They are as real as the gold in Fort Knox.

When we pour out this wealth we ought to get something in return for it. Let us make certain that what we get from our future shipments is a "better" world for our children. They are the ones who will suffer if we fail to obtain a fair return on this forfeiture of national resources.

Triage would seem to be the most clean-cut method of meeting the crisis. Waste not the food on the "can't-be-saved" and the "walking wounded." Send it to those nations which, having it, can buttress their own resources, their own efforts, and win the fight through to survival.

REFERENCES

1. Johnson, President Lyndon B. Feb. 10, 1966. Message to the 89th Cong.
2. Hobson, K. Aug. 1966. The wheat shortage is here. *Farm Journal*, p. 47.
3. Population reference Bureau. Dec. 1965. *World population data sheet*. Washington, D.C.
4. World Hunger. June 1966. *Fortune*, p. 114.
5. *Food for peace 1964 annual report on Public Law 480*, H. Doc. no. 130–89/1. Mar. 1965. Washington, D.C.: Government Printing Office, p. 102.
6. Pearson, D. June 17, 1966. *Washington Post*.
7. United Nations. 1964. *Statistical year book*.
8. Statistics and Reports Division, Agency for International Development. June 1965. *Selected economic data for the less developed countries*. Washington, D.C.
9. Sklarewitz, N. June 7, 1966. *Wall Street Journal*.
10. See n. 4.
11. Adil, E. In Berelson, B., et al., eds. 1965. *Family planning and population programs*. Chicago: Univ. of Chicago Press, p. 125.
12. See n. 8.
13. See n. 4.
14. Bailey, C. H. 1944. *Constituents of wheat and wheat products*. New York: Reinholt, p. 215. Nitrogen figure obtained from LeRoy Voris, National Academy of Sciences, Washington, D.C.

Population and Food in
East Pakistan

ROGER REVELLE and HAROLD A. THOMAS, JR.

ROGER REVELLE *is Richard Saltonstall Professor of Population Policy at Harvard University and Director of the Harvard Center for Population Studies.*

HAROLD THOMAS *is Gordon McKay Professor of Civil and Sanitary Engineering at Harvard University and an associate of the Harvard Center for Population Studies.*

National demographic and economic statistics—for such variables as population, birth and death rates, degree of urbanization, employment, income, and diet—can give much information on the general quality of life. Even in small countries, however, regional differences can be such as to require significant variations in development policies. Breakdown of the data by region then becomes invaluable in the formulation of suitable policy on food, population, education, urbanization, employment, and industrial and agricultural development. The following study of East Pakistan, a province whose area is approximately equal to that of New York State but with three times the population, shows the importance of this kind of disaggregation in considering the problems faced by a poor country.

The most serious population problem in the world exists in the northeastern region of the Indian sub-continent, comprising the Indian States of North Bengal, Bihar, and Assam, and the Province of East Pakistan. Here, some 175 million human beings now live at a bare subsistence level on 75 million acres of farm land. Their numbers are increasing at between 2.5 and 3.5 per cent per year. If sufficient food can be obtained so that death rates do not rise, there are likely to be 500 million people in this area by the year 2000, even if birth control programs are reasonably successful. This is two and a half times the present population of the United States, with about one-fourth as much cultivated land.

In the following discussion, we shall limit ourselves to East Pakistan, both because the most severe problems exist there, and because the data available to us are more adequate for analysis.

Nearly all of East Pakistan lies on the combined delta of three great rivers —the Ganges, the Brahmaputra, and the Meghna. The first two of these rivers drain an enormous area, mainly in India and China, which is several times larger than all of East Pakistan; the third is fed by the highest rainfall in a large region in the world, that of the hills of Assam. The climate of East Pakistan is warm, and crops can be grown throughout the year, though extensive cloudiness in the monsoon season tends to inhibit photosynthesis.

During the monsoon, the volume of flow of the rivers swells to more than twice the volume of the Mississippi in flood. Up to 100 inches of rain fall within the Province itself, and most of this rainwater remains, undrained, on the land surface. At the same time the southwest monsoon winds cause the sea level in the northern part of the Bay of Bengal to rise 2 to 3 feet(16), greatly slowing the velocity of flow in the main rivers and their distributaries. The swollen, backed-up rivers spill over their banks and flood large areas of the countryside, while other areas are flooded by undrained rainfall. During most years, 30 to 40% of the Province is inundated. The kinds of crops that can be grown are limited by the floods and crop yields are sharply reduced.

After the monsoon season the rivers recede; their flow during February and March is only 5 to 10% of the flood flow. Either supplemental or full irrigation is necessary for crop growth over most of the country from November through April.

The problems of human ecology in East Pakistan are as serious as the physical ones. The average density of population in rural areas is already about 1,300 persons per square mile, and could rise within two decades to 2,500 per square mile. Modern agricultural development could prove to be incompatible with such a crowded rural population, and urbanization on a very large scale would then be necessary. The present urban base is very small; only 6 to 7% of the people now live in cities and towns (Table 9, p. 348). Most of the people are illiterate, and the status of women is low. Small boats powered by sail or by oar are the chief medium of transportation throughout half the year. The pattern of culture can almost be described as an amphibious one. The poverty and dispersed character of the population impose great difficulties on the government in collecting taxes. Ways must be sought to enlist the ability and enterprise of the people themselves in economic and social development for their own future welfare. Among the most important aspects of any development program should be a lowering of present extremely high birth rates as rapidly as possible.

DEMOGRAPHY AND AGRICULTURE

Most of the land in East Pakistan is arable and most of the arable land is cultivated. In twelve out of sixteen Districts in 1960–65 (see Figure 1), the ratio of total land area to net cultivated area was small, ranging from 1.26 to 1.65 (Table 1). In four Districts, Chittagong, Sylhet, Khulna, and Noakhali, there were higher proportions of uncultivated land. Much of the

FIGURE 1

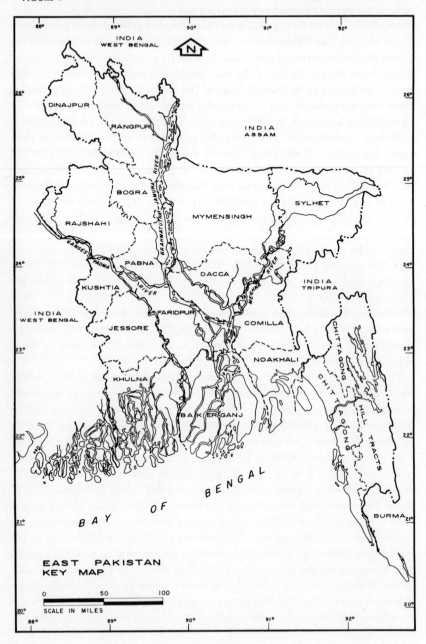

hilly and variable area of District Chittagong is not arable; part of Sylhet consists of a depression in which a lake forms during each monsoon season; a major part of Khulna is covered by the complex of mangrove swamps and forests called the Sunderbans; and considerable areas of Noakhali are apparently too low and marshy to be cultivated. The least developed region of the Province are the Hill Tracts east of Chittagong, which contain less than 0.4% of the population. They will be left out of the following discussion.

There are large differences among the Districts of East Pakistan in population density, agricultural land utilization, rate of population increase, and per capita food production. In five Districts in the central and eastern part of the Province (see Figure 1)—Chittagong, Comilla, Dacca, Noakhali, and Faridpur—there were, in 1961, three to more than five persons per net cultivated acre, an average of 4.25 per acre (Table 2), or 2700 per square mile of cultivated land. The comparable figure for the United States is about 400 persons per square mile of cultivated area. Four Districts on the western edge of the Province—Dinajpur, Rajshahi, Jessore, and Kushtia—averaged only 1.8 persons per net cultivated acre (1160 per square mile of cultivated land). The northern border Districts of Rangpur, Mymensingh, and Sylhet; the southern coastal Districts of Khulna and Barisal; and two Districts on the west bank of the Brahmaputra, Bogra and Pabna, had intermediate population densities of 2.2 to 2.6 persons per net cultivated acre.

The Five Crowded Districts
In the Districts of high population density the intensity of cultivation is also high; multiple cropping is practiced wherever flood conditions allow. On the average, in 1960–65, two crops were grown on each cultivated acre in Comilla and Chittagong, and on 60% to 80% of the cultivated land in Noakhali and Faridpur (Table 1). In Dacca less than 40% of the land was double-cropped, probably because of serious flooding in the south-western part of the District. The average size of farms in these Districts was only 2.25 cultivated acres, ranging from 1.6 to 2.7 acres, and there were 2 to 3 persons per gross cropped acre (Table 2). (The gross cropped acreage is the total number of cultivated acres multiplied by the average number of crops grown per acre.) This was true of the rural parts of these districts as well as of the combined rural and city populations. If the 1961 population of Chittagong City is subtracted from that of District Chittagong, the number of persons per gross cropped acre is 2.6. Similarly, subtracting the populations of the cities of Dacca and Narayanganj from that of District Dacca gives 2.7 persons per gross cropped acre in rural areas.

The 1961 census in these five densely populated Districts counted 18 million persons—over 35% of the population of the Province (Table 2). The proportion of the total population in 1951 was even larger, because, as Table 2 shows, population growth during the decade from 1951 to 1961 averaged only 18% (less than 17%, if the rapidly growing cities of Dacca, Narayanganj and Chittagong are omitted) versus 21% for the province as a whole. Further demographic analysis might show how much of this relatively slow growth resulted from emigration out of these Districts and how much, if any, was due to a lower rate of natural increase (higher mortalities and/or lower birth rates) related to relatively poor nutrition and possibly to somewhat more practice of birth control.

In spite of the high intensity of cultivation there was a deficit in food production in the five Districts during 1960–65 (Tables 5 and 6). Cereals, almost all rice, make up 80% to 85% of the average diet in East Pakistan. The average cereal supply per person from food grown locally was less than 350 gms per day while the estimated per capita cereal consumption was

50% larger, about 465 gms per day. The total deficit in cereal production
was probably more than 750,000 tons, equivalent at retail prices to 630
million rupees or about 35 rupees per person. This was between 10% and
15% of per capita incomes in rural areas.

In Dacca, Chittagong, Comilla, and Noakhali, rice yields per acre were
somewhat higher than for the Province as a whole and the deficit in cereal
production was due to their high population densities, even when the city
populations, which clearly must draw their food supply from a large area,
are excluded. In Faridpur the estimated yield of rice per acre was only about
75% of the average for the Province; probably poor drainage and severe
flooding were more important reasons for the deficit in cereal production
in this District than population density.

The Four Sparsely Populated Districts

Dinajpur, Kushtia, Jessore, and Rajshahi contained only 16% of the population of the Province in 1961 despite the fact that they had a larger cultivated
area than the five most densely populated Districts. The average population
density on cultivated land was 1.8 persons per acre, less than half that of
the five crowded Districts, and the average size of farms was twice as large,
ranging from 3.9 to more than 5 cultivated acres (Tables 1 and 2). Multiple
cropping was practiced to a much smaller extent. Two crops were planted
on only 10% to 46% of the cultivated land, averaging 21%. The population
density per gross cropped acre, while markedly lower than the average for
the Province as a whole, was about three-fifths of that in the most crowded
Districts. This difference is much less than the difference in population
density per cultivated acre.

The rate of population growth between 1951 and 1961 was from 30% to
50% higher than the average for the Province (Table 2). This was probably
in large part the result of in-migration from the more crowded districts.
It is also possible that death rates may have been lower and fertility rates
somewhat higher in the sparsely populated Districts because of better
nutrition, and perhaps somewhat less practice of birth control.

Per capita cereal production in Dinajpur, Rajshahi, and Jessore was
considerably in excess of the food requirements of the local population,
averaging about 650 gms/person/day, while the requirements were probably
less than 500 grams. In Kushtia rice yields per acre during 1960-65 were
10% lower than the average for the province, and cereal production, after
allowing for non-human use and losses, about matched requirements.

In these four Districts, considerably more than the average amount of
land was devoted to food crops other than cereals. This should mean that
human diets were more varied and of better quality than in the rural areas
of the crowded Districts. Perhaps because of poor transportation and
marketing facilities, the percentage of land devoted to non-food cash crops,
such as tobacco, tea, jute, betel leaf, and betel nut, was only about half
the average for the Province.

Seven Districts of Intermediate Population Density

Of the remaining Districts—Sylhet, Mymensingh, Rangpur, Bogra, Pabna,
Khulna, and Barisal—only Pabna appears to have had a deficit in cereal

production in 1960–65, owing largely to its low yields of rice per acre (850 pounds of milled rice compared to the average of 980 pounds for the Province as a whole). This may well be due to extreme flooding each year during and subsequent to the monsoon season. Pabna lies in the triangle made by the confluence of the Ganges and Brahmaputra Rivers. Spill from the Brahmaputra and backed-up rainwater cover most of the District for seven months of the year. However, the percentage of the gross sown area devoted to food crops other than cereals is 80% greater in Pabna than the average for the Province, so that the average diet may be fairly adequate.

Per capita cereal production in the other six Districts ranged from 550 to 660 gms per day, well above the local food requirements. An average of 40% of the cultivated land in all seven Districts was double-cropped, slightly less than the Province average. Population densities on both cultivated land and gross sown acreage were also lower than the average for the Province, and remarkably similar in all seven Districts.

Implications of District Differences for Development
The demographic and other differences among Districts illustrated in Tables 1, 2, 3, and 5 need to be carefully considered in formulating strategies for economic and social development. They suggest that emphasis should be placed on inter-regional transportation, particularly if an increase of agricultural production by irrigation and multiple cropping is to be sought in the western Districts, which already produce a surplus above their local needs. The farmers in these Districts will need the incentive of being able to purchase manufactured products if they are to be persuaded to increase their production. Internal migration from the more crowded to the less crowded Districts may exacerbate the problem of increasing numbers of landless laborers. Reduction of the rate of population growth through family planning and other fertility control measures may occur sooner and more rapidly in the crowded Districts. Finally, the problem of draining off a large part of the growing agricultural population into cities and towns will continue to be much more severe in the crowded Districts.

Present Levels of Nutrition in East Pakistan
We have three kinds of data to estimate the adequacy of nutrition in East Pakistan: computed physiological requirements for calories and protein based on internationally accepted standards for human beings of different age, sex, and weight; nutrition surveys of household food consumption; and estimates of food production and imports in East Pakistan. Tables 4, 6, and 7 show, respectively, estimated food production in East Pakistan during the early 1960's, the results of nutrition surveys, and the computed physiological food requirements per capita.

Computation of Physiological Requirements
for Calories and Protein
Adult males in East Pakistan are small compared to the "reference man" used in the usual computations of physiological requirements for food(5, 15). The average man in his twenties weighs only 101 pounds (45.8 kg) and the average woman of the same age, about 88 pounds (Table 7). Thus their

physiological requirements for both calories and proteins are much less than those of European and American men and women, whose average weights are about 160 and 130 pounds. Moreover the proportion of children under 15 years of age in East Pakistan is relatively high, over 47%, as compared to less than 30% for Europeans and Americans, and 75% of these children are less than 10 years old. Children at these young ages require less than half the food needed by adults. East Pakistani children are smaller than children in Europe and the United States. The average ten-year-old boy weighs 23 kg while boys of the same age in Europe and North America weigh over 32 kg. The effects on food requirements of small adult size and the high proportion of young and small children are somewhat offset by the fact that among the adult population 51% are males and less than 49% females (men require about 40% more food than women) whereas in the developed countries there is an excess of women over men. Also the proportion of persons over 50 years old, whose food requirements are lower than those of young adults, is much smaller in East Pakistan than in the developed countries.

As Table 7 shows, the net of all four of these factors gives a total daily per capita calorie requirement of only 1727 calories, whereas the computed per capita requirement for the world population in 1965 is close to 2400 (10) calories and over 2700 calories for western Europe and the United States. The computed requirement for protein in East Pakistan is 23.5 gm/person/day compared to the world average of 35.2 gm/person/day. Both these figures refer to protein with an amino-acid balance equal to that of egg protein. For the kinds of protein available in the East Pakistan diet the protein requirement is about 40 gm/person/day in contrast to about 57 gm for the average diet of all people on earth.

Nutrition Survey
A nutrition survey of East Pakistan was conducted from March 1962 to January 1964 in cooperation with the United States Public Health Service (12). The 24-hour food supplies in samples of households were weighed before cooking. At least one sample of households was studied in each District. The weighted average of all samples indicated a daily per capita intake of 2200 calories and a protein intake of about 50 gm/day. The reported calorie intake was 27% higher than our computed per capita physiological requirement.

The discrepancy between the computed food requirement and the results of the nutrition survey may be partly due to an undercount of children and adolescents in the sample populations. The recorded age and sex distributions are considerably different than would be expected from census data, and the distributions are inconsistent within themselves. We have attempted to correct for the population undercount in each sample in Table 6. When this correction is made, the average per capita calorie intake is reduced to 2070 calories/day.

In 10 out of the 16 Districts, the measured cereal consumption in the nutrition survey exceeded the estimated supply from cereal production within the District. As we have shown earlier this would be expected for the Districts of high population density, namely Chittagong, Comilla, Dacca, Noakhali and Faridpur, and the low yield District of Pabna, but not in other Districts. In particular, the cereal consumption given in Table 6 for the sample populations in Kushtia and Dinajpur is 33% and 13% higher, respectively, than the estimated supply from local production, even when corrected for undercounting of the sample populations. The recorded per capita calorie intakes in the samples from these two Districts are over 2700 calories, about equal to the requirement of the average American and not much less than actual household consumption in the United States. The number of people in the samples of households in Kushtia and Dinajpur was smaller than in any of the other Districts, and these Districts are on the western border of the Province, far removed from the headquarters of the survey in Dacca. We conclude that the measurements from these Districts are unreliable and should not be included in the averages.

The weighted average of the samples from the other 14 Districts gives a per capita cereal consumption of 489 gm/day, or about 17 ounces, and an energy intake of 2020 calories/day. This corrected average cereal consumption is still at least 20 gm/person/day higher than the estimated cereal supply from food grown in the Province. The latter was computed by subtracting 10% for seed, feed, and wastage from the per capita cereal production in each District given in Table 5.

Food Production in 1960–65
In Table 4 we show the estimated total food production in East Pakistan during the early 1960's, computed from detailed data for each District and each crop given by H. E. Rashid(11). Cereal production was somewhat less than 10 million tons, of which about 99% was rice. The weight of all other foods produced was close to 6 million tons. The calculated available food energy of all crops was 117.6 billion food calories/day(13). Of this, 82% was in cereals. Total protein production was 2755 tons/day, of which about 73% was in cereals. If we reduce the calorie and protein production by 10% to allow for seed, feed, and losses, and divide by an estimated population of 52.5 million in 1962–63 (population of 50.8 million given by the 1961 census plus 3% for one and a half years population growth) we arrive at a per capita intake of 2020 cal/day, very close to the corrected values from the nutrition survey given in Table 6.

Two corrections should be made to this calculation of food supplies per capita. In the early 1960's, about 1 million tons of food grains were imported each year into East Pakistan(14). This would increase the estimated available calories by nearly 9%, to 128 billion food calories/day, or to about 115 billion daily calories after correcting for seed, feed, and losses. Secondly the 1961 census results probably suffer from a significant undercount, estimated by the Planning Commission of Pakistan to be about 8%(2). If the true population in 1961 was 55 million, as estimated by the Planning Commission, the population in 1962–63 would have been about 57 million. These two corrections almost exactly cancel each other and we again arrive at an intake of 2020 cal/day/person.

A third correction, of unknown magnitude, may be warranted. Studies of estimated food grain production in West Pakistan indicate that the estimates may be considerably lower than the actual production(8). Whether this is likewise true for East Pakistan is not known. It should also be emphasized that our 10% deduction for seed, poultry and livestock feed, and losses is very uncertain. The true value could be twice or half this figure.

Estimated Food Supplies and Nutrition in 1970

Estimated cereal supplies in 1970 will be about 12.7 million tons, made up of 11 million tons of production and 1.7 million tons of imports(7). If these cereal supplies constitute 82% of the total supply of calories, which is the proportion represented by cereal production in the early 1960's, food production plus imports would correspond to 152.5 billion food cal/day in 1970. Corrected for losses and non-human uses, this amounts to 137 billion food calories available for human consumption. The population of East Pakistan in 1970 is probably between 70 and 75 million people. The corresponding per capita calorie intakes are between 1960 and 1830 food calories/day. This is still 13% to 6% above the calculated physiological requirement given in Table 7.

There is some evidence that the calculated requirement is low. Studies of caloric intake as related to body weight in six Asian countries show an apparent genetic difference from South Americans or Europeans(6). Using the regression equations derived in these studies, the calculated daily calorie requirement for East Pakistan is about 1830 calories/day. This is identical with the estimated food availability for 75 million people in 1970.

If caloric and protein requirements are met on the average, a considerable fraction of the population must be receiving less than the requirement. Such a deficiency would manifest itself through overt evidence of protein-calorie malnutrition in children and through reduced levels of physical activity and greater susceptibility to illness in adults. The 1962–64 nutritional survey did not find much evidence of protein-calorie malnutrition, expressed as kwashiorkor or marasmus, and this is confirmed in 1970 by travelers' observations. Clearly, however, there is little if any excess food in East Pakistan, and more than likely a deficiency for the poorer classes, even after the large quantities of imports are taken into account.

FUTURE POPULATION AND FOOD NEEDS

At present some 70–75 million people are attempting to feed themselves on about 20 million acres of farm land. The area of cultivated land cannot be much extended, but at present rates of growth the population will be about 125 million by 1985. There will then be 6 persons per net cultivated acre, in contrast to 1.5 persons in the United States.

In Table 8, we have given approximate projections of population size in 1985 and 2000, 15 and 30 years from now, assuming modest declines in fertility and the probable increase in life expectancy at birth. Needed food supplies have been estimated from these projections. We have assumed that the Provincial income will increase by 5.25% per year. About 70% of present very low per capita incomes goes for food; we believe this proportion will be about constant during the next 15 years. After that time diets may have sufficiently improved so that a somewhat smaller proportion of income, say 60%, will be spent for food.

The needed food supplies are stated in terms of tons of "milled rice equivalent"—that is, the tonnage of milled rice (approximately $\frac{2}{3}$ of the rice as harvested, which is usually called paddy) that would provide the daily calorie supplies in the Table. In actuality, as shown in Tables 4 and 6, rice makes up only about 80 to 85% of the present diet.

As diets improve with rising incomes, the proportion of rice may be expected to diminish. The figures of 2140 and 2570 calories per day, shown in Table 8 for 1985 and 2000, do not give the actual daily calorie intake per person, which will, on the average, remain close to physiological requirements, but rather the primary plant calories that would be utilized directly, or indirectly through feeding livestock and poultry, or alternatively the higher priced vegetables, fruits and other food products that would be equivalent in cost (at 1970 prices) (Table 4) to the quantity of rice which would provide the stated number of calories.

With the assumptions underlying Table 8, food supplies would need to be doubled by 1985 and redoubled by the year 2000. Such an increase in production is possible because of the recent development of new varieties of wheat and rice, which produce three to six times as much grain per crop as the previously used varieties. But the potential of these new varieties cannot be attained without expensive irrigation development and the use of large quantities of chemical fertilizers. This demands a shift from subsistence to market agriculture, and hence, industrial and over-all economic development, so that there will be customers outside the agricultural sector who have enough income to be able to buy part of the farmers' crops, and who can produce goods that the farmers want to buy. Large capital investments, including a large component of foreign exchange (dollars, pounds, marks, rubles or yen) will be needed, plus technical assistance from the developed countries on a generous scale.

If the rate of increase of provincial income is no greater than the rate of population increase, then demand for food will grow at a rate of 3.4% per year, and by 1985 would be 65 per cent larger than at present. It might well be impossible to supply this demand because the farmers would be unable to purchase the needed fertilizers and other inputs unless they could sell a larger part of their crops outside the agricultural sector. And such sales would depend on rising total income in these other sectors.

Irrigation and Other Means of Increasing Agricultural Production

With a rapidly growing population it is desirable to increase agricultural employment as well as food production. This could be accomplished by placing already cultivated land under irrigation so that an additional crop could be grown during the winter (Boro) crop season. Supplemental irrigation of the Aus and/or Amon crops would also make it possible to use higher yielding varieties during these seasons. The following calculation indicates the amount of cultivated land that should be placed under irrigation.

In 1970, 14 million tons of food (milled rice equivalent) will be grown on about 30 million gross cultivated acres. The average yields of paddy rice (1.67 x the weight of milled rice) are 0.7 tons per acre. The deficit in food production, which is made up by imports of food grains, is estimated at 1.5 million tons. By 1985, needed food supplies will be 28 million tons (Table 8) and production, allowing for seed, feed, and wastage, should be 30.8 million tons. This represents an increase of 16.8 million tons of milled rice above the present levels of production, or 25 million tons of paddy. With the new rice varieties and sufficient chemical fertilizers, about 2.5 tons of paddy per acre can be obtained for the additional Boro crop under irrigation. Supplemental irrigation of the Aus or Amon crops, using the new varieties, would give an increase in paddy yield of 1.8 tons per acre. Thus each acre put under irrigation would produce 4.3 tons more paddy than at present. To meet food needs in 1985, therefore, about 6 million acres should be irrigated, using 10 to 15 million acre feet of water on the fields. This represents a rate of increase of irrigated area by about 400,000 acres a year, far greater than the rate of development during the past two decades. If the irrigation requirement were supplied by pumping ground water, 75,000 to 100,000 tube wells of one cu. ft./sec. capacity would be required.

Other possibilities exist for increasing food production, including measures to ameliorate flood conditions or reduce the flooded areas. It may be feasible also to introduce higher yielding varieties of "floating rice," which can grow successfully in areas that are not too deeply flooded. More intensive cultivation of present crops would increase both employment and yields, but it is hard to predict the extent of this increase.

PROBLEMS OF EMPLOYMENT AND URBANIZATION

Finding employment for the rapidly growing labor force may prove to be a much more serious problem than increasing food production. The increase of numbers of workers cannot be affected during the next 15 years by family planning or other fertility control programs, because the persons who will be entering the labor force during this period are already born.

In 1961 about 34% of the population were in the labor force in East Pakistan(11). Accepting the Planning Commission estimate of 55 million for the population in 1961, the labor force consisted of 19.2 million people. Of these, 84.5%, or 16.2 million, were farm workers, and 15.5%, or 3.0 million, worked outside of agriculture, as shopkeepers, skilled and semi-skilled industrial workers, unskilled laborers, fishermen, transport workers, domestic servants, office workers, and professional and technical personnel. We estimate that about 40% of these 3 million non-agricultural workers, or 1.2 million people, had jobs in cities and towns, and 60%, or 1.8 million, were non-agricultural workers in the villages. As shown by the fact that there were 3 males for every 2 females in cities and towns (Table 10), the proportion of the urban population in the labor force was about 45%, much higher than that of the rural population. Approximately 10% of the rural workers had jobs outside agriculture. There were 1.67 gross cultivated acres for every farm worker, or 1.16 net cultivated acres.

Observations by Akter Hameed Khan and his associates in the Comilla Academy (personal communication) show that in District Comilla approximately 95 man-days are required per gross cultivated acre of unirrigated land. Extrapolating these figures to the Province indicates that in 1961 the average farm worker had around 150 days of employment. An additional irrigated crop provides at least 60 man-days of added employment.

With a 1970 population of 75 million, the labor force is probably close to 25.7 million workers. Assuming that the gross cultivated area is about 30 million acres and that farm labor intensity has increased to the extent that there are now 1.5 gross cultivated acres per farm worker, the agricultural labor force would consist of 20 million people, or 78% of the total. Non-agricultural workers would make up 22%, or 5.7 million people. With the estimated population of cities and towns given in Table 9 and the same proportions of males and females as in 1961 (Table 10) there should be 2.2 million urban workers. This leaves 3.5 million who are either seeking employment or working outside agriculture in rural areas, about 18% of the rural labor force.

For the same land/man ratio on the gross cultivated area in 1985 as in 1970, there would be 24 million farm workers, and the non-agricultural labor force would be 18.5 million, or 43.5% of the total of 42.5 million. If cities and towns grow as indicated in Table 9, urban employment might be about 7 million. This leaves 11.5 million people who would need employment outside agriculture in the countryside. It is hard to see how more than 4 million could find jobs. The rate of unemployment plus underemployment would thus be about 18%. Either urbanization and industrialization must proceed much more rapidly then we have supposed in Table 9, or labor intensity on the farms must be considerably increased. For example, if the gross cultivated area per farm worker were reduced to 1.2 acres, the agricultural labor force would be 30 million and the non-agricultural workers in the countryside only 5.5 million, about the same proportion to farm workers as in 1970.

A continuing increase in farm labor intensity is said to have taken place in Java with the rapid growth of its rural population(17). It may well have occurred during the past few decades in East Pakistan. But such "agricultural involution" may be incompatible with the modernization of agriculture which is essential if the people of East Pakistan are to feed themselves.

PROSPECTS FOR SLOWING POPULATION GROWTH

Pakistan began a broadly planned and highly organized family planning program in 1965, with strong sponsorship from the highest levels of government. Three years later, in 1967–68(1), nearly 40,000 full and part-time workers were employed, and over 50,000 retail agents had been recruited for distribution of contraceptives. Some 3 million, or 13%, of the 23 million couples of reproductive age were protected against conception. The most popular methods were condoms, followed by IUDs, and by vasectomies.

The program was more effective in West Pakistan than in the East Wing. In the West, over 16% of vulnerable couples were protected; in the East, about 10%. In East Pakistan there was a relatively stronger preference for male methods—condoms and vasectomies, which won little acceptance in West Pakistan, and particularly vasectomies. In East Pakistan 71.5% of protected couples used male methods; in West Pakistan only 65%.

The increase in the number of acceptors from 1966–67 to 1967–68 in East Pakistan was 4.7% of the number of couples of reproductive age, but the size of the reproducing population increased by about 3% during the year. Hence the number of births was diminished by not more than 1.7%. This is probably a high figure, because the average age of wives among couples accepting contraceptives or sterilization is probably close to 30 years and they have already had at least five live births. Both factors tend to reduce the fecundity of these women.

One might expect that the large differences among Districts in population density, size of farms, and potential for raising food production by increasing multiple cropping would be reflected in differences in the effectiveness of the family planning program. Data from District Comilla support this expectation. According to A. H. Khan (personal communication) some 60,000 condoms per month were sold in 1969 in the Thana served by the Comilla Academy, and 3,500 IUDs had been inserted during the last 5 years. Using the accepted ratio of 100 conventional contraceptives for one couple-year of protection, and the expected removal rate of IUDs, this means that over 8,000 couples, or about 27% of the 30,000 families in the Thana, were protected against conception in 1969, in contrast to perhaps 13% for the Province(4).

It will be remembered from the previous discussion that the rate of population growth in the 5 most densely populated Districts of East Pakistan was markedly less in 1961 than for the Province as a whole. We suggested that this was probably mainly due to out-migration. That there is a marked sex difference in this migration is indicated by Table 10, which shows that in the cities and towns where many of the migrants go, there are about 3 males for every 2 females. The complete and accurate demographic data obtained by W. H. Moseley and his colleagues in Matlab Thana of District Comilla(3)(9) show that these males are, as would be expected, young men between the ages of 20 and 34 who have left their villages to seek employment in the cities and elsewhere, leaving their wives and families behind. For this age group in Matlab Thana there are nearly 3 females for every 2 males. Such an economically forced separation of couples should have a significant effect in lowering birth rates, and should be further studied as a part of the complex of village-community and family-level motivation for family planning.

Future planning of population-influencing policies for fertility reduction in East Pakistan should give special attention to small land-owning farmers in the high population-density Districts. Here, the average size of farms is already so small that further subdivision among several male children is highly undesirable. Throughout the male-dominated society of East Pakistan, special attention should be paid to the male heads of farm families, and every effort should be made to provide them with contraceptive methods of their choice and with the opportunity for vasectomy.

The benefit/cost ratio of family planning efforts will probably be much lower in the sparsely populated Districts, where there is less pressure on the land and more food per person, than in the crowded Districts. In both types of Districts, a relatively low payoff can be expected for family planning efforts among landless laborers, who have little incentive to limit the numbers of their children, because the children are capable of earning rupees to help support the family.

Where husbands desire, results may be attained by promoting IUDs, but experience in Comilla Thana indicates that this should be a relatively minor part of the total program. On the other hand, every effort should be made to improve the status of women, and to increase their opportunities for education, jobs, and satisfying alternatives to child-bearing.

In the cities and the new industrial towns, with their considerable excess of males over females, educational campaigns in factories and in voluntary organizations of various kinds may be at least as effective in the long run as direct efforts to dispense contraceptives or other means of fertility control.

REFERENCES

1. Adil, E. 1969. *Annual report on the working of Pakistan's family planning programme 1967-1968.* Rawalpindi: Pakistan Family Planning Council.
2. Brackett, J. W. and Akers, D. S. 1965. *Projections of the population of Pakistan by age and sex; 1965-1968, a measure of the political impact of a family planning program.* U.S. Department of Commerce, Bureau of the Census, pp. 1-63.
3. Chowdhary, A. K. M. A., Aziz, K., and Moseley, W. H. 1969. *Demographic studies in rural East Pakistan, second year, May 1967-April 1968.* Dacca: Pakistan-SEATO Cholera Research Laboratory.
4. Corsa, L. October 1969. Consequences of population growth for health services in less developed countries—an initial appraisal. Manuscript prepared for National Academy of Sciences, Study of Consequences of Population Change and their Implications for National and International Policies.
5. Food and Agriculture Organization of the United Nations, Calorie Requirements. 1957. *Report of the Second Committee on Calorie Requirements,* pp. 1-65.
6. Frish, R. and Revelle, R. May 1969. Variation in body weights and the age of adolescent growth spurt among Latin American and Asian populations in relation to calorie supplies. *Human Biology* 41, no. 2: 185-212.
7. Harvard Pakistan Advisory Group. 1970. *Project Report, July-December 1969.*
8. Hufbauer, G. C. April 1968. Cereal consumption, production, and prices in West Pakistan. Manuscript in files of Harvard Development Advisory Service.
9. Moseley, W. H. et al. June 1968. *Demographic studies in rural East Pakistan, preliminary analysis of the results of daily registration of births, deaths, and migrations in 132 villages in the cholera vaccine field trial area in Comilla district, East Pakistan, May 1966-August 1967.* Dacca: Pakistan SEATO Cholera Research Laboratory.
10. President's Science Advisory Committee, The World Food Problem, Population and Nutritional Demands. May 1967. *Report of the Panel on the World Food Supply,* vol. II, pp. 5-135.
11. Rashid, H. E. 1967. *East Pakistan, a systematic regional geography and its development planning aspects* (2nd ed.). Lahore: Ghulam Ali.
12. U.S. Public Health Service. May 1966. *Nutrition survey of East Pakistan. March 1962-January 1964.* U.S.

Department of Health, Education and Welfare.

13. Watt, B. K. and Merrill, A. L. December 1963. Composition of foods. *Agriculture Handbook*, no. 8 (rev ed.). Agricultural Research Service, U.S. Department of Agriculture. Washington, D.C.:

14. White House Interior Panel on Waterlogging and Salinity in West Pakistan. January 1964. *Report on land and water development in the Indus Plain*, pp. 19–95.

15. World Health Organization, Protein Requirements. 1965. *Report of a joint FAO/WHO expert group*. Geneva: World Health Organization, WHO Technical Report no. 301, pp. 1–71.

16. Patullo, J. G., et al. June 30, 1955. *The seasonal oscillation in sea level*. Sears Foundation Journal of Marine Research.

17. Geertz, C. 1966. *Agricultural involution: Process of ecological change in Indonesia.* Berkeley and Los Angeles, California: University of California Press.

TABLE 1.   East Pakistan land utilization, 1960–65

DISTRICT	(1) TOTAL LAND AREA	(2) NET SOWN AREA	(3) GROSS CROPPED AREA	(4) CROPPING IN-TENSITY	(5) AVERAGE NET CULTIVATED AREA PER FARM	(6) RATIO OF TOTAL LAND AREA TO NET SOWN AREA
	MILLIONS OF ACRES			%	ACRES	
Chittagong	1.675	.528	1.028	194	2.0	3.17
Comilla	1.570	.953	1.923	202	1.6	1.65
Dacca	1.710	1.190	1.636	137	2.6	1.43
Noakhali	1.040	.575	1.023	178	1.7	1.81
Faridpur	1.553	1.084	1.745	161	2.7	1.43
Sylhet	3.025	1.348	2.054	152	3.4	2.25
Pabna	1.086	.767	1.106	144	3.4	1.41
Barisal (Bakarganj)	2.300	1.660	2.472	149	3.3	1.38
Mymensingh	3.940	2.786	4.191	150	3.1	1.41
Khulna	2.615	1.020	1.266	124	3.4	2.56
Hill Tracts	3.065	.163	.185	113	3.8	18.80
Bogra	.936	.681	.910	133	3.3	1.37
Rangpur	2.145	1.707	2.239	131	3.3	1.26
Kushtia	.849	.539	.788	146	5.2	1.57
Jessore	1.598	1.211	1.335	110	3.9	1.32
Rajshahi	2.285	1.599	1.963	123	4.4	1.43
Dinajpur	1.660	1.038	1.216	117	4.9	1.60
Totals	33.10*	18.85	27.08	144	3.3	1.61†

*Area of East Pakistan excluding 2.24 million acres of inland waters

†Omitting Hill Tracts

Source: Columns (1), (2), (5) from Tables XII, XV, and XIV, respectively, of H. E. Rashid, "East Pakistan, A Systematic Regional Geography and Its Development Planning Aspects," Ghulam Ali and Sons, Lahore, etc., 1967. Column (3) compiled from data given in H. E. Rashid, Op. cit. chapter VIII, pp. 140-247. Column (4) = (Column (3) ÷ Column (2)) × 100.

TABLE 2. East Pakistan population density and growth

DISTRICT	(1) POPULATION 1961 CENSUS	(2) ON TOTAL LAND AREA	(3) ON NET SOWN AREA	(4) ON GROSS CROPPED AREA	(5) POPULATION GROWTH 1951–61
		POPULATION DENSITY, PERSONS/ACRE			
	MILLIONS				%
Chittagong	2.98	1.80	5.65	2.90	18
Comilla	4.39	2.80	4.60	2.30	16
Dacca	5.10	3.00	4.30	3.10	25
Noakhali	2.38	2.30	4.15	2.30	15
Faridpur	3.18	2.05	2.95	1.80	14
Sylhet	3.49	1.15	2.60	1.70	14
Pabna	1.96	1.80	2.55	1.75	23
Barisal (Bakarganj)	4.26	1.85	2.55	1.70	17
Mymensingh	7.02	1.80	2.50	1.70	21
Khulna	2.45	.95	2.40	1.95	18
Hill Tracts	.38	.10	2.35	2.05	34
Bogra	1.57	1.70	2.30	1.70	23
Rangpur	3.80	1.75	2.20	1.70	30
Kushtia	1.17	1.40	2.20	1.50	32
Jessore	2.19	1.35	1.80	1.65	34
Rajshahi	2.81	1.25	1.75	1.45	27
Dinajpur	1.71	1.05	1.65	1.40	24
Totals	50.84	1.55	2.70	1.85	21

Source: Columns (1) and (5) from Tables XCV and XCIV, respectively, in H. E. Rashid, "East Pakistan, A Systematic Regional Geography and Its Development Planning Aspects," Ghulam Ali and Sons, Lahore, etc., 1967. Column (2), (3) and (4) computed by dividing column (1) by columns (1), (2) and (3) of Table 1.

TABLE 3. Proportion of gross sown area in rice and other crops in East Pakistan, 1960–65
Source: Computed from data in Chapter VIII of H. E. Rashid, "East Pakistan, A Systematic Regional Geography and Its Development Planning Aspects," pp. 140–259, Ghulam Ali and Sons, Lahore, etc., 1967.

DISTRICT	RICE	OTHER CEREALS	OTHER FOOD CROPS	NON-FOOD CROPS
	PER CENT OF GROSS SOWN AREA IN			
Chittagong	92	—	5	3
Comilla	81	1	8	10
Dacca	75	1	13	11
Noakhali	86	—	7	7
Faridpur	76	2	13	9
Sylhet	91	—	4	5
Pabna	71	3	18	8
Barisal	88	—	6	6
Mymensingh	77	—	11	12
Khulna	88	—	8	4
Hill Tracts	79	1	19	1
Bogra	79	—	14	7
Rangpur	76	2	9	13
Kushtia	71	2	22	5
Jessore	80	1	14	5
Rajshahi	79	3	13	5
Dinajpur	81	1	15	3
Totals	81	1	10	8

Notes on percentage areas for specific crops included in totals.

Rice: 54% Amon; 23% Aus; 4% Boro.

Other Cereals: 0.5% Wheat; 0.3% Barley and Maize

Other Food Crops: 2.9% Pulses; 0.9% Potatoes and Sweet Potatoes; 1.7% Vegetables; 2.8% Oil Seeds; 1.4% Sugar; 0.8% Fruits

Non-Food Crops: 0.4% Tobacco; 0.3% Tea; 6.4% Jute; 0.8% Betel Leaf and Betel Nut.

TABLE 4. Food production in East Pakistan, 1960–1965

	(1) MILLION METRIC TONS	(2) THOUSANDS OF FOOD CALORIES PER TON	(3) PROTEIN KG PER TON	(4) BILLION FOOD CALORIES PER DAY	(5) PROTEIN TONS PER DAY	(6) VALUE MILLIONS OF RUPEES	(7) % OF TOTAL CALORIES	(8) % OF TOTAL PROTEIN	(9) % OF TOTAL CASH VALUE
Cereals	9.76	3600	75	96.4	2006	7900	82.0	72.8	60.4
Pulses	0.23	3500	225	2.2	140	172	1.9	5.1	1.3
Tubers	0.67	950	19	1.7	35	480	1.4	1.3	3.7
Vegetables	(1.44)	290	14	1.2	55	(755)	1.0	2.0	5.8
Oil seeds	0.15	5600	200	2.2	81	120	1.9	2.9	0.9
Sugar	0.53	3700	0	5.5	0	990	4.7	0	7.6
Fruits	1.39	810	10	3.1	39	630	2.6	1.4	4.8
Eggs	0.02	1630	129	0.1	7	40	0.1	0.3	0.3
Meat and Poultry	0.15	2410	183	1.0	77	305	0.8	2.8	2.3
Milk	0.80	650	35	1.4	77	530	1.2	2.8	4.1
Fish	(0.50)	1800	175	2.5	238	1100	2.1	8.6	8.4
Butter and Ghee	0.01	8760	3	0.3	0.1	60	0.3	0	0.5
Totals	15.65			117.6	2755	13082	100.0	100.0	100.1

Sources Column(1) compiled from data given in H. E. Rashid, "East Pakistan, A Systematic Regional Geography and Its Development Planning Aspects," Chapters VIII and IX, pp. 140–259, Ghulam Ali and Sons, Lahore, etc. 1967. Numbers in parentheses are our estimates based on Rashid and other data. Columns (2) and (3), B. K. Watt and A. L. Merrill, "Composition of Foods," Agriculture Handbook No. 8, Agricultural Research Service, U. S. Department of Agriculture, Washington D.C., Revised 1963. Column (6) Retail values in rupees estimated from data given in "Nutrition Survey of East Pakistan, March 1962–Jan. 1964," U.S. Public Health Service, 1966.

TABLE 5. East Pakistan Districts in order of per capita cereal production 1960–65

(1) DISTRICT	(2) POPULATION DENSITY ON GROSS CROPPED AREA	(3) PER CENT OF GROSS SOWN AREA IN CEREALS	(4) AVERAGE RICE YIELDS	(5) PER CAPITA CEREAL PRODUCTION
	PERSONS/ACRE		TONS/ACRE	GMS/PERSON/DAY
Dacca	3.10	76	.452	299
Faridpur	1.80	78	.339	394
Chittagong	2.90	92	.478	416
Comilla	2.30	82	.455	429
Pabna	1.75	74	.388	438
Noakhali	2.30	86	.453	457
Hill Tracts	2.05	80	.460	491
Kushtia	1.50	73	.400	535
Rangpur	1.70	78	.442	550
Mymensingh	1.70	77	.455	575
Jessore	1.65	81	.433	580
Bogra	1.70	79	.456	586
Khulna	1.95	88	.484	606
Sylhet	1.70	91	.445	651
Barisal	1.70	88	.475	660
Dinajpur	1.40	82	.425	680
Rajshahi	1.45	82	.442	682
Totals	1.85	82	.443	529

Source: Column (2) from Table 2. Column (3) from Table 3. Column (4) from data in Tables XIX, XX, and XXI of H. E. Rashid, "East Pakistan, A Systematic Regional Geography and Its Development Planning Aspects," Ghulam Ali and Sons, Lahore, etc., 1967. Column (5) = (Column (4) × Column (3)) ÷ (100 × Column (2) × 365).

Note: Underlined numbers in Column (2) indicate high population density on cultivated land; in columns (3) and (4), relatively small proportion of land planted in cereals and/or low yields per acre; in column (5), per capita cereal production inadequate to supply District requirements.

TABLE 6. Estimated per capita food energy consumption in East Pakistan, early 1960's nutrition survey

DISTRICT	(1) 1961 CENSUS POPULATION MILLIONS	(2) 1962–64 SAMPLE NUMBER	(3) POPULATION ESTIMATED UNDERCOUNT %	(4) CEREAL CONSUMPTION GMS/PERS/DAY PUBLISHED	(5) CEREAL CONSUMPTION GMS/PERS/DAY CORRECTED	(6) ENERGY FROM CEREALS KCAL/PERSON/DAY	(7) ENERGY FROM CEREALS %OF TOTAL CALORIES	(8) TOTAL FOOD ENERGY KCAL/PERS/DAY	(9) DISTRICT CEREAL SUPPLY GMS/PERS/DAY
Chittagong	2.98	587	12.8	539	478	1690	89.4	1890	374
Comilla	4.39	655	5.2	486	461	1630	76.3	2120	386
Dacca	5.10	945	2.7	498	485	1715	86.1	2000	269
Noakhali	2.38	1,293	4.6	506	484	1710	85.1	1965	411
Faridpur	3.18	520	4.8	440	420	1490	83.9	1775	355
Barisal	4.26	631	3.2	507	490	1730	86.2	2005	594
Pabna	1.96	542	9.8	548	498	1765	85.3	2070	394
Mymensingh	7.02	581	8.6	528	486	1720	89.7	1915	517
Sylhet	3.49	677	6.3	526	493	1745	84.3	1965	586
Bogra	1.57	571	6.7	581	594	1920	84.3	2285	527
Khulna	2.45	702	5.3	469	444	1570	87.4	1795	545
Rangpur	3.80	616	5.2	641	608	2155	84.3	2555	495
Kushtia	1.17	453	7.7	690	640	2265	83.5	2715	481
Jessore	2.19	682	5.6	460	435	1540	83.9	1835	522
Rajshahi	2.81	670	3.4	592	571	2020	86.9	2330	614
Dinajpur	1.71	479	4.6	721	695	2440	87.1	2800	612
Totals	50.46	10,599	Weighted Averages	537	502	1777	85.6	2070	476
Less Kushtia and Dinajpur	47.58	9,667			489	1730	85.5	2020	469

Sources: Column (1), Population Census of Pakistan, 1961. Columns (2), (4), (7), "Nutrition Survey of East Pakistan, March 1962–Jan. 1964," U.S. Public Health Service, 1966. Column (3), Estimated undercount of sample population based on analysis of age and sex distribution. Column (5), Per capita cereal consumption from Nutrition Survey corrected for sample undercount. Column (6), Corrected per capita cereal consumption × 3540 kcal/kg. Column (8), Column (6) × 100 ÷ Column (7). Column (9), District cereal supply per capita taken as 90% of estimated cereal production per capita given in Table 5, assuming seed, feed and losses = 10% of production. If production estimates are correct, these numbers are probably 5 to 10% too high because the population in 1962–63 was greater than indicated in Column (1).

Note: Numbers underlined in Column (5) indicate that cereal consumption measured in nutrition survey exceeds estimated supply from District production.

345

TABLE 7. Physiological requirements for calories and protein in East Pakistan, 1961-65

AGE YEARS	SEX	(1) AVERAGE WEIGHT KG	(2) PER CENT OF POPULATION	(3) DAILY CALORIE REQUIREMENTS[2] CAL/KG	(4) CAL/PERS	(5) DAILY PROTEIN REQUIREMENTS GM/KG	(6) GM/PERS	(7) TOTAL DAILY CALORIES/ HUNDRED PERSONS	(8) TOTAL DAILY PROTEIN GMS/100 PERS
0-1	m & f	5.8	4.5	164[1]	950	2.00[1]	11.6	4275	52.2
1-4	m	10.0	7.8	105	1050	1.06	10.6	8190	82.7
1-4	f	9.8	7.5	105	1030	1.06	10.4	7725	78.0
5-9	m	16.8	7.9	82	1375	0.94	15.8	10860	124.8
5-9	f	16.1	7.6	82	1320	0.94	15.1	10030	114.8
10-14	m	28.5	6.1	68	1940	0.86	24.5	11835	149.4
10-14	f	29.2	5.8	64	1865	0.86	25.1	10815	145.6
15-19	m	43.1	4.1	65	2820	0.77	33.2	11560	136.1
15-19	f	39.5	3.8	48	1880	0.77	30.5	7145	115.9
20-29	m	45.8	7.7	55	2495	0.71	32.5	19210	250.2
20-29	f	39.7	7.1	46	1810	0.71	28.2	12850	200.2
30-39	m	45.9	5.9	53	2420	0.71	32.6	14280	192.3
30-39	f	39.6	5.4	44	1755	0.71	28.1	9475	151.7
40-49	m	45.7	4.1	51	2340	0.71	32.4	9595	132.8
40-49	f	38.7	3.7	43	1680	0.71	27.5	6215	101.8
50-59	m	45.0	2.7	47	2130	0.71	32.0	5750	86.4
50-59	f	38.2	2.6	40	1530	0.71	27.2	3980	70.7
60+	m	44.2	2.6	41	1830	0.71	31.4	4760	81.6
60+	f	36.4	3.2	35	1285	0.71	25.8	4110	82.6
			100.1						
Per Capita Requirements:								1726.6	23.5[3]

Sources: Column (1) Estimated from data given by Rose Frisch and Roger Revelle, "Variation in Body Weights at the Age of the Adolescent Growth Spurt among Latin American and Asian Populations, in Relation to Calorie Supplies" Human Biology, Vol. 41, No. 2, May 1969, page 196. (2) From Figure 6 and Table E3 in James W. Brackett and Donald S. Akers, "Projections of the Population of Pakistan by Age and Sex, 1965–1986" U.S. Department of Commerce, Census Bureau, 1965. (3) Calculated according to methods given in "Calorie Requirements," Food and Agriculture Organization of the United Nations, 1957, except for ages from 1 to 14, where calories/kg computed from listed requirements for children of these ages were used. (5) Daily protein requirements in gm/kg from Table 13, of "Population and Nutritional Demands" by Grace A. Goldsmith, Roger Revelle, et al, Chapter 1 of "The World Food Problem," President's Science Advisory Committee, Vol. II, The White House, May 1967. (7) Column 2 × Column 4. (8) Column 2 × Column 6.

Notes: 1. Includes requirements for pregnancy and lactation.
2. No allowance for average environmental temperature, in accordance with recommendations in Goldsmith and Revelle, et al, op. cit.
3. Requirement of "reference protein" (egg). Multiply by 1.7 for average protein in East Pakistan diet.

TABLE 8. Demographic, food, and income projections for East Pakistan

	1970	1985	2000
Population size, millions(1)	75	125	205
Birth rate/1000	47	50	41
Death rate/1000	16	14	11
Rate of increase/1000	31	36	30
Total fertility rate(2)	8	7.5	6
Life expectation at birth, yrs.	52	55	59
Percent population less than 15 yrs.	47	46	44
Sex ratio, 100 M/F	104	104	104
Regional income, $10^9$$	4.5	9.9	21.4
Per capita income, $	60	78	106
Food requirements, 10^6 tons(3)	14	28	55
Ann. rate of incr. of income per cap, %	1.85	1.95	
Ann. rate of population increase, %	3.4	3.3	
Ann. rate incr. regional income, %	5.25	5.25	
Ann. rate of incr. in food demand, %(4)	4.7	4.5	
Per Cap. food requirement, tot. cal/da	1,800(5)	2140	2570

(1) Brackett, J. W. and Akers, D. S. "Projections of Population of Pakistan by Age and Sex 1965-1968." U.S. Bureau of the Census, Department of Commerce, June 1965. Demographic Projections are median values of projections of Series B (declining fertility, constant mortality) and Series C (constant fertility, declining mortality).

(2) The total fertility rate is the sum of the age-specific birth rates and indicates the hypothetical number of children a woman would have during her reproductive life if the age-specific rates remained constant.

(3) 75×10^6 persons $\times$ 1800   calories/day $\times$ 365   day/yr/3.54×10^6 cal/ton $= 14 \times 10^6$ tons, milled rice equivalent.

(4) Assume 0.7 for food-income elasticity (1970-1985). Rate of population increase + (income elasticity for food)(rate of increase of income per capita) = rate of increase in food demand.
$$3.4 + 0.7(1.85) = 4.7\%/\text{year} \ (1970\text{-}1985)$$
$$14(1.047)^{15} = 28 \text{ million tons/year, 1985 A.D.}$$
Assume 0.6 for food-income elasticity (1985-2000)
$$3.3 + 0.61(1.95) = 4.5\%/\text{yr}$$
$$28(1.045)^{15} = 55 \text{ million tons/year, 2000 A.D.}$$

(5) Based on calorie requirement suggested in text.

TABLE 9. Estimated urban population, 1951-1985

	NUMBER IN 1961(2)	POPULATION, THOUSANDS				ANNUAL % INCREASE		
		1951(1)	1961(2)	1971(3)	1986(3)	1951-1965	1961-1971(4)	1971-1985(5)
Cities > 100,000	4	748	1,211	2,800	11,600	5.6	8.4	9.5
Large Towns 25,000-100,000	20	716	846	1170	1,760	1.6	2.4	2.7
Medium Towns 10,000-25,000	21	245	338	545	1,210	3.2	4.8	5.4
Small Towns 5,000-10,000	32	150	219	385	1,030	3.8	5.7	6.5
Total	77	1,859	2,613	4,900	15,600	3.4	6.3	7.7
East Pakistan		45,300(6)	55,300(6)	75,000(7)	125,000(7)	2.0	3.0	3.4
Per cent of Population Urban		4.1	4.7	6.5	12.4			

Sources: (1) Compiled from data in Census of Pakistan, 1951; Vol. 3, Table 2. (2) Compiled from data given by A. Rashid, Census Bulletin 2, Table 5; Population Census of Pakistan, 1961. (3) Estimated: 1961 population in each urban category multiplied by e^{rt} where r = estimated annual rate of increase and t = time interval in years. (4) Estimated: 1951-61 rate of increase in each urban category multiplied by ratio of annual rates of increase of East Pakistan population from 1961-1971 to annual rate of increase from 1951-1961. (5) Estimated: 1961-1971 rate of increase in each urban category multiplied by ratio of estimated annual rate of increase of East Pakistan population from 1971-1986 to annual rate of increase from 1961-1971. (6) Based on estimate by East Pakistan Planning Commission. (7) From Table 8.

TABLE 10. Urban and rural sex ratios in East Pakistan, 1961

	URBAN PLACES SIZE	NUMBER	POPULATION, THOUSANDS MALE	FEMALE	TOTAL	RATIO F/M	EXCESS MALES
Cities	>100,000	4	754.5	456.5	1211.0	.605	298.0
Large towns	50,000–100,000	5	165.8	129.4	295.2	.781	36.4
	25,000–50,000	15	298.8	251.0	549.8	.838	47.8
Medium towns	10,000–25,000	20	172.9	153.1	326.0	.885	19.8
Small towns	5,000–10,000	26	97.0	91.0	188.0	.938	6.0
New Industrial Settlement		7	34.3	8.8	43.1	.258	25.5
Total Urban		77	1523.3	1089.8	2613.1	.715	433.5
Rural			26800	25900	52700	.965	900
Total East Pakistan			28300	27000	55300	.952	1300

Source: Urban Populations from H. E. Rashid, "East Pakistan, A Systematic Regional Geography and Its Development Planning Aspects," Ghulam Ali and Sons, Lahore, etc., 1967. Population of East Pakistan from James W. Brackett and Donald S. Akers, "Projections of the Population of Pakistan by Age and Sex, 1965–1986," U.S. Department of Commerce, Census Bureau, 1965.

THE ENVIRONMENTAL CRISIS

Eco-Catastrophe!

PAUL EHRLICH

PAUL EHRLICH *is a professor of biology at Stanford University.*

In order to meet the needs of our rapidly growing population, it is necessary to increase the production of food and other necessities. Yet the further exploitation of the earth's resources also threatens man's survival because of the undesirable by-product of agricultural intensification and industrialization — pollution of the environment. Just as on the issues of population and natural resources, there is considerable disagreement on how serious the environmental crisis is today. Ehrlich has become one of the chief spokesmen of the view that our environment is being rapidly ravaged beyond recovery. In the following scenario he predicts what our world will be like in ten years if the present course of environmental destruction continues.

I

The end of the ocean came late in the summer of 1979, and it came even more rapidly than the biologists had expected. There had been signs for more than a decade, commencing with the discovery in 1968 that DDT slows down photosynthesis in marine plant life. It was announced in a short paper in the technical journal, *Science,* but to ecologists it smacked of doomsday. They knew that all life in the sea depends on photosynthesis, the chemical process by which green plants bind the sun's energy and make it available to living things. And they knew that DDT and similar chlorinated hydrocarbons had polluted the entire surface of the earth, including the sea.

But that was only the first of many signs. There had been the final gasp of the whaling industry in 1973, and the end of the Peruvian anchovy fishery in 1975. Indeed, a score of other fisheries had disappeared quietly from over-exploitation and various eco-catastrophes by 1977. The term "eco-catastrophe" was coined by a California ecologist in 1969 to describe the most spectacular of man's attacks on the systems which sustain his life. He drew his inspiration from the Santa Barbara offshore oil disaster of that

Ramparts 8(3): 24–28, September 1969. Reprinted with the permission of the author and the Editors of *Ramparts.* Abridgment by the editors of the present volume.

year, and from the news which spread among naturalists that virtually all of the Golden State's seashore bird life was doomed because of chlorinated hydrocarbon interference with its reproduction. Eco-catastrophes in the sea became increasingly common in the early 1970's. Mysterious "blooms" of previously rare micro-organisms began to appear in offshore waters. Red tides—killer outbreaks of a minute single-celled plant—returned to the Florida Gulf coast and were sometimes accompanied by tides of other exotic hues.

It was clear by 1975 that the entire ecology of the ocean was changing.

A few types of phytoplankton were becoming resistant to chlorinated hydrocarbons and were gaining the upper hand. Changes in the phytoplankton community led inevitably to changes in the community of zooplankton, the tiny animals which eat the phytoplankton. These changes were passed on up the chains of life in the ocean to the herring, plaice, cod and tuna. As the diversity of life in the ocean diminished, its stability also decreased.

Other changes had taken place by 1975. Most ocean fishes that returned to fresh water to breed, like the salmon, had become extinct, their breeding streams so dammed up and polluted that their powerful homing instinct only resulted in suicide. Many fishes and shellfishes that bred in restricted areas along the coasts followed them as onshore pollution escalated.

By 1977 the annual yield of fish from the sea was down to 30 million metric tons, less than one-half the per capita catch of a decade earlier. This helped malnutrition to escalate sharply in a world where an estimated 50 million people per year were already dying of starvation. The United Nations attempted to get all chlorinated hydrocarbon insecticides banned on a worldwide basis, but the move was defeated by the United States. This opposition was generated primarily by the American petrochemical industry, operating hand in glove with its subsidiary, the United States Department of Agriculture. Together they persuaded the government to oppose the U.N. move—which was not difficult since most Americans believed that Russia and China were more in need of fish products than was the United States. The United Nations also attempted to get fishing nations to adopt strict and enforced catch limits to preserve dwindling stocks. This move was blocked by Russia, who, with the most modern electronic equipment, was in the best position to glean what was left in the sea. It was, curiously, on the very day in 1977 when the Soviet Union announced its refusal that another ominous article appeared in *Science*. It announced that incident solar radiation had been so reduced by worldwide air pollution that serious effects on the world's vegetation could be expected.

II

Apparently it was a combination of ecosystem destabilization, sunlight reduction, and a rapid escalation in chlorinated hydrocarbon pollution from massive Thanodrin applications which triggered the ultimate catastrophe. Seventeen huge Soviet-financed Thanodrin plants were operating in underdeveloped countries by 1978. They had been part of a massive Russian "aid offensive" designed to fill the gap caused by the collapse of America's ballyhooed "Green Revolution."

It became apparent in the early '70s that the "Green Revolution" was more talk than substance. Distribution of high yield "miracle" grain seeds had caused temporary local spurts in agricultural production. Simultaneously, excellent weather had produced record harvests. The combination permitted bureaucrats, especially in the United States Department of Agriculture and the Agency for International Development (AID), to reverse their previous pessimism and indulge in an outburst of optimistic propaganda about staving off famine. They raved about the approaching transformation of agriculture in the underdeveloped countries (UDCs). The reason for the propaganda reversal was never made clear. Most historians agree that a combination of utter ignorance of ecology, a desire to justify past errors, and pressure from agro-industry (which was eager to sell pesticides, fertilizers, and farm machinery to the UDCs and agencies helping the UDCs) was behind the campaign. Whatever the motivation, the results were clear. Many concerned people, lacking the expertise to see through the Green Revolution drivel, relaxed. The population-food crisis was "solved."

But reality was not long in showing itself. Local famine persisted in northern India even after good weather brought an end to the ghastly Bihar famine of the mid-'60s. East Pakistan was next, followed by a resurgence of general famine in northern India. Other foci of famine rapidly developed in Indonesia, the Philippines, Malawi, the Congo, Egypt, Colombia, Ecuador, Honduras, the Dominican Republic, and Mexico.

Everywhere hard realities destroyed the illusion of the Green Revolution. Yields dropped as the progressive farmers who had first accepted the new seeds found that their higher yields brought lower prices—effective demand (hunger plus cash) was not sufficient in poor countries to keep prices up. Less progressive farmers, observing this, refused to make the extra effort required to cultivate the "miracle" grains. Transport systems proved inadequate to bring the necessary fertilizer to the fields where the new and extremely fertilizer-sensitive grains were being grown. The same systems were also inadequate to move produce to markets. Fertilizer plants were not built fast enough, and most of the underdeveloped countries could not scrape together funds to purchase supplies, even on concessional terms. Finally, the inevitable happened, and pests began to reduce yields in even the most carefully cultivated fields. Among the first were the famous "miracle rats" which invaded Philippine "miracle rice" fields early in 1969. They were quickly followed by many insects and viruses, thriving on the relatively pest-susceptible new grains, encouraged by the vast and dense plantings, and rapidly acquiring resistance to the chemicals used against them. As chaos spread until even the most obtuse agriculturists and economists realized that the Green Revolution had turned brown, the Russians entered.

In retrospect it seems incredible that the Russians, with the American mistakes known to them, could launch an even more incompetent program of aid to the underdeveloped world. Indeed, in the early 1970's there were cynics in the United States who claimed that outdoing the stupidity of American foreign aid would be physically impossible. Those critics were, however, obviously unaware that the Russians had been busily destroying their own environment for many years. The virtual disappearance of sturgeon from Russian rivers caused a great shortage of caviar by 1970. A standard joke among Russian scientists at that time was that they had created an artificial caviar which was indistinguishable from the real thing—except by taste. At any rate the Soviet Union, observing with interest the progressive deterioration of relations between the UDCs and the United

States, came up with a solution. It had recently developed what it claimed was the ideal insecticide, a highly lethal chlorinated hydrocarbon complexed with a special agent for penetrating the external skeletal armor of insects. Announcing that the new pesticide, called Thanodrin, would truly produce a Green Revolution, the Soviets entered into negotiations with various UDCs for the construction of massive Thanodrin factories. The USSR would bear all the costs; all it wanted in return were certain trade and military concessions.

It is interesting now, with the perspective of years, to examine in some detail the reasons why the UDCs welcomed the Thanodrin plan with such open arms. Government officials in these countries ignored the protests of their own scientists that Thanodrin would not solve the problems which plagued them. The governments now knew that the basic cause of their problems was overpopulation, and that these problems had been exacerbated by the dullness, daydreaming, and cupidity endemic to all governments. They knew that only population control and limited development aimed primarily at agriculture could have spared them the horrors they now faced. They knew it, but they were not about to admit it. How much easier it was simply to accuse the Americans of failing to give them proper aid; how much simpler to accept the Russian panacea.

And then there was the general worsening of relations between the United States and the UDCs. Many things had contributed to this. The situation in America in the first half of the 1970's deserves our close scrutiny. Being more dependent on imports for raw materials than the Soviet Union, the United States had, in the early 1970's, adopted more and more heavy-handed policies in order to insure continuing supplies. Military adventures in Asia and Latin America had further lessened the international credibility of the United States as a great defender of freedom—an image which had begun to deteriorate rapidly during the pointless and fruitless Viet-Nam conflict. At home, acceptance of the carefully manufactured image lessened dramatically, as even the more romantic and chauvinistic citizens began to understand the role of the military and the industrial system in what John Kenneth Galbraith had aptly named "The New Industrial State."

At home in the USA the early '70s were traumatic times. Racial violence grew and the habitability of the cities diminished, as nothing substantial was done to ameliorate either racial inequities or urban blight. Welfare rolls grew as automation and general technological progress forced more and more people into the category of "unemployable." Simultaneously a taxpayers' revolt occurred. Although there was not enough money to build the schools, roads, water systems, sewage systems, jails, hospitals, urban transit lines, and all the other amenities needed to support a burgeoning population, Americans refused to tax themselves more heavily. Starting in Youngstown, Ohio in 1969 and followed closely by Richmond, California, community after community was forced to close its schools or curtail educational operations for lack of funds. Water supplies, already marginal in quality and quantity in many places by 1970, deteriorated quickly. Water rationing occurred in 1723 municipalities in the summer of 1974, and hepatitis and epidemic dysentery rates climbed about 500 per cent between 1970–1974.

III

Air pollution continued to be the most obvious manifestation of environmental deterioration. It was, by 1972, quite literally in the eyes of all Americans. The year 1973 saw not only the New York and Los Angeles smog disasters, but also the publication of the Surgeon General's massive report on air pollution and health. The public had been partially prepared for the worst by the publicity given to the U.N. pollution conference held in 1972. Deaths in the late '60s caused by smog were well known to scientists, but the public had ignored them because they mostly involved the early demise of the old and sick rather than people dropping dead on the freeways. But suddenly our citizens were faced with nearly 200,000 corpses and massive documentation that they could be the next to die from respiratory disease. They were not ready for that scale of disaster. After all, the U.N. conference had not predicted that accumulated air pollution would make the planet uninhabitable until almost 1990. The population was terrorized as TV screens became filled with scenes of horror from the disaster areas. Especially vivid was NBC's coverage of hundreds of unattended people choking out their lives outside of New York's hospitals. Terms like nitrogen oxide, acute bronchitis and cardiac arrest began to have real meaning for most Americans.

The ultimate horror was the announcement that chlorinated hydrocarbons were now a major constituent of air pollution in all American cities. Autopsies of smog disaster victims revealed an average chlorinated hydrocarbon load in fatty tissue equivalent to 26 parts per million of DDT. In October, 1973, the Department of Health, Education and Welfare announced studies which showed unequivocally that increasing death rates from hypertension, cirrhosis of the liver, liver cancer and a series of other diseases had resulted from the chlorinated hydrocarbon load. They estimated that Americans born since 1946 (when DDT usage began) now had a life expectancy of only 49 years, and predicted that if current patterns continued, this expectancy would reach 42 years by 1980, when it might level out. Plunging insurance stocks triggered a stock market panic. The president of Velsicol, Inc., a major pesticide producer, went on television to "publicly eat a teaspoonful of DDT" (it was really powdered milk) and announce that HEW had been infiltrated by Communists. Other giants of the petrochemical industry, attempting to dispute the indisputable evidence, launched a massive pressure campaign on Congress to force HEW to "get out of agriculture's business." They were aided by the agro-chemical journals, which had decades of experience in misleading the public about the benefits and dangers of pesticides. But by now the public realized that it had been duped. The Nobel Prize for medicine and physiology was given to Drs. J. L. Radomski and W. B. Deichmann, who in the late 1960's had pioneered in the documentation of the long-term lethal effects of chlorinated hydrocarbons. A Presidential Commission with unimpeachable credentials directly accused the agro-chemical complex of "condemning many millions of Americans to an early death." The year 1973 was the year in which Americans finally came to understand the direct threat to their existence posed by environmental deterioration.

And 1973 was also the year in which most people finally comprehended the indirect threat. Even the president of Union Oil Company and several other industrialists publicly stated their concern over the reduction of bird populations which had resulted from pollution by DDT and other chlorinated hydrocarbons. Insect populations boomed because they were resistant to most pesticides and had been freed, by the incompetent use of those pesticides, from most of their natural enemies. Rodents swarmed over crops, multiplying rapidly in the absence of predatory birds. The effect of pests on the wheat crop was especially disastrous in the summer of 1973, since that was also the year of the great drought. Most of us can remember the shock which greeted the announcement by atmospheric physicists that the shift of the jet stream which had caused the drought was probably permanent. It signalled the birth of the Midwestern desert. Man's air-polluting activities had by then caused gross changes in climatic patterns. The news, of course, played hell with commodity and stock markets. Food prices skyrocketed, as savings were poured into hoarded canned goods. Official assurances that food supplies would remain ample fell on deaf ears, and even the government showed signs of nervousness when California migrant field workers went out on strike again in protest against the continued use of pesticides by growers. The strike burgeoned into farm burning and riots. The workers, calling themselves "The Walking Dead," demanded immediate compensation for their shortened lives, and crash research programs to attempt to lengthen them.

It was in the same speech in which President Edward Kennedy, after much delay, finally declared a national emergency and called out the National Guard to harvest California's crops, that the first mention of population control was made. Kennedy pointed out that the United States would no longer be able to offer any food aid to other nations and was likely to suffer food shortages herself. He suggested that, in view of the manifest failure of the Green Revolution, the only hope of the UDCs lay in population control. His statement, you will recall, created an uproar in the underdeveloped countries. Newspaper editorials accused the United States of wishing to prevent small countries from becoming large nations and thus threatening American hegemony. Politicians asserted that President Kennedy was a "creature of the giant drug combine" that wished to shove its pills down every woman's throat.

Among Americans, religious opposition to population control was very slight. Industry in general also backed the idea. Increasing poverty in the UDCs was both destroying markets and threatening supplies of raw materials. The seriousness of the raw material situation had been brought home during the Congressional Hard Resources hearings in 1971. The exposure of the ignorance of the cornucopian economists had been quite a spectacle—a spectacle brought into virtually every American's home in living color. Few would forget the distinguished geologist from the University of California who suggested that economists be legally required to learn at least the most elementary facts of geology. Fewer still would forget that an equally distinguished Harvard economist added that they might be required to learn some economics, too. The overall message was clear:

America's resource situation was bad and bound to get worse. The hearings had led to a bill requiring the Departments of State, Interior, and Commerce to set up a joint resource procurement council with the express purpose of "insuring that proper consideration of American resource needs be an integral part of American foreign policy."

Suddenly the United States discovered that it had a national consensus: population control was the only possible salvation of the underdeveloped world. But that same consensus led to heated debate. How could the UDCs be persuaded to limit their populations, and should not the United States lead the way by limiting its own? Members of the intellectual community wanted America to set an example. They pointed out that the United States was in the midst of a new baby boom: her birth rate, well over 20 per thousand per year, and her growth rate of over one per cent per annum were among the very highest of the developed countries. They detailed the deterioration of the American physical and psychic environments, the growing health threats, the impending food shortages, and the insufficiency of funds for desperately needed public works. They contended that the nation was clearly unable or unwilling to properly care for the people it already had. What possible reason could there be, they queried, for adding any more? Besides, who would listen to requests by the United States for population control when that nation did not control her own profligate reproduction?

Those who opposed population controls for the U.S. were equally vociferous. The military-industrial complex, with its all-too-human mixture of ignorance and avarice, still saw strength and prosperity in numbers. Baby food magnates, already worried by the growing nitrate pollution of their products, saw their market disappearing. Steel manufacturers saw a decrease in aggregate demand and slippage for that holy of holies, the Gross National Product. And military men saw, in the growing population-food-environment crisis, a serious threat to their carefully nurtured Cold War. In the end, of course, economic arguments held sway, and the "inalienable right of every American couple to determine the size of its family," a freedom invented for the occasion in the early '70s, was not compromised.

The population control bill, which was passed by Congress early in 1974, was quite a document, nevertheless. On the domestic front, it authorized an increase from 100 to 150 million dollars in funds for "family planning" activities. This was made possible by a general feeling in the country that the growing army on welfare needed family planning. But the gist of the bill was a series of measures designed to impress the need for population control on the UDCs. All American aid to countries with overpopulation problems was required by law to consist in part of population control assistance. In order to receive any assistance each nation was required not only to accept the population control aid, but also to match it according to a complex formula. "Overpopulation" itself was defined by a formula based on U.N. statistics, and the UDCs were required not only to accept aid, but also to show progress in reducing birth rates. Every five years the status of the aid program for each nation was to be re-evaluated.

The reaction to the announcement of this program dwarfed the response to President Kennedy's speech. A coalition of UDCs attempted to get the U.N. General Assembly to condemn the United States as a "genetic aggressor." Most damaging of all to the American cause was the famous "25 Indians and a dog" speech by Mr. Shankarnarayan, Indian Ambassador to the U.N. Shankarnarayan pointed out that for several decades the United States, with less than six per cent of the people of the world had consumed roughly 50 per cent of the raw materials used every year. He described vividly America's contribution to worldwide environmental deterioration, and he scathingly denounced the miserly record of United States foreign aid as "unworthy of a fourth-rate power, let alone the most powerful nation on earth."

It was the climax of his speech, however, which most historians claim once and for all destroyed the image of the United States. Shankarnarayan informed the assembly that the average American family dog was fed more animal protein per week than the average Indian got in a month. "How do you justify taking fish from protein-starved Peruvians and feeding them to your animals?" he asked. "I contend," he concluded, "that the birth of an American baby is a greater disaster for the world than that of 25 Indian babies." When the applause had died away, Mr. Sorensen, the American representative, make a speech which said essentially that "other countries look after their own self-interest, too." When the vote came, the United States was condemned.

IV

This condemnation set the tone of U.S.-UDC relations at the time the Russian Thanodrin proposal was made. The proposal seemed to offer the masses in the UDCs an opportunity to save themselves and humiliate the United States at the same time; and in human affairs, as we all know, biological realities could never interfere with such an opportunity. The scientists were silenced, the politicians said yes, the Thanodrin plants were built, and the results were what any beginning ecology student could have predicted. At first Thanodrin seemed to offer excellent control of many pests. True, there was a rash of human fatalities from improper use of the lethal chemical, but, as Russian technical advisors were prone to note, these were more than compensated for by increased yields. Thanodrin use skyrocketed throughout the underdeveloped world. The Mikoyan design group developed a dependable, cheap agricultural aircraft which the Soviets donated to the effort in large numbers. MIG sprayers became even more common in UDCs than MIG interceptors.

Then the troubles began. Insect strains with cuticles resistant to Thanodrin penetration began to appear. And as streams, rivers, fish culture ponds and onshore waters became rich in Thanodrin, more fisheries began to disappear. Bird populations were decimated. The sequence of events was standard for broadcast use of a synthetic pesticide: great success at first, followed by removal of natural enemies and development of resistance by the pest. Populations of crop-eating insects in areas treated with Thanodrin made steady comebacks and soon became more abundant than ever. Yields plunged, while farmers in their desperation increased the Thanodrin dose and shortened the time between treatments. Death from Thanodrin poisoning became common. The first violent incident occurred in the Canete Valley of Peru, where farmers had suffered a similar chlorinated hydrocarbon disaster in the mid-'50s. A Russian advisor serving as an agricultural pilot was assaulted and killed by a mob of enraged farmers in January, 1978. Trouble spread rapidly during 1978, especially after the word got out that two years earlier Russia herself had banned the use of Thanodrin at home because of its serious effects on ecological systems. Suddenly Russia, and not the United States, was the *bête noir* in the UDCs. "Thanodrin parties" became epidemic, with farmers, in their ignorance, dumping carloads of Thanodrin concentrate into the sea. Russian advisors fled, and four of the Thanodrin plants were leveled to the ground. Destruction of the plants in Rio and Calcutta led to hundreds of thousands of gallons of Thanodrin concentrate being dumped directly into the sea.

Mr. Shankarnarayan again rose to address the U.N., but this time it was Mr. Potemkin, representative of the Soviet Union, who was on the hot seat. Mr. Potemkin heard his nation described as the greatest mass killer of all time as Shankarnarayan predicted at least 30 million deaths from crop failures due to overdependence on Thanodrin. Russia was accused of "chemical aggression," and the General Assembly, after a weak reply by Potemkin, passed a vote of censure.

It was in January, 1979, that huge blooms of a previously unknown variety of diatom were reported off the coast of Peru. The blooms were accompanied by a massive die-off of sea life and of the pathetic remainder of the birds which had once feasted on the anchovies of the area. Almost immediately another huge bloom was reported in the Indian Ocean, centering around the Seychelles, and then a third in the South Atlantic off the African coast. Both of these were accompanied by spectacular die-offs of marine animals. Even more ominous were growing reports of fish and bird kills at oceanic points where there were no spectacular blooms. Biologists were soon able to explain the phenomena: the diatom had evolved an enzyme which broke down Thanodrin; that enzyme also produced a breakdown product which interfered with the transmission of nerve impulses, and was therefore lethal to animals. Unfortunately, the biologists could suggest no way of repressing the poisonous diatom bloom in time. By September, 1979, all important animal life in the sea was extinct. Large areas of coastline had to be evacuated, as windrows of dead fish created a monumental stench.

But stench was the least of man's problems. Japan and China were faced with almost instant starvation from a total loss of the seafood on which they were so dependent. Both blamed Russia for their situation and demanded immediate mass shipments of food. Russia had none to send. On October 13, Chinese armies attacked Russia on a broad front. . . .

V

A pretty grim scenario. Unfortunately, we're a long way into it already. Everything mentioned as happening before 1970 has actually occurred; much of the rest is based on projections of trends already appearing. Evidence that pesticides have long-term lethal effects on human beings has started to accumulate, and Robert Finch, when Secretary of the Department of Health, Education and Welfare, has expressed his extreme apprehension about the pesticide situation. Simultaneously the petrochemical industry continues its unconscionable poison-peddling. For instance, Shell Chemical has been carrying on a high-pressure campaign to sell the insecticide Azodrin to farmers as a killer of cotton pests. They continue their program even though they know that Azodrin is not only ineffective, but often *increases* the pest density. They've covered themselves nicely in an advertisement which states, "Even if an overpowering migration [sic] develops, the flexibility of Azodrin lets you regain control fast. Just increase the dosage according to label recommendations." It's a great game—get people to apply the poison and kill the natural enemies of the pests. Then blame the increased pests on "migration" and sell even more pesticide!

Right now fisheries are being wiped out by over-exploitation, made easy by modern electronic equipment. The companies producing the equipment know this. They even boast in advertising that only their equipment will keep fishermen in business until the final kill. Profits must obviously be maximized in the short run. Indeed, Western society is in the process of completing the rape and murder of the planet for economic gain. And, sadly, most of the rest of the world is eager for the opportunity to emulate our

behavior. But the underdeveloped peoples will be denied that opportunity—the days of plunder are drawing inexorably to a close.

Most of the people who are going to die in the greatest cataclysm in the history of man have already been born. More than three and a half billion people already populate our moribund globe, and about half of them are hungry. Some 10 to 20 million will starve to death *this year.* In spite of this, the population of the earth will increase by 70 million souls in 1969. For mankind has artificially lowered the death rate of the human population, while in general birth rates have remained high. With the input side of the population system in high gear and the output side slowed down, our fragile planet has filled with people at an incredible rate. It took several million years for the population to reach a total of two billion people in 1930, while a *second two billion will have been added by 1975!* By that time some experts feel that food shortages will have escalated the present level of world hunger and starvation into famines of unbelievable proportions. Other experts, more optimistic, think the ultimate food-population collision will not occur until the decade of the 1980's. Of course more massive famine may be avoided if other events cause a prior rise in the human death rate.

Both worldwide plague and thermonuclear war are made more probable as population growth continues. These, along with famine, make up the trio of potential "death rate solutions" to the population problem—solutions in which the birth rate-death rate imbalance is redressed by a rise in the death rate rather than by a lowering of the birth rate. Make no mistake about it, *the imbalance will be redressed.* The shape of the population growth curve is one familiar to the biologist. It is the outbreak part of an outbreak-crash sequence. A population grows rapidly in the presence of abundant resources, finally runs out of food or some other necessity, and crashes to a low level or extinction. Man is not only running out of food, he is also destroying the life support systems of the Spaceship Earth. The situation was recently summarized very succinctly: "It is the top of the ninth inning. Man, always a threat at the plate, has been hitting Nature hard. It is important to remember, however, that NATURE BATS LAST."

Ecology: Government Control of the Environment

GARY ALLEN

GARY ALLEN *is a contributing editor to* American Opinion.

Allen challenges the view that our environment is so threatened that only immediate, large-scale intervention by the federal government can solve the problem. He sees the present interest in ecology largely as another tactic by the Left to extend socialistic controls over the American people.

When the Establishment shifts into a new propaganda campaign it does so with the subtlety of an inebriate elephant trying to dance the Watusi in a china closet. First it was poverty, and every imaginable bureaucrat was out searching for government-certified poverts; then it was the "peace" movement, with its angry legions of Castroite pacifists; now the "in" thing is "conservation" or, as it is known among the usual "Liberal" press agents and phonies, "ecology." Check almost any recent issue of such Establishment slicks as *Life* or *Look* or *Time* or *Newsweek* and you will find at least one doomsday article about the grisly state of the American environment.

For those too hypnotized by the anesthetube to read, the federally licensed television networks are now devoting hours to promotion of the idea that man is poisoning his streams, polluting his atmosphere, brutalizing his environment, absorbing natural resources at a crippling rate, becoming engulfed in his own refuse, and at the same time multiplying his numbers like over-sexed rats to further the destruction of his environment. On September 14, 1969, the National Council of Churches presented a series called "High Rise Living" on the N.B.C. network's *Frontiers Of Faith*. The first guest was identified Communist Pete Seeger, introduced in feigned innocence as a "conservationist and well-known folk singer." The frontiers of the Kremlin's favorite bard know no bounds. On March 20, 1969, the Xerox Corporation sponsored another nationwide television special on ecology, also featuring Comrade Seeger.

American Opinion 8(5): 1–16, May 1970. Reprinted by permission of *American Opinion* © Robert Welsh, Inc. 395 Concord Avenue, Belmont, Massachusetts 02178. Subscription price: $10. per year. Abridgment by the editors of the present volume.

Meanwhile, wide-eyed youths in our nation's high schools and colleges are being enthralled with horripilant tales from such fearmongers of ecology as Stanford's Dr. Paul Ehrlich, author of *The Population Bomb*, probably the biggest bestseller on college campuses in a decade. "It is already too late to avoid famines that will kill millions, possibly by 1975," Dr. Ehrlich declares. He also predicts the total pollution and death of the world's oceans by 1979.

Oh, it's scary stuff.

Rudy Abramson of the *Los Angeles Times* and *Washington Post* proclaims that the ecology movement will be "our Sputnik for the 1970s." In referring to "America the Ugly," the Establishment's *Time* magazine croaks with its usual homogenized similies: "The environment may well be the gut issue that can unify a polarized nation in the 1970s." Even the pedagogous John Kenneth Galbraith has declared: "Pollution may well be the nation's most broadly based and democratic effort." And, of course, chief Establishmentarian Richard Nixon agrees. The President announced in his State of the Union message:

> The great question of the '70s is: Shall we surrender to our surroundings or shall we make our peace with nature and begin to make reparations for the damage we have done to our air, to our land and to our water?

In his 1971 Budget message the President delighted "Liberal" pundits by co-opting their ecology issue. Conservatives would, of course, applaud the President for cutting the ground from under "Liberal" issues if the Marxist solutions proposed by the "Liberals" were not adopted in the process. After all, the problems of our environment *are* genuine. But ecology is an issue on which the "Liberals" and radicals have, for the most part, seized the initiative.

Through the use of highly emotional rhetoric, and by playing upon fears of impending social and environmental chaos, the Left is hoping to convert sincere and legitimate concern over the quality of our environment into acceptance of government control of that environment. The object is to make the "Green Revolution" part of the Red Revolution by using the Establishment media to stimulate the usual over-reaction among the American masses through exaggeration, magnification, and distortion of a genuine problem. The object is federal control of the environment in which we all must live.

While the problems of pollution have been with us for centuries, it is only in recent months that the Establishment has begun to feed the issue through its propaganda machines. A few Americans with highly sensitive proboscides have already smelled a rodent. As Guy Wright of the *San Francisco Examiner* observed:

> . . . there's something about the ecology kick that disturbs me. Most of this enthusiasm was artificially induced. And it is being deliberately manipulated. Like the teenie-boppers who squeal for a favorite singer, the people being manipulated don't know it and will swear it isn't true. But it's there.

In early 1969 hardly anyone knew what ecology meant. Yet, by the end of the year, Lynn Sherr of Associated Press was writing: "American youth has found a new supercause . . . The young are mobilizing with some of the same intensity that has gone into antiwar movements, against the pollution of air, land and sea." The radical *Berkeley Tribe* tipped off the objective in its issue for January 2, 1970:

> *The peace movement, which revived briefly this past fall, has sunk again into a lethargy that is more than seasonal. No one realizes this more than the Moratorium leaders, who have watched their constituency slip away as the months go by. In order to broaden their base in 1970, they extended their program to include environmental control . . . as well as immediate withdrawal.*

You will notice that while the student radicals have shifted gears in unison with the Establishment against which they think they are revolting, the radical student leadership remains constant. Ecology is to be the great umbrella of the Seventies, with every radical issue from the governing of private property to population control tied to environment. *Newsweek* of December 20, 1969, informs us:

> *While front pages still report that the major student protests are centered on the war and the draft, concerned college students are enlisting increasingly in the fight for a cleaner, purer, less ravished environment. . . .*
>
> *Joined by former antiwar activists, young Democrats, crew-cut fraternity members and so-called hippies, the environment movement on campus is a response to alarms as varied as pesticides, oil slicks, . . . and car-exhaust pollution. . . .*
>
> *Still, the tone of the antiwar movement has influenced the fight against pollution. "Many students," says Wayne Miyao, a social-science major, "view environment problems and Vietnam as manifestations of the same political and economic situation."*
>
> *Elsewhere as well, the movement cuts across political lines. Half the members of the month-old Ecology Action organization at Columbia are former members of SDS. But the other half, said a radical, "are un-political freaks. . . ."*

Ecology radicals have donned gas masks to invade auto shows, picketed campus recruiters for oil companies and manufacturers of pesticides, and developed a rhetoric for ecology of which Lenin would have been proud. Harvard's underground *Old Mole* recommends:

> *In order to localize and focus the environmental crisis, ecological radicals can engage in exemplary actions: plug up a belching smokestack with cement. Radical students can make radical ecological demands on universities—the laboratories of death technology, the ivory towers of technocratic ideology. . . .*
>
> *Sporadic eco-guerrilla actions and local piecemeal demonstrations can be effective and revolutionary. . . . Ecology by definition cannot be reformist. Ensuring an inhabitable earth requires an international revolution in order to establish a worldwide planet of human life which conforms to the organic requirements of the planet.*

The new ecology game provides the radicals with a whole new audience of potential recruits. After all, the "peace" movement had its limitations. No American with any knowledge of Communism, or any sense of patriotism, would participate in a demonstration led by schoolboy Lenins carrying the Vietcong flag. But concern about the quality of our environment bridges social, political, and religious lines. It presents an opportunity for the greatest con since W. C. Fields passed himself off as a temperance leader and the happy father of ten.

When a "scientist" carrying the prestige of a Ph.D. starts throwing "facts" and "figures" at students, how can they assess their validity? On most issues it takes another scientist to refute the fearful projections made by the radical professors shouting of ecology. But, of course, it is only the radicals who are invited to address student assemblies.

Following in the wake of the Leftist intellectuals are the Leftist politicians, as usual pitching their con to youth. Typical of the ecology bunk being aimed at students is an article by Senator Gaylord Nelson in the Marxist *Progressive* magazine of November 1969:

> The real loser in man's greedy drive is the youth of this country and the world. Because of the stupidity of their elders, the children of today face an ugly world in the near future, with dangerously and deadly polluted air and water; overcrowded development; festering mounds of debris; and an insufficient amount of open space to get away from it all.
>
> Since youth is again the great loser, perhaps the only hope for saving the environment and putting quality back into life may well depend on our being able to tap the energy, idealism, and drive of the oncoming generation that, otherwise, will inherit the poisonous air and deadly waters of the earth.

Senator Nelson is a founder of "The First National Environmental Teach-In." Denis Hayes, the national coordinator of this effort, says that on April 22, 1970, ecology teach-ins will be held at nine hundred colleges and four thousand high schools across the country. The program, employing the same techniques as those used to promote the cause of the Vietcong among American students, was evolved from a meeting of student ecology radicals financed and sponsored by the Department of Health, Education and Welfare. According to Guy Wright in the *San Francisco Examiner:*

> Last October 100 student leaders, mostly activist types, were invited to Washington for a four-day conference on environmental pollution. All their expenses were paid from a $50,000 fund Bob Finch put up as Secretary of Health, Education and Welfare.
>
> On the second day Senator Gaylord Nelson (D.-Wis.) made an unscheduled appearance. He just happened to hear about the conference, he said, and decided to drop in. For a casual visitor he came curiously prepared with a concrete proposal. He promised the student leaders $25,000 and office space if they would try to close down their schools one day next spring for a nationwide teach-in on environmental pollution.

Nobody is willing to admit who selected the date of April twenty-second for the "Earth Day" teach-ins. That is, after all, the one-hundredth anniversary of Lenin's birth. A coincidence you think? The student activists just picked a convenient weekend? Hardly. April twenty-second falls on a Wednesday. For months the radical and Communist Press has been detailing plans to celebrate Lenin's centennial birthday with worldwide demonstrations. April twenty-second is as familiar a date to these people as Washington's Birthday is to real Americans. The selection of this date as "Earth Day" provides an excellent indication of who is running the campus ecology movement.

I telephoned the Teach-In's national coordinator, Denis Hayes, to ask him how April twenty-second happened to be selected for the ecology festivities.

Mr. Hayes, late of Harvard's Graduate School of Government, had obviously memorized his answer: "It also happens to be William Shakespeare's birthday, Queen Elizabeth's birthday, Maryanna Kaufman's birthday and her Aunt Ann's birthday, but I am sure that none of those entered into Gaylord Nelson's thoughts when he and the steering committee or whoever it was chose that date."

Mr. Hayes should avoid lying about matters so easily checked. The date settled upon as the natal day of William Shakespeare is April 23, 1564; Queen Elizabeth was born on April 21, 1926. Which leads one to suspect that even Hayes' friends Maryanna Kaufman and her aunt (if they exist) might well have been born on some Friday the thirteenth for all he knows. What else do you suppose Mr. Hayes lies about?

This ecology business has a particular attraction for hippies, who live in filth but claim to love the beauties of nature. According to Professor Paul Ehrlich, a good deal of the success of the ecology revolution is to be attributed to the "much despised 'hippie' movement ... a movement wrapped up in Zen Buddhism, physical love and a disdain for material wealth. It is small wonder that our society is horrified at hippies' behavior—it goes against our most cherished religious and ethical ideas."

The pseudo-philosophy which attracts hippies to champion the "Green Revolution" is projected in their anthem *This Is The Age of Aquarius*, from the hip-tease show, *Hair*. The hippie subculture is very big on astrology, and the astrologers tell us that we have left the 2,000-year "Age of Pisces" and have entered the "Age of Aquarius." The hippies interpret this as an end to the tiresome "work ethic" of the age of Christianity and the beginning of the age of collectivism. As Vera Reed declares in *Towards Aquarius*:

> Up to now the most valuable factor to evolve in world states is the immense fusion of peoples created by the United States of America and the United States [sic] of Soviet Russia.... The contribution of the U.S.S.R.... is more immediately progressive and valuable. In face of strenuous opposition from the rest of the world [sic] Russia has had the vision to create a new order more in line with the symbolism of Aquarius than any so far attempted .... From Russia the Aquarian note of hope rings crystal clear and from her may come a yet finer expression of human progress.

Ah yes, astrology, ecology, and Communism. The antipathy to Christianity, capitalism, and patriotism is written in the stars. This is *some* con game!

What particularly bugs these self-worshipping Humanists is Genesis 1:28, which states: "And God said unto them, Be fruitful and multiply, and replenish the earth, and subdue it; and have dominion over the fish of the sea, and over the fowl of the air, and over everything that moveth upon the earth." In "The Historical Roots Of Our Ecologic Crisis," Professor Lynn White of U.C.L.A. maintains:

> What we do about ecology depends on our ideas of the man-nature relationship. More science and more technology are not going to get us out of the present ecologic crisis until we find a new religion, or rethink our old one. The beatniks who are the basic revolutionaries

*of our time, show a sound instinct in their affinity for Zen Bud-
dhism. . . .*

*Hence we shall continue to have a worsening ecologic crisis until
we reject the Christian axiom that nature has no reason for existence save to serve man. (The Environmental Handbook, p. 24–25.)*

Stanford's Professor Ehrlich, a favorite of the slick Establishment magazines, contends that in order to survive in the coming years:

*. . . somehow we've got to change from a growth-oriented exploitive
system to one focused on stability and conservation. Our entire system
of orienting to nature must undergo a revolution. And that revolution
is going to be extremely difficult to pull off, since the attitudes of
Western Culture towards nature are deeply rooted in Judeo-Christian
tradition. . . .*

*Before the Christian era trees, springs, hills, streams and other
objects of nature had guardian spirits. These spirits had to be ap-
proached and placated before one could safely invade their territory.
As [Lynn] White says, "By destroying pagan animism. Christianity
made it possible to exploit nature in a mood of indifference to the
feelings of natural objects."**

Another theme which pervades the ecology movement is the idea that
"capitalism is the cause of all our pollution problems." Ignoring the fact
that much of our pollution is the fault of ineffective government sewage
and trash disposal, the Lenin Day *Environmental Handbook* declares boldly:
"Pollution is somebody's profit." Lynn Sherr of Associated Press observes:

*Indeed, to the young ecologists, capitalism is Ecology Enemy
No. 1. They criticize the growth motive—America's annual attempt to
push the Gross National Product higher and higher.*

Writing in Harvard's radical *Old Mole*, ecology activist Tom Gallagher
claims:

*One of the functions of the left in the United States is to show how
environmental destruction is based upon a system of human exploitation and how only the abolition of capitalism will provide the
probability for the preservation of the earth as an inhabitable
place. . . .*

*Ecological destruction on a global scale is a direct product of
American imperialism. . . .*

---

*Part of this anti-Christian attitude of the leading ecologists is reflected by U.C.
Berkeley instructor Clifford Humphrey in an attack on Christmas trees. Honest!
Humphrey, who has worked closely in anti-American activities with Communists like
Bettina Aptheker and Peter Camejo, emphasizes in *Politics of Ecology:* "I want to
mention one specific consumer habit that has outlived whatever usefulness it may
have had—Christmas trees." In December, Berkeley radicals actually held ceremonial
burial services for Christmas trees. It is interesting to recall that one of the first moves
after the Communists' November Revolution in Russia was the banning of Christmas
trees (*100 Things You Should Know About Communism And Religion*, Report of the
House Committee on Un-American Activities, page 8.)

> *Not until imperialism is defeated in the third world and is replaced by socialism at home can we begin to deal with the problem of the environment in a rational way. At this point in history the ecologists' best friends are the Viet Cong.*

The idea that radical socialism is the cure for environmental problems is absolutely absurd. The United States of Russia [*sic*], the Aquarian ideal, has pollution problems as extensive as any in America. Victor Zorza reports in the *Los Angeles Times* of February 15, 1970, that even *Pravda* has confessed: "we are turning the atmosphere of our major industrial regions and large cities into a dump for poisonous industrial wastes." Despite the fact that the U.S.S.R. has only five per cent as many motor vehicles as the United States, that Aquarian Paradise has a severe air pollution problem both because its technology is so far behind ours and because of Communist indifference to the quality of the environment. Victor Zorza notes of the Soviet Union:

> . . . *new factories are still being built without any purification plant, for water or smoke. Indeed where smoke filters are provided, they often* [says Pravda] *"work badly, or not at all." More than half of the Soviet towns discharge their sewage, untreated, directly into nearby waters.*

Clearly the efforts of the "new environmentalists" to create ecology propaganda for the purpose of shoving more socialism down the throat of America are ludicrous. But, while the radical ecologists sow Marxist propaganda below, the politicians above are preparing to reap the socialist crop. There is no secret about all of this. It's right out in the open. Stuart Loory of the *Los Angeles Times* notes:

> Mr. Nixon talked in his State of the Union message last month about developing a "national growth policy" to make certain that new progress is not overwhelmed by new problems. This implies the kind of centralized planning that has long been anathema to the American Way and which has proved economically destructive in the Soviet Union.
>
> But perhaps—with all the beer cans and soda bottles and waste paper and smog piling up in the environment—the time for such planning has come.

The doomsday environmentalists are even using ecology as a ploy to propagandize Americans about the need for world government. "Nations are such an artificial construct from an ecological point of view," says *The Environmental Handbook*, "that any further energies poured into them are almost certain to do more long-term harm than good. Nations . . . must be phased out as quickly as possible and replaced with tribal or regional autonomous economies. . . ." Not surprisingly, the United Nations has developed a sudden interest in environmental problems.

Not only has the ecology movement been perverted into a collectivist One World movement, but many of its most prestigious spokesmen are total regressivists. What the radical ecologists are calling for is an abandonment of our high standards of living and a return to the primitive drudgery from which our ancestors worked so hard to escape. In a chapter in *The Environmental Handbook* entitled "Suggestions Toward An Ecological Platform," Keith Murray declares:

> *The runaway U.S. growth economy must be stabilized to halt the destruction of the world resource base before we choke in the waste products of our affluence. There should be a thorough reassessment and reversal of unlimited economic growth as a national goal. The first and most crucial step is a guaranteed income, to break the compulsory link between jobs and income that has been a principal stimulus to growthmanship.*
> *Ways must be found to curb the U.S. appetite for goods....* (pp. 318–319.)

The poverty-stricken, over whom these same Leftists have spilled buckets of crocodile tears, may not be entirely overjoyed if these people are able to put an end to the only real hope of escaping poverty. Naturally the hippies and revolutionaries would love to be supported by a guaranteed annual income while they work to overthrow civilization.

Professor Paul Ehrlich says in his best-selling *Population Bomb:*

> *Working people should insist on a reduction in working hours.... People would then have more time to repair their own appliances, grow some of their own food, and mend their own clothes, rather than having to pay others. . . .*
> *But in the long run, it is questionable whether large factories can be scaled down and decentralized without dismantling the corporate investment and profit system.* (Reprinted in *The Environmental Handbook,* pp. 245–246.)

One wonders how many hours Dr. Ehrlich has spent lately mending a dollar T-shirt, or whether the average worker would not prefer to work another twenty minutes on the job to buy a new one rather than spend an hour with thread and needle repairing his tattered underwear. And how would you like to repair your color TV set?

Much of this regressivism is simply a pretext for an attack on free enterprise. Gary Snyder is a self-professed Communist who was recently featured in a laudatory article in *Look* magazine. The author of this little screed, who failed to mention Comrade Snyder's advocacy of Communism, explains the game:

> *If everyone in this country refused to buy a new car in 1969, the American economy would collapse. That would be enough to do it all in. That's sort of like an unimaginable utopian kind of revolution, but it's absolutely true. By consumers refusing to consume, you destroy the whole roots of the capitalist economy overnight.*

The automobile is a particular target of the environment radicals, many of whom drive to their demonstrations in new sports cars paid for by their capitalist parents. Students at San Jose State College collected $2,500 earlier this year to buy a new Ford Maverick *for burial.*

Air pollution caused by the internal combustion engine is a genuine problem of great magnitude, but the environment radicals do not want technological solutions to that problem. "The automobile industry's recent announcement of pollution control programs for the private automobile merely prolongs the agony of the private transportation system," argues Professor Ehrlich. You see, these boys want to take away your car so *government* can own our transportation system.

Another facet of the ecology movement closely inter-woven with the anticapitalist mentality is its anti-urbanism. In his widely reprinted article "The Four Changes," Peace and Freedom Party radical Clifford Humphrey predicts:

> *Some communities can establish themselves in backwater rural areas and flourish. . . . Ultimately cities will exist only as joyous tribal gatherings and fairs, to dissolve after a few weeks.*

While preparing to dismantle urban areas, the radical ecologists intend to manipulate the cities politically. Ehrlich says, "We must now begin to integrate ecological reasoning into all community and political organizing for social change." He further advocates forming tenants' unions and "Community Development Corporations"—which amount to nothing less than soviets—to confront local businesses and city hall. Then the author of *The Population Bomb* declares:

> *The most effective mechanism for obtaining community control of the environment is to organize around specific issues in neigh-borhoods, getting media coverage of newsworthy events and building energy to the point of an implicit threat of the possibility of direct action and confrontation in order to negotiate for community control. The community development corporation [soviets] through its self-governing capability will be able to ritualize and maintain whatever control is taken from downtown.* (The Environmental Handbook, page 251.)

Dr. Ehrlich has some quaint ideas for these soviets he wants to impose on the cities. He wants them to "freeze downtown highrise development. There is no need for any new highrise structures. . . . We don't need more shelter, rather we must learn to use our existing buildings more efficiently, to justly redistribute our shelter resources. No more new suburbs should be built until we are prepared to build semi-rural self-sufficient communities from re-claimed, rather than virgin building materials. . . ."

> *Close off streets for orchards, vegetable gardens, parks, market places. Close the city center to private automobiles. . . . Groups [soviets] should organize to take down fences separating yards to make truck gardens and neighborhood sheds for storing shared [property of the collective farm] tools. . . . Experimental living groups should construct their shelters from used building materials (church windows [sic], old car ports—hoods and trunks make beautiful domes). . . .* (The Environmental Handbook, page 243.)

The radical ecologists are arguing for replacement of modern urban civilization with rural communes. *Anarchos Magazine* maintains in an article called "Ecology And Revolutionary Thought" that "the factory floor must yield to horticulture and gardening." *The Environmental Handbook* insists we must accept "the inherent aptness of communal life." And, it continues: "It is hard to even begin to gauge how much a complication of possessions, the notions of 'my and mine,' stand between us and a true, clear, liberated way of seeing the world."

The "back to nature" tribal communes are no joke to these people. The movement has historical parallels with the teachings of Rousseau and Weishaupt, and with the pre-revolutionary Nihilists in Russia. The head guru of this movement is Gary Snyder, whose book *The Earth Household* has been referred to by the Communist S.D.S.'s Tod Gitlin as a "green arsenal." Snyder is an admitted Communist who maintains that "political repression" by the "fascist police," combined with ecological disaster, will make living in rural communes necessary for revolutionaries. According to Snyder:

> *The country is revolutionary territory. . . . What Castro and Che later had to say about the Cuban experience was that you can't trust the city comrades or rely on the city comrades for anything and you just give up depending on them for anything because they'll never understand the situation of the guerrilla camp in the mountains. . . . Also Castro and Che felt that the guerrilla camp provides real training in being a communist.*

In pointing out the military implications of the ecology commune movement, Comrade Snyder notes:

> *What if the Pentagon had to deal with thousands of small tribes scattered across the American landscape? Tribes interiorly gentle but exteriorly capable of good offense and defense. Knowing Indians' techniques and capable of Indian mobility. The suburban whites thus find themselves surrounded—in fact opposed simultaneously from front and rear. The strategic situation changes so much that possibly few shots will have to be fired.*

During the past year a large number of these radical communes have been established in the Western States. Many are comprised of hippies (and nothing pollutes an area like flooding it with hippies) who want to get into the country where they can grow marijuana. Others are guerrilla bands preparing for revolution. A group in Northern California calling itself L.A.R.G.O. (Liberation Army Revolutionary Group Organizations of the National Liberation Front) notified the Mendocino County Board of Supervisors on March 11, 1970, that as of March 15, 1970, a state of war would exist and The Revolution will have begun. On March 13, 1970, Charles W. Bates of the Federal Bureau of Investigation in San Francisco sent the following message to law enforcement authorities throughout all of Northern California:

> *Request for information re black commune* [sic]. *Information has been developed from an informant of unknown reliability that there is a black commune located a few hundred miles north of San Francisco consisting of thirty to fifty male Negroes with no children allowed. This commune is allegedly located in a mountain area near*

*a swift moving river in a densely wooded area inaccessible by heli-
copter and can be reached only by road and any vehicle traveling
the road would be under observation by members of the commune
for some distance prior to the arrival at the site [sic]. Members except
for a chosen few are transported in and out of the site blindfolded
in either trucks or vans. Informant indicated there was a small town
where food was purchased for the commune. The members of the
commune according to the informant possess and maintain a quantity
of firearms and dynamite and they carry out paramilitary exercises
on a daily basis. Another commune consisting of both Negroes and
whites is supposed to exist a short distance from the above commune
and several members are believed to be federal and local fugitives. . . .*

The ecology movement is not only deeply involved in revolution, it is
up to its neck in efforts to control population. The leader of the overpopulation hysteria is Paul Ehrlich, author of *The Population Bomb,* president of a group calling itself Zero Population Growth, and recently appointed as an associate at the radically Marxist Center for the Study of
Democratic Institutions. According to Ehrlich, civilization will during the
next decade collapse in famine as millions of people starve to death. Ehrlich
is not especially concerned about the population growth of Asia, Africa,
or South America. What bothers him is the growth of families in the United
States. "Each American child," he says, "is 50 times more of a burden on
the environment than each Indian child." He claims this is because the
wicked United States, with only 5.7 per cent of the world's population,
consumes forty per cent of the world's production of natural resources. The
answer, he argues, is to stabilize our population and level our standard of
living down to that of the rest of the world.

Joining Ehrlich in this push is the entire ecology crowd, including such
Establishmentarians as Robert S. McNamara, President of the World Bank,
who has proclaimed: "The threat of unmanageable population pressure is
very much like the threat of nuclear war." President Nixon has even announced: "One of the most serious challenges to human destiny in the last
third of this century will be growth of the population." Dr. Lee DuBridge,
the President's science advisor, recently told U.N.E.S.C.O.: "Every human
institution, school, university, church, family, government—and international agencies such as U.N.E.S.C.O.—should set [*population control*] as
its prime task. Our spacecraft called the earth is reaching its capacity. Can
we not invent a way to reduce our population growth rate to zero?"

The "people regulators" have devised some ideas for population control
that would make Big Brother blanch. The same "Liberals" who a year ago
were defending the "rights" of Welfare recipients to breed themselves weary
at the taxpayer's expense are now demanding federal controls over the right
of the middle-class to reproduce. Hippies are crying "Freedom for drugs
but not for babies." Scientists like Ehrlich are ridiculing the idea that
American families have a right to decide how many children they should
have.

Professor H. Bentley Glass of Johns Hopkins University has a plan for
all of this, described in the *Los Angeles Times* of June 4, 1964, as follows:

> A man and woman who planned to marry would visit a "genetic
> clinic" where chemical tests would be given to show if they were likely
> to have defective children. . . . If they passed they would be issued
> a marriage license. The right to the first child would be automatic,
> and the family would even get a tax exemption.
>
> A second child would be licensed too, although there would not
> be a second exemption. Instead of gaining an exemption for a third
> child, even if licensed, a couple would have $600 added to their tax-
> able income.
>
> Dr. Glass said penalties for producing an unlicensed baby would
> be severe. He suggested sterilization as a punishment to fit the crime.

The Associated Press carried the following on September 4, 1969:

> A Washington psychologist and sex therapist advocated Wednes-
> day that the world's nations remove "the right to reproduce" from
> their people as the only solution to the global population explosion.
>
> Dr. Robert H. Harper, addressing the 77th annual convention of
> the American Psychological Association said practical maneuvers
> to assure compliance might be available within a few years by such
> means as placing temporary sterilizing chemicals in food and water
> supplies. Under such a compulsory system, he said, "The privilege
> to reproduce could then be granted and the rules governing such
> privilege could be worked out in whatever wholly democratic ways
> people would want."
>
> "But," he added, "the original removal of the right to reproduce
> would have to be done whether or not it was with the individual's
> approval and consent."*

Numerous other environmentalists have proposed variations on, and
combinations of, the above themes. The one thing they all have in common
is government control of human reproduction. Ehrlich advocates free distribution by government of the pill, voluntary legal abortion, a tax on
children in excess of two per family, heavy taxes on cribs, diapers, toys,
etc., and bonuses or tax exemptions for delayed marriages, childless marriages, and sterilization. He calls for a "responsibility prize" for men and
women who allow themselves to be sterilized.

Many of the ecology groups have actually called for a major *reduction*
in population. The Lenin Day *Environmental Handbook* declares: "The goal
would be half of the present world population, or less." Just what form
such genocide should take is not suggested.

Yet, of all the aspects of the environmentalist programs there is no bigger
fraud than the idea that America is threatened with destruction through
over-population. Dr. Donald Bogue, a respected demographer at the University of Chicago, notes that population in the United States is leveling

---

* Conservatives are concerned at the fact that the two most prominent organizations
working in the field of population control are the Ford and Rockefeller Foundations.
See *Congressional Record*, December 29, 1969, Page 11017. John D. Rockefeller III has
already recommended that the U.N. establish a "population commissioner." (U.P.I.,
May 25, 1969.)

off and predicts it will settle at about 220 million. As Professor Ansley Coale of Princeton observes:

> More than half of the counties in the United States have lost population in each of the last two intercensal decades. The density of population is 4.5 times greater in France, 10 times greater in the United Kingdom and 30 times greater in the Netherlands than in the United States; yet pollution, traffic jams, and delinquency are no worse in those countries than here. Even if our population rose to a billion, its average density would not be very high by European standards. (Congressional Record, October 20, 1969, page S12806.)

The fact is that we are not overpopulated. Professor Karl Brandt of Stanford has spoken of our serious *underpopulation* "by any standards we can reasonably apply. This country will not be overpopulated with 350,000,000 or many more people and will have a much higher standard of living."* Dr. James H. Ford commented in the *Los Angeles Times* of April 2, 1969:

> Some "over-population" pundits talk, in their usual hysterical manner, about "standing room only" somewhere in the future. This term might represent some sort of absolute—even though a rather unrealistic and improbable one. Even if the present world population were 4 billion persons, simple arithmetic will show that we could give each person a two-foot square plot for "standing" and we could put the whole of the earth's population within a plot 30 miles square.

The relation between population and poverty is equally absurd. As Diana Sheets, an outstanding young researcher, has noted: "Overpopulation is commonly accepted as the cause for the great poverty of the people of India. However, India has five hundred people per square mile while Japan has seven hundred, Holland eight hundred, and Monaco forty-six thousand. This means Monaco has ninety-two times as many people per square mile as India. Yet, one never hears of these countries being overpopulated or starving."

Virtually every ecology "expert" is now predicting massive famines for America within only a few years. This prediction is totally debunked by the facts. Professor Karl Brandt (who you may be sure does not get one one-hundredth the opportunities to speak on college campuses as does his Stanford colleague, the radical Dr. Ehrlich), comments:

> . . . I reject as illegitimate and invalid the argument that the accelerating pace of population growth is over-taking the rate of growth of food production and that therefore disastrous famine of abhorrent proportions is almost inevitable unless population growth is throttled.
>
> As I shall prove, the famine projections are neither a sound nor a legitimate argument for population control because the world's existing agricultural capacity gives abundant leeway to produce adequate

---

*From the *National Observer*, July 15, 1963, as quoted by the Reverend Rushdoony in his authoritative *The Myth of Over-Population*, Craig Press, 1969.

*food supplies for the growing population. Therefore, using famine
alarm to justify support of government action toward birth control
can only weaken the initiative to promote recognition of the importance of responsible parenthood.*

Dr. Brandt goes on to say that in recent years some of the most densely
populated areas of the world have increased food production beyond all
expectations and against the worst odds. He notes that since the end of
World War II the world's technical, and economically feasible, potential
for food production has expanded at more than a geometrical rate. Even
the United Nation's Food and Agriculture Organization (F.A.O.) has been
forced to confirm the position of Dr. Brandt. In an announcement appearing
in the *Los Angeles Times* of February 12, 1970, that U.N. organization
revealed: "The food problem facing the world in the near future is more
likely to be surpluses than starvation."

Technological advancements have put the lie to neo-Malthusian claims.
"The underdeveloped areas of the world, where the danger had been
foreseen, increased their agricultural production by 5% in 1967 and 2% in
1968, with estimates for the year just ended showing a continuation of the
trend," admits the U.N.'s F.A.O. Food production even in "under-developed"
areas was growing faster than population. As Stanford's Professor Brandt
concludes:

> *If famine should occur, neither scarcity of natural nor man-made
> resources nor the rate of population growth offer valid excuses. Even
> natural calamities like drought, floods, or pests do not necessarily
> cause famine in any properly organized society.*
>
> *If famine should occur in some countries—as it well may—it will
> be primarily "government made" by policies similar to those that
> initially resulted in the starvation of 5 million people and have pre-
> vented for nearly 40 years any proper expansion of food production
> in Soviet Russia and have cost uncounted millions of lives in Red
> China.**

Actually, American politicians have done everything possible during the
past thirty years to limit our *over-supply* of food. If we ever do have a
famine in America it will be because of socialism and government controls.
As the Reverend Rushdoony writes in *The Myth Of Over-Population:*

> *. . . socialism always creates ultimately an imbalance between the
> number of people living and their food supply which results in hunger
> or famine. There is in this sense therefore always a problem of
> over-population under socialism. Hunger is chronic and endemic to
> socialism.*

Who has to be reminded that Russia, which before the Revolution exported a vast surplus of grain, must now import wheat?

Of course, the professional sowers of environmental despair disdain the

---

* *The Freeman,* January 1967. For information on how our government may be creating
a massive famine, see Dan P. Van Gorder, *Ill Fares The Land,* Western Islands, 1966.

free market and capitalist technology as providers of solutions to our problems because they are promoting socialism as the only answer. Actually, our technology is the best hope for ending pollution and continuing to expand the food supply. Great strides are already being made toward solving these problems.

Innovations in the field of agriculture have been enormous. Such advances allow milk, fowl, and egg production in indoor conditions on a scale unimaginable only a few years ago. Development of improved fertilizers has allowed much more food production on far less land. Vastly improved seed grains have multiplied yields tremendously.

Our free technology can easily meet the demands of population growth! As the *Los Angeles Times* recently reported: "Within a short time, you'll be able to buy for five dollars all the protein you'll need for a year." (That breakthrough is with a protein that comes from a fish-powder concentrate.) Plans are already being made to grow fish in underwater "factories" like chickens. Scotland is even now using the warm water produced by power plants to stimulate the growth of fish and shell fish.

The automobile is, of course, the chief polluter of the air; but technical breakthroughs have already been made in the production of less toxic gasolines and auto pollution-control devices. Because of this, the *Los Angeles Times* was able to report on March 16, 1970:

> *Southlanders may be breathing clean air—at least air free of auto emissions—as much as three years earlier than originally anticipated.*

Meanwhile, scientists are hard at work to develop electric, turbine, or steam-driven cars. Corporations are at work developing techniques for recovering pollutants (which are, after all, lost resources) now being pumped into the air by factory chimneys. Literally dozens of top business concerns are at work on processes to remove pollutants from the water and turn them into profits.

The radical ecologists claim the profit motive is responsible for the pollution of America. It is true that some businesses have polluted air and water in their search for the cheapest way to dispose of wastes, but the answer to this problem is to use our technology to turn those wastes into profits. The fact is that much of our pollution is caused by city-operated trash and sewage disposals, which have usurped the field and precluded the opportunity for private initiative to find a way to re-use trash and garbage. A *Japanese* concern has discovered a way to turn trash into building blocks, and a unit is even now being built in Muskegon, Michigan, to turn sewage into valuable fertilizer.* These problems can be solved without Police State methods. According to the *Chicago Tribune*, "On a percentage basis, business is already spending 10 times more money [*to stop pollution*] than the really big polluters of our environment—the municipal governments."

---

*For numerous examples of how elimination of wastes and pollution can be turned into profits see "Use Pollution To Benefit Mankind," by J. Leon Potter, *Congressional Record*, June 16, 1969, page E4962.

Sanity and balance are needed to solve our environmental problems. Ecology isn't a moral crusade, it is a science—a science which is being perverted by an organized campaign to propagandize Americans into accepting government land grabs, bureaucratic population control, and a further proliferation of government bureaus to manage every conceivable phase of our environment. The legitimate purpose of government is the protection of life and property. Since pollution is an attack on another man's life and property, conservatives will support private law suits and local legislation to put an end to it. Only in this way can these problems be dealt with in anywhere near a simple and efficient manner. But this is *not* the way it is going to be handled unless Americans wake up to the fact that they are being propagandized and used by a well organized army of phony environmentalists, self-seeking bureaucrats, and radical politicians.

America has major problems, but the solutions are not the ones the environmental ideologues are talking about. These people are part of the problem, not part of the solution. Many of them don't give a farthing about the problems of pollution, but are using this issue as a pretense to advance Marxist political schemes. The biggest pollution problem we face is the pollution by the collectivist Establishment and Marxist revolutionaries of the minds of a once thoroughly independent and free people.

Pollution and Cities

ROGER REVELLE

ROGER REVELLE *is Richard Saltonstall Professor of Population Policy and Director of the Center for Population Studies, Harvard University.*

Ehrlich has already suggested many of the dangers to our environment from the increased pollution due to urbanization and industrialization. Revelle explores the extent of this problem by examining the consequences of air, water, and land pollution in America. He analyzes possible solutions for these problems and suggests roles the federal government should play in the effort.

Pollution is the harmful alteration of our environment by our own actions. Pollutants are either unwanted by-products of our activities or the obnoxious residues of things we have made, used, and thrown away. Man has always produced pollutants, but until recently the natural processes in his environment were sufficient to change most of them into harmless or beneficial substances. In the modern world, however, pollutants are produced in such large quantities that the capacity of the environment to absorb them is often exceeded, and pollution results. Man is increasing in numbers, productivity, and technology, but the rest of nature remains fixed. As men clump themselves together in cities, the part of the environment that receives most of their pollutants is actually diminishing.

In 1890, some 22 million Americans were city dwellers. Today there are about 130 million, six times as many, and by the year 2000 the number will probably double again. With the growth of cities, we are placing ever heavier pollution pressure on a small fraction of our environment—about 2 per cent of the area of our country. In the megalopolises of the future—the continuous strip cities like Philip Hauser's "Atlanticopolis" extending from Boston to Richmond—the problems of waste removal and avoidance of pollution will be on the same scale as the problems of water, air, and food supply, and of human transportation.

This article appears in James Q. Wilson, ed. *The Metropolitan Enigma.* Harvard University Press, pp. 91–134. Copyright © 1968 by the President and fellows of Harvard College. Copyright © 1967 by the Chamber of Commerce of the United States of America. Reprinted by permission.

In many ways, the quality of our environment has deteriorated with each new advance of the gross national product. Increases in electric power production mean the burning of more coal and fuel oil, and hence the discharge of more sulphur dioxide into the air. The growth of the paper industry has brought a vast increase in trash. The production of new automobiles and the discard of old ones has resulted in unsightly piles of hulks. The growth of urban automobile transportation is choking both the mobility of the city and the lungs of the city-dwellers.

Not only are we making and consuming more things, and consequently producing a larger quantity of residues, but our advancing technology is producing new kinds of poisons. President Johnson has said, "The uncontrolled waste products of our technology are menacing the world we live in, our enjoyment, and our health."(1) The marvelous advance of American agriculture has depended largely on chemical fertilizers and pesticides, substances that were never before present in nature and against which our fellow creatures, the birds and fishes, have no defense mechanisms. Lead and other metallic additives in gasoline accumulate along our roadsides. New products of chemical industry poison our streams. Technological changes have reduced the kinds and amounts of materials that can be economically reused. Aluminum cans and plastic containers are worthless as salvage but virtually indestructible as litter.

In dealing with pollution, we must think about natural resources in two senses, both as raw materials or sources of energy, and as those parts of the environment that can be depleted or worsened by misuse. In our lifetimes and those of our children, the availability of energy and raw materials will not put any serious limits on American society, but we will be limited in human fulfillment—the quality of life will be lessened and dulled—by destructive changes in our environment. And future generations will suffer because of our prodigal methods of waste disposal. The phosphates we dump into streams and lakes are permanently lost to our farm lands; the rusting auto hulks in the countryside are a drain on our metal resources.

At the same time that we are producing more and worse pollutants, our aspirations for a better environment are rising. We now see pollution where before we were able to ignore it. As the national income increases, people are less willing to trade off environmental deterioration for lower costs of goods and services. The "third parties" who do not benefit from these trade-offs are more aware of their position and more impatient to see it remedied by the abatement or elimination of pollution.

In its report, "Restoring the Quality of Our Environment," the President's Science Advisory Committee has urged that "the public should come to recognize individual rights to quality of living, as expressed by the absence of pollution, just as it has come to recognize rights to education, to economic advance, and to public recreation. . . . The responsibility of each polluter for all forms of damage caused by his pollution should be effectively recognized and generally accepted. There should be no 'right' to pollute."(2)

Like education and economic opportunity, removing pollution is costly; we need to remember that the quality of life depends only in part on the quality of the environment.(3) Economic abundance and civilized diversity are also ingredients. We must use our environment in a variety of ways, and limited environmental resources must be allocated optimally among different uses. Hence, the basic issue in considering problems of pollution is to define our goals.(4) In order to do this we need to find ways of balancing aesthetic, recreational, and related aspects of the quality of human life against other values. Stated in economic terms, how much will people pay, and how much should they pay, for these intangibles?(5) How clean should this stream be, at what cost, for what purpose, and at what future time? It is meaningless simply to say that the stream should be "clean."

At present, we are unable to assess the full costs of pollution or the benefits from preventing it because we cannot measure adequately the psychic and physiological effects of a dirty environment. Consequently, our decisions are generally based on estimates of immediate monetary costs rather than on evaluations of the total benefits and costs of different courses of action.

AIR POLLUTION

The Problem

When I was a boy in Pasadena in the 1920's, we were always aware of the San Gabriel Mountains rising clear and steep, nearly a mile above our heads. The great line from "America the Beautiful": *For purple mountains' majesty above the fruited plain* was an ever present reality to us. Now when I return to Pasadena the mountains have disappeared. Of course, they are still there, but they are seldom seen; in their place is a grayish-brown haze.

One can be sure of seeing the mountains only from an airplane. When one flies into the Los Angeles International Airport, they are there, rising through a semitransparent brown blanket a thousand feet thick that stretches across the broad Los Angeles plain. As the aircraft loses altitude and dips into the blanket, distant objects disappear. When it lands, the passengers step out into a bright, diffuse light. Their eyes begin to smart and the air has an acrid smell. They are surrounded by the famous Los Angeles smog.

In December 1952 the city of London became enveloped in a fog which soon covered a large part of England. It was a black fog, visibility was extremely low, the air smelled of brimstone. The fog lasted a week, and during that time 4,000 people died who would otherwise have remained alive. Many of them were elderly; others had been ill with chronic heart or respiratory disease. They were the largest number of victims of a single episode of atmospheric poisoning ever recorded.

Both the mass tragedy in London and the unpleasant experience of travelers arriving in Los Angeles are examples of metropolitan air pollution, but of somewhat different kinds. So far as we know few people die directly from Los Angeles smog, although fatal accidents may be caused by the low visibility that accompanies it and by "freeway fatigue," which could be the initial stage of poisoning from the carbon monoxide in the air.(6) Its most evident ill effects are eye irritation, damage to orange and lemon trees and to vegetable crops and flowers, and the weathering and cracking of rubber. But it is also so unpleasant for so many people that Californians have been willing to spend half of all the money used for air pollution control in the United States(7) in an attempt to do something about it.

Pollutant emissions in Los Angeles from power plants, petroleum refineries, backyard trash burners, and many industrial sources have been greatly lowered since 1950. (See Table 1.) But the effluents from automobiles persist and now make up 88 per cent by weight of the total of air contaminants (Table 4). The number of automobiles has doubled since 1950 (Table 2) and the amount of pollutants from automobiles has also just about doubled, even though the total weight of pollutants emitted each day from all sources has increased by less than 50 per cent. Rush-hour traffic jams on Los Angeles' streets and freeways have become more than a frustrating method of squandering commuters' time; they are also highly effective in multiplying atmospheric pollutants.

In a modern automobile more than three pounds of carbon monoxide and about two ounces of oxides of nitrogen are formed for every gallon of gasoline burned; in addition, a little over 8 per cent of the hydrocarbons in the gasoline escapes without being oxidized, mostly through the exhaust but also through the crankcase vent, the carburetor, and the fuel tank. Together, the carbon monoxide and the unburned hydrocarbons represent a loss of fuel energy equivalent to about 15 per cent of the total amount of gasoline consumed. Since each of the 3.5 million automobiles in Los Angeles uses, on the average, a little over two gallons per day, this loss corresponds to 400 million gallons a year for Los Angeles County alone, and for the nation as a whole it amounts to nearly 5 per cent of the total consumption of liquid fuels.

The hydrocarbons emitted in automobile exhausts are both those originally present in the fuel and new compounds formed by the high temperature of combustion. There are at least 200 different compounds. The nitrogen oxides are produced in the combustion chamber by the high temperature combination of oxygen and nitrogen from the intake air. In a sense, each automobile is a small nitrogen fertilizer plant. The total amount of nitrogen compounds produced by Los Angeles automobiles each year is enough to fertilize the entire county with 70 pounds of nitrogen per acre.

Nitrogen dioxide is a yellow-brown gas which absorbs the blue and ultra-violet rays of the sun and in doing so breaks down to nitrogen oxide and atomic oxygen. The latter combines with atmospheric oxygen molecules to form ozone. The ozone and the atomic oxygen attack the hydrocarbons in the air to produce a variety of highly reactive compounds. These in turn react with oxygen to form more ozone and other poisons such as formaldehyde, and with the nitrogen oxides to form plant-damaging peracyl nitrates (usually abbreviated to PAN).(8) Ultimately, as the end product of the chain of reactions, stable substances are formed, including carbon dioxide, which remains in the air, and compounds and particles that settle or are washed out of it.

Although the observed ozone concentrations near the ground in Los

TABLE 1. Emission of air pollutants in Los Angeles County (tons per day) *Source: Summary of Total Air Pollution Data for Los Angeles County*. A Report of the Engineering Division, Air Pollution Control District, County of Los Angeles, January 1965, pp. i–ii and pp. 1–41.

SOURCE	POLLUTANTS					
	CARBON MON-OXIDE	SUL-PHUR DIOX-IDE	HYDRO-CARBONS	NITRO-GEN OXIDE	AERO-SOLS	TOTAL
1950						
(1) Fuel combustion	1	350	8	140	35	534
(2) Petroleum	770	450	450	50	6	1726
(3) Transportation	5500	25	1100	240	23	6888
(4) Organic solvents	—	—	300	—	4	304
(5) Chemical industry	—	50	—	—	15	65
(6) Refuse incineration	130	12	95	18	90	345
(7) Miscellaneous	100	2	9	5	150	266
Total	6501	889	1962	453	323	10128
1965						
(1) Fuel combustion						
(a) Electric power generation	—	270	8	145	25	448
(b) Domestic and commercial	1	—	—	55	9	65
(c) Industrial	—	1	6	25	2	34
(Subtotal)	(1)	(271)	(14)	(225)	(36)	(547)
(2) Petroleum						
(a) Production	—	—	60	10	—	70
(b) Refining	170	85	55	70	11	391
(c) Marketing	—	—	105	11	—	116
(Subtotal)	(170)	(85)	(220)	(91)	(11)	(577)
(3) Transportation						
(a) Gasoline powered motor vehicles	10330	30	1930	490	45	12825
(b) All other	153	2	39	21	14	229
(Subtotal)	(10483)	(32)	(1969)	(511)	(59)	(13054)
(4) Organic solvents	—	—	550	—	7	557
(5) Chemical industry	—	65	—	—	8	73
(6) Refuse incineration	1	—	—	1	—	2
(7) Miscellaneous	4	3	1	10	18	36
Total	10659	456	2754	838	139	14846
1970 (PROJECTED)						
(1) Fuel combustion	1	500	16	450	35	1002
(2) Petroleum	100	95	220	100	11	526
(3) Transportation	7860	35	1530	590	68	10083
(4) Organic solvents	—	—	125	—	4	129
(5) Chemical industry	—	65	—	—	8	73
(6) Refuse incineration	1	—	—	1	—	2
(7) Miscellaneous	4	3	1	15	15	38
Total	7966	698	1892	1156	141	11853

TABLE 2. Population and other statistics for Los Angeles County *Source: Summary of Total Air Pollution Data for Los Angeles County*. A Report of the Engineering Division, Air Pollution Control District, County of Los Angeles, January 1965, pp. i–ii and pp. 1–41.

	1950	1965	1970 (PROJECTED)
Population, millions of persons	4.3	6.82	7.75
Gasoline powered vehicles, millions	1.7	3.45	4.00
Gasoline consumption, thousands of tons/day	12.3	22.8	26.0

Angeles are often more than ten times the normal background concentration in rural areas, they are still only a few tenths of a part per million, and these low concentrations hold for all the reacting substances in the air (Table 3). PAN, for example, may be present in a few parts per billion.(9) Because of the extreme dilution, reactions which would proceed to completion in a second under ordinary laboratory concentrations take minutes or even hours in the atmosphere. This results in a complex of processes and a diversity of materials existing simultaneously, which are extremely difficult to study or to reproduce experimentally. Photochemical pollution of the Los Angeles type is probably self-limiting in intensity, because higher concentrations of the reacting substances would result in more rapid production of stable compounds. This is not true of carbon monoxide, most of which does not take part in the chain of photochemical reactions, and instead slowly combines with atmospheric oxygen to form carbon dioxide.

Automobiles are everywhere one of the principal sources of atmospheric pollutants, but their over-all importance in other United States cities is less than in Los Angeles. As Table 4 shows, transportation accounts for only about 60 per cent of air pollution in the country as a whole, while pollutants from electric power generation and industry make up more than 30 per cent. Sulphur dioxide and other odorous and corrosive sulphur compounds from the burning of sulphur-containing coal and fuel oils, together with ash and soot particles, are the principal pollutants produced by electric power utilities and industry. The 1952 tragedy in London, and similar catastrophes elsewhere, were the result of high and persistent concentrations of sulphur compounds and soot in stagnant, foggy air. Los Angeles partly escapes these materials because natural gas, which is low in sulphur and produces no fly ash, is the major fuel for utilities and industry.

TABLE 3. **Daily maximum concentrations of air pollutants in Los Angeles County** *Source: Summary of Total Air Pollution Data for Los Angeles County*. A Report of the Engineering Division, Air Pollution Control District, County of Los Angeles, January 1965, pp. i–ii and pp. 1–41.

	POLLUTANTS (PARTS PER MILLION)				
	CARBON MON-OXIDE	SULPHUR DIOXIDE	HYDRO-CARBONS	NITROGEN OXIDE	OZONE
Median value, May–October	20	0.10	0.60	0.30	0.25
Exceeded on 10% of days, May–October[a]	30	0.20	1.05	0.60	0.40
Median value, November–March	30	0.20	1.90	0.75	0.15
Exceeded on 10% of days, November–March[a]	45	0.40	2.55	1.25	0.25
Exceeded on 10% of days during highest month[a]	55	0.40	2.80	1.40	0.30
Highest observed	72	2.49	40	3.93	0.90
First "alert" stage[b]	100	3.00	—	3.00	0.50

[a]Maximum pollutant concentrations are higher than the indicated values on an average during three days per month.

[b]"Alerts" are called when a pollutant concentration reaches the indicated value. Certain industrial operations are curtailed during an alert stage, and other actions are taken to reduce emission of pollutants. All alerts called to date have been due to ozone.

TABLE 4. **Average proportion of different air pollutants in United States cities compared with Los Angeles County** *Sources:* For the United States as a whole, Reference 5; for Los Angeles County, Table 1.

| | PERCENTAGE OF TOTAL POLLUTANTS | | | | | | | | | | | |
| SOURCE OF POLLUTION | CARBON MONOXIDE | | SULPHUR DIOXIDE | | HYDRO-CARBONS | | NITROGEN OXIDE | | AEROSOLS | | TOTAL[a] | |
	U.S.	L.A.	U.S.	L.A.	U.S.	L.A.	U.S.	L.A.	U.S.	L.A.	U.S.	L.A.
Electric power generation	0.4	0.0	8.2	1.8	0.1	0.05	1.9	0.9	1.9	0.1	12.6	2.9
Industry	1.4	1.2	7.0	1.1	3.0	5.3	1.3	0.9	4.8	0.3	18.7	8.8
Space heating	1.4	0.01	2.7	–	0.4	–	0.6	0.06	1.0	0.4	6.2	0.5
Transportation	47.6	70.6	0.4	0.2	7.8	13.3	2.5	3.4	1.4	0.4	59.8	87.9
Refuse incineration	1.0	0.01	0.2	–	0.8	–	0.1	0.01	0.5	–	2.6	0.02
TOTAL	51.9	71.8	18.4	3.1	12.1	18.5	6.4	5.7	9.6	0.9	99.9	100.1
Total pollutants (lbs./capita/day)[b]	2.74	3.12	0.97	0.13	0.63	0.81	0.34	0.24	0.51	0.04	5.28	4.85
Total pollutants (thousands of tons/day)	178	10.7	63	0.5	41	2.8	22	0.8	33	0.1	342.0	14.8

[a] U.S. totals include a small percentage of "miscellaneous" pollutants not otherwise considered in this table.

[b] Assuming that "U.S." pollutants are emitted in metropolitan areas with a total population of 130 million people; population of Los Angeles County taken at 6.82 million from Table 2.

Next to water and air, fossil fuels make up the largest single weight of material used in our civilization. About a billion tons of coal and petroleum are consumed in the United States each year and 2% of this weight is sulphur dioxide, practically all of which is discharged into the atmosphere.(10)

Atmospheric pollutants reduce visibility and thus create hazards for airplanes. They damage crops, injure livestock, corrode metals, rot masonry, depress property values, and cost the community large cleaning bills for everything from dusty draperies to smoke blackened buildings. The growth of miniaturization in the electronics industry places increasing emphasis on the quality of the air. In many such plants elaborate air filtering systems, special clothing, and other procedures are required. These are much easier to use in areas which have clean outside air.

Common sense suggests that pollutants capable of darkening house paint, disintegrating stone statues, corroding metals, dissolving nylon stockings, and embrittling rubber must also be injurious to delicate bronchial and lung tissues, but there is little hard evidence at present. Acute exposures are clearly hazardous. Community catastrophes like the one in London in 1952 and previous incidents in Donora, Pennsylvania, in 1948 and in the Meuse Valley of Belgium in 1930 are grave warnings for the future. At lower concentrations, urban atmospheric pollution aggravates asthma and some other chronic respiratory illnesses and it can cause transient eye and respiratory tract irritations. The effects would undoubtedly be more serious if it were not for the fact that poisonous gases such as sulphur dioxide are largely absorbed in the nose and upper air passages, and only a small fraction of the amount in the air reaches the lungs.

The incidence of lung cancer is greater in cities than in the country. Urban air pollution may be a contributory factor, but its role is uncertain and cigarette smoking is apparently a greater hazard. In this connection, one little known atmospheric pollutant warrants special attention. This is asbestos, produced by the wear of automobile brake linings, and in other ways. Many city dwellers are now known to have asbestos fibers in their lungs. Industrial experience shows that some types of asbestos are strongly associated with lung cancer and other respiratory diseases.(11)

Large amounts of lead are discharged into the atmosphere from motor vehicle exhausts. This lead is widely dispersed—even the lead content of the surface waters of the ocean has doubled in the past thirty years—but it tends to concentrate in soils and plants located close to heavily traveled highways. Today every American citizen carries a burden of lead in his body, although the average levels are lower than those generally deemed hazardous. No one knows what the human body burdens were before the introduction of lead additives to gasoline. Phosphorus and boron are now being added to motor fuels, and nickel is beginning to appear. These may be hazards for human beings who have to breathe polluted city air.(12)

In general our knowledge of the effects of atmospheric pollutants on either human beings or animals is limited, particularly under conditions where pre-existing disease may enhance the effects or increase susceptibility. Research is especially needed on the results of chronic exposures to comparatively low levels of lead, asbestos, nitrogen oxides, carbon monoxide, and sulphur compounds.

The atmosphere is not a sink for most of the pollutants it receives, but only a temporary reservoir which contains these substances until they become oxidized or are swept out by rain or snow. There is one pollutant, however, that is relatively inert chemically and tends to remain in the atmosphere for long periods. This is carbon dioxide. Because it is the ultimate product of combustion, carbon dioxide is produced by our worldwide industrial civilization in very large quantities—some twelve billion tons a year at the present time. Part of this "new" carbon dioxide, like that already in the air, is utilized in plant photosynthesis, and a fraction enters the ocean, but about half of it stays in the air. By the year 2000 the amount of carbon dioxide in the atmosphere will probably have increased by 25 per cent. Many people believe this will have a significant effect on the world's climate, but nobody has been able to make a convincing guess as to just what the effect will be. It probably will not be disastrous, but it will certainly represent an important geophysical experiment on an earthwide scale.(13)

There is some evidence that atmospheric pollution is also increasing the turbidity of the atmosphere, that is, the concentration of very small particles suspended in the air. Between 1961 and 1964, the atmospheric turbidity index in Boston rose from 0.06 to 0.17, in Chicago from 0.05 to 0.10, and in St. Cloud, Minnesota, from 0.05 to 0.09. Thus in all three cities the turbidity roughly doubled in four years. A 25 per cent increase in atmospheric turbidity over the earth as a whole might result in a cooling of the air near the ground by several degrees Fahrenheit.(14)

Air pollution is a sickness of cities. The amount of air on earth is very large, a million and a half tons for every human being, and its total capacity for containing pollutants is great, but cities occupy only a small area—in the United States about 2 per cent of the land—and the weight of air available to them at any instant is correspondingly small. At the same time most sources of pollution are concentrated in the cities. A single electric generating plant using fossil fuels may emit several hundred tons of sulphur dioxide per day. The weight of particles suspended in city air is commonly ten times higher than in rural areas.

Pollution of city air is by no means a new phenomenon. In the beginning of the 19th century Shelley wrote: "Hell is a city much like London, a populous and smoky city." Nearly 2,000 years earlier Seneca complained of the heavy air of Rome and the stench of its sooty chimneys. Drastic anti-pollution measures were taken in London in the Middle Ages; at least one man was hanged for burning coal.(15)

The modification of the air over an urban area is comparable to the effects of an active volcano. Pollutants tend to create their own climate. Over New York City, for example, atmospheric inversion layers a hundred feet or so thick, high in particles and sulphur dioxide, form and spread as a result of the absorption and re-radiation of sunlight by the pollution particles themselves.(16)

A city affects the wind patterns in its vicinity. With high wind speeds it acts like a conical hill, while in light winds the excess heat produces a thermal circulation. But larger scale meteorological processes are the prin-

cipal cause of variations in pollutant concentrations. These are the fluctuations in speed and direction of the winds, related to barometric pressure variations, that ventilate the city, and the naturally occurring thermal inversions—conditions in which the air aloft is warmer than at lower levels. The warm air forms an effective lid over the colder air beneath, and as a result pollutants are held close to the ground in relatively high concentrations. In much of the United States an inversion at heights of 500 to 1,500 feet occurs about half the time.

With an inversion at 1,000 feet over a crowded city, the weight of the column of air available at any given time near the ground is about a hundred tons per person. If the air is to remain breathable (carbon dioxide concentration less than 1 per cent), the amount required each day for combustion of gasoline, fuel oil, diesel oil, coal, and natural gas at rates of use prevailing in 1965 is close to 6 tons per person. Thus, if the inversion persists, the city air needs to be completely changed at least once every 17 days. Periods of near stagnation lasting four or five days occur several times a year over large parts of the United States. It is clear that, even with present population densities and rates of use of fossil fuels, our cities are coming uncomfortably close to using up all their available air.

Some Solutions

Under these circumstances, we can no longer think of urban air as a "free good." Instead, it must be thought of as a natural resource—that is, as part of the natural environment for which the demand is liable to outrun the supply, and to which a cost can be attached. It is not a resource in the older sense of a raw material for manufacturing, but rather one of the "new" renewable resources we have become aware of only in recent years—a limited part of the environment whose quality has great economic and social importance. It is a common property resource which must be used by all the citizens, and, as such, it requires public regulation or management. Perloff(17) has pointed out that, "Invasion of the [common] domain [of city air] by polluters then may be regarded as trespass, and the cost of control assigned to the polluter. . . ."

Four ways of dealing with the principal source of metropolitan air pollution, the automobile, may be suggested: (1) control of emissions from present internal combustion engines; (2) lowering of the number of automobiles operating at any given time in the city; (3) treatment of the air into which the pollutants are emitted; and (4) a radical change in the kind of energy conversion used in automotive transport.

Both crankcase and exhaust emissions can be lowered by such devices as the direct-flame afterburner, which should remove 60 to 80 per cent of the carbon monoxide and hydrocarbons, though it does not affect the emission of nitrogen oxides. The cost of these devices has been estimated at around $100 per vehicle, and their lifetime at five years. Annual maintenance cost should be around $5, and increased fuel requirements perhaps $10 per year.(18) Total costs for Los Angeles County with its present 3.5 million automobiles would be $350 million every five years for purchase and installation of the device, plus annual operating and excess fuel costs of approximately $50 million. These figures must be multiplied by about 20 to account for all the metropolitan areas of the country. In Table 1 it is assumed that half the automobiles operating in Los Angeles County in 1970 will be equipped with exhaust and crankcase emission control.

Because of the continuing increase in motor vehicle numbers and in gasoline combustion, installation and use of such partially effective emission control devices will, in the long run, only limit the rate of increase of city pollution. More drastic measures are needed. Also, reduction of hydrocarbon emissions without a reduction of nitrogen oxides will free the latter for direct irritating effects, and hence may not be as helpful as one would hope.

The number of automobiles operating in the city at any one time might be lowered by greatly enlarging the area covered by freeways and parking lots, which would speed up traffic and reduce the time spent in cruising the streets, looking for a place to park, but such structures would destroy much of the beauty of the city and many of its values. Development of publicly acceptable mass transportation is perhaps a more promising means of creating conditions under which automobile traffic within the city can be controlled.

Perhaps in the future our cities could be divided into two layers, one for automobiles and one for people. All vehicle traffic would be in tunnels and other enclosed spaces from which the air could be rapidly pumped and treated to remove noxious substances.

Alternatively one might conceive of a system for penetrating the atmospheric inversion layers and replacing the polluted air with fresh air sucked from aloft. The construction of many very high stacks equipped with enormous pumps has sometimes been discussed by engineers for the Los Angeles area, but the costs and amount of energy required, not to mention the hazards to air traffic, seem prohibitive.

Perhaps ultimately the most satisfactory solution will be the development of means for energy conversion at low temperatures that would be inexpensive and light enough to be used in private automobiles. Low-temperature energy conversion probably is the only feasible means of eliminating the nitrogen oxides. These are inevitably formed when ordinary air is heated to the high temperatures prevailing in internal combustion engines. Both fuel cells and rechargeable electric batteries appear promising, but the development work required to make them economically competitive with internal combustion engines will take many years.

Although an increasing portion of the nation's new electric generating capacity is nuclear-powered, the capacity of fossil fuel generating plants may well double by 1980 and redouble by 2000. At present there are no effective and inexpensive processes for removing sulphur dioxide from flue gases, but several fairly promising methods are being investigated. If these were installed in all new plants, sulphur dioxide emission could be held at its present level up to 1980 and perhaps reduced by 20 per cent or more between 1980 and 2000. Research and development are urgently needed to find more economic processes. The cost of the most promising of present devices, the alkali-alumina process, is estimated at a capital investment of about $11 per kilowatt of installed capacity and an additional operating cost of close to $4 per kilowatt per year.(19) Within the United States as a whole, the cost of installing these devices in new fossil fuel generating plants would be about $2 billion by 1980, and the annual operating costs would be around $750 million.

Air pollution raises some of the problems of government in the United States. Polluted air masses do not recognize political boundaries. In the eastern megalopolis, for example, the prevailing winds blow contaminants from New Jersey's oil refineries, smoke belching factories, and smoldering trash dumps right over New York City. A charge on polluters for use of the public air supply as an atmospheric sewer has been widely advocated, but this must be national or at least regional in scope, otherwise polluting industries may simply move from one state or municipality to another one which uses its carelessness about pollution as a recruiting inducement for industry.

WATER POLLUTION

The Problem in General

Most of the rain and snow that falls on the United States evaporates or sinks into the ground. About a fourth of the total precipitation, averaging 1,100 billion gallons per day, runs off or seeps through the ground to rivers, where it is available for use. In 1954, 300 billion gallons per day were withdrawn from lakes and rivers and it is estimated that by the year 2000 daily withdrawals will be close to 900 billion gallons, or 80 per cent of the average river flows.(20) Only 150 billion gallons per day will be actually "consumed," that is evaporated. The remainder will be returned to rivers, lakes, and estuaries, carrying a burden of pollutants from its contact with human beings and their farms and industries.

Though much of the river water will need to be reused several times, the principal water problem in the years ahead will not be quantity but quality. Without a radical change in sewage disposal methods or enormous expenditures for dams and other flow regulation devices it will be impossible to prevent serious deterioration of our bodies of water. Even to maintain enough water at acceptable standards for public health and industrial purposes will be difficult. The problem of water pollution in the heavily populated states could become overwhelming in the next few decades unless we adopt many technological and sociological innovations.

Under conditions of balance between men and their environment human wastes discharged into rivers are metabolized by bacteria and changed into nutrients for other organisms, plus carbon dioxide, water, and other harmless substances. The river cleanses itself, and the water may be used over and over again. But streams have only a limited capacity to handle waste materials, and they can be disastrously affected by overloading, particularly if the stream bed is affected. Organic sludges and other suspended solids settling to the bottom eliminate many higher forms of life from the bed of the river and stimulate the bacterial production of such stinking toxic substances as hydrogen sulfide and mercaptans. Oil accumulated in suspended particles and settling on the stream bed can destroy bottom-living aquatic life for several decades.

Highly toxic substances discharged into a river often cause spectacular fish kills and a public outcry. Low-grade toxins are more insidious. The continued addition of low-grade pollutants results in an increase in the population of certain species, while others, which cannot tolerate contamination, disappear. Clear streams usually contain a large number of species, but the number is greatly reduced in a polluted stream. This reduction of diversity tends to lower the dynamic balance of the river system and to produce instabilities that result in further deterioration. Governor Rockefeller has thus described the Hudson River: "For ten miles south of Albany there are no fish but only sludge worms, leeches, rattail maggots, the larvae of flies—the handwriting on the wall that warns us to stop treating our waterways as if they were open sewers."(21)

Typically, American cities have turned their backs on their rivers. In Hartford a high wall hides the Connecticut River from the nearby streets and buildings. In other cities the banks are lined with factories and warehouses or they are used as a cheap source of land for freeways. Recently, some of our cities have recognized that a river in the city is a priceless asset. Boston was among the first; fifty years ago it laid out miles of parks and grassy slopes along the Charles, and in the last decade, Chicago has decided that the Chicago River can be used for recreation and beauty rather than as an open sewer.

With this new view of the river (which, of course, has long prevailed in many European cities) there has also arisen a strongly felt need to reduce or remove the pollution that has made our rivers unpleasant and useless for many human purposes.

Because of the large and specialized water requirements of different industries, the quality of water is also of direct economic importance. Most industrial uses of water are for cooling, washing, or transport of materials. Water is a raw material in some processes and as steam it is used for energy conversion. Avoiding scale formation from dissolved solids is necessary for the economic operation of a steam boiler, and rigorous control of water quality is essential in a brewery. Thus, while many industries are heavy contributors to water pollution, others must have water of good to very high quality. It may be necessary in a metropolitan area to zone different sources of water for different uses and to establish control of polluting industries for the benefit of others that need water of good quality. Usually, however, industries requiring water of very high quality must treat their water supply, no matter what its source, and their incremental cost for handling polluted water is not high.(22)

A new set of economic demands is arising in many parts of the country, represented by the service industries associated with tourism and the recreational uses of water. Fishermen, swimmers, and scuba divers all demand clear and pure water.

There are special problems related to pollution of the seashore. Here we are dealing not with a two-dimensional area but with an essentially one-dimensional boundary zone between the land and the sea. Nearly half of all Americans live within a hundred miles of the ocean, and this proportion will probably increase in future decades. By the end of the century, some 150 to 200 million people may be struggling for places on the beaches and in the narrow coastal waters. With our present length of shoreline, this would mean about two people per foot, even if the entire coastal strip were a public beach.

Today, only a fraction of the shoreline is available for public recreation, which must compete with factories, power plants, shipping, and military uses. Much of the shoreline is privately held, and long stretches are already too polluted to be safe for swimming or water sports. Bays and estuaries, which are at the lower end of river basins and receive their undigested waste products, are the most seriously threatened parts of the coastal zone.

Varieties of Water Pollution

Eight kinds of water pollutants are recognized by the U.S. Public Health Service: organic sewage, infectious agents, plant nutrients, organic chemicals, inorganic and miscellaneous chemicals, sediments from land erosion, radioactive substances, and waste heat.

(1) Organic Sewage   This is our most obvious water problem. Under favorable circumstances, organic matter in sewage is oxidized to carbon dioxide, water, phosphates, nitrates, and other plant nutrients by aquatic bacteria which utilize the dissolved atmospheric oxygen in the water. For this reason, sewage is said to have a biological oxygen demand—that is, a certain amount of dissolved oxygen is required to transform its contained organic matter into innocuous substances. Most sewage is "treated" to a greater or lesser extent before being dumped into our rivers, lakes, and estuaries and its organic matter content and biological oxygen demand are thereby lowered.

The volume of sewage waters produced in American cities usually ranges from 100 to 150 gallons per person per day. Typically, the suspended solid content of this sewage, and its biological oxygen demand, are 200 parts per million.(23) The amount of organic wastes entering municipal sewage treatment plants is only a few ounces per person per day. This is reduced by 80 to 90 per cent in conventional primary and secondary treatment.

Rivers and other natural waters typically contain about ten parts per million of dissolved oxygen when this gas is close to saturation. For a stream of typical depth, say 15 to 30 feet, natural rates of re-aeration with oxygen are from one to two parts per million per day, depending on the turbulence of the stream and the degree of oxygen undersaturation. This is somewhat less than the rate of oxygen consumption by the sewage. Hence raw sewage with an oxygen demand of 200 parts per million must be diluted about forty-fold when it is dumped into a river if the oxygen supply in the receiving water body is not to be seriously depleted. Two-thirds of the U.S. population, about 125 million people, are served by domestic sewers. Sewage from about a tenth of these people is discharged raw, and that from more than another quarter after only primary treatment. In total, sewage discharges correspond to the raw sewage from 50 million people.(24) To avoid oxygen depletion, these discharges must be diluted with 200 to 300 billion gallons of river, lake, or ocean water per day.

About a third of the biological oxygen demand in municipal sewage comes from industrial wastes. In addition, industries discharge directly into our water bodies waste materials with an oxygen demand greater than that of all municipal sewage. The food processing industries, especially smaller operators, tend to be heavy polluters. Typical oxygen-demanding discharges include the offal from meat packing plants, sugar-beet wastes, whey from dairies, pesticide-carrying cannery washings, and inedible parts of fruits and vegetables. Oil refineries discharge oils, waxes, and complex organic chemicals. The textile industry contributes fatty and oily residues from the bleaching of cotton, flax, and jute, and emulsions of dirt, bacteria, soap, and proteins from the washing of wool. Both the sulphite and kraft processes of the paper industry produce large residues of organic material—in the case of the sulphite process, about 500 pounds of oxygen demand per ton of pulp.(25) This industry alone probably puts more organic material into United States water bodies, in terms of biological oxygen demand, than is contained in all the municipal sewage in the United States.

In the Great Lakes and in harbors and estuaries on both coasts, the maritime transportation industry is an important source of pollutants. In spite of regulations to the contrary, cargo ships and other craft, including small pleasure boats, often dump raw sewage into harbors and bays. The federal government has also been lax. In 1960, federal installations discharged over 46 billion gallons per day of untreated sewage into surface waters or onto the ground.(26) Pearl Harbor, the principal harbor in our youngest state, has long been filthy with ship sewage.

Industry can handle water pollution in several ways, four of which are especially important: (1) process changes (sometimes called "in-plant abatement"); (2) effluent treatment; (3) closed-cycle operations in which the water is not discharged, but treated and recycled through the plant; and (4) export of wastes to an environment that can receive them without deleterious effects.(27) The chemical companies have made the greatest contributions to in-plant abatement through process changes which have, in many cases, proven economical because they conserve valuable materials. Such changes often reduce the biological and chemical oxygen demand of effluents by more than 90 per cent.

A wide variety of effluent treatment and disposal methods is used by industry, including screening, sedimentation, lagooning, centrifuging, filtration, flotation, flocculation, chemical oxidation, precipitation, polymerization, incineration, anaerobic digestion, deep well disposal, barging to sea, piping to sea or to desert regions, and irrigation spreading. In spite of this diversity, treatment by industry of its waste effluents has apparently been pursued less vigorously than process changes. As Table 5 shows, the volume of industrial effluents discharged into our rivers, lakes, and estuaries is nearly twice as great as the volume of municipal sewage, yet the amount spent on operation of industrial treatment plants is only about a third of that spent by municipalities. Municipal expenditures are more than 5¢ per 1,000 gallons of sewage, while industry spends only about 1¢ per 1,000 gallons.

Perhaps the best known example of a closed cycle for water used in manufacturing is that of the Kaiser Steel plant in Fontana, California. Here the motivation for closed-cycle operation is the shortage of water in a semiarid region. More significant from the standpoint of pollution abatement is the action taken by the Wisconsin Steel Company, which was formerly a heavy polluter of the Calumet River in the Chicago area. The company has designed and installed a circulating water supply that discharges nothing to the river and takes in only moderate amounts of make-up water.(28)

In the so-called "Penjerdel Region" (the three metropolitan areas of Trenton, Philadelphia, and Wilmington on the lower reaches of the Delaware River), the waste materials produced by industry have a biological oxygen demand equivalent to that of the sewage from 2.6 million people.

TABLE 5. Municipal and some industrial expenditures for treatment of waste waters, 1959
Sources: For industrial effluents and expenditures: "Water in Industry," National Association of Manufacturers, January 1965. (Quoted in Appendix 5 to "Waste Management and Control," National Academy of Sciences Publication 1400, 1966, pp. 188 and 194 (Reference 6). For municipal effluents and expenditures: various estimates in "Waste Management and Control." National Academy of Sciences Publication 1400, 1966 (Reference 6); and *Restoring the Quality of Our Environment,* Report of the Environmental Pollution Panel, President's Science Advisory Committee (Reference 2). It is assumed that the equivalent of two-thirds of municipal effluents receive primary and secondary treatment at an average cost of 8.5 cents per thousand gallons.

	RETURN FLOWS, IN BILLIONS OF GALLONS OF EFFLUENT PER DAY	OPERATING EXPENDITURES FOR WASTE TREATMENT (MILLIONS OF DOLLARS)	OPERATING EXPENDITURES IN CENTS PER 1000 GALLONS
Industry			
Steel	10.1	4.8	0.13
Chemical	6.5	40.3	1.7
Pulp and paper	4.3	14.0	0.9
Petroleum	3.3	30.6	2.5
Automobile	0.23	4.5	5.3
Bituminous coal	0.08	4.2	14.3
Total industry	24.5	98.4	1.1 (average)
Municipal sewage	14.6	300	5.7

One-fourth of this material is removed by waste treatment, and three-fourths, equivalent to a population of 1.9 million people, is discharged into the Delaware. However, the municipal sewage dumped into the river is even greater. It corresponds to the raw sewage from 2.3 million people, out of a total population of 5 million.(29)

An instructive contrast to the dismal record of Penjerdel is that of the Ruhr River Basin, which contains a large proportion of the entire industrial capacity of West Germany. The waters of the Ruhr River system are used, processed, and reused, eight times over, yet most of them remain clean enough for fishing and swimming, and, with only mild treatment, for drinking.(30) Their quality is maintained by the semi-governmental Ruhr Valley Administration, which levies an effluent charge, proportional to the amount of pollutant materials dumped into the river system, on every municipality and every industry that uses the waters. Each can choose the most economical trade-off between the level of treatment it will provide for its own wastes and the size of the effluent charge it will pay. The efficacy of the system hinges in part upon the use of the Emscher River as a recipient for the residual and hard-to-treat wastes.(31)

Construction of municipal plants for primary and secondary sewage treatment costs about $60 per capita population equivalent (the average amount of domestic or municipal sewage produced by one person). Annual operation costs decrease with plant size, and range from $3.50 to $2.25 per capita population equivalent.(32) Capital and operating costs of industrial waste treatment plants are apparently somewhat lower. New capacity to make up present deficiencies in municipal sewers and sewage treatment plants would require a capital investment of about $5 billion, and an annual operating cost of perhaps $200 million. These expenditures should be about tripled by 1980. Capital and operating expenditures for treatment of industrial wastes should be of the same order of magnitude.

The oxygen-demanding fraction of domestic and industrial wastes is growing more rapidly than the rate of installation and effectiveness of conventional waste treatment. Unless remedial measures are taken, the oxygen demand of sewage effluents will be great enough in future decades to consume the entire dissolved oxygen content of all the waters in all the U.S. rivers during the stage of dry weather flow.(33)

A quantitative insight can be gained by considering the total municipal sewage flow in the 1950's of about 15 billion gallons per day, and its projected increase to 37 billion gallons per day by 2000. If all the sewage in the 1950's had been dumped raw into the nation's streams it could use up the oxygen content of 600 billion gallons per day. Adding on equal biological oxygen demand from industrial wastes would raise the total amount of oxygen used to that contained in 1200 billion gallons per day, whereas the average daily river flow in the United States is only 1100 billion gallons. Fortunately, most of the sewage is treated so that the flow required at present for oxidation is only a few hundred billion gallons per day. But industrial wastes may increase seven-fold by 2000, and as we have seen, the municipal increase may be 250 per cent.

(2) Infectious Agents   Typhoid and other disease-causing bacteria have been virtually eliminated from domestic water supplies in the United States, but a danger persists from infectious viruses—for example, hepatitis.

(3) Plant Nutrients   Conventional sewage treatment greatly reduces the content of dissolved and suspended organic matter, but the effluents contain dissolved nitrates, ammonia, phosphates, vitamin B complex, and other plant nutrients. The phosphate concentrations in treated effluents have actually increased in recent years, probably because of the wide use of phosphate-containing detergents. When discharged into a lake, or a sluggish river such as the Potomac, these nutrients cause a damaging over-fertilization, or "eutrophication" of the water body. Livestock and poultry wastes and flows from heavily fertilized farm fields and suburban lawns also contribute to the process. As a result, many streams, lakes, and estuaries in the United States have become filled with objectionable growths of blue-green algae and other water plants. Particularly on cloudy days, the algal growth near the surface shuts off the supply of sunlight from deeper growing algae and other plants. The latter die and in their decay use up the oxygen dissolved in the water, so that fish and other water animals suffocate. The process is contributed to by variations in nutrient supply, by sporadic release of toxins into the water, and by the excess supply of certain nutrients. The water is made unsatisfactory for domestic and industrial uses, and its recreational values are destroyed. Hundreds of water bodies scattered across the nation are affected; much public attention has been given to some of them, including Lake Erie, Lake Washington, and the Potomac. In Lake Mendota, near Madison, Wisconsin, about a quarter of the added nitrogen oxides comes from the air via rain and snow. Automobiles are probably the source of most of these atmospheric nitrogen oxides.(34)

Possible control measures include removing nutrients from municipal and industrial wastes by so-called tertiary or advance treatment. This is both difficult and expensive, costing 20 to 30 cents per thousand gallons.(35) Alternatively, waste waters can be diverted to streams below a lake, or to a well-flushed water body. Treatment of the lake itself by removal of weeds and debris and dredging of putrescent bottom material is also sometimes tried. Much research is needed on the nutrient requirements of different kinds of water plants. Perhaps addition of particular micro-nutrients or growth-promoting substances to the waters entering a lake would encourage the growth of desirable plants and diminish the obnoxious blue-green algae.

(4) Organic Chemicals Such as Insecticides, Pesticides, and Detergents

Technological advances have caused much of the problem of water pollution. Rachel Carson called ours the "age of poisons" and with good reason, for many of the 500 or so new chemical compounds produced each year are not only highly toxic to living creatures but dreadfully persistent. Until recently, detergents were among these persistent new chemicals. They contaminated lakes and streams because they were impossible to break down in ordinary sewage disposal plants. Soap manufacturers are now producing new "biologically degradable" detergents that disappear by bacterial activity as other garbage does.

But the pesticides, herbicides, and related poisons we are spreading through the environment are more rugged. They are dispersed over the fields and washed into rivers by runoff from rain and irrigation, only to be gathered again in the bodies of wild animals, birds, and fishes, with consequent destruction of our fellow creatures and hazards to our own health.

(5) Inorganic and Miscellaneous Chemicals—Chemical Residues, Salts, Acids, Sludges

Chemicals such as alkyl disulphate do not usually kill fish, but they affect the gill structure and cause a slow loss of blood. Sulphates and ammonia may change the predominant species in a river's flora from diatoms, which are valuable links in the food chain, to blue-green algae, which are noxious and nearly worthless to other organisms. Some substances such as copper and lead accumulate over time and eventually become lethal to fish and other desirable animals.(36) Coal mine effluents flowing into rivers and harbors are often so acid they corrode ships' hulls and destroy aquatic life. Other chemicals, such as phenols, may cause unpleasant tastes or odors that must be specially handled in treating municipal water supplies.

(6) Sediments from Land Erosion

Particles carried in suspension and as bedload, produced by the accelerated erosion of mistreated land, bring destruction to stream channels and reservoirs. They reduce a stream's ability to assimilate oxygen-demanding wastes and prevent sunlight required by aquatic plants from penetrating the water.

(7) Radioactive Substances Present techniques for handling these substances largely prevent contamination of our water bodies at today's levels of production of radioactive substances. But a great increase in nuclear wastes can be anticipated within the next few decades as atomic electric power generation grows, and the problem of disposal will become more serious.

(8) Waste Heat from Electric Power Plants and from Industry When river waters are overheated they can hold less oxygen, while the rate of oxidation is increased; thus, introducing heat into a stream has the effect similar to introducing oxygen-demanding wastes. Thirty years from now, the amount of water required for cooling could be larger than the entire present use of water for all purposes in the United States. Waste heat disposal may have serious consequences for fish and other aquatic organisms, because most of them are highly sensitive to temperature change.

About half the heat energy in the fuel used for electric power generators must be dissipated in the cooling system. For a 1000-megawatt plant which disposes of this heat by dumping it in a river or other water body, 850 million gallons per day are required if the temperature of the water is to be increased no more than 15 degrees Fahrenheit. Heating of river waters can be entirely avoided by the use of large cooling towers, which are estimated to cost about $4 per kilowatt, with an operating cost of $2.50 per kilowatt per year.(37) For all new generating capacity in the United States, the capital cost of cooling towers would be about $800 million by 1980, and the annual operating cost around $500 million.

The Special Problem of Storm Drains
Even after adoption of sophisticated waste treatment methods, many cities continue to be major sources of water pollution, because of the nature of their drainage systems. The drains of a city carry two kinds of liquids: storm water from streets, roofs, lawns, and paved areas, and used or spent water from dwellings and industry. Storm water is sometimes collected, transported, and disposed of through a storm drainage system, while the spent water or sanitary sewage is carried by separate sanitary sewers. In most older cities, however, both types of waste water are collected in a single set of underground drains, called combined sewers. Such sewers have been in use ever since cities began. The problems they cause are still to be solved.

Before the development of sewage treatment plants, city sewers discharged directly into rivers or other water bodies through numerous outfalls. New York City has 218 of these old outlets, Chicago, 362, and Cleveland, 420.(38) When it was decided that sewage should be treated, interceptor sewers were built along the water fronts beneath the outlets to collect their drainage and carry it to a central treatment plant. These interceptors are large enough to collect all the drainage during dry weather. Regulating devices and weirs of several kinds are used to admit measured amounts of liquid to the interceptors. When it rains, the excess flow goes overboard through overflow or relief drains directly into a river, lake, or bay. The volume of storm runoff is 10 to 100 times as large as ordinary sewage flows, hence nearly all sewage during heavy rains enters the river raw and un-treated with the storm water. Even if the interceptors were large enough to carry the storm water to the treatment plants, the capacity of these plants would be overwhelmed. Storms usually occur only four or five times a month, primarily in summer, and consequently a small percentage of the total sewage produced during the year is lost through overflows, but these may carry 20 to 30 per cent of the organic solids, which tend to deposit in the drains during dry weather and to be scoured out during storms.

The Chicago Sanitary District collects and subjects to a high degree of treatment over 99 per cent of the dry weather flow in the combined sewers of the city. During the summer season, however, raw sewage overflows four or five times a month, and as a result the dissolved oxygen becomes com-pletely depleted in parts of the river and canal system. To abate the nui-sance, the District must draw large amounts of water from Lake Michigan to flush out the canals, and the entire flow is subsequently discharged into the Illinois River, where it creates further pollution problems. The operation of the system results in an average diversion of about two billion gallons of water per day from the Great Lakes-Saint Lawrence River basin to the Illinois and Mississippi Rivers.(39)

It is possible to separate, completely or partially, the two systems, provide holding reservoirs and large settling tanks from which the excess runoff can be released gradually, reduce storm drainage, or install treatment devices in the larger combined sewers themselves. The technology is avail-able for any of these approaches, but all are expensive. For complete separation, existing sewers can be used either for storm runoff or sanitary sewage and a new system built to carry the flows that are to be excluded. The direct costs are some $10 million per square mile, or $1,000 and above per household(40), plus the economic loss and agony to the city caused by entering all the streets, properties, and buildings to break existing connec-tions and install new drains.

Partial separation by construction of a new storm water system to drain streets, yards, parking lots, and new buildings would greatly reduce over-flows without the necessity of tearing into existing buildings.

Newly developing suburban areas are nowadays almost universally provided with separate sewers even though the old city may be on the combined system. Separate drains can be installed also in redeveloped areas. Over the years as the city is rebuilt, the entire system will then gradually become separated. In the meantime, new "express sewers" can be built from the separated areas to carry sanitary sewage directly to the treatment plant.

The dust, oil, debris, and filth that settle in a city are usually swept or flushed into the drains, where they lie until the first good rain carries them to the outfall. Thus in many situations, partial treatment (as by sedimenta-tion) of combined sewage might be more effective in reducing pollution than separation of the system.

Large shallow tanks can be built beside the combined sewers in such a way that the tanks must fill as the sewer fills. This damps out peak flow rates and allows a higher portion of the total surface runoff and contained solids to be handled by the interceptors. Columbus, Ohio, and communities in the Detroit area have such tanks; Halifax, Nova Scotia, is studying them.(41) Treatment by settling of solids from excess storm water flows has been practiced in England for many years. Storm standby tanks go into operation when the capacity of treatment facilities is exceeded. These stand empty in dry weather and serve both as storage tanks and settling basins during storms. The overflows from the tanks can be chlorinated.

The problems of combined sewers could be eliminated by reducing sufficiently either the rate or the amount of storm runoff. Urbanization usually greatly increases runoff rates, but it need not. At least one county is now requiring developers to provide designs that will not alter the natural runoff rate. The water should be stored, detained, and where possible allowed to soak into the ground to replenish ground water. In the humid regions of the United States, enough rain and snow fall on a city to supply all the water it needs. Unfortunately, the water is usually carried away as rapidly as possible. Roofs are steepened, yards graded, and streets sloped, to ensure rapid drainage. Planning for new or rebuilt cities should look toward conservation and use of the water that falls on them.

A possible effective technological solution would be the use of large existing sewers as auxiliary treatment plants. This could be done, for example, by aerating them through perforated plastic tubing stretched along the bottom of the sewers.(42)

POLLUTION OF THE LAND

Archaeologists, digging through the layers of old, long-inhabited cities, have found that these ancient settlements were rebuilt many times on their own debris. Evidently civilized man has always cohabited with trash. Today we try to get most of our trash out of sight. But our methods of ultimate disposal have advanced very little over those of ancient times, while the weight and volume of refuse have increased several-fold.

Solid wastes produced each day in the households and offices of United States cities are probably equal to the weight of air pollutants—around 4.5 pounds per person, or 125 million tons per year for the country as a whole. Refuse production is believed to be increasing at about the same rate as our gross national product, roughly 4 per cent per year.(43) This is not surprising because a large fraction of consumer goods ends up as solid waste. Although estimates from different cities vary widely, the average household trash can will contain, by weight, 40-60 per cent paper, 10-20 per cent grass, brush, and garden cuttings, 5-15 per cent garbage, 5-20 per cent ashes and dirt, 8 per cent metal cans and tubes, 3-9 per cent glass bottles and jars, and 2-6 per cent of various odd bits of plastic.(44) The proportions of ashes and garbage are diminishing, while other kinds of refuse are increasing.

In a less affluent society, much of this material would be separated and salvaged, but today in the United States it is mainly a source for pollution of city and suburban land, and to a lesser extent of our air and water.

In addition to household and office refuse, tens of millions of tons of solid wastes are produced by industry—12 to 15 million tons of metal scrap, around 20 million tons of scrap paper, perhaps a million tons of plastics and rubber. Although some of this industrial scrap ends up as an environmental pollutant, a large part of it, together with a small fraction of municipal wastes, is salvaged and recycled. Copper recovery equals 80 per cent of newly mined domestic copper; reclaimed lead is almost twice domestic mine production; reused aluminum is 25 per cent of the total aluminum supply.(45)

The junk and scrap industries are said to gross $5 to $7 billion a year. However, because of technological and other changes, the fraction of salvaged waste materials is diminishing. Replacement of natural fibers with synthetics in clothing has reduced the usefulness and value of rags. Market changes have almost ruled out the collection of waste paper by the Boy Scouts and the Salvation Army. Urban zoning and high labor costs are eliminating junk collectors; Baltimore lost 50 per cent of its junk yards in the last ten years.(46)

Demolition of old structures for freeway construction and urban redevelopment is yielding a growing mass of wastes. In some cities the weight of these materials produced each year is about equal to that of household and office trash. A fraction of demolition waste is burnable; part of it is salvageable (for example, bricks and steel girders), but much of it consists of large, awkwardly shaped pieces of concrete, masonry, plastic, glass, metal, and tile. These are useless for salvage and expensive to dispose of.

Solid wastes can be burned, buried, flushed, reused, or simply thrown away in more or less open country in the hope that they won't be noticed. The first three methods tend to produce problems of air, land, and water pollution, respectively. The fourth is becoming less and less widely used, for economic and other reasons. The fifth method, though condemned by many right thinking people, has always been and still remains very popular. It finds one of its latest expressions in the piles of junk automobiles that disfigure open spaces around our cities.

Data on the amounts of solid wastes disposed of in various ways in American cities are spotty, inaccurate, or nonexistent. Some of the best estimates come from Los Angeles County(47) and the city of New York. In New York, up to 7,000 tons of wastes are burned each day in eleven separate municipal incinerators.(48) About 800 tons of waterfront and harbor debris are hauled out to sea on giant barges and burned by private contractors. The residue from both the municipal incinerators and the barges is dumped by the city on 3,000 acres of tideland fill at Fresh Kills on Staten Island. The number of private incinerators in New York apartment houses is unknown, but it is probably on the order of 12,000(49), serving two million people and burning perhaps 2,500 tons a day. Ashes from these incinerators are routinely collected by the city, while oversized and noncombustible items are collected on the request of householders. It is estimated that 40 per cent of the municipal solid wastes produced in New York are transported directly to municipal dumps and land-fill sites without passing through any incinerators. At least until very recently, some of this material was subjected to open burning at the city dumps.

From these fragmentary figures, we arrive at an estimate of 16,000 tons per day of solid waste disposed of in apartment houses or by the city government.(50) This is 4 pounds for each of New York's 8 million inhabitants. Slightly more than half the total is deposited on municipal land-fill sites. The remainder is burned and disappears into the air, and in the process contributes to the serious air pollution problems of the city. This is particularly true of the emissions from private incinerators and open dumps. Besides the municipal wastes, a large but unknown mass of demolition materials, probably at least 5,000 tons per day, is hauled by private contractors across the Hudson River and dumped in the New Jersey marshlands.

Over-all, the city is using up lands available for "sanitary fill" at a rate of between one and two square miles per year. This large area is necessary because of the low density of the waste materials and the fact that the fill cannot be much more than ten feet thick without creating serious drainage problems.

In New York City, the Sunday *Times* often weighs eight pounds and formerly cost 35¢. To get rid of it through the municipal system cost 10¢. Three-quarters of the money went for collection and transportation to the city incinerator, about a fifth for operation and amortization of the incinerator, and the remainder for transport and burial of the residual ash.

The total annual cost per person for municipal solid waste disposal is about $20. (The cost per ton is $19 to $29, including $15 to $20 for collection costs, $3 to $6 for incineration, and $1 to $3 for land fill.) These figures include about $1 per ton for amortization of the capital cost of the incinerators and for the purchase of vacant land for sanitary fill. Extrapolating to the country as a whole, annual expenditures on municipal solid waste disposal must be on the order of $2.5 billion, eight times the operating costs for municipal sewage treatment. This should increase to $4.5 billion by 1980. If we include in our comparison the amortization of capital costs for municipal sewer and sewage treatment systems, annual costs of solid waste disposal will still be twice the costs of handling municipal sewage by 1980.

Collected trash may be transported ten to fifty miles to a disposal site, but most of the cost is incurred in the first fifty feet from the household trash can. It is hard to see how the latter cost can be reduced without a radical change in the collection process—for example, development of home or apartment trash shredders which would allow paper and other dry solid wastes to be disposed of in the sewage system, much as garbage is now handled.(51) Experience with garbage grinders, which were at first viewed with great uneasiness by sanitary engineers, emphasizes both the potentialities of sewage waters as a medium for waste collection and transport, and the low loads of solid material they carry at present. Substitution of a mechanical method such as shredding and sewage disposal for present trash collection may become necessary in the future, because it may be impossible to find anyone willing to take a job as a trash collector at a wage anyone is willing to pay.

Air pollution from solid wastes can be reduced to negligible proportions by proper design and operation of municipal incinerators. But this kind of disposal is expensive compared to sanitary land fill. In any case, the residue from incineration is 10 to 20 per cent by volume of the initial material, and this, plus the refuse that cannot be incinerated, must be got rid of somehow, either by burial on land or dumping at sea. For most cities, at least some land disposal is necessary. The problem is to find satisfactory sites, and here, just as with air pollution, we come up against the difficulties posed by the many small municipal jurisdictions in the metropolis. The tradition has been for each city or town to find sanitary fill sites within its own boundaries. In the Boston area, with 79 separate jurisdictions, 61 dump wastes locally. Some municipalities will not even allow others to haul refuse through their streets on the way to a burial site. Organization of a metropolitan or regional waste disposal agency such as those in the Detroit and San Francisco Bay areas(52) would benefit all concerned. An agency of this kind could cooperate with metropolitan planners in selecting and laying out future recreational open spaces that could in the meantime be used for sanitary land fill. With the right kind of planning, solid wastes can serve to fill and improve areas for later use as parks, golf courses, and green belts.

The principal pollution problem of sanitary land fill comes from the dumping of garbage, sewage sludge, and other putrescible materials. Besides obnoxious odors and the formation of breeding grounds for flies and rats, there is a danger of ground water contamination, especially when the water table is close to the surface, as well as a hazard from toxic or explosive decay products if the filled area is later built upon. In general, putrescible matter forms only about 10 to 15 per cent of the solid wastes produced in the city, and this proportion can be reduced to less than 5 per cent by the use of household garbage grinders feeding into a sewage system and a treatment plant. In order to avoid pollution, putrescible wastes can be separated from other solids and incinerated, buried in especially selected areas, fed to pigs, or composted.

One of the unpleasant problems of solid wastes is the visual pollution produced by beer cans, glass bottles, plastic containers, and pieces of paper that litter the countryside. Because it is virtually indestructible, this trash accumulates from year to year. A most welcome innovation of modern technology would be a "biodegradable beer can," a container with satisfactory storage properties and adequate shelf life that would be attacked and disintegrated by bacteria as soon as it was discarded. Steel cans have the virtue, in contrast to aluminum, that they disappear relatively quickly. This is an example of one of the key points of attack on the solid waste problem: product design needs to take into account, together with other factors, the possibilities of either reuse or easy disposal.

Another kind of visual pollution is the national eyesore constituted by scattered piles of junk automobiles and auto hulks that have been or are being processed for removal of spare parts. These unsightly objects have greatly increased in number and size during the last ten years.

About 5 million motor vehicles, each containing on the average a ton of salvageable scrap steel, are discarded each year. Although nominally a source of valuable metal, junk cars are now a surplus commodity. The cost of collecting, processing, and transporting auto hulks is more than the price

of the #2 steel scrap into which they can be converted. Not only is this kind of scrap much less desirable than other grades, but changes in the steel-making process have resulted in a smaller demand for scrap of any kind.(53) At the same time, the rapid increase in motor car production has been followed by a steady rise in the number of automobiles junked each year.

To reduce the number of stored or abandoned automobile hulks, it has been suggested that the federal government support a price differential that would assure the recycling of hulks to the steel furnaces. In small or remote communities, this might include government financing of a "cleanup train"(54) which would collect and compress junked automobiles and other outsized steel objects.

Alternatively, a tax could be devised to provide an incentive for quicker salvage of spare parts and disposal of the hulks. An annual federal or state license might be imposed on all automobiles, except those currently licensed for road use, or a personal property tax might be placed on junk cars. Possibly a purchase excise tax could be imposed which would provide a sinking fund for ultimate disposal of the car at the end of its useful life. An excise tax equal to 1 per cent of the purchase price of a new car would amount to about $20 per ton of metal, and this should be ample to ensure the reuse of automobiles as raw materials by the steel companies. Federally conducted or sponsored research is needed on means for producing more uniform scrap from auto hulks, on methods of storage of hulks in excess of current market demands, and on uses other than for scrap steel. For example, it has been suggested that auto hulks might be combined with taconite ore, in order to produce a magnetic material of improved characteristics.

ROLES IN POLLUTION CONTROL

The problems of air, water, and land pollution have little regard for political boundaries, are a national concern, require large expenditures for their solution, and affect the quantity and quality of our natural resources. For all these reasons, the federal government must take a leading role in pollution abatement. Among the things it can and should do are:

1. Avoid being a polluter in all operations it conducts, supports, or controls.(55)
2. Provide tax incentives for pollution abatement by industry—for example, allowances for rapid amortization of waste treatment equipment, and credits for sums spent on research or development.(56)
3. Establish environmental quality criteria and standards for maximum allowable amounts of pollutant discharges. Among other benefits, such standards may effectively create markets for advanced abatement equipment and processes.(57)
4. Carry out and support those kinds of pollution research that are not likely to benefit individual firms, including determining the effects of pollutants on human beings, animals, and plants, studying dispersion

processes in the environment, and developing techniques for measurement and analysis.(58)

5. Underwrite industrial research and development on abatement devices that may later be widely sold. By establishing control regulations, the government creates a market for the successful developer, and it should be able to recoup its share of the costs.(59)

6. Test and demonstrate advanced control methods in its own operations. An army base could be used to test tertiary sewage treatment and complete recycling of water; the Tennessee Valley Authority might install a promising new device for sulphur dioxide removal in its coal burning electric plants.(60)

7. Underwrite large-scale demonstrations of new control systems. Many developments in pollution control cannot be adequately tested or demonstrated on a small scale. It is not sufficient for a method to serve satisfactorily a single dwelling or neighborhood. New systems must be demonstrated in a complete community which has a complex mix of waste problems. The average city administrator feels that he cannot use the local taxpayers' money to take a chance, and consequently he is likely to recommend only economically proven systems. Hence demonstrations and full-scale trials of new systems need to be ensured or partly paid for with federal funds.(61)

8. Support the advanced training of technicians, engineers, economists, and scientists for many kinds of tasks in pollution control. Federal fellowships, training grants, and institutional support are needed to ensure that persons of ability and imagination are drawn into this broad field and trained in its intricacies.(62)

9. Provide meeting grounds for discussion and agreement on pollution problems and abatement measures among state, county, and city officials, industrial managers, and public representatives.(63)

10. Stimulate formation of special governmental or quasi-governmental agencies designed to handle metropolitan or regional waste disposal and pollution control on an integrated basis.(64)

11. Provide information and educational materials that can be used by all governmental and private agencies to create better public understanding of pollution problems.(65)

In recent federal legislation, the Congress has expressed its conviction that programs for pollution control should be progressive and continuously developing and that they should be collaborative, engaging all levels of government and both public and private institutions. There is a strong reliance on both carrots and sticks: authorizations to establish federal standards and appropriations for programs of enforcement; subsidies to state and local governments for construction of abatement facilities and provisions for the conduct or support of research, technical assistance, and training. Formal lines of responsibility from the federal government down through state governments and local bodies of general jurisdiction are emphasized.(66)

At the moment, federal legislation may have outrun the development of administrative machinery for action and the knowledge on which action must be based. This legislation is directed almost entirely at the abatement of pollution after it has occurred. There has been little attention given to the prevention of pollution before it happens.

Control of water pollution was formerly considered to be solely a state and local responsibility. Legislation in the states developed as a public health program, and enforcement authority was vested in state health departments. In recent years, however, such legislation has recognized the need to protect all beneficial uses of water. The legislation of 35 states and Puerto Rico now gives a single state agency the responsibility for developing comprehensive programs to deal with all aspects of water pollution, including establishing stream classification and water quality standards.

About two-thirds of the states also have some type of legislation for air pollution control, but on widely varying bases.(67) Only 12 states provide for any form of state financial aid to help communities control air or water pollution. Federal legislation dealing with solid wastes (Public Law 89–272) came into effect in 1965. Sixteen states have action programs.(68)

The new federal law authorized expenditures on solid waste problems of $7 million in fiscal 1966 (rising to $20 million in fiscal 1969) to finance surveys, technological development, pilot plant and full-scale demonstration of improved disposal methods, engineering feasibility studies of new methods, encouragement of interstate and local cooperation, graduate teaching grants to universities, and research grants to universities, states, and research agencies.

Regional organizations for water-quality management have a traditional standing in the United States—from the early, single-purpose sewage, irrigation, or drainage districts to such modern multi-purpose organizations as the Ohio River Sanitary Commission (ORSANCO) and the Delaware River Basin Commission (DRBC).(69) In Germany, the Ruhr Valley Administration has shown that integrated regional management based on systems analysis and economic optimization can be carried very far in practice, through cooperative organization, wise engineering, and ingenious use of workable but theoretically sound rules of thumb. ORSANCO and DRBC have shown that impressive progress toward basin-wide planning and management can be attained in the United States.

A regional agency needs a competent technical, planning, administrative, and legal staff. In addition, it must have adequate authority and resources to deal effectively with its responsibilities.(70) These include:

1. Investigation of actual or potential pollution problems and development of effective plans. To do this, the agency needs to obtain and interpret physical, biological, and economic data to forecast the occurrence and extent of pollution, and to analyze the economic and other consequences of alternative courses of action.
2. Control and regulation of pollutants emitters—for example, industrial discharges into a river system or combustion exhausts into the air.
3. Taxation and assessment, both for control purposes, through charges on polluters, and for raising funds to carry out the purposes of the

agency. The effluent charges levied in the Ruhr Valley are an example. Besides such revenues, the agency may also need to raise money by issuing bonds or by obtaining grants from other branches of government.

4. Establishment and operation of treatment or disposal facilities.
5. Cooperation with and advice to other governmental agencies, especially municipalitiés and counties, which have authority over land use.

Water, air, and land in part are a common resource, and in part are subject to individual possession or ownership. Traditionally in the United States, individual rights to water and air have been tied to the ownership and use of land. For pollution, as for other aspects of land-use control, planning, zoning, and standards have become the most commonly employed tools to attain a reasonable compromise between private property rights and the public interest.(71)

Under our system, the authority to implement these land-use controls is firmly lodged in local governments—counties and municipalities. This fragmentation of land-use controls is a hard fact of our political life, and it means that the federal government, the states, and regional authorities concerned with pollution must develop cooperative devices to deal with local governmental jurisdictions.

A pollution control unit, to be successful needs the support of a constituency that can help it establish and enforce sanctions against pollution, particularly voluntary sanctions based on publicity and public opinion. An effective constituency must be "grown" through a continuing program of education. The public needs to be supplied, in readily understandable form, accurate and objective information on problems and opportunities. A nongovernmental organization can be especially effective within "problem sheds" that include a number of political units. An example is the Water Resources Association of the Delaware River Basin, which works with industry and community advisory groups to support the work of the Delaware River Basin Commission.(72)

SOME CONCLUSIONS

As pollution problems become steadily more serious, we need both to consider balances and choices within the environment as a whole and to take full advantage of its natural processes. For example, garbage disposal by incineration, land fill, or household grinding adds pollutants to the air, the soil, or the waters. Our choice of which method to use should depend on the character of the local environment and the total burden of pollutants we are adding to different parts of it. In windy areas that are steadily ventilated, a higher proportion of waste products can be disposed of to the air than in regions of light winds and frequent temperature inversions. Different streams may be devoted to different purposes. Some can be kept clean and sparkling, others used to oxidize relatively large quantities of organic matter.

We have seen that air and water pollutants do not recognize conventional

TABLE 6. **Summary of estimated annual costs of pollution control in United States cities dur-ing the next 15 years** *Source:* Except where noted, computed from estimates of unit costs and growth of pollutant emissions given in this paper. Operating costs are averages over the next 15 years. Capital costs for water pollution control are annual investment costs for con-struction, assuming a discount rate of 4% and a 25-year useful life for the structures.

| | ANNUAL COSTS (BILLIONS OF DOLLARS) | | |
	CAPITAL	*OPERATING*	*TOTAL*
Air pollution			
Automobile afterburners	$1.5	$1.0	$2.5
Sulphur dioxide removal from stack gases[a]	0.3	1.0	1.3
Industrial control equipment[b]	0.3	NA	0.3
	(2.1)	(2.0)	(4.1)
Water pollution			
Reservoirs for seasonal equalization of river flows for waste oxidation	0.4	—	0.4
Municipal sewage collection and treatment	0.9	0.6	1.5
Industrial effluent treatment	1.1	0.5	1.6
Separation of combined sewers and storage of storm waters[c]	0.5	—	0.5
Electric utility cooling towers[d]	0.1	0.6	0.7
	(3.0)	(1.7)	(4.7)
Solid waste disposal			
Collection of municipal wastes[e]	—	2.6	2.6
Incineration of municipal wastes[e]	—	0.7	0.7
Land fill of municipal wastes[e]	—	0.3	0.3
Junk auto disposal[e]	—	0.2	0.2
Demolition wastes disposal[f]	—	0.9	0.9
	—	(4.7)	(4.7)
Total	$5.1	$8.4	$13.5

[a] Assuming that all present and future fossil fuel generating plants will install equipment for re-moval of sulphur dioxide.

[b] Los Angeles County expenditures from *Summary of Total Air Pollution Data for Los Angeles County,* A Report of the Engineering Division, Air Pollution Control District, January 1965, pro-jected to 1980 and multiplied by 20.

[c] Based on an estimated population of 40 million people served by combined sewers, and an assumed cost of $200 per person for sewer separation and/or storage of storm waters.[74]

[d] Assuming that all present and future electric utilities will construct cooling towers.

[e] Assuming that the amount of municipal wastes and junk autos will increase by 80% during the next 15 years.

[f] Assuming that amount of demolition wastes and unit costs of disposal are each half those of municipal wastes.

demarcations. They move across city and county lines and ignore state boundaries. To limit or prevent pollution, therefore, control measures are needed over regions determined by meteorological and hydrologic realities, rather than by legal artifacts. We need to treat the entire urban-suburban-rural complex that constitutes a modern metropolis as an entity. Existing levels of government need to cooperate in new ways, and it may be necessary to invent and test new types of governmental organizations.

The problem of pollution has many aspects—public-health, economic, sociological, political, and institutional. But in all aspects it is related to human beings. It would not exist except for man's activities. All living creatures are affected by pollution; only man has the ability to control or eliminate it. The sciences that deal with man, with his behavior and his institutions, are therefore central.(73)

Many kinds of social scientists and social engineers, as well as chemists, biologists, statisticians, and sanitary engineers, must be involved in handling the pollution problems of the future. Economists are needed to determine the real costs of pollution and its abatement, and the economically "efficient" allocation of these costs among different elements of society. Urban and regional planners should keep the goal of minimal pollution constantly in mind. Political scientists, public administrators, and lawyers will have the task of devising new forms of governmental organization, intragovernmental cooperation, and public-private interaction. They must find both incentives for right action and legal sanctions against wrong actions—carrots and sticks—and ways to apply them.

When stated in the aggregate, the sum of the costs estimated in previous sections of this paper for reduction of air, water, and land pollution is large. But even if all measures were taken to meet existing as well as future needs, the total per person per year on the average during the next fifteen years would represent only a small fraction of the national income—less than 3 per cent (Table 6). As incomes continue to rise, it should be possible to increase the absolute amounts spent on waste disposal, even if the fraction of income for these purposes is not increased. With growing affluence, moreover, our people may be willing to allocate a larger fraction of their resources to maintain the quality of their environment, just as the fractions for education, health, and recreation are increasing.

REFERENCES

1. Johnson, Lyndon B. February 1965. Natural beauty message to the Congress.
2. Environmental Pollution Panel of the President's Science Advisory Committee. November 1965. *Restoring the quality of our environment*, pp. i–xii, 1–317.
3. U.S., Congress, House, Report of the Research Management Advisory Panel through the Subcommittee on Science, Research and Development to the Committee on Science and Astronautics. 1966. *The adequacy of technology for pollution abatement*. Washington, D.C.: U.S. Government Printing Office, pp. i–ix, 1–17.
4. *Loc. cit.*
5. Kneese, A. *The economics of regional water quality management*. 1964. Published for Resources for the Future by Johns Hopkins Press.
6. Committee on Pollution of the National Academy of Sciences, Report to the Federal Council for Science and Technology, National Research Council. *Waste management and control*. 1966. Publication 1400. Washington, D.C.: National Academy of Sciences, National Research Council, pp. i–vii, 1–275.
7. *Loc. cit.*
8. Tilson, S. June 1965. Air pollution. *International Science and Technology* 22–31.
9. *Waste management and control. Op. cit.*
10. *Loc. cit.*
11. *Restoring the quality of our environment. Op. cit.*
12. *Loc. cit.*
13. *Ibid.*
14. *Waste management and control. Op. cit.*
15. Griggin, C. W., Jr. May 22, 1965. America's airborne garbage. *Saturday Review* 32–34, 95–96.
16. *Waste management and control. Op. cit.*
17. Perloff, H. S. January 1966. New resources in an urban age. Paper presented at the ACTION Symposium on the Future American City.
18. *Waste management and control. Op. cit.*
19. *Loc. cit.*
20. *Ibid.*
21. Rienow, R. and L. T. May 22, 1965. Last chance for the nation's waterways. *Saturday Review* 35–36, 96–97.
22. Federal Water Pollution Control Administration. 1961. *Delaware*

estuary comprehensive study preliminary report and findings.

23. Restoring the quality of our environment. Op. cit.

24. Loc. cit.

25. Ibid.

26. Carr, D. E. May 1966. Death of the
sweet waters; the politics of pollution. The Atlantic 93–106.

27. Delaware estuary comprehensive
study preliminary report and findings. Op. cit.

28. Loc. cit.

29. Ibid.

30. Carr. Op. cit.

31. Kneese. Op. cit.

32. Waste management and control. Op.
cit.

33. Loc. cit.

34. Nutrient Sources Subcommittee of
the Technical Committee of the Lake
Mendota Problems Committee. January 3, 1966. Report on the nutrient
sources of Lake Mendota.

35. Waste management and control.
Op. cit.

36. Loc. cit.

37. Ibid.

38. Restoring the quality of our environment. Op. cit.

39. Waste management and control.
Op. cit.

40. Restoring the quality of our environment. Op. cit.

41. Loc. cit.

42. Fair, G. M. and Geyer, J. 1958. Water
and waste water treatment. John
Wiley and Sons.

43. Restoring the quality of our environment. Op. cit.

44. Loc. cit.

45. Ibid.

46. Ibid.

47. Sanitation District of Los Angeles
County. September 1955. Planned
refuse disposal.

48. Department of Sanitation, The City
of New York. Annual Report,
1963–64.

49. Mayor's Task Force on Air Pollution
in the City of New York. 1966. Freedom to breathe.

50. Loc. cit.

51. American Public Works Association. Proceedings, National Conference on Solid Waste Research.

52. Association of Bay Area Governments. July 1965. Bay area regional
planning program refuse disposal
need study.

53. Restoring the quality of our environment. Op. cit.

54. Loc. cit.

55. Ibid.

56. U.S., Congress, House, Report of the
Research Management Advisory
Panel through the Subcommittee on
Science, Research and Development
to the Committee on Science and
Astronautics. 1966. The adequacy of
technology for pollution abatement.
Washington, D.C.: U.S. Government
Printing Office, pp. i–ix, 1–17.

57. Loc. cit.

58. Ibid.

59. Ibid.

60. Restoring the quality of our environment. Op. cit.

61. Loc. cit.

62. Ibid.

63. Waste management and control.
Op. cit.

64. Restoring the quality of our environment. Op. cit.

65. Waste management and control.
Op. cit.

66. Loc. cit.

67. U.S., Congress, Senate, Staff Report
to the Committee on Public Works.
September 1963. A study of pollution—air. Washington, D.C.: U.S.
Government Printing Office.

68. Waste management and control.
Op. cit.

69. Loc. cit.

70. Ibid.

71. Ibid.

72. Ibid.

73. Ibid.

74. U.S., Congress, Senate, Staff Report
of the Committee on Public Works.
June 1963. A study of pollution—
water. Washington, D.C.: U.S. Government Printing Office.

Conference on the Ecological Aspects of International Development

JULIAN McCAULL

JULIAN McCAULL *is Program Co-ordinator of the Center for the Biology of Natural Systems, Washington University, St. Louis.*

Whereas Revelle in the previous article focused on the problems caused by urban life in industrial states, McCaull, summarizing a series of case studies of the ecological effects of economic transformation performed by an international group of experts, focuses on the consequences of development in the Third World.

CONFERENCE STUDY

The world situation was surveyed in case histories by experts from around the world in a three-day conference early in December [1968] sponsored by the Center for the Biology of Natural Systems and the Conservation Foundation. The meeting, entitled 'Conference on the Ecological Aspects of International Development,' was held in Warrenton, Virginia. Persons attending the conference included the authors of some fifty papers and representatives of the World Bank, the United States Agency for International Development, the Inter-American Bank for Development, Unesco, the International Biological Programme, and the United Nations Department of Economic and Social Affairs.

HYDROLOGICAL PROJECTS

The biggest and, perhaps, the most consequential projects are those to control the great rivers of the world. The dangers of instituting such gigantic enterprises without adequate ecological, social, and public health planning is illustrated by the Kariba Dam on the Zambezi River near the Kariba Gorge between Zambia and Southern Rhodesia. Although no ecological surveys

Nature and Resources 5(2): 5–12, June 1969. Copyright © 1969 by Unesco. Reprinted by permission.

were made, observed Dr. Thayer Scudder of the California Institute of Technology, government officials realized that provisions were necessary for the 29,000 Tonga people on the north bank of the Zambezi. The plans, however, did not make due allowance for the farming system and the cultural practices of the Tonga.

Before the Kariba Dam, most of the people lived within a mile of the Zambezi river or its major tributaries. They planted crops twice a year primarily for local consumption. Cereals, legumes, and cucurbits were planted at the start of the rainy season in November in alluvial soil and harvested before the flood season in April. The second crop was planted after the flood water receded. Seed was sown just behind the retreating water from late April until September, then harvested before December.

The situation changed after the dam was constructed. The alluvial soil was flooded. From 1958 to 1963, even cultivation of the lake-shore margin was impossible because of rising water, and the Tonga had to depend on a single crop grown in the rainy season.

The margin around man-made tropical lakes has potential for both dry and wet crops, particularly rice, but little research was available on the subject. The Tonga set about planting on their own in November, 1963, shortly after the high-water mark was reached. As a result of their initiative, one of the best maize crops ever was harvested in February and March, but that was not the case thereafter.

Before the dam, agricultural activities in the wet and dry seasons did not overlap. After the dam, the low-water period for dry season planting was August to December rather than April to November as before. This change interfered with ploughing in the rainy season. Even more exasperating to the Tonga farmers was the erratic rise and fall of the water-level, which was controlled to facilitate power-plant operations, not farming. In the 1964–65 season, the low point was reached in December, rather than in March as in the 1963–64 season. In the 1965–66 season, the level declined gradually for four months after the July peak, then plunged 10 feet in two months after November. But persons who planted the large area that became clear in December and January were deceived. The lake level reversed itself and rose rapidly during February and March, 1966. The high point that year was in July, three months after the usual peak before the dam. These fluctuations in the water-level destroyed the crops. Agriculture down-river from the dam was hindered by even greater fluctuations.

Despite uncertainties which are greater under the artificial conditions created by man than under natural conditions, the people will probably continue farming the margin of the river, predicted Dr. Scudder. The potential, however, in terms of agricultural production and job opportunities will be lost since the designers of the dam failed to accommodate regulation of water for power production to the needs of farmers.

FAILURE OF FISHING

Government officials predicted that up to 20,000 tons of fish would be taken annually from Lake Kariba, but the predictions did not materialize. In 1963, an estimated 4,000 short tons of fish were taken by more than 2,000 fishermen. By 1964, the annual catch had dropped to 2,100 short tons. The amount has declined ever since. In 1967, the lake supported only 500 fishermen.

The downward trend, which has been noted in impounded water elsewhere, was due to ecological factors that are only partially understood. Apparently, predator fish multiplied after being dispersed initially by the altered river conditions. Furthermore, chemical and biological stabilization of the lake may have reduced the phytoplankton food available to the fish. In addition, dense shrubbery was left in much of the basin which shielded the fish from the nets. When not fighting to clear their equipment from the snags, fishermen often had to fight clear of the aquatic fern, *Salvinia auriculata,* which flourished in the lake and formed mats that boats could not penetrate.

TSETSE FLY

The new fisheries, while they lasted, contributed to another problem related to the new lake. Fish traders moved from camp to camp or from camp to village with fresh and dried fish, and tsetse flies rode along. The threat of human and bovine trypanosomiasis was increased by this activity and by at least three other factors: (a) disturbance of flies centred in the area flooded, (b) provision of new fly refuges in the lush vegetation along the shore-line, and (c) introduction of cattle into areas known to harbour the fly.

Despite control measures aimed at the flies and prophylactic treatment of cattle, bovine trypanosomiasis produced a crisis in some areas after the lake was formed. In Munyumbwe, for example, officials counted 8,139 cattle, or about one per person, in 1962. The number had been reduced by half in 1966, mostly due to bovine trypanosomiasis. Insecticide spraying eventually brought the outbreak under control, but the threat of tsetse fly invasion from focal areas not under control still remains.

THE NILE

The Aswan High Dam is the most recent and largest of the dams constructed this century near Aswan.

From observations based on his association with Egypt 10, a schistosomiasis control project sponsored by the World Health Organization, Dr. Henry van der Schalie, Curator of Molluscs at the Museum of Zoology, University of Michigan, expressed the opinion that the spread of schistosomiasis through irrigation projects associated with the dam could outweigh the benefits.

The objective of the Egypt 10 project was to develop control techniques in a 5,000-acre tract on the Nile with 32,000 people and six villages. Experience in the programme emphasized the difficulty of introducing measures aimed at reducing contact between people and irrigation waters from the Nile. Throughout history they have depended upon the river in an otherwise barren land, and fishing, farming, and the ablution practices of Islam make

artificial protection such as rubber boots impractical. The larvae of the parasite cercaria emerge from the infected snails in huge numbers and are quick to burrow into exposed human skin.

Efforts at sanitation also foundered. For example, bore-hole latrines became open cesspools because of the high-water table. Medical control of the disease was difficult. The drugs had serious side effects and people were reluctant to lose working time by visiting government clinics.

The most promising approach appears to be control of the intermediary host snails by molluscicides such as copper sulphate. The cost of such a programme on a national scale, however, is beyond the economic means of the country. The poisons also endanger fish which may be of major food importance, observed Dr. C. J. Shiff of the Blair Research Laboratory, Salisbury (Southern Rhodesia).

SPREAD BY IRRIGATION

The incidence of the disease is related to the type of irrigation. In the delta region, perennial irrigation which may support up to four crops a year produces an extremely high incidence of both intestinal schistosomiasis, caused by *Schistosoma mansoni*, and urinary schistosomiasis, which is caused by *Schistosoma haematobium*. By contrast, the incidence is much lower along the river between Cairo and Aswan, where basin-type, or one-crop irrigation is practiced. Intestinal schistosomiasis, the more severe form of the disease, generally is imported from the delta. The incidence of urinary schistosomiasis in the nonperennial region usually is no more than 5–10 per cent.

In addition to electrical power, the Aswan dam is intended to provide a resource for extensive perennial irrigation. The result may well be an upsurge in the incidence of urinary schistosomiasis as well as the invasion of intestinal schistosomiasis along the entire 500-mile river flood-plain between Aswan and Cairo.

Other participants at the conference reported that irrigation without parallel sanitation features has been associated with a rise in the incidence of schistosomiasis in many other regions of Africa, including Southern Rhodesia, Upper Volta, Gambia, Tanzania, Ghana, Uganda, Nigeria, and the Republic of South Africa. Schistosomiasis control must be combined with a general attack on other water-borne diseases in connexion with development of water and soil resources, urged Drs. Charles C. Hughes and John M. Hunter of the African Studies Center, Michigan State University. They called for an integrated approach featuring environmental sanitation, sterile water supplies, and urban sanitation.

FLOOD CONTROL

Another effect of the Aswan dam has been virtually to halt the flow of sediment and nutrients that once were carried during the flood season to the delta and the sea. Before the annual flood was controlled by the dam in 1966, from 50 to 100 million tons of sediment were carried past Cairo each year, estimated Dr. Carl J. George of the Department of Biological Sciences, Union College, Schenectady, N.Y.

The control of the flood makes life less threatening for people along the Nile, but the halt of nutrients reaching the ocean has destroyed the coastal sardine fishing industry. Five delta lakes fished commercially also appear to be less productive without the food nutrients.

Although the lives of the fishermen have been disrupted, the balance sheet in this case may be more favourable. Lake Nasser may produce catches which far exceed those lost at the delta. A parallel was drawn between these expectations and the unfulfilled expectations at Lake Kariba, however, by participants at the centre meeting reviewing the conference proceedings.

THE DWINDLING DELTA

The delta gained ground against wave and current action of the sea before this century. Sediments from the Nile contributed to the build-up, explained Dr. M. Kassas of the University of Cairo. These deposits compensated for erosion, and the delta shore slowly extended northward. Now, with the sediment flow cut off by the dam and other river control structures, the shore-line diminishes by several metres each year. Narrow sand-bars which separate two of the delta lakes from the sea are likely to collapse. This will transform the lakes into bays and endanger hydrological drainage systems into the lakes which support land reclamation projects farther inland.

COMPREHENSIVE PROGRAMME URGED

A number of speakers stressed the need for programmes based on integrated measures to counter problems in public health, sociology, and ecology. Reliance on one approach exclusively is short-sighted, observed Drs. Hughes and Hunter of Michigan State University. They offered the example of campaigns to eradicate the vector mosquito *Anopheles gambiae* in certain areas of Africa with insecticides.

In the area of Thies, Senegal, the incidence of the parasite among children younger than 14 years of age was reduced from 22 per cent to 1 per cent during a four-year campaign of spraying with DDT and Dieldrin. One year later, however, the incidence had risen to 16 per cent due to transmission by insecticide-resistant mosquitoes.

A similar situation developed in the Para region of Tanzania. Six months after the spraying, the incidence of parasites in children was 5 per cent; seven months later, the rate had soared to 30 per cent among children of 2 to 9 years of age. The cause was a new strain of *Anopheles gambiae*.

In Ethiopia a successful insecticide campaign all but eliminated malaria by about 1960, reported M. Taghi Farvar, Research Assistant at the centre and one of the conference co-ordinators. In 1962, the disease recurred and caused 150,000 deaths. The epidemic was traced to complex factors including possible resistant strains of *Anopheles* mosquitoes as well as migration of infected human hosts. A conjecture by some investigators was that periodic exposure to the parasites produced immunity in people before the insecticide campaign. The campaign interrupted this exposure for about two years, during which time immunity decreased. Thus when the disease increased, many people were susceptible to acute cases who had had a certain level of resistance before the eradication campaign.

LACTOSE INTOLERANCE

Powdered milk and milk products for food-aid programmes in Asian countries provided the focus for another example of the complex relationships in public health programmes. Lactose intolerance among adults in Asia has received recent publicity, and further medical verification of this discovery was outlined by Drs. A. E. Davis and T. D. Bolin of the University of New South Wales, Kensington (Australia).

In lactose tolerance tests, eighteen out of twenty-one healthy Chinese students, four out of five Indian students, and eight New Guinea natives had lactose intolerance. The criteria were: diarrhoea and a rise in blood sugar of less than 20 mg per 100 ml after ingestion of 50–80 gm of lactose, normal tolerance curves for glucose and galactose, low levels of the enzyme lactase in the intestinal mucosa, and an end to diarrhoea after elimination of lactose from the diet. With minor exceptions, all of these criteria were noted in the lactose-intolerant patients.

Jejunal mucosal specimens from six Chinese students showed no evidence of significant abnormalities in the intestinal villi. As determined by the biopsy, the mean lactase level was 0.3 U/g in specimens from six control subjects.

The limited evidence available to date suggests that only children younger than 6 years of age would benefit initially from the programmes introducing milk into the Asian diet. A comprehensive survey of lactose intolerance in Asian communities is needed to determine the incidence and whether the cause is congenital or acquired.

If congenital, other ways to improve the nutrition of Asian diets should be developed. If acquired due to lack of continued substrate challenge, a possibility which the investigators favour, milk tolerance might be increased by gradually increasing the lactose content of milk product.

INSECT CONTROL

Before the Second World War, traditional but effective methods of biological control were used against pests, observed Kevin P. Shea, Scientific Director of *Scientist and Citizen* and guest speaker at the centre meeting to discuss the conference. After the war, availability of chlorinated hydrocarbon compounds such as DDT made such methods seem anachronistic. Complete chemical control of insect pests appeared to be at hand.

As was discovered in the control of *Anopheles* mosquitoes as well as other insect pests, the insects showed generally unanticipated ability for genetic adaptation to insecticides. Insecticide resistance kept pace with the newer organophosphorus and carbamate compounds. Furthermore, in controlling pest populations, the insecticides also upset natural control mechanisms. The need for an integrated attack on malaria had a parallel in the development of an integrated approach to control crop pests. This concept featured mechanical, biological, and ecological measures, with localized low-level application of insecticides as a last resort.

DILEMMA IN MALAYSIA

The problem came to a head at the Cocoa Research Station in Sabah, one of the Borneo states of Malaysia. Where certain insecticides were used without sufficient regard to ecological factors, pest problems were thus aggravated and even new ones created.

Spraying with high-concentration insecticides began in 1959. First, a high-volume spray of Dieldrin or DDT was used against the Ring Bark Borer and the Branch Borer in cocoa trees. Then, early in 1960, general spraying was done as a prophylactic measure against other insect pests. The results were described by Gordon Conway, entomologist in the Sabah Department of Agriculture from 1961 to 1966 and now with the Institute of Ecology, University of California, Davis.

Despite the extensive spraying, infestation by the Branch Borer increased. Soon afterward, serious damage was done by three other pests: leaf-eating caterpillars, nettle caterpillars, and plant-hoppers. In July, 1961, several species of bagworms damaged the trees. Silk cases protected the bagworms against the weather and also, apparently, against the insecticides.

After reviewing the situation late in 1961, personnel at the research station decided to stop most of the spraying. They suspected that the broad-spectrum, contact-type insecticides actually did the most harm to parasitic and predatory insects which otherwise would have reduced the pests.

Soon after the spraying ended, the number of leaf-eating caterpillars was diminished by braconid parasites. Then the plant-hoppers and the Branch Borer declined under the pressure of predators and parasites.

The Ring Bark Borers were brought under control by selective measures. New borings were treated periodically with a jet spray of 1 per cent Dieldrin, and a secondary forest tree, Trema cannabina, which was an alternate host of the borer, was cleared from the cocoa fields and much of the surrounding area.

Regular spraying with the short-lived insecticide trichlorphon eventually brought the bagworm infestation under control. By 1963, the parasitic trachinid flies had suppressed the bagworms, and trichlorphon application was discontinued.

The experience at nearby commercial cocoa plantations was similar to that at the research station. At the urging of station personnel, most planta-tion operators discontinued use of contact insecticides in 1962. Pest infesta-tion has been low ever since. The selective control measures for the Ring Bark Borers and bagworms also were successful in other plantations.

DEVELOPMENT OF PROBLEM

In retrospect, Mr. Conway suggested that the original clearing of primary forest and planting of cocoa in Sabah may have produced a chain of events leading to the infestation. The cleared areas supported secondary forest plants and the transplanted cocoa seedlings, but insect species which had well-developed powers of dispersal and reproduction colonized the new sites quickly. They were attracted to the secondary growth plants and also fed on the cocoa trees. At this point, the situation was complicated by heavy application of contact insecticides which killed or otherwise excluded natural enemies. Thereafter, the pests continued to multiply and produced prolonged infestations, hypothesized Mr. Conway.

Older, traditional methods of pest control can compete economically with modern pesticides if the biology of the pest is thoroughly understood, he pointed out. In rubber plantations of Malaya, for example, an integrated programme controlled cockchafer beetles, which fed on the roots of rubber trees in the grub stage. As developed by B. S. Rao of the Rubber Research Institute at Kuala Lumpur, the programme was tailored to the age of the trees. Insecticides were applied locally in the case of young trees. Where the trees were older but still immature, limited insecticide application was combined with capture of the adult beetles in traps that had attractant fluorescent black lights. If the trees were mature, Heptachlor was applied to the soil to kill the emerging adult beetles.

SIDE EFFECTS

The State of Sabah was the site of unexpected side effects from insecticides. In 1955, the World Health Organization began a malaria control programme in co-operation with local medical departments in Sabah, Sarawak, and Brunei. DDT and Dieldrin were applied inside the dwellings to kill mosquitoes. Aside from the development of some strains resistant to Dieldrin, the programme was effective. In 1957, the objective was switched to eradication, and this was nearly achieved.

The insecticides poisoned cockroaches in Sarawak and small lizards in Sabah, however. These were eaten by domestic cats. The cats died, and, in turn, the rats multiplied in the villages, heightening the fear of rat-borne diseases.

To solve the new problem, cat owners in the large towns of Sabah donated cats and litters of kittens to persons in the upland areas to kill the rats. This generosity eased the difficulties in Sabah, but the problem in Sarawak was complicated by the difficulty of delivering the cats to remote areas. Finally, WHO and the Royal Air Force in Singapore teamed up. The donated cats were packed in special containers and dropped by parachute to the upland villages.

Fortunately, outbreaks of rat-borne disease apparently did not occur. The major casualty was the confidence of villagers who were reluctant to have their houses sprayed again.

TUTORIAL SUBJECT

Back in St. Louis, the report by Mr. Conway was discussed in the tutorial on Technology and the Environment of Developing Nations.

The effect of the insecticides on the insects at the Sabah Cocoa Research Station probably was quite complex, stressed Mr. Shea of *Scientist and Citizen,* who visited the tutorial. The population densities of both host and parasite probably were lowered by insecticides. A time-lag may have developed, however, in which the host was reproducing at a relatively faster rate than the parasite, he suggested.

CROP FAILURE

In the controlled conditions of the Sabah Research Station, mistakes were made and corrected without hardship to farmers. In the Canete Valley of Peru, however, similar mistakes produced grave economic crises. Wide-scale spraying of insecticides to combat cotton pests during 1949–56 proved to be disastrous, declared Teodoro Boza Barducci, agricultural engineer from Lima, Peru.

The pattern was similar to that in Malaysia and elsewhere. At first, compounds like DDT and BHC led to increased cotton yields in 35,000 acres of farmland. By 1952, three years after the programme began, pests were resistant to the insecticides and many natural enemies had been killed. The result was a decline in cotton production.

The farmers, who had meagre incomes under any circumstances, followed the recommendations of the Canete Valley Experiment Station and countered with organo-phosphate insecticides. At great expense, they used numerous, heavy applications. Nevertheless, whereas there had been seven major pests before 1949, the number increased to thirteen in 1952 even though United States techniques were followed to the letter.

In 1956, a second and devastating crop failure occurred. As a result, a farmers' association in the valley introduced a series of reform measures. Insecticides were prohibited except for mineral or natural organic insecticides such as calcium and lead arsenate and nicotine sulphate. Introduction of parasites and predators reinstituted biological control. Measures such as hand collection of infected fruit or bolls and agricultural reforms such as seed disinfection were introduced. Crops also were diversified.

As a result, the cotton crop was restored. The same procedures were introduced with success in other cotton-growing areas of Peru damaged by insecticides, reported Mr. Boza Barducci.

The unrelenting cycle threatens to repeat itself, however. New generations of farmers have not been taught the bitter lessons of the seven years' experiment. As a result, the insecticides are again being used and the situation already is critical, reported Dr. Ray Smith, Chairman of the Department of Entomology and Parasitology, University of California, Berkeley.

UNITED STATES SITUATION

Parallel development of insecticide resistance in cotton and other crop pests were reported in a study by Dr. L. D. Newsome, Department of Entomology, Louisiana State University. Insecticide control has been an important factor in increased yields of cotton, rice, and sugarcane in Louisiana during the past two decades. On the other hand, fifteen major pests species now have insecticide resistance. Certain cabbage loopers and the two spotted spider mite cannot be controlled by even the most advanced, experimental insecticides.

In addition, Dr. Newsome observed, damage to non-target organisms has been severe. Most seriously affected have been insect predators and parasites, fish, crustacea, and pollinating species such as honeybees.

ANIMAL PESTS

The hazards of wide-scale chemical attack on animal pests were highlighted in a report from Israel by Dr. H. Mendelssohn, Tel Aviv University. A campaign utilizing thallium was begun to eradicate field mice. Most seriously affected, however, were birds of prey which fed on the poisoned mice. Partially as a result of diminished predation, the mice continue to be a threat to grain, despite the poisoning.

Another project that failed was aimed at jackals, which damaged fruit and vegetables and were a possible cause of rabies. Under the influence of wholesale distribution of bait containing 15 per cent fluoroacetamide, the jackals nearly disappeared, but so did some birds and predators such as foxes, mongooses, and wild cats. Without the predators, hares increased at an enormous rate and did more damage to agriculture than the jackals. In addition, the killing of the mongooses led to proliferation of the Palestine viper in the agricultural settlements.

THE ATOM

Expansion of the nuclear power industry in the United States has been the natural outgrowth of increased power demands and governmental programmes for the peaceful use of nuclear energy, observed Dr. Dean E. Abrahamson of the University of Minnesota. As a result, more than one hundred nuclear-fueled electric-power plants are now planned in the United States, and the Atomic Energy Commission is pressing for major power and desalinization plants in other countries.

These plans have included studies of problems in engineering, economics, industry, and international relations. The same attention has not been given to ecological effects or to the consequences for human health, Dr. Abrahamson declared. For background he reviewed the workings of the nuclear generating plant. The plant actually is similar in many respects to a conventional steam plant, but the heat source for steam production depends upon fission reaction in uranium instead of fossil fuel.

The profound difference for the environment, however, is in the discharge of the plant. The disruption of aquatic biology by excessive discharge of power plant cooling water has received attention in recent publications. Although thermal waste is common to both conventional and nuclear power plants, about 50% more heat is dispersed by the less efficient nuclear plant.

HEALTH THREAT

The direct threat to human health, however, is radio-active material. How are radio-active wastes released into the environment? The answer requires a look into the core of the reactor. There, the fuel, usually pellets of uranium dioxide, is stacked in long, small-diameter, thin-walled fuel rods. A common configuration is four rectangular fuel assemblies each containing dozens of rods. Each assembly is separated from the other by one side of the control rod, which actually is in the form of a beam with four quadrants that runs the length of the rods when fully extended. The core that was described by Dr. Abrahamson would have about 120 of these four fuel-assembly combinations containing approximately 23,000 fuel rods.

In the single-cycle, boiling-water reactor, heat is generated in the reactor core and transferred to primary coolant water, which circulates through the space between the fuel rods. The water is converted to steam, passed through a pipe into the turbine-generator, then condensed and pumped back into the primary reactor vessel to complete the cycle. Cool water from outside the system, called the secondary coolant, passes into the condenser and removes the waste heat without coming into direct contact with the primary coolant.

Radio-active contaminants enter the environment in the liquid and gaseous wastes of the nuclear power plant. The primary coolant becomes contaminated in two ways. First, some fission products pass through the fuel rods by diffusion or other processes or directly through defects in the walls of the tubes. Second, activation products are produced by reactions between contaminants and the high neutron flux in the primary coolant.

The primary coolant usually is exchanged for fresh water gradually over a one-month period. The coolant drained off in this process is, of course, contaminated with fission products and generally undergoes a waste treatment process before being mixed with a secondary coolant and discharged. The quantity of radio-active contaminants in the discharge thus depends upon the effectiveness of the waste treatment system. Gaseous radio-active wastes discharged from the nuclear-power plant are primarily radio-active fission and activation products that are carried from the core into the turbine with the steam and then discharged from the stack.

AMOUNT OF RADIO-ACTIVE WASTE

Estimation of the environmental or public health hazards due to radio-active wastes is hindered by inadequate measurements of wastes from the plants. Manufacturers do estimate the quantities of wastes, however. A large boiling-water reactor with 1 million kw of electrical power capacity would discharge a minimum of 12,000 curies of radio-activity in gaseous wastes each year. The reactor core has about 250,000 linear feet of tubing only 0.02 to 0.04 inches thick, and some defects occur in fabrication. As a result, the waste-disposal system of a nuclear-power reactor plant is designed on the basis of a maximum of 1 per cent of the fuel rods having defects, although some cores have had no significant leaks after a year or more of operation. In the case of leaks from 1 per cent of the fuel rods, the gaseous wastes would be primarily fission products that would be discharged at a rate approaching 20 million curies of radiation per year. By comparison, the explosion of the atomic bomb at Hiroshima released only a few hundred thousand curies of long-lived radiation, Dr. Abrahamson observed.

IONIZING RADIATION

Radio-active isotopes which are particularly serious from the health standpoint, such as Sr_{90}, I_{131}, and Cs_{137}, are produced in large quantities in reactors and must be kept out of the environment because of the dangers associated with ionizing radiation. This is not always being done successfully, however, as indicated in a report from the University of Nevada which links a constant level of I_{131} in the thyroid glands of cattle with emission of radio-isotopes from nuclear reactors and fuel processing plants.

Furthermore, one radio-active substance, tritium, or radio-active hydrogen, is released into the environment without control, since no waste treatment yet devised will remove the substance. As another example, if the release of Kr_{85} from new reactors continues at the level of that from existing reactors, by the year 2000 exposure from this one isotope will approximate the exposure from all natural ionizing radiation in the environment.

LAKE VALENCIA

Ironically, one measure of the state of technological progress seems to be the degree to which water resources are damaged.

The destructive process has become far advanced at Lake Valencia during the past 250 years. A number of detailed historical records about the lake trace its decline. The best evidence points to agricultural, industrial, and urban activities as the cause of the damage, according to Dr. Alberto Bockh, Instituto para la Conservacion del Lago de Valencia, Valencia (Venezuela).

The major problem was the diversion of river tributaries which once supported a positive hydrological balance, causing the lake to flow west through El Paito Gorge and on to the Orinoco River. This flow kept the water fresh. The tributaries were diverted for farming and industries, and indiscriminate deforestation destroyed a considerable portion of the lake's upper watershed.

Interruption of the watershed and tributary system has slowly strangled Lake Valencia. Originally, the lake was at the level of the El Paito spillway, 426 metres above sea level. A drop in that level was recorded in 1727, soon after the development of agriculture under Spanish colonization. Now the surface of the lake is 405 metres above sea level and still dropping. Thus, in less than two and a half centuries, the lake surface has dropped 21 metres, or the height of a seven-storey building. By comparison, 1,000 years would be required for the bottom of the lake to rise 1 metre due to natural deposition of solid material, once carried to the lake by the tributaries.

Shrinking Surface

The surface of the lake has been reduced accordingly. In the early nineteenth century, the lake surface area was 643 square kilometres; now, the area is only half that. So rapidly has the shore-line receded that a yacht club and a restaurant built on the lake only ten years ago are today abandoned and in ruins hundreds of metres from the shore.

Salinity Increase

When the hydrological balance was positive, lake water was constantly renewed, and the saline content was roughly that of the average of the saline content of tributaries. Conversion to a negative hydrological balance, however, brought radical change. Water which still drains into the lake carries small quantities of dissolved salts which remain as the water evaporates. In the last two and a half centuries, salinity has increased eightfold, according to one investigator. The more recent increase in salinity of the lake is apparent in the accompanying table.

TABLE 1. Lake Valencia salinity increase

SALTS	YEAR				
	1920	1939	1950	1960	1966
Brackish solids (ppm)	785	935	1,012	1,050	1,270
Sulphates (ppm)	—	324	372	400	478

ECOLOGY AND CONTROL

The meshing of ecological, political, and economic considerations was stressed by Dr. P. T. Haskell of the Anti-Locust Research Centre, Ministry of Overseas Development, London. These elements have been combined effectively in control of Red Locusts, less so in control of the wider-ranging Desert Locusts.

The broad ecological approach has been stressed in other technological programmes during the past fifty years, observed Senior Fellow Owen Sexton at the centre discussion of the conference. 'Thirty or forty years ago, the Tennessee Valley was an underdeveloped region in the same sense that many of the African countries are today,' he pointed out.

Electrical power was only one of the considerations that went into the eventual construction of the dam system on the Tennessee River. Flood control and recreation were considered as well, and the ecological implications were studied carefully. For example, the incidence of malaria in the area was high, and the Tennessee River control system had built-in features to counter this problem. The water levels were varied systematically to destroy breeding sites of vector mosquitoes.

CONTINUING COMMITTEE

At the end of the three-day meeting, participants formally requested that a continuing committee be established to carry on the work of the conference. The centre and the Conservation Foundation will co-operate in the organization of the committee. A major objective will be preparation of information on the biological consequences of technical development programmes for use at the 1972 United Nations Conference on Human Environment.

Another joint project of the centre and the Conservation Foundation will be publication of the proceedings of the conference through the Natural History press.

Controlling the Planet's Climate

J. O. FLETCHER

J. O. FLETCHER *is an employee of RAND Corporation.*

Our environment is threatened not only by the direct, immediate effects of pollution, but also by long-range indirect effects. For example, man probably has already inadvertently caused significant changes in the world climate. Fletcher summarizes what is known about this area and about the possible ways of altering climate for the benefit or the detriment of mankind.

As* internationally pursued research efforts continue to improve our knowledge of climatic processes and the possibilities of deliberately influencing them, we are also becoming increasingly aware of the disturbing fact that human activity may already be inadvertently and irreversibly doing so. Furthermore, the inadvertent consequences of human activity will increase manyfold in only a few decades, precisely at a time when rapidly growing pressures on world food production make the social consequences of climatic variation ever more serious. The inescapable conclusion is that purposeful management of global climatic resources will eventually become necessary to prevent undesirable changes. That such capabilities could be used to improve existing climatic conditions is obvious.

Recent years have seen an upsurge of research in the fields of weather modification and climate control. Substantial improvements in the accumulation and analysis of environmental data, coupled with a better understanding of the nature and interrelationship of climatic processes, have provided researchers with theoretical insights into how global climate can be modified and what some of the resulting consequences might be. Man already has the technological capability to carry out many climate-influencing schemes, such as the creation of large inland seas, the

---

From "Impact of Science on Society," 1969, Vol. XIX, no 2. Reproduced with the permission of Unesco.

*Any views expressed in this paper are those of the author. They should not be interpreted as reflecting the views of his employer, the RAND Corporation, or the official opinion or policy of any of its governmental or private research sponsors.

deflection of ocean currents, the seeding of extensive cloud or surface areas, and perhaps even the removal of the arctic pack ice.

Still unresolved, however, is the uncertainty about the possible global effects of such large-scale weather modification efforts, which, in addition to bringing about major environmental changes, would give rise to many complex economic, sociological, legal, and political problems.

Let us proceed now to examine more fully the nature of the physical problem, the depth of our present understanding of it, the feasible influencing capabilities available to us, and the prospects for future progress.

THE INADVERTENT INFLUENCING OF GLOBAL CLIMATE

Whether human activity has played a significant role in climatic shifts of the past century is a question which cannot yet be answered with any confidence. The complexities of global climate are still too poorly understood to assess the dynamical response of the system to a given change. Some investigators have argued that the effects of man's activities are already significant, or even dominant, in changing global climate. The influencing factors most frequently suggested are carbon dioxide pollution, particulate pollution (smog and dust), and heat pollution. The physical arguments advanced have to do with the effects of these pollutants on the heat balance of the atmosphere.

Carbon dioxide is one of the three important radiation-absorbing constituents in the atmosphere (the other two being water vapour and ozone). There is no doubt that the carbon dioxide concentration in the atmosphere has been increasing in this century, apparently by some 10–15 per cent, due primarily to the increased combustion of carboniferous fuels.

The physical effect of a greater CO_2 concentration in the atmosphere is to decrease the radiative loss to space. Thus, an increase in CO_2 increases the so-called 'greenhouse effect' and causes global warming.

Some have suggested that the general warming that took place from 1900 until about 1940 was due to just such an increase in the atmospheric content of CO_2. Plass, in 1959, estimated that a warming of 0.5° C during the last century could be attributed to this cause, and this is comparable to the warming that actually did occur.

It is further estimated that, by the year 2000 a further warming of three times this amount could be caused by the increase of CO_2 in the atmosphere. Other estimates have predicted an even greater warming.

Notwithstanding these arguments, the sharp global cooling of the past decade indicates that other, oppositely directed factors are more influential than the increasing atmospheric content of CO_2. For example, Möller (1963) estimates that a 10 per cent change in CO_2 can be counter-balanced by a 3 per cent change in water vapour or by a 1 per cent change in mean cloudiness.

Let it also be noted that the oceans have an enormous capacity to absorb CO_2, this varying according to their temperature with colder oceans being able to store more of the gas. Thus, a warming of the oceans could also be a primary cause of the increase of CO_2 in the atmosphere.

In summary, it appears that, other factors being constant, the CO_2 generated by human activity could bring about important changes of global climate during the next few decades. But other factors, of course, are not constant, and have apparently been more influential than the CO_2 increase in affecting the climate of recent years.

With regard to heat pollution, Budyko (1962, 1966) points out that, although the yearly production of man-made energy on Earth is now only about 1/2,500 of the solar radiation arriving at the Earth's surface which is not returned to space, it could increase to equal the retained solar radiation if compounded annually at 10 per cent for 100 years, or 4 per cent for 200 years. (The present growth rate is about 4 per cent). From these numbers we may conclude that, sometime during the next century, the problem of heat pollution will become important on a global scale. By then we must be able to compensate for it or face the possibility of a sharp global warming which could, in turn, trigger additional reinforcing transformations such as a melting of the polar ice. But, for the time being, and for the next few decades, the effects of heat pollution will not be sizable enough to exert a significant influence on global climate.

One of the most rapidly increasing forms of man-made atmospheric pollution is smog, which embodies all forms of industrial pollution. Bryson (1968) reports a turbidity increase of 30 per cent per decade over Mauna Loa Observatory, which is far from all sources of pollution. This is thus indicative of the general increase. He further argues that a reduced atmospheric transparency, even by only 3–4 per cent, could decrease the global mean temperature by 0.4°C. This is due to the fact that a more turbid atmosphere will reflect back more of the sun's radiation, thus allowing less heat to penetrate through to the Earth.

Bryson believes that the increasing global air pollution, through its effect on the reflectivity of the Earth's atmosphere, is currently the dominant influence on climate and is responsible for the temperature decline of recent decades. Budyko (1968) also attributes climatic changes primarily to the decreased transparency of the atmosphere, caused in the past by volcanic eruptions and in recent decades by man-made pollution. If this interpretation is correct, mankind faces an immediate and urgent need for global climate management, especially in view of the fact that smog production is increasing everywhere at an exponential rate and no means of curbing this increase are in sight.

Curve 4 in Figure 1 shows the observed trends of atmosphere transparency since 1890 and a general correlation with some of the other variations in the global system—such as those of northern hemisphere temperatures (Curves 1, 2) and sun-spot activity (Curve 3)—can be seen. The sharp decrease in transparency early in this century can be attributed to a series of volcanic eruptions. However, the decrease since 1940 cannot be attributed to this cause although the eruption of Agung in Bali, in 1963 did cause a noticeable world-wide effect. Thus, man-made pollution may have been the most important cause of recent climatic changes.

On the other hand, there also appears to be a connexion between solar activity and atmospheric transparency. Curve 3 in Figure 1 shows the trends

FIGURE 1. Comparison of annual variations in several climatic factors. In each case the ordinates are the deviations from an annual mean established over a long term. Curves 1 and 2 (from Budyko, 1968) show the mean annual temperature in the northern hemisphere, curve 1 depicting the annual figures and curve 2 being smoothed by taking a ten-year moving average. Curve 3 depicts total number of sun-spots (from Nazarov). Curve 4 (from Budyko, 1968) depicts atmospheric transparency as percentage of a mean. The transparency was determined by measuring direct solar radiation with cloudless sky at several stations in Europe and America. Since atmospheric transparency can be affected by volcanic eruptions the dates of five major eruptions are indicated.

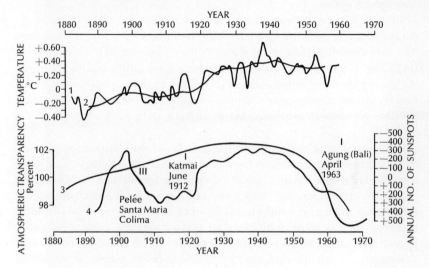

of sun-spot activity and one can see that much of the recent decrease in atmospheric transparency might be accounted for on this basis. If this is true, a reversal should become apparent during the next decade, when fewer sun-spots are expected.

Still another form of growing pollution, and one whose possible effects have received little study, is the creation of cirrus cloudiness (vapour trails) by the exhaust products of high-flying aircraft. Increased cloudiness of any form tends to increase the reflectivity (albedo) of the Earth and, according to Bryson's calculations, a 1 per cent increase in mean albedo would cool the Earth by 1.6°C. On the other hand, it should be noted that increased cloudiness at high levels greatly reduces radiative loss to space, and this would have a warming effect on the Earth. Thus, the dual effects of more or less cloudiness are great, but the direction of the net influence depends on the type and height of the clouds, and on whether they are in a dark or sunlit region of the Earth.

From the foregoing considerations, we may conclude that man is probably inadvertently influencing global climate at the present time. Certainly several products of man's activity are theoretically influential enough to do so within a few decades. However, there are so many variables and degrees of freedom in the global system that specific cause and effect estimates in this regard are still very uncertain. In order to better understand this uncertainty, let us take a brief look at the dynamic and multifaceted nature of global climate.

THE CHANGING PATTERN OF GLOBAL CLIMATE

The climate of a particular region is determined by a number of relatively static factors such as elevation, latitude, topography, type of surface, and also by the properties of the air which passes over it. The dynamic factor which brings about weather changes is the circulation of the atmosphere, which, in turn, is strongly influenced by the interaction of the ocean/atmosphere system.

Substantial world-wide changes of climate have occurred, even in the course of a few decades, and have been described by many investigators. The data show that the general vigour of the global atmospheric circulation undergoes significant variations, with associated latitudinal shifts of the main wind currents and changes in the nature of their disturbances. Variation in the global atmospheric circulation pattern is the factor which makes possible a coherent interpretation of climatic data from all parts of the Earth.

For example, during the first three decades of this century, the general trend was toward a growing strength of the northern hemisphere circulation, a northward displacement of polar fronts (outer boundaries of cold masses) in both the atmosphere and the ocean, a northward displacement of pack-ice boundaries and cyclone paths (movements of large, rotating wind currents), a weaker development of blocking air masses over the continents, and a pronounced aridity of the south central parts of North America and Eurasia. Conversely, recent decades have exhibited opposite trends: a weakening circumpolar circulation, southward shifts of ice boundaries and cyclone paths, and increased rainfall in the south central parts of the continents.

These trends were underscored in 1968. It was a year in which Icelandic fishermen suffered losses due to the most extensive sea ice in the last half century, while phenomenal wheat yields from the plains of both Asia and North America due to increased rainfall pushed world wheat prices to a 26-year low. In a happier vein, the predicted 1968 famine in India did not occur, with favourable climate and better strains of grain as the important offsetting factors. In the southern hemisphere, the southward displacement of the Chilean rainfall region created severe droughts.

Yet such small variations of climate, though of growing importance to our complex pattern of human activity, are minor compared to the more pronounced variations that have occurred in the relatively recent past. Less than 20,000 years ago, an ice sheet still covered North America and stretched from the Atlantic to the Pacific with a thickness of up to two miles. The last major ice sheet disappeared from Scandinavia only about 8000–7000 B.C., while in North America the ice retreated even later. During the period of ice retreat and somewhat after, rainfall in the Mediterranean area and probably over much of the hemisphere was less than at present, possibly due to cooler oceans. The post-glacial warming culminated in a 'climatic optimum' about 4000–2000 B.C., during which world temperatures were 2°–3°C warmer than they are now and rain was much more plentiful in North Africa and the Middle East.

The decline from the warm optimum was abrupt from about 1000 B.C., with cooling continuing to about 400 B.C. This was a period of maximum

North African rainfall, which was accompanied by the rapid development of human activity partly induced by climatic stress. By this time, renewed warming had set in and continued until a secondary climatic optimum of A.D. 800–1000, a period characterized by a relatively rainless, warm and storm-free North Atlantic, which made possible the great Viking colonization of Iceland, Greenland and Newfoundland.

The subsequent climatic decline, during which arctic pack ice advanced southward in the North Atlantic, was abrupt from about A.D. 1300, with one partial recovery around 1500. It culminated in the 'little ice age' of 1650–1840.

Since about 1840, a new warming trend has predominated and appears to have reached a climax in this century, followed by cooling since about 1940, irregularly at first but more sharply since about 1960. The periods of general warming were accompanied by increasing vigour of the westerly circulation in both hemispheres, bringing a more maritime climate to the continents, a northward displacement of cyclone paths, and a pronounced warming of the Arctic. The recent cooling trend exhibits a reverse pattern: weakened westerly circulation, more variable and southerly cyclone paths, and a colder Arctic.

The pattern of change in the southern hemisphere is more obscure. No reliable index has been found for the strength of the southern hemisphere trade winds and even the indices of mid-latitude westerlies are not adequate. Temperature patterns for the 80 per cent of the southern hemisphere covered by oceans are almost non-existent. Even since the International Geophysical Year (1957–58), year-to-year variations in sea-ice extent in the Southern Ocean are largely unknown. However, the meagre data that are available show that corresponding climatic variations are evident from pole to pole.

THE GLOBAL 'CLIMATE MACHINE'

It is increasingly apparent that climatic change can be explained only in terms of the behaviour of the atmosphere and ocean on a global scale. Net heating at low latitudes and net cooling in polar regions forces the motion of the atmosphere, which, in turn, drives the surface circulation of the ocean. On the average, the atmosphere and oceans transport heat vigorously enough to balance the difference in heat loss between equator and poles, with atmospheric motion transforming potential energy into kinetic energy at a rate which balances frictional dissipation.

Climatic variations seem to be associated with variations in the vigour of the whole global circulation, but why the global system varies is still a mystery. It follows that the fundamental problem in the study of climatic change is the development of a quantitative understanding of the general circulation of the atmosphere and, since three-quarters of the heat which forces the atmospheric motion comes by way of the ocean surface, a quantitative understanding of oceanic heat transport and ocean/atmosphere heat exchange is especially vital.

Such an understanding should begin with the planetary distribution of heat loss and gain by the atmosphere and ocean. Fundamental physical laws should then enable us to predict the global distribution of temperature, pressure, motion, water vapour, clouds, and precipitation, together with resulting moisture and heat transports. In practice, this presents enormous difficulties. However, with the development of modern computer technology, rapid progress is being made. Already it is becoming possible to mathematically simulate certain large-scale processes in more detail than we can now observe them in nature.

For further progress in simulating atmospheric dynamics we need a better understanding of the processes of atmospheric heat losses and gains which force the motion of the real atmosphere. Variations in equatorial heating and polar cooling are poorly understood and have received little study, largely because of the paucity of relevant data.

Nevertheless, it has been discovered that significant year-to-year variations in ocean/atmosphere heat and moisture exchange do occur and that these anomalies are closely related to observed variations in the dynamical behaviour of the atmosphere.

For example, one very influential ocean/atmosphere interaction which is subject to large and sudden anomalies, is associated with the zone of up-welling cold water at the equator. This zone is created by the opposite deflection of warm surface water north and south of the equator in response to the easterly trade winds. In the eastern Pacific, the temperature difference between this up-welling water and the warm waters on either side is normally several degrees and extends for several thousand miles.

During some years, these cold tongues weaken or vanish as the equatorial trade winds wane. Bjerknes (1966) has documented several such cases for the Pacific, showing that the resulting variation of evaporation and subsequent condensation influences the atmospheric circulation of the whole northern hemisphere.

Similar studies for the Indian Ocean have not yet been conducted due to the lack of data, though a 1963-64 expedition found a cold equatorial tongue there nearly 10°C colder than the surrounding waters at 28°C. Yet it seems likely that such processes are associated with the rise of East African rainfall since 1961-63. Indeed, the frequency of such occurrences may be closely connected with the changes in the global system since 1961-63 (Lamb, 1966c).

The interaction of large-scale atmospheric and oceanic circulation in the Indian Ocean is known to vary from year to year. Understanding this interaction is not only necessary for understanding global climate, but has immediate application for forecasting the south-west monsoon, which directly affects the crops and economy of one of the most densely populated areas in the world.

Our present state of knowledge cannot yet explain why the equatorial trade winds wane, though we have some surmises. There is growing evidence that variations of the northern hemisphere circulation may be influenced by variations of the much stronger southern hemisphere circulation, but the basic cause of the planetary variation is still obscure.

Impressive statistical correlations between various indices of climatic change and various indices of solar activity (including sun-spot activity, as in Figure 1) have been presented by many investigators (Fairbridge, 1961; Rubinstein and Polozova, 1966), but no one has yet been able to advance a physically plausible cause-and-effect explanation.

Variations in the quantity of radiation received from the sun (expressed as the 'solar constant') are usually judged to be too small to account for the relatively large observed variations of global climate. Therefore, much attention has been directed towards searching for mechanisms by which upper atmosphere processes, triggered by very small changes in the energy from the sun, can in turn influence much more energetic processes, in the lower atmosphere (troposphere). However, a better understanding of ocean/ atmosphere interactions may reveal that feedback processes at the surface can amplify the effect of small solar variations to produce large changes in the behaviour of the planetary system. One such 'thermal lever' is the variable extent of ice on the ocean (Fletcher, 1969).

OCEAN ICE AS A CLIMATE 'TRIGGER'

The presence of sea ice effectively prevents the transfer of heat from ocean to atmosphere in winter, thus forcing the atmosphere to balance the radiative heat lost to space. For example, in January the mean surface temperature in the central Arctic is about—30°C, while a few feet below the pack ice, the ocean water is near—2°C. The ice and its snow cover are such good insulators that relatively little heat reaches the surface from below. The

surface radiates heat to space, and this heat loss simply cools the surface until it is cold enough to drain the needed heat from the atmosphere. The thermal participation of the ocean is greatly suppressed. If the ice were not there, the needed heat would be obtained from the relatively warm ocean.

In summer, on the other hand, an open polar ocean would absorb around 90 per cent of the solar radiation reaching the surface, instead of the 30–40 per cent presently absorbed by the year-round pack ice. Thus, the presence of the ice suppresses heat loss by the ocean in winter and suppresses heat gain by the ocean in summer. For the atmosphere, of course, the reciprocal relation applies; over pack ice, the atmosphere cools more intensely during winter and warms more intensely in summer.

In this way, variations in the extent of ice can amplify the effect of small variations in solar heating. Thus, a decrease in solar radiation causes cooling, which causes ice extension, which in turn cools the atmosphere more, causing further ice growth and stronger thermal gradients. The causes and effects are self-reinforcing, and provide 'positive feedback.'

How far such a process must go before it triggers other instabilities in the ocean/atmosphere system, such as the sudden variation of equatorial temperature described above, cannot be judged at this time. Clearly, there are many complex feedback processes, both positive and negative, in the ocean/atmosphere 'climate machine,' and many thresholds beyond which the direction of the feedback can change.

For example, suppose that the warming of the Arctic, which by 1940 had greatly reduced the thickness of the pack ice, had continued? As the ice receded farther in summer and the thinner ice became more fractured in winter, evaporation would have increased, thus increasing the density of the surface waters both by increasing the salt concentration and by cooling; this would tend to decrease the vertical stability of the upper layers of the ocean.

If this process had continued to the point of destroying the present strong stratification of ocean surface layers and inducing deep convection, then refreezing at the surface would have been impossible until the whole water column had cooled to freezing temperature—a process which would take many years at the least. After the whole ocean had cooled to the freezing temperature, additional cooling would have then refrozen the surface, thus recreating surface stratification and reformation of surface ice, namely, the initial condition. Thus, a 'threshold' exists in each direction: destruction of stratification whose effect is to prevent refreezing, and the eventual depletion of heat content which triggers refreezing.

Budyko (see Fletcher, 1966) has argued that, under present conditions of solar heating, the arctic pack ice would not reform if it were removed. Instead, a new and stable climatic régime would be established in which the Arctic Ocean would remain ice-free.

To answer such questions with more certainty we really need to make a model for the entire planetary circulation under the assumption of an ice-free Arctic Ocean, but as yet this has not been adequately done. However, detailed calculations of zonal temperature distribution at various levels under conditions of an ice-free Arctic have been made by Rakipova (see Fletcher, 1966) using a theoretical model of zonal temperature distribution. According to these calculations, the intensity of atmospheric circulation would decrease, but much more so in the winter than in the summer, so that seasonal contrasts would be much smaller than at present. In high latitudes, poleward atmospheric heat transport would decrease by about 25 per cent during the cold half year, and the Arctic Ocean would remain ice-free.

In summary, it appears that a sufficient warming of global climate would lead to the disappearance of the arctic pack ice, at which time a new and relatively stable climatic régime would be established. Such a régime, while bringing a more temperate climate to the subpolar areas, could make other parts of the world considerably more arid.

Budyko (1968) used a similar empirical approach to estimate the influence on global climate, during planetary cooling, of the interaction of variable solar radiation, changing ice extent, and mean global surface temperatures. For his highly idealized model he concludes that, in the event that mean solar radiation over the earth decreases by 1 per cent, the mean global temperature would drop by 5°C, the cooling being reinforced by an advance of the ice boundary by about 10° of latitude in both hemispheres. Should the solar radiation decrease by 1.5 per cent, the global temperature drop would be 9°C, and the ice advance would be 18° of latitude. If the radiation decrease were more than 1.6 per cent the ice boundary would advance past the 50° latitudes in both hemispheres, and the cooling due to the large ice area would cause continued ice growth until all the oceans were frozen. Once such a condition was established, melting would not occur even with a substantially higher solar radiation intensity.

It should be noted that the empirical dependencies used by Budyko were calculated from northern hemisphere climatic data and he assumes that the southern hemisphere would respond similarly. This assumption probably exaggerates the sensitivity of global climate to solar variations, but Budyko's dramatic conclusions illustrate the necessity of taking such feedback processes into account.

Ice extent is probably the most influential factor capable of quickly transforming the large scale thermal properties of the earth's surface. Thus, understanding the interaction of ice extent, radiation variations and atmospheric circulation is fundamental to understanding global climatic changes.

POSSIBILITIES FOR DELIBERATELY INFLUENCING GLOBAL CLIMATE

Theoretical perspectives for modifying global climate by influencing large-scale atmospheric circulation have been discussed by Yudin (1966), who emphasizes that since the energies in nature are so vast compared to man's capabilities, ways must be found to trigger natural instabilities using relatively small energy inputs. He points out that, in theory, it should be possible to influence the velocity of air masses with much less energy than is needed to effect local changes in either atmospheric temperature or pressure.

Moreover, in influencing velocity, energy should be applied evenly over a broad area in order to minimize its dissipation.

Yudin then proposes that, following these precepts for the application of energy, emphasis should be placed on identifying critical 'instability points' in the natural development of cyclones. For example, only slight deflections of certain winds are associated with a faster movement of cyclone centres.

These brief criteria clearly identify one difficulty associated with large-scale weather modification, namely that the theoretically most effective approaches involve actions that we do not know how to produce efficiently. On the other hand, various ways of influencing the heat losses and inputs to the atmosphere, although theoretically inefficient from the viewpoint of immediate dynamical consequences, are much more achievable with present technology. It has, for example, already been noted that the creation or dissipation of high cloudiness has an enormous influence on the heat budget of the atmosphere and of the surface. Moreover, under certain conditions, only one kilogram of reagent can seed several square kilometres of cloud surface. It is estimated that it would take only sixty American C-5 aircraft to deliver one kilogram per square kilometre per day over the entire Arctic Basin (10 million square kilometres). Thus, it is a large but not an impossible task to seed such enormous areas.

Assuming that such seeding were effective in creating or dissipating clouds, it is of interest to estimate the effect of such cloud modification on the heat budget of the surface/atmosphere system. It is estimated that the average cloud cover over the Arctic in July decreases the radiative heat loss to space by about 350,000 million calories per square kilometre per day from what it would be without clouds. By comparison, total cloud cover at 500 metres would decrease radiative loss by only one-third as much, whereas total cloud cover at 5,000 metres would decrease radiative loss by three times as much. These numbers demonstrate not only the enormous thermal leverage that might be exercised by influencing mean cloudiness, but also the range of influence that might be possible, depending on cloud type, height, and its influence on the regional heat budget. This conclusion is further underscored by noting that mean monthly values of radiative heat loss at the surface have been observed to vary by more than 100 per cent in different years at some Arctic stations, possibly due to variations in cloudiness.

Similarly, it may be noted that, under certain conditions, influencing the surface reflectivity of arctic pack ice is not beyond the capability of present technology. Since the presence of sea ice severs the intense heat flux from the ocean water to the cold atmosphere, regulating the extent of sea ice is still another possible way of exercising enormous leverage on patterns of thermal forcing of atmospheric motion.

Influencing the temperature of extensive ocean surface areas by changing the courses of certain ocean currents has also been proposed (Rusin and Flit, 1962). These schemes involve large, but not impossible, engineering efforts, some of which are discussed in the next section. The principal difficulty, however, is that the present understanding of ocean dynamics is too rudimentary to reliably predict the effects of such projects and, even if this were possible, the dynamic response of the atmosphere to the new pattern of heating could not be predicted until more realistic simulation models have been developed.

These various examples demonstrate the following essential conclusions:

1. It does appear to be within man's engineering capacity to influence the loss and gain of heat in the atmosphere on a scale that can influence patterns of thermal forcing of atmospheric circulation.
2. Purposeful use of this capability is not yet feasible because present understanding of atmospheric and oceanic dynamics and heat exchange is far too imperfect to predict the outcome of such efforts.
3. Although it would be theoretically more efficient to act directly on the moving atmosphere, engineering techniques for doing so are not presently available.
4. The inadvertent influences of man's activity may eventually lead to catastrophic influences on global climate unless ways can be developed to compensate for undesired effects. Whether the time remaining for bringing this problem under control is a few decades or a century is still an open question.
5. The diversity of thermal processes that can be influenced in the atmosphere, and between the atmosphere and ocean, offers promise that, if global climate is adequately understood, it can be influenced for the purpose of either maximizing climatic resources or avoiding unwanted changes.

SPECIFIC SCHEMES FOR CLIMATE MODIFICATION

Many engineering proposals have been advanced for improving the climatic resources of particular regions. All of these schemes share the common defect that their influence on the global system cannot yet be reliably judged. Some are on a scale that could well influence the global system and possibly even trigger instabilities with far reaching consequences. Sooner or later, some such schemes may be carried out, and it is of interest to consider them in the larger perspective discussed here (Rusin and Flit, 1962).

Ice-free Arctic Ocean

The largest scale enterprise that has been discussed is that of transforming the Arctic into an ice-free ocean. As was noted earlier, this has been very carefully studied by the staff of the Main Geophysical Observatory in Leningrad. The central question is the stability of the ensuing global climatic régime. This question cannot be adequately evaluated until global climate simulation models are better developed and suitable simulations performed.

There is also a certain amount of uncertainty in regard to the engineering feasibility of removing the arctic pack ice. It is possible that the capacity of present technology may be sufficient to accomplish this task, but this has not yet been established. Three basic approaches have been proposed: (a) influencing the surface reflectivity of the ice to cause more absorption of solar heat; (b) large-scale modification of Arctic cloud conditions by seeding; and (c) increasing the inflow of warm Atlantic water into the Arctic Ocean.

Bering Strait Dam

The Soviet engineer, Borisov, has been the most active proponent of the much-publicized Bering Strait dam. The basic idea is to increase the inflow of warm Atlantic water by stopping or even reversing the present northward flow of colder Pacific water through the Bering Strait. The proposed dam would be 50 miles long and 150 feet high. The net climatic effect of the project, if it were carried out, is still highly uncertain. A good argument can be made that the effect would be less than that of naturally occurring variations in the Atlantic influx.

Deflecting the Gulf Stream

Two kinds of proposals have been discussed, a dam between Florida and Cuba, and weirs extending out from Newfoundland across the Grand Banks to deflect the Labrador current as well as the Gulf Stream. None of these proposals has been supported by detailed engineering studies or reliable estimates of what the resultant effects would be.

Deflecting the Kuroshio Current

The Pacific Ocean counterpart of the Gulf Stream is the warm Kuroshio Current, a small branch of which enters the Sea of Japan and exits to the Pacific between the Japanese islands. It has been proposed that the narrow mouth of Tatarsk Strait, where a flood tide alternates with an ebb tide, be regulated by a giant one-way 'water valve' to increase the inflow of the warm Kuroshio Current to the Sea of Okhotsk and reduce the winter ice there.

Creation of a Siberian Sea

Dams on the Ob, Yenisei and Angara rivers could create a lake east of the Urals that would be almost as large as the Caspian Sea. This lake could be drained southward to the Aral and Caspian Seas, irrigating a region about twice the area of the Caspian Sea. In terms of climatic effects, the presence of a large lake transforms the heat exchange between the surface and atmosphere. Of equal or greater importance in terms of climatic effects, is the land region transformed from desert to growing fields, with accompanying changes in both its reflectivity and evaporation.

Creation of African Seas

This is the largest known proposal for creating man-made lakes. If the Congo, which carries some 1,200 cubic kilometres of water per year, were dammed at Stanley Canyon (about 1 mile wide), it would impound an enormous lake (the Congo Sea). The Ubangi, a tributary of the Congo, could then flow to the north-west, joining the Chari and flowing into Lake Chad, which would grow to enormous size (over 1 million square kilometres). This large lake (the Chad Sea) would approximately equal the combined areas of the Baltic Sea, White Sea, Black Sea, and Caspian Sea. The two lakes would cover 10 per cent of the African continent. They could then be drained north across the Sahara, creating an extensive irrigated region, similar to the Nile Valley.

NAWAPA Project

The proposed North American Water and Power Alliance is a smaller scale scheme. It would bring 100 million acre-feet* per year of water from Alaska and Canada to be evaporated by irrigation in the western United States and Mexico. The possible climatic effects are highly speculative. For example, would the increased moisture in the air fall out again over the central United States, or would it be transported to some other region?

PROSPECTS FOR FUTURE PROGRESS

It is convenient to think of progress toward climate control in four stages—observation, understanding, prediction, and control. We must observe *how* nature behaves before we can understand *why*, we must *understand* before we can *predict*, and we must be able to *predict* the outcome before we undertake measures for *control*.

From the foregoing examples it is evident that modern technology is already capable of influencing the global system by altering patterns of thermal forcing, but the consequences of such acts cannot be adequately predicted. The global system is a single, interacting 'heat engine' in which a substantial action anywhere may influence subsequent behaviour everywhere. At present, we do not understand the system well enough to predict this behaviour. Much progress in observation, understanding, and prediction is needed before purposeful climate modification can become feasible, but a more rapid progress can now be anticipated.

In theory, it should be possible to solve the equations which describe the behaviour of the atmosphere and the ocean, given the conditions of thermal forcing and the initial state of the system. Such a quantitative analytical approach was formulated by V. Bjerknes in 1904 and expanded by Richardson in 1922. But, since neither the means to observe the state of the system nor the necessary computational power existed, such an approach had little immediate impact. Recent technological break-throughs are removing these barriers and we are now entering a period of rapid progress.

As recently as the Second World War, not more than about 20 per cent of the global atmosphere was observed at one time. With the advent of satellite observing systems, some quantities are now observed over the entire planet every day. This observational break-through makes possible the surveillance of the entire global system, and the sophistication of the observations that can be made by satellite is rapidly increasing.

---

*One acre-foot is the quantity of water which covers 1 acre (0.4 hectare) to the depth of 1 foot (0.3 metre).

Modern computer technology is rapidly overcoming the computational aspects of the problem. Mathematical simulation of the interacting ocean/atmosphere system has already been demonstrated. With computers now being developed that are 500 to 1,000 times faster than existing models, we can reasonably hope that such simulation can be performed in enough detail to reliably evaluate the consequences of specific climate modification acts. With a straightforward means of testing hypotheses, we can expect a surge of new interest in theories of climatic change.

Such simulation capability also provides a means for making long-range forecasts, such as for a season or longer, based on observed and predicted conditions of thermal forcing. This will lead to a shift of emphasis in observing the global system. A short-range forecast can be based largely on the inertial behaviour of the atmosphere, and the 'machine forecasts' of the last decade have basically been of this type. The needed input data for such a forecast is a detailed description of the initial state, especially the field of motion. Patterns of thermal forcing are too slow-acting to be important in this short-range context.

On the other hand, for a very long time period, we may expect that the mean behaviour of the system will depend primarily on thermal forcing and be relatively independent of the initial dynamical state. It follows that the growing capability for climate simulation and long-range forecasting must also place new emphasis on observing and understanding the processes by which heat is exchanged between the ocean and the atmosphere. Today, we are not yet able to observe the global system in enough detail to know whether or not we are simulating realistic patterns of thermal forcing.

The presently-foreseeable ways by which global climate may be influenced all reduce to changing, in one way or another, the pattern of thermal forcing of atmospheric circulation. Such changes occur naturally for a variety of reasons. Understanding how and why they occur is the key to explaining observed changes of climate and also a necessary step toward being able to evaluate the consequences of man-induced changes.

Climatically important variations in surface characteristics and surface heat exchanges occur naturally and to some extent may be influenced by man. In ocean areas, anomalies of surface temperature occur as a result of the wind-driven oceanic circulation. In land areas, the reflectivity and moisture capacity varies with the extent of vegetation. In ice areas, the reflectivity falls abruptly when melting begins.

Of special importance is the variable extent of ice on the sea, for the presence or absence of ice determines whether the thermal characteristics of the surface will resemble those of land or those of ocean. The climatic significance of this factor can be appreciated by noting that about 12 per cent of the world ocean is ice-covered at some time during the year, but only about 4 per cent is ice-covered during the entire year. That is to say, the thermal behaviour of some 8 per cent of the world ocean area is ocean-like for part of the year and land-like for part of the year, a variable factor of possibly great climatic influence.

Figure 2 shows available observational evidence of this relationship (Fletcher, 1969). It shows that variations in iciness of the Antarctic waters (lower curves) have a high correlation with variations in the character of

FIGURE 2. Comparison of iciness of Antarctic waters and atmospheric circulation. Bottom pair of curves (from Schwerdtfeger) shows the number of days per year that Scotia Bay in the Weddell Sea, Antarctica, was closed by ice (jagged curve-annual figures; flat curve-figures smoothed by taking a ten-year moving average). Upper pair of curves (from Dzerdzeyevskiy) indicates the number of days per year in northern hemisphere in which there was air circulation of the zonal type (dominant air movement is east-west, as opposed to meridional circulation, which is dominantly north-south), expressed as number of days more or less than a long-term annual mean (jagged curve = annual deviations; flat curve = ten-year moving average). Examination of lower and upper smoothed curves suggests that iciness of antarctic waters affects northern hemisphere air circulation patterns five years later.

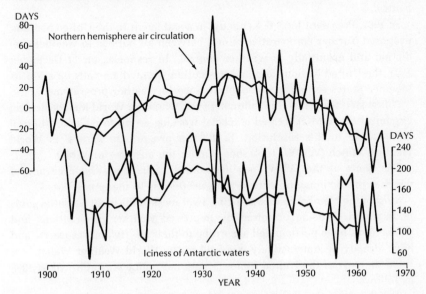

northern hemisphere atmospheric circulation about five years later. We might surmise that five years is comparable to the circulation time for waters moving from the Southern Ocean to the equator, that variations in the Southern Ocean cause variations in the tropical ocean a few years later, and that these variations in ocean temperatures influence northern hemisphere circulation. However, without more complete observational data, or a realistic simulation model, such a hypothesis cannot be easily tested.

Only in 1968 are ocean temperature patterns and the extent of ice on the seas beginning to be observed on a regular basis. A suitable ocean/atmosphere simulation model will probably be available within five years.

Finally, it may be noted that an understanding of contemporary and future climatic changes can hardly be achieved without understanding the large climatic changes of the more distant past. Defining the patterns of these changes is a way of observing nature's own 'climate control experiments.' The collection and systematization of palaeoclimatic evidence is a task of great practical importance.

From the foregoing considerations one arrives at the significant conclusion that *we are reaching, or perhaps have already reached, a technological threshold from which progress can be proportional to the investment of effort.* This conclusion, combined with the proposition that sooner or later purposeful climate modification is inevitable, deserves the attention of scientific and government leaders who must organize the needed resources.

INTERNATIONAL CO-OPERATION

The management of global climatic resources is a problem shared by all nations. So far, international efforts in climatic research have been directed toward *observation* and *understanding*, and co-operation has been good. It is a challenge to political and scientific leadership to preserve this spirit of co-operation as further progress is achieved toward *prediction* and *control*.

In 1961, President John F. Kennedy, in a statement to the United Nations, proposed 'further co-operative efforts between all nations in weather prediction and eventually in weather control.' In response, on 11 December 1961, the United Nations adopted Resolution 1721, which calls on all of its Member States to join in a cooperative world weather programme.

A first step was taken the following year, when the World Meteorological Organization (WMO) created a special working group to make a proposal in response to this resolution. In 1963, a programme known as World Weather Watch (WWW) took shape under the auspices of WMO.

The goals of the WWW are immediate: to improve the accuracy of weather predictions and extend their usefulness to many new areas.

Most of the Member States, showing awareness of the great potential gains in human well-being promised by improved weather observations and predictions, have participated according to their ability and resources, and have already become actively involved in the World Weather Watch.

On the part of the United States, a national policy was affirmed in 1968 as follows:

'*Resolved by the Senate of the United States* (The House of Representatives concurring).

'That it is the sense of Congress that the United States should participate in and give full support to the world weather program which included (1) a world weather watch—the development and operation of an international system for the observation of the global atmosphere and the rapid and efficient communication, processing, and analysis of world-wide weather data, and (2) the conduct of a comprehensive program of research for the development of a capability in long-range weather prediction and for the theoretical study and evaluation of inadvertent climate modification and the feasibility of intentional climate modification. . . .' *

The ongoing observational programmes emphasize certain typical regions, studying them in great detail and for a limited period, in order to understand the heat exchange processes taking place and their influence on the atmosphere and the ocean. This is especially important in regions which play an important role in the thermal forcing of atmospheric and oceanic circulation, and where large year-to-year variations can occur. In the equatorial heat-source regions, variations in the tropical convergence zone, where rising warm air carries moisture and heat up into the atmosphere, seem to be associated with changing global climate. In the two polar heat-sink

---

* *Congressional Record (Senate),* 1 April 1968.

regions, variations in extent of ice cover on the ocean also seem to be associated with changing global climate. In all cases, both the causes and the effects of these variations are obscure.

The progress achieved by co-operative international efforts will bring us closer to a realistic capability for managing global climatic resources. Let us hope that the spirit of international co-operation will continue to grow.

REFERENCES

Bjerknes, J. 1966. A possible response of the Hadley Circulation to variations of the heat supply from the equatorial Pacific. *Tellus* XVII: 820–29.

Bryson, R. A. 1968. All other factors being constant. *Weatherwise* 21, no. 2.

Budyko, M. I. 1962. Certain means of climate modification. *Meteorologiia i gidrologiia,* no. 2: 3–8.

——. 1968. The effect of solar radiation variations on the climate of the Earth. *Proc. international radiation symposium, Bergen, Norway, August 1968.*

——; Drozdov, O. A. and Yudin, M. I., 1966. Influence of economic activity on climate. *Contemporary problems of climatology.* Leningrad.

Fairbridge, R. W. ed. 1961. Solar variations, climatic change, and related geophysical problems. *Ann. N.Y. Acad. Sci.,* vol. 95, p. 1–740.

Fletcher, J. O., ed. 1966. *Proceedings of the symposium on the arctic heat budget and atmospheric circulation.* Santa Monica, California: The RAND Corporation (RM-5233-NSF.)

——. 1969. *The interaction of variable sea ice extent with global climate.* Santa Monica, California: The RAND Corporation (RM-5793-NSF.)

Lamb, H. H. 1966a. *The changing cli-*mate. London: Methuen.

——. 1966b. *On climatic variations affecting the far south.* Geneva. (WMO Technical Note, no. 87.)

——. 1966c. Climate in the 1960's. *Geophys. J.* 132, part 2.

Mitchell, J. M., Jr. 1963. On the world-wide pattern of secular temperature change. *Changes of climate. Proc. Rome symposium.* Paris: Unesco.

Möller, F. 1963. On the influence of changes in the CO_2 concentration in air on the radiation balance of the earth's surface and on the climate. *J. Geophys. Res.* 68, no. 13.

Rubinstein, E. S.; Polozova, L. G. 1966. *Contemporary climatic variations.* Leningrad: Hydrometeorological Publishing House.

Rusin, N. P.; Flit, L. A. 1962. *Methods of climate control.* Moscow.

Willet, H. C. 1961. Solar climatic relationships, *Ann. N.Y. Acad. Sci.* 95, art. 1: 89–106.

——. 1965. Solar climatic relationships in the light of standardized climatic data. *J. Atmos. Sci.* 22: 120–36.

Yudin, M. I. 1966. The possibilities for influencing large-scale atmospheric processes. *Contemporary problems in climatology.* Leningrad.

From Lake Erie to Lake Baikal— From Los Angeles to Tbilisi: The Convergence of Environmental Disruption

MARSHALL I. GOLDMAN

MARSHALL I. GOLDMAN *is a professor of economics at Wellesley College and an Associate of the Russian Research Center, Harvard University.*

There are critics who maintain that pollution is an inevitable result of private enterprise. Goldman argues on the other hand that pollution is more a by-product of industrialization than of capitalism. He analyzes the situation in the Soviet Union and concludes that state ownership of all the productive resources has not eliminated the problem of environmental deterioration.

By now it is a familiar story: rivers that blaze with fire, smog that suffocates cities, rivers that vomit dead fish, oil slicks that blacken sea coasts, prize beaches that vanish in the waves, and lakes that evaporate and die a slow smelly death. What makes it unfamiliar is that this is not only a description of the USA but also of the Soviet Union.

Most conservationists and social critics are unaware that the USSR has environmental disruption that is as extensive and severe as ours. Most of us have been so distressed by our own environmental disruption that we lack the emotional energy to worry about anyone else's difficulties. Yet, before we can find a solution to the environmental disruption in our own country, it is necessary to explain why it is that a socialist or communist country like the USSR finds itself abusing the environment in the same way and to the same degree that we abuse it. This is especially important for those who have come to believe as basic doctrine that it is capitalism and private greed that are the root cause of environmental disruption. Undoubtedly private enterprise and the profit motive account for a good portion of the environmental disruption that we encounter in this country.

A similar version of this article appeared in *Science* 170(3953): 37–42, October 2, 1970. Copyright 1970 by the American Association for the Advancement of Science. Reprinted by permission.

However, a study of pollution in the Soviet Union suggests that abolishing private property will not necessarily mean an end to environmental disruption. In some ways, state ownership of the country's productive resources may actually exacerbate rather than ameliorate the situation.

THE PUBLIC GOOD

That environmental disruption is a serious matter in the Soviet Union usually comes as a surprise not only to most radical critics of pollution in the West but also to many Russians. It has been assumed that if all the factories in a society were state owned, the state would insure that the broader interests of the general public would be protected. Each factory would be expected to bear the full costs and consequences of its operation. No factory would be allowed to do anything if it meant that the public would have to suffer or bear the expense of that action. In other words, the factory would not only have to pay for its *private costs* such as expenses for labor and raw materials; it would also have to pay for its *social costs*, such as the cost of eliminating the pollution of the air and water it had caused. It was argued that since the industry was state-run, including both types of costs would not be a difficult thing to do. At least that was what was assumed.

Soviet officials continue today to make such assumptions. B. V. Petrovsky, the Soviet Minister of Public Health, finds it perfectly understandable why there is environmental disruption in a capitalist society: "... the capitalist system by its very essence is incapable of taking radical measures to ensure the efficient conservation of nature." By implication he assumes the Soviet Union can take such measures. Therefore it must be somewhat embarrassing for Nikolai Popov, an editor of *Soviet Life* to ask, "Why, in a socialist country, whose constitution explicitly says the public interest may not be ignored with impunity, are industry executives permitted to break the laws protecting nature?"

Behind Popov's question is a chronicle of environmental disruption that is as serious as practically any that exists in the world. Of course in a country as large as the USSR, there are many places that have been spared man's disruptive incursions. But as the population grows in numbers and mobility, such areas become fewer. Moreover, as in the United States, the most idyllic sites are the very ones that tend to attract the Soviet people.

Just because human beings intrude on an area, it does not necessarily follow that the area's resources will be abused. Certainly the presence of human beings means some alteration in the previous ecological balance, but the change need not be a serious one. Nonetheless many of the changes that have taken place in the Soviet Union have been major ones. As a result the quality of the air, water and land resources have been adversely affected.

WATER

Comparing pollution in the USA with the USSR is something like a game. Any depressing story that can be told about an incident in the USA can be matched by a horror story from the USSR. For example, there have been hundreds of fish kill incidents in both countries. Rivers and lakes from Maine to California have had such incidents. In the USSR, effluent from the Chernorechensk Chemical Plant near Dzerzhinsk killed almost all the fish life in the Oka River in 1965 because of uncontrolled dumping. Factories along major rivers such as the Volga, Ob, Yenesei, Ural and Northern Dvina have committed similar offenses and these rivers are considered to be highly polluted. There is not one river in the Ukraine whose natural state has been preserved. Like the Molognaia River in the Ukraine, many other rivers throughout the country are officially reported as dead. How dangerous this can be is illustrated by what happened in Sverdlosk in 1965. A careless smoker threw his cigarette into the Iset River and like the Cuyahoga in Cleveland, the Iset caught fire.

Sixty-five per cent of all the factories in the largest Soviet republic, the RSFSR, discharge their sewage without bothering to clean it up. But factories are not the only ones responsible for the poor quality of the water. Mines, oil wells and ships freely dump their waste and ballast into the nearest water body. Added to this industrial waste is the sewage of many Russian cities. Large cities like Moscow and Leningrad are struggling valiantly like New York and Chicago to treat their waste, but many municipalities are hopelessly behind in their efforts to do the job properly. Only six out of the twenty main cities in Moldavia have a sewer system and only two of those cities make any effort to treat their sewage. Similarly only 40% of the cities and suburbs in the RSFSR have any equipment to treat their sewage. For that matter, according to the last completed census of 1960, only 35% of all the housing units in urban areas are served by a sewer system.

Conditions are even more primitive in the countryside. Often this adversely affects the well and groundwater supplies, especially in areas of heavy population concentration. Under the circumstances it is not surprising to find that major cities like Vladimir, Orenburg, and Voronezh do not have adequate drinking water supplies. In one instance reported in *Pravda*, a lead and zinc ore enriching plant was built in 1966 and allowed to dump its wastes in the Fragdon River. This was done even though the river served as the sole source of water for about 25 miles along its route. As a result the water became contaminated and many people were simply left without anything to drink.

Even when there are pure supplies of water, many homes throughout the country are not provided with running water. This was true of 62% of the urban residences in the USSR in 1960. The Russians often try to explain this by pointing to the devastation they suffered during World War II. Yet it is still something of a shock, 25 years after the war to walk along one of the more fashionable streets in Kharkov, the fifth largest city in the USSR, and see many of the area's residents carrying a yoke and two buckets of water around their shoulders. The scene can be duplicated in almost any other city in the USSR.

Again like the USA, the Soviet Union has not only had trouble with its rivers, but with its larger bodies of water. Like Cape Cod and the California coast, oil slicks have coated the shores of the Baltic, Black and Caspian Seas. Refineries and tankers have been especially lax in their choice of oil-disposal procedures.

Occasionally it is not only the quality but the quantity of the water that causes concern. The Aral and Caspian Seas have gradually been disappearing. Because both seas are located in arid regions, large quantities of their water have been diverted for use in crop irrigation. Moreover, many dams and reservoirs have been built on the rivers that supply both seas for the purpose of generating electric power. As a result of such activities, the Aral Sea began to disappear. From 1961 to 1969 its surface dropped by $5\frac{1}{2}$ feet. Since the average depth of the sea is only 50 feet, some Russian authorities fear that at the current rate of shrinkage, by the turn of the century the sea will be nothing but a salt marsh.

Similarly during the past twenty years, the level of the Caspian Sea has fallen almost eight feet. This has drastically affected the sea's fish population. Many of the best spawning areas have turned into dry land. For the sturgeon, one of the most important fish in the Caspian, this has meant the elimination of one-third of their spawning area. The combined effect of the oil on the sea and the smaller spawning area reduced the fish catch in the Caspian from 1,180,400 centners in 1942 to 586,300 centners in 1966. Food fanciers are not so much worried about the sturgeon however, as they are about the caviar that the sturgeon produce. The output of caviar has fallen even more than the height of the sea, a concern not only for the Russian consumers of caviar but for foreigners. Caviar had been a major earner of foreign exchange. Conditions have become so serious that the Russians have now begun to experiment with the production of artificial caviar.

The disruption of natural life in the Caspian Sea has had some serious ecological side effects. Near Ashkhabad at the mouth of the Volga a fish called the belyi amur also began to disappear. As a consequence, the mosquito population which had been held in check by the belyi amur grew in the newly-formed swamps where once the sea had been. In turn the mosquitoes began to transmit malaria.

Perhaps the best known example of the misuse of water resources in the USSR has been what happened to Lake Baikal. This magnificent lake is estimated to be over 20 million years old. There are over 1200 species of living organisms in the lake including freshwater seals and 700 other organisms that are found in few or no other places in the world. It is one of the largest and deepest fresh water lakes on earth with depths of over a mile. It is five times deeper than our Lake Superior and contains double the volume of water. In fact, Lake Baikal holds almost one fortieth of all the world's fresh water. The water is low in salt content and is highly transparent so that one can see as far as 40 yards underwater.

In 1966, first one and then another paper and pulp mill appeared on Lake Baikal's shores. Immediately limnologists and conservationists protested this assault on an international treasure. Nonetheless, new homes were built in the vicinity of the paper and pulp mills and the plant at the nearby town of Baikalsk began to dump 60 million cubic meters of effluent a year into the lake. A specially designed treatment plant had been erected in the hopes

that it would maintain the purity of the lake. Given the unique quality of the water, however, it soon became apparent that almost no treatment plant would be good enough. Even though the processed water is drinkable, it still has a yellowish tinge and a barely perceptible odor. As might be expected, a few months after this effluent had been discharged into the lake, the Limnological Institute reported that animal and plant life had decreased by one-third to one-half in the zone where the sewage was being discharged.

Several limnologists have argued that the only effective way to prevent the mill's effluent from damaging the lake is to keep it out of the lake entirely. They suggest that this can be done if a 42-mile sewage conduit is built over the mountains to the Irkut River which does not flow into the lake. So far the Ministry of Paper and Pulp Industries has strongly opposed this since it would take close to $40 million to build such a bypass. They argue that they have already spent a large sum on preventing pollution. Part of their lack of enthusiasm for any further change may also be explained by the fact that they have only had to pay fines of $55 for each violation. It has been cheaper to pay the fines than worry about a substantial cleanup operation.

Amid continuing complaints, the second paper and pulp mill at Kamensk was told that it must build and test its treatment plant before production of paper and pulp would be allowed. Moreover, the lake and its entire drainage basin have been declared a "protected zone" which means that in the future all timber cutting and plant operations are to be strictly regulated. Many critics, however, doubt the effectiveness of such orders. As far back as 1960, similar regulations were issued about Lake Baikal and

its timber without much results. In addition, the Ministry of Pulp and Paper Industries has plans for yet more paper and pulp mills along the shores of Lake Baikal and is lobbying for funds to build them.

Many ecologists fear that even if no more paper mills are built, the damage may have already been done. The construction of the mills and towns necessitated the cutting of trees near the shore line which inevitably increased the flow of silt into the lake and its feeder streams. Furthermore, instead of being shipped by rail as was originally promised, the logs are rafted on the water to the mill for processing. Unfortunately about 10% of these logs sink to the lake bottom in transit. This not only cuts off the feeding and breeding grounds on the bottom of the lake, but the logs consume the lake's oxygen which again is a strain on its purity.

There are those who see even more dire consequences from the exploitation of the timber around the lake. The Gobi Desert is just over the border in Mongolia. The cutting of the trees and the intrusion of machinery into the wooded areas has destroyed an important soil stabilizer. Many scientists report that the dunes have already started to move and some fear the Gobi Desert will sweep into Siberia and may destroy the taiga and the lake.

AIR

The misuse of air resources in the USSR is not much different from the misuse of water. Despite the fact that the Russians presently produce less than one-tenth of the number of cars each year that we do in the United States, most Soviet cities have air pollution. It can be quite serious especially when the city is situated in a valley or a hilly region. In the hilly cities of Armenia, the established health norms for carbon monoxide are often exceeded. Similarly Magnitogorsk, Alma Ata and Cheliabinsk with their metallurgical industries frequently have a dark blue cap over them. Like Los Angeles, Tbilisi, the capital of the republic of Georgia has smog almost 6 months of the year. Nor is air pollution limited to hilly regions. Leningrad has 40% less sunlight than the nearby town of Pavlosk.

Of all the factories that emit harmful wastes through their stacks, only 14% were reported in 1968 to have fully equipped air-cleaning devices. Another 26% had some treatment equipment. Even so there are frequently complaints that such equipment is either operating improperly or of no use. There have been several reported instances of factories that spew lead into the air. In other cases, especially in Sverdlosk and Magnitogorsk, public health officials ordered the closing of factories and boilers. Nevertheless, additional complaints have appeared periodically that some public health officials have yielded to the pleadings and pressures of factory directors and agreed to keep the plants open "on a temporary basis."

One particularly poignant instance of air pollution is occurring outside the historic city of Tula. Not far away is the site of Leo Tolstoy's former summer estate, Yasnaya Polyana. Now it is an internationally-known tourist attraction with lovely grounds and a museum. Due to some inexcusable oversight, a small coal gasification plant was built within view of Yasnaya Polyana in 1955. In 1960 the plant was expanded as it began to produce fertilizer and other chemicals. Now known as the Shchkino Chemical Complex, the plant has grown so that it employs over 6000 employees and produces a whole range of chemicals including formaldehyde and synthetic fibers. Unfortunately the prevailing winds from this extensive complex blow across the street onto the magnificent forests at Yasnaya Polyana. As a result a prime oak forest is reported near extinction and a pine forest is similarly affected.

LAND

Like other nations of the world, environmental disruption in the USSR is not limited to air and water. For example the Black Sea Coast in the Soviet Republic of Georgia is disappearing. Since this is a particularly desirable resort area, there has been a good deal of concern expressed over what is happening. At some places, the sea has moved as much as 44 yards inland. Near the resort area of Adler, hospitals, resort hotels and of all things, the beach sanitarium of the Ministry of Defense collapsed as the shoreline gave way. Particular fears have been expressed that the mainline railway will also be washed away shortly.

New Yorkers who vacation on Fire Island have had comparable difficulties, but the cause of the erosion in the USSR is unique. Excessive construction has loosened the soil (as at Fire Island) and accelerated the process of erosion. But in addition, much of the Black Sea area has been simply hauled away by contractors. One contractor realized that the pebbles and sand on the riviera-type beach were a cheap source of gravel. Soon many contractors were taking advantage of nature's blessings. As a result as much as 150,000 cubic yards a year of beach material have been hauled away. Unfortunately the natural process by which those pebbles are replaced was disrupted when the state came along and built a network of dams and reservoirs on the streams feeding into the sea. This provided a source of power and water but it stopped the natural flow of pebbles and sand to the seacoast. Without the pebbles, there is little to cushion the enormous power of the waves as they crash against the coast and erode the shoreline.

In an effort to curb the erosion, orders have been issued to prevent the construction of any more buildings within two miles of the shore. Concrete piers have also been constructed to absorb the impact of the waves and efforts are being made to haul gravel material from the inland mountains to replace that which has been taken from the seacoast. Still the contractors are disregarding the orders—they continue to haul away the pebbles and sand and the seacoast continues to disappear.

Nor is the Black Sea Coast the only instance of such disregard for the forces of nature. High in the Caucasus is the popular health resort and spa of Kislovodsk. Surrounded on three sides by a protective semi-circle of mountains which keep out the cold winds of winter, the resort has long been noted for its unique climate and fresh mountain air. Whereas Kislovodsk had 311 days of sun a year, Piatagorsk on the other side of the mountain had only 122. Then shortly after World War II, an official of the Ministry of Railroads sought to increase the volume of railroad freight in the area. He arranged for the construction of a lime kiln in the nearby village of Podkumok. With time, pressure mounted to increase the processing of lime so that now there are eight kilns in operation. As the manager of the lime kiln operation and railroad officials continued to "fulfill their ever-increasing plan" in the name of "socialist competition," the mountain barrier protecting Kislovodsk from the northern winds and smoke of the lime kilns has gradually been chopped away. Consequently, Kislovodsk has almost been transformed into an ordinary industrial city. The dust in the air now exceeds by 50% the norm intended for a *nonresort* city.

Much as some of our ecologists have been warning that we are on the verge of some fundamental disruptions of nature, so the Russians have their prophets of catastrophe. Several geographers and scientists have become especially concerned about the network of hydroelectric stations and irrigation reservoirs and canals that have been built with such fanfare across the country. They are now beginning to find that such projects have had several unanticipated side effects. For example, because the irrigation canals have not been lined, there has been considerable water seepage. The seepage from the canals and an overenthusiastic use of water for irrigation has caused a rise in the water table in many areas. This has facilitated salination of the soil especially in dry areas. Similarly the damming of water bodies apparently has disrupted the addition of water to underground water reserves. There is concern that age-old sources of drinking water may gradually disappear. Finally it is feared that the reduction of old water surfaces and the formation of new ones has radically altered and increased the amount of water evaporation in the area. There is evidence that this has brought about a restructuring of old climate and moisture patterns. This may mean the formation of new deserts in the area. More worrisome is the possibility of an extension of the ice cap. If enough of Russia's north flowing rivers are diverted for irrigation purposes to the arid south, this will deprive the Artic Sea of the warmer waters that it receives from these rivers. Some scientific critics also warn that reversing the flow of some of the world's rivers in this way will have disruptive effects on the rotation of the earth.

REASONS FOR POLLUTION

Because the relative impact of environmental disruption is a difficult thing to measure, it is somewhat meaningless to say that the Russians are more affected than we are or vice versa. But what should be of interest is an attempt to ascertain why it is that pollution exists in a state-owned, centrally planned economy like the Soviet Union's. Despite the fact that our economies differ, many if not all the usual economic explanations for pollution in the noncommunist world also hold in the Soviet Union. They too have been unable to adjust their accounting system so that each enterprise pays not only its direct costs of production for labor, raw materials and equipment, but also its social costs of production arising from such by-products as dirty air and water. If the factory were charged for this and had to take such costs into account when trying to make a profit on its operations, presumably factories would throw off less waste and reuse or recycle their air and water. However, the precise social cost of such waste is difficult to measure and allocate under the best of circumstances be it in the USA or the USSR. (In the Ruhr Valley in Germany, industries and municipalities are charged for the water they consume and discharge, but there are many shortcomings in their system.)

In addition almost everyone in the world regards air and water as free goods. Thus even if it were always technologically feasible, it would still be awkward ideologically to charge for something that "belongs to everyone," particularly in a communist society. For a variety of reasons, therefore, air and water in the USSR are treated as free or undervalued goods. When anything is free, there is a tendency to consume the item without regard for future consequences. But like free love, there is a limit to how much water and air there is to consume and after a time there is the risk of exhaustion. We saw an illustration of this principle in the use of water for irrigation. Since water was treated virtually as a free good, the Russians did not care how much water they lost through unlined canals or how much water they used to irrigate the soil.

Similarly the Russians have not been able to create clear lines of authority and responsibility for pollution enforcement. Like the United States, various Russian agencies from the Ministry of Agriculture to the Ministry of Public Health have some but not ultimate say in coping with the problem. Frequently when an agency does attempt to enforce a law, the polluter will deliberately choose to break the law. As we saw at Lake Baikal, this is especially tempting when the penalty for breaking the law is only $55 a time while the cost of eliminating the effluent may be in the millions of dollars.

The Russians also have to contend with an increase in population growth and the concentration of much of this increase in urban areas. In addition, this larger population has been the beneficiary of an increase in the quantity and complexity of production that accompanies industrialization. As a result not only is each individual in the Soviet Union as in the United States provided with more goods to consume, but the resulting products such as plastics and detergents are more exotic and less easily disposed of than goods of an earlier, somewhat less complicated age. The transformation of nature that accompanies industrialization is like cooking. To make an omelet you have to crack the eggs. Moreover you then have the egg shells to discard. Unfortunately there are few containers as ideal for recycling for conservation purposes as the ice cream cone.

Like their fellow inhabitants of the world, the Russians have to contend with something even more ominous than the Malthusian Principle. Malthus observed that the population increased at a geometric rate but that food production grew at only an arithmetic rate. If he really wants to be dismal, the economist of today has more to worry about. It is true that the population seems to be increasing at multiple rates, but whereas food production at least continues to increase, our air, water, and soil supplies are relatively constant. They can be renewed just like crops can be replanted, but for the most part, cannot be expanded. In the long run, this Doomsday Principle may prove to be of more consequence. With time we may simply run out of fresh air and water. Then if the damage is not irreversible, a portion of the population will be eliminated and those who remain will exist until there is a shortage once again or until the air, water, and soil are irretrievably poisoned.

INCENTIVES TO POLLUTE UNDER SOCIALISM

In addition to the factors which confront all the people of the earth, regardless of their social or economic system, there are also some reasons for polluting which seem to be peculiar to a socialist country like the Soviet Union in its present state of economic development. First of all, state officials in the Soviet Union are judged almost entirely by how much they are able to increase their region's economic growth. Thus, government officials are not likely to be promoted if they decide to act as impartial referees between contending factions on questions of pollution. State officials identify with the polluters, not the conservationists because the polluters will increase economic growth and the prosperity of the region while the antipolluters want to divert resources away from increased production. There is almost a political as well as an economic imperative to devour idle resources. The limnologists at Lake Baikal fear no one so much as the voracious Gosplan officials and their allies in the regional government offices. These officials do not have to face a voting constituency which might reflect the conservation point of view such as the League of Women Voters or the Sierra Clubs do in this country. It is true that there are outspoken conservationists in the USSR who are often supported by the Soviet press, but for the most part, they do not have a vote. Thus the lime smelters continued to smoke away behind the resort area of Kislovodsk even though critics in *Izvestiia, Literaturnaya Gazeta, Sovetskaia Rossiia, Trud,* and *Krokodil* protested long and loud.

At one time state governments in our country often reflected similar one-sidedness. Maine, for example, was often cited as an area where industry did what it wanted to do to nature. Now as the conservationist voting bloc has grown in size, the Maine state government finds itself acting as referee. Accordingly it has passed a far-reaching law which regulates the location and operation of all new industry. Failure to have voted for such legislation may have meant defeat at the polls for many politicians. No such device for transmitting voting pressure presently exists in the USSR.

Second, industrialization has come relatively recently to the USSR and so the Russians continue to emphasize the increase in production. Since pollution control tends to be nonproductive, there is resistance to the diversion of resources from productive to nonproductive purposes. This is even reflected in the words used to describe the various choices. "Conserve" generally seems to stand in opposition to "produce."

Third, until July 1967, all raw materials in the ground were treated by the Russians as free goods. As a result whenever the mine operator or oil driller had exploited the most accessible oil and ore, he moved on to a new site where the average variable costs were lower. This has resulted in very low recovery rates and the discarding of large quantities of salvageable materials which increase the amount of waste to be disposed of.

Fourth, as we saw, it is as hard for the Russians as it is for us to include social costs in factory-pricing calculations. However not only do they have to worry about the social cost accounting, but also they are unable to reflect all the private cost considerations. Because there is no private ownership of land, there are no private property owners available to protest the abuse of various resources. Occasionally it does happen that a private property owner in the United States calculates that his private benefits from selling his land for use in some new disruptive use is *not* greater than the private cost he would bear as a result of not being able to use the land any more. So he retains the land as it is. The absence of such private property holders or resort owners and the failure to make such a calculation seems to be the major reason why erosion is destroying the Black Sea Coast. There is no one who can lay claim to the pebbles on the shorefront and so they are free to anyone who wants to cart them away. Of course private land-owners often do decide to sell their land especially if the new use is to be for oil exploitation rather than pebble exploitation. Then the private benefits to the former owner are high and the social costs are ignored as always. The Russians, however, now only have to worry about accounting for social costs, they lack the first line of protection that would come from balancing private costs and private benefits.

Fifth, economic growth in the USSR has been even more unbalanced and in some cases more one-sided than in the USA. Thus occasionally change takes place so rapidly and on such a massive scale in a state-run economy that there is no time to reflect on all the consequences. In the early 1960's, Khrushchev decided that the Soviet Union needed a large chemical industry. All at once chemical plants began to spring up or expand all over the country. In their anxiety to fulfill their targets for new plant construction, few if any of the planners were able to devote much attention to the disruptive effects on the environment that such plants might have. We saw one result at Yasnaya Polyana. In fact, the power of the state to make fundamental changes may be so great that irreversible changes may frequently be inflicted on the environment without anyone realizing what is happening until it is too late. This seems to be the best explanation of the meteorological disruption that is taking place in Siberia. It is easier for an all powerful organism than a group of private entrepreneurs to build the reservoirs and reverse the rivers. Private enterprises can cause their own havoc as our own dust bowl experience indicates, but in the absence of private business or property interests, the state's powers can be much more far reaching in scope. In an age of rampant technology where the consequence of ones actions are not always fully anticipated, even well-intentioned programs can have disastrous effects on the environmental status quo.

THE ADVANTAGES OF A SOCIALIST SYSTEM

Amidst all these problems, there are some things the Russians do very well. For example, the Russians have the power to prevent the production of various products. Thus Moscow is the only major city in the world that does not put ethyl lead in most of the gasoline that is produced. This may be due to technical lag as much as to considerations of health, but the result is considerably more lead-free gasoline. Similarly the Russians have not permitted as much emphasis on consumer-good production as we have in the West. Consequently there is less waste to discard. Russian consumers may be somewhat less enthusiastic about this than the ecologists and conservationists, but in the USSR there are no disposable bottles nor disposable diapers to worry about. It also happens that because labor costs are low relative to the price of goods, more emphasis is placed on prolonging the life of various products. In other words it is worthwhile to use labor to pick up bottles and collect junk. No one would intentionally abandon his car on a Moscow street as 50,000 people did in New York City in 1969. Even if a Russian car is 20 years old, it is sill valuable. Because of the price relationships that exist in the USSR, the junk man can still make a profit. This facilitates the recycling process which ecologists tell us is the ultimate solution to environmental disruption.

It should also be remembered that while all Russian laws may not be observed, the Russians do have an effective law enforcement system which they have periodically brought to bear in the past. Similarly they have the power to set aside land for use as natural preserves. The absence of private land ownership makes this a much easier process to implement than in the United States. As of 1969, the Soviet government had set aside 80 such preserves encompassing nearly 25,000 miles.

Again because they own all the utilities as well as most of the buildings, the Russians have stressed the installation of centrally-supplied steam. Thus heating and hot water are provided by central stations which make possible more efficient combustion and better smoke control than if each individual building were to provide heat and hot water for itself. Although some American cities have similar systems, this approach is something we should know more about.

In sum, if the study of environmental disruption in the Soviet Union demonstrates anything, it shows that not private enterprise, but industrialization is the primary cause of environmental disruption. This suggests that state ownership of all the productive resources is not a cure-all. The replacement of private greed by public greed is not much of an improvement. Currently the proposals for the solution of environmental disruption in the USSR seem to be no more advanced than they are in the USA. One thing does seem clear, however, and that is that unless the Russians change their ways, there seems little reason to believe at this point that a strong centralized and planned economy has any notable advantages over other economic systems in solving environmental disruption.

Aesthetic Power or the Triumph of the Sensitive Minority Over the Vulgar Mass: A Political Analysis of the New Economics

AARON WILDAVSKY

AARON WILDAVSKY *is a professor of political science at the University of California, Berkeley.*

Many of the advocates of increased governmental control over polluters argue in terms of a "new economics" which takes into account the public's welfare as well as the profits of the producer. Wildavsky argues that the "new economics" is mainly politics rather than economics. He examines the assumptions and the dilemmas of those advocating further investments in improving the quality of the environment. Though he agrees with the objectives of "new economics," he cautions its advocates against self-deception by distorting traditional economic analysis in order to rationalize their own goals.

How does the "old economics" of natural resources differ from the "new economics"? The old economics was mostly economics. The new economics is mostly politics. The agonizing question confronting the new economics has troubled political theorists from the time of the Hebrew prophets to this very day: How shall society be organized so that the preferences of the morally or aesthetically sensitive minority will triumph? Where majorities are rarely mobilized, the question may be rephrased to ask how our *good* minority may prevail over their *bad* minority. If only a superior few truly love the remote and virgin wilderness, for instance, how may this opportunity for solitary communion with nature be preserved against hostile masses or rival elites? The new economics of natural resources appears to be designed to answer this question indirectly without quite raising it to a conscious level.

This paper appears in Roger Revelle and Hans H. Landsberg, eds. *America's Changing Environment.* Houghton Mifflin Company, pp. 147–60. Copyright © 1967, 1970 by the American Academy of Arts and Sciences. Reprinted by permission.

The terms new economists use to describe the deterioration of the natural environment are sufficiently expressive to convey the feeling behind them. The landscape has been assaulted and degraded, if not raped; genocide has been practiced against certain animal species; the air threatens to become a poisonous gas; the odor of dead fish testifies to the pollution of our water; human marauders invade and despoil isolated areas. The tone is strident; the mood, a mixture of rage and disgust. The metaphors belong more to the battlefield than the market place. It is not surprising, then, that Athelstan Spilhaus urges us to take risks in enhancing the environment comparable to those we would take in war; nor that Nathaniel Wollman suggests a political structure with administrative environmental boards possessing "the power and authority that is now accorded the military establishment . . . because the penalty of inexpert decisions may be just as disastrous for the human race as the effect of military weapons." Unfortunately, the old economics does not provide the necessary weapons for what many evidently see as the war for environmental quality.

In the beginning, the rationale for the Conservation Movement was one of preserving basic resources that were becoming increasingly scarce. Wood, coal, and iron were essentially fixed in given lumps; use was a kind of desecration. As demand increased and supply decreased in an industrial society, these resources would become more and more valuable. The larger the part played by natural resources in the economy and the higher their price in comparison with other goods, the easier it was to make an economic case for protecting them. To the extent that the votes of a misguided or ignorant people would not protect these precious resources through the political arena, the symbolic casting of ballots in the more rational economic market place would restrict use by raising prices. If politics were involved at all, it would be not for economic reasons, but merely to undo the evil restrictions upon the free market that special interests had worked out with conniving politicians.

Even when economic theorists arrived at a justification for governmental intervention to overcome certain imperfections in the market place, the political arena proved vexing. When a large dam would impose costs on those who did not benefit from it, for example, it was deemed appropriate for the government to intervene to rectify the situation. But, as it turned out, the politicians marched to music of their own and were only remotely interested in following the lead of economic science. The interest rate, that old puritan arbiter between present consumption and future desires, was kept artificially low so that many projects were justified on economic grounds without valid reason. Cost-benefit analysis, designed to increase national income by assuring that the benefits to whoever received them would exceed the costs to whoever paid them, was twisted out of shape in notorious fashion. Things were arranged so that general taxpayers received less and the direct beneficiaries far more than their economically justifiable shares. A project with a low benefit-cost ratio might be joined with another having a much higher ratio so that the "new" combined project could qualify. So-called intangibles like recreation values were credited with increasingly large shares of the benefits, thus representing a "finagle factor" that could be enlarged almost at will to provide justification. A decentralized party system and a highly fragmented national political system with strong regional interests proved resistant to making decisions on economic grounds. Comments about narrow local interests, selfish minorities, and violations of the public interest filled the economic literature. While politics was proving so disappointing, the former economic rationale for protecting resources suffered severe blows.

The market mechanism, together with man's remarkable technical ingenuity, drastically changed the supply-and-demand relationships for many natural resources. New sources of supply were continuously discovered, and new products substituted for old. Industrial and farm production grew exceedingly large and immensely more efficient. Consequently, the prices of resources commodities continually decreased in comparison with those of other goods and services. The contribution of natural resources to Gross National Product showed a corresponding, proportionate drop. The decline in the price of resource commodities made it more difficult to justify special treatment on the grounds of economic efficiency. The contribution that these resources made to production was too small, and it is getting smaller. This change in the economic importance of resources lies behind the plaintive cry that it is not possible to justify on economic grounds most large programs designed to improve the quality of the natural environment.

Re-evaluations of the abundance of natural resources illustrate another aspect of their new position. We now know that we have more forest resources than we had thought and that new growth may exceed demand. Although water may be in short supply in some areas, technological advance and the shift of existing supplies to more productive uses should provide amounts more than adequate for the future. Despite the hue and cry about the advancing tentacles of the monster called urbanization, only 2 or 3 per cent of the nation's land is or will be devoted to urban uses in the next few decades. The immediate conclusion is all too evident. Resource problems will, by and large, not be critical for economic purposes. A technological advance here or a local adjustment there will take care of the worst difficulties. From a strictly economic viewpoint, nothing much need be done.

The terrible difficulty for economists is that problems of environmental quality do not look so bad as they ought. If present modes of economic justification are used, there is no way of preserving the basic values these men hold as users of the natural environment. To have personal values done in by professional values is no fun at all. Hence, a "new economics" has emerged to get around the old. If the old economics will not let you have what you know is right, it follows that a new economics is evidently needed. The term *new economics of natural resources* is used to designate an emerging trend, and permits economists to avoid direct confrontation with political problems by bringing in aesthetic factors to make economic analysis come out "right."

Since the new economists of today are the old economists of yesterday, a certain ambivalence about their enterprise might be expected. It is tempting to retain an economic vocabulary for essentially non-economic processes. The deep woods with clear lakes, white-water streams, and rare animal species may be called unique and irreplaceable, like the White House or the Liberty Bell or a man's children or his sweetheart. One could say that no price is too high for these treasures except that the concept "price" is really inapplicable. These treasures are not to be bought and sold at all. They are literally "priceless"—that is, outside any market. The usual system for determining what is allowable in the market place is political or in some sense deeply traditional or social, but in no case may it be called economic. The old economist considers it ridiculous for a society to spend $20 billion to rid itself entirely of water pollution when marginal benefits of spending the largest fraction of that sum elsewhere would be much higher. The new economist says "why not" and invents rationales. After all, at current rates of economic growth, $20 billion a year represents only a few months delay in reaching a GNP that much higher. This marginalist fallacy, a variant of the old argument that for want of a nail a war was lost, suffers from a fatal defect. We can all think of huge expenditures to accomplish highly cherished ends that could be justified if only people would wait a little while longer to become richer. All the wilderness areas and fine old buildings might be preserved for even less, and many experimental cities might be built. The wealth is here. Presumably, all that is required is the will. We undoubtedly can have some of the things some of us want, but not all the things all of us want. Otherwise, there would be no problem of scarcity, no need for allocation. This is not a new economics but a "non-economics."

The old economists cried out against the use of "finagle factors" that might in some sense be important, but that could not be measured in the market place. In preference to having such factors expanded or contracted at will, they preferred that these be brought to the attention of decision-makers who could take them into account. To do otherwise would be to compromise fatally the economic part of the analysis. The new economists are tempted to abandon this position. Maintaining the wilds may be justified, without being able to specify size or cost or conditions, on the grounds that people like to leave a legacy to their children. Outdoor recreation may be alleged to have great psychic benefits, though demonstrating its dimensions or comparing it with television or people-watching on crowded streets is another matter. Yet alternative expenditures may also serve some values people hold, and the economic problem is to justify one expenditure rather than another on something more than personal grounds. Surely economics is not to become a parody of a parody, the social-science version of Saul Bellow's *Henderson the Rain King* who plunges throughout time and continents shouting ever more loudly, "I want, I want."

No one will argue that the values of economic man in the market place are the only ones that count. Who is so vulgar and insensitive as to claim that only what is objectively demonstrable is important? Will progress be made, however, by undermining the rationale for economic analysis or by concealing intransigent political problems under an economic guise? The new economics poses for itself essentially political problems. Which decisions shall be made through the market and which not? What decision structures will best assure environmental quality? How can aesthetic feelings be translated into public policy? What happens if strong aesthetic impulses are shared by only a small minority? Consideration of the problems surrounding public preferences will help throw the many political dilemmas into sharper focus.

Let us assume, for the moment, that all problems of directly measuring public preferences in regard to the quality of the environment were solved through opinion surveys or other devices. Would our problems of allocating resources then be solved? In one sense, they would be solved all too well. The problem of the interpersonal comparison of utilities, the relative preferences among different people for shares in things like housing, transportation, space exploration, or ballet, must be solved before environmental quality may be given its place. If the results of the survey are accepted, then all allocation problems in society have been solved. Such a state of affairs is usually called utopia.

Suppose, however, that some people prefer a different mix of goods than was provided in the grand allocation mechanism. Perhaps they are among the relatively small groups that intensely desire long canoe trips through completely wild areas and have been outvoted (or "outpreferenced") by others who want skin diving near where they live or who prefer large indemnities to black people to repay them for decades of service in slavery. These minorities would certainly challenge the existing state of preferences. They might argue, as democratic theorists have through the ages, that strict majority rule should not prevail. Minorities like themselves should be given some proportionate share of good things (though it is doubtful whether they would agree that every minority, including ones opposed to their desires, should get similar consideration regardless of what they wanted). The wilderness minority might say that people should not get what they want, but what they ought to have, according to the principles of the sensitive few. Perhaps many people decide in ignorance and ought to be educated before their preferences are counted or weighed equally with those of the more knowledgeable. Things might be different if people were encouraged through subsidies to experience elementary contact with nature, which would in turn alter their previous preferences. What turns out to be crucial is not merely knowledge of preferences but a set of rules for putting them together so that policy decisions emerge. Yet we have not even mentioned the knotty problems of accounting for intensity of preferences. Should the intense minority triumph over the apathetic majority? Should we satisfy the widespread norm of equality by treating all citizens equally or only equals equally? Extraordinary difficulties arise when public preferences must be translated into public policy.

Should their sensitivities be sufficiently outraged, the wilderness minority might question the procedures through which public preferences for governmental expenditures are determined. The use of opinion polls to derive a rank order of public preferences is suspect in many ways. The process of seeking preferences may create preferences where none existed before. People may feel they have to respond to a questionnaire without ever having thought of the matter before or having any real preference. Many citizens may discover that they have preferences only after an act to which they can respond has taken place. It is difficult to get people of low education to understand the wording of questions and the complex choices involved. Highly educated people will also have trouble sorting out their feelings if they are required to make a series of comparisons leading to a ranking of some fifteen or twenty major areas of public policy. If the ranking is

performed by a survey analyst, the rules for determining the hierarchy of preferences may be challenged as inadequate or controversial. Political leaders like the President are known to influence the determination of public preferences from time to time. What a President may get from a survey, therefore, is an echo of his own voice. Since opinion is mutable, the opposition can say that if they will just work harder, public preferences will come closer to their values in the future. Although the temptation is understandably great, the hard problems of making interpersonal comparisons of utility cannot be avoided by fobbing off the task on other people through an opinion survey.

For the old economics, the political system unfortunately did not produce decisions that met the strict criteria of economic rationality. It was desirable economically, for example, to take into account as many measurable consequences for others as possible. The larger the area covered, the greater is the number of externalities that can be internalized within the analysis. If economic criteria were to be followed, bargaining, horse-trading, logrolling, or other practices that might introduce inconsistencies had to be kept to a minimum. Thus, a unitary government with highly centralized parties and powerful hierarchical leadership would appear to be preferable to a federal system with extremely decentralized parties and fragmented leadership continuously engaged in bargaining to accommodate the most diverse range of interests. But the desirability and feasibility of abolishing the federal system, the separation of powers, and decentralized parties are not usually considered because such matters go beyond economic analysis.

The new economics need not face the same problems. It is concerned, after all, with getting away from rigid economic analysis and the strict application of efficiency criteria. Its practitioners are committed to values favoring the enhancement of environmental quality. The new economists are advocates as well as scholars. For them, policy outcomes cannot simply be the result of a set of analytic procedures. They want some results and not others. They want to develop the best arguments they can for securing the results they favor. In cases of doubt and indeterminacy, the new economists want the values they favor included rather than excluded. But they are inhibited by a nostalgia for the credibility accorded to the old economists they once were. Caught between the desire to insure certain outcomes and the pull of their economist's conscience, they risk being neither economists nor effective advocates.

The new economics is in danger of misconstruing its mission. Its goals are laudatory (that is, I share them), but they cannot be achieved by self-deception. Little is to be gained and much lost by compromising the old economics. It should be perfected according to its own lights, so that at least part of the spectrum of values will be properly illuminated. What is first required is an accurate statement of the political problems involved in realizing environmental values.

There is no evidence to suggest widespread and intense support for drastically improving the quality of the environment. Most people are probably indifferent. Some care a little, but are unwilling to sacrifice much. Only a relatively small minority cares deeply enough to make significant sacrifices. The best available evidence comes from a survey of attitudes toward government programs conducted in 1961 by Eva Mueller through the Michigan Survey Research Center.(1) The survey is especially valuable because people were asked whether they would give up income in the form of higher taxes in order to pay for expenditures they believed desirable. Of fourteen types of public policy mentioned, the item called "Parks, recreation facilities" provides a fair test of public support for improving the environment. No doubt more people care about parks than about the remote backwoods, but 10 per cent of the people interviewed have no opinion on these resource programs, and 48 per cent think that existing governmental expenditure is about right. Thus, 58 per cent of the population is essentially indifferent to a change in public policy. It is true that a larger minority favors more rather than less expenditure (27 to 15 per cent), but the favorable minority declines by almost 400 per cent (27 to 7 per cent) when asked if they would pay higher taxes to support this resource policy. Larger proportions of the population are willing to pay through higher taxes for help for the old and needy, education, defense, and highways. Indeed, the number of people willing to pay to explore outer space is twice that willing to pay to improve the earthly environment (14 per cent as compared to 7 per cent).

Public sentiment may have changed since 1961. Perhaps people would now be willing to pay more to deal with water pollution. When a candidate for governor of California suggests selling part of the state's wilderness areas, however, and still receives overwhelming endorsement by the electorate, it is difficult to believe that the wilderness minority is very large. Though

TABLE 1. Attitudes toward government programs.

PROGRAM	MORE	LESS	SAME	NO OPINION	TOTAL	MORE EVEN IF TAXES HAD TO BE RAISED[2]
	%	%	%	%	%	%
Help for older people	70	3	23	4	100	34
Help for needy people	60	7	28	5	100	26
Education	60	7	25	8	100	41
Slum clearance, city improvement[1]	55	9	24	12	100	[3]
Hospital and medical care	54	9	28	9	100	25
Public works[1]	48	11	31	10	100	[3]
Defense, rearmament[2]	47	6	34	13	100	30
Support for small business[1]	37	11	31	21	100	[3]
Highway construction	36	10	45	9	100	13
Unemployment benefits	29	14	45	12	100	10
Parks, recreational facilities	27	15	48	10	100	7
Space exploration[2]	26	32	28	14	100	14
Support for agriculture	20	26	34	20	100	6
Help to other countries[2]	7	53	28	12	100	2

[1] Question asked only in June, 1961.

[2] Question asked only in November, 1961.

[3] Unavailable.

small, the wilderness minority is not always impotent. Yet the victories recorded here and there all appear to stem from an intense campaign run by a few dedicated individuals. When this middle- and upper-class effort fails to materialize, nothing happens, except the loss of another site of scenic splendor.

The provision of subsidies on behalf of the aesthetic minority—subsidies like the British Broadcasting Company's Third Programme—might suggest that a unitary and centralized political system would be more receptive to demands of this nature. But this result depends on the existence of a privileged minority to which great deference is accorded. The cultural conditions for this phenomenon do not exist in the United States, nor, on other grounds, would many of us prefer such a situation. In America, a centralized political system that registered immediate majority demands could well wreak havoc with the policies preferred by the aesthetic minority. Bigger and better highways might always be preferred to clean air, or parks, or refuges for wildlife.

A system like the American one that provides special opportunities for skillful and well-organized minorities would appear well suited to the characteristics of the aesthetic few. How should they go about realizing their preferences? How can they mobilize their forces? What organizational structures and strategies are best suited to translating their preferences into public policy? What kinds of administrative arrangements will help obtain favorable results in the future? Although satisfactory answers are not likely to be immediately forthcoming, these questions are foremost among the right ones to ask.

There is no reason to suppose that the most aesthetically interested members of society are politically disadvantaged. They probably do not suffer from being denied the right to vote or from low educational attainments or poor family backgrounds that would deny them the skills necessary to compete in political life. Like those with special interests in theater or ballet or sailing, the aesthetic minority is likely to be composed of middle- or upper-class people who do not have to struggle for the necessities of life and can afford to be sensitive. Their problems of political mobilization are likely to be quite different from those of the poor and downtrodden. Given a choice between political activity in behalf of their preferences for environmental quality or individual economic action, they may well choose the latter. They can move to the suburbs to get away from air pollution or travel to where the remote wilderness still exists. Things may have to get worse before they find it less costly to spend time in political activity than in raising income to satisfy their aesthetic preferences. Yet they are also capable of reasonably long-run perspectives. The leaders of this minority must first convince people who share their preferences that political action is necessary now if they want their children to be able to enjoy a natural environment of higher quality in the future.

Political elites are far more likely to share the preferences of the aesthetic minority than are the mass of people. While long-term efforts of mass education may be desirable, short-term results depend on the men in power. Since various interests oppose certain specific measures, and alternative objects of expenditures compete for existing resources, ways must be found to enable public officials to support the policies most of them would like to see implemented. The questions of who will pay and how are crucial. In the best of all possible worlds, a new process is discovered that produces a good like wood pulp more cheaply and with far less noxious waste than before. Everyone gains, and no one loses; or those who win in one transaction compensate the losers in another. In most cases, however, the questions of who will pay and how much loom large. Costs can be transferred to large industries or to those who consume their products, to general taxpayers or to specific industries, to citizens or to foreigners, from one region or class of citizens to another. Citizens with low incomes are notorious for their willingness to seek greater public benefits, and their unwillingness to pay more taxes. The wealthy are famous for the ingenuity with which they escape the full burden of the income tax. The acknowledged principles of the public-finance literature—ability to pay and benefits received—are inadequate when there are severe disagreements over the justice and applicability of each principle. The difficulties are compounded when a desired objective, say reduction of air pollution, can be accomplished if and only if an objectionable mode of assigning costs is accepted. If it turns out to be much easier to pass the burden on in the form of hidden consumer taxes than to assess the polluters or desecraters of the wilderness, difficult choices must be made.

In the past, there has been considerable public support for conservation in some western states. Mass support may now be generated in various areas in regard to water and air pollution, but the possibilities of support may be slim for a subtle policy specifying so much reduction of pollution here, a little less there, and none someplace else (the kind of policy favored by the old economics). The price of mass support may be massive programs to wipe out pollution entirely. Again, a difficult choice may have to be made between too little effort to reduce pollution and too much.

Presently we do not have the knowledge that would enable us to choose the kinds of organizational structure that would lead to decisions in favor of improving environmental quality. We can, however, identify critical choices. The number of governmental organizations concerned with natural resources is already large and growing. These agencies traditionally perform specialized functions for a particular clientele and are closely tied to local interests and their congressional advocates. To these divisive forces are then joined narrow organizational loyalties. The legitimization of new functions by society, such as desalinization, pollution abatement, and highway beautification, has been accompanied by the creation of separate organizations to devise and implement programs. For people concerned with rationalizing policy in the resource field, the rapid proliferation of autonomous organizations is alarming. It points to the need for larger units or co-ordinating structures that will presumably produce decisions which take into account a wider range of values. Leaving aside questions of the feasibility and cost of such a change, it is not clear whether it would further the cause of the aesthetic minority. New and "narrow" agencies supporting environmental quality with ever greater determination might be preferable. Sub-units within larger multipurpose agencies dealing with extensive geographical areas might be used to great advantage in the cause of the aesthetic minority. We do not know and are hardly in a position to guess.

Another critical issue involves the choice between setting-up or strengthening a regulatory agency or trying to enact legislation that contains automatic incentives making it advantageous for the affected parties to do the right thing. When outrage over pollution or destruction of forests bursts out, it is tempting to pillory the offenders and to control their future conduct by establishing a regulatory commission of some sort. But the history of regulation has not been an entirely happy one. With the best of motives, the original regulatory passion begins to wane. The people whose interests are most directly affected maintain constant vigilance, while the rest of us turn to other pursuits. The regulatory agency is surrounded by the interests it is supposed to regulate. The inevitable accommodations may leave little regulation intact. Moreover, the existence of friendly regulatory bodies is used as a rationale for avoiding the necessity of other and possibly more stringent measures. We have little evaluated experience in developing incentives in the form of tax measures, bonuses for keeping land or water in certain conditions, support for competitive products, or other devices that might accomplish the task.

If action is to be based on some knowledge, the consequences of varying institutional arrangements for major values must be specified. In different times and places, there has been considerable variety in organizational arrangements and legal patterns. Knowledge of what results ensued under different conditions might give direction to future judgments. New techniques of organizational analysis also provide splendid opportunities for current research. The development of computer simulation models is especially promising. These models view organizations as problem-solving mechanisms that use certain rules for arriving at decisions in a complex environment. These rules can be derived from interviews and observations, and programmed on computers. By recapitulating the processes of decisions on computers, it should be possible to explain how the organization works. One can then experiment with alterations in the assumptions guiding the organization, its specific rules for decisions, and its environment, and determine how these changes affect its policy outputs.

There is, in general, an appalling lack of information on the causes and consequences of environmental deterioration. If environmental quality is broadened to include the design of urban living (and hence poverty and race relations), the absence of knowledge is even more startling. The availability of better information might reveal a wider range of choice and thus result in different political decisions. There is overwhelming need for experimentation. We could use more than one experimental city. Thus, there is an important role for the man who does not find it becoming to devote his talent to direct political questions of mobilizing support to preserve the wilderness or the cultures of the city. He may feel that his desires are not more worthy than those of other men. Such a man may be prepared to have his minority preferences overridden. But by working to improve the information base for decision-making, he may hope to make everyone wiser about the scope of their interests and the possibilities of reconciliation with others.

We do not wish to restrict ourselves to the values appropriate to economic man in the market place. (Failure to preserve superb redwoods because the economic worth of the income produced by cutting them down exceeds their presently known aesthetic value would be tragic.) Nor do we wish to become mere schemers who, so long as they can muster the political power necessary to achieve their personal objectives, do not care about other people's feelings. (Failure to alleviate the psychic deprivation suffered by people who will lose their jobs if the redwoods are protected, and whose identity is bound up with the lumber trade rather than selling souvenirs to tourists, would be cruel.) Yet, like Dostoevski's underground man, whose appreciation of the endless depths of every question rendered him unfit for any action, the cost of taking everyone's preferences into account may be paralysis. Worse, it may result in grand opportunities foregone or in irreversible damage to the environment. Weak and frail as we are, beset by doubts and anxieties, undoubtedly partial in our views, we must act. If those who love the wilderness will not save it, who will?(2)

REFERENCES

1. Mueller, E. May 1963. Public attitudes toward fiscal programs. *The Quarterly Journal of Economics* 77: 210–35. For questions, see Table I.

2. Having come late to this symposium, I have had the opportunity of profiting from and reacting to the other papers. My obligation to the authors of these papers is gratefully acknowledged. I would like to thank Irving Fox, Jerome Milliman, Vincent Ostrom, Jeffrey Pressman, David Wentworth, and Carol Wildavsky for their valuable comments. All of these people disagree with me in significant ways and are not responsible that I often did not take their excellent advice.

Agricultural Pest Control and the Environment

GEORGE W. IRVING, JR.

GEORGE W. IRVING, JR. *is the Administrator of the Agricultural Research Service, U.S. Department of Agriculture.*

Increased agricultural production is essential if we are to avert world-wide famines in the near future. One of the major requirements of improvements in agricultural production is the elimination of harmful pests. Irving describes the different ways of controlling pests and the ecological problems created by the use of pesticides.

The quality of the environment stands high among the problems demanding attention today. As we cope with the needs and complexities of a faster moving, more populous world, we must at the same time prevent pollution of the air, the land, and the water beyond a level that man can and will endure. One of the greatest needs is production of food for billions of people. At present such production requires the use of pesticides, but in turn this use carries with it the possibility of environmental pollution.

Because the Agricultural Research Service (ARS) is responsible for an important share of the nation's research on pests and pesticides, for federal registration of all pesticides, and for administration of a large number of federal programs for pest control in cooperation with the states, it is in a unique position to observe and participate in the scientific and legal controversies that now abound on the subject of pesticides. Accordingly, it may be useful to present the ARS rationale: why we try to control agricultural pests at all; the circumstances that dictate our doing it as we do; and the reasonable alternatives and outlook for doing it differently.

WHY CONTROL AGRICULTURAL PESTS?

Man controls pests because they compete with him for the means of survival. This is a deliberate choice; when pests threaten man with plague or

Science 168 (3938): 1419–24, June 19, 1970. Copyright 1970 by the American Association for the Advancement of Science. Reprinted by permission.

starvation, he fights them as best he can. Some people of the world are being threatened in these respects right now. Fortunately, the United States is a nation of relatively healthy and well-fed people. We can afford to be—and should be—circumspect about the ways in which we control pests, and the effects of these controls on other elements of our environment. However, we do not hold such an edge over malaria mosquitoes and boll weevils that we can seriously contemplate attaining a natural balance between man and his pest enemies. The balance of nature is not an achievable ideal, if it is an ideal at all.

From the time he gave up his nomadic existence, man has increasingly upset the balance of nature, until today it is hardly a meaningful term. Man has constantly tried to tip the balance in his favor. His decisions have not always been wisely made. History is replete with instances where short-range objectives or more often, ignorance, has led to missteps.

Whether or not man has relied excessively on chemical control of pests is now being debated. That there are both benefits and problems accruing from the use of chemicals is quite clear. However, the pertinent fact is that, at this time, pesticides are essential to the abundance, quality, and variety of agricultural production which our nation has come to expect.

American agriculture has evolved a monoculture system. It is an efficient system wherein food and fiber crops and livestock are produced in regions of the country best suited in climate and soils for the optimum in quality and quantity. However, the large acreages of wheat, corn, or citrus orchards provide inviting environments for pests and diseases of the crops, and big broiler flocks and cattle-feeding operations increase greatly the opportunity for animal diseases and pests to survive and spread. Thus, the balance of nature would be heavily weighted on the side of the pests were it not for pesticides. The synthetic organic pesticides, which can be applied over large areas in a matter of hours, fit our efficient agriculture. Along with fertilizers, irrigation systems, and complex machinery, they have made it possible for only 5 per cent of the American work force to meet the nation's food and fiber needs. Pesticides have helped to make possible production of the cheapest food in the world, in terms of percentage of take-home pay, and to free the manpower that now provides the other goods and services our high standard of living demands.

Contributions of pesticides have been worldwide. The National Academy of Sciences—National Research Council Committee on Persistent Pesticides states (1):

> During the past quarter of a century, nations in all parts of the world have benefited from increasing use of the synthetic organic pesticidal chemicals. Through use of these chemicals, spectacular control of diseases caused by insect-borne pathogens has been achieved, and agricultural productivity has been increased to an unprecedented level. No adequate alternative for the use of pesticides for either of these purposes is expected in the foreseeable future . . . . Modern agricultural productivity depends on coordinated increase in the use of pesticides, fertilizers, machinery, and better crop varieties.

This does not mean that use of pesticides is the only available method for combating pests and diseases. Nor does it mean that current pesticides must continue to be used in present quantities. It does mean that chemicals are now the most effective weapons for pest control the farmer has and that in the future chemicals will continue to be an essential part of the integrated program for pest control. The use of some pesticides will decrease, and some will cease to be used altogether; but the total amount of chemicals used for pest control in agriculture can be expected to increase as the need for agricultural production increases.

QUARANTINE, ERADICATION, AND CONTROLS

The first step in avoiding pest problems is quarantine—keeping pests out of the country. To that purpose, ARS maintains quarantine and inspection at U.S. ports of entry in order to intercept pests and diseased materials that might be brought here from other countries. This is an operation of some magnitude. Last year inspectors examined the cargo of thousands of trains, ships, and airplanes; millions of passenger automobiles; nearly 76 million pieces of baggage; and over a million imported animals. Without this first step of control, the pest problem in this country would quickly be staggering. Just one illustration from among the many exotic insects and diseases that might be taking their toll from our agriculture—the Mediterranean fruit fly, or Medfly—makes this point.

Medflies attack citrus fruit and a wide range of other soft fruits and vegetables. Despite vigorous quarantine and inspection, the United States has been invaded by Medflies four times in the past 14 years. One invasion cost $10 million to eradicate; the others were discovered and eradicated more quickly and cheaply.

To have been invaded four times in 14 years is not good, but it is not nearly as bad or as costly as it might be. Plant quarantine inspectors intercept the Medfly in incoming cargo and baggage as many as 148 times a year. Without inspection and quarantine we could have 148 infestations of the Medfly every year. At the very least, we know that we would have many more frequent and expensive battles with this and other exotic pests than we now face.

Quarantine, then, is a necessary and remarkably effective precaution, but it is far from sufficient. Quarantine programs can never be completely effective, and their weaknesses are being increased by several factors. We have for some years now been in an era of rapid and frequent international travel. Ever faster jet planes, and increasing plane capacity for both passengers and freight, tax our inspection system, which must also cope with the understandable impatience of travelers and shippers with any delays occasioned by the inspection process. As a result, the inspection for unwanted pests and disease organisms has already become selective and can only be less effective than complete inspection. This means that we can rely less now than formerly upon quarantines to provide more than a thin, but still essential, front line of defense. Foreign pests and diseases can and will gain entrance into the United States more frequently in the future.

What do we do when this occurs? First, a cooperative network of federal and state personnel, working with all of the legal chemicals and other tools available, tries to stamp out the invasion at the incipient stage, as has been done several times with the Medfly. Sometimes, as is the case with the cereal leaf beetle, the attempt is unsuccessful, and infestation becomes established. Again, the federal-state network tries to contain the infestation, control its spread by intra- and interstate quarantines, and suppress numbers to levels that can be tolerated. This "living with" the insect continues until research develops new tools, and experiments indicate that eradication is feasible. Then the ARS and the states eradicate the U.S. infestation as we did with the screwworm in the southeastern states, as we are trying to do now with the fire ant, and as we believe we might be able to do with the boll weevil. Once eradicated, the insect again becomes a target for our quarantine inspectors who try to prevent its reentry.

As a practical matter, however, "living with" the insects we have long had, as well as with the more recent invaders, is more nearly the normal way of life for agriculture. It is for this reason that much of the research on pest containment and control is focused on development of resistant crop varieties; improvement of cultural practices; the use of insect parasites, predators, and pathogens as biological agents; the development of genetic defects such as sterility; physical devices; and more selective chemicals such as attractants and hormonal insecticides.

RESISTANT CROP VARIETIES

In combating pests and diseases we prefer to use a method that is specific to the target organism, that interferes only with its welfare, and that does not introduce new contaminants into the environment. Ideal in this regard is the immune or resistant crop variety. By growing crops that are naturally immune or substantially resistant to pests and diseases, we compound our benefits. We avoid crop losses from insect and disease damage, save the cost of preventive chemicals, and reduce contamination of the environment.

Many plant varieties resistant to disease have been developed and are in use. However, less progress has been made in developing plant resistance to specific insects. Farmers do not yet have the alternative of using resistant plant strains in fighting insects that they do in combating diseases. Accordingly, pesticides have been the principal weapons for controlling plant insect pests.

Breeding plant resistance to diseases or insects is not a simple undertaking, because the relationship between the host and the parasite is intricate and their physiologies are complex. The plant scientist and the cooperating scientists working on the pests must know the elements of heredity of the particular plant involved, the habits of the disease or insect pest, and the factors that control its behavior, before they can find and combine genes to confer the type of resistance desired. Resistance to a specific pathogen or parasite is also a delicate characteristic. A plant resistant to one disease or pest may be quite susceptible to another.

In many cases, there are wide gaps in the existing knowledge about the relationships of hosts and parasites. Until these gaps are closed, the development of resistant plants continues to be tedious and time-consuming. Scientists have searched the world for more than 75 years to find crop-breeding materials that might carry identifiable and usable hereditary factors for resistance. They have made worldwide collections of germ plasm and comprehensive assemblages of varieties and strains of crop plants and their related species. Crop specialists of ARS and other scientists continue to seek the wild forbears of the cultivated plants at the places where the species originated. They are combing the countries where the particular diseases and pests are endemic in search of strains and individual plants which, through operation of natural selection, may have developed factors of resistance. Once found, the selections and strains from the collected germ plasm must be tested under exposure to a wide range of diseases and conditions in many areas at the same time. Such tests will determine whether or not the plants do have resistance to pests and diseases in this country. If the resistance of the imported plants is satisfactory, the proper genes from these plants are incorporated into varieties of acceptable commercial yields and retested to determine adaptability to various climates and regions.

Plant breeders have been successful in developing varieties, notably of wheat, corn, alfalfa, and potatoes, resistant to certain diseases. But in some cases even the best of the varieties so far developed are unable to resist massive infestation by insects, and chemical pesticides are required to provide effective protection. In addition, it is possible for a variety to demonstrate satisfactory pest resistance for several seasons, and then become susceptible again as the insect adapts itself, just as a disease-resistant variety can become susceptible to a mutant of the pathogen. In such cases the plant breeder and the pathologist or entomologist must begin again(2).

The contribution that successful pest-resistant varieties could make is so attractive, and the promise that developing knowledge holds for eventually accomplishing it is so encouraging, that plant breeders in laboratories of the world are eager to continue vigorous research in this field. Even so, it is apparent that we cannot depend solely upon plant resistance to pests as a reliable method for pest control for some time to come.

Meantime, cultural practices, the chief resort of farmers before other sophisticated methods were available, continue to be exploited for insect control. These practices include sanitation, early planting of crops, destruction of crop residues, tillage, crop and animal rotation, strip-cropping, destruction of volunteer plants, and specific harvesting procedures(3). These practices are still used to the extent that circumstances warrant it, but in the current system of monoculture they are totally inadequate unless used with other methods. Most frequently chemical control is also used.

BIOLOGICAL CONTROLS

For many years, we have been attempting to develop ways to use insect parasites, predators, and diseases to prey upon damaging pests and thus control their numbers. The work includes world exploration to discover

parasites and predators that might be useful; introduction of these organisms into the United States; evaluation of the effectiveness of pest control
provided; and the distribution and establishment of the organisms so that
they become part of the environment and contribute to the control of
destructive insect pests. We have also explored ways of protecting native
beneficial insects which aid in counteracting destructive pests. A few
examples will illustrate the extent of progress.

Over a period of more than 80 years, attempts have been made to introduce parasites and predators of about 80 pests into the United States. Of
about 520 species imported, 115 have become established, but only about
20 have provided significant control of some of the most destructive pests(4).

Recent research is aimed at mass production and release of parasites or
predators in order to make sufficient numbers available at the critical time
for effective control. For example, recent tests have shown that the release
of 200,000 aphid lions (*Chrysopidae*) per acre for a sustained period was
as effective against the bollworm as the available insecticides(5).

In another study, 100 million parasitic wasps were produced and released
on 18,000 acres of alfalfa to control the pea aphids which are vectors of
pea enation mosaic virus and pea streak virus that overwinter in alfalfa.
The parasites suppressed populations of winged aphids, delaying their
migration to pea plantings, and thus protecting some 130,000 acres of peas
from the virus diseases(6, 7).

Current studies are evaluating a special strain of *Bacillus thuringiensis,*
which, under laboratory conditions, is about 100 times more virulent to
bollworm and certain other insects than strains now commercially avail-
able(8). The effectiveness of this new strain under field conditions must be
determined before its practical value can be properly assessed. So far,
results from applications of the commercially available bacterium to cotton
have not been entirely satisfactory.

Field studies of a polyhedrosis virus for control of the cotton bollworm
and the cabbage looper have shown that this highly selective disease
organism is potentially just as effective and economical as insecticides.
However, until criteria are established for standardization of formulations
and the registration and approval for exemption from tolerance for this
insect virus, its use must be held in abeyance. Experimental evidence to
date indicates that this virus poses no hazard to man or other forms of life(9).
However, more extensive toxicological data must be submitted to provide
complete assurance of safety before this and other insect viruses can be
approved by the Food and Drug Administration and the U.S. Department
of Agriculture for use on food crops.

An ARS entomologist explored Argentina in search of insect enemies of
alligator weed, a pest in the southern region of the United States that chokes
reservoirs, canals, and other waterways, spoiling their use for recreation,
wildlife, and commercial activities. He found that a flea beetle (*Agasicles*)
is a damaging enemy of the weed. Tests were made to determine that it
would not be harmful to other plants, and the beetle was released in 1964
in Florida and South Carolina. This insect has multiplied sufficiently to make
important contributions to the control of alligator weed in some areas(10).

The potential value of such biological controls is promising. Parasites are usually specific in action, and so far there have been no known damaging effects on the environment from those already released. The prognosis for various disease-causing organisms is good enough to encourage continuing research. However, the relatively meager successes demonstrated over the years and the complex obstacles to be overcome—notably the difficulty of mass-producing biological agents—indicate that we are still a long way from being able to depend on these methods for practical pest control.

INSECT STERILITY

The manipulation of insects for their own destruction, by inducing sexual sterility or introducing other harmful genetic traits, is a relatively new approach to insect control and holds considerable promise. Two distinct methods of using sterility as a control are being studied. One method is based on rearing massive numbers of a pest species, sterilizing them with gamma radiation, and releasing the insects to compete for mates in the natural population. The resulting eggs do not hatch and the insect population dwindles. The second method involves the application of chemosterilants to native populations at a central source; the treated insects then disperse and serve to reduce the reproduction of target pests in the environment.

The first method was used to eradicate the screwworm from the southeastern United States and is now employed to suppress this livestock pest throughout the southwestern region of the United States. In view of the long flight range of the insect, a continuous barrier of sterile flies must be maintained against reentry of the screwworm from Mexico. Before these programs for eradication and suppression were undertaken, beginning in 1958, this pest was costing livestock producers up to $120 million a year(11).

The sterility method is also being used to replace insecticide spraying in preventing the entry of the Mexican fruit fly into Southern California. The sustained release of sterilized flies has also been proved effective experimentally in eradicating the melon and oriental fruit flies from islands in the Pacific. Considerable work is now being done to develop this method for use against the pink bollworm. Preliminary investigations are under way to determine the potential of the sterility method for suppression of the boll weevil, corn earworm, tobacco hornworm, tobacco budworm, cabbage looper, fall armyworm, and hornfly(12).

The sterility principle and other genetic methods for insect control are most attractive, but before such methods can be developed for practical use, scientists must have a thorough knowledge of the biology, ecology, and population dynamics of each target insect. They must study the problems of mass-rearing and sterilizing the billions of insects that are often needed to flood adequately the target insect population. One of the obstacles to achieving successful mass-rearing and sterilization is the difficulty in preserving healthy and aggressive characteristics in the released insects to enable them to compete for mates in the native population. Another limiting factor is the fact that the method is effective only when the target population is at a natural low ebb or when the population is first reduced by insecticides or other methods of control. The sterility technique is usually successful as a tool for eradication or continuous suppression of an insect only when used in conjunction with other methods of pest control or when insect populations are reduced by natural causes.

In explaining how and why the sterility technique is most useful, Dr. E. F. Knipling, originator of this technique in pest control and director of entomology research for ARS, describes it as follows(13):

> In most situations, the natural population of a pest, even at the lowest level in the population density cycle, may be so high that it would not be practical to rear and release enough sterile organisms to start a downward population trend. In such event the prior use of an insecticide or some other method of control would be more efficient and practical than the release of sterile organisms. However, the release method should become more practical than insecticides at some point in the natural population density level. We may illustrate this by citing some hypothetical figures. A 90 per cent kill of a million insects in a population would mean the destruction of 900,000 insects the first treatment. In terms of numbers killed this would be highly efficient. The second treatment, however, would destroy only 90,000; the third, 9,000; the fourth, 90; the fifth, only 9. Thus, as the population declines each insecticide treatment becomes less efficient in terms of the number of individuals killed.
>
> At some point in the population density level, the rearing and release of sterile insects should become more efficient and perhaps more desirable than the continued use of an insecticide.

ATTRACTANTS AND HORMONES

One of the newest trends is research to identify and develop attractants and hormones for insect control. Scientists are investigating insect responses to various chemical substances in the plants the pests feed upon, to chemical sex attractants, to light, and to sound.

Naturally occurring attractants are highly specific and active in infinitesimal amounts. Intensive effort is being devoted to the isolation, identification, and synthesis of several sex pheromones so as to obtain sufficient amounts for practical use in the control of important pests(14). Sex attractants have already been demonstrated for such major pests as the cabbage looper, pink bollworm, tobacco hornworm, Japanese beetle, lesser peach tree borer, European corn borer, fall armyworm, corn earworm, boll weevil, and gypsy moth(15). Field studies on the use of appropriate sex pheromones in combination with black-light traps for the control of the tobacco hornworm and cabbage looper have been encouraging(16, 17).

The synthetic lure, methyl eugenol, was used experimentally to eradicate the oriental fruit fly on the island of Rota. The chemical attractant was fortified with the insecticide named and incorporated into small squares of fiberboard. The squares were distributed by aircraft, about 125 per square mile, every 2 weeks. Such releases were supplemented by treated pieces of cane fiber suspended from trees in village areas. The fly was eradicated within 6 months(18).

Another recent trend is research on hormones and hormone-like materials that may be used as insecticides to disrupt insect development rather than to cause immediate death. Sterility in adult insects may result soon after treatment with molting hormones or their analogs, but juvenile hormones act by interrupting insect development and producing monster insects that eventually die or, if they become adults, cannot reproduce because of their physical abnormalities(19).

Certain of these hormonal materials, which would not be expected to have a detrimental effect on nontarget organisms, are effective against specific pests at fantastically small dosages.

Recently, several new "hybrid" synthetic ethers, similar to juvenile hormones, were tested for their ability to block normal insect growth and development. These compounds are fairly easy to synthesize and are far more potent than the insect's own hormones(20). In addition, the antifertility effect of a synthetic molting hormone called triol was intensified 10 to 20 times when combined with synergists such as sesamex or piperonyl butoxide.

Insect physiologists of ARS and industrial scientists are working separately and cooperatively to push developmental research on juvenile and molting hormones and their analogs. There are at least two dozen chemical and pharmaceutical companies that are studying insect hormones, and perhaps half of them have under way extensive screening programs involving hundreds of compounds.

These examples indicate some of the interesting leads being followed in the development of useful hormones and attractants; at present they are hardly more than that. It will be some time in the future before some of these chemicals will be ready for practical and general use.

INTEGRATED CONTROL PROGRAMS

The opportunities for experimentation provided by the wide variety of insect control methods now available and the limitations of most of them have prompted investigation of integrated methods to place maximum pressure on insect populations. Integrated control is a compatible system of insect control in which various methods are used in proper sequence and timing so as to create the least hazard to man and the environment and to permit maximum assistance from natural controls. The objective is to keep the numbers of key insects in a given area below the level that can cause economic damage or, in some instances, to eliminate the population if feasible and advantageous. The development of techniques required for such integrated control programs on a practical scale is costly. Because there is limited profit in developing these techniques, they may not be of immediate interest to industry; thus, it is likely that most of the development will have to be undertaken by public agencies. Research by ARS is directed toward certain important insects in which this method of control seems practical.

Much research is needed, because for several major insect pests pertinent information is lacking on the life history, host plants, flight habits, population dynamics, role of natural enemies, numbers of different stages of insects per acre, nutritional requirements, requirements for mass rearing, comparative vigor and competitiveness of reared insects and native strains.

Much more information about the insects is required for development and application of integrated control methods than is generally required for use of insecticides. Areawide programs in which billions of sterilized insects, or biological control agents, or large quantities of natural sex attractant are used, will require housing facilities, development of suitable rearing media, and automated techniques for mass production of insects.

After the basic data have been obtained areawide control procedures for each insect must be tested in an isolated area, preferably an island. Then, with the cooperation of state agencies and growers, it will be possible to carry out a substantial experimental test. If results are favorable, it will be necessary to conduct a significantly large field test supported by a large-scale pilot test for production of the agent to determine the practicality of the entire procedure. At the conclusion of the testing, we decide whether the federal government should continue the work or turn the project over to private enterprise for further development. An obstacle to the rapid advancement of such means of insect control is the high cost. For example, such a test for integrated control of the boll weevil is estimated to cost nearly $2.5 million a year for 2 years.

PROBLEMS AND HAZARDS OF PESTICIDES

Although we have high hopes and great enthusiasm for the eventual development of effective alternative means of pest control, for the present we must depend on chemicals, used selectively and prudently. As we continue to use pesticides in agriculture we must be aware of the problems and the hazards that they can create for man and his environment.

Pesticides have their shortcomings. One of the first problems to be recognized in the use of the most effective organochlorine pesticides was the development of resistance by insect pests. Differing reactions of individual insects to insecticides was recognized as early as 1897(21), and the possibility that insects can develop resistance was pointed out in 1914(21).

Development of resistance to DDT and related compounds was most spectacular. The repeated and widespread use of such insecticides created an intolerable environment for many species of insects, and some species evolved a stronger resistance with each succeeding generation. Finally, certain insects, including the housefly and the boll weevil, became almost impervious to the originally potent effects of these insecticides. Some 224 species of insects and acarines in various parts of the world have developed resistance to one or more groups of insecticides; of these, 127 are agricultural pests and 97 are pests of medical and veterinary importance(22).

The more effective persistent pesticides are said to have a "broad spectrum" in that they often affect many organisms other than the target pest. Some of the more specific pesticides in use today are more acutely toxic to man; the use of the more specific chemicals requires use of a different pesticide for almost every different pest that attacks a given crop or area. The long-term result of shifting away from broad-spectrum pesticides may be creation of greater immediate hazards to man and the need for more chemicals than are now used.

A report on pesticides made to the Secretary of the U.S. Department of Health, Education, and Welfare by a special commission(22) included the following findings in relation to human health:

> *The available evidence concerning such human exposure to pesticides derives from three main sources: planned and controlled administration of pesticides to human subjects; case reports of episodes of accidental or other acute poisoning; and epidemiological studies, which in turn comprise surveys of occupationally-exposed groups (in accordance with a variety of retrospective and prospective approaches), and studies of the general population. . .*
>
> *A detailed survey of case reports of incidents involving accidental poisoning by organochlorine pesticides reveals that their general action is to increase the excitability of the nervous system. Some of these compounds also damage the liver. Their capacity to penetrate intact human skin varies from one compound to another; in the case of endrin, for example, percutaneous penetration plays an important part in clinical intoxication. With the organochlorine group of compounds there is a wide range of potentials for acute toxicity. DDT is relatively safe in terms of acute intoxication, while dieldrin and endrin have produced many cases of serious poisoning. Lindane presents a special problem, inasmuch as it has been implicated, largely on the basis of circumstantial evidence, in the causation of hematological disorders. A characteristic of organochlorine poisoning is the difficulty of establishing the correct diagnosis. This is especially true in cases of mild poisoning that result in nonspecific symptoms and signs, since except in the case of dieldrin there are no established criteria for diagnosis on the basis of blood levels. Specific therapeutic measures do not exist. . . .*
>
> *. . . The longest studies on record have lasted less than four years and the results can only reflect the period of study. Consequently, the findings, especially when they are negative, are open to question when taken by themselves. It appears, however, that present levels of exposure to DDT among the general population have not produced any observable adverse effect in controlled studies on volunteers. The same is true of aldrin-dieldrin. These findings acquire greater force when combined with observations on other groups, such as occupationally-exposed persons.*

Despite the lack of unequivocal evidence of harmful effects upon man, public concern over the use of DDT and its relatives has continued to grow, largely because another problem has become increasingly apparent as the experience with the pesticide has lengthened. Residues of DDT and related pesticides do not readily break down; therefore they dissipate very slowly. Residues have been accumulating in the environment, in adipose animal tissue, and in milk. Residues of DDT have been found many miles from any point of known use, for example, in tissues of polar bears and other wildlife in the Arctic.

The residues of DDT and several other chlorinated hydrocarbons are harmful to certain beneficial insects, including pollinators and parasites or predators of pests. Some fish and birds have been harmed by residues of persistent pesticides.

The previously cited commission reporting to the Secretary of the U.S. Department of Health, Education, and Welfare, and other competent scientific study groups have noted additional reactions of nontarget organisms to persistent pesticides in the environment. Species react differently to specific pesticides. For example, DDT can cause thinning of eggshells in ducks and falcons, but not in pheasants and quail(22). Pesticides from the air, water, and soil may be absorbed and concentrated in the bodies of organisms. The concentration in the tissue is frequently increased as one species feeds on another and passes the pesticide from one link to another one higher in the food chain. In this sequence some predators, like birds and fish, may be exposed to levels several thousand times the concentration in the physical environment.

INCREASED PRECAUTIONS

In the light of all this, a guideline is emerging with which most agree: Persistent pesticides should be released into the environment only when necessary—that is, when the need is immediate to protect human health or life-supporting food supplies and when no satisfactory alternative is available. Most also agree that research on the long-term effects of persistent pesticides in the environment should be intensified since, even with this guideline, we will continue to need and use some persistent pesticides.

We are moving in the direction indicated by the guideline. Actions are being taken to accomplish an orderly reduction in the use of persistent pesticides without sacrificing essential uses. One of the safeguards is the Federal Insecticide, Fungicide, and Rodenticide Act (FIFRA) administered by ARS. The original federal legislation on pesticides was enacted in 1910 and amended in 1947 under the designation FIFRA. Additional amendments have been added as needs have arisen. The purpose of the Act is to assure the safety and efficacy of pesticide products sold in interstate commerce.

In making decisions concerning the registration of chemicals proposed for specific uses, our scientists carefully evaluate the detailed data submitted with each application and consult with scientists in other agencies concerned with public safety—most frequently the Department of Health, Education, and Welfare and the Department of the Interior.

The following are examples of the actions taken in recent months relating to FIFRA and other ARS responsibilities concerned with pesticides:

1) On 20 November 1969, registration of DDT was canceled for use against pests of shade trees, tobacco, house and garden, and aquatic sites such as marshes and swamps. As provided under the law, five manufacturers have appealed this decision through a request for either a review by a panel of experts, nominated by the National Academy of Sciences–National Research Council, or a public hearing. On 25 November, the Department announced its intention to cancel all other uses of DDT except those needed for prevention or control of human disease and other essential uses for which no alternative means of pest control are available.

2) On 23 April 1970, the Department of Agriculture announced that pesticide manufacturers and formulators had been notified that federal registration of certain 2,4,5-T products used for weed control is suspended. The suspended products include liquid formulations for use around the home or recreation areas; and all formulations for use in lakes, ponds, or on ditch banks. The action was taken because 2,4,5-T was reported to cause birth defects when injected at high doses into experimental pregnant mice. Pregnant rats were unaffected. No data on humans are available.

3) A review of uses of all persistent pesticides in federal-state pest-control programs was made, with the result that less persistent chemicals will be used wherever possible in all such programs.

As we continue increasing our criteria for safety—particularly for keeping the use of persistent pesticides to the minimum—judgments will be made on the basis of the best scientific knowledge available. But decision-making cannot always wait until all scientists agree. In the traditional and leisurely scientific winnowing process, scientists argue their data and conclusions with each other and discuss and test them until shreds of truth can be aggregated to establish fact. In the case of pesticides, this process is now being hastened under the glare of the public spotlight in which controversial and complex scientific issues are being debated by scientist and layman alike.

Basic to the speedy resolution of these controversial issues is knowledge, now lacking, that can come only through research. We do not know, for example, what the long-term effects of persistent pesticides upon man will be nor their ultimate fates in soil, water, and other parts of the ecosystem. Crucial to the resolution of questions of environmental pollution—particularly, as they concern pesticides—is the establishment of the significance in man of the results of toxicological experiments on laboratory animals. We need to have settled, among other things, some questions concerning cancer and carcinogens, species specificity, significance of dose size and route, and the effect of substances to which the living organism is concomitantly exposed. We need knowledge to enable us to cut through the present scientific complexities and arrive at an acceptable practical answer to the question, "How safe is safe enough?"

This is far from an academic question, but it is one that must be faced repeatedly in administering programs for pest control and in regulating the use of pesticides. These decisions, based on scientific knowledge, must be made in the light of what is best for the overall welfare of man, his environment, and the creatures with which he chooses to share the environment.

SUMMARY

Agriculture is expected to maintain and increase efficiency of production in order to feed the increasing millions in our country; the needs in underdeveloped countries are even more drastic. Meeting these needs requires more than ever effective control of agricultural pests. We can no longer afford to give up so large a share of the potential world food supply to pests and diseases. At the same time, with more people crowded closer together the need for protecting the environment from pollution is more acute. We must have an effective program for combating the diseases and pests that plague mankind and his food supply, but we must also preserve and protect the quality of our environment.

REFERENCES

1. *Report of Committee on Persistent Pesticides, Division of Biology and Agriculture, National Research Council, to U.S. Department of Agriculture.* 1969. Washington, D.C.: National Academy of Sciences, p. 2.
2. Luginbill, P. 1969. Developing resistant plants—the ideal method of controlling insects. *USDA Prod. Res. Rep. no. 111.*
3. *Principles of plant and animal pest control,* vol. 3. 1969. Washington, D.C.: National Academy of Sciences, pp. 208–42.
4. Data taken from speech presented by Under Secretary J. Phil Campbell to the National Agricultural Chemicals Association, White Sulphur Springs, W. Va., September 15, 1969.
5. Ridgway, R. L. and Jones, S. L. 1969. *J. Econ. Entomol.* 62: 177.
6. Halfhill, J. E. and Featherston, P. E. 1967. *J. Econ. Entomol.* 60: 1756.
7. Henneberry, T. J. 1968. *Nat. Canners Assoc. Inform. Lett. no. 2149*: 52–55.
8. Dulmage, H. T. *J. Invertebr. Pathol.,* in press.
9. Heimpel, A. M. 1967. In *Proceedings of Joint U.S.-Japan Seminar on Microbial Control of Insects (Fukuoka, Japan),* pp. 51–61.
10. Zeiger, C. F. 1967. *Hyacinth Control J.* 6: 31.
11. Baumhover, A. H. 1966. *J. Amer. Med. Assoc.* 196: 240.
12. Knipling, E. F. 1966. *Alternative methods of controlling insect pests.* Washington, D.C.: U.S. Government Printing Office, pp. 16–18, 23–24.
13. Knipling, E. F. 1963. *Agricultural Science Rev.* 1: 2.
14. Jacobson, M. 1965. *Insect sex attractants.* New York: Wiley.
15. Hoffman, C. H. and Henderson, L. S. 1966. *Yearbook of agriculture.* Washington, D.C.: U.S. Government Printing Office, pp. 26–38.
16. Wolf, W. W., *et al.* 1969. *Trans. Amer. Soc. Agri. Eng.* 12: 329, 335.
17. Henneberry, T. J. 1968. *Nat. Canners Assoc. Inform. Lett. no. 2149*: 52.
18. Steiner, L. F., et al. 1965. *J. Econ. Entomol.* 58: 961.
19. Williams, C. M. and Robbins, W. E. 1968. *BioScience* 18: 791, 797.
20. Bowers, W. S. 1969. *Science* 164: 323.
21. Porter, B. A. 1952. *Yearbook of agriculture.* Washington, D.C.: U.S. Government Printing Office, pp. 317–18.
22. *Report of the Secretary's Commission on Pesticides and Their Relationship to Environmental Health.,* parts I and II. 1969. Washington, D.C.: U.S. Government Printing Office, pp. 59, 231–33, 179.

Victory on San Francisco Bay

JUDSON GOODING

JUDSON GOODING *is an Associate Editor of* Fortune *magazine.*

Wildavsky's article discussed the importance of political considerations in seeking solutions to our environmental crisis. Gooding recounts how a conservationist movement mobilized public opinion and political support to prevent the further filling of San Francisco Bay.

The tactics used in winning the Battle of San Francisco Bay will long be studied as a textbook example of how to wage a successful campaign in defense of the environment. Conservationists opposed to filling the bay found that the path to victory in the struggle to save natural resources leads from the mimeograph machine and the telephone through newspaper columns and radio stations to the halls of the legislature. There, after a campaign of an intensity unprecedented in California, they succeeded in bringing about passage of a bill that prohibits any indiscriminate bay filling. Henceforth only projects of priority importance to the community as a whole will be permitted. The work done by the conservationists to save the bay has a dual benefit for the rest of the country: it assures the preservation of a great national scenic asset, and it illustrates how citizen power can be mobilized to preserve other endangered wonders.

At stake had been the future of an immense, extraordinarily lovely series of inland seas stretching fifty miles from north to south, and extending inland to the great Sacramento delta where the waters from sixteen rivers flow down from the Sierras. The bay's opening to the sea, the Golden Gate, was carved out by the Sierra waters grinding their way through the coastal mountain range two hundred thousand years ago, but it was discovered only in the eighteenth century. An early explorer traveling with Juan Bautista de Anza wrote in 1776: "If it could be well settled, there would not be anything more beautiful." He described the harbor as "so remarkable and so spacious that in it may be established shipyards, docks and anything that may be wished." What man wished, it slowly became clear, was to

From the February 1970 issue of *Fortune Magazine*. This article has appeared in a book, *The Environment: A National Mission for the Seventies*, published by Harper and Row.

fill the bay where he needed more shoreland, and to use its waters as a dump for garbage, sewage, and industrial wastes.

The first bay fill occurred in what is now downtown San Francisco, where ships that had brought prospectors in the 1850's gold rush were turned into wharfside houses and offices as the city grew explosively. A new type of fill operation began as hydraulic gold mining up the rivers washed hundreds of millions of tons of silt downstream to the bay floor, where it destroyed rich oyster beds and silted channels so that water-flow patterns were altered. At the northern and southern extremities of the bay, thousands of acres of bay and marshland were set off from the ebb and flow of the tides, for use as salt-evaporating ponds and as game preserves. By 1960 diking and filling had reduced the water area by one-third, from 680 to 400 square miles. A report by the Army Corps of Engineers showed that two-thirds of the bay was less than twelve feet deep, and "susceptible of reclamation," and that half belonged to private owners or local governments.

Complacency about the preservation of the bay was hard to understand, even before the engineers' alarming report was published. It was true that pollution of bay waters had been reduced markedly, so that swimming was once again possible in some areas. However, both San Francisco and Oakland were developing their waterfronts, and building up their big bayside international airports—relying on fill for new land. All around the bay, waterfront housing developments and marinas were being built. New refineries and other industries were under construction, or being planned, adding to the economic base of the thirty-two towns abutting the bay.

This rush of development threatened to destroy the bay. Studies showed that the bay-area population would double within thirty years, and would reach thirteen million by the year 2020. Pressures to convert bay waters to valuable land were certain to increase enormously. Garbage dumping into diked-off areas became a commonplace solution to disposal dilemmas. During the late 1950's and early 1960's one city after another announced plans to expand its land areas into the bay, and private developers proposed numerous schemes of their own. In the south bay, Foster City was planned to accommodate 35,000 people on 2,600 acres, a scheme that required dredging 18 million yards of sand from the bottom of the bay.

One of the most startling proposals was advanced by the city of Berkeley, which planned to double its size by filling 2,000 acres of the bay. This plan alarmed many east bay residents, including Mrs. Clark Kerr, whose husband was then president of the University of California. She and two friends, Mrs. Donald McLaughlin, whose husband was chairman of the university regents, and Mrs. Charles Gulick, wife of a professor, investigated the Berkeley proposal. They quickly became convinced that conservation groups should be mobilized, and soon aroused the Sierra Club, the Save the Redwoods League, the Audubon Society, and others in defense of the bay. With this encouragement, Mrs. Kerr and her friends decided to form the "Save San Francisco Bay Association." They mailed out 700 letters and got 600 replies, many with contributions. This overwhelming consensus indicated that although concern over the bay had not been particularly visible, it was wide and deep.

The association persuaded the University of California's Institute of Governmental Studies to carry out a detailed study of the bay's future. The report, published in 1963, pointed out that fill reduced the amount of tidal flux and diminished the oxygenation of the water. The findings helped to defeat the Berkeley Bay fill proposal after the association made it a local election issue. The group then broadened its attack and, working through Assemblyman Nicholas Petris of Oakland, tried to get the state legislature to enact a moratorium on all bay fill. Petris (who subsequently became a senator) offered two bills, but opponents crippled them with amendments providing for exceptions to the moratorium, and the bills died in committee.

Renewing the attack at the state level, the association decided to convert a powerful politician to its cause instead of working through an already convinced conservationist with a narrow power base. Mrs. Kerr settled on Senator J. Eugene McAteer, who was planning to run for mayor of San Francisco. She urged him to head the fight for the bay bill. "If you take the lead on this," she said, "you will be 'Mr. San Francisco' himself." McAteer threw himself into the struggle with vigor. (He was to die of a heart attack before the fight was won.) He and Assemblyman Petris proposed legislation creating a Bay Conservation and Development Commission (BCDC) to look into ways in which San Francisco Bay might be developed to its maximum usefulness without harming its scenic or recreation potential. The study would also report on the effects of fill on the bay. A crucially important provision prohibited any new fill during the group's three-year study period without a public hearing and authorization by the commission.

There was strong opposition to the bill in the legislature. But Save the Bay Association members flocked to Sacramento, where they packed the legislative chambers, and some Oakland activists even mailed small bags of sand to their legislators with tags saying, "You'll wonder where the water went, if you fill the bay with sediment." With this kind of highly visible and audible support, McAteer was able to get the bill passed.

The language of the McAteer-Petris act was direct. "The bay is the most valuable single natural resource of an entire region," it said. "The present uncoordinated haphazard manner in which San Francisco Bay is being filled threatens the bay itself and is therefore inimical to the welfare of both present and future residents of the area."

The law created a commission of twenty-seven members to be appointed from federal, state, and local agencies and governments, and the public. The commission was to present a plan for bay conservation and development to the legislature in 1969. If that plan was approved, it would be put into effect and the commission would become permanent. If the legislature demurred, the commission was to go out of existence—and there would be no curb on filling the bay.

The commission went to work on the plan, breaking down the study into twenty-five topics, such as recreation, water front housing, fish, and wildlife. The finished report, submitted in January, 1969, stressed that the bay should not be treated as "ordinary real estate," but as an asset belonging to the area, the state, and the nation, an asset to be protected for present and future generations. The commission held that since any change in the bay might affect other parts, this protection could be afforded only through a regional approach.

The report, bearing out earlier findings, declared flatly that "any filling is harmful to the bay" because it upsets the ecological balance, diminishes the bay's ability to assimilate pollution by reducing the water volume exchanged by the tides, and cuts down the surface area, thus limiting oxygenation. Commission jurisdiction over development of shoreline areas was one of the most controversial elements of the plan. The commission sought to reserve prime shoreline sites for what it termed "priority uses": ports, water-related industry, airports, wildlife refuges, water-related recreation, and public access to the bay (only ten miles of the entire 276-mile shore was at that time open to the public).

To carry out their recommendations and to continue surveillance of fill proposals the commissioners sought the creation of a limited regional government body. They estimated the costs of acquiring 7,400 acres of submerged land deemed of particular importance for recreation and wildlife at between $30 million and $50 million. If it became necessary to compensate private owners of submerged land for keeping their property as open water (rather than developing it profitably, which the commission could prohibit), the extra cost could go as high as $285 million.

The lobbying effort against BCDC constituted the heaviest offensive mounted against any legislation proposed at the 1969 session of the legislature. A conspicuous opponent of certain provisions was Westbay Community Associates, a firm that owns 10,000 acres of the bay and presented a plan for development of twenty-seven miles of peninsula shoreline below San Francisco airport, including 4,700 acres of fill. The Westbay design included residential, industrial, and recreation areas. The meetings at which Westbay tried to present its plans were "all packed with articulate and rabid conservationists," a company spokesman, Warren Lindquist, recalls, and as the debate continued, the issue "became a matter of right or wrong—if you didn't agree with the BCDC you were wrong." Another Westbay representative, Richard Archer, told a legislative committee plaintively that the BCDC plan was unsatisfactory. "The plan should have teeth," he said, "but this one has fangs."

Strong opposition to specific aspects of the plan came from other firms with large holdings in or along the bay. Against the platoons of lobbyists for the opponents, which included the Leslie Salt Co. and the Atchison, Topeka & Santa Fe Railway Co., the tax-exempt conservation groups could not field even one lobbyist, since taking a political position could cost them their tax status. Accordingly, seventy conservation groups joined to form the Planning and Conservation League, which did not claim tax exemption and which hired a lobbyist to work for the bill.

But the main effort in support of the bill came from thousands of concerned citizens. The Save the Bay Association had worked uninterruptedly for three years to support the commission, sending out communiqués on new developments, ringing hundreds of telephones, promoting the cause on radio and television, and expanding its support from 5,000 to 22,000 dues-paying members as the crucial vote drew near. In addition, two

vigorous, deeply committed San Mateo women, Janet Adams and Claire Dedrick, formed the Save Our Bay Action Committee. The committee sold bumper stickers, ran a succession of full-page ads in local papers urging citizens to "demand a halt to 122 years of destruction of San Francisco Bay," and organized charter bus trips to attend committee hearings in Sacramento.

More than 200,000 signatures were gathered on petitions asking Governor Reagan to support the bill. When he was not available to receive the mass of documents, the committee, with a keen eye for publicity, strewed them—they totaled 3.4 miles in length when volunteers had stuck them all together—across the capitol lawn and steps, then like true conservationists picked them all up. Meanwhile the Sierra Club had thrown its full national weight behind the campaign, the first urban conservation issue the club had endorsed nationally.

Passage of the BCDC bill remained uncertain right up to the end of the session. Volunteers continued to pack the hearings, and letters poured in to legislators. So many telephone calls were made in support of the bill that the president pro tem of the senate had to plead with conservation groups to cut them off so that state business could be transacted.

The bill passed, with its provisions for control over fill and dredging preserved intact. There were a few modifications: most important, one reducing commission authority over the shoreline from 1,000 feet to 100 feet back from the water's edge. Another alteration provided that some commission members were to be elected county supervisors or city councilmen rather than conservationist-appointed city and county representatives. This change reflected the behind-the-scenes battle between "home rule" supporters and those who favored a truly regional government, responsible to the area rather than to specific communities. It was a modest but significant victory for the developers, since it gave them some election-time leverage over commission members.

The commission was given three years to select and acquire privately owned lands it believes are needed for public purposes, under the law. It has no funds for these purchases, but BCDC executive director Joseph Bodovitz hopes state or federal monies will become available. At present the annual operating budget of $200,000 is being met out of the state's general fund. But Governor Reagan does not approve of the state footing the bill for this regional function; he believes it should be paid for by bay-area citizens. Various methods of financing are being considered, including a special bay-area income tax.

Conservationists across the country agree that this pioneering effort provides many lessons for other groups determined to protect other estuaries and natural resources, and that the plan developed for the bay furnishes an excellent pattern for management of a major natural resource. "But the battle is not now, and never will be, won," says Bodovitz. "Maintaining a high degree of continuing public interest is crucial."

Pittsburgh: How One City Did It

TED O. THACKREY

TED O. THACKREY *is the editor of* Better Times, *published by the Community Council of Greater New York.*

The Revelle article discussed the pollution problems facing American cities today. Most of the cities are only beginning to deal with these problems. However, one city, Pittsburgh, has already made a concerted effort to clean its air and water. Thackrey briefly describes its efforts and results.

It's possible in Pittsburgh, Pennsylvania, these days to wear a white shirt, or a white dress, from dawn to dusk and come home almost spotless. Housewives are able to hang out a wash on a sunny morning in Pittsburgh, if they are so minded, without having the load to do over by noon because of sootfall and dust. The downtown skyscrapers, or most of them at any rate, appear newly constructed, though it may have been five years or more since the surface was washed or blasted. Since the middle or late 1940s, a generation has grown up in Pittsburgh that on any day could look up and see, of all urban wonders, the sky.

Before the 1940s, however, generations lived in Pittsburgh—once known as the Smoky City—that often found it difficult to see the opposite side of the street. Today Pittsburgh, the once murky steel-town at the junction of the Allegheny and Monongahela Rivers, is one of America's cleaner cities. It has, for example, only half the dustfall registered in New York City: thirty tons per square mile per month on the average, compared with New York City's current sixty tons.

The story of the Pittsburgh renaissance reaches back over more than three decades and is by no means concluded. It has been and continues to be a bitter, emotionally charged battle to keep the atmosphere pure enough to breathe and clean enough to see through. The struggle to rid the mighty rivers of pollutants and to halt the despoiling of the land has barely begun.

Coal and steel interests, along with the railroads, were not only the job-giving lifeblood of Pittsburgh but were also the chief despoilers of air,

land, and water in the old days. But Pittsburgh also had many men of determination and vision who foresaw that Pittsburgh could choke itself to death on the smoke and fumes belching from factory and locomotive chimneys. The fight for clean air really began late in 1939, but it was seven grimy years before any specific results could be seen.

Leading industrial and business executives, including representatives of the steel industry, sparked the renaissance through formation of the Allegheny Conference on Community Development. By 1942 another civic group, the United Smoke Council, was formed by 142 men and women from seventy-one organizations. World War II was on—and the United Smoke Council entered the battle on patriotic grounds; smoke control, it proclaimed, was essential to save fuel needed for war production.

By 1943 an antismoke ordinance had been passed. It provided that as of October 1 of that year private homes were to burn only smokeless coal, fed to furnaces by stokers. But the effective date of the ordinance was eventually postponed to March 1945, partly because of opposition from soft-coal interests and partly because there weren't enough stokers and other smoke control equipment to go around. Meanwhile, rallies, meetings, and membership campaigns in the fight for smoke control were almost continuous. Finally, in 1945, the United Smoke Council became a part of the Committee on Smoke Abatement, a subdivision of the Allegheny Conference on Community Development.

But something else took place in 1945 that dramatized the struggle for clean air so prominently that most of Pittsburgh's population had to take sides: David L. Lawrence, an independent and well-to-do civic leader, campaigned for the Democratic nomination for mayor, and his major appeal was to those who wanted smoke control.

Not everyone wanted smoke control by any means. Householders were told that smokeless fuel would cost them dearly and that smoke control would drive industry from Pittsburgh; that it would become a jobless ghost town if the Lawrence supporters had their way. "Remember Little Joe," read the opposition placards. ("Little Joe" was a personification of

"the little man" who would have to buy smokeless coal, stokers, and other conversion equipment if smoke control laws were enforced.) It was a tough battle, but Lawrence won the nomination and the election. And he proved to be a man who kept his campaign promises, particularly where smoke control was concerned.

One key to Lawrence's campaign was an impressive fact sheet about the high cost of atmospheric pollution. Respected physicians said flatly that Pittsburgh was not a healthy place to live, and statistics on respiratory diseases appeared to bear them out (in 1945, for example, Pittsburgh led the nation in deaths from pneumonia). It was disclosed that forty industrial firms had decided to leave Pittsburgh because of smoke, smog, and impure air, as well as because of a recurring danger from floods and contaminated water. A department store estimated that on one winter day alone smog soiled merchandise and home furnishings so seriously that the loss in cleaning bills and markdowns was $25,000. Nevertheless, the coal industry and the railroads continued to oppose clean-air efforts on economic grounds.

In 1946, the Pittsburgh Chamber of Commerce, the League of Women Voters, and other civic groups joined the Allegheny Conference fight to extend air-pollution efforts to all of Allegheny County. Pittsburgh had discovered what many other regions have still failed to grasp: that polluted air knows no political boundaries; it drifts over borders and chokes communities impartially. Mayor Lawrence was deep into the fight by now, meeting around the clock with industrial leaders. In 1947, during a stalemate in the General Assembly in Harrisburg over legislation to permit county-wide control of air pollution, one of the major opponents capitulated. The Pennsylvania Railroad, which not only hauled but burned coal, feared a loss of freight tonnage and was also worried about the enormous cost of converting coal-burning locomotives to Diesels. At that point Richard King Mellon, most powerful of the city's financial and industrial giants, was persuaded to use his influence with the Pennsy's directors. The opposition died away, and the legislation passed.

By this time Pittsburgh was basking in some of the benefits of air pollution control. Two years after its smoke control ordinance went into effect, visibility in downtown Pittsburgh had improved 67 per cent, and there was a 39 per cent improvement in days of sunshine observable. The pall of smoke was thinning out.

Under the ordinance, factories, homes, steamboats, and locomotives were required to burn smokeless fuels or install smoke-consuming devices. River boats, which had once fouled the atmosphere, converted to diesel burners. Apartment houses, churches, hotels, and office buildings converted to gas fuel. Schools installed stoking equipment and went to smokeless coal. Private homes, however, were once more exempted for a year, chiefly because of the combined opposition of the owners and unions involved in soft-coal production.

By 1952 industry, public utilities, railroads, and municipalities in Allegheny County were at work on a $200,000,000 air pollution control program. In that year a saving of $26,000,000 was estimated for Pittsburgh in cleaning bills alone. Household laundry bills dropped $5,500,000. Visibility was up

77 per cent over 1945. And no one even tried to estimate the benefits to physical and mental health. In the ten years from 1955 to 1965, the 132 open-hearth furnaces in Pittsburgh found out how to limit smoke and fly ash, and are now working on methods of screening dust from open-hearth gas.

The Bureau of Air Pollution Control of the Allegheny County Health Department reports that despite record steel production in 1964 and in the first quarter of 1965, the basic downward trend in dustfall continues (though in April of 1965 the dustfall registered thirty tons per square mile per month, compared with 1962's average of only twenty-seven tons.) And a ten-year report made available by Thomas E. Purcell, chief engineer for the Bureau of Air Pollution Control, shows an almost continuing drop from 1954 through 1964.

Sunny Pittsburgh has come a long way since the 1940s. Most residents and industries now believe in pollution control—at least in the atmosphere. But other troubles persist. Disposal of rubbish, garbage, and waste by municipalities is still a major problem. Sulfur contaminants, carcinogens, and other airborne health hazards are just coming under serious study by health department laboratories, aided by federal grants. And the state is only now preparing legislation to eliminate the privileged status of mines and make acid drainage subject to the same regulations as other industrial waste pouring into Pennsylvania's streams and rivers. The mining industry is, of course, opposed. The cost of avoiding such drainage, it says, would bankrupt every mine.

To anyone who was around thirty years ago, the arguments sound somewhat familiar. But the participants in the struggle have at least one advantage this time: On good days they can enjoy Pittsburgh's fresh air and bright sunshine.

Education for Environmental Concerns

ROBERT S. MORISON

ROBERT S. MORISON *is Director of the Division of Biological Science at Cornell University.*

If the current concern for preserving the environment is to be translated into action, there will be a need for a large number of trained specialists and an educated public willing to support their efforts. Unfortunately, our present educational system is not geared to fulfill this task. Morison outlines some of the problems and possible solutions for altering our school system to educate the needed experts and the general public.

To write an essay on education for environmental management is to write an essay on the future of the university. Nothing is alien to our environment, and, thus, nothing can be alien to the environmental manager. Almost without exception, the separate parts of a modern American university's curriculum yield some angle of perspective on the environment. The university exists, in part, to train specialists for intensive study in the various branches of modern knowledge. At the same time, the university remains dedicated to the proposition that life is coherent and can be understood within a single frame. Both attitudes must be kept clearly in mind as we educate ourselves to be responsible stewards of our environment.

The management of the environment will require specialists of all kinds: the geologist to tell us about the nature of the earth and the derivation and future of its watercourses; the soil specialist to tell us about the thin layer of degraded rock and accumulated organic matter on which life depends; the biologist to describe living things and the means by which their variety is maintained in a dynamic, constantly changing state of equilibrium; the conservationist to maintain, restore, and alter the face of nature so that it can best minister to the complex fancies of man. Finally and perhaps most important, we need the anthropologist, the sociologist, the economist,

This paper appears in Roger Revelle and Hans H. Landsberg, eds. *America's Changing Environment.* Houghton Mifflin Company, pp. 285–98. Copyright © 1967, 1970 by the American Academy of Arts and Sciences. Reprinted by permission.

and the philosopher to tell us about man and his ways, for it is man, the most "successful" of all the species, who occupies, exploits, and pollutes the largest number of ecological niches.

Supplying these specialists is, however, only the first and much the easiest part of the problem. It is becoming increasingly obvious that ordinary run-of-the-mill specialists by themselves are of limited value. The collaboration of several different technologies is required to solve all but the simplest of environmental problems, and most of these problems are far more complex than they seem to be at first glance. As soon as we begin to analyze our purposes, we find that the goals that seemed obvious at first are not nearly so easy to define as we had thought. Moreover, once the possible goals are defined, it becomes painfully apparent that there is little unanimity about which goals to choose.

For purposes of analysis, let us consider the collaboration between specialists that is required to reach an already defined and chosen goal— cleaning up the river that runs through a town. The major source of contamination is domestic sewage. The standard objectives of sewage disposal involve the removal of solids, partly by physical settling and partly by conversion of organic matter with the help of bacterial fermentation. The professional sanitary engineer has long enjoyed some training in biology as well as civil engineering because biological methods are used in sewage disposal. Moreover, he is concerned with removing organisms dangerous to health. Nevertheless, no single profession can now be expected to command all the biology, the physics, and the chemistry, not to mention the economics and the sociology, necessary to cope with the many problems involved in the disposal of domestic sewage. The time-honored removal of solids and elimination of pathogenic bacteria, and the addition of sufficient oxygen to render the final effluent clear, odorless, and innocuous to health are increasingly found to be inadequate. The remaining inorganic materials—nitrogen, phosphate, potash, and certain as yet ill-identified trace elements—remain to feed a luxurient growth of algae and other aquatic weeds. Alive, these organisms render the water unattractive and make water sports dangerous; dead, they essentially replace the organic matter so laboriously removed from the original sewage. The decaying weeds release noxious gases that disturb the passer-by and rob the water of its oxygen so that it can no longer support animal life. For many practical purposes, the river so contaminated is as badly off as it would have been had we not tried to deal with the original sewage problem.

Although we now understand in broad outlines the events leading to the overgrowth of aquatic plants, the details of the process differ from place to place. The control of these plants requires the co-operation of biologists, chemists, and physicists, as well as sanitary engineers. Such collaboration presupposes that each specialist has had a certain degree of familiarity with the disciplines of the other specialists involved. Each must also develop a certain sympathy and understanding of the current weaknesses and inadequacies of his sister specialties. A successful collaborative friendship can be easily ruined if the chemist is obviously contemptuous of the biologist's inability to determine whether the overgrowth in a particular pond is primarily due to an excess of nitrogen, of phosphorus, or of some unexpected trace element. Some other quite different factor may be responsible: the unusually high temperature of the water, the speed with which the water circulates vertically, or the unusual distribution of light intensities. Conversely, the biologist should not be too obviously incredulous when he hears that the chemist has no feasible, cheap way of removing phosphate.

The requirements for breadth of understanding and sympathy become even greater when we come to the matter of goal selection. A thoughtful conservationist shows his sensitivity to this problem by beginning a recent article on education for conservation with the following anecdote:

> *The scene was rural, but only an hour's drive from an urban center. The attractive gray-haired lady from the city listened at length, and with some patience, to the "farm planner" as he expounded the merits of birdsfoot trefoil as a crop on the field from which he had just extracted his soil auger. "No, no, young man," she admonished as she led him to a spot where they could survey a neighbor's rocky pasture covered with Queen Anne's lace and chickory: "There! That's what I want. How do I get it?"(1)*

This charming story is true not only for little old ladies but for almost everybody else. The industrialist who once looked upon the stream flowing by his factory as a source of power and, later on, as a drainage ditch is now beginning to wonder if the stream would not be more useful as a recreational area, which would also attract scarce personnel. Once restored to recreational quality, it could support a small fishing industry, which would incidentally delight the palates of the sophisticated with the shellfish that are now rapidly disappearing. Before we make such choices, however, we must know a great deal more than we do now about the differential benefits to be gained from the extraordinary costs that must be incurred.

Squarely in the center of our problem is the need to develop more sensible ways of thinking about and more persuasive ways of talking about value judgments. In the past, humanists and philosophers have tended to assert a more or less exclusive right to deal with problems of value. The rest of the scholarly world has been glad enough to acquiesce, since the relevance of theoretical studies of value to practical affairs is not always obvious. We must now realize that what we decide about value will determine to a very great measure what we do with our environment. If, for example, "one impulse from a vernal wood may teach you more of man, of moral evil and of good, than all the sages can," it becomes immediately more important to preserve green belts in the neighborhoods of cities than to increase the budget for the municipal university. How we can validate Wordsworth's statement is unclear, but we are going to have to try. Now that we have the power and the resources to abolish woods altogether, or to make new ones spring up where no tree has grown for a thousand years, we must be sure about why we like to walk in the woods and listen to vernal impulses. Conversely, we must become more explicitly aware of the motives of those who have cut down forests in the past and more vigorously analytical of the benefits and costs of alternate uses of forest products.

As we begin to come to grips with some of our more obvious environmental problems, we discover how little thought we have given to the ultimate goals toward which we are racing with ever increasing speed. The United States and, in varying degrees, all the Western democracies have concentrated on means rather than ends. The general idea has been to develop those conditions under which each individual can pursue his particular happiness. Underlying this procedure is the assumption that each individual would have little difficulty selecting his own objectives and that it would be meddlesome of society to talk about such matters in public. This generally laudable respect for private purposes has provided an insecure philosophical basis from which to undertake common action for common purposes. At this point we may pause only to notice the embarrassment we feel when we try to explain to ourselves why we should try to reduce smog or why some of us do not like automobile graveyards. Nowhere is our awkwardness more apparent than in the discussion of standards.

Although one's instinctive personal reaction is that even one junk automobile in a neighbor's front yard or any noxious fumes in the air we breathe is bad and should be avoided, any sophisticated person knows that you cannot approach the problem in this way. This matter came into painfully sharp focus as the "zero tolerance" problem, after Congress passed a law stating, in effect, that foods should contain no substances capable of causing cancer. Scientists find it impossible to prove the absence of something. About the best they can do in regard to potential carcinogens in food is to say something like: "Contains no more than one part per million of any known substance which when given to rats at a concentration of one part per 10,000 for three months is followed by an increase in the incidence of malignant tumors of the liver of less than 1 per cent."

In attempting to control pollution, we must begin by recognizing that some pollution is inevitable. One automobile crossing the empty Dakota Bad Lands changes the composition of the air; one privy on an Appalachian hillside pollutes the Ohio River. The practical engineering question remains: "When does the pollution become intolerable?" This question in turn raises philosophical, ethical, and aesthetic questions of the greatest moment. But curiously we are so embarrassed discussing such matters in public that we quickly turn the problem into one of public health. As was pointed out at a recent meeting of environmental policy-makers, we do this for two reasons. The American people "have already been sold on health as a value and are prepared to pay a lot for it." Moreover, although it is at least theoretically possible to correlate so many parts per million of pollution with some measurable increase in morbidity or mortality, it is presumably less easy to measure how much the total sum of human welfare has been reduced merely because smog has obscured the view of the North River for one million office workers and caused their eyes to burn on the way home. Sooner or later, we may need to ask ourselves whether good health is an end in itself or a means to something else. Can we go on indefinitely equating the goodness of life only with its length?

We are now in a position to ask what kinds of educational arrangements are necessary to prepare us for dealing more consciously and more effectively with our environment. If our analysis of the problems to be solved is correct, the educational requirements are of two rather different kinds.

There is, first, a need to train substantial numbers of environmental specialists to develop and operate the technologies necessary for modifying, restoring, and maintaining the environment in accord with whatever goals we set. The second and more challenging task is to devise ways of educating and guiding the entire population to make informed and satisfying choices of goals.

The modern well-rounded university already provides adequate opportunities for mastering the basic knowledge necessary for managing the environment. Basic biology, physics, chemistry, economics, and sociology are all readily available. As one approaches the specific problems of the environment, existing knowledge appears to be less adequate. Thus, everyone is more or less aware of the rapid progress in basic genetics and the less spectacular but still steady advances in animal and plant nutrition and metabolism, including photosynthesis. Much less work has been done, however, on how these basic factors combine in a given lake or stream to determine the growth of a particular species of algae. This lag in application can be traced, in part, to the individual scientist's lack of motivation to enter the necessary "applied" fields. It also reflects the very real inability of modern scientific methodology to deal with what Warren Weaver has called "organized complexity." The two factors work together in a vicious circle (itself a primitive example of organized complexity). Young people are not attracted to complex problems because they recognize the lack of an adequate methodology, and the methodology remains inadequate because few first-rate people are motivated to improve it. The present state of affairs in ecology illustrates the nature of the difficulty and suggests a possible solution.

Although there is a great deal of talk about the importance of "ecosystems," no such system has been adequately described even in qualitative terms. Quantitative analysis of ecosystems is in its infancy. Some scholars are beginning to foresee dimly the outlines of how modern systems analysis and computer simulation may be applied to some of these problems. Challenging though these possibilities may be to a few experts, they have not reached the stage where they can be presented in an exciting and convincing way to students. The freshman or sophomore with a head for mathematics and a love of precise definitions is much more likely to go into molecular biology where provocative personalities have blazed a clear trail to the understanding of several interesting and very basic matters. The only discernible and not very satisfactory path to a more productive future for community biology may be through the encouragement and support of those few individuals who can develop effective methods of analysis and simulation, so that the secrets of community action become as accessible as those of the genetic code now are.

If difficulties are encountered in attracting sufficient student interest in ecology, those difficulties are only intensified as we reach the applied and professional levels. Here the purpose is not so much to understand the environment as to do something about it. In view of the now obvious importance of maintaining the integrity of the environment, surprisingly few young people are stimulated to take up these vocations. It seems quite obvious to an urban planner that a mass transport system provides a more rapid and comfortable form of transportation to and from work than the individual automobile. Moreover, it would also stay the conversion of productive land into highways and reduce one of the primary sources of smog. To the average young engineer, however, designing anything as old hat as a subway train is an unexciting prospect. In addition, the solution to the problem involves a number of economic, social, and psychological variables—the kind of thing he went into engineering to avoid.

Unhappily, bright young men and women tend to select careers that seem exciting to them rather than those that are demonstrably needed by society. In this, they are only following their teachers, for scholars, scientists, and artists have all proclaimed that the best work is done when the inspired individual follows his curiosity and need for self-expression. Indeed, there is convincing evidence that knowledge advances according to the rules of some inner dynamic that interacts with the tastes and curiosities of the knowledge-seekers. A particularly fertile hypothesis or the development of a particularly powerful methodology determines where the progress will be; the demonstrated need for a new type of knowledge plays rather a small role in the process.

In recent years, however, public awareness of the importance of science to our civilization has resulted in efforts to harness the scientific process so that it can be driven toward foreseeable ends. Whatever can be done to modify the direction by providing money and facilities will probably be done and have some influence, but the over-all effect is likely to be limited. Money can hasten development of an existing idea or technique; its role in stimulating an original idea is less clear. The National Foundation for Poliomyelitis, with the large sums at its command, developed the Salk vaccine some years earlier than would have been possible without such aid. On the other hand, the key element was the invention of a method for growing the virus in tissue culture, and this came about largely through the efforts of an individual who was attracted to the investigation of viruses a decade before the foundation was established.

The proportions of students electing to enter a given branch of knowledge have remained remarkably constant even though financial support has increased sharply in some areas and not in others. In spite of the enormous publicity given to science since World War II and especially since the first Sputnik, the percentage of people going into the natural sciences after they are graduated from college has remained level. Indeed, a somewhat smaller percentage of students is taking high-school physics. Confronted by these unsettling facts, one can only point to the need for more people with better and more exciting ideas about environmental studies and hope that the ways to attract first-class students into the area will be found. A first step might be to free some of the rare leaders from the many committee meetings called to map out programs in environmental management, so that they may return to classroom and laboratory where they can develop their ideas and attract more students.

Finally, we must improve the status of the environmental professions. A rather musty civil-service atmosphere still clings to sanitary engineering, public health, toxicology, conservation, and even urban planning. Once a generation, perhaps only once a century, a Christopher Wren, a Baron

Haussmann, or a Frederick Law Olmstead shows us that a genius can apply himself to the urban environment and incidentally satisfy a personal need for public recognition if not glamour. (*Si monumentum requiris; circumspice.*) More rarely, a man acquires immortality simply by cleaning up a city and making it more livable, as Sir Edwin Chadwick and John Snow did in the last century. Society seems even less prepared to recognize those who would preserve the natural rural environment, although one of the acknowledged merits of Theodore Roosevelt was his encouragement of Gifford Pinchot. Democracies have been slow in finding suitable incentives and rewards for those who would make the general conditions of living more healthful, comfortable, and beautiful for all.

Even when we succeed in encouraging prospective environmental managers to seek professional training, we quickly discover that the prestigious professional schools associated with most universities come out of ancient traditions. The universities of the Middle Ages had their schools of theology, law, and medicine, and these are still the principal professional schools operating at the graduate level. The newer professions have not succeeded in developing recognizable traditions and have, therefore, borrowed rather awkwardly from the tradition of the university in general. Nowhere is this more clear than in the tendency to turn the Ph.D. into a kind of jack-of-all-trades. Not so long ago, one expected to find a person with a doctorate to be engaged in the traditional business of uncovering new knowledge and teaching it to students. Now perhaps as many as half of the holders of the degree are practicing other professions. The typical Ph.D. in the agricultural sciences, for example, is not so much a teacher and contributor to knowledge as he is a developer and promoter of new agricultural technology. A large, industrialized chicken farm may have several Ph.D.'s on its staff to guide the breeding program and to keep up with the ever advancing knowledge of nutrition. Such men do need to be trained well beyond the level available in an undergraduate agricultural college, so that they know how new knowledge is developed and how to evaluate the results of experimentation. It is less clear, however, that they need to spend much time in learning to do basic research. Much the same could be said for the large number of Ph.D.'s in engineering who are now being absorbed into the more progressive kinds of manufacturing. Perhaps even more analogous to the classical profession is the Doctor of Philosophy in psychology who spends his life practicing clinical psychology on a more or less individual basis.

The characteristics of professional, as opposed to strictly academic, education are the training to *do* as well as to think and a somewhat broader approach to the subject than is strictly necessary for most researchers and teachers. Conversely, professionals have somewhat less obligation to contribute new knowledge of a theoretical sort or to qualify as teachers.

One of the difficulties in attracting young people into the newer professions arises because the prestige of professions varies almost directly with their age. Holders of degrees in law, medicine, and theology do not feel particularly inferior to holders of the Ph.D. Some of them may, in fact, feel a trifle superior. Nobody has succeeded in transferring this type of dignity and self-confidence to a degree that might be suitable for those practicing such professions as clinical psychology, advanced agricultural technology, engineering, or environmental management. The matter may be most acute as we begin to think seriously about preparing people to manage the environment. It is more unlikely that a Ph.D. in any of the recognized disciplines could provide adequate preparation for the people who must make the environment more suitable for human needs. The two existing professions that seem most likely—public health and civil engineering—are for various reasons not so promising as they look. Competitors like regional and urban planning are almost certainly too specialized.

We should probably be looking toward a six- or seven-year program leading to some definite graduate degree that would confer dignity and prestige, but not necessarily testify to the ability to make original contributions to knowledge. The curriculum should contain enough biology so that the candidate would emerge with some understanding of how biological systems work, enough engineering to give a sense of man's power to alter the physical environment in both adaptive and nonadaptive ways, and enough of the humanities and social sciences to give a feeling for what men think they want, what they really want, and how human institutions work to forward or frustrate human desires. This is a large but, perhaps, not impossible order; anything less is inadequate to the purpose. The engineer without familiarity with both biology and the humanities cannot go very far in meeting the need. The conventional engineer is too used to problems that are in a sense easy to solve because they are posed in a limited frame.

Modern engineering technology can make drastic changes in the environment before we have had time to assess their ultimate results. The topsoil it has taken centuries to accumulate can be removed in a few years. A marsh can be drained before anyone weighs the benefit of its increased agricultural production against its recreational value to bird-watchers, Sunday walkers, and October hunters who utilized it in its pristine state. On the other hand, left to himself, the biologist or ecologist is likely to become so bemused by the mystical beauty of the balance of nature that he underestimates the importance of human needs or the power of modern engineering technology to compensate for what may at first glance seem to be wanton destruction. The economist and the sociologist are likely to develop too abstract a picture of both man and nature in a pseudo-scientific search for order in human affairs. A more balanced view is needed that recognizes man as a part of nature—a somewhat peculiar part since he can modify the direction in which natural forces operate in order to reach objectives different from those which nature might produce if he were not there.

In the long run, changes in the environment will evolve from the conscious or unconscious choices of the majority of ordinary people. Ordinary people alter the environment directly by building houses, clipping hedges, and throwing beer cans out of cars, and indirectly by voting to build roads, sequester wildlife areas, or control smog. The future of the environment will be largely what we choose it to be. These choices will, in turn, depend in large part on what we think life itself ought to be. In the past it has been customary to describe the American standard of living in terms of the amount of food, clothing, real estate, and chattels available to each individual. No longer, however, can this quantitative enumeration be directly equated with happiness or personal welfare. The cherished automobile loses much of its value if caught in a continuous traffic jam; the lovely cruiser or the beautifully designed fishing rod are left at the dock when rivers and lakes lose their oxygen and give off methane and hydrogen sulfide; even food loses some of its savor when its production entails the inadvertent poisoning of birds and fish.

John Kenneth Galbraith has described the many ways in which members of the affluent society have focused production on individual rather than community welfare. In spite of the clarity of his presentation, we have difficulty in adjusting ourselves to its implications largely because of the accounting problems involved. To a large extent, the shift from an individual-centered to a community-centered economy is a shift from a system of bookkeeping that easily adds innumerable objects like washing machines, to one which tries to give a value to the feelings of people about things they enjoy in common. Our thoughts and judgments must turn from the individual and the material to the moral and the aesthetic. The morality will doubtless remain basically utilitarian, but the perspective from which the utility is measured is likely to be broader and to involve more individuals. Most modern democracies have attempted to duck the moral and the aesthetic issues by concentrating on means while leaving value judgments to the individual.

Insofar as moral judgments are a matter of religion, the democratic state *must* abstain because of its dedication to religious toleration. As a practical matter, it has been *able* to abstain because in matters of individual morality, such as those covered by the Ten Commandments, most men hold astonishingly similar views, even though their religions may vary considerably. The ethical base of most democracies is, therefore, utilitarian rather than transcendental, and legislative bodies, as well as individuals, make most of their moral choices after a reasonably careful appraisal of the probable results of various courses of action.

This tradition seems to leave no alternative to assuming that an informed electorate will make the proper choices when exposed for a long enough time to the best evidence available. To become suitably informed on a modern program for the environment will require considerable sophistication in the weighing of scientific evidence, most of it presented in a statistical way. Few things of significance to the environment happen as the inevitable result of a single definable cause. Just as the smog in Los Angeles is the result of hundreds of thousands of motorists driving hundreds of thousands of cars, each with its own rate of emitting pollutants, and the weather conditions, a result of additional thousands of factors, so the effect of the smog on any given individual depends upon his basic constitution, health, the degree and duration of his exposure, and other unidentifiable factors. Weighing all these factors simply to make a prediction requires considerable training and experience in the natural sciences and in the use of statistics.

On various occasions, it has been recommended that the teaching of statistics and probability begin earlier and go on longer than has been usual in our educational system. Indeed, the argument for replacing the study of plane geometry in high school with a course in probability and statistics is a persuasive one. Today we have largely abandoned the thought that the right decision can be arrived at by a process of logical deduction topped off by a Q.E.D. Right action almost always depends on the weighing of probabilities. Even the most basic scientific generalizations are expressions of probability rather than inescapably logical conclusions. Nevertheless, a statement of probabilities is not yet wholly convincing, even to the most sophisticated. Relatively few people feel as safe in an airplane as they do in an automobile, even though the odds against accidents are far higher in the first case. We will not be modern men until we believe our statistics the way we now believe our eyes.

In addition, the average man must become aware of statistical realities in another, more subtle way. It is not enough to *know* what is going to happen to others as a result of an overt act of neglect; one must *care* about it as well. One must become statistically moral in the sense that one *cares* about what happens to numerous unseen people as much as one cares about the welfare of the few who are close enough to be seen and heard. Other people in other places and in future times will benefit most from our efforts to preserve the environment. Many of the benefits will be discouragingly intangible—a blue sky instead of a gray one, trees and green fields instead of barren hillsides, bird songs instead of a silent spring, clean streets, well-proportioned façades, and quiet walks instead of ugliness, traffic jams, and noise. The educational system for tomorrow must not only make it clear how these presumable goals can be achieved but why they are worth achieving.

Quite possibly, and perhaps quite shockingly to some, this increased concern for goals may mean that certain branches of knowledge will have to renounce a part of their highly cherished objectivity and return to an earlier interest in ends as well as means. In many instances, the answer to why a particular goal is selected will be found in personal taste and feeling. Formal education and scholarship once directed a substantial part of their efforts to cultivating "sensibility" and refining tastes. In recent years, the apparent success of objective or scientific methods has tended to erode the dignity of subjective approaches and to cast doubt on their effectiveness. Consequently, we are better prepared to describe and improve our means than to choose satisfactory ends. Much of recent literature concerns the individual's difficulty in discovering valid personal goals. The difficulty is many times greater when the goals of an entire group or society must be set. Trained as we are to doubt the validity of our own feelings, we can scarcely be blamed for not giving much weight to the feelings of others. Nevertheless, the collective feeling about the consequence or inconsequence of clean air, pure water, and graceful cities will decide the way in which we employ our energies in the future. If the educational system is to prepare the oncoming generations for collective aesthetic decision-making, it will have to develop more self-confidence in its ability to deal effectively with questions of taste and other nonquantitative matters. Above all, it must recognize that aesthetic choice can no longer be regarded entirely as an individual matter with consequences safely limited to inner experience.

The need for a reorientation toward a greater concern with the social consequences of aesthetic choice is probably strongest at the university level. The elementary and secondary schools, being less sophisticated about the epistemological problems involved and less squeamish about appearing to dictate in matters of taste, have always had far less trouble taking positions on the good, the true, and the beautiful. On occasion, they have even indulged in outright propaganda for conservation of natural areas and beautification of cities. The universities must, of course, continue to deal with such matters with considerably more circumspection and to give special attention to the difficulties involved in arriving at group decisions in matters of feeling. They must, nevertheless, leave their students with a conviction of the importance of these matters in everyday life.

The educational system of the future must ensure that the decision-makers—and in a democracy that includes almost everybody—know enough of science to understand the consequences and the costs of different courses of action and enough of philosophy, the humanities, and the arts to appreciate their value. Only the urgency of this plea for a unified or "general" education for the whole population is new. When society commands the means to do almost anything it wants, value judgments of ends are crucial.

It is not nearly so easy to explain why the study of philosophy, history, and literature prepares one for making discriminating judgments about the significance and beauty of life as it is to point out what physics and chemistry have to do with the practice of engineering. To an embarrassingly great extent, advocates of the liberal arts as a preparation for life in the real world find it hard to go much beyond Matthew Arnold's view that it is good to know the best that has been thought and said in the world and that somehow this will contribute to sweetness and light. In a rapidly industrializing society bent on supplying the means of subsistence and creature comforts for all and dominated by the austerities of a remnant puritanism, there often seems to be something a little irrelevant, if not actually frivolous, about a preoccupation with sweetness and light. In the crudest possible terms, "Who but a starry-eyed do-gooder would try to weight the integrity of the West Virginia landscape against the ten-foot seam of coal one could get by tearing it up?"

By an interesting paradox, the progress of science and technology has now demonstrated that it is not inevitable and certainly not desirable that we do everything we can do, that the choice of what to do is, in fact, our most important problem, and that the ultimate basis of choice is aesthetic. We must have faith that the soundest base for aesthetic judgment is the cultivation of the best that has been known and thought.

REFERENCES

1. Hamilton, L. S. Education for the changing field of conservation. *Science Education* 51, no. 2.

Picture Credits

ABCDEFGHIJ— H —7654321